LETTERS OF
ARNOLD BENNETT

Edited by
JAMES HEPBURN

VOLUME IV

Family Letters

Translations from the French by
ROSAMUND HOWE

Oxford   New York

OXFORD UNIVERSITY PRESS

1986

v. 4

Oxford University Press, Walton Street, Oxford OX2 6DP
Oxford New York Toronto
Delhi Bombay Calcutta Madras Karachi
Kuala Lumpur Singapore Hong Kong Tokyo
Nairobi Dar es Salaam Cape Town
Melbourne Auckland
and associated companies in
Beirut Berlin Ibadan Nicosia

Oxford is a trade mark of Oxford University Press

British Library Cataloguing in Publication Data
Bennett, Arnold
Letters of Arnold Bennett.
Vol. 4: Family letters
1. Bennett, Arnold—Biography 2. Authors,
English—20th century—Biography
I. Title II. Hepburn, James
823'.912 PR6003.E62/
ISBN 0–19–212207–X

Library of Congress Cataloging in Publication Data
(Revised for vol. 4)
Bennett, Arnold, 1867–1931.
Letters of Arnold Bennett.
Contents: v. 1. Letters to J. B. Pinker.—v. 2.
1889–1915.—[etc.]—v. 4. Family letters.
1. Bennett, Arnold, 1867–1931—Correspondence.
2. Authors, English—20th century—Correspondence.
I. Hepburn, James G., ed. II. Pinker, James B.
III. Title.
PR6003.E6Z48 1966 828'.91208 85–21510
ISBN 0–19–212207–X

Set by Wyvern Typesetting Ltd.
Printed in Great Britain by
Biddles Ltd.
Guildford and King's Lynn

CONTENTS

ILLUSTRATIONS

Between pages 74 and 75

Arnold Bennett, 1911
Miss Mary Kennerley

Sarah Ann Bennett
Miss Ruth Bennett

Dorothy Cheston Bennett, 1932
Mme V. M. Eldin

Marguerite Bennett, 1907, with Arnold Bennett at the piano. Painting by Eugene Paul Ullman.
Professor Pierre Ullman

Tertia Bennett, later Mrs Kennerley, 1903
Miss Mary Kennerley

Plaque of Enoch Bennett, by Septimus
Miss Ruth Bennett

Virginia Bennett, 1951
Mme V. M. Eldin

Septimus Bennett with two friends, 1890s
Miss Mary Kennerley

Marguerite and Richard Bennett with Marguerite's sister and mother
Miss Mary Kennerley

The Bennett family: Sarah Ann, Frank, Fanny Gertrude, Arnold, Tertia, Emily, Enoch, Septimus
Miss Ruth Bennett

ACKNOWLEDGEMENTS

This final volume of Arnold Bennett's letters has been delayed for many years by copyright and other problems. It is now published with the kind permission of the present owner of the copyright, Bennett's daughter, Mme V. M. Eldin. I wish to express my appreciation for her generous and sympathetic support of the volume.

Work on the collection has been supported in a material way by the Guggenheim Foundation, the American Council of Learned Societies, the American Philosophical Society, the National Endowment for the Humanities, and Bates College. I am very grateful to the authorities of these institutions.

The letters printed here were generously made available by several persons and institutions. Mme Eldin lent letters to herself, to Bennett's brother Septimus, to May (Beardmore) Marsden, and to Joan Marsden (Ells). She also provided information about her mother for the Introduction. Miss Mary Kennerley very kindly lent letters to herself and her sister Margaret; to her mother and father, Tertia (Bennett) and W. W. Kennerley; and to Bennett's mother, Sarah Ann. Miss Ruth Bennett very kindly lent a letter to herself and letters to her father, Septimus. I am grateful to Miss Kennerley and Miss Bennett for reading unreadable words in Bennett's letters and for providing much information about the Bennett family, relatives, and friends. Miss Kennerley gave me permission to use Bennett's biographical sketch of her father, Bennett's first formal example of calligraphic writing, and a letter from her mother to May Beardmore. Miss Bennett gave me permission to quote from her father's war journals.

The letters to Marguerite Bennett (née Soulié) are used with the permission of the University of Keele Library. I am especially indebted to Dr Ian H. C. Fraser, the former archivist, for his courtesies over several years. I am also obliged to Miss Margaret Morris and to Mrs Christine Fyfe, the present archivist. The letters to Dorothy Cheston Bennett and to George Cedric Beardmore come from the Henry W. and Albert A. Berg Collection, the New York Public Library, Astor, Lenox, and Tilden Foundations. Unpublished portions of Bennett's journals that are quoted from in the Introduction are also held in the Berg Collection and used with permission. I would like to express my appreciation for the helpfulness of Mrs Lola Szladits, the curator. The letters to Richard Bennett are used with the permission of the Syndics of Cambridge University Library. I wish to thank Mr A. E. B. Owen, Senior Under-Librarian, for his courtesies. The remaining letters in the collection come from the City Museum, Stoke-on-Trent. They include letters to Sarah Ann, Septimus and Frank Bennett, Florence (Wooldridge) Bennett, Emily Hancock Beardmore, Margaret Beardmore (Shingler), and Stella Lisle. I would like to thank Mr Arnold Mountford, Director of Museums, and Mr J. H. Kelly, Keeper of Social History, for their helpfulness on several occasions.

Among other people I must first mention the late Frank Swinnerton, who with this volume as with the three previous volumes was always ready to answer questions and to obtain answers elsewhere when he did not have them himself. Mr Swinnerton lent me a number of manuscripts containing helpful background information. Mr John Ford very kindly provided information about Stoke-on-Trent and Bennett's books. Mr Thomas R. Roberts and the late W. Hartmann Hoult very kindly provided information on Bennett family history. I am also very grateful to Mrs Joan Ells, Mrs Victoria Knowles, Mr Roger Beardmore, and Mr Richard Beardmore for providing information about the Beardmore families and friends. Mr Patrick Quinn put at my disposal his extensive information on Bennett's visit to America. Mr Cyril Shingler and Mr J. H. Cheston generously answered questions about the Bennett family and relatives.

I am also obliged to Professor Dan Laurence for giving me information about several people. Professor Pierre Ullman and Martha Ullman West provided information about the Ullman–Bennett circle in Paris. Other help was kindly given by Mr R. A. Randall (Editor of the *Evening Sentinel*), Professor John Tagliabue, Professor Antony Patti, Mrs Felicité Wilkinson, Professor James Dayananda, Mr Derek Beard (City Central Library, Stoke-on-Trent), Mr Thomas Hayward (Ladd Library, Bates College), James Bettley (British Architectural Library), Professor Matthew Bruccoli, Mr E. Parker Hayden, Mr Omar Pound, the Keeper of Records of the Public Record Office, the Secretary of the Royal Society of Painters in Watercolour, the Dean and Archivist of Balliol College, the Librarian of the University of Oslo, and the Registrars of the Law Society, the General Medical Council and the General Dental Council.

Initial transcription and translation of letters in French was undertaken by Judith Seraikis, with assistance by Lisa Quintal, Allison Johnson, and Betsy Dower. English transcription and proof-reading were done in part by Ana Maria de Garavilla and Rebecca Jones.

I am especially indebted to my two assistants at Bates College:

Susanna Burger, who faithfully and cheerfully transcribed a great many letters and typed a great many notes, and Kelli Armstrong, who helped to put the manuscript in final order. I am also obliged to Diana Grant for doing some genealogical research, and to Sue Foster for typing parts of the final manuscript.

I must thank Sir Rupert Hart-Davis for permission to quote from a letter to Frank Swinnerton.

Lastly I must thank my wife, who with all four volumes helped with research and with preparing the manuscript and reading proof.

EDITORIAL MATTERS

This volume of 448 letters is culled from more than two thousand surviving letters to family. Inevitably the selection is unbalanced, just as the surviving letters are. When Bennett left the Potteries in 1889 to go to London, he began a sequence of letters to his mother that continued up to her death in 1914. Apparently for at least twelve years he wrote every day, as he was to do with his two wives whenever he was away from them. He must sometimes have written twice a day, as he did with his wives, and often enough he was likely to have added a picture-postcard. The letters would have numbered above five thousand, and they were all burnt at his mother's death save for one, and several dozen postcards. The record of Bennett as a family man is thus inescapably deficient in the aspect of him as a son, most regrettably so in the earlier years. Printed here are the one letter, six postcards that comprise most of a letter, and two further postcards. They are hitherto unpublished. No letters to Bennett's father are known.

More than a hundred letters survive to his favourite brother, Septimus, mainly from the years 1915–20. Thirty-six are published here; none have been published before. Some sixty letters survive to his favourite sister, Tertia, and her husband, W. W. Kennerley; twenty-three are printed here; portions of ten appeared in Reginald Pound's biography. Four of the few known letters to his brother Frank are reproduced here, as is one letter that survives to his sister Emily. A single brief postcard is known to survive to his sister Fanny Gertrude. He was effectively head of the family from the late 1890s onward, and took his position seriously, and it is probable that a large number of letters to his brothers and sisters are lost.

The three major surviving groups of letters are those to his two wives and his adopted son. In the years 1907–30 he wrote more than four hundred letters to his first wife, Marguerite, mainly during the fifteen years of their courtship and marriage, until their separation in 1921. Almost all of the correspondence has been preserved, along with a large body of letters from Marguerite. Portions or all of 110 of these letters were printed in *Arnold Bennett in Love*, edited by George and Jean Beardmore. The Beardmores printed translations instead of the original French in which most of the letters were written. Printed here are 147 letters, in French where Bennett wrote in French, with translations in footnotes. The Beardmores censored a few erotic passages.

In 1935 in *Arnold Bennett, A Portrait Done at Home* Dorothy Cheston Bennett published portions or all of 170 letters that Bennett wrote to her. She drew them from a total correspondence of 300 items that cover the years 1922–30. Many of the letters in her collection are badly truncated, and they characteristically omit passages that are seriously critical of her. She deliberately damaged two holographs irretrievably with India ink (see pages 476–7). Perhaps we are lucky to have any of the letters to her, for Bennett wanted her to destroy them. Printed here are ninety-one letters.

Bennett and Marguerite had no children, and he died before his daughter Virginia, by Dorothy, was five years old. Among an unknown number of postcards and letters he wrote to Virginia, two postcards survive and are printed here. In 1916 he and Marguerite undertook the adoption of Frank Bennett's oldest son, Richard, and in the years 1916–31 he wrote perhaps eight hundred letters to Richard, seven hundred of which survive. When Richard was away at school, at university, and then at a job, there was a regular weekly letter, and often enough there was another letter or two as well. In 1935 Richard Bennett published portions or all of 400 of these letters in *Arnold Bennett's Letters to His Nephew*. These letters were censored to delete all references to Marguerite and Dorothy. Eighty-three letters to Richard are printed here.

Bennett wrote another few hundred letters to other nephews and nieces; some thirty are printed here. Among the few other letters in this collection, one group requires mention. May Beardmore was the daughter of John and Emily Beardmore, friends of the senior Bennetts (her brother Frank married Fanny Gertrude). She was a close friend of Bennett's rather than an official relative, but it seems appropriate to print ten letters to her, along with a letter to her mother.

At an early stage in the preparation of this volume it was hoped to include letters to Annie Wood, who likewise was no formal relative but a member of the large Wood clan in Stoke-on-Trent with whom the Bennetts and Beardmores were intimate. Some forty letters to Annie Wood came to light after the first three volumes were published. They are mainly from the nineties and the first decade of the century, and they show Bennett's characteristic kindness in helping a young friend with journalistic ambitions. They also have special interest in that some of them come from his editorial office on *Woman* and give details about his career there that are not otherwise known. Regrettably there is no space for these letters here.

All letters are printed in full except for four that have small deletions to avoid pain to people. Three letters were not printed for the same reason. The censorship does not affect the picture of

Bennett. An unreadable word is indicated by a bracketed question mark. Uncertain words are bracketed with a question mark preceding them. The very few slips of the pen—omitted word, repeated word, wrong word, misspelling—have been silently corrected unless of some apparent significance. Translation of Bennett's French is given in the footnotes to the letters, with addresses, salutations, and closes characteristically omitted. Isolated passages in French of less than four or five lines are not translated. Ellipses used in the translations indicate that succeeding material in a letter is in English. Ellipses used in the original French are all Bennett's. Bennett's French is uncorrected except for slips of the pen.

Addresses from which Bennett wrote are given in full the first time and in abbreviated form thereafter. No distinction is made between points and dashes that Bennett used in separating day, month, and year: dashes are used. Presumed dates and addresses are placed within brackets. Points are always supplied for Bennett's initials, even though sometimes he did not supply them or supplied them so lightly that they did not clearly register. Commas are provided after all salutations, though Bennett characteristically used a downward flourish with the last letter of the addressee's name. Punctuation and printing of titles of short stories, novels, and periodicals have been standardized, as likewise have the spellings of a name or two. Another standardization is size of type: unshown is the fact that when Bennett was angry with Dorothy his handwriting tended to become smaller.

Ownership of each letter is indicated in the heading by one of the following symbols:

BENNETT (Miss Ruth Bennett)
BERG (Henry W. and Albert A. Berg Collection, New York Public Library)
CAMBRIDGE (Cambridge University Library)
ELDIN (Mme V. M. Eldin)
KEELE (University of Keele Library)
KENNERLEY (Miss Mary Kennerley)
STOKE (City Museum, Stoke-on-Trent)

The symbol MS indicates that the letter or postcard is in Bennett's hand, TS that the letter is typed, and S.Tr. that the letter is a shorthand transcription. The numeral in the heading gives the number of the letter in the sequence of the collection.

Quotations from Bennett's journals as published in 1932–3 are indicated as *Journals*, quotations from the 1907 journal as published in the Penguin edition of 1971 are indicated as *Journals 1971*, and quotations from unpublished portions are indicated as journals.

INTRODUCTION

To anyone who thinks of Arnold Bennett as the businessman of letters, it may come as a surprise to see him as the family man of letters. Yet it should not be. He was 'Uncle Arnold' to a multitude of people who sought his advice and aid on matters private and public, ethical and monetary, sexual and legal. He wrote pocket philosophy in several volumes for further multitudes on 'how to make the best of life'. He was wise, commonsensical, kind, and generous. How could such a man—uncle to the world, as it were—be less than a family man?

The letters give a powerful answer, if by no means a perfect one. It is the common view that he chose his wives badly, and the letters sometimes show him dealing with them badly—unwisely, naïvely, mean-spiritedly. He seems to believe, in the face of insistent evidence to the contrary, that if he tells them how to behave properly (according to his lights) they will learn to behave properly. Though anything but a complaisant husband, he encourages a freedom of conduct in Marguerite that leads directly to her infidelity with Pierre Legros. Occasionally the tone of his letters is that of a harsh prosecuting counsel—though he thinks he is merely being direct and open. On the other hand, he gives the two women the attention of a devoted lover and husband. He embellishes his long letters with hearts and arrows and kisses. He forgives hysterical violent words and wakings of him in the night to quarrel. He offers energy and money towards the artistic careers they think they want. And when Marguerite chooses her lover and separation, he makes an absurdly generous settlement and writes her kindly letters thereafter. So too with others of his family, along with the occasional admixture of unpleasantness. He offers unreserved help to May Marsden when her husband is killed in the First World War, he keeps his brother Frank out of prison and keeps his brother Septimus solvent, he manages investments for his sister Tertia, he supervises the early writing career of his nephew George Cedric, and he entertains nephews and nieces on his yacht and sees to it that they are outfitted for the occasion without expense to themselves.

I. FIRST YEARS IN PARIS

There are new things in the letters, or new perspectives on them—Bennett in America in 1911 and visiting the Western Front in 1915, the circumstances of the collapse of Frank Bennett's law firm, the relationship between Bennett and Septimus. Of paramount importance is the picture of Bennett in his sexual relationships; for the letters to the two wives, Marguerite and Dorothy, dominate the volume, and the picture contradicts the picture that has hitherto been offered. Bennett's very good friend H. G. Wells may have been initially responsible. In *Experiment in Autobiography* in 1934 he portrayed Bennett as a sexually inhibited man: 'He never gave the effect of being welded, even temporarily, with the woman he was with.' He supposed the inhibition to stem from some unknown childhood shock, that likewise accounted for Bennett's stammer. Perhaps other people inferred that a philanderer like Wells was sure to know an inhibited man when he saw one. At any rate, Reginald Pound in his biography in 1952 was content to accept the Wells opinion. He added some stories in confirmation: Bennett impotent with a prostitute in his early days in London, Bennett speechless before the gibes of friends about the lack of sex in his novels, Bennett boasting unconvincingly to Mrs Belloc Lowndes about 'a little book in which he kept careful notes of his amorous adventures'.

But if Wells and a somewhat careless biographer are to be discounted, it is harder to dismiss Frank Swinnerton, who was without doubt Bennett's closest friend, and who was explicit in private conversation in saying that Bennett lacked normal sexual drive. Then too Margaret Drabble in her critical biography in 1974 asserted that Bennett was unable to form sexual relationships in his years in England to age thirty-six. She thought that even in Paris he remained ill-informed on sexual matters and that when told about them was perhaps unlikely to have acted on his knowledge. And in 1978 several reviewers of Frank Swinnerton's memoir, *Arnold Bennett, A Last Word*, thought that Bennett must be undersexed. Anthony Burgess wrote, 'Of Bennett's sexuality we know little. He worked too hard, one would say, to be able to find time for it.' An inhibited man indeed!—especially seeing that he said to his literary agent in 1904, during which year he wrote three novels along with weekly journalism: 'You would be under a false impression if you imagined that I am working at pressure. I am not. I could do lots more. I have vast leisure.'

It would of course be useful to have the little book that Reginald Pound implies was fictitious, for it did exist, and it might settle the matter readily. Bennett kept it for a year, beginning in mid-April 1905, and there is an allusion to it in the published *Journals* on 27 April of that year. But it is lost. However, the regular journals survive, and though there is a gap in them from 27 May 1901 through 27 September 1903, the succeeding material tells a suggestive enough story. Bennett left England for France in March 1903, and the day after he resumed the journal he made the following entry. It indicates prior acquaintance with the woman involved, and unless Bennett was far more detached than anyone has hitherto suspected, it suggests intimate relationship.

Concerning sexual perversions, Chichi gave me several of her own experiences. As of the man who always wished to make love on the floor in a corner of a room, *more canino*. The man who had his *fesses* beaten with a cane till they bled.... These men insisted on going through a comedy. They had to cry: 'Pardon, pardon, I entreat.' And she had to say: 'No, no, I won't pardon you', & had to hurt them more and more. The pain must have been really intense, yet they said: 'If you don't hurt me more, I can never finish.' Afterwards, they were absolutely exhausted, and wept.... Yet once she said to me when we were discussing sexual perversions: '*Mais tout est naturel.*' The force of this observation struck me. I had been protesting, rather conventionally perhaps, against certain common practices. I explained to her the philosophy of the passion for pain in the enjoyment of love, & how it grew on a man like drink.

Beginning in October 1903 there are references to an actress who is identified as 'C'. The conversations reported between them concern theatre, and only occasionally and slightly do they incline towards sexual matters. But Bennett dines at her place and she at his, and on 9 December he says he has had 'a hell of a row' with her. The relationship seems rather more than casual or platonic. References to 'C' continue until July 1904. An entry on 4 May 1904 very probably concerns her, but she is not named.

> *Hier. Soirée de reconciliation.* According to my theory expressed in my Xmas article in *T. P. 'S Weekly*, I must have lived more fully during the last 3 days than for a very considerable time past. In fact I had not suspected such possibilities in myself. Unfortunately, to work under such circumstances is impossible.

(In his Christmas article he indulged in a Pateresque enthusiasm for sensation: 'Only celebrate the intense consciousness of being alive. Revel in every manifestation of your being alive.') In 1905 and early 1906 there are references to 'Cosette', whom he describes as a cocotte. He portrays her in *A Great Man*.

On 2 July 1904 he reports a conversation with his friend Mrs Devereux (Margaret Rose Roy Pember-Devereux), who wrote for him when he was editor of *Woman* (1896–1900).

> She could talk of nothing but her heart, & I wanted to talk of nothing better. I said it was singular I had never got up a passion for her, & she said she supposed it was singular: 'Because in some ways, I suppose,' she said, 'I must be the most attractive woman you have ever known in your life.' To that I sincerely agreed. When she had told me all about her affairs (I don't know why I should tell you all these things, she said), I told her all about mine, & pretty considerably astonished her. She said she thought I had done very well for myself.

A long *Journals* entry on 8 July 1904 records a conversation with two young Englishmen about the sexual lives of dons at Oxford and Cambridge. They assured Bennett that the majority of dons were chaste. 'I said that I was astounded. I said I had never heard tell of such a class of men before.' Later he said to one of them: 'Don't you think women are the most interesting thing in the world?'

During the succeeding two years there are a number of like entries. Two are intriguing. They concern a woman named May Elliott, otherwise unknown but apparently a member of the circle of English and American expatriates in Paris. No other entries mention her. The first entry is of 24 May 1906 and alludes to the American painter Eugene Paul Ullman (see pp. 10–12); the second is of 19 April 1907.

Tonight Ullman dined with me & I told him at great length the whole history of the May Elliott episode (not giving the name), the crucial & final scene of which occurred between her & me in this flat here in Paris yesterday between 1 & 2 in the afternoon.

I acceded to the desire of May Elliott last Friday afternoon. En voilà ma préoccupation! There was an accident, and for aught I know consequences may follow in the shape of the younger generation. The affair gave me no satisfaction. I sent for her to come & see me on Monday night, and in 3½ hours of talk made it fairly plain to her what I thought. I was as careful as I could be, but she wept again and again.

The latter entry turns from May Elliott to note that he has just brought Marguerite Soulié down to his country flat at Les Sablons. 'Voilà une affaire qui me plait infiniment.' He had met Marguerite in January.

2. ELEANOR GREEN

It was in this atmosphere that Bennett seems to have contemplated marriage seriously for the first time. A *Journals* entry of 27 May 1904, his 37th birthday, says that he has now warned Tertia and his mother that he will marry by the age of 40. Such a plan presumably foresees agreeable arrangement rather than romantic compulsion. In a letter of 30 September 1905 to H. G. Wells, he says that he has never yet been in love. But he then very shortly fell in love romantically, not with Marguerite but with a young woman who preceded her. The time was that of the first May Elliott episode.

Eleanor Green's family were Americans from Georgia, and her father was an executive in the cotton industry who handled his firm's European affairs. They had lived in Paris for some years, long enough for Bennett not to be able to detect an American accent in the mother. Eleanor's younger brother Julian became a distinguished novelist. First mention of them by Bennett is in a journal entry on 2 July 1904, when he records being introduced to the mother at Mrs Devereux's flat. The Greens were intimate with another friend of Bennett's, Agnes Farley, wife of an American dentist in Paris. Reginald Pound asserts, presumably on Eleanor Green's authority, that it was

Agnes Farley who introduced Bennett to the Greens. Be that as it may, it seems probable that Bennett and the Greens met occasionally during the next year or so, but no further mention is made of the family in his *Journals* until 1 April 1906, when he says that 'Miss Green' told him some tales about operatic careers. Perhaps Eleanor was away from Paris for a year or more. At all events the rather formal 'Miss Green' of 1 April becomes the rather romantic 'Eleanora Green' of 12 April, in which entry he tells of taking her to the Grand Guignol. On 15 June they became engaged. On 3 August the engagement was broken off.

The affair is described at some length by Pound. He was able to use a private memoir by Eleanor Green, written perhaps some years before Bennett died, and he obtained a further account from her about 1950. In his narration Eleanor was a vivacious red-headed girl of 18, just out of school and with dreams of becoming an opera singer, and she was introduced to Bennett a few months after he met her mother. She was not impressed by him, for he was more than twice her age, but he was by her, and he 'begged Mrs Farley to arrange another meeting'. In such a chronology the relationship must have simmered in Bennett's mind for more than a year before the crucial events of 1906. During this time, others became aware that he was in love, but not Eleanor. She never thought of him in terms of love; she thought he was nice, clever, and avuncular; she left his letters lying around unopened—and had to be made to open them by her mother. When his proposal came in 1906, she did not even think it was serious, and she was unaware that he then began to make plans for the wedding date. Six weeks later the two of them finally understood each other.

Eleanor Green has clear recollections of the final scene but thinks it unfair to Arnold Bennett's memory to recall them publicly in detail. It is sufficient to say that his speech difficulty appeared at its worst, that every aspirate deserted him in this extremity, and that he was reduced to uttering comically pathetic threats of social excommunication for Miss Green. 'You'll lose the respect of the 'ole world—and Mr. and Mrs. Farley too.'

All of these things are what Eleanor Green told Pound in 1950, with perhaps some embellishment from him. In her earlier memoir she was mainly concerned to give a dispassionate glimpse of Bennett at the time.

Agnes and I frequently had tea with Bennett, in spite of its being China tea, 'the delicate perfection of which' I was incapable of appreciating, according to my host. He was quite right. I preferred good strong Ceylon, which Bennett said was stewed.... And after tea he played Mozart sonatas.... One day he read us a paraphrase he had just finished of a poem of Verlaine's and which was very good indeed. Bennett's conversation was varied and amusing; he was a charming companion, never dull, and I like to remember the long happy afternoons we spent together.

Her only reference to the affair in the memoir is an oblique one, unexplained in any way.

Once he asked Agnes if I liked his books. 'Not all of them', Agnes said tactfully. 'I should not care for her to like them all', was his comment. At that time I did not really care for any of them but later ... I read and admired *The Old Wives' Tale*. All through the years since I have wished we might have been friends again, he and I, and talked together. I do not flatter myself that he went on loathing me.

Against this account is an account by Eleanor's younger sister Anne, in her memoir *With Much Love*. Here Eleanor is consciously involved, consciously engaged to be married. She has yielded to the engagement because of Agnes Farley's promptings, Bennett's charm, and her own weakness of character. She thinks she will go through with the marriage because she cannot break his heart. Besides, he is looking for an apartment. She brings his letters to her mother to ask for help in answering them, and gets help reluctantly. Secretly she is interested in someone else, and she finally finds courage and occasion to make the break, on a day when she comes upon Bennett examining the contents of her handbag.

The difficulty with these two accounts is less their contradiction of each other than their individual implausibility with regard to Bennett—not merely the Bennett of considerable sexual and other experience of women but also the Bennett who at the age of 39 was within a year and a half of sitting down to write that wise book *The Old Wives' Tale*. This is to say nothing of the fact that he was never known otherwise to make plans for people without consulting them or to go through women's handbags without permission. The only other account of the affair is by Bennett himself, and sparse though it is, it deserves credence. In it Eleanor Green is not a schoolgirlish figure of 18, of whom wilful and ignorant behaviour might be expected, but a woman of 25. (All that is otherwise known to suggest her age is that her parents married in 1880, and she was the first child.) After the two *Journals* entries of 1 and 12 April, there are three further references to her and her family prior to the engagement. On 3 May he tells of a three-hour conversation with Mrs Green about the women in his novels. On 10 May he records going to the theatre with Eleanor, but the entry is concerned with the play rather than with her. On 24 May he records going to an exhibition and having tea with her. The entry on 15 June is a single sentence: 'At 5 P.M. on this day in the forest of Fontainebleau I became engaged to marry Eleanora.' There are no further entries until the entry of two sentences on 3 August: 'At 11 A.M. on this day, at Caniel, my engagement to Eleanora was broken off. In the meantime I had, with the utmost difficulty, finished my novel, *Whom God Hath Joined.*' There are no further journal entries for another three months.

The rest of the affair as described by Bennett appears in his letters, one of them printed in this volume, the others in Volumes I and II. On 20 June he writes to thank James Pinker his literary agent for his 'kind and sagacious letter', presumably about the engagement, and goes on to say, 'I do not often give vent to my feelings, but I am in a highly emotional state just now, & I use the chance to tell you what I think. Pinker, I will write you some *books* in the future!' On 21 June he writes to thank Emily and Eden Phillpotts for their letters of congratulation. 'Your letters gave me the keenest pleasure, & Eléonora also.... I may tell you that this courtship has been rather violent. Eléonora is recovering with her mother in the country, & I have been near collapse. One doesn't know what one has been through till afterwards.... I hope to marry in October.' On the same date he writes to Violet Hunt to say that he owes much of his success in the courtship to Agnes Farley and that he has been 'tasting the extremely mixed sensations of love, honestly for the first time in my life'. On 29 June he informs Wells of the engagement, gives Eleanor's age, and says that she has spent most of her life in Paris. A few days later he writes to

Wells again to say that he has read parts of Wells's reply to Eleanor, and he says that he and she plan to marry at the registry office in Folkestone, and Eleanor will bring a friend over as witness. He asks if he and she can spend a few days with the Wellses in order to meet the residency requirement. On 9 July he writes to his brother Frank (p. 13) to describe reading parts of *Whom God Hath Joined* to Eleanor and to say that the first introduction to a member of his family, Tertia, has taken place.

Then there is nothing until a brief note to Wells on 4 August. 'My engagement exists no longer. Can't write to you about it now, but it's right bang off, anyhow.' Then he writes to Pinker again, on the 7th or 14th, implying that he himself broke the engagement.

A great calamity has overtaken me, & it is a good thing my book is done. I had made all arrangements for my marriage, taken a flat, bought a lot of furniture, and accepted various responsibilities, & given up my old flat, and now my engagement is broken off. A piece of pure ill-luck—or perhaps good-luck—who knows? Anyhow I had no alternative but to bring the affair to a sudden & definite end.

Lastly, at about the same time, he wrote twice to Violet Hunt.

Her feelings, violent enough at one time, did not ultimately justify marriage. Rather desolating, isn't it? However, such is life.... I am up here on the Moor with Eden Phillpotts & his wife.

I may tell you that in spite of everything I wouldn't blot out the last six months even if I could. I knew a devil of a lot about women before. I know more now, & I have never yet bought knowledge too dearly. Besides that, I know more about myself, & can write infinitely better books. And I am a writer first; all the rest comes afterwards.

It is clear that the affair meant a great deal to him, clear that the break was very hurtful—regardless of who made it. No doubt he stammered in the final scene. Dorothy Cheston Bennett, who was not a reliable reporter about him, said that he bore the scar for the rest of his life. He himself reported in October 1906 (*Journals 1971*) that by mental discipline he recovered from the affair in six weeks. What seems certain is that he did not fall romantically in love again until he met Dorothy in 1922.

3. MARGUERITE

Marguerite Soulié came into Bennett's life as a prospective secretary. So she herself described their meeting. But she came better prepared to be his mistress, and he needed a mistress more than he needed a secretary. In less than a month he was setting up a lover–mistress relationship in a most formal way, but it took him another five years to hire a genuine secretary.

George and Jean Beardmore have told the tale of Marguerite's origins and background in *Arnold Bennett in Love*. She was born Marie Marguerite Soulié on 17 September 1874 in Negrepelisse in the south-west of France. The Soulié family in the district were well off, and her father, Jean, was a baker. He made a small fortune on the side with the invention of a stove, but lost the fortune and then deserted the family. Her mother, Juliette, is described on pp. 96, 103. Marguerite was educated at a convent-school in Toulouse, and at an early age she began sewing in a dressmaker's workshop in St Antonin. Presently she became a companion to a woman with homes in Paris and Luchon in the Pyrenees, but had difficulties with the husband and returned to the shop. Then she became a model and a seller in a fashion-house in Paris, and she left that job to go to England for an uncertain time, first as a governess in Suffolk, later as a teacher of French at a girls' school in Richmond, Surrey. She returned to Paris, and at some point opened a dress-shop with her aunt, Hélène Bion, and at another point worked in a fashion-house in the rue de la Paix.

She then became the mistress of a law student. He came of a moneyed family, and he kept her for three years. Then he died. Bennett records the sequel in *Journals 1971* for 24 April 1907, by which time she was well established as his own mistress.

How she saw nothing but the path to the cemetery for months. How his family left her to starve, giving her, after a long delay, 2,000 francs. How other women came to her & instead of sympathising, said: 'You must expect to lose your lover. That might happen to anyone. Why not to you?' Etc. And how they were secretly vexed when she retained her *chic* and got onto her feet again.

Her recovery meant in part going to a school of elocution to train to become an actress. Whether she had any career as an

actress is uncertain, but at the elocution school she met Blanche
Albane, who later married the novelist Georges Duhamel, and
through her she was introduced into Parisian literary and
artistic circles and met people who knew Bennett. One of these
people was M. D. Calvocoressi, critic, writer on music, and
linguist, and it was he who recommended her to Bennett.

The first meeting occurred at Bennett's flat on 16 January
1907. He recorded it in *Journals 1971*, using the form Solié that
she used at the time.

> When Mddle Solié called to see me today she sat after tea on the
> end of the chaise longue. 'Won't you find an easier seat?' I suggested
> to her. 'No', she said, 'I prefer uncomfortable seats. Besides, it gives
> one a feeling of liberty. One is more at one's ease.'

Three days later he noted a fragment of her conversation
concerning an acting job that she had refused. On the 21st they
dined together at a restaurant where, as *Journals 1971* says, 'We
recounted to each other our chagrins. Hers appeared to me
much worse than mine.' It seems clear that sexual intimacy
occurred within the first two weeks of their meeting, for on 1
February he went away to San Remo for two months to write
The Statue with Eden Phillpotts, and on 15 February, in
response to a letter from her, he set forth his credentials as a
reliable lover (p. 16).

Nothing in his letters or journals of the time suggests great
passion or great love. Nevertheless, it was 'une affaire qui me
plait infiniment'. She was a woman of character, intelligence,
and handsome appearance. She could be exceedingly agreeable
in a feminine, sexual way—no woman more so to him, as he
remarked to Dorothy many years later (p. 445). Doubtless, in
the months of courtship and early marriage she exerted her
charms to the full. And she was well enough experienced
sexually to accommodate and enjoy the variety of Bennett's
sexual interests—as Dorothy at the age of 33 was not (p. 424).

April and May were the crucial time in which the mistress
showed her possibilities as a wife. On 12 April Bennett had his
unpleasant sexual encounter with May Elliott at his flat. On
the following Monday, the 15th, he had her there again to talk
with her. On the 16th he took Marguerite to Les Sablons, where
they stayed until the 21st, and then they returned together to

his flat, where Marguerite remained for another two weeks. On the 25th he, and possibly she, dined at the Ullmans, where he became ill. Three subsequent *Journals 1971* entries tell the tale.

Friday 3 May. Marguerite nursed me all the time, and not once has that creature (who is clearly a born nurse) made a gesture or used a tone that grated on my nerves. This is one of the most wonderful things that ever happened to me.

Tuesday 7 May. Marguerite departed yesterday, after 3 weeks, including my illness. I felt like a widower; and that ten years would elapse before Wednesday.

Sunday 12 May. Les Sablons. I came down . . . with Marguerite. . . . If I had simple, narrow tastes, what an ideal existence I could live down here with this ideal mistress.*

Bennett seems not to have realized immediately how deeply he was involved. A *Journals 1971* entry of 27 May merely records how deeply Marguerite felt involved.

One thing she said the other day rather surprised me: 'Now that I belong absolutely to you, and my decision is final, and I am full of happiness and security, still I feel a little sad. I do not regret my decision—very far from that—but it seems to me that my life is over. . . .' This is exactly the sentiment men have on the morrow of even a happy marriage. . . .

But perhaps he saw his situation as soon as he wrote his words. On 4 June he wrote: 'On Friday last [i.e. 31 May] I decided I would marry M. That is to say I openly decided. I had decided, without admitting to myself that I had done so, several days before.' His decision involved asking his Parisian friend Émile Martin whether he thought Marguerite was suitable, and he got yes for an answer. In *Arnold Bennett, A Last Word* Frank

---

* That the nearly ideal existence had another side to it is suggested by an entry in a cashbook that Bennett kept for the year. The entry is from 21 May, and it has been mistakenly thought to be a journal entry, but it is clearly a notation for a story. Nevertheless the story presumably drew to a degree from personal experience. The entry reads in part: 'When I take you in my arms I am not there. I always think of other things, & even of nothing. I am preoccupied. I want to love. No I do not want to love. I have a slight scorn for love. I can't give myself up to it completely. I should be rather ashamed of myself if I did. Yes, disdain for a whole-hearted love, as something silly, or rather infantile. It would rob me of my egoism. Nevertheless I want you there. I enjoy your gestures, your grace, your love, your passion. . . . I only lend myself, in a dream. I must be free to think, to observe, to work. . . .'

Swinnerton recalls the proposal as described to him by Bennett several years later.

Bennett said in his abrupt way: 'Do you know what my friends are telling me? They are saying I ought to marry you.' Marguerite's response . . . was: 'Oh, don't dazzle me with such a prospect if you are not serious.'

In *My Arnold Bennett* Marguerite provides further detail.

He himself told me that his friend's opinion of me was high, that he valued his opinion and that, together with his own conclusions about me, he had made certain that I was the wife for him.

'You are wrong,' I had said, 'I am so thoroughly French you will not be happy with me.'

'It might be you who might not be with me!'

When this dialogue took place we were both in love with each other and we decided to marry.

Perhaps on this point, if not elsewhere, the two memoirs are reliable enough.

The letters in this volume tell the story of the marriage, and little more need be said here. It is evident enough from both letters and journals that for some years Bennett was very happy with Marguerite. The first fourteen months of their marriage saw the writing of *The Old Wives' Tale*, *Buried Alive*, *The Human Machine*, and much else. Even when the marriage was moving towards breakdown, he retained strong affection, sexual interest, and admiration. He was not a person to commit himself lightly, or to withdraw commitment lightly, either on the moral or on the emotional plane. Once when he was away for some weeks in 1913, Marguerite suggested that he indulge himself sexually with a woman. He replied (p. 113) that he was 'the slave of one woman'. Not until 1920 does he give attention to other women that could be called culpable from a strict standpoint. There is no evidence that he was ever unfaithful in a technical sense. When Reginald Pound was writing his biography, Dorothy tried to persuade him to her own understanding of the marriage. She quoted Bennett as having said to her, 'There was never anything in it for me after the first year— or few months . . .; I stuck it for 14 years.' No doubt there was much sticking it, for Marguerite was egotistical, volatile, and intemperate; but there was much sticking it as well with Dorothy, who was a similar sort of woman. In 1925 Bennett wrote to his nephew Richard, then aged 24: 'You "must have women—they unbend the mind". Of course also you have to "stick it". That is part of the business' (p. 482).

He and Marguerite had no children. The reason is not known. Two letters suggest answers, but they are contradictory and unclear. In the first (p. 62), four and a third years after marriage, Bennett says that his chief reservation about having children has been the fear that he and Marguerite are too radically opposed in their views on bringing up children. Her conduct with Richard has delighted him, and he withdraws his reservation. There is a possible implication that Marguerite herself has not wanted to have children for reasons of health. Then in 1917, when the marriage is unhappy, there are recriminations about the absence of children. Bennett writes (p. 198) that he has never hitherto mentioned his fundamental objection to having children, namely the history of mental disorder in both his and her families. He recalls that when he did accede to her desire to have children she herself then refused.

The subject was discussed publicly after his death. In January 1933 Dorothy wrote an article for the *Sunday Chronicle* about her life with him, and asserted in it that he was 'a born father'. She had borne his child out of wedlock (Marguerite having refused divorce); she had not been welcomed by his family, some of whom thought she had got herself pregnant to secure Bennett's attachment; and she had been dropped by his friends after his death. The phrase 'born father' must have been salve to her conscience and ego; it must have been meant to give offence to her enemies—just as did her subtitle to her book on Bennett, *A Portrait Done at Home*. One of the enemies replied in the *Chronicle* the following week. Fanny Gertrude Bennett was a truculent, moralistic woman. She detested Dorothy, and detested much else in Bennett's life. In her reply she rejected Dorothy's claim, and recalled a conversation with Bennett and Marguerite just before the War. The conversation suggests her truculence, but it does not clearly suggest Bennett's reciprocal dislike of her. He may have suited his words to the occasion—assuming accuracy in the report of them.

With proper Five Towns outrightness, I turned to Arnold, saying, 'Well, you seem now to have almost everything life can give you—wealth, fame, a lovely home, and the wife of your choice. Almost everything.'

'What more would you wish me, sweet sister?' (This was his particular name for me.)

'You have no children,' was 'sweet sister's' reply.

'Children!' said Arnold, 'True, true, I have no children. I have no use for them. They do not enter my horizon, for they upset the easy running of a household. . . .'

Bennett then withdrew from the scene, and Fanny Gertrude was left with Marguerite, who among her other qualities possessed talents for self-pity and for making up facts as she went along.

Later . . . his wife spoke to me in heartfelt tones of her wish for children . . . and of Arnold's refusal. 'He warned me before our marriage,' she said, 'and now, therefore, I cannot complain. Alas!'

What does seem certain from the letters in this volume is that Bennett was immensely pleased (if worried) when Dorothy became pregnant and that he was an affectionate father to Virginia. In his memoir Frank Swinnerton notes that he saw Bennett and Virginia together on a number of occasions. 'The understanding between them was amusingly notable. Virginia sat on his knee, and sometimes jogged his elbow, as he wrote; and Bennett insisted that her supposed naughtiness was natural and a sign of strong character.'

4. DOROTHY

Dorothy Muriel Cheston traced her ancestry back to the Chestons of Mildenhall, East Anglia, in the sixteenth century. Her father, Chester Cheston, trained as an architect, and became estate agent to Lord Amhurst in East London and elsewhere. Her mother was Amelia, née Coppen. She was born on 31 August 1891 at Summit House, Clapton Common, London, much the youngest of four children. Her brother Harry became a naval officer. Her brother Charles became a painter; he was made a vice president of the Royal Water-Colour Society in 1950. Her sister Gladys is described briefly and unflatteringly by Bennett (p. 605).

In her memoir, *Arnold Bennett, A Portrait Done at Home*, Dorothy gives glimpses of her youth. She lived in a large house, with many servants and haphazard order. She was a lonely child, but she was close to her father, and she describes breakfasts alone with him when she was between 9 and 12 years of age. She received part of her education at Queen's College, Harley Street, and at some point studied the piano. She lacked interest in domestic and social matters, and as a girl and young woman she rebelled against home and society, especially with regard to the role of women as commodities to be sold on the marriage market. At the age of 18 she thought that in an ideal marriage husband and wife should live apart for the first two years, to avoid settling into the pettiness of domesticity.

Presently she broke away from her family—whether formally or not is unclear—and went first to live in Cornwall. The break seems to have meant that she lived largely or wholly on her own resources for the next fifteen or more years, and that she lived mainly alone, in furnished rooms. It seems probable that fairly soon she turned to acting as a career, for she speaks of having 'toured up and down the world'. In 1915 she was in America. Overall she spent several years there, and became acquainted with J. C. Powys and Theodore Dreiser in New York. Powys was an influence on her life, and Dreiser tried to be.

Theodore Dreiser had lectured me in New York on the subject of my wilful and wrong way of life. Dreiser had described to me very powerfully the 'withering' process which would result from such a way of living, and its final diminishing of the capacity to love at all, or alternatively, ending in a passionate need to cherish cats and parrots.

Her response to Dreiser was to ask what was to be done if one did not love.

She met Bennett on 8 March 1922 in Liverpool, where she was playing one of the two female leads in his play *Body and Soul*. She had read his books and had found wisdom in them, and she and Powys had argued about his merits. A year earlier, on 6 March 1921, she had performed in a playlet at a party at Mrs Ralph Hammersley's. Bennett was there, and reported in his journal that party, playlets, and food were good, and that there was dancing afterwards: 'All was for the best at this party.' At Liverpool there was a supper in honour of Bennett after the performance, and before the guests sat down to it Dorothy was introduced to him, and he said to his hosts that he would be very much hurt if Dorothy Cheston and the other lead, Viola Lyel, did not sit with him. So Dorothy sat beside him and talked about Dreiser and Dostoevsky. Bennett admired Dreiser, and Dorothy could tell him that one day in New York Powys had showed her a telegram just received from 'Bennett and Wells' to protest against an action to suppress *The Genius*. She also talked about theatre. '"The theatre is a gloomy subject," he said—giving very nearly three o's to gloomy—"And, you know, it always makes me *feel* gloomy." ' Thus the relationship began. It moved slowly for several months, not, apparently, for lack of interest on Bennett's part, but perhaps through plans already made that kept him in London or on his yacht for much of the time.

What sort of woman was she? She was generally accounted to be beautiful. She was blonde and had an extraordinarily fine complexion. Bennett described her to his sister Tertia and to H. G. Wells as 'a hefty wench', and Richard Bennett in an unbuttoned moment many years later said she was 'a magnificent specimen of humanity'. Richard shared the family dislike of her, and also called her a 'bloody bitch'—'the B.B.D.C.B.'. That dislike seems to have encouraged tales that her beauty could lend credence to: that she was Beaverbrook's mistress before she became Bennett's, that even as Bennett lay dying she was casting about for another generous man. There is no substantial evidence to support such tales. In one letter here (p. 495) Bennett alludes to her suggestion that she take a second lover, but in all probability it was a rash fancy, designed to hurt his feelings. Her life after Bennett's death seems to have been as lonely as her life before him.

She had abundant energy and subtle intelligence, and she impressed Bennett and other people with them. One need only compare her memoir with Marguerite's two slim volumes to see how much more interesting her mind was. Unluckily both energy and intelligence lacked sustained control except by egotism. Had her letters to Bennett survived, they would be seen to be four or five times longer than his, with scrawlings up and down all margins, with heavy underlinings and many cross-outs, looking a great mess but nevertheless interesting.

She had read Freud and Jung, and above all else she was interested in nuance, and she analysed character, motive, and action at Jamesian length. On one occasion in later life she wrote a 9,000-word letter to Frank Swinnerton mainly to set him straight on a single sentence in his introduction to the 1971 Penguin edition of the *Journals*.

Her nuances too often developed into flights of fancy, coloured here and there with fact. One of the flights was a theory about the meaning of Shakespeare's plays. The major flight, which preoccupied her for many years, concerned Bennett's death-wish. She did not suppose that everyone had a death-wish, nor did she suppose that to end *The Old Wives' Tale* and *Lord Raingo* with death was necessarily to betray a death-wish, nor did she think it unreasonable for a man whose father died in mental decay in his early sixties to feel apprehensive in approaching the same age. What she saw in Bennett was a special self-destructive urge that took hold of him and led him to rash actions and indeed to his death. She, with her superior perception of hidden forces, understood what was going on, and she tried to save him.

The outline of this fancy is in the memoir, where in the second chapter she says:

I am writing of the drama which for eight years I saw unfold, and of the fateful essences that were contained in the very composition of that drama's heroic principal character. To me it always seemed inevitable—for I came up against the workings behind the scenes—that under the strain of his existence he must be destroyed. All those eight years I lived with a sense of impending death. . . . The sense of death's nearness left me after Arnold died.

She alludes later to his apprehension that he might die in the same way as his father, and sees him in such thoughts as 'a man living in a peculiar hell of twisted spun glass'. Her major evidence concerns three episodes: of his gambling with utter recklessness at Le Touquet, of his determination to retain their new flat at Chiltern Court even though it was damaging their health, and of his insisting upon drinking unsafe water in Paris and so contracting the typhoid fever that killed him. Bennett did gamble, not very often, in an amused, detached way, and he wrote an engaging little essay on its compulsions and vanities

('Monte', reprinted in *Sketches for Autobiography*). Something of his attitude towards the sport can be seen on pp. 253, 322, and 566. His satisfaction with Chiltern Court is evident on pp. 607–8 and 609–10. As for the unsafe water, other people offered another first cause of Bennett's death: Dorothy herself (pp. 617–18).

It is clear that she was an exceedingly difficult woman to live with. Frank Swinnerton argues in his memoir that Bennett came back from Paris in 1931 convinced that he would have to separate from her. Swinnerton admits that his evidence is uncertain, but he drew it from things said by Bennett's secretary, Winifred Nerney, a shrewd and sensible woman who knew the domestic scene intimately. The letters, though, seem to say that in spite of all difficulty Bennett remained deeply in love with Dorothy. Right up to the final minute before Marguerite's choice of separation and Legros, he had been willing to take her back and continue with the marriage. Would he have been less honourable, less generous with Dorothy? Would he have countenanced breaking up the home of the child to whom he was devoted? He seems too much the family man for such action.

5. OUR WOMEN

There were those who knew that Bennett chose his wives badly. There were others who knew the sort of woman he should have married—reasonable, orderly, selfless—like Winifred Nerney, to whom he once wrote (p. 318 n.), 'You understand that my feelings towards you are not precisely cold.' There were others (George and Jean Beardmore) who understood his dilemma with fixed psychological insight: 'he could only enjoy sexual freedom with women of the theatre'. Still others realized that he was a born bachelor. There is modest truth in all these views.

In proposing his lover–mistress relationship to Marguerite in 1907, Bennett said that he was in part a solitary man. The greater portion of every day went to writing—in a long morning before and after breakfast, often in the afternoon, sometimes in the middle of the night. When he was not writing he might be reading. At other times he liked society, disliked solitude, and much of the society he liked was male. He was interested in

politics, business, industry, law, power; and these domains
were almost exclusively male. When after a year or two of
intense strain he broke with Marguerite, he felt intense relief to
have his bachelor freedom. It must have called to mind his
years until the age of 39 when he was unimpelled by love or
sexual need to bind himself to one woman.

So much for Bennett the bachelor. There is an amusing
moment in his play *The Honeymoon* in which the beautiful bride
acknowledges to the ambitious bridegroom the unimportance
of women compared with men. He is a famous aviator, and he
wants to abandon the honeymoon in order to be the first man to
fly over Snowdon and beat out a German (the time being 1909).

I fully admit that if Hyde Park were full of aviators and Battersea
Park were full of charming young women, rather pretty and—er—
chic [gesture to show off her frock]—I fully admit that not a man
among you would *dream*—of crossing the river. I fully admit that if
every aviator in Europe gave up business tomorrow the entire world
would go into mourning, whereas if all the charming women retired
from business they'd never be missed. Still—

The importance of women to Bennett is evident in the many
volumes of his novels, plays, short stories, and essays. Think of
his early novels about women—*Anna of the Five Towns*, *Leonora*,
Sacred and Profane Love—that lead up to his major novel about
women, *The Old Wives' Tale*. Think that his other major work,
the Clayhanger trilogy, gives one book to Edwin, one to Hilda,
and one to their joint lives. The greater emphasis is given to
Edwin; nevertheless he is a man in love. Think that the last
major novel, *Imperial Palace*, concerns Evelyn Orcham's conflict
between love and work, love represented spectacularly by
Gracie Savott who is drawn after Dorothy, with the conflict
resolved by Evelyn's abandoning her but only because in
choosing work he can have Violet Powler with it, a woman of
the Nerney sort. Sex and love between men and women are the
dominant themes of the novels, and of his writing generally,
and the focus is upon women to a high degree. That supposed
lack of sex in the novels refers to a convention of his time and of
his literary style. His novel *The Pretty Lady*, whose leading
character is a prostitute, seemed indecent and corrupt to some
people, and attempts were made to suppress it (see Volumes I

and III). For that matter he did write some portion of a pornographic novel (p. 523).

Of special interest is a small book he wrote in 1919 entitled *Our Women*. Some of his views in it are not likely to do him credit in certain quarters in the 1980s. He thinks that women are less rational than men and more emotional, less progressive and more cautious, less possessed of humour and wit and more tenacious, and so forth. He thinks that no theory of suppression will account for female failure to achieve greatness comparable to men in philosophy, science, painting, music, sculpture, and literature.

The truth is that intellectually and creatively man is the superior of woman, and that in the region of creative intellect there are things which men almost habitually do but which women have not done and give practically no sign of ever being able to do.

Small wonder that he enjoyed his luncheons with his brilliant male friends. On the other hand, he thinks that every girl ought to be taught to earn her living and that every wife ought by right and by law to own a share of the family income even if the income is technically earned only by the husband. He sees that female economic independence will transform women and transform the relations between the sexes. The idle woman, the helpless woman, the sheltered woman, the ornamental woman, the deferential woman, the ignorant woman will cease to preoccupy the ideal imaginings of either sex.

At the outset of the book he acknowledges that his views and evidence are partial.

I adore 'particulars' and consider that one 'particular' is quite sufficient material for so abstract and poor a thing as a 'general'. I dare say that I hold the record for the long jump to conclusions. I live by impressions and emotions. I am not averse from prejudices when they suit my enterprise. If conviction for inaccuracy involved penal servitude I should have passed my whole existence in prison. I have no exact knowledge on any subject whatever.

His partial material exists within the framework of two opposed beliefs he holds. For the first he quotes Lady Mary Wortley Montagu: 'I have never in all my various travels seen but two sorts of people, and they very like one another: I mean men and women.' The second belief is that the discord between the sexes is 'fundamental and eternal'; it can change its form, improve its quality, but it will not disappear.

And who wants the sex-discord to be resolved? The sex-discord may be the most exasperating thing in existence, but it is by general agreement the most delightful and the most interesting.

Of course in the end Bennett must be judged by the attitudes he took rather than by the attitudes he professed. There are aspects of his letters to Marguerite and Dorothy (not least 'mon enfant', 'petlet', and 'fawn' of his addresses to them) that contradict the advanced views in *Our Women*. At one time or another both Marguerite and Dorothy took offence at such language. But set aside the offence, or even allow the most extreme bias and impercipience: the point is that he was preoccupied with women. One person, Mrs Belloc Lowndes, went against the common view and said that he was sex-obsessed. He would have admitted the charge. (In 1925, when he was 58 years old, and Dorothy just 34, he wrote to her, 'I suppose that my desire is about six times, or more, as frequent as yours.' Page 476.) In his obsession what did he want for a wife? Someone as like himself as possible, sane, detached, orderly? It does not seem so. Rather he wanted unlike, unknown: female beauty, female excitement, female discord. And what more probable place to find them than on or near the stage (even though he once said that as a rule he did not like actresses)? It is impossible to imagine that he regretted his choices: 'I wouldn't blot out the last six months even if I could.'

Yet no view of him avoids distortion. Give those who thought he was inhibited their due. In his *Journals*, ten months after marriage to Marguerite, he writes:

> I see that at bottom I have an intellectual scorn, or the scorn of an intellectual man, for all sexual–physical manifestations. They seem childish to me, unnecessary symptoms and symbols of a spiritual phenomenon.

And just as he is touching bottom he adds a contradiction: 'Yet few Englishmen could be more perversely curious and adventurous than I am in just those manifestations.' The last word must be contradictory too, or perhaps it explains everything. He wrote to an American woman in 1911, just as he was returning from America: 'I am partly a woman, à mes heures'.

In 1899 Arnold Bennett was 32, with an uncertain literary career ahead of him. Ten years earlier he had left the Potteries to come to London to work in a solicitor's office and in his spare time to write paragraphs and occasional stories for the popular press. In 1894 he joined the staff of Woman, *a lively weekly journal, and in 1896 he became editor. He wrote book and theatre reviews, fashion articles, and sentimental and sensational stories for* Woman *and for other journals, and occasionally, on the side, he wrote serious fiction such as 'A Letter Home', published in the* Yellow Book *in 1895 and* A Man from the North, *published by John Lane in 1898. Both story and novel made favourable impressions upon literary London, and they encouraged his serious intentions. But they did not make money; and if he was to abandon the editorial office, the way seemed to lie with popular fiction. To that end he wrote two sensational novels,* The Ghost *and* The Gates of Wrath, *the first in late 1898, the second in the summer of 1899.*

One of the chief encouragers of his ambitions was Eden Phillpotts, five years his senior and already a successful author of both popular and serious novels. The two men met in 1897 and presently became friends. During the next decade they wrote several plays and novels in collaboration. The first letter reprinted here was written from Phillpotts' home, where Bennett was staying for a weekend. The recipient of the letter, May Beardmore (1878–1945) was a young friend in the Five Towns, daughter of John Beardmore, a close friend of Bennett's father. John Beardmore was an ironmonger in the firm of Pidduck and Beardmore of the Market-place, Burslem. May's brother Frank married Bennett's sister Fanny Gertrude. May was a bright woman, and Bennett often sent her his books for criticism.

ELDIN / MS / 1
(*To May Beardmore*)   Cosdonne
                                                        Torquay
                                                        30 Oct 99

My dear May,

Your 21st birthday may have passed; I never could get any precise information as to the day; but do not imagine that I have forgotten it. Indeed I lay awake thinking in the night what I could say to you of an inspiring nature. I asked Eden Phillpotts this morning whether he could give me any hints as to what to say to a woman of 21, & he offered me Marcus Aurelius. I said that wouldn't do. He said, 'Is she beautiful?' I said: 'Divinely.' 'Then' he said 'begin by telling her so, & then follow your instincts.'

However, I find I haven't any instincts to follow. I wish you a long life, continuance of beauty, ever-increasing tidiness, and contentment, and an energy which will enable you to go to bed every night with the feeling that you have exhausted yourself in the day's work. This is the best I can do for you. As for happiness, very few people are happy & they wouldn't be happy if they were. (This is bad English, but I love to make errors in letters; it is such a relief from the 'company manners' which one has to practise in articles.) I have at home for you certain volumes which will be forwarded on Wednesday. I am just going out now with Phillpotts to a village about 3 miles off which is to be the scene of his next novel but one. I perceive more & more that the life of a successful novelist, though it is a strain, has immense advantages. The hours are short, for one thing. We write *The Pagan* (which is to succeed *Children of the Mist*) only between 11 & 1 in the morning, & another 1 or 1½ hours at odd things completes our day's work—except thinking. We have a huge house, a charming wife, two children, simple tastes & an ample supply of money. And when critics from London come down to see us we give ourselves up entirely to recreation.

I can see myself in this role with much satisfaction.

Kindest regards to all, & to the Poker Club, & Porthill; & to yourself best wishes.

Yours, E.A.B.

P.S. I won't come in, I shall mess your clean steps.

1. For letters and other references to the Phillpottses—Emily, d. 1928; Eden, 1862–1960; Adelaide, b. 1896; Henry, 1895–1976—see the other volumes. Phillpotts published *Children of the Mist* in 1898. *The Pagan* became *Sons of the Morning*, 1900. In 1900 he and Bennett dramatized the former novel. In September 1900 Bennett resigned his editorship of *Woman*, and went to live at Trinity Hall Farm in Bedfordshire, and henceforward earned his living by his pen.

Porthill: presumably Porthill House, home of the William Wood family. Members of the Bennett, Beardmore, and Wood families were close friends. Porthill was the district outside Stoke-on-Trent where the Beardmores lived.

ELDIN / MS / 2
(*To May Beardmore*)

9, Fulham Park Gardens
17 Augt 1900

Dear May,

To acknowledge your sweet & brilliant note. We are having rather a various time. William has just been in to get me to draw up a will for Thomas Smith (I don't know if you know him, but Tertia does—Art master) who may or may not be alive tomorrow morning. William is staying for a meal here. Smith's collapse is due to overwork, against which he has been warned for years. Let this be a lesson to you. I have drawn the will. Also I have just been upstairs where (with Pa's assistance) Sep is doing a mighty fine equestrian statuette of Joan of Arc on a most rampageous horse. It really is excellent. His sculpture, which did *not* win the scholarship, came back yesterday. It is fine work. Sep wants to become a sculptor, & I fancy he may actually make a splash in time. Anyhow his work gives me much satisfaction. By the way, if Sep *does* come to Llanfair etc, it will be due to my persistent advocacy. At first he said he couldn't wouldn't & shouldn't, & Pa opened not his mouth. I have jawed it out at every meal, & this morning I think it was settled that he should go. He is hard up. Tomorrow morning I am going down to Sandgate to spend the weekend with H.G. Wells & Catherine his wife. To this I am looking forward. There are only two things I should like as well—to go to

Llanfair etc, & to see the portraits of Mrs. Bourne, Amy, &
Marion Longson in the *Methodist Recorder*, where, I am told,
they are veritably to be seen. Tonight after supper I go to play
through the third act of *Die Meistersinger* with Dr. Farrar. I
expect I shall get home about 1 a.m. We are having good meals
from Emily: that is a blessing; but she is very cross with the
laundry. I spent 1½ hours last night with Mrs. Pet going
through a short story which she has written, a most pleasing
period for both of us, as you can guess. Ma is well, but she is
inclined towards pessimism for some reason or other. Possibly
it is the amount of the rent of Mr. & Mrs. Pet's new flat that has
started her. She says Pa is 'low', & that it is Auntie Sarah's
birthday tomorrow & no one has written to her (but I had, by
pure chance) & the cast-off furniture at 205 won't fetch so much
money now because it is so dirty, & Frank & Florrie will have a
bad passage tonight. (I think they will.) I have written 12,000
words in the first four days of this week, & even now my hand
aches.

You may be interested to know that the region of Llanfair etc
is the region I have in mind for my final house. Alas! 'Time,
which hath an art to make dust of all things,' may make dust of
that too.

With respectful regards to all,

E.A.B.

2. Bennett lived at 9 Fulham Park Gardens from February 1898 to October 1900.
William: William Wood Kennerley (1870–1969). He was courting Tertia, Bennett's
youngest and favourite sister (1872–1949). A Five Towns man, he became a barrister
and worked for the Board of Education.
Pa and Ma: Enoch Bennett (1843–1902) and Sarah Ann Bennett (née Longson,
1840–1914). Enoch Bennett's health failed in 1900, and Bennett took both father and
mother to live with him.
Sep: Septimus Bennett (1876–1926), Bennett's youngest and favourite brother. He
was educated at the Middle School, Newcastle-under-Lyme, and began his career with
J. Marsh of Burslem as an apprentice modeller. He studied at the Burslem School of Art
and then at the Hanley Art School. In the middle nineties he won a national scholarship
to South Kensington, and he studied there with Professor Edouard Lanteri. He began
business as a pottery designer and modeller in London, and returned to Stoke-on-Trent
in 1903. He designed for some of the well-known firms there. His studio was illustrated
and described in the *Pottery Gazette and Glass Trade* some years before 1926.
Llanfair etc: Llanfairfecham. One or another of Bennett's early letters to May
Beardmore was addressed to her there.
H. G. Wells (1867–1946), like Phillpotts, had an earlier literary success than
Bennett. For the Wells–Bennett correspondence see Harris Wilson, ed., *Arnold Bennett
and H. G. Wells*, London 1960, also Vols. II and III of this collection. Included are
letters to Catherine (Jane) Wells (d. 1927).

Mrs Bourne: Frances Edna, née Longson (d. 1913), Bennett's maternal aunt, married to Ezra Bourne; model for Auntie Hamps in the Clayhanger trilogy. Amy Bourne was her stepdaughter. Marion Longson (b. 1882) was the daughter of John Longson (b. 1838), brother of Frances Edna and Sarah Ann. John Longson took over the draper's shop in St John's Square (original of the shop in *The Old Wives' Tale*) from his father Robert. The portraits in the *Methodist Recorder* are apparently to be seen in a group photograph of some twenty-five 'lady assistants in the conference tea-room' of the great Wesleyan conference that began in Burslem on 1 August.

Dr John Farrar: a Yorkshire man who was Bennett's physician at this time.

Emily: Emily Edge, née Bennett (1871–1953), another sister of Bennett's, married to Spencer Edge who was associated with Edge Malkin & Co. (later Malkin Tiles). At this time he was a designer and potter's factor in London. Bennett often referred to Emily as Mrs Pet.

Auntie Sarah: Sarah Barlow, née Bennett (d. 1924), Bennett's paternal aunt.

Frank and Florrie: Francis Clayton Bennett (1868–1938), Bennett's middle brother, and his wife Florence (née Wooldridge). They married in 1899. Frank was a solicitor. He took over his father's law firm.

205: the Bennett family address on Waterloo Road, Cobridge, from 1880. It was now being abandoned.

Bennett was doing a lot of journalism for *Woman, Hearth & Home*, and the *Academy*. He was also rewriting *Anna of the Five Towns*.

KENNERLEY / MS / 3
(*To W. W. Kennerley*)   Trinity Hall Farm
                                          Hockliffe (Bedfordshire)
                                          17th Jan 1902

My dear William,
    The Pater finished his course in perfect quietness at 8:40 last night.

                                          Yours, E.A.B.

3. Trinity Hall Farm, where Bennett lived from October 1900 until January 1903, provided the setting for his novel *Teresa of Watling Street*. An article by Simon Houfe in the *Bedfordshire Magazine*, summer 1970, describes his life there in interesting detail.

When Darius Clayhanger dies in *Clayhanger*, son Edwin writes to Big James, 'My father died quietly at eight o'clock tonight.' The detailed description of Darius's rapid mental and physical decline is usually taken to be an accurate description of Enoch Bennett's decline. It involves depression, silence, tears, inability to feed or dress himself, and bizarre plans such as growing mushrooms in the cellar. At the end he develops the paroxysms of Cheyne–Stokes breathing. In his journal in 1897 Bennett says that for the first time he has noticed signs of ageing in his father. By 1900 he is writing to George Sturt (Vol. II), 'My father's health . . . will gradually get worse till he loses all his faculties and dies.'

For many years within the family there was talk of an inherited streak of insanity or severe mental trouble, and Bennett himself may have feared it (see pp. 198 and 443). Emily was certainly eccentric, Fanny Gertrude had senile dementia, and there were troubles in the next generation. Dudley Barker in *Writer by Trade* implies that Enoch suffered from general paralysis of the insane. G. D. Perkin, consultant neurologist at Charing Cross Hospital (Fulham), suggests that there is little evidence to support either the family fear or the Barker diagnosis. He suggests Pick's Disease instead, which might or might not be a familial disorder. (*British Medical Journal*, December 1981.)

On the memorial card sent to Kennerley, Bennett quoted *Antony and Cleopatra*: 'The miserable change now at my end / Lament nor sorrow at; but please your thoughts / In feeding them with those my former fortunes / Wherein I lived.' On other memorial cards he quoted the Bible: 'In a little wrath I hid my face from thee for a moment: but with everlasting kindness will I have mercy on thee.'

Bennett describes his father in his essay 'The Making of Me' (reprinted in *Sketches for Autobiography*):

My father began, and failed, as a pottery manufacturer. Then he took to pawnbroking, and cared not for it.... My father was ambitious. At the age of nearly thirty, he did what to me has always seemed a marvellous thing—he decided to become a solicitor, and at the age of thirty-four he became one and set up practice in the Potteries.... Beyond doubt my father's influence was the main factor in making a home in which the 'humanities' flourished more brightly than in any other home of my acquaintance.

KENNERLEY / MS / 4
(*To W. W. Kennerley*)

Trinity Hall Farm
8 April 1902

My dear William,

I could write an article about this, but not a letter. See? I experience a feeling of profound satisfaction, & that is the end of it, in words. These upheaving affairs, of which the importance & beauty can only be slowly ingurgitated, leave me dumb for about a month, & then I begin to chirrup. And me only a spectator! Two people could scarcely be more at variance in temperament & ideals than you & me or Tertia & me. But the longer I live the less I think of temperament, ideals, intellect, & the more I think of one quality, which we all three possess & which I will name to you in due course.

Yours, E.A.B.

P.S. I perceive that owing to this abduction & rapine I shall be under the necessity of starting life afresh, before the century is much older. The mater will certainly return to the native heath. This aspect of the case may not have presented itself to you as vitally important, but to me it has a certain faint interest. I shall have about 5 times as much money as is good for me & no one to spend it on except your brother-in-law. However, don't mind me. Gather your roses.

4. Kennerley's father was from Cheshire, and married into the Wood family of the

Potteries, where William himself grew up. He and Bennett were friends in the nineties if not before, and he was with Bennett in France in 1897 when Bennett learned of the death of Tertia's fiancé (see the *Journals*). He studied science and art at London University and was called to the Bar in 1904. He belonged to the circle of friends in London who gathered for musical evenings. Bennett wrote a series of 'Biographies of the Great' about them. His account of Kennerley reads:

William Wood Kennerley, President of the Court of Appeal, was born, with a caul, on the Judicial Bench in 1870. He has never left it, except to take his daily walk under the Mimosa trees in the forecourt of Solomon's Temple. At the age of three months, upon the close of the Franco-Prussian war, he was consulted by both parties as to the amount of indemnity which ought to be paid by France to Germany. He replied, on Science and Art paper, that it was a nice question, and returned thoughtfully to his bottle. He studied balance under Cinquevalli, who advised him to part his hair in the middle. He thenceforth made a practice of doing so, with the result that his decisions are never reversed on appeal—a consummation which he assists by his invariable custom of reserving judgment *sine die*. His naturally fine presence is slightly marred by the bulging of his clothes, due to a prudent habit of carrying *pros* in one pocket and *cons* in the other. On this account he is sometimes called the pro-consul. He spends the Long Vacation partly in passing exams—on the other side of the street—and partly in superintending other people's honeymoons. His chief title of fame is his discovery of the Law of Gravity.... His motto is: 'Least said soonest mended, but when I ope my lips let no dog bark.' Club: A.B.C. Authorities: Kant's *Critique of Pure Reason*. Young's *Night Thoughts*. [Young refers in part to Charles Young, one of the group.]

Bennett brought Tertia to London after her fiancé's death. In the *Journals* he describes her arrival there and her coming up to his landlord and friend Frederick Marriott.

As we drove up to 6, Victoria Grove, Marriott came to the front door and stood on the steps. His face was working.

'Well,' Tertia exclaimed, with a desperate pitiful effort at self-control and cheerfulness, 'here I am—bicycle and all.' Marriott burst into tears, but not Tertia. Tertia stayed in London and kept house for Bennett. She may have studied singing there. She wrote stories for *Woman* and *Hearth & Home* for him. Over the years she published three small children's books (see Vol. I). She and Kennerley married on 4 March 1903. Very likely the quality that Bennett thought they all three possessed was strength of character.

STOKE / MS / 5
(*To Sarah Ann Bennett*)   [4, rue de Calais]
                                            [Paris]
                                            [postmarked 10–12–03]
[no salutation]

Here you have a photo of the restaurant where I usually take my lunch. It does not exaggerate the size of it, which is enormous. I always have the same table; it is on the left. I have marked it with a cross. I am working enormously today on my new humorous book.

With love, E.A.B.

5. Bennett left England to live in France in March 1903. From September 1903 until December 1906 he lived at 4, rue de Calais, Paris.

Sarah Ann (Longson) Bennett grew up in Glossop, where the Longsons had lived for three generations. Her family were strict Methodist. Her father kept a draper's and tailor's shop. When she was 20, the family removed to Burslem, and the home and shop there, in St John's Square, became the home and shop in *The Old Wives' Tale*. Something of Sarah Ann's character is seen in that of Constance in the novel. She married Enoch Bennett in 1866, when she was 26 and he 23. She bore him nine children in twelve years. Three died in infancy. In their first years she and Enoch were poor, and she did occasional work for her father. To her children she was S'ran. Bennett describes her in his essay 'The Making of Me'.

My mother during the lifetime of my father was my father's wife. But when he died we immediately discovered that she, too, had a most powerful individuality. She had also the great merit of being 'interested in people'. Her curiosity about them was inexhaustible, detached, and her judgment sound—if harsh. Nearly all her children were great humorists and teasers before the Lord, but she never in her life really saw a joke.

Often at family meals, when we were all adult and independent, I would commit some naughty witticism, and then, seeing her face, would walk round the table and kiss her. This reassured her. She read a lot, but only as most other people read, to pass the time. The mere mention of some of my books at table invariably caused her to play nervously with her bread.

The restaurant was one of the Duval chain, in the rue de Clichy in Paris. Bennett conceived *The Old Wives' Tale* there a few weeks earlier. His *Journals* for 18 November record his seeing a repulsive old woman in the restaurant the previous evening and thinking that she had once been young and attractive. He imagined a sister for her, and imagined contrasting lives for them. See his Preface to *The Old Wives' Tale*. See also his essay 'A Tale of Tyranny' in the collection *Sketches for Autobiography* for an account of his relationship with one of the waitresses.

The humorous novel was *A Great Man*, written from December 1903 to 13 March 1904 (with an interruption of five weeks), and published that May.

STOKE / MS / 6
(*To Sarah Ann Bennett*)

[Aberdeen]
[postmarked 31–8–04]

[no salutation]
/ exhausted, & me particularly. Happily this dinner was excellent. There is an Italian chef. I slept tremendously & woke up with a headache, which is going off. It is a pouring wet day. I am / working all day. The town is rather fine, as it is all built of granite, & looks clean. Granite is cheaper than brick here. But the place does not compare with Glasgow. Like Glasgow & Inverness it is a tremendous place / for churches. Scotland is the land of churches & of quarrels about creeds. We have two pianos in the hotel; one of them is a Chickering Grand. Kindly

ask Frank to buy me a certain Steingräber volume of miscellaneous piano duets, including sundry by Weber that I have
never seen in / any other edition. He will know the book I mean.
I am just told that the weather will clear up, & I think it will.
Anyhow both pianos are good. One can play Chopin on them.
Yes I shall miss my French friend. But it will be a great relief to
me / all the same. I have got into such a state that I often talk
French when I mean to talk English. This is a fact. I can do with
a little calm English society. It was an excellent idea of Auntie
Bourne's to give you a postcard album. / I will soon fill it for
you, & then you can ask her to give you another one. I spend
enormous sums every week in supplying my friends with
postcards. And now you will add to the strain. I trust no other
relations will have albums.

[E.A.B.]

6. Bennett was in Scotland during August in part to have treatment (unsuccessful)
for his stammer. The therapist was M. Berquand, who had treated him in Paris as well.
    The letter is made up of seven postcards, the first missing, all written on the same
day. The first five cards end in mid-sentence, as indicated by the strokes.
    In 'The Making of Me' Bennett describes his Aunt Bourne as possessing 'one of the
most powerful, attractive and formidable personalities I have ever encountered. She
adored me, and burnt my first book in Wesleyan horror'. A letter from Tertia to May
Beardmore tells of a holiday in Aberystwyth in 1907 with Aunt Bourne, 'a perfect
terror', a 'great Ego & doesn't know it'. The letter describes grace before and after each
meal, and a "reading" at the breakfast table.

> The annoying parts are when Auntie insists on its being bed-time for *everybody*—
> not even Ma has strength to oppose her.... We had a very wet morning yesterday,
> 'not fit for *any*one to go out' says Auntie in her tone which means that nobody must
> think of going out.... This afternoon I am going to bathe. I announced it at dinner-
> table—it needed announcing—why, I don't know, only there is a feeling against
> bathing....

    All this subtle nonsense emanates from Auntie Bourne & simply from a notion that
she is representing God. She will keep a tight grip as long as there is a breath in her.

STOKE / MS / 7
(*To Sarah Ann Bennett*)

[4, rue de Calais]
[postmarked 22–9–04]

[no salutation]

   I now begin my series of artistic & topographical postcards
to you. No more coloured prettinesses. And first you will have a
series of 'old Paris' intermingled with reproductions of classical

works of art. I am fairly well, but my stomach has not yet got over London & the restaurants thereof.

With love, E.A.B.

KENNERLEY / MS / 8   Les Sablons
(*To Tertia Kennerley*)   [près Moret]
                                       [S. & M.]
                                       21 Sept 1905

My dear Tertia,

I now have two letters from you in hand, & nothing to reply. Mrs. Ullman announces daily her intention of writing you, but really the exorbitant demands of the baby deprive her of her dearest satisfactions. The amount of time that woman spends in her bedroom, with the shutters closed, even when the baby is out with the nurse, is amazing. Judging from the appearance of the room she must simply muddle about in it, meditatingly. She says she likes being alone, & I can believe her. She is different from me in that. They have now definitely taken a magnificent apartment just off the Champs Elysées, where they expect to receive you. The new regime will certainly cost Ullman père a lot of money. I forget whether you know or not that she is again enceinte—to their mingled astonishment & horror. The dreadful truth *gradually* burst on them. First, when nature refused to take her course, they thought it *might* be but of course it *couldn't* be. Then when nature kept on refusing to take her course, they said: '*Can* it be? No. Nature is simply being obstinate.' Then when the second moon had nearly died they grew gloomy & sent for their Paris doctor, & the fatal verity was officially announced by him. Deep disgust on the part of Ullman. The fact is held to be rather up against *me*. Aghast at the terrific business of parturition & baby-nutrition, Ullman consulted me some months ago as to the various devices of science to prevent a recurrence of these inconveniences, he having a strong objection to the commonest—that which is called French in English & English in French. I poured the accumulated knowledge of a lifetime into his ear, & he departed impressed. Result: another baby. I am full of sympathy with them, but really I can't help laughing whenever I think of this. Mrs. Ullman's facile ingenuity in explaining the thing away also amuses me. Of course to me she doesn't pretend that it is anything but an extremely amazing mischance. But she forgets that Mrs. Devereux has no secrets from me, & she told Mrs. Devereux that they always meant to have two children & thought it best to get over the infancy business as much at one stroke as possible. Mrs. Devereux believed her, & it is greatly to my credit that I have not undeceived Mrs. Devereux.

Ullman has painted a small full-length portrait of Mrs. Devereux, & it is a strikingly distinguished success. He is going to do a life size in the autumn. She has simply taken the Ullmans by storm. They are enchanted with her, & Ullman raves about her handsomeness, at which, really, I was rather surprised—artists are so capricious & unexpected in their likes & dislikes. Ella D'Arcy, who has been down once or twice, objected to meeting Mrs. Devereux; she was sure from what she had heard that she should not like her. However, she too fell an instant victim to those complex charms. Mrs. D'Arcy, whom I asked down here before I had seen her, had a great success here. Lanchester also was a terrific success, & Webster much endeared himself. I wish I could say the same of Rickards. I must say Rickards got himself seriously disliked, by everyone. When I had him alone, on a day when he didn't happen to be in need of apérients, I thought he was finer & maturer than ever. But as a person to eat with twice a day for a fortnight he is right bang off. That fact I am unable any longer to conceal from myself. He is as he was at Hockliffe, quadrupled. I am bound to say it was an eye-opener for me. And when all the people, including Mrs. Devereux, who is as careful as Eden Phillpotts in what she says, put themselves to the trouble of *informing* me that Rickards, though obviously a genius, had no manners and was mainly impossible, I realised that I had made a mistake in thrusting him on strangers. Yet now and then he had immense success with his stories. I have come to the conclusion that I haven't got to show him about in future. It isn't good enough. His old friends must enjoy him on the quiet & suffer him ditto. I have now forced him on the attention of the following people: the Phillpottses, the Wellses, Murray Gilchrist, the Ullmans, Mrs. Devereux, Mrs. Le Gallienne, the Davrays, Doctor Vallée, Emily Symonds, Mrs Rawson, & various respectable young & old women whom you don't know. I think he got on

well with Gilchrist; at any rate he, Rickards, thinks so. Dr.
Vallée regards him as one of the greatest jokes in the world.
Wells's language about him is merely unfit for publication.
Phillpotts got furious & told me such behaviour was inexcus-
able. Ullman is unprintable on the point; Mrs. Ullman vicious;
Mrs. Devereux pained, & surprised at *me*; the rest mildly
inimical. So you see I am not encouraged. As you are to see
Webster soon, you will be able to compare his notes.

The canoe is really a fine success, but I am awaiting a new
paddle from London. You are, with luck, to have a photo of the
craft. We have put a centre board on it, & by keeping one's
hand on the boom of the sail, one can sail it even in a high wind
within ½ an inch of filling it with water. I leave my watch on the
bank, as a second's negligence in a squall would cause the ruin
of the watch. No upsets yet, & I don't expect any now. I began
to work again last Saturday, & so I am now canoodling less. I
have just written the 'Mandarin' short story, & am now half
way through another one, very funny, in which a sort of
Edward Beardmore senior is compelled, while sitting with his
feet in hot mustard & water owing to a severe cold, to relate to
his nephew how he has secretly run away with an actress. The
divorce novel is simmering along. I have "got up" all the law of
it. Just now of course I am secretly preoccupied about the
reception which will be accorded to *S. & P. Love*. It is a very
good fiction season, much better than for a long time past, but I
have got into my head that my book is just the one that isn't
going to sell. On Monday I expect the views of the mater about
it, or as much of them as she thinks well to tell me. Much
depends on the success of that book. If it had any decent
success, I would carry out my half-resolved design never to
write any more sensational stuff. But there, I never have any
real luck (Rickards, vols I–XXXIII). Love to all. You ought to
be hearing from America soon.

E.A.B.

8. Les Sablons: Bennett took rooms here in October 1904 to have for occasional use.
Eugene Paul Ullman (1877–1953) was an American artist living in Paris. See Vol.
III for a letter to him. His first wife was Alice Woods (1871–1959), novelist and
illustrator. His painting of Marguerite Bennett is reproduced between pages 74 and
75. On Roy Devereux (Margaret Rose Roy Pember-Devereux, b. 1877) see the Introduction, p. xx. Ella D'Arcy published a novel and a short story collection in 1898 with
John Lane, who published Bennett's *A Man from the North* and *Journalism for Women* in
the same year.

Dr H. V. Lanchester (1863–1953) was a partner of Bennett's close friend E. A. Rickards (1872–1920) in the architectural firm of Lanchester, Stewart and Rickards. On Rickards, see previous volumes. Alexander Webster (d. 1919) was a friend from Bennett's London days. Murray Gilchrist, the novelist (1868–1917), became known to Bennett through the Phillpottses. Mrs Richard Le Gallienne (née Julia Norregaard) was the second wife of the author. Henry Davray (1873–1944) was on the staff of *Le Mercure de France*; he had a cottage at Les Sablons. Dr Vallée was Bennett's physician. Emily Symonds (d. 1936), better known as the author George Paston, had been a friend of Bennett's since 1896. Mrs Rawson is not otherwise known; *Journals* on 6 January 1904 alludes to Rawson coming to lunch.

Canoodling: a humorous word with several meanings for Bennett and his friends, here canoeing. See also pp. 182, 277.

'The Murder of the Mandarin' appears in the collection *The Grim Smile of the Five Towns* (1907). The uncle/nephew story is unknown. Edward Beardmore senior was brother of John Beardmore; see p. 1.

The divorce novel was *Whom God Hath Joined*, the actual writing of which was accomplished between December 1905 and July 1906, with an interruption to write *The Sinews of War* with Eden Phillpotts. *Sacred and Profane Love* was published on 21 September. For its time it was rather free in its moral stance and was doubtless one of Bennett's novels the mention of which made his mother play nervously with her bread. Bennett was apparently trying to place one of Tertia's children's stories with an American publisher.

STOKE / MS / 9
(*To Frank Bennett*)

4, rue de Calais
9 July 1906

My dear Frank,

I enclose cheque for 19/-, with many thanks to you & D'Arcy. Your work on my novel is now over, I am thankful to say, & so is mine too, nearly. I trust it will be done by the end of next week. I never was so sick of anything before in my life. Had to read it aloud to the sex. So nice & cheerful to read aloud your most secret & unsentimental thoughts on the relations of the sexes, and particularly on divorce, to your betrothed during the first month of your engagement! No wonder the tragical parts drew tears, whether of sorrow or fury God knows.

I trust your summer is arranged. I'm damned if mine is.

Yours, E.A.B.

P.S. The first shock of the meeting of the two families occurred last week. Tertia conducted her share of it to perfection; though, except for their common hatred of sentimentality & their keen sense of humour, it would be difficult to imagine two women more violently different than Tertia & Eléanora. Tertia confirmed my opinion that the mater will probably without much difficulty be able to refrain from going into ecstasies over her youngest daughter-in-law. Still, as she is only marrying *me*, that doesn't gravely matter. I am genuinely enthusiastic about *her* family, & am prepared to marry it entire.

9. Frank Bennett did some legal research for the divorce novel, *Whom God Hath Joined*, which was published at the end of October. D'Arcy Ellis was a solicitor in the Five Towns. Many years earlier Enoch Bennett was articled to the Ellis firm.

The story of Bennett's brief engagement to Eleanor Green is told on pages xxi–xxv. Her family were expatriate Americans, and had lived in the Potteries for some while. Bennett was perhaps especially prepared to marry the mother. In an unpublished journal entry of 2 July 1904 he describes meeting her for the first time.

Mrs. Green is a youngish American wife, with no trace of the accent; a rather fatigued face & manner of talking. She was wearing a superb rose-coloured gown, & looked extremely luxurious, especially when she stooped to replace a highly ornamental slipper on her small foot. I talked to her for two hours about literature, art, women, & so on. She is a cosmopolitan, knows nothing really, but can converse very neatly.

KENNERLEY / MS / 10
(*To Tertia Kennerley*)

4, rue de Calais
18 Oct 1906

My dear Tertia,

This is the most exciting news that I have received for many years. To me it is merely exciting. I mean it doesn't after all give me any feeling of pleasure. One never knows what sort of an unfortunate rascal or tearsheet one may bring into the world, or what complications may ensue even with a pattern child. As to the actual event itself I have no apprehensions; smoothness in these matters is largely a matter of temperament, and yours is not the sort of temperament to turn the thing into a dangerous comic-opera. Well, if you are not deceived, your life will be completely changed.

About buying a house, I much doubt whether I would buy any house in London before I had lived in it. London is in a transition period just now. By the time you are forty it will have settled down somewhat. Who would have had the effrontery to say a few years ago that Sharpes would find their house uninhabitable in 1906? It seems to me they are going to lose over that. No, in your place I would not buy a house. It means a slight annual saving, of course, but the saving is not in my opinion worth the fettering. Mind you, in your place I would not live in London at all. In spite of the bother of getting from Euston on the Great Central, I would live out on the north. Putney can only get worse. It is a fine roaring picturesque place now, but not habitable. The more I stay in the country (& I go regularly every week) the more I see the folly of *not* living in the country when one isn't alone. Even quite alone I enjoy myself in the country. In searching for a house you must remember that your partiality for the house you want will impair the justness of your views of other houses. If you *feel* you must move, that very fact makes it wise, but to move between now & next May seems audacious, unless you have already given notice, or unless you want to pay two rents. Not knowing anything really of the circumstances, I can't say anything really. All I can say is that it is most amazing that just at the moment when I wanted to épater everyone with my new flat, everyone should be either buying palaces or having babies, & naturally therefore in a mood to damn my flat. Here Frank is turning his house inside out. Impossible for him to get up the least interest in my flat while he is contemplating the immensity of the drawing-room he is going to have!

It is a risky thing to say, but I think I have never been so busy as I am now. The casual Whitten wrote last Saturday to ask if I could let him have two drawing-room plays by the 1st prox! Of course I replied yes. Yet I had as much as I could do before. There is what I consider a pretty good 5 Towns story in the October *London Magazine*. But they have given it a rotten air by splitting it up into two short paragraphs, & by the vilest illustrations. I hate to be published in that desolating publication. It humiliates me. Still, new flats have to be paid for.

I should say there is about an 80 per cent chance that that presumptive (or it is presumed?) child *will* be all right in every way. It may become the Director of Harrods Stores or the Queen of Sheba. Mr. Q. has my profound sympathies. But he must be a little man & try to practise philosophy, I mean about the exam.

With love, E.A.B.

10. Mary Kennerley was born on 3 June 1907. The Kennerleys first lived at 31 Spencer Road, Putney; they moved to 37 Clarendon Road, Putney, which they rented, just before Mary was born.

Herbert Sharpe, the musician (1861–1925) was a good friend of Bennett's.
Bennett moved into his new flat at 3, rue d'Aumale in December 1906.
Wilfred Whitten (d. 1942) was editor of *T.P.'s Weekly*. 'The Power of Love, a Dining
Room Play' and 'The Fortress, a Drawing-Room Dialogue' appeared in the Christmas
issue and the 14 December issue 1906.
  The *London Magazine* published 'From One Generation to Another', reprinted in *The
Grim Smile of the Five Towns*, 1907.
  Mr Q: W.W.K.

KEELE / MS / 11
(*To Marguerite Soulié*)

                                        Nice
                          [postmarked 2 February 1907]
[no salutation]
  I had a very good journey yesterday; the train was quite
prompt, and my friend came to meet me at the station. I send
you many kisses, and I shall write in a day or two. It was very
nice of you to come to the station.

                                        Your Nold

    11. For Marguerite Soulié's origins and background see the Introduction, pp. xxvi–
xxxi. This first note to her was written on the way to San Remo, where Bennett spent
several weeks with Eden Phillpotts, probably writing *The Statue*. In *My Arnold Bennett*
Marguerite tells of how she surprised Bennett by coming to see him off at the Gare de
Lyon in the morning. 'Just before his train left he said calmly, "I shall write to you from
San Remo." '

KEELE / MS / 12   Hotel Royal
(*To Marguerite Soulié*)   San Remo
                                        Italie
                                        Friday night
                                        [15 February 1907]
My dearest girl,
  I appreciate your letter very much indeed. I have never
asked you about your private life, because I did not think it
discreet to do so; but more because, whatever your private life
was, my ideas about you would not have been affected by it.
You see, I am a novelist, and a good judge of character; and I
very soon saw that you had a good heart and were sympathetic;
ce qui est toujours l'essentiel. As you have been frank with me, I
will be frank with you. I earn a pretty good income, about
20,000 francs a year; but I have to pay a certain sum to my
mother and one of my sisters, and I am afraid I shall soon have

to find a lot of money for my other sister, who wants a divorce from her husband. I have also spent a great deal of money on my flat, and my tastes generally are expensive. If I asked you to 'lâcher' the 200 francs a month which you have, I should consider myself entirely responsible for you, and I do not feel justified in doing this in my present circumstances. If I had more money, and if I had not to think of my family, I should urge you to place yourself entirely under my protection. And I hope, one day, to be able to do this. But I will not do it now. You are able to judge by this time what my character is, and so I will not tell you anything, except that I am absolutely reliable, and to be trusted.

Let me give you 200 francs a month for your clothes. That will help you a little. And few things give me more pleasure than pretty clothes on a woman who knows how to dress. If you are free to change your flat, will you change it! But I do not want you to run any risks. I will pay the expenses of the déménagement, of course.

I myself always act slowly. But I really do think that we should agree very well. I like you very much, and I think I should like you more and more. And probably you would have no cause to regret being my friend. But I always keep my promises, and therefore I do not make any promises that I am not quite sure of being able to keep.

Est-ce que tu as compris ce que je t'ai dit en anglais? Je t'aime beaucoup ma petite; mais je suis un type à part, très réfléchissant, très égoiste, très prudent, très débrouillard, et, avec ça, absolument sûr. Qui a affaire avec moi peut compter sur moi, et sur ma fidélité et ma franchise. Je t'embrasse sur tes lèvres. Tu es une femme d'un tempérament rare, et tu me plais infiniment. J'attends une lettre.

Ton Nold

Le travail marche bien. Je peux te dire une chose. Un de ces jours j'aurai beaucoup de la galette. J'ai commencé avec 100 francs par mois, et personne ne m'a jamais aidé.

---

12. [Have you understood what I said in English? I love you very much, my pet; but I am a solitary sort of chap and I think a lot. I am very selfish, very careful, very resourceful and absolutely reliable. Whoever has anything to do with me can count on me and my faithfulness and candour. I kiss your lips. You are a woman with an

exceptional temperament and I find you infinitely pleasing. I am expecting a letter....
Work is going well. I can tell you one thing. One of these days I will have a lot of money.
I started off with 100 francs a month and I've never had any help from anyone.]

    With the exchange value at £1 = 25 fr., Bennett's income was £800. In the year 1906
the income he received through his literary agent, J. B. Pinker, was £712, and he would
have received certain payments that did not go through Pinker. In the next three years
his earnings received through Pinker dropped precipitately to £303, £532, and £276. He
made occasional payments of £50 to Tertia. On Emily's divorce see below.

KENNERLEY / MS / 13
(*To Emily Edge*)
                                  3, rue d'Aumale
                                  [Paris]
                  [2, 12, or] 22 June 1907
My dear Em,

    My motives in asking you to come to the Riviera were
complicated, as most motives are. But certainly one of them
was that I might get to know something about you & *of* you,
with a view to seeing whether your existence might not be put
on a better basis. For of course it has been a matter of common
knowledge among a small circle of perceptive people, such as
Tertia, Liza, May, me & others, that your present existence
was highly unsatisfactory—in fact nothing but an armed truce.
It is certainly over four years ago since I became acquainted
with facts that were decidedly stirring. I also thought that a few
weeks complete absence from Spencer might help things. In the
face of your letter this morning I now think exactly the
contrary. My notions arrange themselves thus:—

    The chances are about 100 to 1 that a separation, if not a
divorce, must ultimately occur.

    That being so, we have to take care that from your point of
view the events that lead up to it are managed, so far as you can
control them, in an unexceptionable manner. It is extremely
important that no one should be able to accuse you of indiscre-
tion, haste, or lack of restraint; and that everything you do
should be marked by conventional correctness.

    If he is given sufficient rope, poor Spencer (for whom I really
have a great deal of sympathy—he is so bereft of common
sense) will mismanage this affair as he has mismanaged his
whole life. He is bound to play into your hands. He is cunning,
but fools often *are* cunning.

You have the advantage of him in this, that he is more *impatient* for the separation than you are. The separation will not give him more pleasure than it will give you, but he is more impatient, & less able to control his desire.

Having regard to his perfect unscrupulousness, it would be very unwise of you to leave his house now. He might make it extremely awkward for you to get back again. He would be certain to invent something; he couldn't help it. And then you would be placed in a false position. In his house you are unassailable. You must therefore stand it a bit.

There are two things he is afraid of: the money question, & his mother. You say he doesn't care for *anyone's* feelings. Perhaps he doesn't. But he is afraid of his mother. His mother is a superstition with him. These two things must be held over him.

He must be gradually made to see that a separation will cost him a considerable amount of money, directly and indirectly. And that if he is not reasonable his mother is bound to know of his performances; indeed that his mother's feelings will not be in the least considered. He will soon perceive that a separation will cost him money anyhow; his mind will get accustomed to the idea, and his impatience will cause him to consent to legal terms which he will no doubt afterwards much regret. That is what I think.

I much doubt if a divorce can be arranged as things are. There is nothing to go on. But if you have reason to think that he is straying, we can have him followed and the facts ascertained. This is the only sensible course. Indeed I would much sooner you waited for opportunities for a divorce, rather than accept a separation, even a properly-arranged one, at once. Having divorced Spencer, you would be able to recommence your life with a man who would no doubt please you better. And you are still young—younger than your years.

If a discussion arises between you as to a separation, do not give *any* opinion as to any terms he may offer, except to say that they are entirely inadequate. Tell him you are not capable of deciding yourself and refer him to me or Frank. Frank is a good lawyer, but not a good diplomatist. Any terms of separation must include a proper allowance, the leaving of the furniture to you, the payment of all expenses by him, and a written statement by him that the separation is at his desire.

Do not raise the discussion yourself. Do not say any cutting things at all. Do not regard the whole affair as anything but a calamity—for which no one is to blame. I needn't say that you can always count absolutely on me. But you must do *nothing* without consulting me.

Yours, E.A.B.

13. 3, rue d'Aumale was Bennett's new address in Paris. He moved there in December 1906.

In the manuscript the letter is clearly dated 22 June, but Bennett was in England from 16 June until 1 July. Of alternative dates 2 or 12 June seem most likely. Bennett characteristically crossed out addresses that he was not writing from.

Bennett's journal on 14 May 1907 reads (*Journals 1971*): 'On Sunday night I received from Emily the first letters sent to her by Spencer's solicitors, and was horribly embêté to find myself right in the middle of a matrimonial row that did not concern me.' Divorce ensued. Afterwards Emily went under the name Emily (or Emilie) Vernon (her middle name), sometimes Mrs Eve (for Emily Vernon Edge). She earned her living as a dressmaker, and for a time kept lodgings. She was an excellent cook, and her brother Septimus used to say that if you gave her a tomato skin and a sardine she could produce a five-course meal. In the early 1930s when Septimus's son John stayed with her for a while she pestered him to take her dancing. She always assumed that the character Emily Vernon in Bennett's play *What the Public Wants*, written in 1903, was based upon her. The character is described thus in the notes preceding the play:

Beautiful; but conscious that her youth is passing. Charming. Her moods change rapidly. She is dressed with distinguished taste, but not expensively. Her face is sad when she isn't alert. She has been through sorrow and through hard times. Age 29.

Whatever Spencer Edge's fault may have been, Bennett's letter does not reveal the fact that Emily was a difficult, eccentric person. Bennett helped her financially over many years, but in 1950 she told his biographer, Reginald Pound, that he was not generous to her.

Liza: Elizabeth (Wood) Tennant, who was Emily's great friend over many years. She was the daughter of Absalom Wood, architect, one of four Wood brothers. He was a friend of Bennett's father and the original for Osmond Orgreave in *Clayhanger*. One of his brothers was Thomas Francis, JP and mayor of Burslem. Another was William Wood, master potter (see pp. 555–6). May: May Beardmore.

In 1921, when Marguerite was involved with Pierre Legros, Bennett could not bring himself to have her followed.

KEELE / MS / 14   Golden Cross Hotel
(*To Marguerite Soulié*)   Charing Cross
                                London
                                Lundi
                                [17 June 1907]

Chérie,

Révolution dans mes habitudes quotidiennes aujourd'hui! Je me suis habillé avant de prendre mon thé. M'habiller seul, sans toi, ça me prend très longtemps. Je ne puis plus m'habiller vite

sans interruptions. Il me faut des interruptions. Des, 'pardon
— est ce que je peux entrer,' 'pardon, veux-tu m'agrafer mon
corsage?' 'pardon, où as-tu mis le etc. etc.' Une heure ça m'a
pris ce matin. Puis je suis descendu majestueusement prendre
mon thé dans le restaurant de l'hôtel, avec tous les journaux
anglais à lire. J'aime avoir mon thé comme ça, entouré par des
garçons très bien qui me connaissent et qui me flattent depuis
de longues années. Ayant bu mon thé avec de grande
cérémonie, je viens dans le salon t'écrire un petit mot. Il fait
frais, mais beau. J'ai trouvé ma sœur en très bon état. Elle s'est
levée pendant quelques minutes hier pour la première fois.
Mais il n'y a qu'un sujet de conversation. *C'est toi.* J'ai vu
plusieurs amis hier soir. On m'a demandé de tuyaux pour les
cadeaux de mariage. Et ainsi de suite. Londres est bondé de
monde mais il manque une personne. Qu'est-ce qu'elle a fait
hier. Qu'elle n'oublie pas, l'alliance, et le livre relié. Je suis allé
chez ma sœur hier par l'autobus: il y en a beaucoup, et de très
rapide. La distance, bien que la maison est toujours dans
Londres même, est 9 kilomètres du centre. Voilà une affaire! Je
suis rentré par le même moyen, à 12 moins le quart. Et j'ai bien
dormi pendant six heures. Faut dire que j'étais éreinté tout
simplement.

    Give my kindest regards to your mother, and write to me.

                        Nolitotocheztata, Noliton

14. [A revolutionary change in my daily routine today. I got dressed before I had my
cup of tea. Dressing alone, without you, takes me a very long time. I can't dress quickly
any more when I'm not interrupted. I need interruptions, such as 'Please, may I come
in', 'Please, would you do up my blouse?' 'Please, where did you put the etc. etc.' It took
me an hour this morning. Then I went majestically downstairs to have my cup of tea in
the hotel restaurant, with all the English newspapers to read. I like to have my
breakfast like that, attended by very good waiters who have known me and flattered me
for a long time. Now that I have drunk my tea in grand style, I have come into the
lounge to write you a little note. Today is chilly but fine. My sister seemed in very good
form. She got up for a few minutes yesterday for the first time. But there is only one topic
of conversation. *You.* I saw a few friends yesterday evening. They asked me for hints
about wedding presents. And so on. London is crammed full of people, but I miss one
person. What did she do yesterday? May she not forget the wedding ring and the bound
book. I went to my sister's yesterday by bus: there are a lot of buses and they are very
fast. Although the house is still in London proper, it is 9 kilometres from the centre.
What a business. I got back, the same way, at a quarter to 12. And I slept well for six
hours. I must say that I was quite simply exhausted.]

    Bennett came to England on 16 June, and went first to see Tertia and Mary in
Putney. On Marguerite's family, see the Introduction, p. xxvi.

KEELE / MS / 15
(*To Marguerite Soulié*)

Golden Cross Hotel
Mercredi
[19 June] 1907

Ma très chère Guite,

J'ai reçu ta carte-lettre hier soir. Je ne comprends pas que tu n'avais pas reçu de mes nouvelles à 9½ heures lundi soir. Tu aurais mieux fait de me dire carrément dimanche matin de te télégraphier. (Tu sais comme les hommes sont negligents.) Si tu m'avais demandé ça, je t'aurais expliqué que c'est impossible de télégraphier de Londres le dimanche soir, tout bureau étant fermé. Comme ça tu n'aurais pas attendu inutilement un mot rassurant. Dans le train de Douvres à Londres je t'ai écrit une toute petite lettre, et je l'ai mise à la poste tout de suite. J'attendais que tu l'aurais reçue au plus tard à 7½ heures lundi soir.

Je t'ai écris lundi matin
Je t'ai écris mardi matin
Je t'écris ce matin
　　　　(et pas de carte-lettres!)

Je ne suis pas de ces misérables qui racontent comme ils sont si terriblement occupés et bousculés par des affaires de la plus grave importance qu'ils n'ont que le temps d'écrire des cartes postales. Moi je suis très occupé et bousculé, mais l'affaire de la plus grave importance que j'ai à faire c'est de t'écrire tous les jours, et je la fais.

C'est certainement très difficile pour toi de comprendre et de sentir comme je t'aime, puisque je suis tellement 'bird' et 'bath'. Mais à la fin tu comprendras bien. Si je pouvais d'une façon naturelle te combler avec mes épanouissements, je le ferais. Mais je ne peux pas. Si je l'essayais je le ferais mal. Tandis que je peux éjaculer 'bird' et 'bath' d'une manière épatante et singulièrement bien. Donc, tu m'aimeras de ta façon, et moi je t'aimerai de la mienne (toujours si les jarretelles ne fichent pas trop souvent le camp).

Je comprends parfaitement bien que tu t'ennuies et que ta mère te porte sur les nerfs. Je t'assure sérieusement qu'à chaque instant que je rentre dans moi-même je m'ennuie énormément. J'aimerais infiniment mieux être avec toi à Paris. Et ça me dégoûte que j'ai déjà une quinzaine de jours à attendre avant que je serai marié. Je te prie, ne neglige rien dans cette affaire. Si c'est plus sûr d'aller au Mans, vas-y. Et après que les feuilles seront signées assure-toi tout de suite chez Bodington qu'elles sont en ordre. Fais tous les arrangements. Et demandes à Bodington la prochaine fois que tu le vois qu'il envoye un clerc, ou quelqu'un qui s'y connait, avec moi à la mairie pour la cérémonie, de sorte que je n'aurai pas des embêtements. Des embêtements inévitables je supporte avec du calme, mais des embêtements qui sont évitables — je les supporte aussi avec du calme, mais un calme faux et énervant.

Aujourd'hui j'ai une journée bien remplie:

11. rendez-vous avec mon homme d'affaires

12.45. déjeuner avec un directeur de journal

3. rendezvous avec un directeur de théâtre

4.30. thé avec une romancière

7.45. dîner avec un autre directeur de théâtre.

(Saches que la romancière a 40 ans, un mari, et 2 enfants; et qu'elle est énorme.)

Ecris-moi désormais à la campagne: tu as l'adresse. Hier soir je me suis couché de bonne heure; ce matin je me sens sous l'influence du cachet. Je t'embrasse, mon petit,

Ton Noliton

Mes respects à ta mère.

15. [I received your letter-card yesterday evening. I can't understand why you didn't receive my letter at 9.30 on Monday evening. It would have been better if you had asked me plainly on Sunday morning to send you a telegram. (You know how neglectful men are.) If you had asked me, I would have explained that it's impossible to send telegrams from London on a Sunday evening, as all offices are closed. And then you wouldn't have waited in vain for a word of reassurance. I wrote you a very short letter on the train from Dover to London, and I posted it straight away. I expected you to get it by 7.30 on Monday evening at the latest.

I wrote to you on Monday morning.

I wrote to you on Tuesday morning.

I am writing to you this morning (and no letter-cards).

I am not one of those wretched people who say that they are so terribly busy and hard pressed by things of the utmost importance that they only have time to write post cards. I am very busy and hard pressed but the most important thing that I have to do is to write to you every day, and I am doing so.

Of course it must be very difficult for you to understand and feel how much I love you as I am so very much 'bird' and 'bath'. But you will understand eventually. If I could shower praises on you and make them sound natural, I would do so. But I can't. If I tried, I would do it badly. But still I can bark out 'bird' and 'bath' strikingly and unusually well. So you will love me in your way and I will love you in mine (as long as the suspenders don't disappear too often).

I quite understand how bored you are and how much your mother gets on your nerves. I give you my solemn word that whenever I look into myself, I find I am terribly bored. I would infinitely prefer to be with you in Paris. And I am disgusted at having to wait another fortnight before we are married. I beseech you to leave nothing for the wedding undone. If it's best to go to Le Mans, then go there. And after all the papers have been signed, go straight to Bodington's to make sure they are all in order. Make all the arrangements. And next time you see Bodington, ask him to send a clerk or someone who knows the ropes, to go with me to the town hall for the ceremony, so that I don't have any problems. I can bear unavoidable problems calmly, but problems which could be avoided—I bear them calmly too, but with a false and irritable calm.

I've got a very full day today:

11.   appointment with my business advisor
12.45 lunch with a newspaper editor
3.   appointment with a theatre producer
4.30   tea with a woman novelist
7.45   dinner with another theatre producer.

(Note that the novelist is 40, with a husband and two children and she's huge.)

Write to me in the country from now on: you have the address. I went to bed early last night; I can still feel the effect of the pill this morning. I kiss you, my pet. . . . My regards to your mother.]

Bodington, an English lawyer, handled arrangements for the marriage.

KEELE / MS / 16
(*To Marguerite Soulié*)   Golden Cross Hotel
                                            Jeudi matin
                                            [20 June 1907]

Chérie,

J'ai reçu ta lettre hier soir. À propos de ta mère tu as toutes mes sympathies. Je connais ça! Faut le supporter. Je regrette infiniment que tu serais triste. Je voudrais pouvoir t'embrasser pour te redonner tout de suite la figure gaie et souriante. Ça me tracasse énormement quand je pense que tu t'êmbetes comme ça toute seule à Paris. J'ai l'idée folle de courir à plat ventre à Paris pour te dire que j'existe toujours et que tout est bien, et qu'une quinzaine de jours — c'est un rien. Ça passera comme un éclair (que je mange). Pour Londres, je commence à en avoir assez. Quel journée hier! Tellement j'ai causé que je me suis couché tout enroué. Aujourd'hui ça sera la même chose. Ce matin je serai seul. Je commence avec mes lettres. Puis je visite les expositions de tableaux à 1 heure. Déjeuner avec un directeur de journal dans un club. (Puis un tout petit somme.) Puis 9 kilomètres en autobus pour prendre le thé avec mon docteur, qui va braquer sur moi son appareil photographique. Il devrait faire quelque chose de bien. À 6 heures je serai chez ma sœur, où je dîne. Je lui ai déjà donné tes salutations etc. Et elle me charge de choses vraiment aimables pour toi. C'est une brave femme, et elle est extrêmement impatiente de faire ta connaissance. Elle m'a presque persuadé de te conduire à Londres tout de suite après le mariage. Mais j'ai refusé. À 9½ heures je quitte ma sœur pour finir la soirée chez un autre ami. Voilà ma journée. Demain j'irai chez ma mère. Tu as raison de ne pas aller chez le photographe si tu ne le sens pas bien. Ma petite chérie, reste tranquille. Ne te fais pas de bile à propos de ta mère. D'un peu nous serons ensemble encore une fois, et tout sera bien. Ah! Quel malheur que je ne suis pas démonstratif, pour te convaincre plus comme tu m'es parfaitement indispensable, & comme je suis tendre, au fond! Je t'embrasse tendrement, ma petite Guite.

Lord Arnaudale

16. [I received your letter yesterday evening. About your mother, you have my every sympathy. I know what it is like! You must bear it. I am so very sorry that you are sad. I wish I could kiss you and straight away see your face look gay and smiling. It worries me terribly to think of you being so bored, alone in Paris. I've had the mad idea of rushing to Paris to tell you that I am still alive and that everything is all right and that a fortnight is nothing. It will go by like lightning, like an *eclair* (that I eat). I am beginning to feel I have had enough of London. What a day I had yesterday! I talked so much that I was quite hoarse when I went to bed. Today will be the same. I will be alone this morning. I am starting with my letters. Then I am going to the painting exhibitions at 1 o'clock. Lunch with a newspaper editor in a club. (Then a very short sleep.) Then a 9 kilometre bus journey to have tea with my doctor who will train his camera on me. He should do something good. At 6 o'clock I will go to my sister's for dinner. I have already sent her your regards etc. And she gave me really kind messages for you. She is a good woman and she is longing to get to know you. She almost persuaded me to bring you to London straight after the wedding. But I refused. I will leave my sister's at 9.30 to spend the rest of the evening with another friend. So that's my day. Tomorrow I am going to my mother's. You are quite right not to go to the photographer if you don't feel he's good. My little darling, don't worry. Don't upset yourself about your mother. In a little while we'll be together again and everything will be all right. Oh what a pity I am not demonstrative and can't convince you more firmly that you are absolutely essential to me and show you how tender I really feel. I kiss you tenderly my little Guite.]

KEELE / MS / 17
(*To Marguerite Soulié*)

Golden Cross Hotel
Vendredi
[21 June 1907]

Chérie,

Tu as bien fait de dire ça à Joséphine tout de suite, et je suis sûr que tu l'as dit d'une façon charmante. Ce séjour à Londres commence de me dégoûter. J'en ai soupé. Je suis éreinté. Absolument! Heureusement mes petites visites sont en ordre. Aujourd'hui je vais chez ma mère; elle est un peu mieux. La bas je me reposerai. Toute la journée d'hier j'ai causé avec des amis. J'ai une dame (romancière) pour le déjeuner aujourd'hui. C'est la dernière affaire. Je fiche mon camp à 4 heures. Tu sais, ça ne me dit rien, d'être loin de toi. Tu es devenue ma plus chère habitude (et aussi ma plus élégante). Au fond je m'ennuie ici, bien que je suis très animé avec mon monde. Mon docteur a fait mon portrait hier. Il a opéré même 6 fois. J'aurai les épreuves d'ici peu. Il est très fort pour ça. Donc ai-je des espoirs d'avoir quelque chose qui ne te dégoûtera pas. Bouscule les notaires tout ce que tu peux. Je les connais, les imbeciles. Ils font un tas de chichis, et passent 4 jours à la selle pour pondre rien (c'est une façon de parler). Assure-toi que les bans seront publiés dimanche. S'ils ne sont pas publiés j'assassinerai Bodington; on me guillotinera, & il n'y aura pas de mariage. Tu vois alors ton intêret — où il sied. Dieu que j'ai besoin de me reposer dans les bras d'un être qui sait me choyer! Faute de toi, ça sera ma mère. La pauvre femme, elle ne s'y connait pas dans ces arts-là. Petite, je regrette infiniment que tu t'ennuies. Tu as de quoi t'occuper, tout de même. J'attends avec impatience voir tes nouvelles robes et fanfreluches. Ici il fait un vent terrible, mais qu'est-ce que ça me fiche? Le temps m'est parfaitement égal. Penses à moi et sois en beauté pour mon retour.

Ton Noliton

Oui, tu laisseras la chambre à Joséphine, puis que tu me demandes mon avis. On me demande des chroniques. Je sais bien que ça ne te regarde pas, mais veux-tu que je les écrive? J'exige absolument que si je m'occupe de Joséphine et ses sœurs, toi tu t'occuperas de mes chroniques.

17. [You did well to tell Josephine immediately and I am sure you told her charmingly. This stay in London is beginning to disgust me. I'm fed up with it. I'm worn out. Quite worn out. Luckily my little errands have all been arranged. I'm going to my mother's today. She is a little better. I will rest there. I spent all of yesterday chatting with friends. I am having a lady (the novelist) to lunch today. This is my last engagement and I will get off at 4. You know, there is no pleasure for me in being away from you. You have become my dearest habit (as well as my most elegant). The truth is I am bored here although I am very lively in my own circle. My doctor took my portrait

yesterday. In fact he carried out the operation 6 times. I will have the prints soon. He is very good at it. So I am hoping to have something which won't disgust you. Keep on at the lawyers as much as you can. I know those fools. They fuss over everything, they sit for 4 days and produce nothing (so to speak). Make sure the banns are published on Sunday. If they are not, I will murder Bodington: I will be guillotined and there will be no wedding. So you see where your interest lies. God how I need to rest in the arms of someone who knows how to pamper me. As I can't have you, it will be my mother, who, poor woman, is no expert in those arts. My pet, I am endlessly sorry that you are bored. But all the same, you have got things to do. I am longing to see your new dresses and frills and furbelows. It is terribly windy here, but what do I care? The weather means nothing whatever to me. Think of me and be beautiful for my return.... Yes, give Josephine the room, since you ask my opinion. I have been asked to write articles. Of course it is nothing to do with you, but do you want me to write them? I absolutely insist that if I take an interest in Josephine and her sisters, you should take an interest in my articles.]

Josephine was Bennett's maid at 3, rue d'Aumale.

KEELE / MS / 18
(*To Marguerite Soulié*)

179, Waterloo Road
Burslem
Stoke-on-Trent
Samedi
[22 June 1907]

Chérie,

Ta lettre que j'ai reçue ce matin m'a fait beaucoup de plaisir. J'espère bien que les arrangements pour les consentements continueront de bien marcher. J'ai peur qu'il y aura un délai à Brest. Enfin, en tout cas je serai inquiet jusqu'au moment de *quitter* la mairie. Tes paroles pour ma mère lui font un plaisir énorme. C'est étonnant comme des paroles charment. Ah ma pauvre petite, quelle *fusillade* de questions à propos de toi quand je suis arrivé ici. C'était de la grêle. Je suis arrivé à 7.15 hier soir. Ma sœur ainée (sérieuse mais riante, et fichue comme 2 clous), et mon frère (barbu) m'ont pris à la gare. Ma mère va beaucoup mieux — tout simplement parce qu'elle s'est arrangée avec sa fidèle domestique qui voulait la quitter. Il y avait naturellement du monde pour le diner, et après. Plus tard ma mère et moi nous sommes allés chez mon frère. Le docteur est venu. Il est très lié avec mon frère, et aussi avec moi, et il est très noctambule. Je me suis arraché à la maison à minuit. J'étais éreinté, plus que jamais. J'avais une névralgie magnifique. Je ne pouvais pas dormir. Je me suis reveillé à $2\frac{1}{2}$ heures, et à $4\frac{1}{4}$ heures, toujours avec la névralgie, mais après ça j'ai bien dormi, et je me sens très bien ce matin, reposé, moins énervé, dans un calme, et la névralgie disparue. J'ai tout de même beaucoup à faire. Plusieurs chroniques etc. Heureusement les petites [?] sont épatantes. J'ai pris des grains de Noly deux fois. Tu ne me dis rien de ta santé, je suppose donc que c'est bien. Nous allons être heureux d'une façon tout à fait particulière, j'en suis sûr. Nous nous comprenons. Ma mère est déjà très contente de toi. Elle t'envoie des amabilités de toutes sortes, et aussi ma sœur. Quand tu viendras ici tu auras des expériences plutôt embêtantes avec tout ce monde, dans ce sale pays ouvrier. Ma petite je t'embrasse de ma façon, et je te quitte. Sois sûr que je me porte très bien, et que je m'ennuie infiniment dans mon cœur.

Nold

18. [Your letter which arrived this morning gave me a great deal of pleasure. I do hope that the arrangements about the wedding will continue to go well. I am afraid there will be a delay at Brest. Whatever happens I will go on being anxious until we *leave* the town hall. Your message to my mother gave her tremendous pleasure. It is amazing how charming words can be. When I arrived here, I was hit by a *volley* of questions about you, my poor pet. It was like a hailstorm. I arrived at 7.15 yesterday evening. My elder sister (who is serious but cheerful and as plain as can be), and my (bearded) brother collected me at the station. My mother is much better—just because she has come to an understanding with her faithful servant who wanted to leave. Of course there were people to dinner, and afterwards. My mother and I went to my brother's later. The doctor came. He is a close friend of my brother's and of mine, and is a nightbird. I dragged myself away at midnight. I was exhausted, more so than ever, and I had a grand attack of neuralgia. I couldn't sleep. I woke up at 2.30 and again at 4.15, still with neuralgia, but after that I slept well and I am feeling very well this morning, rested, less strained, relaxed and the attack of neuralgia over. But I have a lot to do. A few articles etc. Luckily the little [?] are wonderful—I have taken grains of Noly twice. You say nothing about your health, so I imagine you are well. We are going to be happy in a very special way, I'm sure. We understand each other. My mother is very pleased with you already. She sends all kinds of best wishes, so does my sister. When you come here you will have rather annoying experiences with all these people in this dirty workers' country. My pet, I kiss you in my special way, and I must leave you. You can be sure that I am very well, but I am deeply bored in my heart.]

179, Waterloo Road was Bennett's mother's address during her last years.

Fanny Gertrude Bennett (1869–1939) was married to Frank Beardmore, May Beardmore's brother, a potter. She had trained as a nurse at the West London Hospital, and then as a midwife, but did not practise. She was active in affairs concerning women and children—swimming clubs, temperance societies, infant welfare associations. During the War she was District Food Officer in Fenton, and she organized a National Kitchen. In 1920 she became JP for Stoke-on-Trent. She bore three sons and a daughter. In 1911 when Bennett and Edward Knoblock were writing *Milestones* and casting about for a name for a character who was 'staunch, loyal, unafraid, sees the truth and speaks it' (Bennett's words, according to Knoblock), they lighted upon the name Gertrude because they both had sisters of such quality with that

name. Another side of Fanny Gertrude's character is given in the Introduction, p. xxx.
  The bearded brother: Frank.
  Dr John Russell (d. 1926) was the Dr Stirling of the novels.

KEELE / MS / 19
(*To Marguerite Soulié*)
179, Waterloo Rd.
Dimanche
[23 June 1907]

Ma chérie,
  J'ai été très occupé aujourd'hui. J'ai été forcé d'écrire une longue chronique. Et voici le moment de sortir chez mon frère pour le diner. C'est très embêtant, tous ces chichis pour la publication des bans. Je t'envoie sous ce pli un petit chèque, que tu toucheras quand tu en auras besoin. J'attends avec impatience ta lettre de demain pour savoir si tu as réussi avec les bans. Si ça ne marche pas je prendrai mes dispositions tout de suite. Bodington ne peut pas 'faire des impossibilités,' mais il aurait dû savoir que ma présence était nécessaire à la mairie. Il m'a dit, au contraire, très nettement, qu'il pourrait tout faire sans moi. Et c'était sur ça que je suis venu en Angleterre.
  Enfin tout ça — c'est rien. Tout sera bien. Tout s'arrangera. Je suis fatigué. Le jour arrivera quand je ne serai plus fatigué. Nous serons ensemble. Nous serons mariés. Et nous nous aimerons toujours. Tes lettres sont ma joie, le matin, ou le soir. Je ne pleure pas mais je suis très touché. Il fait horriblement froid ici. Je suis très pressé. Ma mère m'attend. Elle t'envoie mille choses. Embrasse-moi bien, et je t'embrasse les oreilles.

Ton Noliton

Faudra signer le chèque au dos.

19. [I have been very busy today. I had to write a long article. And now it's time to go to dinner at my brother's. All this fuss over the announcement of the banns is very annoying. I am sending you a small cheque, enclosed with this letter, for you to draw on whenever you need. I am impatiently awaiting tomorrow's letter from you to know whether you have been successful with the banns. If things have not worked out, I will make my arrangements immediately. Bodington cannot 'do the impossible', but he should have known that my presence at the town hall was essential. He told me quite clearly, on the contrary, that he could do it all without me. And it was at that point that I came to England.
  But none of this really matters. Everything is all right. Everything will work out. I am tired. The day will come when I am no longer tired. We will be together. We will be

married. And we will love each other for ever. Your letters are my joy, in the morning or
the evening. They don't make me cry but I am deeply affected by them. It is horribly
cold here. I am in great haste. My mother is waiting for me. She sends you a thousand
messages. Kiss me nicely and I kiss your ears.... Cheque must be signed on back.]

KEELE / MS / 20
(*To Marguerite Soulié*)   179, Waterloo Road
                                                      Mercredi
                                                      [26 June 1907]
Chérie,

Je suis content que les bans sont publiés. Mais quelle
negligence de la part de Bodington ou du notaire, pour que
l'acte de ta mère est à refaire! J'ai connu dans ma vie pas mal de
notaires et d'avoués, et j'ai toujours trouvé que, comme race, ils
sont négligents, idiots, inexactes, et cocasses — bien que
souvent très polis. Je regrette, my child, que tu souffres. Ça
passera. C'est déjà beau que ta mère est charmante. Ma mère
est décidément mieux; mais je ne crois pas, sérieusement, que
c'est moi qui ai fait le miracle. Une de ses copains lui a indiqué
un vin fortifiant, qu'elle prend tous les jours. Et c'est les
qualités de ce merveilleux boisson qui l'ont guéri. Elle le boit
avec une foi qui est touchante. Hier j'ai pris le thé chez la femme
du directeur du grand journal régional. M. le directeur est aussi
venu, exprès de son bureau, causer avec moi. Il est très bien, le
bonhomme, et grand travailleur (comme ton serviteur); mais il
s'intéresse tellement à son métier qu'il se fiche pas mal de sa
femme, tout en l'aimant de sa façon à lui. Elle se trouve un peu
incomprise. Elle lit beaucoup. Elle est folle de *L'Amour Sacré et
Profane*: Elle a lu *Leonora trois fois*. Et elle pense qu'en invitant
l'auteur de ces chef-d'œuvres à un thé intime, (une heure avant
l'arrivée du mari) elle entendra des choses flattantes, et des
'pronunciamientos' (tu comprends, hein?) sur les secrets du
cœur féminin. C'est infiniment drôle. Parce que moi, comme tu
sais, je ne parle jamais comme mes livres. Je lui ai causé chiffons
tout le temps. Mais elle est bien, la pauvre femme. Le soir j'ai
causé tard avec mon docteur et mon frère. Si tu me voyais, ma
chère petite, tu serais fachée. Je fume 5 cigars par jour. Je fiche
le camp tout de suite. C'est aujourd'hui que je vais à
Manchester.

J'arriverai dans mon Paris (qui contient toi) lundi soir. Je t'embrasse, my dearest girl, très tendrement.

Arnaudale

Il fait horriblement froid ici. On va célébrer Noël demain.

20. [I am glad the banns have been published. But what negligence on the part of Bodington or the notary that your mother's statement has to be made again. I have met a fair number of notaries and solicitors in my life and I have always found that as a breed they are negligent, stupid, inaccurate, and absurd—though often very polite. My child, I am sorry you are unwell. It won't last. One good thing is that your mother is being charming. My mother is decidedly better; but I don't seriously believe that it was I who performed the miracle. A friend of hers recommended a tonic wine which she drinks every day. And it is the qualities of this marvellous drink which have cured her. She drinks it with a touching faith. Yesterday I had tea with the wife of the editor of the main regional newspaper. The editor himself came too, leaving his office especially to have a talk to me. He is a very agreeable gentleman, and a hard worker (like your humble servant); but he is so interested in his profession that he pays little attention to his wife, although he loves her in his fashion. She feels rather unappreciated. She is a great reader. She adores *Sacred and Profane Love*. She has read *Leonora* three times. And she thought that if she invited the author of these masterpieces to an intimate tea (an hour before the arrival of her husband), she would hear flattering things and 'pronunciamentos' (do you understand, eh?) on the secrets of the feminine heart. It is too funny for words. For as you know, I never say the kind of things my books do. I talked to her of fashions all the time. But I liked the unfortunate woman. In the evening I talked to the doctor and my brother till late. You would be cross if you could see me, my darling pet. I smoke 5 cigars a day. I'm getting away immediately. Today I'm going to Manchester.

I will arrive in my Paris (which holds you) on Monday evening. My dearest girl, I kiss you very tenderly.... It is horribly cold here. Our Christmas celebrations are tomorrow.]

Henry Barrett Greene edited the *Staffordshire Sentinel* from 1899 until his death in 1927. The *Sentinel* reviewed the Five Towns novels at length, and usually took pride in Bennett's references therein to the local newspaper, which he called the *Signal*.

KENNERLEY / MS / 21
(*To Tertia Kennerley*)

Les Sablons
29 July 1907

My dear Tertia,

The only worm gnoring at the root of my mind is that this business of being married cannot possibly last as it is. It can last perfectly well on *my* footing; but it can't last on *her* footing. However, it is no use trying to explain to anybody facts about human nature which that body is not ripe for receiving. I am

about a century older than my wife, though she is 32, and has
been through pretty considerable things in the way of misfortune. Marriott put her age at 26, & Mrs. Marriott at 28. The
fact is that she looked her age six months ago, but has steadily
been getting younger during the last three months. So far as I
can judge Marriotts are somewhat taken with her. He said to
me in his solemn serious tone, with that peculiar look which he
can't help wearing at such moments: 'Bennett, your wife is a
beautiful woman.' I was so excited when they came that I could
not eat my dinner slowly, so I had indigestion. M. considers
Mrs. Marriott better dressed than most Englishwomen, but she
objects to her jewels. So do I. There is too much Frederick
about them. I showed Frederick some specimens of the 'hobby'
which William decided I should take up, last summer in
Normandy. He was much impressed, and said I should be able
to do that sort of thing as well as anyone. He understands the
principles of the thing perfectly; but when I got him to design
me some 'units', 'diapers' etc., he instantly lowered the plane
and became awfully New Crossy. A single one of his designs
would ruin a page of my calligraphy. However, I didn't tell him
so; and, as I say, he is very clear and illuminating when he
explains principles. He also approves my furnishing. I
naturally take this as being satisfactory to me; though logically
it ought not to be entirely so.

I do not think this weather would suit you. But it suits me;
incidentally it kills Marguerite. I took my thermometer outside
the house this afternoon, and in five minutes it went up from 80
to 102. If it had gone up to 118 it would have exploded the
machine so I brought it in. I am most frightfully busy. I do
Italian every day. Also piano. And I keep my journal much
better than I used to. I am writing my Five Towns play for the
Stage Society. It only remains for me to do embroidery. By the
way I have no recollection of objecting to embroidery.
Certainly not for years past. But I can never be sure, as my
ideas are always changing. By the way Mrs. Greene told me
that Lizzie Wood told her that I was changeable. I had a great
time with Mrs. Greene responding to the femme incomprise in
her. Then her husband came in, with a copy of the *Sentinel*
containing three columns about me. And I was permitted the
spectacle of seeing how she was incomprise. She never hinted to

me that she considered herself incomprise, nor did I hint to her
that I so considered her. But we understand each other. She
calls on Florence. And as Frank has not yet been at home when
she called she must have had a gay time. I have got hold of a
whole new aspect of the Potteries (this has no connection with
Mrs. Greene), which will result in prodigious books.

The Marriotts are good visitors. The conversation is
extremely intimate, but of course you can't talk to Frederick
really about human nature. He would get frightened. I don't
think Tully would; but *he* would. So we keep off IT. I am doing
him good in politics, I thank God! He needed it badly. He is a
great discredit to William & Charles. I can't help thinking that
both these sound politicians shirk the business of doing their
duty. Perfectly useless to talk to Sharpe, but not useless to talk
to Marriott. Marguerite is continuing to learn poetry and I am
continuing to write it. I shall publish a book of poems next year,
I think. I regret she will never be able to recite them. I get up
now at 6.30. I don't know how long it will last. But I know I
can't keep awake at nights. I can only keep awake at 3 a.m.
Marguerite sleeps like two logs—but not in *my* room. The one
difficulty that I have in marriage is to refrain from looking after
everything. I am so used to controlling every department of my
household, from the washing to the dusting, that I continually
forget it is no longer necessary for me to worry about such
things. I can't write letters now. I have written an enormous
quantity, not one of the slightest interest. Yet my mind is
crowded with unsorted interesting things. Marriage is just as
exciting to me as your baby is to you, though I think I know
perhaps more about women and living with women than you
know about babies. However, I shall get my ideas clearer in
about 2 years' time. At present I am reading Goethe's conversations with Eckerman. They are nearly as good as Sam Johnson, though in an entirely different vein. You ought to read
Wilhelm Meister—again, if you have already read it. Your
interest in Marguerite is not more acute than hers in you. If I
had time & money, I would come over to England for a week in
September; but I have neither. I may say that Marguerite is
staggered at my expensiveness. She is determined to cure it.
Every now & then she drops a drop of water on the top of my
head, always in the same spot. But as I desire nothing better

than to be economical, provided I don't have to worry about it myself, she will certainly have her way. I shall be delighted, and I may become rich. She has already settled to live on half my income. In fact I believe she has already begun. She sends her compliments. Love to all.

Yours, E.A.B.

21. Bennett and Marguerite were married on 4 July. A few days afterwards they went to stay at Les Sablons for several months. In an account book for the year Bennett noted that the expenses of the marriage were 21 francs, 55 centimes, with sundries at 6 francs, 75 centimes.

Frederick Marriott (1861–1941) was born in Stoke-on-Trent but grew up in Shropshire. He was art master at Goldsmiths' College, New Cross. Bennett described him to Frank Swinnerton as the worst artist in the world. Bennett was very fond of him and he of Bennett. He wrote a memoir of Bennett that the University of Keele published in 1967. His wife Margaret Hannah (d. 1938) was known familiarly as Tully. Bennett had lived with them in Chelsea from spring 1891 to February 1898. For letters to them see Vol. II.

For examples of Bennett's calligraphy see Vol. II, p. 257, Vol. III, facing p. 24. His first formal effort is dated 26 October 1906, and reads:

> This is the first
> attempt I have
> made—and
> it is pretty damn
> bad—to produce
> in a free manner a more
> or less—chiefly less—art-
> istic effect by means of a
> formalised method of hand-
> writing. It is achieved
> without ruling or other gu-
> ide for the untrained and
> infantile pen, and the eff-
> ect is more free than it is
> lovely.

Cupid and Commonsense, dramatized from *Anna of the Five Towns*, was Bennett's first play to be produced. Eight other full-length plays (most of them written in collaboration with other people) and several shorter plays preceded it.

Lizzie: Elizabeth Wood (Tennant).

The *Sentinel* editions available for this period show a one-column review of *The Grim Smile of the Five Towns* on 18 June, reprinted the following Saturday, and slightly more than one column on 24 June reprinting reviews from the *Nation* and the *Daily Mail*.

Florence: Frank Bennett's wife.

William: Kennerley.

Charles: Charles Young (1861–1940), manager of Lamley & Co., South Kensington. For fuller details see Vol. II.

For several of Bennett's poems see Vol. II. He never published a collection.

KENNERLEY / MS / 22
(*To Sarah Ann Bennett*)   [Villa des Néfliers]
                                                  [Avon S/M]
                                                  [24 April 1908]

My dear Ma,

This is just an experiment that I am making as to the form and look of a page in double column that I mean to adopt for a future manuscript that I have in mind. So I thought that I might as well kill two birds with one stone, and use the stuff for a letter to you.

It is raining this morning. Or rather it has been. I don't think the change will last long as there has been scarcely any fall in the temperature. I walked across the park to the town in a fine drizzle, which stopped soon afterwards. Today it is the municipal elections, and the cafés have extra tables and chairs put outside. Also there is a movement to and from of well-dressed and conceited tradesmen and others—doubtless candidates or friends and supporters thereof. Soldiers were knocking about as usual on their morning errands. In the morning they appear to be chiefly employed in attending to their officers. You meet them carrying letters, packets, newspapers, despatch cases, and even coffee-breakfasts in baskets specially made for this work. Also leading horses. Etc. Etc.

I wrote to Madame Lebert yesterday saying that I had meant to go over and see them today, but could not as Calvocoressi was coming down for the day. Naturally we receive a letter this morning from Calvo to say that he can't come till next Sunday. It is the annual fête at Les Sablons today. There is a superstition that it always rains for this wakes. In these cases of superstition 'always' means merely often. Certainly it rains today. Rose has gone off to it with a clear day's holiday. Her new dress ought to have come yesterday afternoon, but it didn't. However her mother brought it this morning at 8 a.m., and the entire household breathed again. So that we are spending today alone. But if it clears up we might go to Les Sablons after all.

We are very glad that you have not been chopped to pieces by a mad chop-woman. Mr. Jones ought to keep his servants on chains, or in safes. What with Savage's servants to front, and Jones's at the side, you haven't a chance.

On Tuesday week we are going to Paris for one night. To buy carpets, visit the theatre, lunch with Davrays, dine with Martin and tea with Mrs. Farley and others. Violet Hunt is coming over. By that time I shall have finished half the big novel, and more than half of the Human Machine articles for T.P. Those articles continue to make a stir in the world. Last night we had our first meal in this house. It was very simple, as I have got back to my old habit of eating very little at night. I have convinced myself that my sleeping depends on my stomach. I trust your eyes continue to get better, and that you can decipher this. It has taken me 53 minutes to rule and to write. It probably conveys no impression of beauty to you, as it is only a sketch; but it does to me, because I see it as it ought to be.

Best love, E.A.B.

22. Bennett and Marguerite moved into the Villa des Néfliers, rue Bernard Palissey, Avon-Fontainebleau, on 23 April.

The letter is printed in double columns, in Bennett's calligraphic hand, with enlarged and decorated capital letters at the beginnings of paragraphs.

Madame Lebert and her husband, a gardener, owned Les Sablons. Bennett wrote an article about them that is reprinted in *Things That Have Interested Me, First Series*, 1921.

On M. D. Calvocoressi (1874–1944) see the Introduction, p. xxvii. For letters to him see Vol. II.

Émile Martin and Agnes Farley were friends in Paris. See the Introduction, pp. xxviii and xxi. Martin is described by Marguerite in *My Arnold Bennett* as a wealthy Parisian dilettante and patron of the arts of whom Bennett was very fond. For other references to Agnes Farley see Vol. II.

Violet Hunt (1866–1942) was one of Bennett's literary friends in Paris. See the Introduction, p. xxiv. For letters to her see Vol. II.

The big novel was *The Old Wives' Tale*, 200,000 words, begun 8 October 1907 and finished 30 August 1908, with time off to write *Buried Alive* at the turn of the year.

The human machine articles were written in the first months of 1908 and published in *T.P.'s Weekly* beginning on 20 March. The collection *The Human Machine* was published in November.

STOKE / MS / 23
(*To Emily Beardmore*)

Villa des Néfliers
5th Oct 1908

My dear Mrs. Beardmore,

I have just had news of Mr. Beardmore's death. Your feelings, & the feelings of everyone, must be very complicated. I know that mine are. The fact is, I don't know how to express them. I know from the mater something of the strain which all

of you—& especially you & Edward & Agnes have been
through since the illness began, & I can guess how sorrowful
you are now, though what has happened is the best that could
happen. I can only just tell you that my sympathy with you is,
and has been, very keen indeed. As I saw very little of Mr.
Beardmore when he was ill, I still see him most clearly as he
was when he was well. In that I have an advantage. When I
first left home, in 1889, the pater was rather shy of saying to me
all those things that fathers are supposed to say to their sons in
such circumstances, & he got Mr. Beardmore to do it. This is
the scene in which I best remember him, standing on the
hearthrug at 205 & talking to me, while the pater sat silent in
the easy-chair. It was the sort of thing that he could do very
well. When he was at his best he had an immense personal
charm and persuasiveness. These things, & his impulsive
generosity, and his extraordinarily clear grasp of problems, will
be remembered. My dear lady, I will not say any more to you.
Accept my deep sympathy, & also my wife's,—for you,
Edward, Agnes, & all of them.

Yours sincerely, Arnold

23. Emily (Hancock) Beardmore (d. 1922) and John Beardmore (b. 1845) were
married in 1862. Their children were Edward Harry (1869–1932), Frank (1870–1936)
who married Fanny Gertrude Bennett, May, and Agnes (1886–1969).

KENNERLEY / MS / 24
(*To Tertia and W. W. Kennerley*)

Villa des Néfliers
7th Oct 1908

Dear people,

Having rearranged my daily life once more, after this most
strenuous holiday, I now in the appointed order sit down to
write you a few lines. Except for a general slight creeping
carelessness, and the difficulty of entertaining, I see no reason
why we should ever have a new servant, Laurence being so
comforting. But I daresay when the weather changes I shall
think differently. This district stands very well the ordeal of
coming back to it after the Midi. I have walked out two
mornings, at length, in search of ideas for my fine new play, and
really the forest and the park are not easily to be sat on. I have

found ideas with extraordinary certainty and ease. I must now be in my prime, I suppose. I shall never be any more efficient, but may hope to keep as I am for another 9 years. I feel as if I could write a book or a play once a month. This play is to be entitled *What the Public Wants*. And Harmsworth is the hero, & the press & the theatre the subjects. What *my* Harmsworth wants is: not to be continually slighted by intellectual people. The play is the story of his disappointment in this desire. I shall call it 'a tragedy in five acts'. But it will be externally a farce. Among other people to be guyed in it is A. B. Walkley. I like him, but I owe him one, and in a coin more golden than his own I will pay. I tell you all this because *What the Public Wants* promises to be a very gay lark. I have corrected all the proofs of *The Old Wives' Tale*—578 pp. I am sure Tertia is wrong about those two chapters. I deliberately lowered the tension in the last part of the book, in obedience to a theory which objects to violent climaxes as a close; and, now I have done it, I don't know that I am quite satisfied. I know the public will consider the fourth part rather tame and flat, if not dull. And I am not sure whether I don't slightly share this view. This is annoying. Still, I must say it's a bit of honest work. And the effect as you finish the last page is pretty stiff—*when you begin to think things over*. It isn't in many books that you can see people growing old. I read *Un Vie* again (than which I meant to try and go one better) and was most decidedly disappointed in it. Lacking in skill.

I don't know whether you understood my letter to the mater about Xmas. As it is about 75 % certain that I shall have to come to England anyhow in March, I do not want to come at Xmas too, and I certainly do not want to stay in England from December to March, much as I adore that country. So I think you might arrange to go to the Potteries at Xmas for a change. A visit to Burslem, for us, taking it altogether, is a costly affair, & two visits close together in addition to being costly would be an infernal nuisance. It is our intention to go to Vevey on the Lake of Geneva just before Christmas & stay there while I write a humorous book. Mrs. Ullman stayed for 7 months at the hotel I have in view, & still came away enthusiastic about it. I have heard others say that it is the most comfortable hotel in Switzerland. 3000 ft. above the lake, innumerable excursions, constant sunshine, close to Montreux, and prices from 6 and 7 francs a day, with central heating. You pay 1½ frs. a week for electricity. You get there from Paris in 8 hours, without changing. It will probably cost us slightly less than staying at home. Certainly much less disturbance than going, for instance, to Toulouse etc. Thus we hope to take advantage of your kind suggestions about March, & also to go to Burslem. There is one thing: I can see a great deal more of the Potteries in March than I can at Xmas.

Marguerite is not sure for the moment whether she wants to engage a definite servant now, for so short a time. The only difficulty is that she has 2 costumes to 'create', and she can't do this while preoccupied with the house, no more than I could write under similar circs. I have now minutely studied her in her creative crises. It really is a bit of an accouchement. As Sep magnificently said of Maud: 'The woman's an artist!'

No, I have not forgotten that it is your birthday. I have eminently remembered it, and I now desire you the highest good—that is to say, freedom from earthly desires and a will stronger than Mary's. I must say that the Ullman children are very good, & getting even better. But their nurse is a pearl. Old man Ullman has been cutting up rough about money, and as they are absolutely dependent on him the situation is the least in the world delicate. It will smooth itself, I believe. A father has no right to set up a son in a career such as Eugene's, and then begin to bully. However, it has given Eugene a fillip. My own artistic labours have under Providence been greatly blessed. I think I fair staggered Mrs. Ullman. But I must wear a semblance of humility, and stick to work. I am determined to do something glittering of the dog. You cannot conceive how fine he is. Laurence (the femme de ménage) has trained him admirably.

I could tell you lots of interesting things about life in London and Torquay—which it appears is very complex. 'I could keep you amused for hours—days,' but somehow I can't put it in a letter. I can't begin. *The Virgin in Judgment* is a prodigious success. My impression is that the *New Age* will be sold soon, though they are trying to form a company. But it is too damnation clever to last long. I have the written certificate of the editor that commercially 'Jacob Tonson' is the most

important contributor to the paper. But the question in my
mind is: How long am I going to continue making him a present
of £150—a year, at least? There is no virtue in me, because I
only do it for the amusement of self and a few others. Young de
Selincourt, having ascertained who J.T. was, wrote to me the
other day in these terms: 'Damn you, Bennett, what hideous
fun you must be having!' Rather cryptic. It is now about time
that Tertia read *La Chartreuse de Parme*. Marguerite has just read
it. Balzac said there were only 1200 people in Europe capable of
appreciating it. And I was much pleased to find that
Marguerite behaved to it as a dog to a bone. I couldn't get her
off it. It is very long, quite worthy of Tertia. Assuredly there is
nothing in fiction more *distinguished*. I have subscribed to the *M
Guardian*, & it is a great comfort to me. About a year ago
Marguerite had a fit of 'keeping up' with the papers. But it has
happily passed, though she continually laments that she lives
'comme une oie'. By immense efforts I keep her abreast of
Wilbur Wright's performances and the more salient adulteries.
We are still deeply attached to the Godebskis. Calvo & Martin
& the Davrays are to pay visits soon—servant permitting. I
have forgotten all that I wanted to say. You ought to receive the
novel on Oct 23rd.

Our loves, E.A.B.

24. Bennett went on a cycling tour of France in September after finishing writing *The
Old Wives' Tale*. In his Preface to the novel he remarks on his intention of going one
better than Guy de Maupassant in *Une Vie* by relating the histories of two women.

On Alfred Harmsworth (Lord Northcliffe, 1865–1922) and *What the Public Wants* see
Vol. I. The play was produced at the Aldwych Theatre and then at the Royalty Theatre
in May 1909. Max Beerbohm described it as 'one of the best comedies of our time'. A. B.
Walkley (1855–1926), the critic, appears as Simon Macquoid in the play. In a note on
the characters, Bennett says that Macquoid should be angry throughout his scene.
Bennett has an article on Walkley, 'The Dramatic Critic', reprinted in *Things That Have
Interested Me, Second Series*, 1923.

The new humorous book was *The Card*, which Bennett wrote from 1 January to 1
March 1909 at Vevey.

Maud Mary Marsden (1877–1946) married Septimus in 1905.

The Virgin in Judgment, Eden Phillpotts's new novel.

'Jacob Tonson' was Bennett's pseudonym for a series of weekly articles that he wrote
gratis or for a token fee of one guinea for A. R. Orage's *New Age* in 1908–11. For further
details see Vols. I and II.

Hugh de Selincourt (1878–1951), author and critic.

Cepa and Ida Godebski were Parisian artistic friends of Bennett's introduced to him
by Calvocoressi. He was a painter. They were close friends of Ravel's.

BENNETT / MS / 25
(*To Ruth Bennett*)

Villa des Néfliers
27 Oct 1908

Dear Niece,

We are much touched by this mark of your regard. We did not expect you till Christmas morning at 5 a.m., & we had in fact arranged everything to greet you with parcels at that day and almost hour. This early arrival flatters us the more, though finding us unprepared. You will certainly have a certain amount of difficulty with your parents; but you must excuse their youthfulness and inexperience. They know not what they do. Happily you have any number of uncles, aunts, & even more elderly relatives who will be ever ready to explain to this pair of children, several days or weeks before they are asked, exactly how they ought to treat you in every conceivable crisis. If you suffer it will be because God, seeing that he has no longer a monopoly of all wisdoms, has decided in self defence to abandon you to the sole care of the most Capable Family on earth. We cannot help thinking all the time that you are out of an opera, set to music by Sullivan and conducted by your uncle, your aunt superintending rehearsals. What makes us solemn is the thought that you might have been twins, as there is no knowing what people will do once they begin.

Our warmest blessing is upon your baldness, and our curious sympathy with your parents in the new, disconcerting, and marvellous sensations which you are now causing them.

Yours affectionately,
The Barren and Lady Bennett

25. Ruth Bennett was born to Septimus and Maud on 25 October 1908.

KENNERLEY / MS / 26
(*To Tertia and W. W. Kennerley*)

Villa des Néfliers
22nd Oct 1909

People,

Thanksgivings for letters. No, I have received very few letters about the book. I am not convinced about the second part myself, but I am sure that the 1st and 3rd parts are as good as

the best I can do. Some people who like the 2nd don't care for
the 3rd: which unfortunately shows that they have not understood the second. Also I am now supposed to be a Theosophist,
a Hegelian, and all sorts of things. The second part is simple
Theosophy, nothing else, and taken bodily therefrom (with
improvements); but I have now made Theosophy serve my
turn, & have done with it. I read Mrs. Besant three times, and
made fresh notes every time, in order to do the second part; a
fearful grind; & the Theosophical Society ought now to reprint
my second part as one of their official publications; it is
infinitely more graphic and coherent than any of their own
tracts. I am glad you liked 'Bond Street'. I did. Enough. What
chiefly interests me now is the sales. I am up to the neck in my
play. Trench has signed the contract & forked out a preliminary 100 quid. So I suppose he is likely to produce it. Also the
Manchester Gaiety has forked out a preliminary 20 for darling
old *Cupid & Commensense*: which is a great triumph for the just
man, for they refused it 18 months ago. It will now be done in
Hanley. All our plans depend on plays. If we stay in England
for the winter I see nothing but Bournemouth; it is dear. And I
much want to go to Florence, which is cheaper & funnier, only
for the travelling. We certainly can't be always crossing
Europe. I shall positively appear in the Five Towns early in
December, and remain there at least 2 weeks. I must have at
least two weeks with Mr. Dawson. My next hero's father is the
pater+Mr. Beardmore = a steamprinter. And the hero is a sort
of Edward Harry. This novel has to be begun on Jan 1st, either
in Bournemouth or Flo. I don't think Margharita will come to
England till about the 7th or 8th Decr. And I suppose as the
mater will be in London for Xmas, we shall too. We have
arranged a state visit to Frank's opera. A state visit to Jennings
will also be necessary for me. I have had dreadful frights with
the Income Tax people, and am greatly joyed to find today that
I have emerged with only £10 odd to pay. I wouldn't pay it;
they couldn't make me—& I pay all French taxes; only if I
come back to live in England any time, there would then be a
hell of a row if I couldn't produce my papers in order. I may tell
you that Marguerite's catarrh is really not better. Chronic. We
find that Pauline Smith (who is here) also has a chronic
catarrh, but she never says anything about it. She is beginning

a novel, and has half an hour's remarks from me every night. My remarks are really rather good. Strange girl. She *can* write. But she won't talk. However, we make her. At least Marguerite does. She says: 'Now Pauline, you have let the conversation fall.' She is already better. But we had a friend down on Sunday, who talks rapidly in English, French, German, Italian, Spanish, and Servian. And she didn't speak a word the whole day, except 'Yes' and 'No' to his direct addresses. So we took her to task afterwards. The timid little thing worships Marguerite. Still she is no chicken. 27. What about Emily? As I haven't heard anything from her I assume she isn't in immediate need. I know something about Mary, I do, that you don't know. *Ann Veronica* is not very good. You really ought to buy Kropotkin's *Memoirs of a Revolutionist*, remainder from the New Age Press 2/8d. It is the book of a great man, and not unhandsome as a volume.

Loves, E.A.B.

26. *The Glimpse* was written from 18 May to mid-August 1909, and was published on 7 October. It offered an aesthete's protracted glimpse into reincarnation, and was largely based upon a reading of the works of Annie Besant (1847–1933). H. G. Wells described it as 'a glimpse into an empty cavern' of Bennett's mind. 'Bond Street' was a chapter in it. For other details see Vols. I and II.

The new play was *The Honeymoon*, written during the autumn. Herbert Trench (1865–1923) accepted it for the Haymarket Theatre but did not produce it.

Cupid and Commonsense was produced for the Stage Society on 26 and 27 January 1908. There were productions in Glasgow in 1909 and in Manchester, Hanley, and Glasgow again in 1910.

Bennett went to the Potteries on 27 November. The trip was in part to gather material for *Clayhanger*. Joseph Dawson (d. 1911) was a bookseller and printer. He printed the three Christmas books that Bennett gave his friends in 1906, 1907, 1908. He was also a magistrate, and was a prime source of information about the Potteries. *The Grim Smile of the Five Towns* (1907) is dedicated 'to my old and constant friend Joseph Dawson, a student profoundly versed in the psychology of the Five Towns'. For an anecdote about him see p. 376. Bennett began writing the novel on 5 January.

Frank Bennett was a keen and capable musician. He was conductor of the Stoke-on-Trent Amateur Operatic Society, of which the principal contralto was Maud Bennett. They were doing both *The Mikado* and *The Yeoman of the Guard*.

F. C. Jennings was Bennett's tailor. His shop appears as Shillito's in the Five Towns novels.

On Pauline Smith (1882–1959), the South African novelist, see the other volumes.

Wells's *Ann Veronica* was published in October 1909.

Prince Peter Kropotkin (1842–1921).

KEELE / MS / 27
(*To Marguerite Soulié Bennett*)   [179, Waterloo Road]
                                                    Mardi
                                                    1 Dec 1909

Chérissime,

J'y suis. Il pleut sans cesse. Il fait 9 degrés au thermomètre à coté du lit. J'occupe la grande chambre. Tout le monde demande où tu es. Florence avait déjà arrangé tout un programme pour la 'semaine'. Tu es prise tous les soirs. On t'attend vendredi au lieu de samedi. Ma mère se porte assez bien. Elle a pleuré ce matin au petit déjeuner en me racontant que Frank ne voulait pas lui acheter exactement le charbon qu'il lui fallait. Mais elle est assez bien. Je mange chez Frank. Avec papa, mama et les enfants. Il y a un enfant alité. Je l'ai vu. Richard veut bien venir chez nous. Il est terriblement laid, le pauvre. J'ai été chez le dentiste ce matin 1½ heures. Il m'a mastiqué une fissure. J'y vais encore lundi. Grand dîner municipal ce soir. J'y assiste. J'ai été invité aussi à distribuer les prix à l'école des beaux arts et à faire une conférence sur le socialisme. Pas besoin de te dire que je ne marche pas. J'ai tout commandé chez Jennings. Chic pardessus. Chic complet! Tout est embêtant ici, mais je m'amuse. Faut pas oublier de te dire que je me porte très bien aujourd'hui. J'ai commencé le sanatogèn. J'ai beaucoup raconté la perte du pépin. Tout le monde est très sympathique. Tout le monde veut te voir. J'espère que tu as bien déjeuné chez Ida, et que le pepin est retrouvé et que tu n'as pas [?] avec la patronne de l'hôtel. Il y avait un tas de lettres qui m'attendait. Bref je suis énormément [?] pressé et j'ai laissé à Fontainebleau le plus important de tous les livres dont j'avais besoin. Je file maintenant [several words unreadable] vendredi à Manchester. Et je t'embrasse.

                                                    Ton A.B.

27. [Here I am. It rains incessantly. The temperature is 9 degrees according to the thermometer by the bed. I am in the big bedroom. Everyone asks where you are. Florence had already prepared a whole programme for the week. You have engagements every evening. You are expected on Friday instead of Saturday. My mother is fairly well. She cried during breakfast this morning as she told me that Frank wouldn't buy her exactly the kind of coal she needed. But she is fairly well. I have my meals with Frank. With papa, mamma and the children. One of the children is ill in bed. I saw him. Richard would like to come and stay with us. He is terribly ugly, poor thing. I spent 1½ hours at the dentist this morning. He put a filling in a cavity. I'm going again on Monday. Tonight there is a grand municipal dinner. I am going. And I've been

asked to give out prizes at the art school and make a speech on socialism. Needless to say, I refused. I have ordered everything at Jennings's. A smart overcoat! A smart suit! It is dull here, but I'm having a nice time. Mustn't forget to say that I'm feeling very well today. I have started the sanatogen. I have frequently told the story of the loss of the brolly. Everyone is very congenial. Everyone wants to see you. I hope that you enjoyed your lunch with Ida, that the brolly has been found and that you didn't [?] with the proprietress. A pile of letters was waiting for me. In short, I am terribly busy and I left the most important of all the books I needed in Fontainebleau. I am rushing off now [several words unreadable] Friday in Manchester. And I kiss you.]

Richard (1906–76) was Frank's eldest son. The other two children were Clayton (b. 1903) and Vernon (b. 1905).

KEELE / MS / 28   Midland Hotel
(*To Marguerite Soulié Bennett*)   Manchester
                                        vendredi soir. 10½ heures
                                        [3 Dec 1909]
Chérissime,

J'étais très content, même extrêmement content, de recevoir ta lettre hier après-midi; je venais de t'écrire. En te disant que tu retrouverais peut-être ton pépin je n'ai pas été, après tout, si terriblement simple, ingenu et maboule que ça. Enfin c'est très bien, ainsi que ton sommeil de 14 heures! I am very glad that you are not coming to England today. The sea-passage would have been terrible. But I suppose that there has been just as much rain & wind in Paris as here. It was an extremely rough night, and today it has rained & snowed & hailed all day. It is still raining. I came to Manchester this morning. J'ai été reçu d'une façon absolument épatante par la direction du journal de Manchester. Ce sont tous des types particulièrement intellectuels, fins, et charmants. Il y avait 4 qui m'ont offert un déjeuner dans le plus chic hôtel hors de Londres. Puis ils m'ont fait les honneurs de leurs salles de direction etc. (majestueuses). Ils m'ont fait voir tous les numéros des années 1872 - 1882 dont j'avais besoin pour mon roman. Puis ils m'ont reconduit à l'hôtel pour un thé, avec d'autres rédacteurs également spirituels et admirateurs. Bref, j'ai été extremely touched. Plus tard je suis allé au théâtre; j'ai dîné avec le directeur (homme bizarre et fin) à son club, et il a passé la soirée avec moi au balcon. Spectacle très artiste. Je suis rentré seul à l'hôtel pour t'écrire ce mot. À 11.15 je vais à la rédaction du journal pour voir l'imprimerie, l'expédition, etc. J'espère me coucher vers 1

heure du matin. Hier soir, après quelques bouts de causette
avec le docteur Russell et Frank, je me suis couché à 1 heure
également. You will get this letter on your arrival in London. I
fear the passage will be very bad and you ill. However you will
be all right at Tertia's. I return to Burslem tomorrow for lunch.

Bref, et laconiquement, je t'aime, et il me tarde assez de te
revoir.

Ton A.B. Époux

28. [I was very glad, indeed extremely glad, to receive your letter yesterday
afternoon; I had just written to you. When I told you you might find your brolly again, I
wasn't being so terribly simple, ingenuous, and batty as all that after all. It's a good
thing anyway and so is your 14 hour sleep.... I was given the most terrific welcome by
the management of the Manchester newspaper. They are all unusually intellectual,
clever and charming fellows. 4 of them took me out to lunch in the smartest hotel
outside London. Then they showed me all the backnumbers of the years 1872–82,
which I need for my novel. Then they took me back to the hotel for tea, with other staff
writers who were just as witty and admiring. In short, I was extremely touched. Later I
went to the theatre; I had dinner with the producer (an eccentric, clever man) at his
club and he spent the evening with me in the dress circle. It was a very artistic
performance. I have come back to the hotel alone to write this note. I'm going to the
newspaper offices at 11.15 to see the printing works, dispatch, etc. I am hoping to go to
bed by about 1 o'clock in the morning. Yesterday night I went to bed at 1 as well, after a
bit of a chat with Doctor Russell and Frank.... To be brief and laconic, I love you and
am longing to see you again.]

Bennett visited the offices of the *Manchester Guardian*. He said of *Clayhanger*, 'Never
before have I made one-quarter so many preliminary notes and investigations.'

KEELE / MS / 29
(*To Marguerite Soulié Bennett*)

179, Waterloo Road
Lundi
[6 December 1909]

Chérissime,

I write this morning at Mr. Dawson's shop, as I shan't have
time this afternoon. We spent last night at Frank's, and I went
to bed at one o'clock as usual. The Sanatogen has had a
wonderful effect on me. I am perfectly well in every way. The
weather is very bad, very dirty, but *not* very cold. I have been
talking politics all morning, and I am going to write a manifesto
for the liberal candidate. And also an article on the operatic
society for the *Sentinel*. The mater was unwell yesterday morning but today she is better. Tu m'excuseras si j'écris une lettre
parfaitement inepte, mais ma tête est tellement bouillant avec

des idées politiques, opératiques, et puis aussi avec tous les tuyaux que je ramasse continuellement pour mon livre que je ne peux pas écrire une lettre convenable à ma pauvre enf.

Je file maintenant à la gare à la rencontre de Florence qui m'accompagne chez Patty pour le déjeuner. Avant le dîner ce soir j'écris une chronique pour le *Sentinel* pour Frank. Et ce soir après le dîner je ferai la connaissance de ce musicien Havergal Brian qui m'a envoyé ses œuvres.

Donc, ma pauvre chérie, je te quitte. Je n'ai rien reçu de toi aujourd'hui, mais j'ai quitté la maison à 9.30 heures. Probablement une lettre arrivera plus tard dans la journée.

Les dactylographes de la pièce sont arrivées.

Mes amours à tout le monde.

Ton A.

29. [I am sorry if I am writing an utterly inept letter, but my brain is so simmering with ideas on politics and opera, as well as all the hints I'm picking up all the time for my book that I can't write a proper letter to my poor child.

Now I must rush to the station to meet Florence who is coming with me to have lunch with Patty. Before dinner this evening I am going to write an article for the *Sentinel* for Frank. Also this evening after dinner, I am going to make the acquaintance of the musician Havergal Brian who sent me his works.

So I must leave you my poor darling. I haven't heard from you today, but I left the house at 9.30. A letter will probably arrive later in the day.

The typists for the play have arrived.

Love to everyone.]

The manifesto, 'The Present Crisis: Plain Words to Plain Men', was published by Joseph Dawson, and also printed in the *New Age* on 30 December. It was a harsh attack on Toryism and the House of Lords.

The article on the operatic society appeared in the *Sentinel* on the 8th. It was an interview with the chairman of the managing committee, who was F. C. Jennings.

Patty: Pattie Bourne, daughter of Ezra Bourne by his first wife.

Havergal Brian (b. 1876), composer, was a Staffordshire man. He had just begun reviewing for the *Sentinel*.

KEELE / MS / 30
(*To Marguerite Soulié Bennett*)

[179, Waterloo Road]
[7 December 1909]

Ma sposa carissima,

J'ai eu ta lettre par le premier courrier, et j'en étais très content. Continue de bien dormir et de te porter bien, et tout sera parfait. Par le deuxième courrier j'ai eu la carte que je t'envoie. C'est embêtant. J'ai écrit tout de suite au plombier, à Mario, et à M. Deiro. Je pense donc que la chose s'arrangera sans délai.

Florence veut que tu prennes le train de midi quinze, vendredi. Tu arriveras ici à $3\frac{1}{2}$ heures. Le train après ça sera trop tard parce que, à cause des répétitions de Frank, on soupe ici à 6 heures ou $6\frac{1}{2}$ heures. Ici on ne parle que des représentations de la semaine prochaine. Je dine avec plusieurs copains chez le Dr. Russell demain soir; pas de femmes. Il t'invite pour le souper après la représentation de mardi prochain. Il y tient beaucoup, et j'ai accepté pour toi.

Yesterday we had a very fatiguing day. Lunch at Patty's. It was necessary to take two trains and then to walk a mile. To come home we had to walk 2 miles, and take 2 more trains. The weather was disgusting, but Patty was charming. Her husband est plus qu'un peu scie. I was going to bed early last night, but Russell came in to Frank's. Il racontait des histoires scabreuses jusqu'à une heure du matin. Pourtant j'ai très bien dormi. J'ai passé une heure avec M. Dawson ce matin, à propos de mon roman. Puis une heure avec le dentiste. Il a plombé ma dent avec de l'or. Ça a l'air d'être très bien fait. Deux longues séances. Prix 25 francs. L'or brille dans ma bouche. Après le déjeuner j'ai dormi (très peu) et puis j'ai écrit une assez longue chronique pour le *Sentinel*, histoire de faire une réclame pour l'opéra. Puis j'ai écrit douze lettres. Puis souper à $6\frac{1}{2}$ heures. À neuf heures j'irai passer une heure au music hall à Hanley. Frank est sorti pour une répétition. Ma mère est chez Auntie Bourne qui a une bronchite très accusée. Florence est ici avec moi. J'espère rentrer à $10\frac{1}{2}$ heures, et puis j'essayerai de roupiller. Toutes mes journées sont horriblement remplies. J'ai essayé la plupart de mes nouvelles toilettes. Demain je continuerai à chercher les tuyaux pour mon roman. Jeudi et vendredi je consacrerai à la politique. Demain thé chez Ethel. Soirée tranquille. Véritablement je m'embête en cachette sans toi. Il me tarde de te tâtonner, de t'écouter, de te taquiner délicatement, et de voir une femme bien mise. C'est très bien que tu t'amuses. Tertia dit que tu te portes très bien.

Mon enf., je t'embrasse avec tendresse.

A.

30. [I got your letter by the first post and was very pleased with it. Go on sleeping

and feeling well and everything will be perfect. I got the card which is enclosed by the second post. It is annoying. I wrote immediately to the plumber, Mario and M. Deiro. So I think the matter should be sorted out without delay.

Florence wants you to take the 12.15 (midday) train on Friday. You will arrive here at 3.30. The next train would be too late as we have dinner here at 6 or 6.30 because of Frank's rehearsals. The only topic of conversation here is next week's performances. Tomorrow evening, I am having dinner at Dr Russell's with several pals; no women. He has invited you to supper after next Tuesday's performance. He sets much store by it and I have accepted on your behalf.... He told scabrous stories until one in the morning. But I slept very well. I spent an hour with Mr Dawson this morning, on my novel. Then an hour at the dentist. He gave me a gold filling. It seems to be well done. Two long appointments. Cost—25 francs. The gold shines in my mouth. After lunch I slept (very little) and then I wrote quite a long article for the *Sentinel*, giving a plug for the opera. Then I wrote twelve letters. Then supper at 6.30. At nine o'clock I will spend an hour at the Hanley music-hall. Frank has gone to a rehearsal. My mother is visiting Auntie Bourne who is having a bad attack of bronchitis. Florence is here with me. I hope to be back at 10.30, and then I'll try and have a nap. All my days are horribly full. I have tried on most of my new clothes. Tomorrow I'll go on looking for hints for my novel. I will devote Thursday and Friday to politics. Tea with Ethel tomorrow. A quiet evening. I am really bored hidden away without you. I'm longing to put out my hand and find you, listen to you, tease you gently and see a well-dressed woman. I'm glad you are enjoying yourself. Tertia says that you are well. My child, I kiss you tenderly.]

KEELE / MS / 31
(*To Marguerite Soulié Bennett*)

179, Waterloo Rd
Mercredi
[8 December 1909]

Chérissime,

I had your long & excellent letter this morning. I shall be at Stoke on Friday. So will Florence. As regards Emily, you are quite right to do exactly as pleases you. I learnt one thing from Frank a long time ago, and that is not to try to interfere in difficulties between a wife and a sister. Des scènes terribles se passaient, dans le temps, entre Florence et Tertia. Frank restait toujours absolument coi. Naturellement il prenait la part de sa femme, mais il était tout ce qu'il y a de plus aimable avec Tertia. Donc, c'était très bien. Je ne reconnais qu'une chose c.à.d. que Emily est infiniment embêtante; mais ça n'empêche en rien que je sois le chef de la famille. I slept very badly last night, but I am very well. Il est indiscutable que je m'embête seul. Today we have been to tea at Port Hill House. Beaucoup de 'Woods,' May, et Patty. Last night I went to the music-hall. C'était très bien. J'y ai rencontré un ami, qui m'a reconduit chez Frank. Went to bed at 12 o'clock. I was with M. Dawson this morning for three hours. J'ai assisté à la séance des juges de paix. (Il y a toujours plusieurs.) On m'a mis avec les juges sur leur banc sacré, et ce soir, naturellement le *Sentinel* dit que M. Bennett était avec les juges. Un des juges c'est M. Dawson. Frank et Florence sont terriblement pris par les répétitions. Aussi les costumes ne sont pas arrivés, et tout le monde est bouleversé, surtout le metteur en scène, qui s'écoute trop. Je vais passer une soirée tranquille dans les jupes de ma mère. J'ai des machines politiques régionales à étudier, et puis aussi une lettre à la *Sentinel* à propos de la critique musicale. M. Greene a trouvé un nouveau critique, compositeur et vrai artiste. Sa première critique a offusqué tout le monde, mais c'est très bien. M. Greene est pour son critique et contre son public, et moi, 'à la demande générale des vrais amateurs,' je vais donner un appui moral au critique qui a été si critiqué. C'est amusant. Mais, dans son genre, c'est sérieux.

Maintenant je vais chez Frank pour siffler une tasse et tailler une bavette. C'est à dire le souper, qui se passe à 6.30 à cause des répétitions.

Dis, mon enf. Amène toi.

Amitiés de tout le monde.

Ton A.

31. [Florence and Tertia used to have terrible scenes at one time. Frank always stayed quite out of it. Of course he would take his wife's part but he behaved in the most agreeable way to Tertia. So everything was quite all right. I will just acknowledge one thing, that is, that Emily is boundlessly annoying; but that does not stop me being head of the family.... A lot of 'Woods', May and Patty. Last night I went to the music-hall. It was very good. I met a friend there, who took me back to Frank's.

I was present at the magistrates' session. (There are always several magistrates.) I was put with the magistrates on their sacred bench, and this evening, of course, the *Sentinel* says that Mr Bennett was with the magistrates. Mr Dawson is one of the magistrates. Frank and Florence are terribly busy with rehearsals. And the costumes have not arrived and everybody is in a state of confusion, particularly the producer, who takes himself too seriously. I am going to spend a quiet evening, hiding in my mother's skirts. I have to study regional political machinery and then also a letter to the *Sentinel* on musical criticism. Mr Greene has found a new critic, a composer and a real artist. His first review offended everyone but it is very good. Mr Greene is supporting his critic, against his public and I, 'in response to general demand from real enthusiasts', am giving moral support to the critic who has been so much criticized. It is amusing. But serious in its way.

Now I'm going to Frank's to swig down a cup of something and have a chat. That is, for supper, which takes place at 6.30 because of the rehearsals. Well, my child, bring yourself here. Regards from everyone.]

KENNERLEY / MS / 32
(*To Tertia Kennerley*)

Villa des Néfliers
24 June 1910

My dear Tertia,

I have just finished my 160,000 word novel. My opinion as to the mater is worth nothing, as anyone can sway it. On the whole I am slightly inclined to your idea, that she ought not to be alone. But Mrs. Marriott, for instance, always convinces me to the contrary. Assuming that she ought not be alone, there is another point. Would the sum total of unhappiness be unduly increased if she was with someone else? Your suggestion that she ought to be with Emily ne me sourit pas du tout. She wouldn't like it. Emily would absolutely refuse, & after all it wouldn't last. Couldn't. The unhappiness of both would be increased. Nor do I think for a moment she could be at Frank's. If she lived there, all Florence's worst points would inevitably come out & Frank at any rate would be in hades. If she is to be with anyone she ought to be with Sep; she gets on well with Maud, & she could amuse herself by killing a child or two by some senile mistake. The objection to this is that I don't think Sep would consent. *You* might ask him. *I* never dare ask Sep anything. I don't know why. Perhaps it is his mysteriousness that affrights me. I haven't even had courage to inform him that he is dishonest in not paying the mater the interest on the money he owes her. It seems to me that of the family three members Sissie, Emily, & Sep are devoid of any sense of family obligation—except *towards* themselves. If the mater migrates to anyone it will infallibly be to you. The only reason you give against this is not a good one. Mind you, I don't say or think she *ought* to go to you: I only speak of your argument against.

Although, unaccountably, in the most excellent health, I am in a state of extreme temporary exhaustion. I hope you will not object to bringing Richard, as we see no other way of him coming. I am in communication with a hotel at Carantec, & I have stated as an ultimatum that your ménage and ours will each require 2 rooms & 3 beds,—and that we will pay 25 frs. per day in all, that is, ten bob apiece. If these terms are not accepted I shall try somewhere else. Anyhow, *we* shall be in Carantec not later than the 12th & shall arrange convenablement. I think you will enjoy the journey unless by ill-luck you have a thoroughly rotten sea. You must sleep at St. Brieux on the Tuesday night (Hôtel de France). It will be much better if you can start on the 11th, instead of the 18th as the French holiday season really begins on the 13th July (14th July is their August Bank Holiday) & it would be well to be installed then. From all I can gather the district is a fair treat. We shall leave here about the 5th.

Marguerite is sending the robe. She thought it was done with.

Loves, E.A.B.

32. Bennett finished writing *Clayhanger* on 23 June. It was published on 15 September.

Sissie: Fanny Gertrude.

Tertia and the children came for a month-long holiday at Carantec, Brittany. Bennett wrote in his *Journals* on the first day, 'It takes some time to get used to the great central fact that you have nothing to do that must be done.' On 15 August he wrote, 'I have now taken what nearly everybody said I was incapable of taking and never would take, a long holiday. From July 2 to yesterday I did nothing whatever in the way of work except 3 short articles for the *New Age*, which I was obliged to do. Of course I had to attend to my correspondence; but I kept that as short as possible. I wrote an illustrated journal at Carantec, and I also did a number of paintings and sketches.'

KEELE / MS / 33
(*To Marguerite Soulié Bennett*) 179, Waterloo Rd
Dimanche matin
[9 April 1911]

Très chère enfant,

Autrement je me porte très bien. J'ai très bien dormi chaque nuit, & j'ai des cigares que je peux fumer. Aussi ai-je commandé de très chic complets, et je me suis acheté des cravates merveilleuses. Merci de ta délicieuse lettre, qui m'a fait un intense plaisir par sa seule tournure. Je ne t'ai pas écrit hier. C'était inutile, puisqu'il n'y a pas de courrier à Londres le dimanche. Du reste il y avait trop à dire. J'ai écrit hier un précis du dernier livre de *Hilda Lessways*. Doran a télégraphié que le journal en question est prêt à abandonner son règle ordinaire, qui le défend d'acheter un roman dont il n'a pas lu le manuscrit entier!! Donc j'ai envoyé un précis des derniers chapitres, et il y a des chances (maigres) qu'on me prend le feuilleton de l'incomprise Hilda au prix de 250 000 000 000 000 000 francs. (Je veux dire 2 milles.) Ma mère est certainement beaucoup mieux. Mais elle est pourrie des griefs qu'elle raconte tout le temps. La maison a l'air d'être bien tenue par Pattie, mais ma mère n'est pas trop contente. Aussi Pattie a mauvaise caractère, et la réplique très vive. Enfin ça pourra aller, et ça ne pourra pas aller. En somme je suis tout à fait confortable sauf pour la saleté. L'hospitalité de Florence est très franche et très bien. Soirée excellente hier avec des amis. Tout le monde demande de tes nouvelles. J'ai eu un assez bon voyage solitaire de Londres. Le salon de thé à la gare terminus était bondé de femmes. Pas une table. Je me suis installé donc dans un bar de la gare, sur un tabouret haut de 1 mètre 75 c. et j'ai bu une tasse de thé et mangé un plat de poulet et du jambon. Coute — 1 shilling 5. J'aurais bien voulu que les Godebskis me vissent dans ce bar sur ce tabouret. Ecoute un peu; mardi en huit, jour de votre départ, je serai forcé de rester à Burslem jusqu'à l'après-midi pour mes derniers essayages (très important!). Non, je trouverai ça moi-même et je t'écrirai. Je suis très [five words unreadable]. Mille mots idiots mais les paroles très sensées à tes parents. Je t'embrasse tendrement.

A.

33. [Otherwise I am in very good health. I have slept well every night, and I have some cigars which I can smoke. And I have ordered some very smart suits and have bought myself some beautiful ties. Thank you for your delicious letter; its turn of phrase alone gave me intense pleasure. I did not write to you yesterday. It was useless to do so since there is no post in London on Sundays. Besides, there was too much to say. Yesterday I wrote a summary of the last book of *Hilda Lessways*. Doran telegraphed to say that the newspaper in question is ready to abandon its usual rule, which forbids it to buy a novel unless the entire manuscript has been read!! So I sent a summary of the last chapters and there is a (slim) chance that I may sell the serial of the misunderstood Hilda for 250,000,000,000,000,000 francs (I mean 2 thousand.) My mother certainly is much better. But she is festering with resentments that she talks about all the time. The house looks as if Pattie were running it well but my mother is not too pleased. And Pattie is ill-natured and sharp-tongued. So things may work out, or they may not. All in all I am perfectly comfortable except for the dirt. Florence's hospitality is open and very good. An excellent evening with friends yesterday. Everyone asked after you. I had quite a good journey alone from London. The tea-room at the terminal station was chock-full of women. Not a single free table. So I settled down in a station bar, on a stool 1.75 metres high, and I had a cup of tea and a plate of chicken and ham. The cost—1 shilling 5d. I would very much have liked the Godebskis to see me in the bar on that stool. Now listen; on Tuesday week, the day of our departure, I will be obliged to stay in Burslem until the afternoon for my last (very important) fittings. No, I will find that myself and I will write. I am very [five words illegible]. A thousand sweet nothings but thoughtful sentiments to your relatives. I kiss you tenderly.]

Bennett came to England on 8 April, and remained there for two months. Marguerite joined him in Burslem on the 13th, and they remained there until the 18th.

George Doran (1869–1956) became Bennett's principal American publisher in 1909, in part through the enthusiasm of his wife Mary (d. 1951) for *The Old Wives' Tale*. Bennett had little reputation in America in 1909, but within two years Doran made him a famous figure there. See the other volumes for correspondence. The *Saturday Evening Post* negotiated to buy serial rights to *Hilda Lessways*, but did not buy them. Bennett wrote the novel from 5 January to 13 June. It was published on 21 September.

KEELE / MS / 34   [179, Waterloo Road]
(*To Marguerite Soulié Bennett*)   Lundi matin
                                           10. heures
                                           [10 April 1911]

Chérie,

Ta lettre n'est pas encore arrivée. Ma mère est beaucoup mieux. Elle a bien dormi. Elle porte toujours son peignoir, qui est bien, deux châles, et une broche. Quand elle dort sur le canapé, elle a tout ça; en plus une couverture, une boule, et un coussin sur son ventre. Hier après-midi elle a dormi jusqu'à 4 heures presque. Je suis entré dans le salon sans la réveiller, et j'y suis resté une demi heure. Puis j'ai eternué — je ne pus m'empêcher, et ainsi je l'ai reveillée en sursaut. C'était énormément comique, et elle avait largement assez dormi. Hier j'ai visité Madame Beardmore, et j'ai vu le jardin de Sep. qui est épatant comme travail. Ce jeune homme fait de l'argent. Il en met même de côté. Enfin il me l'a dit. Je pense que je suis le seul humain ainsi honoré. Je ne t'ai pas dit qu'il y a une espèce de cousine de Flo qui habite avec les Frank, et qui est très bien (mais ficelée); jeune, pimpante, fière, assez agréable à voir, et bonne cuisinière. Elle est fiancée, et passe toutes ses soirées avec son type dans la salle à manger. Avec elle, Florence n'a besoin que d'une domestique; et tout le monde s'aime beaucoup. Elle s'appelle 'Fan'. Encore une soirée très bien hier. Mary Ellen, Edward, Sep, Maud, Frank Beardmore, Sissie (énorme) et Russell. Russell et moi sommes restés les derniers — une heure. Je dors très bien, et je fume trop, et je ne fiche rien sauf des notations. Galsworthy et Madame sont à Manchester pour les répétitions d'une petite pièce, un acte. Je les verrai demain soir, chez M. Mair à dîner. Maintenant, t'ayant préalablement embrassée, je sors pour mes petites affaires.

                                                   Ton A.

Quand tu m'écriras *mardi* tu te serviras de l'enveloppe ci-incluse. Tous les autres jours tu m'écriras ici.

P.S. Une heure. Je viens de lire ta lettre qui est arrivée à midi. Ma pauvre enfant, tu aurais dû savoir qu'il n'y a pas de courrier à Londres le dimanche. Donc c'était impossible que tu eusses une lettre dimanche écrite samedi; donc j'ai écrit seulement dimanche. Je suis très content que tu viennes avec Gertrude.

A.B.

34. [Your letter still hasn't arrived. My mother is much better. She is sleeping well. She always wears her dressing-gown, which is nice, two shawls and a brooch. When she sleeps on the sofa she has all that on; and a blanket, a hot water bottle, and a cushion on her stomach. She slept until nearly 4 o'clock yesterday afternoon. I went into the drawing-room without waking her and stayed there for half an hour. Then I sneezed—I couldn't stop myself—and I woke her up with a start. It was tremendously comical and she had had easily enough sleep. Yesterday I called on Mrs Beardmore and I saw Sep's garden, which is a marvellous piece of work. That young man is making money and can even put some aside. Or that's what he told me. I think I am the only person alive to be so honoured. I haven't told you that some kind of cousin of Flo's lives with the Franks. She is very nice (but overdresses); she is young, neat, proud, fairly pleasant to look at, and a good cook. She is engaged and spends every evening in the dining-room with her young man. With her there, Florence only needs one maid; and everyone likes each other very much. She is called 'Fan'. Another very pleasant evening yesterday. Mary Ellen, Edward, Sep, Maud, Frank Beardmore, Sissie (who is huge), and Russell. Russell and I were the last to leave—at one. I am sleeping very well and I smoke too much and the only thing I think about is notations. Galsworthy and Mrs are in Manchester for rehearsals of a short play, one act. I will see them tomorrow, at dinner with Mr Mair. Now after I have kissed you, I am going out on my little errands.... When you write to me on *Tuesday*, you will use the envelope I have enclosed. All the other days, write to me here.

P.S. One o'clock. I have just read your letter which arrived at noon. My poor girl, you should have known that there is no post in London on Sunday. So a letter written to you on Saturday couldn't reach you on Sunday; so I wrote on Sunday only. I am very glad you're coming with Gertrude.]

Fan, Mary Ellen, and Gertrude: unidentified.
For letters to John Galsworthy (1867–1933) see Vols. II and III.
G. H. Mair (1887–1926) was on the staff of the *Manchester Guardian*.

KEELE / MS / 35
(*To Marguerite Soulié Bennett*)

Authors' Club
2, Whitehall Court
22 avril 1911

Très chère enfant,

Ta lettre m'a fait plaisir. Or, je vais te dire quelque-chose qui te fera plaisir. J'ai relu presque tout ce que j'ai écrit de *Hilda*; et c'est vraiment assez bien. Il y a des pages épatantes. Si seulement je peux l'achever d'une façon assez brillante!

Alors tu étais à Londres hier! Moi aussi. Extrêmement. J'ai déjeuné avec Wells et un autre au Reform Club — plantureusement. Wells boit trop de porto, habituellement. Puis je suis allé chez le photographe. Je me suis idiotement trompé d'adresse. *Gower* Street au lieu de Baker St. Donc, étant en retard, j'ai pris un taxi. Le photographe est un jeune allemand, avec sa femme — très convenable et un peu précieux et trop serieux. Il m'a pris dans trois poses, plastiques. Tu auras les épreuves, et le type dit qu'il aime mieux être sévèrement critiqué! Puis je suis rentré au Club pour le thé et le somme. J'ai rencontré Rickards au Café Royal, où nous avons bien dîné dans un atmosphère infectissime. Il attendait des amis qui ne sont pas arrivés. Plus tard nous voilà au Palace Music-hall, pour voir les danseurs russes. Pavlova est vraiment très bien. Les Galsworthy étaient là. Aussi une cocotte mulâtresse avec qui Rickards couche actuellement. Il dit qu'elle est très bien, et que ses épaules sont d'une couleur très belle. Je lui ai dit que j'ai toujours eu envie de coucher avec une négresse. Il m'a offert la mulâtresse. Peureux, je n'ai pas marché. Nous n'avons causé ni avec les Galsworthy ni avec la rouleuse. Plus tard — Café. J'ai demandé de la camomile. Inconnue! J'ai pris du thé. A une heure et quart je n'étais pas encore endormi. J'ai bien dormi jusqu'à 8 heures. Je me sentais fatigué mais bien portant. Toute la matinée j'ai travaillé. Je suis très discuté dans ce club. J'en suis même l'étoile. A chaque instant je surprends des couples qui chuchotent: 'He ... *The Old Wives' Tale* ... Very good ... Very fine.' Et quand je m'approche ils se taisent, confus. Dans le *Manchester Guardian* ce matin, réproduction de la caricature de Max. Je te l'adresse sous ce pli. Elle n'est pas très bien, je pense. Mais les caricatures politiques sont très bien. Je vais au vernissage cet après-midi. Puis chez Tertia. Je compte absolument sur toi mercredi. Maintenant, pour mon âme et tout ça, tu sais; donc je ne te le dis pas.

Ton A.B.

35. [Your letter gave me pleasure. Now I will tell you something which will give you pleasure. I have read through almost all that I have written of *Hilda*; and it is really quite good. There are some smashing pages. If only I can give it a sufficiently brilliant ending!

So you were in London yesterday! So was I. Very much so. I had lunch—a lavish lunch—with Wells and one other at the Reform Club. Wells habitually drinks too much port. Then I went to the photographer. Like a fool, I mistook the address. *Gower* Street instead of Baker Street. So as I was late, I took a taxi. The photographer is a young German, with a wife. He is very respectable, a little precious and too earnest. He took me in three sculptural poses. You will have the prints and the fellow says he likes to be harshly criticized. Then I returned to the Club for tea and a nap. I met Rickards at the Cafe Royal, where we had a good dinner in the most horrible atmosphere. He was expecting friends who did not arrive. Later, there we were at the Palace Music-hall to see the Russian dancers. Pavlova is really very good. The Galsworthys were there. Also a half-caste tart whom Rickards sleeps with at present. He says that she is very fine and that her shoulders are a very beautiful colour. I told him that I have always wanted to sleep with a negress. He offered me the half-caste. I took fright and went no further. We did not get into conversation either with the Galsworthys or with the whore. Later we went to a Cafe. I asked for camomile tea. Unheard of! I had ordinary tea. I was still awake at a quarter past one. Then I slept until 8 o'clock. I felt tired but healthy. I worked for the whole morning. I am talked about a great deal in this club. Indeed I am its star member. I constantly come across couples whispering 'He ... *The Old Wives' Tale* ... *Very good* ... *Very fine.*' And they fall into embarrassed silence when I approach. Max's caricature was reproduced in this morning's *Manchester Guardian*. I have enclosed it with this letter. It is not very good. I am going to the vernissage this afternoon. Then to Tertia's. I am absolutely counting on you on Wednesday. Now I won't tell you about my soul and all that, as you know about it already.]

E. O. Hoppé (1878–1972) was the photographer.

The cartoon by Max Beerbohm (1872–1956) shows Bennett standing with one arm extended to a cradle, the other to a grave. Terrace houses are in the background. The legend beneath reads: 'Mr. Arnold Bennett. Personally conducted tour from the cradle, through Bursley, to the grave.' Bennett and Beerbohm had been friends since 1909, when Beerbohm wrote to Bennett about *The Old Wives' Tale* to express his appreciation 'to the man who had laid so large an aesthetic debt on me'.

KENNERLEY / MS / 36
(*To Tertia Kennerley*)

Villa des Néfliers
29 July 1911

My dear Tertia,

We have perused your document with the greatest satisfaction, & I have filed it. I didn't think I would do any more parturitions in novels, but I will do one more, now. We haven't yet heard that kid's name; but we have heard that Mary has been ill in bed. We have your American publisher here & his wife. I have seen a dummy copy of *Dash*. I may say I don't like Jowett's specimen picture at all. I expect he has been silly enough to do something that he thought would suit them. Don't alter the book any more, & if you have any further trouble let me know. Mrs. Doran is a very decent & handsome woman. It

is an absolute fact that she pours out adjectives the whole time.
Oh! My! Lovely! De-licious! First time she has been to Europe.
Still I like her. She is perfectly mad on children (has a girl of
$13\frac{1}{2}$) & strokes Richard all the time she can get near him.
Richard is easily the most Bennetty Bennett that I ever struck.
But he carries off his singular selfishness with great skill, & he is
never disobedient. He never exaggerates. When Marguerite
was giving him his French lesson, there was the sentence,
'J'aime ma tante.' Asked in an aside if he did, he wouldn't give a
definite yes. He said: 'Anyhow I like you better than mother.'
He is most apprehensive about everything, & a perfect terror
for dovetailing together a long programme that has to be kept
to. When I told him I should be ready to go out with him in a
quarter of an hour, & not before, he went off gloomy & then
came back & said: 'If you're going out in a quarter of an hour, I
shall just have time to look through the paper.' Emily is treating
us with great severity. I arranged to pay her rent for her, & was
much crushed by a letter later saying that I pretended to be in
favour of women, but that if I really was I should give her the
£60 all at once instead of doling it out untrustfully once a
quarter! This rent was supposed to free me from liabilities.
However, she wrote me that she had been expecting £33 from
someone & had only got £5. So I told her to go to Pinker and ask
for what she wanted. She went & obtained £50. We are showing
the Dorans round. Marguerite has been indisposed in the
bladder but is better. Today we motor all day. 100° in the kiosk
& 91° in my bedroom.

Our loves, E.A.B.

36. Margaret Kennerley was born on 4 July 1911.
Doran published Tertia's children's tale, *Gentleman Dash*, in 1912, with illustrations
by P. H. Jowett.
On Bennett's agent, J. B. Pinker (1863–1922) see Vol. I.

KEELE / MS / 37
(*To Marguerite Soulié Bennett*)   Authors' Club
                                                     Friday
                                                     8 Sept 1911
Dearest,
    I get your letters in the evening, & I had the last, last night,
after coming from Sharpes. While I was at Sharpes your letter

to her arrived, & Mrs. Sharpe was enchanted at the idea of you staying with her. I send you by book-post a special early copy of *Hilda* which I have obtained from the publishers for you. There was no difficulty yesterday at Marie Tempest's. She was at home with Graham Browne, her lover. It had been arranged that he should play the principal male part, and then he thought he couldn't do it, and they were thinking of getting an unknown actor to play the part, & wanted my advice. I advised them to keep Browne in the part, because Marie Tempest will play better with him than with a stranger. I then returned to London in her car, having had an agreeable lunch and chat. She is a very nice woman, & the lover is all right too. *The Great Adventure* is now definitely sold to the Little Theatre and the contract is to be signed on Monday. Marie says that *The Honeymoon* is to be produced on Thursday Oct. 5th *certain*. I shall therefore leave Liverpool on October 7th Saturday. The Sharpes will be delighted to have you at any time. My boil is slowly getting better. I have to dress it myself now, 3 or 4 times a day. Et c'est assommant au plus haut degré. I go to Manchester this afternoon. Your letter due this evening will be forwarded to me. I expect to return on Tuesday.

Well, good luck to your story. Je te bise tendrement.

Ton A.

37. Bennett came to England for the month of September.

Marie Tempest (1864–1942) produced and starred in *The Honeymoon*. Dion Boucicault played the leading male role. The play opened at the Royalty Theatre on 6 October and ran for four months. It was Bennett's first commercial success in the theatre. Graham Browne (d. 1937) married Marie Tempest after the death of her second husband.

The Great Adventure was produced provincially in 1911, and in London at the Kingsway Theatre in 1913. It ran there for 673 nights.

KEELE / MS / 38
(*To Marguerite Soulié Bennett*)

Burslem
Monday
[11 September 1911]

Darling,

I may tell you that I have been ill; but I am now better. Diarrhoea! I went out in a large motor car yesterday, il y avait une panne, which lasted 4 hours. During this time I had bread-

and-cheese & ginger ale for lunch, & then at tea I had Ceylon tea & cake, & then the editor of the *Manchester Guardian* entertained Mair & me to dinner at the Midland Hotel—très chic. My diarrhoea began before that, & went on all the evening, & began again this morning at 5 o'clock. I got some medicine at 8 o'clock, & began to be better. I was just well enough to leave Manchester at noon, & I got here to Burslem at 1.30. I had cornflour for lunch, & I have just had tea with the mater. I sleep at Frank's. Frank est toujours dans la dêche. They cannot move into a better house because they cannot afford. C'est très extraordinaire. Faut que je lui parle un peu. J'ai beaucoup parlé avec Florence, qui a ses idées. I go to London tomorrow morning. Mrs. Mair returns tomorrow. The doctor has forbidden her to go to the United States. So I hope she will be able to play in *Milestones*. Mair is very anxious to come & live in London. The mater is fairly well, but the social atmosphere of this place is *appalling*. I quite understand the severity of Tertia towards it. If you have not enough money you must let me know. Il y en a — comme toujours. Je ne m'appelle pas Frank.

Ton A.

Tendrement te bise-je!

38. *Milestones* was Bennett's greatest theatrical success. He wrote it in August 1911 in collaboration with Edward Knoblock. It opened at the Royalty Theatre on 5 March 1912 and ran for 609 nights. There were many productions elsewhere. The cast included Haidée Wright, Mary Jerrold, and Gladys Cooper but not Mrs G. H. Mair (1887–1952), whose stage name was Maire O'Neill. She was originally Molly Allgood, J. M. Synge's fiancée, and actress in his plays.

KEELE / MS / 39
(*To Marguerite Soulié Bennett*)

Whitehall Court,
Tuesday
[12 September 1911]

Dearest girl,

I have just got back to London and my diarrhoea is cured. I have found 2 letters & one post card from you. Many thanks. Je suis content que tu as été contente d'être Madame Arnold Bennett. I enclose a cheque for two hundred francs which you can cash in Paris. Burslem est infecte. Je suis heureux de l'avoir quitté, mais je pense que je peux arranger un peu les affaires de Frank. Il n'a aucun initiatif, cet homme. Je trouve les deux autres enfants terriblement gauches, rustres, et malhonnêtes. Ça sera terrible pour Richard quand il réintégrera sa maison. Tout le monde a été très hospitalier. Madame Anne a failli de mourir. Son fils se marie samedi — encore un cadeau à donner. J'ai trouvé un tas de lettres ici. La première du *Great Adventure* est remise à lundi, parce que l'actrice choisie pour Janet était impossible dans ce rôle si important. Lee Mathews est un idiot; il se croit tellement rusé qu'il arrive à l'idiocie. J'ai une chronique sur Blackpool à écrire. Aussi me demande-t-on un conte très court que je pourrais écrire dans une matinée — 525 francs — je ne sais pas si je l'écrirai. Je souffre de ton absence, mais je m'en tirerai. J'avais un rêve compliqué et polisson l'autre nuit. Tu étais dans une robe ultra élégante, mais sans absolument rien dessous. Alors, tu levais la dite robe pour faire une délicieuse petite crotte qui est tombée dans un cendrier, et puis il y avait la chaise longue... à la fin la robe était complètement dechirée, et tu étais desolée mais contente. N'en dis rien à Madame Bergeret — elle serait sans doute choquée. Écris toujours ton conte et t'en fiches pas mal de *Hilda*.

Je te bise dans la robe sans rien dessous, un peu brutalement.

Ton A.

39. [I am pleased that you were pleased to be Mrs Arnold Bennett.... Burslem is vile. I am glad to have left it but I think I can do a little to sort out Frank's affairs. The man has no initiative. I find the two other children terribly uncouth, loutish and rude. It will be terrible for Richard when he returns home. Everyone has been very hospitable. Madame Anne nearly died. Her son is getting married on Saturday—another present to give. I found a pile of letters here. The first night of *The Great Adventure* has been put off till Monday because the actress chosen to be Janet was impossible in this important part. Lee Mathews is an idiot; he thinks himself so cunning that he verges on idiocy. I have an article on Blackpool to write. And I am being asked for a very short story that I could write in one morning—525 francs—I do not know whether I will write it. I am missing you but I will survive. I had a complicated and licentious dream the other night. You were in an ultra-elegant dress, but with absolutely nothing underneath. Then you lifted up the afore-mentioned dress to make a lovely little turd which fell into an ashtray, and then there was the chaise longue...; in the end the dress was quite torn and you were devastated but satisfied. Don't tell Madame Bergeret—she would certainly be shocked. Go on writing your story and don't worry about *Hilda*. I kiss you in the dress with nothing underneath, rather roughly.]

Madame Anne: unidentified.

The Great Adventure, dramatized from the novel *Buried Alive*, 1908, opened in Glasgow on 18 September, with Frederick Lloyd and Helen Haye. The review in the *Glasgow Herald* praised both of them. The play was not produced in London until 1913. On Lee

Mathews (d. 1931) see Vols. I and II. He was Bennett's theatrical agent for some years.

'Ten Hours at Blackpool' was published in *Eyewitness* on 21 September, and reprinted in *Paris Nights* in 1913.

Madame Bergeret: an acquaintance with whom Marguerite stayed from time to time.

KEELE / MS / 40
(*To Marguerite Soulié Bennett*) Authors' Club
           Mercredi soir 11.30
           [13 or 20 September 1911]
Dearest,

Je suis totalement désolé parce que je suis sûr qu'avec ton chien, ton neveu, et ta bicyclette, tu as eu une mauvaise traversée, peut-être très mauvaise. Remets-toi vite, et viens me voir vendredi. Je serai à la gare de Victoria, mais je ne peux pas t'accompagner à Euston, parce qu'il y aura une répétition à 11 heures et quart. C'était fixé pour onze heures, mais j'ai changé ça pour pouvoir venir à Victoria. Je te rencontrerai de nouveau au déjeuner. J'ai assisté à une répétition ce matin. Marie Tempest est *épatante*, et je pense que ça sera très bien. Le metteur en scène, quoique un peu vieux jeu est admirable. Enfin, tout le monde en est enthousiasmé. Tout le monde demande de tes nouvelles. Au téléphone j'ai causé avec Mdme. Lowndes ce matin. Elle m'a demandé l'état de ta santé! Je lui ai dit que tu avais été un peu souffrante toute l'année, mais que maintenant tu es mieux. Elle m'a dit: 'Elle devrait avoir un enfant. C'est ça qu'il lui faut.' Je lui ai dit 'Non.' Elle m'a répondu 'Nonsense!' etc. Beaucoup de personnes me soufflent à peu près la même chose. Je n'en crois rien. Mais il faut dire que ma principale raison contre la maternité est disparue. Je craignais, tout en ne disant rien, que nos idées sur la façon d'élever un enfant seraient tellement différentes que nous aurions des histoires serieuses là-dessus. J'avais tort, complètement. Ta façon avec Richard m'a charmé et enchanté. C'est tellement la mienne que j'en suis bleu. Je ne pense pas un instant que la maternité changerait ta santé en quoi que ce soit, mais je ne voudrais plus te priver du plaisir (c.à.d. des peines et des embêtements) d'être mère.

Il me tarde horriblement et péniblement de te revoir. Encore 36 heures. C'est assommant.

Je te bise, mère, mais a-t-on le droit de biser une mère?
Love to all at Bellevue.

Ton A.

40. [I am utterly devastated because I am sure that with your dog, your nephew, and your bicycle, you had a bad crossing, perhaps a very bad one. Recover quickly and come and see me on Friday. I will be at Victoria station, but I cannot go to Euston with you, because there will be a rehearsal at 11.15. It was to have been at eleven, but I changed it so as to be able to go to Victoria. I will meet you again for lunch. I attended a rehearsal this morning. Marie Tempest is *terrific*, and I think it will be very good. The producer is admirable, though a bit old-fashioned. In fact he has made everyone enthusiastic. Everyone asks after you. I had a talk with Madame Lowndes on the telephone this morning. She asked after your health! I told her that you had been rather unwell all this year, but that you are better now. She said: 'She should have a child. That's what she needs.' I told her 'No.' She answered 'Nonsense!' etc. A lot of people mutter much the same thing to me. I don't believe a word of it. But I must admit that my main reason against motherhood has disappeared. Although I did not say anything, I was afraid that our ideas on how to bring up children would be so different that we would have serious quarrels about it. I was completely wrong. Your way with Richard has charmed and delighted me. It was so much what I would want that I am speechless. I don't think for a moment that motherhood would change your health in any way, but I would not want to deprive you any longer of the pleasure (that is, of the burdens and annoyances) of being a mother.

I long terribly and painfully to see you again. 36 hours more. It is unbearable. I kiss you, mother, but is one allowed to kiss a mother!]

Mrs Belloc Lowndes (1868–1947), author of many popular books, was a friend of Bennett's, probably from the turn of the century, and became a close friend of Marguerite's. For a letter and other references to her see the other volumes.

Bellevue was the home of Bennett's friend Fred Alcock in Newhaven. Alcock was a customs officer and a musician.

KEELE / MS / 41
(*To Marguerite Soulié Bennett*)

On Board the Cunard
R.M.S. *Lusitania*
7th Oct 1911

Dearest Girl,

Immediately I got on this boat, I was struck by a *new* sense of my own importance. Seats at the purser's dining table had been reserved for me, & deckchairs also. The Chairman of the Cunard had given orders that I was to be looked after, and Mr. Hoblyn, the Liverpool manager, came & showed Knoblock & me over the ship, & offered me another berth if I wanted it. I didn't. My berth is in the steadiest part of the ship. It is quite a small room, but with every convenience, except a writing table. There *may* be a writing table, among all the *trucs* that fold up,

but I haven't yet discovered it. I have arranged to take my bath
at 7 a.m. each day (if I am not ill). The ship is enormous. The
sea is so far down below the promenade deck that it is like a
mere incident, in another world. The lifts are continually
ascending & descending. But no tea is served till after the boat
starts. She is just starting & I am scribbling this in 5 minutes or
less. I have been talking with Forbes Robertson in the train. He
is a great admirer of

Ton mari, A.B.

41. Bennett was now a famous figure in both England and America, and by some
people was reckoned to be the major English novelist of the day. George Doran
arranged an American tour for him. He travelled to America with Edward Knoblock
(1874–1945), who himself was American. Knoblock collaborated with Bennett on
several plays. For letters to him see Vols. II and III.
   Sir Johnston Forbes Robertson (1853–1937) was an actor-manager.

KEELE / MS / 42   On Board the Cunard
(*To Marguerite Soulié Bennett*)   R.M.S. *Lusitania*
                                       Friday 10 p.m.
                                       7th Oct 1911

Dearest Girl,
   This is the second letter I have written to you today. It will be
posted at Kingstown (Ireland) at 7 a.m. Sunday. I shall not
come to America again without you. The ship is simply
magnificent. The only difference between it and a first-class
grand hotel is that no first-class grand hotel is so spacious. The
night weather is most beautiful. In the drawing-room (which is
much larger than the Royalty Theatre) you cannot even feel the
vibration of the screw. We had a very good dinner. It is like
being in a restaurant where there is nothing to pay. (You pay
beforehand—for the ticket!) You order whatever you like, and
it comes, and the waiters are all English and very polite and
quick. I am in the *writing*-room and library (my books in it, and
people reading *Hilda*!). It is as large as the dining-room of the
United Arts Club. When you have walked round the deck you
have walked half a kilometre. I like my room because it is full of
drawers and hooks and places for putting things away. The top
of the washstand makes a writing desk, and there is a beautiful
electric light over the bed. There are about 3,000 people on
board altogether. 430 first-class passengers. In fact the boat is

quite full. Knoblock is an exceedingly polite and agreeable travelling companion. Forbes Robertson now wants to have a special dining-table for him & us & his friend. You would like him; and from the way he pronounces French words I should say he can speak French very well. I hope you won't forget to send notices of the play to Martin and the Godebskis. You might send the criticisms from the *Express* and the *Times* and the *Daily Telegraph*. The last is very bad. Silly old Malcolm Watson wrote it. I have read all the morning papers. It is evident that half of them don't see the point of the play at all. Some say that the last act saves the play, & others say the last act damns the play. What are you doing? I fear that you were very sad when you went back to our bedroom to pack up the things. I have not seen a single chic woman. I wish you were here to show them. Tu ferais sensation. Never mind. Though far away, I adore you still. I am now going to my solitary little bed. Much love; many kisses.

Ton A.

Affection for all the Sharpes.

42. Except in the *Manchester Guardian* and the *Daily Express*, the critics were fairly cool towards *The Honeymoon*. Malcolm Watson (1853–1929) wrote for the *Daily Telegraph* for many years. He was also the author of plays.

KEELE / MS / 43
(*To Marguerite Soulié Bennett*)

On Board the Cunard
R.M.S. *Lusitania*
Sunday afternoon
8 Oct 1911

Dearest Girl,

We got to Queenstown this morning & I received a lot of telegrams, which I enclose. I ought to have had them at the theatre on Friday night. But I expect everybody was too excited or too busy to think of giving them to me. I think we left Queenstown about 7.15 or 7.30. I was dressed just as we left. At noon we had done 108 miles. Lovely weather. Sunshine all day. It takes about twenty-four hours to perceive how big this ship is. The dining saloon is so big that the faces of people on the opposite side are not clear. And up the corridors you can see figures of stewards walking along long before they get to you. I made a lot of notes this morning. And they are not like any other notes that anybody ever made on board ship. The food is very good indeed. And you can order whatever you like. I had an omelette chasseur for lunch. Then Knoblock & I thought we would have a grilled chicken. It was done specially for us and very good. You can make up your own menu in advance, and it will be prepared for you. We had a lot of talking this morning with Forbes Robertson & his agent Burton. Forbes is extremely agreeable. He is 58 & looks 50. A friend of his, Innes, in the diplomatic service, is at our table. He is a decent sort of ass, and always asking questions, asking what you think of so-and-so. He began talking about the Russian ballets & Nijinsky, & what I thought thereof. So I said I knew Nijinsky, & told him all about it. Then he got on to *Jean Cristophe*, & I said I knew Romain Rolland, & told him all about that. Then he asked if *Marie Claire* was really written by Marguerite Audoux, & I said I knew Marguerite Audoux, & told him all about *that*. I fancy he thinks I am a bit of a liar. Church service this morning in the drawing-room. The band played Handel—very nice. I slept after breakfast in the smokeroom. I went to bed after lunch, and slept for *2 hours*. I could have slept more, but I wanted my tea. It is a great mistake to suppose that these enormous boats do not roll and pitch. They do. The sea is not rough, but there is the Atlantic 'swell' (you must ask Mrs. S. the meaning of these words), and the whole mighty boat goes up and down. However I have felt perfectly well. It is now dinner time.

I write to mater on a different coloured paper, so as not to mix up the two letters. Goodnight.

Monday. 9 Oct 1911
Good morning Mrs. Bennett. The weather is even calmer than it was yesterday. I must say I had a very agreeable evening last night in the Lounge talking with 5 or 6 men. Every now & then a girl or two in white wrap would show her face at the outside of one of the windows, mysteriously. People walk round & round on the deck outside till late at night. Knoblock & I just took a few turns before going to bed. I was in bed at 10.30. I have read about a hundred pages of *Nicholas Nickleby*. But I am being magnificently idle. Beyond making notes for my article on the ship, & thinking somewhat about the sequel to *Hilda* &

Clayhanger, I do absolutely naught. The ship's daily paper was published this morning at 8.30. I must try to remember to send you one. There is not a great deal of news, but there is *news*. I think I eat less breakfast than any healthy man on board. Coffee & cold toast. So that I feel a little hungry most of the day. I sleep each day after breakfast, and again before lunch, and again after lunch. Knoblock has not got a room to himself, & he was very afraid that he might have an annoying companion. But his companion is a most charming man, a German composer & conductor named Schindler, in New York. I had a long talk with him this morning. He admires Ravel's music immensely, so I was able to tell him something about Ravel, Schmitt, and so on. Then I walked on the topmost deck, where the dogs are kept, to think about *Clayhanger*'s sequel. This made me so sleepy that I had to come down to the drawing-room and sleep. I write this in my berth before lunch. I have just been talking with the purser (littéralement — boursier). He keeps all the accounts & is a great mandarin. He is going to show me over the whole ship tomorrow at 10.20. They are very particular to a minute. Not 10.30. But 10.20. The Captain himself has received a letter from headquarters to say that I must be attended to. I feel rather pleased, especially as men are reading my *Mental Efficiency* all over the blessed ship.

Goodnight.

Tuesday 10.10.11
10.30.

Is my bath ready auntie? Knoblock & I went over the third class & second class parts of the ship yesterday. There are 1,000 people in the third-class, & they are extremely comfortable. We saw their tea served. It is a very big tea, with fish and meat. I never saw such a healthy & independent set of working people in my life. The mothers with infants were splendid. I should say they would do America a great deal of good. You should see the cooks faire la vaisselle. Il y a des machines pour ça. Et toute la vaisselle pour un repas de 330 couverts est faite dans quelques minutes et bien faite. Infiniment mieux que Martha! Then the kitchens for the first-class passengers are superb. All the petit fours et cakes de toutes sortes are made on board. The bakery goes on day and night—all the 24 hours. The mechanical egg-boilers too, are most amusing. These egg boilers cannot make mistakes. If you want an egg boiled three & ½ minutes, the machine lifts it out of the water at the end of 3½ minutes, and there you are! The second-class accommodation is simply magnificent: not quite so large as ours, but very fine. Only it is over the four 'hélices', which make a devil of a racket. The band plays for them as for us. With the Chief steward it took us exactly two hours to see all this, and I was quite exhausted and enfeebled through being in the hot kitchens & descending into the wine cellars and so on & so on. Still, I sat down and wrote all my notes at once, before dinner. After dinner we had the usual talk, but I was too tired. The sea was rather rougher, and all the windows were closed, so that even the saloon, which is as big as a concert-hall, was stuffy. I went to bed at 10.30. Dans ma chambre il fait toujours 20 dègres, ce qui m'est très agréable. Avec ça il y a toujours un courant d'air frais dans le haut de la chambre. C'est très bien. I did not sleep well. I had smoked two cigars. I had to smoke an extra one with a man from the British Embassy in Washington. I said I shouldn't be able to go to Washington, but he said I must, & that I should stay in his house, & he would give a dinner-party for me & invite the British Ambassador. Que veux-tu? J'ai dit que je ferai mon possible. Ces choses ne se refusent pas.... I was up at 6.30. While I was having breakfast at 8, a wave came in at an open window (30 feet above the water) and soaked a table & several chairs. Yet the dining-room was quite steady. At 10.30 I had an appointment to see the captain & the Chief officer. I have just left them. I shall see a lot more of the ship this afternoon. Je regrette, presque, que le voyage sera bientôt fini. Je t'embrasse. Bonne nuit.

[A.]

43. Mitchell Innes was *chargé d'affaires* at the British Embassy in Washington.

Waslaw Nijinski (1890–1950): Bennett saw him dance in Paris in 1910 and wrote in his *Journals*, 'I understood a little for the first time the possibility of a man charming another man sexually.'

Romain Rolland (1866–1944): the *Journals* of 22 January 1911 describe a visit with him.

Marguerite Audoux (1863–1937) was a seamstress who wrote a popular account of her childhood, *Marie-Claire*. Bennett wrote an introduction to the English translation, 1911.

Mrs. S.: Mrs Sharpe. Marguerite was now staying with the Sharpes.

These Twain was the third volume of the Clayhanger trilogy. Bennett did not begin writing it until 1914, owing to illness and the pressure of other work.

Kurt Schindler (1882–1935) was a German-American conductor and composer.
Maurice Ravel (1875–1937) and Bennett had been acquainted for several years.
Florant Schmitt (1870–1958) was a French composer.

Mental Efficiency was an enlarged version of the first of Bennett's pocket philosophies,
The Reasonable Life, 1907.

Bennett signed this letter and several subsequent letters with hearts instead of initials
or name.

KEELE / MS / 44
(*To Marguerite Soulié Bennett*)

On Board the Cunard
R.M.S. *Lusitania*
Wednesday
11th Oct 1911

Je t'embrasse, ma cocotte x x x x x x x x x x x x x x x x x x
x x x x x x x x. You will not understand the meaning of all this,
but I will tell you. I had the idea of sending you some kisses by
telegraphe sans fil this morning. I thought of *three* kisses. I wrote
out the telegram, & they said it would cost 26 shillings. I
thought this rather dear, so you must take it that I sent 26
kisses—one shilling apiece—not too dear, I think. I sent off that
telegram on Wednesday about noon London time (9 a.m. on
the boat). I wonder when you will get it. It is the first
marconigram I have ever sent off, and I suppose the first you
have ever received. I had a most busy day yesterday. I was
writing most of the morning, & at 2.30 the First Officer took
Knoblock & me over all the navigating part of the ship and also
through the engine-rooms. This occupied nearly two hours. I
can't describe this now. I shall describe it in an article. But I
can tell you it was absolutely astounding. Then while we were
promenading on the deck the Captain, who was with Forbes
Robertson, asked us into his parlour, & we smoked cigars and
told stories there for nearly two hours. I had a tremendous
dinner. I think that baked ham is one of the most indigestible
things I ever ate. And then a friend across the table was having
a welsh rarebit, so I said I would have a welsh rarebit too; you
don't know what a welsh rarebit is, but Cedric will tell you in
French. Then I had some pudding & an ice! Why I should do
this I cannot imagine. I felt rather uncomfortable all the
evening, & I woke up this morning at 3 o'clock with a bad
headache. However it went off during my next sleep, & I am all
right this morning. There is such a strong breeze this morning

that, at the front of the boat, you literally cannot stand up against it. It would blow you down. Yet the boat is very steady, & I am writing this as if I was in my study. I am now on very friendly terms with a lot of people in this boat. This is the sort of thing that goes on. A man comes up to me & says: 'Excuse me, but are you Mr. Arnold Bennett.' I say that I am he. Then he says: 'Well, I should like to shake your hand, & tell you what pleasure I've had from your books. But I suppose that you've had so many compliments that you're tired of them.' I say: 'Never! And I never shall be tired of them. What do *you* think?' Then laughter. Then the man begins to talk, not about me & my work, but about himself and what *he* is doing.

It is not certain whether we shall land tomorrow night or Friday morning.

I am still wondering with what adventures you got to Sharpes on Saturday afternoon last, & how you managed with all my things. And so good night, my child,

[A.]

44. Cedric Sharpe (b. 1891), son of Herbert. For letters to him see Vols. II and III. He became a distinguished violoncellist.

KEELE / MS / 45   Park Hill
(*To Marguerite Soulié Bennett*)   Yonkers
                                          New York
                                          13th Oct 1911

Dearest Girl,

I am here safe but exhausted. Mary, the daughter of the house, has given me some of her own private notepaper to write on. This is understood to be a great compliment. Mr. Doran, and a man from Harpers, and a lot of journalists came on the government steamer (douanes) which meets the Lusitania in the harbour before she gets to the dock. The crowd of journalists deputed two of their number to interview me on behalf of all of them. This was done very neatly and nicely, and I talked to them at a tremendous rate, being in great form. This was on the ship. Then we got on to the pier. I had no difficulty with the douanes, as the chef des douanes gave me a special permit (I am to give him a signed copy of *Hilda*); so the examination was a mere matter of form. We drove through the city, and saw some of the big streets, and called at two hotels for drinks (water) & cigars; and caught the 11.19 from the Central Station for Yonkers. The house is a 25 minutes drive from Yonkers station. Mrs. Doran was all in white. She is really very nice. She said: 'Oh Mr. Bennett, having you here is just like a dream. I can scarcely believe it's true.' And so on. I didn't sleep much. The climate is beautiful. The house is very like a small English country house, a mixture of various styles and tastes. Mary Doran is a very nice little girl, quiet & modest, not at all like American children generally are. I am resting today. I shall go to New York tomorrow, when I am to see the great 'baseball' (conseille Cedric) match of the year. 60,000 people will be there. I am not writing much today. But my regard for you, my child, is stronger than ever.

Ton A.

Write always to the address I gave you c/o G. H. Doran

35 West 32nd St.
N.Y.

45. The *New York Times* gave Bennett a modest 7 inches of space on his arrival.

Arnold Bennett ... arrived here on the Cunarder Lusitania last night for a two months visit, during which he will tour the country from the Atlantic to the Pacific, writing his observations for a magazine.

Mr. Bennett talks rapidly. When met by the reporters he began by alluding to the suit he wore, as giving him a twelve days residence in a country he had never visited before. He said he had bought the clothes at an American department store in London, and that as he had worn them every day since the purchase he considered himself in a sort of way an American for that period of time....

He was asked about his use of the word 'reckon' to mean 'consider', and he referred to Shakespeare. He was asked what sorts of books he thought the public liked best, and answered that those that seemed dullest to him often proved to be very popular.

KEELE / MS / 46
(*To Marguerite Soulié Bennett*)

George H. Doran
35 West 32nd Street
New York
Tuesday
17 Oct 1911

Dearest Girl,

I write this in the morning at Washington, which is the capital of the United States. We have just seen the Parliament etc. We came down yesterday afternoon, leaving at 3.34. The

Pennsylvania Railway Station in New York is the finest I have ever seen anywhere. The train is magnificent, but I was too ill to enjoy it. I had both tea & dinner on the train, but didn't enjoy either of them. I had only slept about 2 hours the previous night (though I went to bed at 10.30). I had the beginning of a headache, which got worse as the day went on. The journey here takes 5 hours. We arrived at 8.30. At 9 I was in bed. I had been sick. Bref, tu sais d'avance l'histoire. I had a good night, & am very much better this morning. The funny thing is that I have come down here with my two principal publishers, Doran, the publisher of *Old Wives' Tale* etc. & Macrae (of Duttons) publishers of *Clayhanger* etc. These two men are down here because of negotiations with the Government about douanes etc., on books. They knew each other as boys. They call each other by their Christian names. But they had a great quarrel about me, because Macrae thinks that Doran advertises my old books as if they were new books. They are both quite friendly now, & both extraordinarily proud of going about with me. They are both very nice chaps, & I like them both. They are both about my age. We all like the best of everything on railways and in hotels, and we have it. We go back tonight by the night train, leaving at 12.10, but we get into the train at 10.30 & go to sleep—if we can. We arrive in New York tomorrow at 6 am, but can stay in the train till 7.30. I have two other men to dinner tonight, Mitchell Innes, the chargé d'affaires at the British Embassy here, & Maurice Law, the Washington correspondent of the London *Morning Post*.

Things are going very well here for me. In the first 14 days Macrae has sold over 10,000 copies of *Hilda*. This is much better than any of the other books. He has sold over 11,000 of *The Card* and over 12,000 of *Clayhanger*, and all these books are still selling very well. Doran has sold over 25,000 of *How to live on 24 hours a day*. The humorous feuilleton that I shall write in January–March is practically sold for £2,000. I can now give you an idea of how much money we are likely to earn next year.

		frs
Harper articles	serial	20,000 minimum
,, ,,	American book rights	2,500 minimum
,, ,,	English ,, ,,	2,500 ,,
Humorous serial	American serial rights	50,000
	English ,, ,,	10,000

		American book rights	12,500	minimum
		English ,, ,,	15,000	,,
written {	Travel book	American book rights	5,000	,,
		English ,, ,,	5,000	,,
written {	book of Short	stories		
		American book rights	2,500	,,
		English ,, ,,	3,750	,,
if not more }		royalties from old Doran books	50,000	,,
than this year }		,, ,, ,, Dutton ,,	15,000	,,
			193,750	frs.

I shall probably make over that. *You notice that I take no account of plays.* A magazine has offered me 25,000 francs for ten chroniques; but I have refused it as I am too busy.

I wonder when the devil I shall have a letter from you. Perhaps when I get back to New York. I will send you a lot more interviews soon. In the papers they print in advance even where I am going to have lunch, and what train I am going to take to Washington etc. I have been made an honorary member of the principal club. But the principal thing that I want to do is to meet Arthur Hooley, & I haven't yet met him.

Est-ce que tu sens mes bras autour de toi? Je l'espère. Si tu étais ici — ... tu aimerais le luxe de New York, mais les chemins de fer, le bruit, et tout ça t'embêteraient énormément. Madame Doran est totalement charmante. Les femmes-journalistes sont tordantes, et ficelées, mais ficelées. — Je te bise tendrement mon amour.

Ton A.

46. Bennett's *Journals* of 17 October read:
    Doran and I took 3:34 Congressional Limited from Pennsylvania Station to Washington. This station is very impressive. Silence. Not crowded.
    Trains a mere incident in it, hidden away like a secret shame. Tunnel under Hudson. Very neat, regular, and well lighted: seen from observation car. Noise from steel. Jolting of smoking car. General jolting when brakes put on.
    Electric sign sticking up high as we passed through Baltimore in the dark: 'Baltimore, the electric city.'
John Macrae was an editor at Dutton's. They published nothing more of Bennett's after *Hilda Lessways*.
    The *Harper's* articles were the serial form of *Your United States* (in England *Those United States*). They began to appear in April 1912. Book publication came in 1912.
    The humorous serial, *The Regent*, sequel to *The Card*, was written from 14 February to 11 April 1912. It began to appear in the *American Magazine* in December 1912 and in the *London Magazine* in November. Doran and Methuen issued it in 1913, Doran under the title *The Old Adam*.
    The travel book is presumably *Paris Nights*, published in 1913, the essays for which were written 1904–11.

The short story collection was *The Matador of the Five Towns*, 1912, which followed two earlier collections, *Tales of the Five Towns*, 1905, and *The Grim Smile of the Five Towns*, 1907.

In 1912 Bennett's income was £16,000, which he reckoned was more than he had earned in all the preceding years put together.

Arthur Hooley (1874–1928) was related to the Kennerleys. He and Bennett wrote two plays together in 1900, *A Wayward Duchess* and *The Chancellor*. Neither was produced. He went to America and became an editor and author there.

KEELE / MS / 47
(*To Marguerite Soulié Bennett*)

> 35 West 32nd Street
> 20 Oct 1911

Dearest girl,

J'étais fortement enchanté de tes trois lettres si pleines de toi. It seemed about a year since I had seen you. Ton rhume est assommant. I hope to hear next que ça n'existe plus. Si tu peux faire passer une de tes pièces à Londres, personne ne sera si enchanté que moi. C'est la main de Laure qui est la meilleure. Your little Jeanne dactylographe is very good. The receipts at the Royalty are very good—better than I expected. I have seen all the criticisms. There are 2 that are good—the *Westminster* & the *Express*. The rest—completely uncomprehending. What pleases me is that *you* are convinced that I can write for the theatre. I know that Tertia thinks the play very good, because she has written & told the mater so. So long as the receipts come to 25,000 frs. a week the play will make a good profit. I could sell here all the stuff that I could do in twenty years. You know the book I am going to do about Hilda's son—a London book, that Doran is to give me £1,500 for on account. Well, I have sold it as a serial to the *Metropolitan Magazine* for £3,000—my highest price up to now. I have also taken a commission for 8 chroniques at 3750 frs. la pièce. Que dis-tu de ça? *I shall accept no more commissions whatever.* I now am certain of 450,000 frs. at least for 3 years' work: c'est assez. I am living at a tremendous speed. I get more & more into the newspapers. Yesterday I lunched with some editors & dined with some others, and then went to see another at midnight—he works on the 23me étage. Doran & I went to bed at 1.15 a.m. Up at 8! Very well in health. Today I lunch with people & dine with people & then go to the theatre,

Sarah Ann Bennett

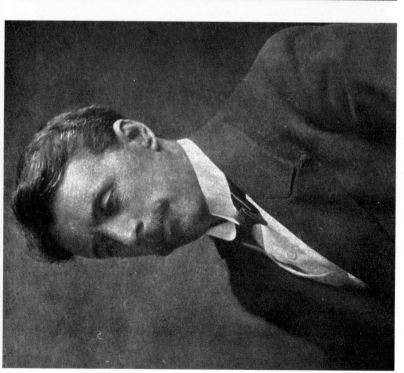

Arnold Bennett, 1911

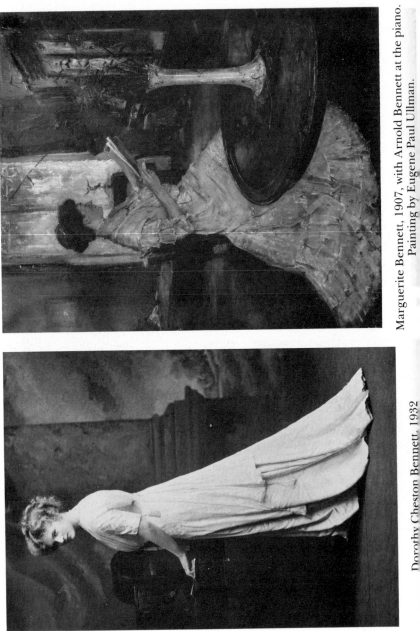

Dorothy Cheston Bennett, 1932

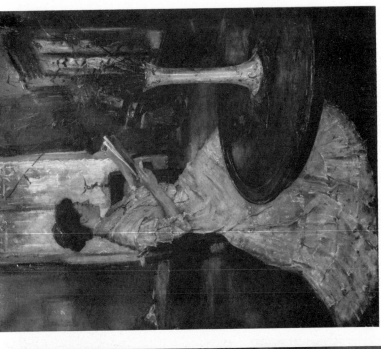

Marguerite Bennett, 1907, with Arnold Bennett at the piano.
Painting by Eugene Paul Ullman.

ertia Bennett, later Mrs Kennerley,
1903

Plaque of Enoch Bennett,
by Septimus

Virginia Bennett, 1951

Septimus Bennett (*centre*) with two friends,
1890s

Marguerite and Richard Bennett (*foreground*) with Marguerite's sister and mother

The Bennett family: (*seated, left to right*) Sarah Ann, Frank, Fanny Gertrude, Arnold, Tertia (*standing*) Emily, Enoch, Septimus

& Doran & I take supper with the principal actor & his wife (who is the author of the play we are going to see, I think). Tomorrow morning we go out of New York to Doran's house in the suburbs for the weekend. Such is life. Have I told you that *Harpers Magazine* invited me to a lunch at which were present the heads of all their departments, including Colonel George Harvey, their president? C'est un très gros chou. He is going to give a grand dinner in my honour on Dec. 7th at which will be present the most important people in New York. The nuisance is that I shall have to make a speech. People in provincial cities write to me and ask me to go and make a speech, & offer to pay all my expenses and any fee that I like to name. I refuse. Next Thursday I am going to Boston for 4 days, with T. B. Wells (of Harper's) who came to see us at Fontainebleau. By the way he sends you his kindest regards. It is very evident that you have made a profound impression on both the Dorans. Mrs. Doran talks of you all the time, & is extremely anxious to see you again. I do *not* think she is of a gloomy disposition. I have become very friendly with her indeed. She is very nice and candid, & I have not found that she has un fond de tristesse. But I think she thinks her husband is too happy in his business, & that she is not necessary to his happiness. I am glad you are inviting people to Cedric's concert. I hope you will do this kind of thing very freely, and be generous in all ways, as we have heaps of money, & money is made (by me) to be spent by my wife in a generous fashion. I am not spending much money here. I want when I come home to go straight away to Cannes with you seule as soon as I can. We must spend 2 or 3 days in Paris. But as little as possible. Il me faudra toi et toi et toi et du calme. Entre des caresses et des conversations et des intimités j'ai du travail à faire. Maintenant tes lettres, surtout les fins de tes lettres m'ont très touché. Je ne peux pas finir une lettre comme toi, mais tu me comprends x x x x

Ton A.

I send some more interviews. They are chiefly quite inaccurate.

47. Laure and Jeanne: unidentified.
    The Roll-Call, which concerns Hilda Lessway's son, was not written until five years later, from 16 October 1916 to 30 April 1917. It was published in *Munsey's Magazine*, beginning in April 1918.

The eight articles were taken by the *Metropolitan Magazine*. They became two slender books, *The Plain Man and His Wife*, 1913, and *The Author's Craft*, 1915. The *Metropolitan Magazine* began publishing the first series in October 1912 (with English publication in the *Strand Magazine* beginning in November) and the second series in June 1913 (with English publication in the *English Review* beginning in April). The *Metropolitan Magazine* was not satisfied with the articles and omitted publication of the first of the four on writing.

For a letter to Colonel George Harvey (1864–1928) see Vol. II.

On Thomas B. Wells (1875–1941) see Vol. I.

KEELE / MS / 48
(*To Marguerite Soulié Bennett*)   Park Hill
                                                    Sunday
                                                    22 Oct 1911

Dearest girl,

Ça fait cinq de tes précieuses lettres que j'ai reçues dans deux jours. C'est une bonne idée de les mettre à la poste tous les jours. Ça vous évite l'embêtement de te tuyauter sur les courriers et les paquebots. Je suis très content que ton rhume disparaît et que tu écris à ma mère. Elle m'écrit des lettres assez mornes. Ici il pleut depuis *cinq jours*. This is the beautiful New York autumn que tout le monde a si vanté! It was raining when we arrived in New York from Washington at 8 o'clock on Wednesday morning. It is raining now, Sunday afternoon, and in the meantime it has scarcely ceased to rain. I have had wet feet twice. It is a most excellent thing that I spend the weekends in this country house doing nothing but eating & sleeping. But I have been sleeping pretty well lately. We return to New York tomorrow, & I go to Boston with T. B. Wells on Thursday till Monday. Lunches & dinners every day. Tomorrow I lunch with Mrs. Ullman, & I expect I shall meet a lot of new people. What I miss most (after you) is people who *understand art*. Nobody does that I have met. I also miss Paris tremendously, where people understand *life* and talk about it freely. Here nearly everything is puritanical—even les cocottes—as in London. Mais les affaires sont perfectionnées. C'est un pays merveilleux pour les affaires. Visiter les bureaux, comprendre l'organisme, et l'organisation de ces affaires, c'est un vrai plaisir. J'ai le goût des affaires. La preuve — nul agent, ni ici ni à Londres, pas même le célèbre Pinker — n'a pu m'obtenir plus que 62,500 frs. pour un feuilleton. J'entame une affaire personellement. Je la dirige, je prends le dessus, je dis à tous les autres de se taire, et j'obtiens 75,000 — et pour *les droits américains seulement*. J'avoue que j'en suis fier, et j'ai écrit à Pinker dans ce sens. Le même jour M. Doran a vendu pour moi un autre feuilleton. Il m'a dit 'Je peux vous avoir 37,500 frs. pour ce court feuilleton.' Je lui ai dit '50,000.' Il a réussi. Mais je le regrette, parce que je suis sûr que moi-même j'aurais pu avoir 62,500 frs. I think the receipts at the Royalty are pretty good— for a failure! But compared to New York there is *no* money in London. J'ai rencontré l'autre soir un couple, youpin: Selwyn. Le mari est dramaturge et acteur et agent dramatique. En ce moment il joue dans une pièce qu'il a écrite. L'année dernière il a presenté une autre sienne pièce, que trois troupes différentes jouent en ce moment en tournée. Sa femme (Margaret Mayo, auteur de *Baby Mine*, pièce complètement idiote, mais un gros succès actuel de Londres et un peu gros succès de New York) m'a dit que quatre troupes différents jouent *Baby Mine* en tournée en ce moment aux États-Unis, et que la moins fructueuse de ces quatre lui rapporte plus que la troupe de Londres. La recette à San Francisco pour une semaine, dépassait la recette de Londres pour deux mois. Je calcule que ce couple, fort aimable et assez amusant, gagne au moins 25,000 frs. par semaine — peut-être beaucoup plus. C'est eux qui m'avaient invité voir la pièce du mari (pièce sotte) et puis après à un souper dans un restaurant ultra-chic. Je n'ai rien mangé, mais j'ai fait tordre tout le monde pendant deux heures comme si tout le monde s'appelait Godebski! C'était un succès éclatant, et je ne sais pas pourquoi. Mais tout les interviewers disent que je suis extrêmement humouristique. Il est évident que mon côté 'humour' est mieux compris ici qu'en Europe. Le couple Selwyn nous a invité (moi et les Doran) aller avec eux en auto voir je ne sais pas quel beau pays. J'ai refusé. Aussi la dame m'a-t-elle téléphoné hier m'invitant aller avec elle à la plus chic première de la saison. J'ai refusé ça également. Demain je t'enverrai encore des interviews que je te prie envoyer après à ma mère. N'oublie jamais qu'au moins la moitié des choses attribuées à moi dans ces interviews sont complètement fausses et inauthentiques. La plus grande insulte — il y en a un qui dit que je porte 'detachable cuffs.' Raconte ça à n'importe qui à Londres, et tu entendras le rire!

Je suis très confortable dans cette maison, and the way the Dorans look after me is positively amazing. *It is astounding.* À toi mon enfant et chère, *tout* mon moi.

Ton A.

Je suis content que tu sors, et que tu dînes chez les Vaughan etc.

48. [Now I have received five of your precious letters in two days. It is a good idea to post them every day. Then you avoid the bother of finding out about posts and packet-boats. I am very glad that your cold is getting better and you are writing to my mother. She writes me rather gloomy letters. It has been raining for *five days* here. This is the beautiful New York autumn which everyone has so much praised. . . . But business has been brought to perfection. This is a wonderful country for business. It is a real pleasure to visit offices and understand the system and organization of business. I have a taste for business. The proof: no agent, either here or in London, not even the famous Pinker, has ever managed to get me more than 62,500 frs. for a serial. I embark on a deal, I manage it, I take the upper hand, I tell every one else to be quiet and I get 75,000—for the American rights alone. I admit that I'm proud of it and I have written to Pinker to tell him so. The same day Mr Doran sold another serial for me. He said to me 'I can get you 37,500 frs for this short serial.' I told him '50,000'. He got it. But I am sorry, because I am sure that if I had done it myself, I could have got 62,500. . . .

The other evening I met a Jewish couple, the Selwyns. The husband is a playwright, actor and theatrical agent. At present he is acting in a play which he wrote himself. Last year he put on another of his plays, and three different theatre companies are taking it on tour at the moment. His wife (Margaret Mayo, who wrote *Baby Mine*, an utterly idiotic play but a great success in London at present and a great success in New York) told me that four different theatre companies are touring the United States with *Baby Mine* at the moment and that the least successful of these is bringing her in more than the London company. Box-office takings in San Francisco for one week were more than the takings in London for two months. I reckon that this very pleasant and quite amusing couple are earning at least 25,000 frs. a week, perhaps much more. It was they who invited me to see the husband's play (a silly play) and then to have supper afterwards in an ultra-smart restaurant. I ate nothing, but I kept everyone in fits of laughter for two hours, as if they were all called Godebski! I was a tremendous success and I do not know why. But all the interviewers say that I am extremely witty. Clearly my 'witty' side is better understood here than in Europe. The Selwyn couple asked us (me and the Dorans) to go on a car trip with them to see some beautiful part of the country or other. I refused. So the lady telephoned me yesterday asking me to go with her to the smartest première of the season. I refused that too. Tomorrow I will send you some more interviews which I would ask you to send on to my mother. Never forget that at least half the things attributed to me in these interviews are completely false and unauthentic. The greatest insult is that one of them says that I wear 'detachable cuffs'. Tell that to anyone in London and you will hear them laugh.

I am very comfortable in this house, and the way the Dorans look after me is positively amazing. It is astounding. To you my child and beloved, all my self. . . . I am glad that you are going out and having dinner with the Vaughans etc.]

The 75,000 frs. was for *The Roll-Call*, the 50,000 for *The Regent*.

On Edgar Selwyn (1875–1944) see Vols. I and II. He became Bennett's dramatic agent in America. His play was *The Arab*. Margaret Mayo (1883–1951) wrote a number of successful plays, including *Twin Beds* and *Polly of the Circus*.

The Vaughans—Tom Benjamin (d. 1928), producer and manager, and his wife Marian.

On 22 October the arts section of the *New York Times* gave a full page to an interview at Doran's headlined 'Makes Sir Walter Scott responsible for the Backsliding of English Fiction from Realism to Romanticism—How George Moore and Hardy Rescued Literature—Neither Dickens Nor Thackeray a First-Rate Artist'. The whole article was devoted to the subject. The *New York Tribune* of the same date gave eight half-columns to another interview headlined 'Arnold Bennett thinks Thackeray, Dickens, Scott, Eliot and Dumas are Second Raters'. This interview was not so thoroughly serious:

Mr. Bennett is a remarkably fluent and plausible talker. He never seems to have to scramble for the right word. Now and then he stutters slightly, very slightly, but you feel sure it is purely a mechanical, not a mental, hesitation.... He said he had attended the theatre only once since he arrived in New York. [The interview took place before he saw *The Arab*.] An opinion by so successful a playwright would be interesting. He was asked what he had seen.

'Let me see', he pondered, puffing his cigarette. 'It's funny, but I can't think of the name of the piece. One goes somewhere to dinner in this highly exciting city, and someone says something about the theatre, and one gets into an automobile and goes to a theatre. And that's all one knows about it. I haven't the least idea what the name of the play was.'

It was suggested that perhaps if he would tell a little of the plot the title of the play could be discovered.

'Quite right', replied the playwright animatedly. 'The first scene of the play shows a woman sitting at a telephone.' A play was mentioned. 'I dare say you're right', he said. And that was as far as he cared to go in criticising it.

In the *Journals* on 19 October Bennett wrote:

We drove to Republic Theatre (Belasco) to see *The Woman* by William C. De Mille. Telephone girl play. Melodrama plot. Essentially childish. Nevertheless, in spite of too much talk in 1st act, I was not really bored. It appealed to the child in me.

The entry concludes, 'Guggenheim pointed out to me at theatre. Looked like a little grocer.'

KEELE / MS / 49
(*To Marguerite Soulié Bennett*) 35 West 32nd Street
Tuesday
24 Oct 1911

Dearest girl,

There may come a letter from you this evening. I hope so. I am not quite settled down into the routine of a New York Lion. I still see interviewers every day, and the greatest editors of the greatest publications, who come to this little office to try to buy my stuff. One man came this morning & asked me to write an interview with myself! One column and a half of a newspaper—1500 francs. I refused. But I really could have made a great deal of money in America by giving 'conférences'. I receive letters asking me to do this, from all sorts of firms, *every day*. They always offer to pay all my expenses, and to name my own price. The lowest price I have been offered for a conférence is 1,000 francs, and all expenses. I suppose I could easily make 20,000 francs a month if I agreed to do this. Only I don't. Lee Mathews cabled me this morning to say that he has sold *The Great Adventure* in America for 10,000 frs. down in advance, and good royalties. This is excellent. I had lunch with the Mitchell Kennerleys today. Mitchell was very agreeable. Since I last saw him, many years ago, he has become quite humorous. His wife is an excellent creature, but she is commonplace & she talks a lot too much. Mrs. Kennerley senior was looking very well & rosy. Arthur Hooley is exactly the same as ever. He is going to England at Christmas. All these people (except Mitchell, who does not know you, I think) said the very kindest things about you. Last night I dined with millionaires & saw a really *admirable* play, *Bought & Paid For*, by George Broadhurst. This is the best modern play in English that I have seen since *Cupid & Commonsense*. I had a great evening. Tonight we see another play. The Dorans continue to look after me in the most perfect manner. A friend of theirs came to stay in New York at my hotel, from Chicago, yesterday. She is a woman of 44, with a son aged 17. A very close friend of theirs, & extremely bright. They had always mentioned her as 'Adelaide', & so when I was introduced to her I said: 'Well, Adelaide, I know a lot about you, & I'm glad to meet you.' She was startled but delighted. I have called her Adelaide ever since. She dined with us & went to the theatre with us. I asked her to breakfast with me & the Dorans this morning at 8.30. I said if she was late we should begin without her. I got down soon & told the waiter to have everything on the table at 8.30. She was one minute late, & we had begun! She said no man had ever asked her to breakfast before & begun without her. I asked her if she would like to try again at tea, & she said she would. Knoblock is coming. If she is not there at 5, we shall begin without her. She is a very agreeable woman.

Doran has just come & told me there is a courier tonight for England, so I am posting this. I am going to the Columbia University tomorrow. The staff of professors will be there to meet me. It is said that they teach 'the art of writing short stories' there, & I want to see how it is done! Now mon enfant adoré, chéri, et caressé, je te caresse, je t'embrasse, et je te bise, tendrement, brusquement, et cruellement. x x x x

Ton [A.]

49. Mitchell Kennerley (1878–1950) was W.W.'s brother. He went out to America at the turn of the century. He became a publisher, notable for the good design of his books. From 1916 to 1929 he was President of the Anderson Galleries. Arthur Hooley was associated with him there. His wife's name was Helen.
George Broadhurst (1866–1954), American playwright.
Adelaide: Adelaide Ames.

KEELE / MS / 50   Hotel Touraine
(*To Marguerite Soulié Bennett*)   Boston
                                                       Friday
                                                       27 Oct 1911
Dearest girl,
   I have a quarter of an hour & so I write a quarter of a letter. I am very bored of this place, & yet I ought not to be, for I am extraordinarily successful here. I went round to the booksellers here this morning with Mr. Doran's sous-directeur. There are 20 good bookshops, & I am the most popular author in all of them. In some there are entire counters full of my different books. I had a sleep after lunch, & then Mr. Basil King, a very popular novelist himself, came to take us up to Harvard University. C'est le plus *chic* université des États Unis. He made us go in a tram, & I wanted to go in a taxi. The tram-ride was very crowded & uncomfortable. I had to stand nearly all the way. Then he made us walk nearly 2 miles! It had begun to rain. Ass!! Silly!! We got to a club, & I said I would not stir from that club until I had had some tea. They offered me whiskey. However, I had the tea. Then another professor came in a fine motor car. Very polite. But too damned self-possessed. We went in and out of the various buildings. Interesting but fatiguing. There are over 4,000 students living there. Each of them has a private sitting-room, bedroom, bathroom and telephone. The whole place—there are sixty different build-ings—is astoundingly rich. They run a comic paper, and this comic paper has offices, specially built, like a palace. I was nearly dead. The other professor brought us back to the hotel in his car. We have to dine (T. B. Wells, me, & Frank Craig, who is going to illustrate my articles) at Basil King's tonight. It will

be a men's party, and I want some women. Tu n'as pas idée comment j'ai besoin de la société des femmes ici. King is a nice man, but I do not like him. I have only just found out that he used to be a clergyman. That is why I don't like him, I suppose. The people up here have the professional mind: which I hate. La ville est très puritaine. Dans l'hôtel il n'y a pas de bar!! L'hôtel est extrêmement bien. Je serai content de retrouver mon New York. Je t'embrasse, et je te bise mon enfant, bien qu'éreinté. Il faut souffrir pour être célèbre, et je le suis. M....

Ton A.

50. Basil King (1859–1928), author of *The Inner Shrine* and *The Street Called Straight*. In the *Journals* on 27 October Bennett records a fragment of conversation with him: 'He said major vices did not exist in this community of professors, writers, and professional men.

A.B.: "No adultery?"

B.K.: "None." '

Frank Craig's illustrations for *Your United States* were later described by Bennett as 'highly finished, unoriginal, & utterly mediocre'.

The *Boston Evening Transcript* gave Bennett several long columns during his visit. He was asked his views on American literature.

The trouble with America is that it is ashamed, unconsciously, of its material. Criticism here takes an apologetic attitude. I agree with Grierson, however, that the future of the novel is in America, though the bulk of the best writing still comes from England. Even though I do believe the future of the novel belongs in America, I do not yet see proof of it.

Nevertheless he thought that Stephen Crane was a wonderful writer, and he was surprised that no one talked about him. Frank Norris, whom people did talk about, was not in the same class.

Bennett noted in his *Journals* that the Puvis de Chavannes paintings in the Boston Public Library were the most beautiful things he had seen in America so far.

KEELE / MS / 51
(*To Marguerite Soulié Bennett*)

[Park Hill]
Sunday
5 Nov 1911

Dearest girl,

Nous passons une fin de semaine très tranquille chez les Doran, après avoir été au 'football match' hier à Princeton. C'était une journée très remplie at fatigante. Nous étions avec Booth Tarkington, romancier et dramaturge extrêmement riche que je connais depuis mes premières années à Paris. Nous sommes arrivés ici à 7 heures hier soir. J'ai dormi 8 heures presque sans bouger. Tu auras une idée de ma popularité à

New York quand je te dis que dans les tramways il y a des affiches ainsi conçues.

Arnold Bennett
says that literary taste is essential
to right living.
The New York Sun
helps you to form your literary taste. Read it.

The *New York Sun* est un des très grands journaux du monde entier. Malgré tout ça il me tarde d'être en Europe. Je ferai mon possible pour prendre un bateau qui fait escale à Boulogne. Je t'écrirai tout ça dans quelques jours. Mais les courriers sont embêtants. À New York il y a deux courriers principaux. L'un arrive le mercredi après-midi, l'autre le vendredi matin. Donc entre mercredi après-midi et vendredi matin (plus que 5 jours) je n'ai rien de toi. Ce qui me dégôute. Je pense toujours des jours quand nous serons ensemble. Je te vois dans notre petit appartement très particulier dans un hôtel, quand nous serons seuls. Je te vois t'habiller et te déshabiller. Je te vois dans une nouvelle chemise de nuit noire, que tu vas faire faire tout de suite à Paris (même deux) très fine, élégante, et sensuelle. Je te prends. Je t'aime. Je t'abuse. J'abime la dite chemise. Je te regarde, après, faire toutes les petites choses de la vie. Je te vois quand tu fais pi-pi gentiment. Je voudrais même te voir quand tu fais autre chose. Enfin tu comprends ce que tu es pour moi, et que tu es à moi. Je te bise mon enfant chéri, et je voudrais bien partir demain vers toi. Les quelques jours que nous passerons à Paris, nous les passerons dans un chic hôtel, parce que ça sera une lune de miel nouvelle. Disons l'hôtel Meurice.

Je te bise tendrement.

Ton A.

51. [We are spending a very peaceful weekend at the Dorans, after going to the 'football match' at Princeton yesterday. It was a very full and tiring day. We were with Booth Tarkington, an extremely rich novelist and playwright whom I have known since my first years in Paris. We arrived here at 7 yesterday evening. I slept for 8 hours, hardly stirring. You will have some idea of how popular I am in New York when I tell you that there are advertisements in the trams worded as follows. . . . The *New York Sun* is one of the biggest newspapers in the whole world. In spite of all that, I am longing to be in Europe. I will do everything I possibly can to catch a boat which puts into port in Boulogne. I will write to tell you all about it in a few days. But the posts are annoying. In New York there are two main posts. One arrives on Wednesday afternoon, the other on Friday morning. So between Wednesday afternoon and Friday morning, (more than 5 days), I have nothing from you. Which disgusts me. I think all the time of the days

when we will be together. I see you in our own special little room in a hotel, when we are alone together. I see you dressing and undressing. I see you in a new black nightgown which you will have made in Paris immediately (have two made)—very fine, elegant, and sensual. I take you. I love you. I seduce you. I damage your nightgown. Then I watch you going through all the little motions of life. I see you peeing sweetly. I would even like to see you when you do other things. So you must understand what you mean to me, and that you belong to me. I kiss you, my beloved child, and I would love to set off to come to you tomorrow. We will spend the few days that we have in Paris in a smart hotel, because that will be another honeymoon. Let us say the Hotel Meurice. I kiss you tenderly.]

Booth Tarkington (1869–1946) established himself as a popular novelist with *Monsieur Beaucaire* in 1900.

Bennett describes the Princeton football game in his *Journals*.

Coloured effect of hats on stands, heaps of violet colour.

Harvard opposite to us.

Cheer-leaders with megaphones.

Standing up and sitting down. At high moments standing on seats.

Accident at start. Man led off amid cheers.

Several minor accidents.

Naive and barbaric. Merely an outlet for enthusiasm.

Touch and goal scored.

Left at half time.

KEELE / MS / 52
(*To Marguerite Soulié Bennett*)

Park Hill
Sunday
12 Nov 1911

Dearest girl,

It annoys and wearies me extremely to have to wait till the 6th or 7th December before seeing you. When I am with other beautiful women, I amuse myself fairly well, but immediately I leave them I remember with disgust again that I have to wait till the 6th or 7th of December till I see *you*. I was dining at the house of a rich Jew last night where there were fine women, including Mrs. Doran, and three of them were pretty and one was beautiful, and they all spoilt me to the last degree. I had four of them round me after dinner. The fifth was with the other four men. One of the men came up, leading the fifth woman, and said: 'Mr. Bennett, you have kept the other four, you may as well have all of them.'! Which I did. This was a rather agreeable house, with some good taste in it and some bad. It will be a good thing for me to leave America, as I am getting very spoilt. There is no doubt about that. Wherever I am, I am

the principal person. I am always on the right hand of the
hostess, and whenever I speak everybody is silent to listen.
Enfin c'est idiot, surtout de la part des femmes, qui me
regardent, bouche bée, en ecstase. Heureusement en
Angleterre je ne serai encore une fois rien — sauf toujours que
nous aurons, tout en étant rien, 200,000 frs. par an au moins.
Comme tu dis, qu'en dira-t-elle, Hélène? Sa fissure sera
définitivement mastiquée. We came home last night here in a
motor-car, having left the hotel for the week-end. It had rained
a little, & the streets were *very* slippery & dangerous. Bien que le
chauffeur était très prudent, l'auto dérapait tout le temps.
Enfin, crevaison de pneu! Et je t'assure que j'en étais très
content, et M. Doran aussi. Nous avons pris le tramway, &
nous avons téléphoné pour une voiture en arrivant. Coucher à
1½ heures du matin. Aujourd'hui éreinté, naturellement! Il fait
très chaud. Il pleut diablement. Je n'ai rien fait. But I have
slept three times! We dine out at a house just opposite. We shall
go to bed early. We go to Chicago demain. The journey takes
from 4 p.m. to 8 a.m. et c'est le rapide le plus rapide d'Améri-
que. I have decided that it would be cruel if I passed through
England, from Liverpool to London, without spending one
night at the mater's. C'est en route. I must do it. Ça
m'assomme, mais la pauvre femme m'écrit des lettres
extrêmement deprimées. Je me porte, malgré la fatigue, très
bien; parce que je mange avec une discrétion qui dégoûte tous
mes hôtes. C'est Chicago qui sera le plus fatigant de tout. Hier
le président de l'université de Chicago m'a télégraphié
m'invitant à l'université. Doran était bleu de stupéfaction et de
plaisir. C'est un grand honneur, paraît-il. Mais, moi, je n'ai pas
bronché. C'est le troisième président d'université qui m'a reçu.
I shall have several letters from you tomorrow morning. I had
your three letters on Friday morning, et j'en étais ravi. Le jour
de notre rapprochement s'approche ma pauvre chérie adorée et
inoubliable — inoubliée. Je te bise avec toute mon âme.

Ton A.

52. [It really is silly, of the women particularly. They stare at me in open-mouthed
ecstasy. Luckily I will be a nobody again in England, but of course we will have at least
200,000 frs. a year in spite of being nobodies. As you say, what would Hélène say? It
would really stop her mouth up. We came home last night here in a motor-car, having
left the hotel for the weekend. It had rained a little, and the streets were *very* slippery and
dangerous. Although the driver was very careful, the car kept skidding. At last we had a

puncture! I can tell you I was very pleased and so was Mr Doran. We took a tram and telephoned for a car when we arrived. We went to bed at 1.30 in the morning. Today we're exhausted, of course. It is very hot and is raining like the devil. I have done nothing ... It bores me to death, but the unfortunate woman writes me extremely depressed letters. In spite of the tiredness, I am very well; because I eat with a caution that disgusts my hosts. Chicago will be the most tiring of all. Yesterday the president of the University of Chicago sent me a telegram asking me to the University. Doran was speechless with amazement and gratification. Apparently it is a great honour. But I didn't turn a hair. He is the third university president to invite me.... The day is approaching when we will be together again, my poor adored, unforgettable, and unforgotten darling. I kiss you with all my soul.]

Hélène: Hélène Bion, Marguerite's aunt, and a shrewd businesswoman.

KEELE / MS / 53   The Blackstone
(*To Marguerite Soulié Bennett*)   Michigan Boulevard
                                         Chicago
                                         Tuesday
                                         14th Nov 1911

Dearest girl,

We got here this morning. The train was two hours late. C'est pas chic du tout. Pas assez chaud, & pas de déjeuner avant 9½ heures! Idiot! Naturellement j'ai mal dormi, j'ai fait 1,600 kilomètres. C'est déjà ça. L'hôtel ici est très bien. Cher, mais bien. J'ai une chambre magnifique. Il y avait des journalistes à la gare, et des journalistes à l'hôtel, & des cartes et des invitations. J'ai pris un bain; il me faut seulement le coiffeur. La coupure ci-incluse te donnera tout de suite une idée de mon importance à Chicago. La chose la plus importante du vernissage annuel est que je serai là! Deux jours avant mon arrivée j'étais annoncé. Doran a vendu 24,000 exemplaires de mes livres différents depuis mon arrivée. Duttons (*Hilda, Clayhanger, The Card*) ont vendu je ne sais pas combien. Peut-être 10,000. Maintenant un autre journaliste m'attend et je déjeune avec deux autres. Puis le petit somme. Puis vernissage. Puis dîner. Puis théâtre. Et je me coucherai fatigué.

Je te bise, mon petit, tendrement.

Ton A.

53. [It isn't too good. Not warm enough and no breakfast till 9.30. Ridiculous! Of course I slept badly and I travelled 1,600 kilometres. It really is that far. The hotel here is very good. Expensive but good. I have a magnificent room. There were journalists at the station, journalists at the hotel and cards and invitations. I have had a bath and now I only need a barber. The enclosed cutting will give you an immediate idea of my

importance in Chicago. The most important thing about the annual *vernissage* is that I
will be there! I was announced two days before my arrival. Doran has sold 24,000
copies of my various books since I arrived. I don't know how many Duttons has sold
(*Hilda, Clayhanger, The Card*). Maybe 10,000. Now another journalist is waiting for me
and I am having lunch with two others. Then I'll have a little rest. Then the *vernissage*.
Then dinner. Then a theatre. I will go to bed tired. I kiss you tenderly, my pet.]

A reporter named Elia Peattie interviewed Bennett in the Blackstone for the *Chicago
Daily Tribune*.

Mr. Arnold Bennettt ... sat in his room ... and looked out at the gray monochro-
matic day. Snow and smoke swirled about the skyscrapers ... The prospect might
have discouraged another man, but it exhilarated Mr. Bennett.

'I like your architecture', he declared. 'See those walls there—those walls beyond
walls, and those interesting cornices, and the little bare chambers on the tops of those
prodigious buildings. It's like Naples, though different in color, of course. But it's the
right color for the place, and it has its character and its romance. I've been here but a
very short time, but I can see that it is not only a tremendously efficient city but a very
romantic one as well. There is a certain sort of poetry in men who can make a city like
this. They have a vision of their own. Such achievements are impossible without the
vision.'

'It's very good of you to like our gray sky, Mr. Bennett, and still better of you to
admire our utilitarian architecture.'

'Admire it? Why of course I do. Your city is of absorbing interest. But then, all
things are interesting. I might go so far as to say that within limits all things are
equally interesting.'

KEELE / MS / 54
(*To Marguerite Soulié Bennett*)

The Blackstone
Wednesday
15 Nov 1911

Dearest girl,

Chicago est le plus fatigant de tout. La réception à l'Institut
des Arts était compliment fou. Je t'enverrai une coupure pour
te le prouver, mais je ne l'ai pas ici en ce moment. Toutes les
femmes de Chicago se précipitaient sur moi. J'ai serré la main
de 200 femmes. J'étais la seule chose regardée dans l'exposition. Heureusement le président m'a protégé autant que
possible. J'avais pris le thé avant de partir. Madame Adelaide
Ames (*une des meilleures*) et M. et Mdme. Ross ont dîné avec
nous. Très bien, le dîner! Je me suis amusé. Après, le théâtre!
Pas très bien, mais toujours avec mon monde. Après le théâtre
des rafraichissements. Coucher à 12.30. Dormi pendant 6
heures. Tout de suite quand nous sommes sortis ce matin, je me
sentais fatigué. Nous avons visité les plus grands magasins du
monde, et puis nous sommes rentrés. Déjeuner d'honneur au

Press Club de Chicago — le plus grand du monde. Infiniment bien. J'ai dit que je ne ferais pas un speech. Donc, deux membres ont fait des speeches humouristiques, comme si c'était moi. Très spirituellement fait! Nous avons quitté ce lunch à deux heures. Il est maintenant 3.30. J'ai dormi. J'ai écrit 5 lettres et mon journal. À 4 heures le président de l'université de Chicago envoie un auto pour nous. Nous irons là-bas. Nous visiterons l'université et nous prendrons le thé avec la femme du président, laquelle femme est très bien. Je l'ai rencontrée hier. Les interviews ce matin étaient très bien sauf un, fait par une femme à qui j'ai été très gentil hier. C'est très méchant. Le Press Club m'a exprimé ses regrets et son chagrin à propos de cette petite saleté. Tu la verras. C'est probablement à cause de cet interview que quelqu'un (inconnu) a téléphoné à M. Doran ce matin ainsi:

'Vous êtes M. Bennett?'

'Non. Je suis M. Doran, son éditeur.'

'Eh bien, dites à M. Bennett qu'il pue.'

Doran en était absolument furieux.

C'est Chicago. Ou plutôt une partie de Chicago. Chicago est cependant très bien. Je te bise ma petite crotte. Je suis fatigué.

Ton A.

54. [Chicago is the most tiring of all. The reception at the Institute of Arts was an extravagant compliment. I will send you a cutting to prove it to you, but I do not have one here at the moment. All the women in Chicago made a rush for me. I shook hands with 200 women. I was the only thing that was looked at in the exhibition. Luckily the president protected me as much as possible. I had had tea before leaving. Madame Adelaide Ames (*one of the best*) and Mr and Mrs Ross dined with us. A very good dinner. I enjoyed myself. Then, the theatre; not very good but I was still with my group. After the theatre, refreshments. Bed at 12.30. 6 hours' sleep. As soon as we went out this morning, I felt tired. We visited the biggest shops in the world, and then came back here. Lunch in my honour at the Press Club of Chicago, the biggest in the world. Unbelievably good. I had said that I would not make a speech. So two members made humorous speeches, in my style. Very wittily done! We left the lunch at two o'clock. Now it is 3.30. I have had a sleep. I have written five letters and my journal. At 4 o'clock the president of the university of Chicago is sending a car for me. We will go to visit the university and have tea with the president's wife, a very nice woman. I met her yesterday. The interviews this morning were very good, except for one, done by a woman to whom I was very nice yesterday. It is really spiteful. The Press Club expressed its regrets and sadness at this little bit of filth. You will see it. This interview was probably why somebody (unknown) telephoned Mr Doran this morning to say the following:

'Are you Mr Bennett?'

'No, I'm Mr Doran, his publisher.'

'Well, tell Mr Bennett he stinks.'

Doran was absolutely furious about it.
That's what Chicago is like. Or rather one bit of Chicago. Still, Chicago is very nice. I kiss you my little poppet. I am tired.]

Bennett's visit to the Press Club was reported in the *Chicago Daily Tribune*.
    In pursuance of an agreement entered into when he received the club's invitation, he was not called upon to make a speech. Instead his impressions of Chicago were delivered by proxy. The writer explained in his letter that an Englishman 'almost never can speak', to which President Douglas Malloch of the club replied that his wish would be respected, as there were several hundred members of the club who 'almost never could be restrained from speaking'.
    Members of the club, therefore, 'made the speech that Mr. Bennett would have made if he would have made a speech'. Mason Warner described the trip up to the sixth floor of the club building in the elevator with assurances that it would form the subject for but the first series of magazine articles, while the trip down again would comprise the second. Harry B. Darlington testified that we 'have a marvellous city, don't you know. Columbus discovered America in 1492', he said. 'A year later, or to be more correct, 1493, English authors began visiting America and writing their impressions. The shorter their stay the longer their impressions.'

KEELE / MS / 55
(*To Marguerite Soulié Bennett*)

Indianapolis
Sunday
19 Nov 1911

Dearest girl,

    Here I am, staying with Booth Tarkington, one of the most popular authors in America, whom I knew in Paris. He has made enormous sums out of plays. Malheureusement il boit un tout petit peu trop. Mais il est très bien. And extremely hospitable. The house is very comfortable. Mais attends un peu. J'ai appris beaucoup en Amérique. Le célèbre confort anglais — ce n'est rien. Il n'y a que les Américains qui comprennent le confort. Nous aurons, dans notre maison, le confort Anglo-Américain. Tu diras certainement que je suis fou; mais tu céderas gentiment, et tu auras une maison, mon enfant, dont tu seras fière. Et tu souffriras, après, dans toutes les autres maisons du monde! À Fontainebleau, étant donné le pays etc, j'ai fait beaucoup pour avoir une maison bien, mais tu verras — en Angleterre. There was une grande réception hier soir. Indianapolis c'est la capitale d'un état, et rempli de gros choux de toutes sortes. Naturellement c'était moi la grande attraction. C'est complètement fou. C'est un prince, ton simple mari, dans ces pays. Tout le monde se rue dessus. Deux journalistes m'attendaient à la maison. Un autre arrivait tout de suite. M. Tarkington est divorcé il y a 8 jours. Sa femme habite presque dans la même rue. J'irai la voir, puisqu'elle m'est sympathique. Mais pas si sympathique que son mari. Celui c'est un homme qui me plait énormément, malgré son petit défaut (qui grossit naturellement). M. Doran has gone to-day to Toronto pour un procès qui lui concerne. Je le reverrai à Philadelphia. Je quitte ces parages demain soir à 7 heures, et j'arrive à Philadelphia à 3 heures de l'après-midi de mardi. 20 heures de chemin de fer! Le billet, avec salon (que j'exige) coûte 160 frs. Mon courrier m'attend à Philadelphia. C'est assommant. Parce que je n'aurai rien de toi avant mardi. C'était difficile à organiser autrement. J'espère que tout marche bien. Si tu as besoin d'argent, écris à M. Pinker qu'il t'envoie une ou deux mille francs pour des achats spéciaux. Je veux dire pour ta toilette. (Je t'en ferai cadeau.) Il t'enverrait ça en billets français. Je t'aime mon petit, mais tu m'embêtes horriblement en ne pas étant ici. Je te bise tendrement.

Ton A.

55. [Wait a minute, now. I have learnt a lot in America. The famous comfort of England is nothing. Only the Americans understand comfort. In our house, we will have Anglo-American comfort. You are sure to say that I am mad, but you will kindly give in, and then you will have a house you are proud of, my little one. And then you will feel uncomfortable in every other house in the world! In Fontainebleau, considering the country etc., I did my best to have a nice home, but you will see—in England. There was a large reception yesterday evening. Indianapolis is a state capital and full of big fish of all kinds. Of course I am the great attraction. It is quite absurd. Your simple husband is a prince in these parts. Everybody rushes at him. Two journalists were waiting for me at home. Another arrived a minute later. Mr Tarkington got divorced a week ago. His wife lives almost in the same street. I will go and see her as I find her congenial. But not as congenial as her husband. I like him very much indeed, in spite of his little weakness (which is getting bigger of course). Mr Doran has gone today to Toronto for a trial which concerns him. I will see him again in Philadelphia. I am leaving these parts tomorrow at 7 in the evening and I will arrive in Philadelphia at 3 on Tuesday afternoon. 20 hours on a train! The ticket, which includes a private compartment (which I insist on) costs 160 frs. My post is waiting for me in Philadelphia. It is infuriating because I won't hear from you until Tuesday. But it was difficult to make any other arrangement. I hope that everything is going well. If you need money write to Mr Pinker to send you one or two thousand francs for special purchases. I mean for clothes (which will be a present from me). He will send it in French notes. I love you my pet, but I am very cross with you for not being here. I kiss you tenderly.]

KEELE / MS / 56
(*To Marguerite Soulié Bennett*)

c/o George H. Doran Co.
23 Nov 1911

Dearest girl,

Charmed by all your letters, which I received last night on returning. Your description of the wedding (& of Uncle Joe in particular) est épatante. Aussi suis-je très content que tu travailles toujours, et qu'enfin tu envoies des pièces à des 'managers.' Ta lettre d'Alcock est assez bien — pas trop. Tout ce que tu me racontes m'intéresse beaucoup, mais je ne peux pas signaler chaque détail dans ma réponse. En suite je suis très content que tu te commandes des chiffons. Bref je suis content de toi et de tes gestes. En dépensant seulement £24 jusqu'au 10 novembre tu as été très raisonnable. Mais je ne comprends pas la somme de £4. Si c'est le premier chèque envoyé par M. Harrison, cette somme aurait du être renvoyée. Mais ça m'est égal. Je suis rentré hier soir. C'est le concours hippique et les hôtels sont bondés. J'avais une chambre trop petite et trop près d'un des ascenseurs. J'ai mal dormi. J'avais un courrier immense à avaler. Je t'envoie encore des coupures. J'étais à l'Opéra hier soir (*Faust*) dans une des loges les plus chic avec des sommités financières. C'était la belle-fille du célèbre Schiff (seul concurrent de Morgan) qui m'avait invité. Ces femmes jeunes, ultra-riches et paresseuses, se ruent sur moi, parce qu'elles sont convaincues, par mes livres, que je les comprendraient d'une façon spéciale. Elles sont toutes pleines de curiosité sur toi. Je fais manger à cette curiosité affammée, qui me flatte extrêmement. Je compte être embêté ce soir. Je vais visiter le concours hippique avec un autre gros choux et sa femme, que tout le monde me dit embêtante. Deux de ces femmes sont venues à Philadelphia exprès hier, avec le mari d'une, pour me rencontrer et pour causer dans le train et dans l'auto sur la *Vie*. Mais je te raconterai tout ça. Une m'a dit: 'Il parait que vous vous intéressez beaucoup à la toilette des femmes que vous rencontrez, M. Bennett. Est ce vrai?' J'ai répondu: 'Oui, c'est vrai. Voulez-vous que je vous dise la verité sur votre toilette?' 'Oui.' 'Eh bien, votre corsage est mal agrafé à la ceinture. *On voit du blanc.*' Pour un instant elle en était suffoquée. Puis elle a ri. Je lui ai demandé si elle avait chez-elle un jeu de glaces. Elle a dit non!! Je lui ai dit qu'il fallait on un jeu de glaces ou une femme de chambre avec des yeux dans la tête. Étonnantes, ces femmes riches. Elle me traitent toutes comme une espèce de père confesseur. J'étais à l'Opéra de Philadelphia avant hier. Salle énorme, neuve, et laide. Bondée de monde. Quelques toilettes parisiennes. Le reste, provinciale! Hier le *Saturday Evening Post* m'a offert un déjeuner, très chic. Et puis après, le petit-fils du notoire Widener, un des plus riches milliardaires des Etats Unis, est venu me chercher. Il m'a conduit, avec deux femmes et un mari, à la maison de son grand-père pour voir les tableaux. C'est la collection la plus magnifique que j'ai jamais vue. Il y a 150 chefs d'œuvres. Il a payé (le vieux, je veux dire) 2,500,000 frs. pour un seul tableau (*The Mill* de Rembrandt). Maison superbe, d'un goût presque parfait, partout. Le petit-fils est collectionneur de livres. Je lui ai signé son *Hilda* et il était enchanté. En suite il nous a conduit à la gare.

La recette du *Honeymoon* pour la cinquième semaine dépasse la recette de la quatrième, de £112. C'est très bien. On insiste toujours que je refais le troisième acte, et toujours je refuse. Dans une quinzaine de jours je serai (j'espère) dans tes bras, et entre tes seins. Je te reverrai et je saurai si tu es changée, je veux dire physiquement. Autrement tu n'es pas changée, je sais ça par tes lettres. Les fins de tes lettres me charment et m'excitent horriblement. Le fond de ma pensée est que chaque jour ici m'embête, bien que je suis toujours amusé ou intéressé. Avant que je t'aurai vu je n'aurai pas un instant de vrai tranquillité. Pourtant par le plus extraordinaire effort de volonté que j'ai jamais accompli je garde, absolument intacte, toute ma force vitale pour toi. C'est assommant. Ma petite, on se comprend, je pense. Tu ne sauras jamais exactement comme et comment je t'aime; personne ne le saura sauf moi. Mais enfin tu sais presque. Je te bise énormément.

Ton A.

56. [... is terrific. And I am very glad that you are still working and are at last sending plays to 'managers'. Your letter from Alcock is quite good, not very. I was very interested in everything you told me, but I cannot refer to every detail in my reply. I am also very glad that you are ordering clothes. In short, I am pleased with you and what you are doing. You were very economical to have spent only £24 until 10 November. But I do not understand the sum of £4. If it is the first cheque sent by Mr Harrison, it should have been sent back. But I don't mind. I arrived back here yesterday evening. The horse races are on and the hotels are packed. My room was too small and too near

one of the lifts. I slept badly. I had a great deal of post to get through. I am sending you more cuttings. I went to the Opera yesterday evening (*Faust*) and was in one of the most expensive boxes, with some top financiers. I had been invited by the daughter-in-law of the famous Schiff (Morgan's only competitor). These young, ultra-rich, idle women make a rush for me because my books make them feel sure that I will understand them in a special way. They are all very curious about you. I give sustenance to this devouring curiosity, which I find extremely flattering. I am expecting a boring evening. I am going to the horse races with another bigwig and his wife, who everyone says is boring. Two of these women, with the husband of one of them, went to Philadelphia yesterday on purpose to meet me and talk about *Life* on the train and in the car. But I will tell you all about that. One of them said to me 'I have heard that you are very interested in the clothes of the women you meet, Mr Bennett. Is that true?' 'Yes, it is true. Do you want me to tell you what I really think about your clothes?' 'Yes.' 'Well, your blouse is badly fastened at the waist. There is a bit of underwear showing.' She was speechless with rage for a moment. Then she laughed. I asked her if she had a set of mirrors at home. She said no!! I told her she needed either a set of mirrors or a chambermaid with eyes in her head. These rich women are amazing. They all treat me as some kind of father confessor. I went to the Opera in Philadelphia the day before yesterday. An enormous, new, and ugly hall. Crammed with people. Some Parisian outfits, all the others looked provincial. Yesterday the *Saturday Evening Post* gave a very fine lunch for me. Then afterwards the grandson of the famous Widener, one of the richest multimillionaires in the United States, came to fetch me. He took me, with two women and the husband of one of them, to his grandfather's house to see the pictures. It is the most magnificent collection that I have ever seen, with 150 masterpieces. He (I mean the old man) paid 2,500,000 frs. for one picture alone (Rembrandt's *The Mill*). A superb house with almost perfect taste throughout. The grandson is a book collector. I signed his copy of *Hilda* and he was delighted. Then he took me to the station.

The takings for the fifth week of *Honeymoon* were £112 more than the takings for the fourth week. This is very good. I keep being asked to redo the third act and I keep saying no. In a fortnight I will (I hope) be in your arms and between your breasts. I will see you again and I will know whether you have changed. Physically, I mean. You have not changed in any other way, I know from your letters. The endings of your letters charm me and excite me terribly. In the depths of my mind I am bored by every day that I spend here, although I am always entertained or interested. I will not have a moment of real peace until I see you. Still, by the most extraordinary effort of will that I have ever made, I am keeping all my life force intact for you. It is killing me. My pet, I think we understand each other. You will never know exactly how and in what way I love you; nobody will know but me. But you almost know. With an enormous kiss.]

On Fred Alcock see p. 63 n.

Frederick Harrison (d. 1926), manager of the Haymarket Theatre, had been offered *Milestones* by mistake. The play was produced by J. E. Vedrenne and Dennis Eadie at the Royalty.

Mortimer Schiff (1877–1931); J. P. Morgan (1867–1943); and P. A. B. Widener (1834–1915), all financiers. Harry Widener (1885–1912), the bibliophile, went down on the *Titanic*.

The grand dinner given by Colonel Harvey of Harper's, mentioned in the letter of 20 October, took place at the St Regis Hotel on 27 November. The evening included the recital of a poem by Carolyn Wells.

Lord of the English language, master of plot and plan,
Wizard of clever diction, seer of the heart of man;
Sculptor of subtle syntax, scribbler of sapient screed,
We in our breathless interest, quiver with joy as we read

Story or sermon or satire, confessions, reflections, reviews;
Essay or drama or novel—eagerly these we peruse,
All other authors forgotten while his new books we devour;
All other idols dethroning, Bennett's the Man of the Hour!
Have we an author to match him? Is there a writer of us
So vigorous, various, versatile, vivid, voluminous?
No; to our Old World brother we offer the laurel and bays;
His to write magical marvels, ours but to read and to praise.
Loud as Olympian thunders, clear as Pandean Pipes,
May he record his impressions under the Stars and Stripes.
Gladly we give him our homage, hopefully seeking the way
How to Read Arnold Bennett on Twenty-Four Hours a Day.

KEELE / MS / 57   On Board the Cunard
(*To Marguerite Soulié Bennett*)   R.M.S. 'Lusitania.'
                              Samedi
                              [2 December 1911]

Dearest girl,

J'écris ceci dans une orage énorme. Mais ça ne me fiche
absolument rien comme mal de mer, le bateau est si grand. Il
roule beaucoup mais le mouvement en est si lent et si doux
qu'on n'est pas incommodé. Pas moi, au moins. Maintenant, je
ne saurais pas ne pas aller voir ma mère. J'arriverai à Liverpool
à la première heure de *mardi*. Je coucherai mardi soir chez ma
mère. J'arriverai à Londres pour le déjeuner *mercredi*. Je
pourrais venir directement à Paris le même jour, mais je serais
trop fatigué, et je ne veux pas arriver ratatiné et flapi. Donc je
m'occuperai de mes affaires (Pinker, Vernon, etc) mercredi
après-midi, et je passerai la soirée chez Tertia, et je filerai vers
ma fe-femme *jeudi* matin à neuf heures. J'espère la voir à la gare
du nord jeudi soir (le 7 courant) à 4.45. *J'ai écrit* à l'hôtel
Meurice. Il me faut une petite lune de miel plutôt confortable et
chic que chiche. Donc j'ai arrêté une chambre à deux lits, avec
salle de bain particulière, et un petit salon particulier. Ne
t'occupe pas du prix. Je leur ai dit que très probablement tu
arriveras pendant la matinée de jeudi, avec tes bagages. Arrives
donc, Hôtel Meurice, Rue de Rivoli, fièrement, et puis viens à
la gare du Nordette. J'ai une petite idée que peut-être tu ne
resterais pas dans tes Champs Elysées, et j'ai écrit une autre
lettre, semblable à celle-ci mais adressée chez Miss Cravens.
C'est comme ça que je suis prévoyant et prévenant. Je calcule

que tu recevras celle-ci mardi soir. Je le mettrai à la poste à Fishguard, première escale du *Lusitania*.

En attendant,

Ton A.

Avant mon départ j'ai reçu ta délicieuse petite lettre, qui m'a égayé. A.

---

57. [I am writing this during a terrible storm. But I don't feel the slightest bit seasick as the boat is so big. It is rolling a lot, but the movement is so slow and gentle that one is not really upset by it. Not I, at least. Now, I couldn't not go and see my mother. I will reach Liverpool first thing on *Tuesday*. I will spend Tuesday night at my mother's. I will arrive in London in time for lunch on *Wednesday*. I could go straight on to Paris the same day, but I would be too tired and I do not want to arrive dried up and exhausted. So I will see to my affairs (Pinker, Vernon, etc.) on Wednesday afternoon, and I will spend the evening with Tertia and I will slip off to my little wife at nine on *Thursday* morning. I hope to see her at the Gare du Nord at 4.45 on Thursday evening (the 7 of this month). I *have* written to the hotel Meurice. I need a little honeymoon and it must be comfortable and stylish, not stingy. So I have booked a room with two beds, a private bathroom and a private sitting-room. Don't worry about the expense. I told them that you would most probably arrive with your luggage on Thursday morning. So go proudly to the hotel Meurice, Rue de Rivoli, and then come to the Gare du Nordette. I have a sort of feeling that you have not stayed in your Champs Elysées and I have written another letter, like this one but addressed to care of Miss Cravens. You see how far-sighted and attentive I am. I reckon that you will receive this on Tuesday evening. I will post it in Fishguard, the *Lusitania*'s first port of call. In anticipation, . . . Before I left, I received your lovely little letter which cheered me up.]

Bennett cut short his visit to America by a week or more, possibly because he was overtired. While he was in Chicago he announced that he was being called back to Europe and would not complete the two month coast-to-coast visit.

Frank Vernon (1875–1940), produced *Cupid and Commonsense*, and was shortly to be stage director for *Milestones*. For letters to him see Vol. III.

Margaret Cravens (1881–1912/13) was a young woman from Indiana who went to Paris to study with Ravel. She became involved with Ezra Pound, and committed suicide when he left her. Nothing is known of her relationship with Bennett and Marguerite.

KEELE / MS / 58
(*To Marguerite Soulié Bennett*)

Hôtel Californie
Cannes
lundi matin
11 Mch 1912

Dearest girl,

Quand j'ai reçu ta télégramme hier soir à 7 heures, j'ai compris que tu t'étais mise dans la tête d'acheter cette maison. Donc ça m'embêtait de te télégraphier ma pensée. Mais

vraiment, pour moi ça n'est pas une heureuse idée. Posséder
une maison à Toulouse quand on habite l'Angleterre, serait
fatalement un embêtement continuel. Il y a toujours des
histoires avec des propriétés — réparations, contributions,
affaires de commune, de *canton*, quoi! Personne ne sait qui n'a
pas été, comme moi, intendant de propriétés. Et aussi je ne
pense pas que Juliette a un tempérament qui nous éviterait des
ennuis. Et, encore plus fort, tout ça ne servirait à rien! Ta mère
n'a pas besoin d'une maison spéciale, avec des salles de bain, de
la ventilation, et du chauffage centrale. Elle a besoin seulement
d'une maison ordinaire, comme il existe partout. Elle serait
tout à fait aussi heureuse dans une maison louée que dans une
maison à toi. Peut-être plus. Si je pensais que le projet servirait
à quelquechose, je l'entretiendrais, mais je suis convaincu qu'il
ne servirait qu'à causer des ennuis pour tout le monde — même
si Juliette y restait tranquillement. Il ne peut pas être impossible de trouver une petite maison aux environs de la ville. Le
loyer *exacte* — qu'est-ce que ça peut faire — à nous? Trouve la
chose, et payes-en le prix. C'est tout.

plus tard

Je viens d'avoir ta lettre, et celle de Juliette. Pour ce que tu as
à faire, tu as toutes mes symps! C'est assommant, chercher.
Enfin ne t'inquiètes pas de moi. Ce matin je suis *infiniment mieux*.
Et si je n'avais pas des courriers si énormes je pourrais
travailler. Je t'envoie toutes sortes de choses. Je m'étais arrangé
pour aller voir Descaves cet après midi, mais je lui ai télégraphié que je ne peux pas venir. J'aime mieux travailler.

Donc, ma chérissime enfant pas si melancolique que ça, je te
bise tendrement.

A.

58. [When I received the telegram at 7 o'clock yesterday evening, I realized that you
were determined to buy that house. So I didn't want to send you a telegram to say what
I thought. But in my view it really is not a good idea. Owning a house in Toulouse when
we live in England is fated to be a constant problem. Property always means trouble—
repairs, dues payable to the commune, the *canton*, and so on! Nobody could know unless
they have been a property manager, as I have. And I don't think Juliette is the kind of
person who would spare us trouble. And, an even stronger reason, there would be no
point in it! Your mother does not need a special house, with bathrooms, ventilation and
central heating. She only needs an ordinary house, such as there are everywhere. She
would be just as happy in a rented house as in one belonging to you. Perhaps happier. If
I thought there were any purpose in the project, I would consider it, but I am convinced

that it would cause nothing but trouble for everyone—even if Juliette were to stay in it quietly. It cannot be impossible to find a little house on the outskirts of the town. What does the *exact* rent matter—to us! Find what is needed and pay the price. That's all.

Later. I have just received letters from you and Juliette. You have my every sympathy for all you have to do! Searching is deadly. Finally don't worry about me. I am infinitely better this morning. And if I did not have so many letters to answer I would be able to work. I send you all sorts of messages. I had arranged to go and see Descaves this afternoon, but I sent a telegram to say that I could not go. I would rather work. So my dearest child, I am not so gloomy as all that and I kiss you tenderly.]

After brief stays in England and Paris after his return from America, Bennett, with Marguerite, went to live at Cannes for four months. They had settled in their minds before the American trip that they would come to England to live. In his little essay 'Graphic Art in Paris', reprinted in *Sketches for Autobiography*, Bennett describes his decision to leave France.

For several years there had been gradually germinating in my mind the conviction that I should be compelled by some obscure instinct to return to England, where, unhappily, art is not cherished as in France. I had a most disturbing suspicion that I was losing touch with England, and that my (literary) work would soon begin to suffer accordingly. And one day I gave notice to my landlady, and then I began to get estimates for removing my furniture and books. And then I tried to sell to my landlady the fittings of the admirable bathroom which I had installed in her house, and she answered me that she had no desire for a bathroom in her house, and would I take the fittings away? And then I unhooked my pictures and packed my books. And lastly, the removers came and turned what had been a home into a litter of dirty straw. And I saw the tail of the last van as it rounded the corner. And I definitely quitted the land where eating and love are understood, where art and learning are honoured, where women well dressed and without illusions are not rare, where thrift flourishes, where politeness is practised, and where politics are shameful and grotesque. I return merely as a visitor. I should probably have enjoyed myself more in France, only I prefer to live in England and regret France than to live in France and regret England. I think the permanent exile is a pathetic figure. I suppose I have a grim passion for England. But I know why France is the darling of nations.

Lucien Descaves (1861–1949), journalist, novelist, playwright.

KEELE / MS / 59
(*To Marguerite Soulié Bennett*)

c/o F. Alcock
Bellevue
NewHaven
Sussex
[about 1 May 1912]

Chérie,

Deux cartes de toi ce matin! Infiniment merci. Aussi je suis infiniment content que tu aimes tant l'hôtel. Amuse-toi bien. Tu me verras samedi pour le déjeuner. Aujourd'hui j'ai conduit cet auto à Lewes et la plupart du retour. 30 kilomètres en tout! Sans accident. Mes deux professeurs sont très contents de moi. Moi aussi! Il parait que je ferai un bon chauffeur. Je vais être en pourparlers avec deux vrais chauffeurs. En tout cas c'est presque sûr qui j'en aurai un provisoirement à partir de samedi pour Londres. Demain nous allons voir M. Preston sur place. M. Vernon sera avec nous dans la loge lundi soir. Je discuterai la mise en scène avec lui. Il fait un temps merveilleux aujourd'hui. On dit que le pays est très épatant par un temps pareil, mais quand on conduit en auto on ne peut rien regarder sauf la route. La première fois que j'ai rencontré un autre auto, j'avais une frousse. Après ça j'ai rencontré avec sang froid une cylindre à vapeur, un autobus et une voiture de bébé. (Pourtant j'ai encore beaucoup à apprendre.) Il n'y a pas de domestique ici. La servante est souffrante, et il arrive tous les matins une minuscule enfant qui s'appelle 'Flossie'. Elle est bien. Elle m'apporte mon thé à 8 heures et tes lettres et toutes les autres lettres. Le relevé de la semaine théâtrale est extrêmement bien. Jeudi matinée dépassera tous les records. £197. Nous allons prendre le thé, et puis encore une sortie en auto.

Et ta femme de chambre?

Veuilles ouvrir ma malle. L'adresse de Pinker, en cas tu en aies besoin — est Talbot House, Arundel St. Strand.

Tout le monde te salue, amicalement, respectueusement, frénétiquement, et moi amoureusement.

Ton A.

L'adresse de Mdme. Lowndes
    9 Barton St.
    Westminster.

---

59. [Two postcards from you this morning! Infinite thanks. And I am infinitely glad that you like the hotel so much. Have a nice time. You will see me for lunch on Saturday. Today I drove this car to Lewes and most of the way back. 30 kilometres altogether! With no accidents. My two teachers are very pleased with me. I'm pleased too! It looks as if I will make a very good driver. I will be negotiating with two real chauffeurs. In any case I will almost certainly have one temporarily from Saturday to go to London. Tomorrow we will go and see Mr Preston *in situ*. Mr Vernon will be with us in the box on Monday evening. I will discuss the production with him. The weather is beautiful today. People say that the countryside looks terrific in this weather but when driving a car one can look at nothing but the road. I got a fright the first time I met another car but since then I have kept my composure when meeting a steam-roller, a bus and a baby carriage. (I still have a lot to learn, however.) There is no servant here. The maid is ill and every morning a tiny child called Flossie comes. She is sweet. She brings me my tea at 8 o'clock and your letters and all others. The weekly return from the theatre is extremely good. The Thursday matinee will break all records. £197. We are going to have tea and then have another car trip.

How is the chamber maid? Please open my trunk. If you need Pinker's address, it is Talbot House, Arundel St., Strand.

Everybody sends you friendly, respectful, frenetic, and in my case loving, regards....]

Harry Preston (1860–1936) managed the Royal York Hotel in Brighton. Bennett wrote much of *Clayhanger* there, and he and Marguerite stayed there during part of the spring and early summer of the present year.

Milestones, devised by Edward Knoblock and written almost entirely by Bennett, opened at the Royalty Theatre on 5 March. It was Bennett's greatest success in the theatre, running for 609 nights and spawning several provincial productions and production in New York in 1912.

KEELE / MS / 60
(*To Marguerite Soulié Bennett*)   Yacht Velsa
                                                      Wednesday afternoon
                                                      [mid-June 1912]

Chérie adorée,

J'ai fait le premier voyage dans la Velsa. Nous avons voyagé de Ditton à Kingston (2 milles) où nous restons pour la nuit. J'espère avoir un membre de l'équipée ce soir qui vient de Brightlingsea. Le bateau marche admirablement et le capitaine est charmant. Peut-être nous aurons le troisième matelot (cuisinier) à Londres, en passant, mais c'est pas encore sûr. Nous repartirons demain matin à 6 heures et demi, et nous arriverons à Gravesend dans l'après-midi. Gravesend est la fin de l'estuaire de la Tamise. De là je viendrai dans la soirée en auto vers toi. C'est la chose la plus exquise que même Cepa pourrait imaginer.

Tu as parfaitement raison pour l'hôtel. Sois ferme et sévère. Je ne doute pas que tu plaira énormément à ma mère. Si elle te charmait autant comme je serais content!!! Parlant de l'énorme courrier d'hier, c'est justement cette correspondance qui va m'embêter. Enfin, je m'en fiche tout de même. En passant à travers Londres je compte arrêter le bateau en face chez Pinker pour lui faire une visite d'affaire — prendre les papiers du bateau etc. J'ai eu une histoire énorme avec l'ex-propriétaire! C'est fini. Je te raconterai tout ça. Je t'ai télégraphié ce matin. Je me porte très bien. Atkins aussi. Après sa rechute Muriel est ce matin seulement un peu mieux. Atkins a été très embêté. Il allait filer au moment qu'il a reçu la télégramme rassurante.

Je t'aime, et plus que ça.

Ton A. Nouche

60. [I have made my first trip in the *Velsa*. We went 2 miles, from Ditton to Kingston, where we stopped for the night. I am hoping that a member of the crew who is coming from Brightlingsea, will arrive by this evening. The boat goes wonderfully well and the captain is charming. We may pick up the third sailor (the cook) on the way through London, but it is not certain yet. We will set off again tomorrow morning at 6.30 and we will reach Gravesend in the afternoon. Gravesend is at the end of the Thames estuary. From there I will return to you by car during the evening. This is the most exquisite thing that even Cepa could imagine.

You are absolutely right about the hotel. Be firm and severe. I am sure that my mother will be delighted with you. How happy I would be if you felt the same about her!!! On the subject of yesterday's enormous post, all this letter-writing is going to get me down. But the hell with it. On our way through London I mean to stop the boat opposite Pinker's and pay him a business visit—give him the papers about the boat etc. I have had an enormous to-do with the former owner! It is all over now. I will tell you all about it later. I sent him a telegram this morning. I am very well, so is Atkins. Muriel is only a little better this morning after her relapse. Atkins was very upset. He was just about to rush away when he received the reassuring telegram. I love you and more than that.]

Bennett was a keen boatsman all of his life. He kept a small boat in his youth and also later when he came to London. He began negotiations to buy the *Velsa* in 1910. He was able to work on the *Velsa* quite as well as he worked in his home. *From the Log of the Velsa* (1914) records some of his travels in it. The frontispiece is a watercolour by him.

J. B. Atkins (1871–1954), assistant editor of the *Spectator*, owned a yacht as well. He and Bennett often sailed together. Muriel Atkins was his wife.

KEELE / MS / 61
(*To Marguerite Soulié Bennett*)

Yacht Velsa
Ostende
Dimanche matin
[18 August 1912]

Adorée,

Nous avons quitté Boulogne hier matin à 6.15, et nous sommes arrivés à Ostende à 6.40 du soir. Jusqu'à midi il pleuvait à torrents, et il y avait du vent. Au Cap Griz Nez, tempête! Mer très agitée. J'étais content que tu n'y étais pas. Pourtant personne n'a été incommodé. J'ai donné du Mothersill à Gilbert. Moi, j'ai porté la bande. Mais si la bande y était pour quelquechose je n'en sais rien. Je peux te dire que c'est *une sensation magnifique* de contourner le Cap Griz Nez dans son vaisseau à soi. À trois heures il faisait beaucoup plus calme. Nous avions la marée pour nous, & nous faisions 13 kil. à l'heure! Puis le vent est complètement tombé, et nous avons recommencé avec le moteur. La mer était comme une glace quand nous entrions à Ostende. Aussi, la sensation d'entrer tout bonnement dans une ville en bateau est épatante. Nous avons amarré près de la gare, en plein centre! Il y a une demi douzaine d'autres yachts, tous les uns plus chic que les autres. Willem les connaît presque tout. Moi je connais le reste. Gilbert et moi nous sommes allés au Casino hier soir. Concert. Après le Cap Griz Nez c'était un changement! Le temps est toujours infecte. Ce matin il brouillasse. Probablement nous irons à Bruges aujourd'hui. Je ne sais pas. Je n'ai pas encore causé avec mon capitaine. Gilbert est ahuri de son voyage. Je peux te dire que c'est un garçon charmant mais plutôt nul. Il ne sait rien du tout, même artistiquement. Il a des idées arriérées, et il n'a *jamais* la moindre lueur d'originalité. Comme compagnon de voyage c'est parfait. Mais j'ai été un peu deçu dans ce garçon. Je le croyais supérieur. Si vraiment il l'est, ou il le sera, il le cache par timidité ou décidément il n'est pas précoce. Mais je suis à peu près sûr qu'il ne l'est pas.

J'espère trouver une lettre de toi au bureau de poste ce matin. Maintenant je vais écrire à ma mère.

Je t'aime,

Nouche, A.

Mes amours à grand'mère et Gabrielle.

61. [We left Boulogne yesterday morning at 6.15 and reached Ostend at 6.40 in the evening. It rained in buckets until noon and it was windy. There was a storm off Cape Gris Nez! The sea was very rough. I was glad you weren't there. Still no one was unwell. I gave some Mothersill to Gilbert. I wore a bandage, but I don't know whether that helped. I can only say that going round Cape Gris Nez in one's own vessel is a *wonderful feeling*. By three o'clock it was much calmer. The tide was in our favour and we were doing 13 kil. an hour! Then the wind dropped completely and we started again with the engine. The sea was like a millpond when we went into Ostend. And the feeling of sailing straight into a town by boat is terrific. We docked near the station, right in the middle of the town! There are half a dozen other yachts, each one smarter than the others. Willem knows almost all of them. I know the rest. Gilbert and I went to the Casino yesterday evening. There was a concert. What a change from Cape Gris Nez! The weather is still terrible. It is drizzling this morning. We will probably go to Bruges today. I don't know, I have not talked to my captain yet. Gilbert is amazed by the trip. I can tell you he is a charming boy but fairly worthless. He knows nothing, even artistically. He has backward ideas, and never has the faintest spark of originality. He is a perfect travelling companion. But I am a bit disappointed in him. I thought him better. If he really is, or will be, he is either hiding it out of shyness, or else he is decidedly not precocious. But I am almost sure he is not.

I am *hoping* to find a letter from you at the post office this morning. Now I am going to write to my mother. I love you.... My love to grandmother and Gabrielle.]

Bennett was sailing during much of August and September.

Willem: the Dutch captain of the *Velsa*; Gilbert: unidentified; Gabrielle: Marguerite's sister.

KEELE / MS / 62   Yacht Velsa
(*To Marguerite Soulié Bennett*)   Dimanche matin
                                         en mer
                                         [25 August 1912]

Chérissime,

We left Veere this morning at 6.55. Perfectly calm & gloomy. Misty. Foggy. But no rain. We had *one* gleam of sunshine, lasting 2 seconds; the first for 3 or 4 days. We shall soon be at Zierikzee. But we can see nothing but the sea all round, except a few sandbanks. Yesterday it rained nearly all day. We did water-colours in the afternoon (very bad) in a shed with the wide double doors open. Veere is a most beautiful place, but there are too many English people there. I forgot to tell you that when we were crossing from Terneuzen to Flushing on Thursday in a storm, the piano broke loose and jumped into the middle of the saloon & fell forward on to the table!! We put it back. It was not injured. I played Bach on it afterwards. The meals continue to be simple but very good. We have no more tea, & are drinking the crew's tea. Horrible Ceylon stuff! Still eating an apple each morning! I believe I am very well. I expect Gilbert will leave during this week. I shall insist on paying his fare home. I have taught him a great deal. He said the other night, '*I only began to take an interest in art last year.*' He also said that he had not considered sculpture as an emotional art! Il est étonnant. The one & only thing about him that really annoys me is that he puts his knife & fork on the plate silently, avec toutes les précautions possibles, comme Pauline. Ça m'agace. He is very timid. The more I know the Captain the better I like him. He is alive. Compared to him the other two are half-dead. But they are nice chaps. After a week's instruction daily, I have at last persuaded Edward to do the cabins all at once when he begins them. At first he would make the beds, then go to the kitchen & do something else, then come back & sweep, then go away, then come back & empty the slops, then go away, then come back & fill the reservoirs, then go away, & by about 3 in the afternoon he would be doing the carafes, & the lamps at 7 o'clock. I have cured that. He is undoubtedly a good cook. He made us an omelette the other night. It wasn't like any other omelette that I ever tasted. I doubt if it was a real omelette at all; but it was simply delicious. We are now just arriving at Zierikzee & it is nearly ten o'clock.

Quand te verrai-je, cara mia?

Love to all. Je t'aime.

Ton Nouche

KEELE / MS / 63
(*To Marguerite Soulié Bennett*)

Yacht Velsa
Tuesday
27 Augt 1912

Chérissime adorée,

J'ai reçu tes deux lettres avec grand plaisir. Eh bien, tu as du mal avec tes parents. Je suppose qu'il est arrivé des histoires entre toi et Hélène à propos de grand'mère. Pour moi, elle serait plus heureuse à St. Antonin. Le confort ça lui est égal. Mais je reconnais que tu ne peux pas prendre toute la responsabilité morale. Si grand'mère est douée d'une fille dure et sans imagination, il faut bien qu'elle en souffre un peu. Tu n'es que la petite-fille. Et tu ne peux pas t'arroger les pouvoirs pleins sur la destinée de la vieille. C'est une situation délicate et difficile. Et en l'arrangeant tu apprends encore plus profondément ce que c'est la vie. Pour les affaires, je ne pense pas que c'est une très heureuse idée d'embêter Tertia avec les gages de Locker. C'est assommant, aller acheter des mandats de poste. Si Locker change son programme tant pis pour lui. Nous pourrions très bien lui envoyer un chèque toutes les semaines sur Londres. Puisqu'il n'a rien à faire il peut aller chez Cook le toucher. Tertia pourrait lui payer pour samedi prochain et après je te verrai et nous arrangerons ça. Mardi donc, je t'attendrai. C'est mieux que je n'espérais. Je suis énormément content que tu puisses arriver si tôt. Ton voyage sera des plus faciles. Lundi soir tu coucheras à l'hôtel de la Gare du Nord. Tu prendras le train de 8h. 10m. du matin pour la Hollande. Aucun changement de voiture. Wagon restaurant à partir de Bruxelles. Ce train s'arrête à Haarlem, Leyden, et Amsterdam, et dans une de ces villes la *Velsa* sera amarré aussi près de la gare que possible. Laquelle ville, je t'écrirai plus tard. Mais tu vois que tu n'auras aucune difficulté. Tu seras sur le *Velsa* entre 5 et 7 heures de l'après-midi. Je t'envoie sous ce pli un chèque de quinze cent francs sur Cooks Paris. Veuilles le toucher. Prends 40 livres en argent hollandais, et le reste en anglais. Mais naturellement si tu as besoin d'argent tu en prendras pour toi en français.

Le temps reste toujours infectissime. Dimanche après-midi il a fait très beau, et nous espérions. Mais dans la nuit de dimanche-lundi il a plu à torrents. Nous nous sommes amarrés dans le petit port de Zeype dimanche (sur l'Escaut). Nous l'avons quitté lundi matin dans la pluie, le froid, et la tempête. Nous avons déjeuné à Willemstad, et puis dans l'après-midi nous sommes venus ici à Dordrecht. Il faisait du vent. Nous avons fait 23 kilomètres en $1\frac{1}{2}$ heures, sans le moteur. Arrivés près de Dordrecht, nous étions forcés d'attendre 3 heures pour le pont-bascule (chemin de fer). Chic. Mais c'est ça la Hollande. La vue était bien, et la vie de la rivière toujours très intéressante. Mais quel vent. Dans la nuit la tempête était *terrible*. Nous étions dans un bassin en pleine ville, et tout à notre aise; mais ce matin le pont était tapissé de feuilles arrachées aux arbres par le vent. Nous restons ici aujourd'hui. Demain nous irons à Schiedam, où Gilbert me quittera. Ce garçon est exquis mais il est *nul*. La première troupe de *Milestones* a commencé sa tournée à Littlehampton (petite plage) avec des résultats éminemment satisfaisants. C'est tout. Aujourd'hui j'ai reçu toute ma correspondance de Londres. Je me porte très bien. Ma nuque n'est pas encore tout à fait cicatrisée. Je t'embrasse tendrement mon petit.

Ton Nouche, A.

63. [I received your two letters with great pleasure. Well, you are having a bad time with your relations. I suppose you and Hélène got into an argument about your grandmother. In my view, she would be much happier at St Antonin. She doesn't care about comfort. But I can see that you must not take on the entire moral responsibility. Your grandmother is blessed with a hard, unimaginative daughter and she will have to suffer a bit in consequence. You are only the granddaughter. And you cannot assume full powers over the old woman's fate. It is a sensitive, difficult situation. And by sorting it out you are learning ever more of what life is about. As for business, I don't think it is a very good idea to bother Tertia with Locker's wages. Going to buy money orders is deadly dull. If Locker changes his programme, then it's his bad luck. We could easily send him a cheque every week in London. Since he has nothing to do, he can go to Cook's to collect it. Tertia could pay him next Saturday and after that, I will see you and we can make some other arrangement.

So I will expect you on Tuesday, which is better than I thought. I am tremendously pleased that you can come so soon. Your journey will be very easy. You will spend Monday night at the Gare du Nord hotel. In the morning you will take the 8.10 train for Holland. No change of carriage. A restaurant car from Brussels. The train stops at Haarlem, Leyden, and Amsterdam and the *Velsa* will be docked as near the station as possible in one of these towns. I will write to you later to say which. But you see, you will have no trouble. You will be on the *Velsa* between 5 and 7 in the afternoon. I am sending you enclosed a cheque for fifteen hundred francs payable at Cooks, Paris. Please cash it. Take 40 pounds in Dutch money, and the rest in English. But of course take some in French money for yourself if you need it.

The weather continues absolutely rotten. It was very good on Sunday afternoon and we were hopeful. But it rained cats and dogs on the night of Sunday to Monday. We had docked in the little port of Zeype (on the Escaut) on Sunday. We left on Monday morning in rainy, cold, stormy weather. We had lunch in Willemstad and then we arrived here in Dordrecht in the afternoon. It was windy. We did 23 kilometres in 1½ hours without the engine. Just outside Dordrecht, we had to wait nearly 3 hours for the bascule bridge (railway). Great. But that is what Holland is like. The view was good and river life is always interesting. But what a wind. In the night the storm was *terrible*. We were in a dock right in the middle of the town and perfectly comfortable. But this morning the deck was covered in a carpet of leaves which had been blown off trees by the wind. We will stay here today. Tomorrow we will go to Schiedam where Gilbert will leave us. The boy is exquisite but worthless. The first *Milestones* troupe has begun its tour in Littlehampton (a little seaside town) with eminently satisfactory results. That's all. I received all my correspondence from London today. I am very well. The back of my neck has still not healed completely. I kiss you tenderly, my pet.]

Locker: unidentified; presumably not a mistake for Lockyer, who presently became head gardener at Bennett's new home in Essex.

KEELE / MS / 64   14, St. Simon's Avenue
(*To Marguerite Soulié Bennett*)   Putney S.W.
    mardi
    le 22 oct 1912

Nouchette chérie,

Ta lettre. Très bien. Donc, je t'attends samedi. Prends le train de — Enfin prends le train que tu veux. Mais arrives pour le dîner. Les Sharpes seront au théâtre ce soir-là. Ils m'ont demandé des billets pour *Voysey*. Mdme. Sharpe m'a dit: 'Mais Marguerite, ne voudrait-elle aller avec nous?' 'Penses-tu?' j'ai dit (à part). Je sais que tu ne voudrais nullement ressortir le soir. Comme ça, je verrai avant les autres toutes ces choses que tu as achetées, et cette personne et ce corps qui attrayent (à ce qu'il paraît) les regards de tout le monde dans tous les restaurants de Paris. Ce linge, ces déshabillés, ces dessous, et tous ces bijoux de toilette que tu t'es offerts, ainsi que la chair aimée qu'ils sont destinés à voiler. C'est étonnant comme tu me manques, après une semaine, et comment ton absence m'agace à tous les instants. Tu peux te dire que tu as pris une emprise sur moi qui n'est pas ordinaire, étant donné mon caractère etc. Tâche de ne pas t'en abuser, je te supplie. C'est ton souvenir qui m'excite. Pendant ton absence je devrais avoir une petite cocotte pour me soulager. Je suppose que tu reviendras avec les nichons plus énormes que jamais, et toutes les courbes extrêmement potelées et passouillettes. Il me tarde aussi de te voir en déshabille dans notre château. Je me flatte que ces intérieurs-là seront mieux que les pièces de cette sacrée maison sêche, aride, laide, et froide comme une vieille fille. Pourtant je me plais beaucoup dans cette maison, beaucoup. C'est une trouvaille bien trouvée. La nouvelle 'servant' est entrée hier. Elle m'a l'air bien. Mais elle est laide. Godebski m'a écrit, de Paris. Tu devrais y passer. Non, je ne m'amuserai pas avec Roy Devereux. Je refuse. Elle m'a écrit une lettre touchante. Pour les tapis, très bien. Demain j'ai rendezvous avec Rickards pour approfondir la question des prix — de tout! Ça sera terrible. Je déjeune avec Lowndes. Je travaille bien, et je me porte merveilleusement bien. Je te fais supporter les derniers outrages. Ne te defends pas.

Ton Nouche, A.

64. [Your letter. Very good. So I am expecting you on Saturday. Take the train arriving at—well, take whatever train you like. But come in time for dinner. The Sharpes will be at the theatre that evening. They asked me for tickets for *Voysey*. Mrs Sharpe said to me 'But won't Marguerite want to go with us?' 'That's what you think,' I said (silently). I know that you will have no wish to go out again in the evening. I will thus be the first to see all the things you have bought and the person and the body who (apparently) attracts all eyes in all the restaurants of Paris. The underwear, the déshabilles, the undergarments and all the pretty things that you have bought yourself, as well as the beloved flesh that they are to conceal. It is amazing how much I miss you after a week and how much your absence jars on me all the time. You must know that you have taken a hold on me which is very unusual, given my character etc. Try not to abuse it, I beg you. The memory of you excites me. When you are away, I should have a little tart to comfort me. I suppose you will come back with your breasts bigger than ever and all your curves rounded and plumped out. And I am longing to see you *en déshabille* in our *château*. I flatter myself that its interiors will be better than the rooms of this house, which is dry, arid, ugly and as frigid as an old maid. But still I am very well in this house. It is a well-found find. The new 'servant' arrived yesterday. She seems all right. But she is ugly. Godebski has written to me, from Paris. You should go and see him. No, I will not have a nice time with Roy Devereux. I won't. She has written me a touching letter.

Fine about the carpets. Tomorrow I have an appointment with Rickards, to go more deeply into the question of prices—of everything! It will be awful. I am having lunch with Lowndes. I am working well, and feeling remarkably well. I subject you to the worst excesses. Don't defend yourself.]

14, St. Simon's Avenue was owned by the Sharpes. Bennett and Marguerite lived there from July 1912 until February 1913, when their new home in Essex was ready.

The Voysey Inheritance: Granville Barker's play, first produced in 1903 and revived this year.

Rickards was doing the alterations to the new house.

Lowndes: F. S. A. Lowndes (1868–1940), Marie Belloc Lowndes' husband, was on the staff of *The Times*. He and Bennett had been friends for many years.

KEELE / MS / 65
(*To Marguerite Soulié Bennett*)

Yacht Velsa
Samedi matin
le 19 juillet 1913

Enfant chérie,

Je n'ai pas bien dormi. Par contre j'ai réflechi sur le désordre de mes papiers depuis avant-hier. Pourtant la soirée était *exquise* — grise et calme. J'ai tout de suite levé l'ancre. Nous avons regardé bien un beau yacht à trois mâts, avec un vieux et une petite femme à bord et puis nous avons filé si bien que nous étions dans le port de Woodbridge à 8¼ heures!! Je ne m'y attendais vraiment pas. Je comptais partir pour Woodbridge ce matin seulement. Mais Willem est actif; moi aussi. C'est maintenant une certitude que je rentrerai lundi après-midi ou soir. Il y a des certitudes sur terre. Une autre certitude (j'espère) est que la prochaine fois que tu voudras changer la disposition de mes papiers, tu exprimeras tes volontés pre-mièrement à moi et pas à ma clerquette. Hier tu as tenu à me dire quelquechose sur ma clerquette. Moi aussi je tiens à te dire quelquechose sur ma clerquette. Il lui aurait été impossible de me cacher pendant 24 heures le changement dans mes papiers. Elle ne m'a rien dit d'elle-même. Mais naturellement puisque 'je vois tout', j'ai remarqué son premier geste en essayant de t'être agréable. 'Qu'est-ce que vous faites avec ces papiers?' je lui ai demandé. Elle a rougi et puis elle m'a dit que madame voulait avoir le placard. Sache, my child, que le mauvais arrangement de mes livres que tu déplores tant, est le mien et exclusivement le mien. (Ah le bel ordre de tes tiroirs à toi, my sweet child!) Quand j'ai remarqué que la clerquette n'avait pas le don de l'organisation, j'ai surveillé tout ça, et je le surveille toujours. N'importe quel homme d'affaires te dirait que celui que remplit tous ses tiroirs est un idiot et un mauvais organisateur. N'importe quel homme d'affaires te dirait que quand des papiers de toutes sortes arrivent tous les jours il faut avoir de la place. On ne peut pas gagner 400,000 frs par an sans avoir quelques pauvres papiers. N'importe quel homme d'affaires te dirait que l'organisation de mes papiers est merveilleuse. Si tu gagnais 400,000 frs par an avec ta plume, la maison entière ne contiendrait pas tes papiers. Je voudrais bien te voir avec ta clerquette et tes papiers. Je voudrais mieux voir ta précieuse binette si je t'avais joué le même tour avec Suzanne que tu m'as joué avec ma clerquette (toujours avec les meilleures intentions). Ah! Les cris! Les pleurs! Les protestations! Et si j'avais dit 'mauvaise foi'! Fin de monde! Oh la la! Ce qui est malheureux est que, en essayant de t'être agréable, ma pauvre clerquette a fait des choses avec mes papiers qu'il faut rectifier. La disposition actuelle est idiote. Au mois de septembre j'aurai ça à entreprendre. Et il me faudra un autre meuble Empire. Il est toujours possible d'attacher une trop grande importance à ses affaires personelles. Si toutes mes papiers étaient brûlés je m'en tirerais, je suppose. Pourtant les choses sans importance réelle ont des fois une importance morale que les femmes fines finissent par comprendre toujours. Si tu es fine, prudente, et sensée, tu me rendras ce placard que tu m'as chipé, et tu me le rendras sans rien dire. Et tu te rappelleras sagement que quand tu essaies de faire des choses derrière mon dos, surtout des choses qui me touchent de très près, ça ne réussit jamais. On verra. Ce n'est pas question de tes intentions, qui sont parfaites. Après le petit déjeuner nous irons par la rivière à Woodbridge même. 9 miles. Et puis après ça je ne sais pas exactement. Il devrait arriver dimanche ou lundi pour moi un paquet des Stores. Si je te télégraphie lundi 'BRING THINGS' tu seras infinimento amabile de mettre dans le car (1) ce paquet (2) 4 demi bouteilles de champagne sec (3) 4 bouteilles de vin blanc (4) 6 de vin rouge (5) un nouveau pantalon de flannelle dans ma commode (6) mon complet brun de Colchester (avec un seul pantalon) (7) toi-même. En tout cas toi-même, si tu peux! C'est probable que le bateau partira directement de ces parages au continent, et ne retournera pas à Brightlingsea. Je me suis pansé ce matin, mais ce n'est pas la même chose qu'un de tes pansements. Il a plu. Il pleuvra. Love to the mater. Je t'embrasse tendrement.

Le rusé, la ficelle, le mari qui n'est pas un ami. L'homme de mauvaise foi.

A.

P.S. Tu te dis: C'est dégoûtant comme il prend des choses trop au sérieux. Pas du tout. Je sais que [?]. C'est ton droit. Moi aussi je plaisante. C'est mon droit.

65. [I have not been sleeping well. On the contrary, since the day before yesterday, I have been thinking about nothing but the mess that my papers are in. Nevertheless the evening was *exquisite*—grey and still. I raised the anchor immediately. We had a good look at a beautiful three-masted yacht, with an old man and a little woman on board, and then we made such good time that we were in Woodbridge port at 8.15!! I really wasn't expecting that. I did not think we would leave for Woodbridge until this morning. But Willem is energetic and so am I. It is now certain that I will return on Monday afternoon or evening. There are certainties in this world. Another certainty (I hope) is that next time you want to change the arrangement of my papers, you will express your wishes to me first, and not to my secretary. Yesterday, you wanted to tell me something about my secretary. I want to tell you something about her too. She could not have concealed the change in my papers for 24 hours. She said nothing to me herself. But of course, since 'I notice everything', I noticed her first move in trying to be nice to you. I asked, 'What are you doing with those papers?' She blushed and then told me that Madame wanted the cupboard. You must know, my child, that the bad arrangement of my books which you so much deplore, is mine and mine alone. (Oh for the beautiful neatness of your drawers, my sweet child!) When I noticed that the secretary had no talent for organization, I supervised that whole aspect of things, and I still do. Any businessman would tell you that the man who fills up his drawers completely is a fool and a bad organizer. Any businessman will tell you that when you have papers of every kind arriving every day, you have to have space. Nobody can earn 400,000 frs. a year without having a few miserable bits of paper. Any businessman will tell you that my papers are extremely well arranged. If you earned 400,000 frs. a year with your pen, your papers would fill the whole house. I'd like to see you with your secretary and your papers. And I would like to see your precious face if I'd played the same trick with Suzanne that you have played with my secretary (always with the best intentions). Oh what shouts, what cries, what protests! And what if I said 'bad faith'! It would be the end of the world. Oh la la! The unfortunate thing is that my poor secretary, in trying to be nice to you, did things with my papers which will have to be put right. The present arrangement is idiotic. That's something I will have to take on during September. And I will need another piece of Empire furniture. It is always possible to give too much importance to one's own affairs. If all my papers had been burned, I suppose I would get over it. But things which have no real value sometimes have a moral importance which intelligent women always understand eventually. If you are intelligent, prudent and sensible, you will give back the cupboard you have pinched from me, and you will give it back without a word. And you will do well to remember that when you try to do things behind my back, particularly things that touch me closely, you will never succeed. We will see. I am not questioning your motives, which are perfect.

After breakfast we will go to Woodbridge itself by river. 9 miles. And after that I don't know exactly what we'll do. A parcel should arrive for me from the Stores on Sunday or Monday. If I send you a telegram on Monday saying 'BRING THINGS' could you please be so kind (infinimento amabile) as to put into the car (1) this parcel (2) four half bottles of dry champagne (3) four bottles of white wine (4) 6 of red wine (5) a new pair of flannel trousers from my chest of drawers (6) my brown suit from Colchester with only one pair of trousers (7) yourself. Yourself anyway, if you can! The boat will probably go directly from these parts to the continent and will not go back to Brightlingsea. I bandaged myself this morning, but it is not the same as when you do it. It has been raining and will go on raining. Love to the mater. I kiss you tenderly.

The cunning, knowing one, the husband who is no friend. The man of bad faith.

You are saying to yourself: How disgusting that he takes things so much too seriously. Not at all. I know that [?you were joking]. You have the right. I am joking too. I have the right.]

Bennett was sailing in the yacht perhaps for five days from the 16th.

Suzanne: Marguerite's maid at Comarques, Thorpe-le-Soken. Bennett and Marguerite moved in on 24 February 1913.

Winifred Nerney (d. 1964) was Bennett's secretary from 1912 until his death. For letters to her and other references see Vols. I and III. See also the Introduction, p. xxxv.

KEELE / MS / 66
(*To Marguerite Soulié Bennett*)

Yacht Velsa
16th Augt 1913

Mon Enf. chéri,

Ça m'a infiniment soulagé de recevoir enfin, une dépêche de toi. Dans une quinzaine de jours j'avais reçu une dépêche et une lettre. Je t'ai envoyé un tas de télégrammes à Paris, Fontaine-bleau, Royau et Royal. Il doit y avoir un dossier formidable à Royau pour toi, que tu n'as pas eu. Ma dernière lettre, je l'ai écrite mercredi, mais ne sachant point où était ma fefemme, je l'ai gardée. Ta télégramme reçue, j'ai fait mettre tout de suite ta lettre à la poste. Nous voilà à Copenhague depuis avant hier. Nous partirons après demain matin pour Helsingfors, & après ça je ne sais pas — un peu vague. Tu sais que nous avons attendu le yacht *8* jours, et à la fin nous étions forcés de faire un voyage de 130 kilomètres en auto pour le rejoindre! Maintenant je me trouve tellement retardé dans ma croisière que je ne pense pas pouvoir rentrer le 24. Et après tout pourquoi? Il me faut ma croisière. Que le travail attende. (C'est toi qui parle.) Je pense que nous rentrerons par Harwich. Tu viendras à Harwich me prendre? Rickards est déprimé parce qu'il n'a pas de travail, mais autrement il est très bien comme compagnon de voyage. Il exagère tout. Tu vas entendre des histoires sur la beauté et le charme excessifs des femmes de Copenhague! C'est pourtant un peu vrai. Le grand établissement ici (le Tivoli) est vraiment épatant. Vastes jardins avec toutes sortes de théâtres, concerts, etc. etc. Dans aucune ville n'ai-je vu des cocottes simples et charmantes comme ici. Je protège Rickards. Il dit: 'Pour moi les cocottes — ça ne me dit plus rien.' Et puis dans un instant il en voit une qui lui fiche un frisson — et je l'emmène. C'est un enfant, surtout avec les femmes. Nous nous couchons de bonne heure, mais parce que le yacht est amarré en pleine ville nous dormons mal à cause des bruits. C.à.d. moi je dors mal. Rickards dort très bien. Ce soir nous allons mettre le yacht dans le yacht-bassin, à l'extremité de la ville, pour dimanche. Il y a un chic café restaurant en face. Comme ville Copenhague est très sympathique. (Mais les autres villes de Denmark sauf Esbjerg ne sont pas grand'chose.) L'architecture et la vie des rues sont infiniment agréables.... Donc tu es à Paris avec Gaby. Il me semble que vous n'êtes pas restées très longtemps dans les villes d'eau. Pourquoi? Comment es-tu? Ces maux de tête? Les choses marchent bien. Le contrat pour *Don Juan* est arrangé. Je vais avoir la *moitié* des bénéfices brutes. C'est la première fois je pense, qu'un auteur est arrivé à avoir ça. Si j'avais ça pour *La Grande Aventure* je toucherais 8,000 frs. par semaine au lieu de 2000. Il y a une différence! Achète-toi un petit cadeau de ton mari à Paris. Je ne parle pas du sac. A présent, tu pourrais t'acheter de la lingerie. Par exemple la plus chic chemise et le plus chic pantalon qui se trouvent dans Paris. Tu dis que je ne m'intéresse pas à la lingerie. Quelle couche, ma pauvre! D'ailleurs je t'ai toujours dit que tu n'as jamais eu un pantalon assez chic. Achète-toi ces deux choses. Tu me feras plaisir. Et puis tu les porteras quand je t'embrasserai à mon retour. J'examinerai tout ça sur ton joli corps de faux maigre.... Tu n'es pas par hasard devenue énorme depuis le temps, comme tu craignais? J'attends ta lettre. Je t'embrasse et je te caresse et je t'excite.

Ton Nouche

Love to Gabrielle.

66. [I was tremendously relieved to receive a telegram from you at last. In the last fortnight or so, I had received one telegram and one letter. I sent you lots of telegrams,

to Paris, Fontainebleau, Royau, and the Royal. There must be quite a stack of documents which you have not received waiting for you at the Royau. I last wrote to you on Wednesday, but I kept the letter as I didn't know where my little wife was. Once I received your telegram, I posted the letter straight away. Well, we have been in Copenhagen since the day before yesterday. We will leave for Helsingfors the day after tomorrow in the morning, and after that I don't know, it's a bit vague. Do you know, we waited a whole week for the yacht and in the end we had to make a 130-kilometre car journey to reach it! Now I am so far behind in my cruise that I don't think I will be back by the 24th. After all, why should I be? I need my cruise. Let work wait. (As you would say.) I think we will come home via Harwich. Will you come to Harwich to fetch me? Rickards is depressed because he has no work, but otherwise he is a very good travelling companion. He exaggerates everything. You will hear stories about the excessive beauty and charm of the women of Copenhagen! There is some truth in this though. The largest building here (the Tivoli) is really impressive. Huge gardens, with all kinds of theatres, concert halls, etc., etc. In no other town have I ever seen such unaffected and charming-looking tarts as there are here. I am protecting Rickards. He says 'Tarts mean nothing to me.' And then a minute later he sees one who gives him a thrill—and I take him away. He's like a child, particularly where women are concerned. We go to bed early, but as the yacht is anchored right in the middle of town, we sleep badly because of the noise. I sleep badly, that is. Rickards sleeps very well. This evening we are going to take the yacht to a yacht basin, on the outskirts of the town, ready for Sunday. There is a good cafe-restaurant opposite. As a town, Copenhagen is very nice. (But except for Esbjerg, the other towns of Denmark are not up to much.) The architecture and the street life are infinitely pleasing. So you are in Paris, with Gaby. So it seems that you did not stay very long in the watering places. Why? How are you? How are those headaches? Things are going well. The contract for *Don Juan* has been settled. I will get half the gross profits. I think this is the first time that an author has ever managed that. If I had had it for *The Great Adventure* I would be getting 8,000 frs. a week instead of 2,000. Quite a difference! Buy yourself a little present from your husband in Paris. I don't mean the handbag. Now you could buy yourself underwear. For example the smartest slip and smartest knickers to be found in Paris. You say that I am not interested in your underwear. What foolishness, my poor girl! Anyway I have always said that you have never had smart enough knickers. Buy yourself both these things and you will give me pleasure. And you must be wearing them when I kiss you on my return. I will examine it all on your pretty, falsely thin body ... or have you by any chance grown huge in this time, as you were afraid? I am expecting a letter from you. I kiss you and caress and excite you. . . . Love to Gabrielle.]

Bennett was yachting in the Baltic Sea during August.

Don Juan was never produced. From 1911 forward Bennett negotiated for its production with several people—Granville Barker, Gilbert Miller, John Drinkwater, John Barrymore, and others. He wrote it between December 1913 and January 1914. *The Great Adventure* opened at the Kingsway Theatre on 25 March, and ran for 673 nights.

KEELE / MS / 67
(*To Marguerite Soulié Bennett*)   Yacht Velsa
                                                    Mardi
                                                    le 19 août 1913

Chérissime, Infanta,

Qu'est-ce qu'il a dit, le docteur Blanc? J'ai le regret de te dire
que hier après-midi, quand nous sortions de Copenhague, s'est
passé *une panne définitive de moteur.* Un des quatre pistons s'est
cassé, et le krach a démantibulé d'autres parties du moteur.
Willem était dans tous ses états. Moi j'ai conservé le calme
absolu. C'était apparamment la faute des ingénieurs
fabricants. C'est possible qu'on arrivera à repasser la sacrée
chose aujourd'hui ou demain. Sinon, nous continuerons en
voilier. Pourtant c'est assommant. Nous étions à deux lieues de
Copenhague. Nous avons retourné à voile. C'est tout. Il fait
frais. Pas de soleil. Mais le baromètre est plutôt optimiste. On
mange et on boit bien. On est entièrement sage, malgré ton
invitation si aimable et touchante à la débauche. Tu ne sais
donc pas que ça ne me dirait rien de courir un poco? C'est
dommage d'être comme je suis l'esclave d'une seule femme,
mais que veux-tu? Tout ce que je regrette c'est que tu *sais* que à
la fin tu es plus forte que moi, parce que à la fin j'ai une faiblesse
totale et définitive à ton egard. Je le mettrai dans un livre....
Donc tu es forcée de t'embêter avec la question parlourmaid. Je
te conseille de n'accepter qu'une de première ordre. Et de ne
rien changer dans la manière de servir à table. La façon
conventionelle des English parlourmaids est ma meilleure
façon du monde, et j'ai horreur de voir 36 choses sur la table et
de passer les assiettes et tout ça. Déjà tu m'as largement assez
ennuyé avec les histoires de 36 bouteilles et carafes sur la table.
Pour ça je sais que je suis roulé. Mais il y a des limites à mon
roulage et à ma faiblesse, surtout dans les petites choses qui me
touchent de très près et que je comprends. Donc, je te
reconseille de ne changer plus rien. J'ai oublié Comarques et
tout, sauf toi. J'ai complètement oublié mon roman — ce qui est
fort embêtant. Et quand je pense à la vie antérieure, et à la vie
actuelle hors du yacht, c'est à toi uniquement que je pense. Je
lis les feuilles de recette théâtrale comme dans un rêve. Il n'y a
que le yacht pour vous fair oublier tout sauf votre fefemme.
Pourtant si tu nous avais accompagné tu aurais été

certainement malade. J'ai envie de te voir, et de te voir chicment habillée, et moitié habillée (c.à.d. sans robe), and seulement en chemise ou en pantalon, et puis nue. Et j'ai envie de t'embrasser de toutes les façons, et de te noter de toutes les façons. Et c'est dommage que tu ne puisses pas faire guérir ton petit derrière, parce que c'est un petit derrière que j'aime assez, et jamais tu n'as joui comme tu as joui quand je l'ai aimé un peu douloureusement tout en soulageant avec ma main d'écrivain ton minuscule conin... C'est peut-être heureux que je suis arrivé à la fin de la feuille. Ne fais pas voir cette lettre à Gabrielle.

C'est embêtant que je t'ai donné Helsingfors comme adresse, parce que nous ne sommes pas encore là, et une lettre de toi m'aurait plu. However... N'écris pas avant de recevoir une autre adresse.

Et maintenant Dieu te bénisse.

Ton A. Nouche

67. [What did Doctor Blanc say? I am sorry to have to tell you that the engine broke down definitively yesterday afternoon, as we were leaving Copenhagen. One of the four pistons broke and the shock smashed up other parts of the engine. Willem was in the most terrible state. But I remained perfectly calm. It seems to be the fault of the manufacturers. There is some chance of getting the blessed thing mended today or tomorrow. If not, we will continue as in a sailing boat. But it is infuriating. We were two leagues outside Copenhagen. We went back by sail. That's all. It is chilly. No sun. But the barometer looks fairly hopeful. We eat and drink well. Virtue is being perfectly maintained in spite of your kind and touching invitation to debauchery. You don't seem to realize that womanizing *un poco* would mean nothing to me. It is a pity to be as I am, the slave of one woman, but what can one do? The only thing I regret is that in the final analysis you *know* that you are stronger than me, because, in the final analysis, I have a complete and incurable weakness where you are concerned. I will put it in a book. . . . So you are having to go through the tedium of the parlourmaid question. I advise you only to take a first-rate one. And don't make any changes in the way of serving at table. For me, the conventional way of English parlourmaids is the best in the world and I hate seeing 36 things on the table and passing plates and all that. You have already irritated me more than enough with your performances of 36 bottles and carafes on the table. I know you can always get round me over this. But there are limits to my indulgence and my weakness, particularly in little things which touch me very closely and which I understand. So I repeat my advice to you not to change anything else. I have forgotten about Comarques and everything except you. I have completely forgotten about my novel—which is very annoying. And when I think of my former life and of the world outside the yacht, all I think of is you. I read the theatre takings slips as if in a dream. Only yachts can make one forget about everything except one's little wife. But if you had come with us you would certainly have been ill. I want to see you, and see you smartly dressed, and half dressed (that is, without your dress on), and only in a chemise or knickers and then naked. And I want to kiss you in every way and observe you in every way. And it is a pity that you can't have your little bottom cured, because I quite love your little bottom, and you have never enjoyed anything as much as you did

when I loved it a bit painfully while giving your tiny cunt relief with my writer's hand. Perhaps it is lucky that I have come to the end of the page. Don't show this letter to Gabrielle.

It is a pity that I gave you Helsingfors as my address because we haven't got there yet and a letter from you would have made me happy. However ... Don't write until you get another address. And now God bless you.]

―――――

Marguerite is seen in part in the characterization of Hilda in *These Twain*, especially Hilda in her quarrelsome moods.

The new novel was *The Price of Love*, begun on 15 October 1912 and finished on 29 September 1913.

Marguerite had an operation for haemorrhoids in July.

KEELE / MS / 68   Yacht Velsa
(*To Marguerite Soulié Bennett*)   Spothberg
                                        Saturday
                                 23 August 1913

Sweet mistress & wife,

On Monday night or Tuesday morning at Aarlus I really do hope to get a *letter* from you. If it is not there, I shall be desolated. We sailed about 70 k today; heavy sea. We had to have lunch on deck. Ricco was nearly ill, but not quite; so he is proud. We rather liked our glimpse of Sweden yesterday. This place that we have called at on our way to Aarlus is nothing— extremely small, & without interest, except for the little harbour, where a fisherman's daughter in native costume was leaning pensively & picturesquely on her father's arm and gazing at us. 'Pretty girl that!' said Rickard. We went ashore & walked up the hill—nothing. However, we had a fine sail, and we were smilingly saluted by a diligence full of women and girls. I am just going to bed. J'espère que je ne rêverai pas trop, parce que — eh bien, à un de ces jours. Tu t'amuses, mon enfant, avec ta maison, ta sœur, ton chien, et les choses que tu t'as achetées en route? Mci je n'ai rien acheté. Mais je t'amenerai toute suite à Bruxelles. Je te salue avec tout mon corps, si blanc, et je te bise.

Ton Nouche

Nous partirons demain dimanche matin à 6.30.

68. [I hope I will not dream too much because—well, I'll see you one day soon. Are you enjoying yourself, my child, with your house, your sister, your dog, and the things

that you bought yourself on the way? I haven't bought anything. But I will take you straight to Brussels. I salute you with my whole body which is so white, and I kiss you. . . . We will leave tomorrow morning, Sunday, at 6.30.]

KENNERLEY / MS / 69
(*To W. W. Kennerley*)

The Berkeley Hotel
Piccadilly W
11 Dec 1913

Dear William,

I slept 7 hours without moving, so I am all right. I am unable to agree with you on either of the two points. I am not sure if you understand my attitude. It is not at all that I want an extra half per cent. What does it matter to me? My sole idea is that the fact that Frank has been an ass (and therefore almost necessarily dishonest) ought to be brought home to him, & there is only one way of doing it. I have chosen that way. These things can't be allowed to blow over as if nothing had happened. Frank has obtained money by false pretences from me, from the bank, & from American buyers. A sermon would be idiotic, but there are other ways of preaching. There is no question of spoiling a 'generous' action. In these affairs, of which I have had many, my sole idea is to do what I think ought to be done. The notion of generosity does not present itself to me. Anybody can be generous, if he has the money. But to avoid sentimentality in generosity, & to be just all round & think of the future, is not so easy. At least I think so. I take absolutely no credit to myself for helping Frank out of a crisis. In effect, it costs me nothing that I feel. But I do take credit to myself for the way in which I do it & the conditions which I lay down & the regard I have for the personal factor in Frank's future. Frank is a proved fool. I don't blame him, but I shan't pretend he isn't. The weakness of his character has to be invigorated, & that extra $\frac{1}{2}$ is one of the things that will do it. However, I shall tell him that I haven't yet decided as to the rate of interest. Think this over again, & please send me a line tonight. I shall act on what you say. But I repeat that if you hold to your view, I shall act against my own judgment. Still, I shall act on your opinion.

As regards the fares, no! No earthly power can prevent you from returning your fares to Frank if you wish. But I won't. The whole affair is a question of *money*. He is not being asked to pay for that which money can't pay for. He is not even being asked to pay for my time. (My time is worth at least £50 a day, & he has had 2 days.) All he is asked to pay for is that which he can & ought to pay for. But you may bet your boots he will never offer to pay.

Just off.

Yours, A.B.

69. Bennett often stayed at the Berkeley Hotel on trips to London. The trip this time concerned Frank Bennett's financial troubles.

KEELE / MS / 70
(*To Marguerite Soulié Bennett*)

Comarques
Thorpe-Le-Soken
Monday
25 May 1914

Ma chère épouse,

Pour être sérieux, j'ai commencé *Clayhanger III* à 5 h. 50m. ce matin, et j'y ai travaillé jusqu'à 8 heures. C'est un commencement: Énorme! Ce jour a une certaine importance dans notre vie, mon petit coco. Aussi, hier j'ai fait deux aquarelles, chacune plus infecte que l'autre. Il a fait froid hier. Mais l'après-midi a été beau ou belle, comme tu voudrais. Robert a essuyé des observations hier, mais il est agréable. Repas excellents. C'est tout. J'espère que tu as passé une bonne journée. Le petit déjeuner sonne.

N.

Je retravaillerai après le p.d.

70. [Making myself be serious, I began *Clayhanger* III at 5.50 this morning and I worked on it until 8 o'clock. So that's a start—a tremendous one. This is quite an important day in our life, my little sweet. And I did two watercolours, each more appalling than the other. It was cold yesterday. But the afternoon was fine, *beau* or *belle*, whichever you like. Robert had to put up with some criticisms yesterday, but he is being pleasant. The meals are excellent. That's all. I hope you had a good day. The breakfast bell is ringing. I will do some more work after breakfast.]

Comarques was a Queen Anne house, with about three acres of lawn, lake, and garden. Rickards made improvements in it along American lines. Thorpe-le-Soken was twelve miles from Colchester.

These Twain, 128,000 words, was completed 12 February 1915. By one or another contemporary critic it was thought to be 'the very greatest literary achievement of recent years', and by others to mark or confirm a decline in power.

Robert: Robert Bion, Marguerite's nephew.

KEELE / MS / 71
(*To Marguerite Soulié Bennett*)

Comarques
vendredi
10 juillet 1914

Chérie enfant,

Je te griffonne un petit mot ce mat. avant de partir pour Londres. Il n'y a rien à dire. J'ai travaillé un peu mieux hier après-midi. Rien n'arrive, sauf les petites histoires de la maison. Miss Hatchell s'en tire très bien. J'ai eu une '*row*' avec Robert hier. Je lui avais recommandé de ne pas monter pendant que je dormais. Il a monté 3 fois. À la fin je lui ai dit d'aller jouer dans le jardin. Ce qui l'attrayait en haut, c'était la peinture fraiche! Mon somme tout abimé, je suis allé dans le jardin quelques minutes après. J'ai vu Robert qui appelait John vers le monument. Lundi dernier j'avais une histoire avec Robbie à propos du monument. Cette fois je vois Robert qui réussit enfin à faire arriver John au monument, et puis il fait son possible pour faire monter John sur le dit monument!! Il ne m'a pas vu. Il était très attrappé. Il a essuyé une fessée, et je lui ai fait coucher tout de suite. C'était à $3\frac{1}{2}$ heures. Je ne pouvais pas faire autrement. Ce matin il est très gai parce que il a reçu le bateau magnifique que je lui ai offert. Je ne crois plus que cet enfant pêche toujours par oubli. Des fois il oublie, mais des fois il fait exprès. Miss Hatchell dit la même chose. Par le fait, si tu te décides de garder cet enfant jusqu'à septembre, il faut absolument que tu gardes aussi Miss Hatchell. Je ne te permettrai pas d'essayer d'être maîtresse de maison et institutrice à la fois. Il lui faut une surveillance continuelle. Je t'envoie plusieurs lettres, et puis aussi des baisers.

Ton [A.]

Je rentre lundi.

71. [I am scribbling off a little note to you this morning before setting off for London. There is nothing to tell. My work went a bit better yesterday afternoon. Nothing is happening apart from little domestic incidents. Miss Hatchell is coping very well. I had a 'row' with Robert yesterday. I had told him not to come upstairs while I was asleep. He came up 3 times. In the end I told him to go and play in the garden. It was the wet paint that was drawing him upstairs! As my rest had been quite destroyed, I went into the garden a few minutes later. I saw Robert, calling to John to climb on the sculpture. I had a row with Robbie about the sculpture last Monday. This time I saw Robert actually managing to make John come to the sculpture and then doing his best to make John climb on said sculpture. He didn't see me. He was scolded sternly and got a

spanking and I made him go straight to bed. It was 3.30. What else could I do? He is very happy this morning because he has got the lovely boat that I gave him. I no longer think that this child always sins through forgetfulness. Sometimes he does forget, but other times he is naughty on purpose. Miss Hatchell says so too. In fact if you decide to keep the child till September, you absolutely must keep Miss Hatchell too. I will not allow you to try to be mistress of a house and governess at the same time. He needs constant supervision. I am forwarding you several letters, kisses as well. I am coming back on Monday.]

John was a fox-terrier kept by the Bennetts.

KEELE / MS / 72
(*To Marguerite Soulié Bennett*)

Comarques
lundi
13 juillet 1914

Ma petite chérie,

Je suis rentré, et j'ai trouvé tes trois lettres. La première aurait dû être envoyée à Londres, mais je ne l'ai pas eue. Erreur de Miss N.! Pour ta santé, ça a l'air de marcher, mais lentement. J'espère que tu ne souffres pas trop. Hélène m'écrit que tu es très bien. Oui, j'avais oublié pour les cigares. Je te donnerai une autre boîte. Je pensais que j'avais laissé une boîte dans ta chambre un soir, et que tu l'avais mise dans ton armoire, et puis complètement oubliée. Je ne te pensais pas chipeuse de mes cigares. Maintenant il y a une histoire avec le fourneau de la cuisine. La chaudière est pourrie, et le reservoir au 2me fuit. Une autre chaudière est commandée. En attendant on fait la cuisine dans le scullery. On s'en tire. Mrs. Selwyn est déjà partie pour les États Unis. On essaye de lui chiper l'idée mère de sa pièce, et de la devancer avec une autre pièce. Assommant! Edgar est venu me voir sur le yacht. Je lui télégraphierai de venir aussitôt que poss. Probablement il sera reparti avant ton arrivée. Il quitte cette île le 22 je pense. Maintenant pour ton retour, tu auras la voiture si tu la veux, mais le train serait moins fatigant. Enfin il n'y a aucune raison que tu n'aies pas la voiture. Que tu restes allongée dès ton arrivée, je le comprends. Mais es-tu fondamentalement guérie? Est-ce que le mari va pouvoir s'approcher de sa petite légitime. Je voudrais savoir ça avant que tu arrives. Parce que après toutes ces privations j'ai des envies assez rudes de voir et frôler et tatônner et violer ton délicieux corps. Si je sais d'avance que c'est défendu, — bien. Mais si je l'attends, et suis désappointé au dernier instant ça serait pénible pour moi. Pourquoi penses-tu toujours que je ne suis pas content de ton housekeeping. Au contraire je suis très difficile et j'en suis très content. Et puis aussi je te l'ai dit plus qu'une fois. Aussi je suis très content que tu aimes *Le Price d'Amour.* Je te bise tendrement.

Nouche

Voyage très bien avec Swinnerton.

72. [I have come home and found your three letters. The first must have been sent to London but I did not get it there. Miss N's mistake! About your health, you seem to be making progress, but slow progress. I hope that you are not in too much pain. Hélène writes that you are fine. Yes, I had forgotten about the cigars. I will give you another box. I thought I had left my box in your room one evening, and that you had put it in your cupboard and then completely forgotten about it. I didn't think you had been pinching my cigars.

Now there's some problem with the kitchen-range. The boiler is no good and the tank on the second floor is leaking. Another boiler has been ordered. Meanwhile, the cooking is being done in the scullery. We're managing. Mrs Selwyn has already left for the United States. Someone is trying to pinch the main idea of her play and to bring out another play before hers. Infuriating. Edgar came to see me on the yacht. I will send him a telegram to come as soon as poss. He will probably have left again before your return. He is leaving this island on the 22nd, I think. Now about your return, you can have the car if you want, but the train would be less tiring. But there is no reason why you shouldn't have the car. I understand that you must lie down the minute you arrive. But are you actually cured? Will the husband be able to approach his lawfully wedded little wife? I would like to know before you arrive. Because after all these deprivations, I have quite violent longings to see and stroke and feel and violate your delicious body. If I know in advance that I can't—all right. But it would be very painful for me to expect to be able to and be disappointed at the last minute.

Why do you always think that I am not satisfied with your housekeeping? On the contrary, I am very hard to please and I am very satisfied with it. And I have told you so more than once. And I am very pleased that you like *The Price of Love.* I kiss you tenderly.... A very good journey with Swinnerton.]

The Price of Love was the last of the Five Towns novels (aside from *These Twain,* which had been conceived prior to it). It was published on 1 October 1914.

Frank Swinnerton (1884–1982) met Bennett in 1911 and became his best friend of later years. For letters to him and other references, see the other volumes. See also the Introduction.

KEELE / MS / 73
(*To Marguerite Soulié Bennett*)

Comarques
16 juillet 1914

Chérie enfant,

Rien de toi hier. Embêté. Deux lettres par le courrier de midi aujourd'hui. Très bien. Ça se voit que tu vas mieux, et même beaucoup mieux. Je ne saurais pas t'offrir un conseil, mais il me semble que tu ferais beaucoup mieux de rester jusqu'à après tes règles. En attendant tu pourrais faire une sortie ou deux. Je crains beaucoup que tout de suite en arrivant ici tu ne tombes encore malade, ce qui serait très agaçant pour toi, et pour moi aussi. Non, je ne viendrai pas te chercher. Le plaisir de se voir à Paris serait vite dissipé dans les agacements du voyage. Tu me trouves un mauvais voyageur. Moi je te trouve mauvaise voyageure. À quoi bon? Seulement pour la satisfaction de se voir 24 heures plus tôt? Non, si tu avais besoin de moi, si ça servirait à quelquechose, je viendrais tout de suite, et tu le sais bien. Tu seras beaucoup mieux avec Jean qu'avec moi parce que tu seras libre à faire tout ce que tu veux. J'aime mille fois mieux te rencontrer ici qu'autre part. Je suis *sérieusement* embêté dans mon travail. Je ne pense pas que tu t'imagines jusqu'à quel point je suis embêté. Mais ma santé est assez bien, et les jeunes filles très gentilles. Pourtant, habiter avec des jeunes filles ça ne me dit rien. Plutôt ça m'énerve. Néanmoins, je m'entends admirablement avec, et je suis sûr qu'elles te diront comme je suis agréable!! Pour l'argent ça n'a aucune importance. La plus facile ça sera que tu paies, et que je te rembourse. Qu'est-ce-que tu racontes sur *Les Liaisons dangereuses*? Tu parles sur un ton assez dégagé, ma foi. Sais-tu, ma petite, que *Les Liaisons dangereuses* est *un des plus grands romans* jamais écrits? Et tu dis que c'est 'bien mené'. C'est comme si tu disais que Verlaine 'n'est pas mal', ou que Molière 'peut aller'. Quand tu le reliras dans 2 ans, tu seras plus épatée. Il paraît que Methuen est *très épaté* du *Price of Love*, et il veut tout de suite faire un nouveau contrat pour d'autres livres. Jusqu'à ce moment tout le monde est épaté de ce livre. Étrange!

Selwyn vient de me télégraphier qu'il arrivera demain à midi (vendredi). Je fais mon possible pour l'empêcher de venir. Mais il insistait.

Rickards viendra dimanche mais il descendra à l'hôtel. Les enfants sont allés à l'exposition des fleurs à St. Osyth. *Lockyer* espère décrocher tous les premiers prix.

Maintenant ma très petite, tu as toutes mes sympathies et toutes mes affections. Ne fais pas de bêtises avec tes voyages. Et évite la rechute, coûte que coûte.

Je te bise tendrement.

Nouche

Je t'ai écrit tous les jours avec la plus stricte regularité. Muriel m'écrit — mais je t'envoie sa lettre je n'ai pas besoin de te la raconter.

73. [Nothing from you yesterday. Fed up. Two letters by the midday post today. Very good. You are obviously better, even much better. I don't want to give you advice, but it seems to me that it would be much better for you to stay until after your period. You could have an outing or two while you are waiting. I am very much afraid that you may fall ill again as soon as you arrive here, which would be very upsetting for you; and for me as well. No, I will not come to fetch you. Our pleasure at seeing each other in Paris would be dissipated quickly by the irritations of the journey. You regard me as a bad traveller. For my part, I regard you as a bad traveller. What would be the point? The mere satisfaction of seeing each other 24 hours sooner? No. If you needed me, if there were any purpose in it, I would come immediately, as you know well. You will be much better off with Jean than with me, because you will be free to do whatever you like. I would a thousand times rather meet you here than anywhere else. I am having *serious* problems with my work. I don't think you realise what problems I am having. But my health is quite good, and the girls are very sweet. Still, living with girls does nothing for me. On the contrary, it irritates me. Nevertheless I get on perfectly well with them and I am sure they will tell you how nice I am.

About money, it simply doesn't matter. It would be easiest if you pay, and I pay you back. What can you mean about *Les Liaisons Dangereuses?* I must say you are taking a fairly offhand tone. Do you realize, my pet, that *Les Liaisons Dangereuses* is *one of the greatest novels* ever written? And you say it is 'well told'. It is as if you said that Verlaine 'isn't bad' or that Molière 'is all right'. When you read it again in two years' time, you will be more impressed. Methuen seems to be *very impressed indeed* with *The Price of Love* and wants to draw up another contract for other books straight away. So far everybody has been impressed with the book. Strange.

Selwyn has just sent me a telegram saying that he is coming tomorrow (Friday) at midday. I am trying my hardest to put him off. But he is insisting.

Rickards is coming on Sunday but he will stay at the hotel. The children have gone to the flower show at St Osyth. Lockyer is hoping to win all the first prizes.

Now my little pet, you have all my sympathy and all my affection. Don't do anything stupid about your journeys. And whatever happens, don't let yourself have a relapse.

I kiss you tenderly. . . . I have written to you every day with the strictest regularity. Muriel has written to me—but I am sending you her letter—I needn't tell you about it.]

Jean: presumably Marguerite's father, Jean Soulié (d. 1928).

A. M. S. Methuen (1856–1924). For Bennett's relationship with him as a publisher see Vols. I and II.

Thomas Lockyer: head gardener at Comarques.

KEELE / MS / 74
(*To Marguerite Soulié Bennett*)

Yacht Velsa
Friday morning
31–7–14

Mon enfant chérie,

Il fait beau. Mon foie, bien que loin d'être guéri, est sensiblement mieux. J'espère aussi que tu t'es un peu remise de tes airs de pauvre femme martyrisée. Ça ne te va pas. Ce que j'avale avec difficulté, c'est quand tu me dis que je fais des choses derrière ton dos, et que tu as l'air d'une folle. Ceci c'est du toupet, et tu le sais. Tu veux une fruit-house. Très bien. Consultation entre toi et moi, Canham et Lockyer, et tout est arrangé. Prix £15.16 — ou 400 frs. C'est la plus parfaite des fruit-houses, tout le monde en est content. Mais un beau matin l'idée de deux fruit-houses te passe par la tête. Tu commandes une autre sur le champ. Tu donnes l'ordre définitif, sans avoir la moindre idée du prix. Moi je suis à la maison tout le temps, mais tout ça se passe sans que je sache rien. C'est le seul hasard qui m'apprend. Tu dis que tu as oublié de me dire. Soit. Mais c'est un peu fort que tout de suite après tu me dis que je fais des choses derrière ton dos. Inexacte, totalement. Tu me dis que quand je suis surpris comme ça je deviens obstiné. Inexacte, totalement. Les deux fruit-houses ensemble coûteraient certainement 1,000 frs. puisque la deuxième est presque deux fois plus grande que l'autre qui seule coûte 400 frs. Je n'ai aucune intention de dépenser une telle somme cette année. C'est certain que la petite house sera assez pour tout ce que nous aurons cette saison. Pour l'année prochaine, on verra. Personne ne sait encore si la fruit-house sera bien. Tout ça c'est à voir. Quand Marrington m'a dit que tu avais commandé la deuxième je ne lui ai rien dit. J'ai commencé par toi. Je t'ai dit mes idées, et puis après j'ai dit à Marrington: '*Madame a décidé.*' Ça ne sera jamais par moi que tu auras l'air d'une folle. Pour moi, je tiens absolument à être au moins consulté avant que des ordres définitifs soient donnés dans des choses qui coûtent de l'argent supplémentaire. Tu es la maîtresse de la maison, mais moi je suis le maître. C'est moi qui gagne et qui paye, et qui dirige les finances générales, et ça sera toujours moi. 19 fois sur 20 quand tu me consultes je dis oui. Presque toujours tu fais à ta tête. Par exemple tu voulais dépenser 50 frs.

au palier du deuxième. Tu auras dépensé, avec ameublement, au moins 750 frs. C'est très bien. Je n'ai rien à redire là-dessus. Mais c'est une preuve que tu n'es pas la femme martyrisée. Dans ton rayon tu es entièrement libre. Les frais de la maison, les gages des bonnes, l'argent que je te donne regulièrement pour toi-même, et les cadeaux supplémentaires que je te fais de temps en temps, tout ça remonte à 30,000 frs. par an — somme dont tu es la maîtresse absolue. Ça, c'est ton rayon. Tu as parfaitement le droit de sortir de ton rayon, mais en sortant tu devrais au moins me consulter, et les rares fois que je ne suis pas de ton avis tu as tort de me traiter de brute etc. Moi je suis convaincu que je suis *très gentil* avec toi, aussi gentil que toi avec moi, et je mourrai dans cette opinion. Je ne suis pas un ange, mais je n'en connais pas. Dix fois cette après-midi tu m'as coupé la parole; tu ne me laisses pas finir, et souvent tu ne me fais pas l'honneur de m'écouter. Je ne me plains pas. Mais je t'écris, puisque je suis loin. Je sais que tu liras. Romancier, je ne demande pas mieux que ça.

Pour laisser cette écume frivole de la vaste et magnifique mer conjugale, j'ai à te dire que nous sommes maintenant dans la manche. Je compte être à Douvres avant huit heures. Nous avons été retardés ce matin deux heures par un brouillard, qui est tombé subitement au moment que nous levions ancre. Au lieu de partir at 6h. nous sommes partis à 8 heures. Temps assez bien, mais pas assez chaud. J'ai été dehors toute la journée, mais épaissement couvert. Nous avons vu pas mal de navires de guerre en train de s'exercer. Teukema me dit que ce pauvre Sullivan si nerveux n'est pas parti parce que il avait peur d'être capturé par les Allemands. C'est insensé, mais il est capable de ça au fond de son cerveau. Son capitaine nous a dit qu'il pensait partir ce soir. Penses-tu? Ernest a très bien réussi sa cuisine aujourd'hui. Ces petites pommes que tu m'as consacrées sont excellentes en compôte. Je te répète que je suis mieux, mais pas trop fort. J'espère être tout à fait guéri demain. Tu as eu M. Vernon aujourd'hui. Ce type là me prépare des ennuis, avec ma pièce — je vois ça. Il n'a aucune aptitude pour les affaires, et il a la malheureuse manie de tout remettre toujours. Enfin je m'en fiche tout de même. Mon enfant je te respectueusement et affectueusement salue. C'est comme ça. Salue toute cette ribambelle d'enfants pour moi, ainsi que Miss H.

Ton Nouche

Écoute. Pour avoir l'heure du train de Waterloo pour le bateau pour St. Malo le 10 août, tu la trouveras dans *les annonces* du London & South Western Railway vers la fin de l'Indicateur *Bradshaw* pour août, que Miss Nerney devrait avoir demain.

A.B.

74. [It is a fine day. My liver is far from cured but is perceptibly better. And I hope that you are recovering from your poor martyred woman act. It doesn't suit you. What I find hard to take is when you tell me that I am doing things behind your back and that you look a fool. It is cheek and you know it. You want a fruit-house. Very good. You and I, and Canham and Lockyer hold a consultation and it is all arranged. At a cost of £15.16—or 400 frs. It is the most perfect of fruit-houses and everyone is satisfied with it. But one fine morning the idea of two fruit-houses comes into your head. You immediately order another one. You place a definitive order without having any idea of what it will cost. I am at home all the time but all this happens without my knowing anything about it. I find out merely by chance. You say that you forgot to tell me. All right. But it is a bit much for you to tell me straight after this that I do things behind your back. Utterly incorrect. You tell me that when I am taken by surprise in this way I become obstinate. Utterly incorrect. The two fruit-houses together will certainly cost 1,000 frs. since the second is almost twice as big as the first which cost 400 frs. alone. I have no intention of spending so much money this year. The little house will certainly be adequate for everything we have this season. For next year, we'll see. No one knows yet whether the fruit-house will be good. All that remains to be seen. When Marrington told me that you had ordered the second one, I did not say anything to him. I spoke to you first. I told you what I thought and then afterwards I said to Marrington '*Madame* has decided.' It won't ever be me who makes you look a fool. I feel that I absolutely must at least be consulted before final orders are given in matters involving additional expense. You are the mistress of the house, but I am the master. I am the one who earns and who pays and who runs our money matters in general, and I always will be. When you consult me, I say yes 19 times out of 20. You almost always get your own way. For example, you wanted to spend 50 frs. on the second-floor landing. You will end up spending at least 750 frs. counting the furnishings. That's quite all right. I won't repeat anything I have said to you already about it. But that proves that you are not a martyred wife. You have complete freedom in your sphere. The household expenses, the maids' wages, the money I give you regularly for yourself and the additional presents that I give you from time to time, all add up to 30,000 frs. a year—and you are absolute mistress of this amount. That is your sphere. You have every right to go beyond your sphere, but when you do so you should at least consult me, and on the rare occasions when I am not in agreement with you, you are wrong to treat me as a brute etc. I am quite convinced that I am *very nice* to you, as nice as you are to me, and I will think so till I die. I'm no angel, but who is? You interrupted me ten times this afternoon; you don't let me finish what I am saying and often you don't do me the honour of listening to me. I am not complaining. But I am writing to you, as I am far away. I know you will read this. As a novelist, I don't ask anything better.

To get away from this frivolous froth on the vast and magnificent sea of married life, I'll tell you that we are now in the channel. I intend to be in Dover before 8 o'clock. But we were held up for two hours this morning by fog, which fell suddenly, just as we were lifting anchor. We left at 8, instead of at 6. The weather is quite good, but not warm enough. I have been outside all day, but warmly dressed. We saw quite a lot of warships carrying out exercises. Teukema told me that poor nervous Sullivan didn't leave because he was afraid of being captured by the Germans. That's quite absurd, but he is capable of thinking it in the fastness of his mind. His captain told us that he is thinking of leaving this evening. Do you believe it? Ernest has done very well with the cooking today. Those little apples you spared for me are excellent stewed. I am better, I repeat, but not too strong. I hope to be completely better tomorrow. You have had Mr Vernon today . . . That fellow's going to make trouble for me over my play, I can see. He has no flair for business and he has an unfortunate habit of always putting things off. But still what do I care. My child, I respectfully and affectionately greet you. I really do. Give my greetings to the whole bunch of kids and to Miss H. . . . Listen. To find the time of the train from Waterloo to the St Malo boat on 10 August, you must look in the announcements of London and South Western Railways toward the end of *Bradshaw's Guide* for August. Miss Nerney should have it tomorrow.]

Canham: one of the two under-gardeners; Marrington, probably the other.
Teukema: the new Dutch captain of the *Velsa*; Ernest, a crewman.
Sullivan: Herbert Sullivan (d. 1928), nephew of the composer, a yachtsman.
Frank Vernon was proposing a production of *Don Juan de Marana*. See Vol. II.

KEELE / MS / 75
(*To Marguerite Soulié Bennett*)   Comarques
                                                         Samedi
                                                         22–8–14

Ma chère Marguerite,
    L'autre jour tu es redescendue au petit salon exprès pour me dire que si tu avais de la fortune il y a longtemps que tu m'aurais quitté, que tu détestais cette vie de snobisme et de luxe, et que tu serais beaucoup plus heureuse seule avec 500 francs par mois.
    Les maris qui gardent leurs femmes par la seule force des choses matérielles sont des idiots et pires. J'estime que c'est le devoir d'un mari de faciliter le départ d'une femme qui voudrait sérieusement partir. *Si tu étais sérieuse l'autre jour*, je te garantirai une rente — pas de 500 frs., mais de 1,000 frs. par mois. Tu prendras si tu veux tes meubles qui ont coûté plus de 10,000 francs, et je te donnerai en plus 5,000 francs pour les frais de ton installation. Je suis sûr que je pourrais fournir des garanties satisfaisantes. Du reste, je pense que la valeur de ma parole est connue.
    Autre chose. Tu as dit que mon testament est offensant et humiliant pour toi. Je suis prêt à dire à Martin les dispositions de ce testament. S'il pense que c'est offensant et humiliant pour toi, si même il pense que le testament n'est pas tout à fait juste dans les circonstances, je le changerai.
    Cette lettre ne demande aucune réponse *si tu n'étais pas sérieuse l'autre jour*. C'est la simple constatation d'un fait: que si tu veux

me quitter ce n'est pas des raisons matérielles qui empêcher-
aient, une fois les enfants partis et la guerre arrangée. J'écris
sans rancune et sans amertume, et exclusivement par devoir.
C'est vrai que je t'ai déjà dit de vive voix à peu près ce que je
redis maintenant, mais j'aime mieux que ça soit en écrit.

Ton A.B.

P.S. J'ai oublié de dire que je payerai en plus les rentes que tu
sers en ce moment à ta mère et à ta sœur.

A.B.

75. [The other day you came back into the parlour on purpose to tell me that if you
had any money of your own, you would have left me long ago, that you loathe this life of
snobbery and extravagance and that you would be much happier alone with 500 francs
a month.

Husbands who keep their wives through material things alone are fools and worse. I
consider it the duty of a husband to facilitate the departure of a wife who really wants to
leave. *If you really meant what you said the other day*, I will guarantee you an income of not
500 frs. but 1,000 frs. a month. If you like, you can take your furniture, which cost over
10,000 francs and I will give you a further 5,000 francs for your removal expenses. I am
sure I could provide satisfactory guarantees. Besides, I think that my word is known to
be trustworthy.

Another thing. You said that my will is offensive and humiliating to you. I am ready
to tell Martin the provisions of my will. If he considers it to be offensive and humiliating
to you, if he even thinks that the will is not altogether fair under the circumstances, I
will change it.

This letter does not require an answer, *if you did not mean what you said the other day*. I am
simply noting a fact: that if you want to leave me, there are no material reasons to
prevent your doing so, once the children have left and the war is settled. I am not
writing out of resentment or bitterness but solely out of a sense of duty. Of course I have
already said by word of mouth more or less what I am saying again now, but I prefer to
put it in writing.... I forgot to say that I will also pay the allowances that you now give
your mother and sister.]

At the time of her operation in July 1914, Marguerite feared she might die, and she
asked Bennett if he would help support her mother and sister Gabrielle afterwards. She
suggested 75 francs a month plus 360 francs a year for rent for her mother, and 600
francs a year for Gabrielle. It is very likely that Bennett helped to support them from
1907 onwards.

Bennett's stammer made domestic quarrels more than usually difficult for him, and
here and elsewhere he conducted quarrels in writing, though both he and Marguerite
might be at home together. This letter also exists in a draft, without significant
difference.

KEELE / MS / 76
(*To Marguerite Soulié Bennett*)

Comarques
23 août 1914

Mon enfant,

Puisque je t'ai toujours supplié de prendre une housekeeper, et tu as toujours refusé!

Il n'arrivera jamais des histoires entre toi et moi si on me laisse tranquille dans mon sommeil, mon travail, et l'organisation du jardin, que je dirige. Ton malheur, et le mien, c'est qu'avec les meilleures intentions tu oublies. Déjà il était arrivé une histoire sur les bonnes, que tu avais fait lever à 5.30. Je me suis plaint; je t'avais largement expliqué que je ne pourrais pas le supporter, et tu l'as changé tout de suite. Mais il a fallu que ça recommençât. Je me suis plaint encore, mais cette fois tu étais plus dure. Tu m'as dit que si je ne pouvais pas dormir ni travailler, tant pis, — il était absolument nécessaire que les bonnes se levassent à 5.30. Pour que les bonnes ne soient pas genées et la maison marche d'après le programme, tu as même suggeré que je quitte la maison qui existe exclusivement par moi!! Naturellement à la fin ton bon sens a triomphé. Même chose pour les canards. Déjà je les avais fait chasser du lac parce que je ne pouvais pas dormir. Déjà les voisins s'étaient plaints. Mais il a fallu que tout ça recommence. Un canard, puis deux, puis plusieurs, et encore je ne dors pas à cause d'eux. C'est loufoque. C'est absolument comme si mon aise, mon travail, mon sommeil ne comptaient pas. Je sais qu'ils comptent mais on ne le dirait pas.... Tu me dis de faire comme je veux. Je donne des ordres définitifs. Tout de suite, *sans qu'on ne me dise quoique ce soit*, mes ordres sont décommandés. Toujours avec les meilleures intentions, mais le résultat est que je suis encore une fois embêté dans la nuit. Et même maintenant tu voudrais empêcher la vente des canards. Tout ça ne tient pas debout comme idée générale de la vie. Ça ne peut pas continuer. Quand tu réorganiseras cette maison, décide bien si tu veux les services d'un homme, ou non. Si oui, je te donnerai un homme, et j'organiserai le jardin séparément. Les deux choses ne peuvent pas bien marcher quand chaque fois que la maison se trouve à court, elle prend sur le jardin. Que la maison soit suffisante pour elle-même. Je ne dis pas pour le moment;

mais plus tard quand tu réorganiseras, il ne faut pas compter sur un jardinier pour les chaussures et pour massacrer les couteaux, et un chauffeur pour nettoyer le poêle etc etc. *Je répète — je ne dis pas pour le moment.* N'attends pas la fin de la guerre pour réorganiser. La guerre pourrait durer un an. Ça ne sera jamais une économie ici de roquer sur le service ou de me déranger dans les choses qui comptent pour moi. Chaque dérangement coûte dix fois plus que tu pourrais économiser dans un an, et davantage. Nous avons perdu cette semaine au moins 4,000 francs. Je partage tous les sentiments affectueux.

Ton A.B. Nouche

P.S. Je pense que c'est maintenant assez de lettres.

---

76. [But I have always begged you to engage a housekeeper and you have always refused. There will never be any friction between us if I am left in peace as regards my sleep, my work and the organization of the garden, which is my affair. It is your misfortune, and mine, that with the best of intentions, you forget. We have already had one scene over the maids, when you made them get up at 5.30. I complained; I explained to you at length that I could not bear it, and you changed the arrangement immediately. But now this has all started all over again, I complained again, but this time you were less amenable. You told me it was too bad if I couldn't sleep or work—the maids absolutely had to get up at 5.30. You even suggested that I should leave this house which exists exclusively through my doing so that the maids could get on with their work and the house could be run according to schedule!! Of course your good sense triumphed in the end. The same thing happened with the ducks. I had already had them taken away from the lake because they kept me awake. The neighbours had already complained. But we had to go through it all over again. One duck, then two, then several. And again, I can't sleep because of them. It's crazy. It's just as if my comfort, my work and my sleep counted for nothing. I know they do count but no one would think so.... You tell me to do as I like about it. I give definitive orders. Straight away, *without anyone saying a word to me*, my orders are cancelled. Always with the best of intentions, but the result is that I am disturbed during the night again. And now you still want to prevent the sale of the ducks. This does not stand up as a general idea of life. It can't go on. When you reorganize this house, make your mind up carefully whether you want a manservant or not. If you do, I will give you one, and I will organize the garden separately. The two things can't be run properly if each time the house is under-staffed, it takes from the garden. The house must be self-sufficient. I am not saying it must be at the moment, but later, when you do the reorganization, you must not count on a gardener to do the shoes and destroy the knives, and a chauffeur to clean the stove, etc., etc. *I repeat*, I said *not at the moment*. Don't wait till the end of the war to do the reorganization. The war could last a year. It will never be economical here to make the servants change places or to disturb me in things that matter to me. Every disturbance costs ten times more than you could save in one year, even more. We have lost at least 4,000 francs this week.

I share your fond feelings.... I think that's enough letters now.]

Further on the ducks see p. 445. In July 1915 in the *Metropolitan Magazine* Bennett published a story called 'The Muscovy Ducks' (never reprinted) in which two Muscovy ducks that belong to the mistress of Chamfreys Hall are killed by mistake by the gardener. The story concerns the violent antagonism between mistress and gardener, with the husband as innocent, diplomatic, and uneasy protector of the latter. The gardener is described thus:

> He was difficult, touchy, harsh, taciturn, censorious, and opinionated. He had no social charm. He was not liked. Only a dog could have loved him, and he had an intense objection to dogs. And why should he be agreeable, and why should he have social charm? He despised such qualities. He possessed greater. He was not vain; he was not conceited; but he had a calm and just appreciation of his great qualities. He was absolutely honest, absolutely industrious, absolutely reliable, and he knew his job absolutely.

The mistress of the house bears the name Vera Cheswardine, used by Bennett in a group of Five Towns stories that he wrote before he knew Marguerite. In them the mistress is a pretty, vain, selfish, and unscrupulous woman, perhaps modelled upon Eleanor Green. In 'The Muscovy Ducks' the Five Towns are on the distant horizon, and Vera is a vaguer figure of the same stamp as her namesake. As seen by the gardener she is 'his archenemy, bold, powerful, unscrupulous.' Bennett also depicts Lockyer in *The Lion's Share* (1916) and in the last chapter of *Our Women* (1920).

KEELE / MS / 77
(*To Marguerite Soulié Bennett*)

Comarques
10–4–15

Enfant,

Il n'y a aucune espèce de raison que tu n'ailles pas à Ipswich mercredi. Si tu n'avais pas oublié que j'allais à Colchester mardi, tu ne te serais jamais dit mardi. Mais la chose dite, tu t'obstines. Que moi je serais forcé de me promener dans les rues de Colchester une heure et demie avant mon meeting, et plus qu'une heure et demie après, tu ne t'en soucies pas. Mais je n'ai pas le temps de faire ces amusements, et si tu prends la voiture mardi, je ne pourrai pas aller à Colchester. Les conséquences de ton entêtement seront graves. Je prends cette occasion de te dire une seule chose que j'ai beaucoup sur le cœur, — que tu as beaucoup de talent et autant de charme, mais que le prix que tu en exiges est trop cher, et que je ne peux pas continuer de la payer. Il y a trop, et beaucoup trop, de griefs, de renchonnements, et de scènes humiliantes pour moi et pour toi, et ici et à Londres. Je ne peux pas continuer de vivre dans ce monde bizarre où toutes les domestiques sont des imbéciles, tous les jardiniers des coquins, la secrétaire stupide, le chauffeur un être qui ne fiche rien, et la maîtresse de maison un martyre. Tu te plains trop, tu es trop souvent mécontente, tu me critiques trop, et tu fais trop d'histoires. C'est vrai que tu as tes névralgies, et je te plains beaucoup. Mais tu n'es pas la seule qui supporte des maux physiques. Moi comme toi, j'ai mes maladies héréditaires. Je sais aussi que tu as un tempérament difficile et porté vers la mélancholie. Mais il y a des bornes que tu ne devrais pas franchir. Tu n'as vraiment pas le droit de te conduire vers moi comme tu te conduises — sans doute inconsciemment. Les scènes que tu me fais sont inouies, — et pour rien. Il te faut un grief coûte que coûte, si ce n'est pas un grand grief, un petit; mais il t'en faut. Je me rappelle, et je me rappellerai toute ma vie, la scène que tu m'as faite devant Pinker, parceque je ne te donnais pas assez d'argent!! Scène inexcusable et inoubliable. Maintenant c'est la voiture. Si je faisais le martyre comme toi, qu'est-ce que tu en dirais? Un changement est absolument nécessaire, parce que ma vie est empoisonnée, et tout ton charme et tout ton talent ne seront pas assez pour empêcher un catastrophe. Tu grondes, tu critiques, tu renchonnes, tu fais le martyre — et je ne sais pas si tu t'en aperçois! Mais je te prie sérieusement d'y réflechir. Si tu trouves comme toujours que tu as parfaitement raison et que moi j'ai parfaitement tort, tu me forceras à la fin de te quitter. Je ne suis pas un Sharpe, et je ne suis pas exclusivement une machine à gagner de l'argent. Et je te conseille de me ménager un peu, parce que je suis en train de devenir dangereux.

Ton A.B.

77. [There is absolutely no reason why you shouldn't go to Ipswich on Wednesday. If you hadn't forgotten that I was going to Colchester on Tuesday, you would never have thought of Tuesday. But having once thought of it, you can't get it out of your mind. You don't care that I would have to walk up and down the streets of Colchester for an hour and a half before my meeting and more than an hour and a half after. But I don't have the time for these amusements any more and if you take the car on Tuesday, I won't be able to go to Colchester. The consequences of your obstinacy will be serious. I am taking this opportunity to tell you something which is very much in my heart— that you have a great deal of talent and as much charm but that the price you demand for them is too high and I can't go on paying it. There are too many, many too many grievances and complaints and humiliating scenes for me and for you, both here and in London. I can't go on living in this strange world in which all maids are idiots, all gardeners are rogues, the secretary is stupid and the chauffeur someone who never does a hand's turn and the mistress of the house is a martyr. You feel too sorry for yourself, you are too often displeased, you criticize me too much and you make too many scenes. I know you do have your attacks of neuralgia for which I do feel very sorry for you. But you are not the only one to have to contend with physical ills. Like you, I have my hereditary illnesses. I know, too, that you have a difficult temperament with a

depressive tendency. But there are limits and you should not overstep them. You really have no right to behave to me as you do—no doubt unconsciously. The scenes you make are unbelievable—and over nothing. You have to have a grievance whatever happens, if it isn't a big one, a little one will do; but you have to have one. I remember, and will remember all my life, the quarrel you picked with me in front of Pinker, because I wasn't giving you enough money!! An inexcusable and unforgettable scene. Now it's the car. What would you say if I put on a martyr act, as you do! A change is absolutely essential because my life is being poisoned and all your charm and all your talent will not be enough to prevent a catastrophe. You scold, you criticize, you whine, you make yourself out a martyr—and I don't know if you realize what you are doing! But I earnestly beg you to think about it. If, as always, you find that you are completely in the right and that I am completely in the wrong, you will finally force me to leave you. I am not a Sharpe and I am not just a machine for earning money. And I advise you to treat me with a little consideration, as I am becoming dangerous.]

KEELE / MS / 78
(*To Marguerite Soulié Bennett*)

Comarques
13th April 1915

Ma chère Marguerite,

Ce n'est pas question de choisir entre toi et Lockyer. C'est question de décider qui — toi ou moi — va prendre le dessus dans les choses qui me regardent & dont j'ai la responsabilité. Je me fiche de Lockyer, mais je n'ai pas la moindre intention de te laisser me mener par le bout du nez. Je n'ai aucun béguin pour Lockyer. M. Greig m'a dit que Lockyer n'était pas très agréable — je ne sais pas: il est toujours agréable avec moi. C'est certain qu'il manque de tact. M. Greig m'a aussi dit que Lockyer était un admirable jardinier, très honnête, très économe, fidèle de toute confiance. M. Greig avait parfaitement raison. Lockyer est toutes ces choses. C'est un excellent organisateur, et un des meilleurs employés que j'ai jamais eu. Tout ce qu'il fait marche bien, soit le chauffage, soit l'électricité, et c'est reconnu que nous avons le plus beau jardin du pays. Et tout ça ce n'est rien. Ce qui est important, c'est que tu n'as pas le droit de me donner des embêtements dans les choses que je dirige. Si je te faisais la même chose, qu'est ce que tu dirais? Tu dirais comme moi je dis. Je me vois avec toutes les histoires d'un nouveau jardinier, et qui certainement serait inférieur à Lockyer. Et pourquoi? Tu t'es mis dans la tête il y a longtemps que tu perdrais Lockyer. Lockyer m'est égal, mais puisque tu ne peux pas perdre Lockyer sans me rouler et sans me déranger et sans me blesser horriblement dans mes droits, je ne marche pas. 'Choisir entre toi et Lockyer' — de telles choses ne se disent pas. Si tu me dis de choisir entre mon droit de mari et ton caprice, je choisis tout de suite et sans la moindre hésitation pour mon droit. Tout ce que tu dis sur Lockyer, c'est qu'il est 'impoli' et desagréable. Les filles sont impolies et desagréables. Tu me dis toi-même que ta femme de charge est obligée de les admonestrer en ta présence. On est forcé de supporter des choses dans les employés. Si je t'écoutais je changerais les jardiniers aussi souvent que toi tu changes les domestiques. Et si j'avais un autre, ça pourrait bien être la même chose pour toi.

Je ne sais pas si tu as bien réfléchi sur le défi que tu me lances. Je ne pense pas. C'est un défi sérieux, et je l'accepte sérieusement, mais je ne pense pas que tu en as saisi tout le sérieux. Il n'y a qu'une réponse à un tel défi. Et si tu le maintiens, je te le donne. Si je te disais: 'Choisis — ou tu dirigeras la maison d'après mes idées, et flanqueras à la porte des domestiques comme je veux, ou je te quitte.' Tu serais la première, avec ton indépendance, de me dire: 'Quitte moi, alors!'

Ce que tu dis sur nos conversations n'accorde pas avec les faits. Presque toujours quand nous sommes seuls, tu es caline et charmante. Mais quand il y a du monde tu commences de froncer les sourcils. Je suis prêt à écouter, et effectivement j'écoute, à tout ce que tu as à me dire, mais je ne suis pas prêt à accepter des scènes et cetera devant le monde. Si seulement tu avais pu voir ton visage ce matin, tous les traits tirés, la voix cuisante! Naturellement les officiers comprenaient que tu étais furieuse, et que tu te trouvais le martyre et moi la brute, etc etc. Tu n'as aucune idée de ton apparence quand tu es comme ça; autrement tu changeras.

Ce que tu dis sur ce 'coin de Comarques' n'est pas à la page. Les Sablons, Brighton, Londres, la Suisse, l'Italie, la Riviera, et surtout l'hiver à Paris quand tu as renchonné tout le temps, — c'est la même chose. Tu n'es pas contente. Tu n'as jamais été contente, tu ne le seras jamais. Renchonner, avec toi c'est un besoin impérieux. Renchonne comme tu voudrais quand nous sommes seuls, mais ne me fais pas des scènes devant le monde. Et ne me lance pas de défis impossibles.

Je t'avais écrit une lettre samedi, mais je l'ai gardée. Je te la donne maintenant, parce qu'il y a des choses dedans que je voudrais que tu saches.

Ton A.B.

78. [A choice between you and Lockyer is not at issue. What is at issue is which of us—you or I—is to take the upper hand in things which are my business and for which I am responsible. I don't give a damn about Lockyer, but I have not the slightest intention of letting you twist me around your little finger. I have no special love for Lockyer. Mr Greig told me that Lockyer is not very pleasant—I don't know; he is always pleasant with me. Of course he's tactless. Mr Greig also told me that Lockyer was an excellent gardener, and very honest, very economical, and completely trustworthy. Mr Greig was perfectly right. Lockyer is all those things. He is an excellent organizer and one of the best employees I have ever had. Everything he does works well, whether it's the heating or the electricity, and everyone says we have the most beautiful garden in the district. But none of this matters. What matters is that you have no right to make trouble for me in things that I am in charge of. If I did that to you, what would you say? You would say the same as me. I can see myself going through all the problems of having a new gardener, who would certainly not be as good as Lockyer. Why? You got the idea some time ago that you would get rid of Lockyer. I don't care about Lockyer, but since you can't get rid of Lockyer without cheating me, and upsetting me and wounding me horribly in my rights, I won't do it. 'Choose between you and Lockyer'—you can't say things like that. If you tell me to choose between my rights as a husband and your whim, I will immediately and without the slightest hesitation choose my rights. The only thing you have to say about Lockyer is that he is rude and disagreeable. The girls are rude and disagreeable. You told me yourself that the housekeeper often has to scold them in front of you. We have to bear these things from employees. If I listened to you, I would change gardeners as often as you change maids. And if I did get another, you might feel just the same about him.

I don't know whether you have thought carefully about the challenge you are throwing at me. I don't think you have. It is a serious challenge and I take it seriously, but I don't think you have grasped its full significance. There is only one answer to such a challenge. And if you maintain your challenge, I will give you the answer. If I said to you: 'Make your choice—either run the house according to my ideas and dismiss the servants as I want, or else I am leaving you', you, with your independence, would be the first to say to me: 'Then leave me!'

What you tell me about our conversations does not correspond to the facts. When we are alone together, you are almost always fond and charming. But when other people are there, you start to frown. I am ready to listen, and I do in fact listen, to everything you have to say to me, but I am not prepared to put up with scenes etcetera in front of other people. If only you could have seen your face this morning, with all your features drawn, and an imperious tone in your voice! Of course the officers understood that you were furious and that you felt you were a martyr and I a brute, etc., etc. You have no idea what you look like when you are like that; if you had, you would change.

What you say about this 'Comarques backwater' is off the point. It was the same in Les Sablons, Brighton, London, Switzerland, Italy, the Riviera, and particularly the winter in Paris when you whined all the time. You are not satisfied. You never have been satisfied and you never will be. You have an overwhelming need to whine. Whine as much as you like when we are alone together, but don't pick quarrels with me in front of other people. And don't present me with impossible challenges.

I wrote you a letter on Saturday, but I kept it. I am giving it to you now, because there are things in it I would like you to know.]

During the war, officers were regularly entertained at Comarques, and frequently stayed there.

KEELE / MS / 79   Hôtel Meurice
(*To Marguerite Soulié Bennett*)   228, rue de Rivoli
                                    Paris
                                    22nd June 1915

Mon enfant minuscule,

Train very slow, but absolutely prompt. Decent meals. Impression all through England of soldiers & camps. Same impression in France. Nothing but *English* soldiers at Boulogne, & all along the line *English* camps & hospitals as far as Etaples. So that you might as well be in England. At Creil the bridge that was blown up by the English on their retreat has been rebuilt already. The old bridge is laid out in pieces on the banks. The train runs through all the country of the retreat. Not a sign of it from the train, except this new bridge. Fields all cultivated. Line guarded all the way to Paris. I had a police-pass which was very useful to me both at Folkestone & at Boulogne. I wasn't allowed to take my bag in the compartment. Very few people at Gare du Nord. No trouble with luggage. Got a porter & a cab at once. All Paris seems as if it was Sunday & the day after a great funeral. No autobuses. Horse omnibus, Madeleine Bastille, with a woman conductor, nu-tête. Mair & I dined together here. Madame Edwards had got me a most excellent flat, pour à peu près rien. We went to the Godebskis afterward. I told Ida about your dresses. In your letter to Mimi you *had* asked them to get a dress for you. Mimi showed me the letter. Ida s'en occupe to-day. I shall ask Hélène about the hair dye. This morning I go to see Martin. I think Gide is coming to lunch. Tonight we dine with a deputé, je ne sais pas pourquoi. C'est Mair qui arrange tout ça. We are to leave tomorrow for Nancy. We shall return to Paris about Friday, & then go to Arras, where all the big fighting is. And afterwards we go to Alsace. This is what Mair says, anyway.

I am now just going to have my breakfast. J'ai pris mon thé. I hope everything is all right.

                       Respex to darling Edith   B OOOOT
                       Je te bise bien
                                          Ton Nouche
J'ai très bien dormi.

79. Beginning on 21 June, Bennett made a 25-day tour of the battle-front for the government. The essays he wrote about it were published in the *Illustrated London News* and in the *Saturday Evening Post* in America. They were published in book form as *Over There* in November. Bennett's involvement in war-work was extensive. He served without pay on a number of committees, and ultimately entered the government in the Ministry of Information. He also wrote extensively about the war for the *Daily News*, the *New Statesman* and other periodicals. See Vols. I and II. See also Kinley Roby, *A Writer at War* (1972).

G. H. Mair now headed the government's Department of Information. The Department was later merged with the propaganda unit to form the Ministry of Information.

Misia Edwards (1872–1950), born Misia Godebski, half-sister of Cepa Godebski; art patron, painted by Bonnard, Renoir, and others, author of *Réveillon*, 1910.

Mimi: daughter of the Godebskis.

For correspondence with André Gide (1869–1951) see Vols. II and III and also *Correspondance André Gide—Arnold Bennett*, edited by Linette Brugmans, 1964.

Edith: unidentified.

KEELE / MS / 80
(*To Marguerite Soulié Bennett*)   Hôtel Meurice
                                                Thursday
                                                24–6–15

Enfant chérie,

I expect to make an excursion today into the war zone, but it is not yet sure. Meanwhile I am doing an article on Paris. All the Bions, and Gabrielle came for tea yesterday. Gabrielle looks older. Her complexion is decidedly worse. But she was nicely dressed. She says that Madame Bergeret décline *beaucoup*. These people stayed for about 2 hours. Gabrielle m'a fait le récit de son voyage de Mailly à Paris. Effrayant. At night we dined at Misia's. I found that she had asked Philippe Berthelot avec Hélène (maintenant sa vraie légitime) exprès pour faciliter notre voyage, puisque Philippe est presqu'à la tête des Affaires Etrangères. C'était gentil de sa part. Je n'ai jamais aimé Philippe, que je connais depuis 1902, et mes sentiments ne changent pas. J'aime mieux Hélène, qui a commencé sur le trottoir et qui a couché avec toute la bande, et qui finit comme femme du chef du cabinet du Ministre, et que toutes les femmes d'ambassadeurs courtisent. C'est tordant. Elle est gentille mais ignorante. Il y avait aussi Sert, Gide, Legrix (jeune romancier), les God. Moi j'avais la place d'honneur et Mair l'autre. Mais Mair ne parle pas assez bien Français pour pouvoir être à la hauteur de la sit. Aussi Philippe gêne un peu tout le monde, parce qu'il est trop conférencier. Misia a toujours l'air d'une femme qui s'embête mortellement. L'appartement est féérique. Beaucoup mieux que l'autre, avec une terrasse pavée de marbre noir, et une vue sur la Seine. Très épatant. Mais elle s'embête. Sert aussi. Ida n'est pas encore rétablie. On lui a tiré un demi litre d'eau avant hier. Mais elle sort tout de même.

Ce matin j'ai mal à la tête.

Il fait toujours très chaud. Hier des averses torrentielles. Love to Edith.

Je te bise.

Ton Nouche

80. [I found that she had asked Philippe Berthelot and Hélène (now his actual lawfully wedded wife) on purpose to make our journey easier, because Philippe is now almost the head of Foreign Affairs. It was nice of her. I have never liked Philippe, whom I have known since 1902, and my feelings have not changed. I prefer Hélène, who started her career on the streets, has slept with the whole group and ended up as the wife of the Minister's principal private secretary; all the ambassadors' wives pay court to her. It's hilarious. She is nice but ignorant. Sert, Gide, Legrix (a young novelist) and the Gods were there as well. I had the place of honour and Mair had the other one. But Mair does not speak good enough French to be able to cope with the sit. And Philippe rather embarrasses everyone because he has too much the style of a lecturer. Misia always looks bored to death. The flat is enchanting. Much better than the other one, with a terrace paved in black marble and a view over the Seine. Quite wonderful. But she is bored and so is Sert. Ida has still not recovered. Half a litre of water was extracted from her the day before yesterday. But she goes out all the same.

I have a headache this morning. It is still very hot. Torrential downpours yesterday.]

Bennett describes Misia Edwards's flat in more detail in *Over There*: 'a home illustrious in Paris for the riches of its collections—bric-a-brac, fans, porcelains, furniture, modern pictures; the walls frescoed by Pierre Bonnard and his compeers; a black marble balcony with an incomparable view in the very middle of the city'. Philippe Berthelot (1866–1934) is also described:

With tranquility and exactness and finality the high official, clad in pale alpaca and yellow boots, explained the secret significance of Yellow Books, White Books, Orange Books, Blue Books. The ultimate issues were never touched.

Bennett met Berthelot in 1904 and described him at that time as 'absolutely charming ..., with a French face and perfect manners'. The journal for 26 May 1905 reads:

In Philippe Berthelot's 'musée secret' what I chiefly noticed in several indecent prints was the exquisite drawing of the clitoris of prostitutes; realistic absolutely and yet beautiful. It was amusing how Mme B. sent me and another man into the 'musée secret', & left us there, & then asked our impressions.

José Maria Sert (1866–1945), Spanish artist.

Legrix: unidentified.

KEELE / MS / 81
(*To Marguerite Soulié Bennett*)   Hôtel Meurice
Friday
25 Juin 1915

My dear child,

I am now beginning to be very busy. I was up at 7.10 to write my first article, which I have begun. I have now all the material for it. We went to Meaux yesterday. It is the nearest point to Paris reached by the Germans. We saw the battlefield covered with graves. Each grave is marked by a cross. But German graves have black crosses. The effect of these black crosses among the white ones is very sinister. It was a perfect day. Today we go to Senlis, & tomorrow to Reines. I saw lots of interesting things yesterday that I have in my notebook that I haven't time to write to you now. Particularly the village of Barcy. While we were looking at the church *three* [?] came up together. La quantité de femmes en deuil à Paris est effrayante. Pourtant elles sont toutes calmes et de bonne humeur. I went to bed early last night, & slept well. Tonight Mair & I dine chez les God. Je t'ai écrit une lettre hier que j'ai donné à l'Ambassade pour être mise dans une enveloppe ambassadoriale. Parce que je craignais la censure. Il y a dedans des vérités fort désobligéantes pour un gros choux, et si la lettre lui parvenait, il y aurait des histoires. Donc, etc. La lettre sera mise à la poste à Londres par un ami.

Je te bise,

Nouche

Très pressé.

81. [I wrote you a letter yesterday which I gave to the Embassy to be put in an Embassy envelope. Because I was afraid of the censor. In it there are some very unpalatable truths about a bigwig and if the letter were to reach him, there would be trouble. Therefore etc. The letter will be posted in London by a friend. I kiss you.... Great haste.]

In *Over There* Bennett writes:

And then a tomb with a black cross. Very disconcerting, that black cross! It is different not only in colour, but in shape, from the other crosses. Sinister! You need not to be told that the body of a German lies beneath it. The whole devilishness of the Prussian ideal is expressed in that black cross. Then, as the road curves, you see more black crosses, many black crosses, very many. No flags, no names, no wreaths on these tombs. Just a white stencilled number in the centre of each cross. Women in Germany are still lying awake at nights and wondering what those tombs look like.

KEELE / MS / 82
(*To Marguerite Soulié Bennett*)   Hôtel Meurice
                                                    lundi soir
                                                    28–6–15

Enfant chérie,

    Enfin je suis de retour à Paris. Merci de tes deux télé-grammes. Je suis bien fatigué. Autrement je me porte très bien. Je ne pourrais pas supporter plus que 3 jours en suite de ces sensations. On nous a traités comme des princes. Nous avons tout vu. Hier matin nous sommes allés dans les tranchées de première ligne à Bétheny. Les hommes sont *superbes*. Les relations entre les officiers et les hommes sont tout à fait admirables. Nous avons été à 400 mètres des Allemands. Le commandant de la place nous a offert du champagne. Un type épatant! Justement à ce moment un obus allemand est tombé au coin de la cour de ferme où se trouve sa popotte. En nous en allant nous étions forcés de courir dans les endroits exposés. Quand nous étions dans la tranchée de communication un autre obus a éclaté à 60 mètres de nous, et puis un troisième. On l'entend venir. Tout le monde se baisse jusqu'à après l'explosion. Nous avons marché *4 ou 5 kilomètres* dans les tranchées de communication. Nous avons très bien déjeuné à Reims (Hôtel du Nord); la cathédrale avait été bombardé le matin même. Personne n'a l'air d'y penser. On vendait les journaux à l'endroit où un obus est tombé une heure auparavant. Je suis bien éreinté. Je t'embrasse et je te bise tendrement.

               Love to Edith.

                                  Nouche

La censure dans le zone militaire fait des délais énormes pour la correspondance. J'espère tu es bien retournée, contente, de Londres.

Je ne sais pas où nous irons pour notre prochaine excursion.

    82. [I am back in Paris at last. Thank you for your two telegrams. I am very tired, otherwise very well. I could not bear these feelings for more than three days running. We were treated like princes. We saw everything. Yesterday morning we went to the front line trenches at Bétheny. The men are wonderful. Relations between officers and men are quite admirable. We went to 400 metres from the Germans. The man in command there offered us champagne. A terrific chap! At exactly that moment a German shell fell in the corner of the farmyard where the soldiers' mess was. When we

left we had to run through exposed areas. When we were in the communications trench, another shell exploded 60 metres away from us, and then a third. You can hear them coming. Everybody keeps down until after the explosion. We walked *4 or 5 kilometres* in the communications trenches. We had a very good lunch in Rheims (Hôtel du Nord); the cathedral had been bombed that very morning. No one seems to give it a thought. Someone was selling newspapers on the spot where a shell had fallen an hour before. I am quite exhausted. I hug you and kiss you tenderly.... Censorship in the military zone causes huge delays in the post. I hope that you have got back from London happily. I don't know where we will go for our next trip.]

KEELE / MS / 83
(*To Marguerite Soulié Bennett*)   Hôtel Meurice
                                                    Samedi
                                                    4–7–15

Épousette chérie,

Enfin, que j'ai ta lettre écrite jeudi je sais où tu en es. Je pensais que le déjeuner du Savoy s'est passé cette semaine. J'espère que tu auras un aussi beau succès au Savoy qu'à Clacton. Je suis passablement embêté, parce que notre départ est toujours remis. Mail il n'y a rien à faire. Demain nous irons à Compiègne et peut-être Senlis. Je compte partir pour Arras mardi. Tous les journaux anglais sont maintenant remplis de conseils de la part du chancelier de l'Echiquier aux citoyens britanniques d'économiser leurs ressources, de dépenser le moins poss. et ainsi de suite. Donc je fume des cigares très bon marché et nous mangeons dans des restaurants ditto. Hier nous avons dîné chez les God. Gide était là. Cet homme me charme de plus en plus. Il me dit que je lui ai tellement inspiré le désir de travailler, que depuis plusieurs jours il écrit beaucoup plus regulièrement et plus longuement. Cet après-midi je vais voir son 'Foyer Franco-Belge'. J'ai invité Mimi ici pour le petit déjeuner ce matin à 9 heures. Elle a été à l'heure. Cette enfant a de la véneration pour toi. À cause du temps j'ai mal à la tête. Je pense que ça passera. Je ne fiche rien, puisque je ne peux plus, et mes premières chroniques sont déjà expédiées. La censure les a approuvées. Nous déjeunons avec le directeur du bureau de la presse étrangère. Il est très bien, très intelligent. Hier nous avons déjeuné chez Larue avec nos journalistes américains, compagnons de voyage. C'était bien. Il fait chaud et lourd. Si j'ai l'occasion de revenir en France, ce qui est possible (pour aller en Alsace) je t'amènerai à Paris. Ça vaut la peine d'être vu, quoique triste. J'ai écrit 11,000 mots. Tu me crois en voyage et je ne suis pas. Amuse-toi bien. Ton mari te bise.

Nouche

Clayhanger est à sa troisième partie dans *La Revue de Paris*.

J'espère que ta robe est bien arrivée.

83. [Now that I have at last received the letter you wrote on Thursday I know what you are up to. I thought that the lunch at the Savoy had taken place this week. I hope that you will be as great a success at the Savoy as at Clacton. I am fairly bored because our departure is constantly delayed. But nothing can be done about it. Tomorrow we will go to Compiègne and perhaps Senlis. I hope to leave for Arras on Tuesday. Now all the English newspapers are full of advice from the Chancellor of the Exchequer to British citizens to economize their resources and spend as little as poss and so on. So I am smoking very cheap cigars and we eat in ditto restaurants. Yesterday we dined with the Gods. Gide was there. I find the man more and more charming. He tells me that I have so inspired him with the desire to work that recently he has been writing much more regularly and much more. This afternoon I am going to see his 'Franco-Belgian home'. I invited Mimi to have breakfast here at 9 o'clock this morning. She was on time. The child worships you. The weather has given me a headache. I think it will pass. I am doing nothing because I can do no more and my first articles have already been sent. They were passed by the censor. We are having lunch with the director of the foreign press bureau. He is very nice and very intelligent. Yesterday we had lunch at Larue's with the American journalists who are travelling with us. It was nice. The weather is hot and heavy. If I have an opportunity to come back to France, which is possible (to go to Alsace), I will bring you to Paris. It is worth seeing, though it's sad. I have written 11,000 words. You think I am travelling and I am not. Have a nice time. Your husband kisses you.... The *Revue de Paris* is on the third part of *Clayhanger*. I hope the dress arrived safely.]

Clayhanger began appearing in *La Revue de Paris* in May 1915.

KEELE / MS / 84
(*To Marguerite Soulié Bennett*)

Hôtel Meurice
lundi
5–7–15

Chérie enfant,

C'est maintenant arrangé que nous partirons mercredi matin pour Arras. Je compte arriver à Londres, via Boulogne, dimanche ou lundi soir. Tu pourrais peut être m'attendre ou au Savoy ou au Berkeley. Berkeley est mieux. J'espère que ta robe est arrivée, et que ton déjeuner aura un éclatant succès demain. La chaleur ici est intense, accablante. Hier soir à 10 heures il faisait 27 degrés dans la rue. Ça m'a dérangé intestinalement.

Pourtant je ne fiche rien. Je lis seulement. Je lis un roman de Hermant qui me plaît beaucoup. Toute la journée tout le monde est en rage. En même temps, il y a toujours le danger d'attraper froid. L'esprit à Paris est mauvais à présent Chacun l'admet. Il y a un sale esprit pessimiste. Il m'est arrivé de remonter plusieurs personnes qui en avaient bien besoin. Je t'envoie une lettre d'un des plus grands écrivains de cette époque. Note ce qu'il dit sur le soussigné. On est très déprimé à propos des Russes. On attend une forte attaque allemande sur cette partie de la ligne française qui est la plus près de Paris. Si l'attaque réussit, et on prend Paris, la guerre est finie pour la France, parce que toutes les grandes fabriques d'ammunitions sont autour de Paris. C'est contre ce genre de raisonnement que je lutte, pas inutilement. Hier après-midi nous sommes allés voir Sert dans son atelier. Atelier énorme. Sert était habillé en blanc, avec les pattes sales. Nous y sommes restés une heure. Il était très dans le noir. Je l'ai secoué. Il m'a prié plusieurs fois *très particulièrement* de le rappeler à ton bon souvenir. Il a parlé de ses sentiments admiratifs et affectueux pour toi, et je ne sais plus quoi.

Cet atmosphère d'attente, de chaleur, de pessimisme, et de paresse dans lequel je vis en ce moment n'est pas tout à fait désagréable pour moi. Je n'oublierai pas les jours que j'ai passés ici. Et aussi je n'oublierai pas que tous ces êtres ont puisé chez-moi des idées de tranquille bon sens et un peu d'optimisme. En attendant j'ai eu d'excellentes idées pour mon prochain roman.

La première partie de la lettre de Gide réfère à ceci : — Il m'a pris à part samedi, et il m'a dit : 'Bennett, Varsovie est prise.' La nouvelle était inexacte. Pourtant Varsovie sera prise, je pense, bientôt.

Note : À partir d'après demain je serai exclusivement dans la Zone militaire, où il y a des délais terribles pour la correspondance, et même pour les télégrammes. Donc, tu peux compter que j'arriverai à Londres (*Victoria*) à 9 heures du soir, ou dimanche ou lundi. Probablement dimanche. C'est tout ce que je peux dire.

Je te chatouille en te bisant.

Nouche

84. [It is now settled that we will leave for Arras on Wednesday morning. I am

counting on arriving in London, via Boulogne, on Sunday or Monday evening. Perhaps you could wait for me either at the Savoy or at the Berkeley. The Berkeley is better. I hope that the dress has arrived and that your lunch tomorrow will be a dazzling success. The heat here is intense and incapacitating. It was 27 degrees in the street at 10 o'clock yesterday evening. It has upset me intestinally. Still, I am doing nothing. All I do is read. I am reading a novel by Hermant which I think is very good. Everyone is bathed in sweat all day. There is always the danger of catching cold as well. Morale in Paris is bad at present. Everyone admits it. There is a rotten pessimistic spirit. I have had occasion to cheer up several people who certainly needed it. I am sending you a letter from one of the greatest writers of this age. Notice what he says about the undersigned. People are very depressed about the Russians. A heavy German attack is expected on the part of the French line which is closest to Paris. If the attack succeeds and Paris is taken, the war is over for France, because all the big munitions factories are round Paris. This is the kind of reasoning that I am struggling against, not ineffectually. Yesterday afternoon we went to see Sert in his studio. A huge studio. Sert was dressed in white with dirty paws. We stayed there for an hour. He was in a very black mood. I got him out of it. He asked me several times *very specially* to remember him to you. He spoke of his admiring and affectionate feelings for you and I don't know what else. This atmosphere of waiting, heat, pessimism and idleness that I am living in at the moment is not entirely disagreeable to me. I will not forget the days that I have spent here. And neither will I forget that all these human beings have drawn ideas of calm good sense and a little optimism from me. While waiting I have had some excellent ideas for my next novel.

The first part of Gide's letter refers to this: he took me aside on Saturday and said to me: 'Bennett, Warsaw has been taken.' The news was incorrect. But Warsaw will be taken soon, I think.

Note: From the day after tomorrow I will be in the military zone all the time and there are terrible delays in the post, even for telegrams there. So, you can be certain that I will arrive in London (*Victoria*) at 9 in the evening on Sunday or Monday. Probably Sunday. That is all I can say. I tickle you as I kiss you.]

Ariel Hermant (1862–1950), novelist.

The next novel was *The Roll Call*, though Bennett did not begin writing it until October 1916. He was now in the middle of writing a light novel, *The Lion's Share*.

KEELE / MS / 85   Doullens
(*To Marguerite Soulié Bennett*)   Jeudi
                                       [8 July 1915]

Hier Arras. Scène unique de désolation. Nous avons été à 40 mètres des Allemands, et même moins. Aujourd'hui. Notre Dame de Lorette. Nous avons été dans une tranchée Allemande abandonnée. Toute désolation, désordre, du linge sale, des vieux fusils, des courroies, une puanteur écrasante, et des jambes des cadavres qui sortent de la terre. Milliers de mouches. Encore une fois sous le feu! Les soldats étaient en joie de voir des civils marmités. 'Ça, c'est trop rigolo!' Pas si rigolo que ça. Nous avons vu toute la plaine qui commence à Ablains. Les Français font toujours du progrès. Bombardement sans cesse hier et aujourd'hui. Demain, vendredi, nous irons aux lignes anglaises. Je t'embrasse.

A.B.

85. [In Arras yesterday. A unique scene of desolation. We were 40 metres from the Germans, even less. Today—Notre Dame de Lorette. We went into an abandoned German trench. Desolation and confusion everywhere, dirty linen, old guns, straps, an oppressive stink, and the legs of dead bodies sticking up out of the ground. Thousands of flies. Under fire again. The soldiers were delighted to see civilians being shelled. 'It's too funny.' Not so funny. We saw all of the plain which begins at Ablains. The French are still making progress. Shelling all day yesterday and today. Tomorrow, Friday, we will go to the English lines. I kiss you.]

Bennett describes the German trenches in more detail in *Over There*. The ellipses are his.

The sides were delapidated. Old shirts, bits of uniform, ends of straps, damaged field-glass cases, broken rifles, useless grenades lay all about. Here and there was a puddle of greenish water. Millions of flies, many of a sinister bright burnished green, were busily swarming. The forlornness of these trenches was heartrending. It was the most dreadful thing that I saw at the front, surpassing the forlornness of any destroyed village whatever. And at intervals in the ghastly residue of war arose a smell unlike any other smell. . . . A leg could be seen sticking out of the side of the trench. We smelt a number of these smells, and saw a number of these legs. Each leg was a fine leg, well-clad and superbly shod in almost new boots with nail-protected soles. Each leg was a human leg attached to a human body, and at the other end of the body was presumably a face crushed in the earth. Two strokes with a pick, and the corpses might have been excavated and decently interred. But not one had been touched. Buried in frenzied haste by amateur, imperilled grave-diggers with a military purpose, these dead men decayed at leisure amid the scrap-heap, the cess-pit, the infernal squalor which once had been a neat, clean, scientific German earthwork, and which still earlier had been part of a fair countryside. The French had more urgent jobs on hand than the sepulture of these victims of a caste and an ambition. So they liquified into corruption in their everlasting boots, proving that there is nothing like leather.

ELDIN / MS / 86
(*To Septimus Bennett*)

Comarques
9th August 1915

My dear Sep,

I received your previous letter in Paris. I replied to it, only briefly as I was much took up, but I replied. Apparently this did not reach you. I think you are doing very excellently, &—I should say—more good than if you were in the Army, even as general. Do I understand that you work Sundays! 100 hours is a mighty week. I should like to know who the chief people are in Vickers Maxim; if I knew their identity I expect I could get an introduction to them & work an improvement for you. The firm has a bad name for not having kept its contracts, especially with Russia, & it may interest you to know that you are one of the causes of the Russian retreat, & Russia is very sick with you all.

Any money which you want I shall be glad to place at your disposal, or Maud's, at any time. This money will not be a loan. Don't exhaust your resources.

My illness, which was inflammation of the bow-wows, has no connection with the ancient rupture. It is quite manageable so long as it is dealt with promptly; but not otherwise. I am now quite well, but rather enfeebled.

Yours, A.B.

P.S. Don't tell me about Frank's exploits in the legal profession. I could talk your head off on the subject.

A.B.

All letters descriptive of your career, welcome.

86. Owing to the war, Septimus closed his studio in June 1915 and went to work in Sheffield for the Vickers company, where presently he supervised a group of women in the production of shells. He left his family in the Potteries. He worked eleven hours a day on the day shift, thirteen on the night shift (from 5 p.m. to 6 a.m.). In his journal in October 1915 he wrote:

I am mightily sick of the whole business. I could put up with days, but the man who started night work ought to be shot. The strain is too great. The living and working in false light & rotten atmosphere and sleeping while the sun shines is as fatal to the strongest constitutions as it would be to a flower.... The work itself has its picturesque side. The interior, lit up by large electric arc lights, & small individual bulbs on each lathe, the hum of the machinery, the noise of hammers & the anvil, the clink of shells, people going to and fro with trucks loaded with shells & someone active at each lathe, produces a wonderful effect seen through an open doorway from across the yard, on a dark night.

Bennett was ill for some weeks after his return from the Front.

ELDIN / MS / 87
(*To Septimus Bennett*)

Comarques
16th Oct 1915

My dear Sep,

The W.O. sends out official notices by post to families of men, & by telegraph to families of officers. The notices by post are often seriously delayed. I will try to find out myself whether the information is true, but I have not much hope of ascertaining anything. If I do I will let you know at once.

I edited your last two letters & sent them to the Editor of the *Westminster Gazette*, who was much impressed by their value. He will publish them like a bird if the Censor does not turn them down. All such things are submitted to the censor, who has very little sense, and probably *will* turn them down. I have had a proof of the article.

We are all right here, but I am overworked. We saw Florence yesterday at the Waldorf.

Yours, A.B.

ELDIN / MS / 88
(*To May Beardmore Marsden*)

Comarques
24th Oct 1915

My dear May,

I had a vague rumour yesterday morning, & a more precise one when Marguerite returned from London last night. I was very glad, but not surprised, to learn that Tertia had at once gone to Burslem. I have looked at the casualty lists (men) for months now solely for that name. Mixed up with your desolation there must be some rather fine thoughts & sensations. It is a terrible event, but it is also magnificent. I expect you often feel as if everything had broken loose. However, you will soon know what sort of stuff you are made of. It must be some satisfaction to you to think that your individuality has made you some very good friends, and enabled you to keep them for a long period. In any way in which I can possibly be of the least assistance to you, either material or otherwise, I am absolutely & completely at your service, not only now but always, without fail. The same for Joan.

Marguerite sends her kindest thoughts.
Yours, Arnold

88. May Beardmore married Sidney Marsden (b. 1879) in 1905. Maud, Septimus's wife, was his sister. He was a pottery designer and potters' manager in his father's firm, Marsden Tiles. In the army he was a lance corporal, and was being recommended for a commission. He was killed in action on 13 October. His daughter Joan was eight years old.

ELDIN / MS / 89
(*To Septimus Bennett*)

Comarques
8th Nov 1915

My dear Sep,

Many thanks for all these interesting details, & the cutting. You have had all the *I.L.N.* articles. They appeared irregularly, owing to typescript being sunk in the Arabic & again in the Hesperian on its way to America. The articles had to appear simultaneously in England & America. With regard to money, my undertaking of course still holds good. And I am ready to furnish any sums which on reflection you think are necessary. You should of course envisage your expenditure over periods. I sent you £50 on August 19th. I gather this is exhausted. Which means an expenditure of over £4 a week. From previous figures I understand that your total peace expenditure on yourself & family was only about this. I note that you have had extraordinary expenses, but in the end extraordinary expenses must be counted with ordinary & averaged up. One always has extraordinary expenses. I don't know anything of the circumstances concerning the human equation involved, but unless human nature is very different down Waterloo Rd from what it is elsewhere, I should say that the furnishing of money in a lump sum is a mistake, despite all good intentions on the part of the spender. Also I should on the whole prefer to provide the money through you. I think this is better in every way. Do not read any criticism into these remarks. I have no knowledge & therefore can't criticise either favourably or unfavourably. I only offer cautions & suggestions based on general principles.

Let me know just what you decide & I will send you the cheque or cheques. I don't particularly want myself to have to send cheques every week or so, & I should think the weekly amount required will vary with your earnings. If I send a lump sum to you, you could employ it as & when you choose. But all that is for you to decide.

Our loves,

Yours, A.B.

P.S. I didn't write to Maud about Sid. I wrote to May. I thought that was about right.

A.B.

89. The series of articles for *Over There* began appearing in the *Illustrated London News* and the *Saturday Evening Post* on 21 August.

Septimus's home was at 182 Waterloo Road.

ELDIN / MS / 90
(*To Septimus Bennett*)

Comarques
29th Nov 1915

My dear Sep,

The Glasgow strike was due partly to irritation caused by increase of rents & partly to the working of the Munitions Act. I thank God I always said this ridiculous Act would cause trouble & be a failure. Under it employers can dismiss men, whereas men cannot give notice. And if men leave they cannot get work at any other factory without a 'leaving certificate' from the first factory. Employers actually dismissed men, or kept them without work, while withholding the leaving certificate. The Tribunals appointed are for the most part unsuitable, incompetent, biassed, and tyrannic. Men were imprisoned, contrary to a positive promise to the Unions, for breaches of workshop discipline! The Act is to be altered, and quickly. I understand (but I have no details) that the men have won all round at Glasgow. I know that the Munitions Ministry telegraphed to the employers that they must give in to the men's demands. The men have certainly won on the rent question. That is clear from all the comments in the press.

I shall see that the article is all right.

I am now quite well. I am going to have a look at things in Manchester next week, and in Glasgow (I think) the week after. I finish my novel on Wednesday.

Kind regards to the new bureau.

Thine, A.B.

90. Bennett's trip to the Midlands and Scotland resulted in two articles in his long series of articles for the *Daily News*. 'In the Midlands', 15 December, dealt with savings in war-loans by workers. 'On the Clyde', 22 December, attacked parts of the Munitions Act. It laid the conflict between employers and the Amalgamated Society of Engineers to inadequate education of both the rich employers and the poor workers.

Bennett wrote *The Lion's Share* from 22 September to 1 December.

KEELE / MS / 91   Central Hotel
(*To Marguerite Soulié Bennett*)   Glasgow
                                   mardi
                                   14–12–15

Chérie enfant,

J'ai déjà pour ainsi dire construit cette pièce. C'est facile. J'ai dîné au Reform, mais là j'ai été abordé, & je suis resté trop tard pour aller chez Tertia. Du reste je ne voulais pas. Je suis allé à l'Empire. Tout à fait *infecte*. Mais j'ai vu Vedrenne et sa femme dans leur loge. La femme assommante; mais Vedrenne très intéressant. J'y suis resté avec eux jusqu'à 10.45. Assez bonne nuit. Les Vedrenne t'envoient les amitiés les plus empressées.

Il gèle, mais c'est tout.

Tu trouveras, réflection faite, que toutes sortes de choses sont changées dans notre existence matérielle. Plus de yacht. Une domestique de moins. Plus de chauffeur. Petite voiture au lieu de grosse. Frank sera bientôt dans l'armée. Le fainéant nous quitte à la fin de l'année. Et aussi, nous avons dépensé environ 25,000 frs. de moins cette année que dans les 12 mois précédents à la guerre. La dernière chose qu'on devrait changer dans un ménage, surtout le ménage d'un artiste, même de deux artistes, c'est le train de vie de la maison. Et nous avons arrangé ça sur pied si modeste, relativement à nos revenus, que c'est nullement nécessaire. Du reste quand on a une maison, on a une maison. Ou on la garde ou on la quitte. La quitter nous coûterait décidément plus cher que de la garder. L'alternatif est Londres, où nos dépenses seraient doublées. Il me faudrait une pièce pour trav. & une autre pour Miss Nerney, et la valeur de la maison serait perdue: toujours faudrait-il la faire chauffer et soigner etc. etc. Donc nous allons rester dans cette niche, et sur le même pied si les domestiques permettent. Tu es libre comme toujours de dépenser ton argent comme bon te semble. On te demande seulement de ne pas être trop désolée quand par un accident tu es privée d'un auto pour quelques jours. Je pense que après la guerre, s'il n'arrive pas de malheur, nous prendrons un flat à Londrinette. Le voyage a été long mais bien.

Je te bise.

                                   Ton [A.B.]

91. [I have already, so to speak, constructed this play. It is easy. I dined at the Reform, but I got into conversation there, and stayed too late to go to Tertia's. Anyway

I did not want to. I went to the Empire. Utterly *awful*. But I saw Vedrenne and his wife in their box. The wife is deadly but Vedrenne is very interesting. I stayed with them until 10.45. Quite a good night. The Vedrennes send you their warmest regards.

It is freezing, but no worse.

You will find, on reflection, that all sorts of things have changed in our material life. No more yacht. One fewer maid. No more chauffeur. A small car instead of a big one. Frank will be in the army soon. The lazy fellow is leaving us at the end of the year. And we have spent about 25,000 frs. less this year than we did in the 12 months before the war. The way of life of the house is the last thing which should be changed in a household, particularly in the household of an artist, or two artists indeed. And to do so would be quite unnecessary as we have organized our life on such a modest footing in comparison with our incomes. Anyway, once you have a house, you have a house. Either you keep it or you leave it. Leaving ours would definitely cost us more than keeping it. The alternative is London, where our expenses would be doubled. I would need one room for work, and another for Miss Nerney and the value of the house would be lost. It would still have to be heated and maintained, etc., etc. So we will stay in our nook and on the same footing, servants permitting. As always, you are free to spend your money as you like. I would only ask you not to be too disappointed when by some mischance you cannot have a car for a few days. After the war, if there are no disasters, I think we might take a flat in Londrinette. The journey was long but all right. I kiss you.]

The new play was *Sacred and Profane Love*, based upon the novel.

The Empire was a variety theatre, showing *Watch Your Step*, with Joseph Coyne and Blanche Tomlin.

J. E. Vedrenne (1867–1930) produced *Milestones*, and presently he arranged to produce another new play of Bennett's, *The Title*. For other references to him see the other volumes.

The *Velsa* was lent to the government.

Frank was a houseman at Comarques.

KEELE / MS / 92
(*To Marguerite Soulié Bennett*)

Central Station Hotel
mercredi matin
15 Dec 1915

Enfant chérie,

Je suis plus que content que tu trouves bien *These Twain*. Je n'ai pas déchiré ton autre lettre (sur la question conjugale), que je trouve très bien et très gentille. Il faut dire que je suis très bien traité dans mes voyages. Hier soir à la gare Neil Munro, le premier romancier d'Écosse, m'attendait avec Richmond. C'était une attention. Nous avons dîné ensemble avec Richmond au *Conservative* Club. Puis nous sommes allés chez Richmond pour causer et fumer. Sa femme n'était pas là./Elle est dans la nouvelle maison, de campagne, distance — 100 kilomètres. Sa belle-sœur était là — très écossaise et très intelligente. Les écossais en général sont beaucoup plus instruits que les anglais. Mais ils ont un accent terrible. Je ne comprends guère les domestiques de l'hôtel, et ils ne me comprennent guère. L'hôtel est bien, avec de grandes pièces, solide et province. Salle de bain parfaitement agencée. J'ai assez bien dormi, mais pas trop bien. J'ai admirablement supporté le voyage. Aujourd'hui j'ai une journée formidable, dans les fabriques etc, suivie d'une soirée au Arts Club. Richmond m'envoie son auto ici à 10.30. Le plus grand avantage d'être un romancier dont les romans sont aimés par des gens sérieux, c'est qu'on est traité mieux qu'un prince. Note: Je compte rentrer à la maison *vendredi soir*, par le train de 7.45 de Liverpool St. Ça sera mieux si je ne suis pas trop éreinté. Le train de Glasgow doit arriver à London 6.30.

Je te bise tendrement.

Ton [A.B.]

92. [I am more than pleased that you think *These Twain* good. I did not tear up your other letter (on the marital question); I find it very good and very sweet. I must say I am very well treated on my travels. Neil Munro, Scotland's foremost novelist, was waiting for me at the station yesterday evening, with Richmond. It was a courtesy. We dined together with Richmond at the Conservative Club. Then we went to Richmond's to chat and smoke. His wife was not there. She is in the new country house, 100 kilometres away. His sister-in-law was there—very Scottish and very intelligent. In general the Scots are much better educated than the English. But they have a terrible accent. I can hardly understand the hotel servants and they can hardly understand me. The hotel is good, with big rooms, solid and provincial. The bathroom is perfectly equipped. I slept quite well, not too well. I stood up to the journey admirably well. I have the most awesome day today, in factories etc., followed by a party at the Arts Club. Richmond is sending his car here for me at 10.30. The greatest advantage of being a novelist whose novels are liked by serious people is that one is treated better than a prince. NB. I mean to return home on Friday evening, by the 7.45 train from Liverpool St. It will be best if I am not too exhausted. The train from Glasgow should reach London at 6.30. I kiss you tenderly.]

These Twain was published on 14 January 1916. Very likely it annoyed Marguerite in its depiction of her quarrels with Bennett.

Neil Munro (1865–1930), author and journalist. He had recently published *The New Road*.

John Richmond (1869–1963), art collector and partner in the engineering firm of C. & J. Weir, met Bennett in 1909 when *Cupid and Commonsense* was produced in Glasgow. They became good friends. In some brief notes Richmond describes Bennett and Marguerite at Comarques.

He had himself always well under control. I have seen Marguerite irritate him beyond measure yet he always retained command of himself and remained calm outwardly and uniformly courteous.

KEELE / MS / 93
(*To Marguerite Soulié Bennett*)

Comarques
le 28–1–16

Enfant chérie,

Ta lettre, que j'ai trouvée par hasard, était très gentille. Je tâcherai d'y répondre avec la même gentillesse. Je reconnais que des fois c'est assez difficile pour toi, et je le regrette. Mais ceci est rare. 19 fois sur 20 tu viens, en montant, tout de suite dans ma chambre en disant 'Good Night', et tu disparais immédiatement: habitude qui m'est un peu agaçante souvent. Maintenant pour hier soir, tu es venue dans ma chambre et je pensais que c'était pour dire bonne nuit. Tu sais mon idée sur la question de la toilette consacrée, — idée peut-être trop poète et artiste, mais facile à contenter. Tu m'as dit: 'Is it good night, or — ?' J'ai dit 'It is good night.' Tu m'as dit, 'Eh bien je viens dans ton lit pour 3 minutes.' Il faut te rappeler que tandis que toi tu es arrivée de Londres excitée par les plaisirs, moi j'étais souffrant et éreinté — après avoir travaillé toute la journée pour ces soldats que — il paraît — les français aiment beaucoup mieux que les anglais les aiment. Je n'avais aucune idée que tu étais vexée. J'étais extrêmement surpris par tes larmes. Tout ça m'a coûté une très mauvaise nuit, la troisième, et j'étais très innocent.

Je suppose que je ne pourrais jamais t'enlever de la tête cette idée de la jalousie. Donc je n'essaie plus. Pourtant je la trouve quelque peu insultante pour moi — et pour toi aussi. Tu dis que tu me comprends, mais si tu savais mes idées sur la jalousie tu serais peut-être stupéfaite. Loin d'être jaloux, je me trouve extrêmement chic et gentil dans ces affaires. Je suis très bien avec tous tes amis, et très prévenant aussi. Ils sont tous le bienvenu. Et je me plais assez avec eux. Par contre tu n'invites jamais une femme si ça peut s'éviter. Et tu refuses nettement, en tranchant la discussion, d'inviter certains amis — par exemple les Rickards: ce que je trouve assez drôle, dans les circonstances. Mais je ne me plains pas. Même je trouve que c'est mieux comme ça.

Tes balades à Londres, loin de m'offusquer, me font plaisir, surtout quand tu es gentille en rentrant. Mais tu n'as pas le droit de parler de ta vie monotone et solitaire. Ta vie n'est pas monotone, et tu es infiniment moins seule que la plupart des femmes. Tu admets ça toi-même, mais tu dis que parce que la maison marche toute seule sans toi, tu n'as rien à t'intéresser. Il y a des dizaines de milliers de maisons comme la tienne qui marchent toute seules. Qu'en font les maîtresses? Tu as tout ce qu'il te faut pour le bonheur. Tu es belle, tu as un mari qui comprend tes toilettes, tu as de l'argent, tu as, artistiquement, une très grande situation, tu es entourée d'admirateurs ... Mais pour les balades, ça te regarde. Tu ne peux pas rentrer d'une balade en disant que tu es trop pauvre pour faire un beau geste que tu avais contemplé pour les soldats de ce village. Tu n'es pas trop pauvre. Nous sommes en guerre, mais tes revenus ne sont nullement diminués. Tu auras dix mille francs cette année, et le premier trimestre quand tu voudras. Tu aimes les soldats. C'est facile de faire une *vraie* sacrifice pour eux. Je ne payerai pas cette maison de club. Je donne énormément d'argent et de mon temps, déjà. Je suis prêt, comme preuve de bonne volonté, de donner le quart de ce que tu donnes pour la maison, et c'est tout. Je viens de payer 60,000 frs. d'impôt, et je n'aurai pas trop d'argent comptant pendant quelque temps, et je n'accepte aucune responsabilité financière pour le club, hors le quart de ce que tu veux bien payer toi-même. Ayant tout ça au clair, je suis libre de t'embrasser, et de t'assurer de mon amour sérieux.

Ton Nouche

93. [Your letter, which I found by chance yesterday, was very kind. I will try to answer it with the same kindness. I realize that sometimes things are quite difficult for you, and I am sorry. But such times are rare. 19 times out of 20, when you come upstairs you come straight into my room saying 'Good night' and you disappear immediately: a habit which I sometimes find irritating. Now yesterday evening, you came into my room and I thought it was to say good night. You know my idea about the ritual of getting ready for bed—an idea which is perhaps too poetic and artistic, but which is easy to accommodate. You said to me 'Is it good night or—?' I said 'It is good night.' You said 'Well I will come into your bed for 3 minutes.' You must remember that whereas you had arrived from London stimulated by your amusements, I was unwell and exhausted—after having worked all day for these soldiers whom—it seems—the French like much better than the English do. I had no idea that you were upset. I was extremely surprised by your tears. All this cost me a very bad night, the third, and I was in no way to blame.

I suppose I will never be able to get this idea of jealousy out of your head. So I no longer try. But I find it rather offensive to me—and to you too. You say you understand me, but if you knew my ideas on jealousy you might perhaps be amazed. I find that far from being jealous, I am really fine and nice about these matters. I am very well disposed, and even very considerate to all your men friends. They are all welcome. And

I quite enjoy their company. But you never invite a woman if you can help it. And you simply will not invite certain friends, and will not even talk about it—for example the Rickardses: I find this rather strange under the circumstances. But I'm not complaining. I even think it might be better like this.

Your trips to London in no way offend me, but give me pleasure, particularly when you are sweet when you return. But you have no right to say that your life is dull and lonely. Your life is not dull and you are alone infinitely less than most women. You admit it yourself, but you say that the house can run itself without you and you have nothing to occupy yourself with. There are tens of thousands of houses like yours which run themselves. What do their mistresses do? You have everything you need to make you happy. You are beautiful, you have a husband who takes an interest in your clothes, you have money, you are in a great situation from the artistic point of view, you are surrounded by admirers . . . But your trips are your own business. You cannot come back from a trip saying that you are too poor to make a generous gesture which you had been considering for the soldiers in this village. You are not too poor. We are in a war but your income is in no way diminished. You will have ten thousand francs this year, and the first three-monthly allowance when you like. You love the soldiers. It is easy to make a *real* sacrifice for them. I will not pay for this club house. I give away a great deal of my time and money already. As proof of good will, I am ready to give a quarter of whatever you give for the house and that's all. I have just paid 60,000 frs. in taxes and I will not have too much cash for a while, and I will not take on any financial responsibility for the club, apart from a quarter of whatever you pay. Now that I have put all my cards on the table, I feel free to kiss you and assure you of my serious love.]

ELDIN / MS / 94
(*To Septimus Bennett*)

Comarques
8th Feby 1916

My dear Sep,

Thanks for your letter received yesterday. I hope you will do your 2,000, & continue to exceed £4 a week. No such photo of me as you want is extant in Europe. It would take at least a month to get one from New York & the cost of each print is five dollars. I am sending you three Japanese prints, one of which is superlative. Also a number of photogravures (real ones) of famous pictures that have never been reproduced for the public. They are issued to members by the Arundel Club, to which I belong. I could send you some framed things for your room, but the risk of the glass being smashed is great, and all railway parcels now run dangers & you never know when they will arrive. Some of these things simply pinned up on your self-chosen wall paper will give the eye agreeable food. I am not yet well, but I have to go to London tomorrow.

Yours, A.B.

94. In one 3-month period of the following year, Septimus operated on 2,561 shells and received £61. 8s. 6d. in wages.

ELDIN / MS / 95
(*To Septimus Bennett*)

Comarques
6th Mch 1916

My dear Sep,

Yes, this shortage of shells is rather a bore, but it might be worse. I wish I had some hobby such as mounting photos or writing letters. I have absolutely no hobby now, as water-colours are off. Nor have I any time for any. In fact I can't even keep up with my reading—I am miles in arrear with it. I can't take anything up after dinner, as we always have 3 or 4 officers here, & I have to be sociable. We have one youth on a visit who has had a year in the trenches & is on leave with a strained heart. He had a bit of an attack this afternoon & is now in bed. The whole East coast has been in alarm about an alleged possible German naval raid for the last fortnight. Guards doubled. Pass words. Batteries doubled; & so on. I have not believed in it, and still don't. But if one did occur, the coastal defences would simply not have a look in against the picked Germans who would land. They are not only third rate, but they are very badly generalled. Indeed it is comic, & is so regarded by the officers who are intelligent. Still, men *have* been sleeping out night after night on the Clacton shore in rain and snow. It is equal to the front for discomfort for them. We had two batteries in the village last week. They have gone forward, & now we have only an ammunition column of about 96 men, & enough explosives to blow up all Essex in my stables.

I got rid of a concert at the Haymarket a fortnight ago, which I organised alone for my Wounded Committee & got £250 net profit, besides vast stores of experience concerning the antics of celebrated singers. I meant to have a half-rest, but the next day I was called upon governmentally to prosecute official propa-ganda in the U.S.A. press, which meant a solid ten days of my time. I have a play to write for Doris Keane which ought to have been begun last Friday, but which probably now will stand over for a month. It is beginning to occur to me that this

war is rather a bore. I am going to dine with the Chancellor of
the Exchequer on Friday.

Marguerite now rides almost daily on army horse, shaddle,
& is much rejuvenated thereby. I don't.

Our loves,

Yours, A.B.

Oh! By the way, the article has not yet appeared in the
Westminster. There have been great mix-ups. You shall have it in
due course.

A.B.

95. See Vols. I and II for accounts of the Haymarket concert.

On the American actress Doris Keane (1881–1945) see Vols. I and III. The play
intended for her was *Sacred and Profane Love*, which Bennett began writing in April.

Septimus's article seems never to have been published.

ELDIN / MS / 96
(*To Septimus Bennett*)

Comarques
22 Mch 1916

My dear Sep,

Congrats. I meant to have written to you before—after your
previous (depressed) letter: but it was imposs. If I were you I
should leave records alone for a bit. How is the financial aspect
of things now? We are all right here, except that I am suffering
from chronic liver. In fact the doctor came to see me today. It
was not my own doctor, who is in bed with asthma, brought on
by overwork. He sent a locum tenens, who is a medical officer
on sick leave from the front. He has had inflammation of the
smaller intestine for a year, & cannot cure himself! All our
officers left this house at the end of last week. Two others come
in on Saturday. My one personal grievance is that in four
months I have earned just about as much as I give away. This is
not because I have not heaps of remunerative work to do, but
because I have no time to do it in. However, I am going to make
a start on 1st April, or anyhow after Easter, war or no war. If it
wasn't for my forced weekly article in the *Daily News* I should be
earning o. These cheerful persons give me £1,100 a year for a
feature which they do not deny has had an immense &

beneficial influence on their circulation. I do not try to stick them for more lest it should be said that I was trying to batten on the war. However, *Lloyds News*, worried by the terrific competition of the *Sunday Pictorial* & the *Sunday Herald*, are now looking out for a new big feature & they have been ferreting round my way. So I have conveyed to them that money will buy me. They have a circ of two millions. I don't know whether these details interest you, but they have to interest me. Marguerite's sister Gabrielle is very ill with consumption in Paris. I doubt if she will get over it. I have told her for years she would finish herself if she didn't nourish herself better, but there is no dealing with these virgins.

Our loves, A.B.

96. Bennett wrote fifteen articles for *Lloyd's Weekly Newspapers* (which became *Lloyd's Sunday News*) in 1918. He was paid £100 for each article of fifteen hundred words.

KEELE / MS / 97
(*To Marguerite Soulié Bennett*)   Comarques
28 Mars 1916

[no salutation]
   Tu dis que je t'agace et qu'il faut remettre la chose. Mais moi je ne l'entends pas de cette façon. Je me suis déjà donné un mal de chien pour t'être agréable. J'ai mille autres affaires pour m'occuper. Je ne vois pas pourquoi je m'embêterais plus. Arrange-toi avec le conseil. Tu as tes idées. Ce ne sont pas les idées de Cosfield ni de Canham ni de moi. Mais c'est possible que tu as raison. Canham me dit qu'il voulait discuter la chose avec moi au commencement, mais que tu ne voulais pas. C'est très bien, mais arrange-toi donc. Je te préviens seulement que quand l'inspecteur viendra tu seras certainement forcée de changer tes dispositions, et que tu auras très probablement une histoire avec le conseil; une amende, etc. etc. Et il y a des gens dans le village qui seront enchantés. Il est presque certain que c'est ces gens qui se sont déjà approchés de l'inspecteur du conseil. Canham enverra le nouveau plan jeudi. Miss Nerney a tous les documents.

A.B.

You would have had no difficulty over the hut if you had left it to me. But when I tell you something you always contradict. How much trouble did I have with the urinoir!! There is nothing to understand about the thing. The plan has been drawn exactly as the council asked. It has been sent in. You will hear the result. You always think you know better than I do, and you don't learn by experience. That is the pity. I have to suffer. It is *absolutely untrue* to say that you don't get protection from me. You get every protection from me. A great deal more than you deserve, because whenever I protect you you resent it. Je peux te dire que JE SUIS EXTRÊMEMENT IRRITÉ par ton attitude inexcusable. Je fais tout ce que je peux pour ton hut. Je bûche toute une matinée, et à la fin tu me dis que je t'agace, et que tu regrettes de m'avoir demandé quoi que ce soit, et tu m'engueules, et tu contredis tout ce que je dis. Voilà ma récompense! J'ai eu largement assez de ces manières là. Je n'ai pas la moindre intention de discuter des règlements avec toi. J'ai beau t'expliquer, tu me soutiendrais toujours le contraire. Si tu laisses la chose à moi, tu n'auras aucune difficulté. Si tu ne veux pas — eh bien, tu t'arrangeras je suppose. Et je suppose aussi que ta malhonnêteté remarquable vers ton innocent mari continuera.

Pour le 'Temporary' j'ai discuté ça avec M. Canham. Nous étions du même avis. En tout cas le meeting du Conseil se passe aujourd'hui. Il n'y a rien à faire, et il n'y a pas à s'en inquiéter. Je t'avais déjà prévenu qu'il y aurait des histoires, mais ça ne t'empêche pas de prendre au sérieux tout ce que les vieillards les plus idiots et les plus intrigants du pays te disent. Tâche d'être un peu raisonnable et un peu plus juste avec moi.

A.B.

97. [You say that I get on your nerves and that the thing must be put off. But that's not how I see it. I have already given myself a hell of a pain, to be nice to you. I have a thousand other things to attend to. I don't see why I should bother any more. Make your own arrangements with the Council. You have your own ideas. They are not the same as Cosfield's or Canham's or mine. But you may be right. Canham tells me that he wanted to discuss the thing with me at the beginning, but that you didn't want him to. All right then, now you do it yourself. But I warn you, when the inspector comes, you will certainly be made to change your arrangements and you will most probably have a row with the council, a fine etc., etc. And some people in the village will be delighted. It is almost certainly these people who have already had a word with the Council inspector. Canham will send the new plan on Thursday. Miss Nerney has all the documents.... I can tell you that *I am extremely irritated* by your inexcusable attitude. I do everything I can for your hut. I slave for a whole morning, and at the end you tell me

I get on your nerves and that you are sorry you ever asked me to do anything, and you shout at me and contradict everything I say. So that's my reward. I have had more than enough of this behaviour. I have not the slightest intention of discussing the regulations with you. In vain I explain to you, you always take the opposite view. If you leave the thing to me, you will have no difficulties. If you don't want to—well, I suppose you'll make your own arrangements. And I also suppose that your remarkable dishonesty towards your innocent husband will continue.

About the 'temporary', I have discussed it with Mr Canham. We were of the same opinion. Anyway the Council meeting is taking place today. There is nothing to be done about it and there is nothing to worry about. I had already warned you that there would be problems but that doesn't stop you taking seriously what all the stupidest and most scheming old men in the village tell you. Try to be a bit more reasonable and a bit fairer to me.]

Cosfield: presumably another employee.

In his memoir Frederick Marriott describes a visit to Comarques during the war.

Arnold Bennett and his wife were doing everything they could for the benefit of the troops. They had a large wooden hut constructed on their grounds, and equipped it with a stage and piano, tables, chairs, and a good variety of games, such as chess, draughts, cards etc.... There was a plentiful supply of tea, coffee, and soft drinks served by Mrs. Bennett and willing helpers from the village whom she enlisted to assist with the work.

Entertainments were organised which discovered talented performers among the officers and men of the army, and augmented by local talent.... Arnold Bennett was so busily engaged in London on official work that he couldn't actively cooperate in these jolly affairs, which were entirely arranged by his wife. I well remember the pride with which she told me that she had sung an old French popular song at one of the concerts, and that 'the Tommies loved it'. With a characteristic ripple of laughter, she said, 'And now I am the favourite artiste of the company.'

ELDIN / MS / 98
(*To Septimus Bennett*)

Comarques
9th May 1916

My dear Sep,

Thanks for your three letters. Your last, about F. C. B., is exactly right. You did excellently to do your best for the invading girls, and all that you say on this is very interesting. As to the possible effect of the changes on your income you must not worry about that as the matter will be arranged. You must let me know when the state of your balances requires adjustment. The chances of your having to go into the army, though they exist, are in my opinion rather small. I regard both the last Conscription Act & the present Conscription Bill as a mistake on the whole, but you can't make a nation show more intelligence than it has—at any rate in war time. I have been asked by

the French government to write my views about British conscription for the chief French daily (*Le Temps*) & I have done
so—with due discretion. The war may end sooner than many
people think. My view is that the Eastern front is the danger
point. I never have believed in the Russians and still don't. I
should say that the Germans will next try an offensive on the
Eastern front, & if it is at all successful the war may be
prolonged. If it isn't there is a chance of a German cave-in. The
Asia Minor position is all right for the Allies, and the Salonika
people will be doing something soon. In Essex the military are
all on fire preparing for an invasion. The first serious defences
against an invasion are now being made. I have no belief in it
myself, but the civilian part of the organisation falls on me as
War Office representative for over 30 parishes, including about
15 miles of coast. Officers are sitting up nights at the telephones
waiting for alarms etc. I feel sure that if the Germans did
manage to land events for a few days would be in a high degree
disconcerting. Among other trifles for which I have the chief
responsibility is a War-Fair at the Islington Market—with
1,500 stalls, 6,000 helpers; the biggest thing of the kind ever
organised. I am also writing a play, and writing (official)
articles for America about British affairs. Still, we shall open a
sort of tennis season on Saturday next, w.p.

I want to know what you have to say about the £225 lent to
you by the Pater, & regarded by the executors as a debt to the
estate. That the cash will not be forthcoming we vaguely guess.
But ought your share of the estate to be set off against the debt
in your opinion? I desire your views. Frank has a similar debt of
£350 which he admits. I have one of £620 which will be paid
except to those beneficiaries who are in debt to me.

Yours, A.B

98. F.C.B.: Frank Bennett.
Bennett wrote several articles in the *Daily News* attacking conscription.
Le Temps published Bennett's piece without his name on 10 May.
The War-Fair took place on 6 and 7 June. For an account of it see Vol. III.
An article by Bennett on the Irish Easter Uprising appeared in the *New York Times* on
28 May and again in *Current History* in July.
Bennett's mother died on 23 November 1914. The estate was still in process of
settlement.

ELDIN / MS / 99
(*To Septimus Bennett*)

Comarques
31 May 1916

My dear Sep,

Thanks. I return these statements. Strange that you should have handled exactly the same number of shells in each week of the fortnight. In spite of your warning I am bound to be struck by the disproportion between your output and the others'. It is enormous. Financially this change doesn't seem to have done you harm, and surely in other ways the change is an advantage. The new job must be more varied & less slave-like than the old. I don't know how you manage with six girls. It takes me all my time to look after one girl—my secretary. And now you will apparently have no Whit holiday. Evidently they mean to merge Whitsun & August bank into one orgy. It makes no difference to me, as I keep on all the time. I am always being told that I am a tremendous worker & that I work too hard. But I know it is not so, because almost all my work is really a lark & I never under any circs work in the evening. Also I am quite free as to hours, & I am in a position to tell anybody & everybody to go to hell. Occasionally I exercise this exquisite privilege. The tennis season is now in almost full fury here. I play on this lawn, at the Frinton Tennis Club, & also at the Brigade Head-quarters where everybody calls the General 'Sir' in every sentence. He is 60 & a very lively player. His aide de camp & I felt it our duty to beat him & the brigade major yesterday. He is very peppery—no, rather peppery. The preparations to receive the Germans here continually grow, but I don't think much of them, & the immediate consequences of a German landing would still be hideous. But I don't think there'll be any German landing. There is a most powerful rumour that all leave-passes of soldiers are now endorsed: 'If peace should be agreed before the expiration of your leave, you are to report yourself at your regimental depot.' Seeing that leave very rarely exceeds 14 days I have always denied this, & I have heard it authoritatively denied. On the other hand I have seen a man who has seen a man who had it on his pass. I am also positively informed that all postal mails between England & the B.E.F. are stopped for one month henceforward. If this does not mean the offensive

what does it mean? However, experience has taught me to
believe naught, especially from the mouths of ministers & the
higher journalistic nobs and generals. The Caledonian War-
Fair (on behalf of the Wounded Allies Relief Committee), of
which I am theoretically in supreme charge, takes place at the
Islington Cattle Market next week. After which I shall breathe
again. There are about 5,000 helpers. There are 6 military
bands. I have made a bet that the net profits are less than
£10,000, but I may lose. Six girls are nothing to this load, after
all. I send you a good new book of sarcasm.

Yours, A.B.

ELDIN / MS / 100
(*To Septimus Bennett*)

Comarques
11th July 1916

My dear Sep,

   Although losing your lathe would be a considerable bore, &
loss I suppose, I don't mind that so much. What I should mind
would be your being shoved into the army. A piece of folly at
your age. I hope it won't occur. All your details have an
exceeding interest. Give Robert my nephewly sympathies as to
his mother. He will like to have them. My play was sold in the
early part of the year. That was why I decided to write it. It will
be produced by Doris Keane (unless she decides to forfeit her
money rather than produce) & she will play the principal part
but *when* she will produce, & whether she will produce it first in
London or in New York, God knows. I expect to finish it on
Saturday. To my great content. I *did* see the film version of *The
Great Adventure*. In fact I was at the first performance of it in
London. Of course it was tremendously vulgarised, but it was
certainly not so bad as I expected. It contained some ideas that
would have been in the play if I had thought of them. Only I
didn't. The only real news that I know of is that Marguerite & I
have offered to take over the upbringing of Richard, & that the
parents thereof have consented.

Our loves,

Thine, A.B

100. Robert: unidentified.
    Doris Keane did not produce *Sacred and Profane Love*. It was first produced at the

Aldwych Theatre on 10 November 1919, and came off after a hundred performances. It had a considerable success in America the following year.

The Great Adventure was produced by Turner Films, with Henry Ainley and Esmé Hubbard in the leading roles. Public release was on 27 March 1916.

The adoption of Richard was apparently at Marguerite's desire, not Bennett's. Visits by Richard over the preceding years had apparently been successful. He was a bright boy, and it was clear that he could benefit from the material advantages that Bennett and Marguerite could offer him. His home in the Potteries was unhappy—his father's law firm was collapsing and his father drank to excess.

CAMBRIDGE / MS / 101
(*To Richard Bennett*)

Comarques
31 July 1916

My dear Richard,

Your letter was good. I showed it to H. G. Wells, who liked it. I also sent it to the Head Master (F. W. Sanderson, M.A.) of Oundle School. I always thought well of this school. Wells's oldest boy (aged 15) is there, & his other boy has been waiting for a year for a place in the School House (there are several houses—350 boys—School House is the best). The Head wrote me that it was true that School House is full, but he will find room for you. Term begins Sept. 26. I want the date of your birth. I also want a certificate of conduct from Dr Rutter. I think you will like this school. Young Wells will put you up to the tricks of the trade. I think this is about all, except that I believe that your father & mother will be satisfied with the results of Oundle. I hope they will. Of course it will be up to you.

The 1/- a week formerly divided between R., C., & V. will after your departure be divided between C. & V. in the proportion of 66.6 to 33.3 unless they want it otherwise.

Yours, Uncle Arnold

Auntie wants you to come to Thorpe *instantly* the seaside is over,
A.B.

101. F. W. Sanderson, d. 1922.

Dr T. F. Rutter (d. 1957), headmaster of Wolstanton Grammar School (today Marshlands High School) 1907–37.

George Philip (Gyp) Wells, b. 1901; Frank Richard, b. 1903.

R., C., and V.: Richard, Clayton, and Vernon Bennett.

ELDIN / MS / 102
(*To Septimus Bennett*)

Comarques
22 Augt 1916

My dear Sep,

I was just about to write to you when your letter came. I hope you *won't* have to go into the army. It would be too footling. You will inform me how things are at Quarter Day or thereabouts. I can tell you one thing—there are fewer changes and mess-ups in Munition Factories than there are in the Army, where life is nothing else but these things—many of them incredibly silly. I am now at work again. Also I have to cycle, as we have only been allotted petrol for 35 miles a week. We have a reserve of petrol, thanks to my deep sagacity, but we don't use it yet. Also I have a second reserve of petrol, of which nobody knows anything except me & the head gardener. Richard arrived last night at 10 pm. in charge of Captain Mason's sister. Cap Ma's is a cap that lived here for some time & still eats here, while sleeping in a tent. His father is head of one of Robert Heath's works. They evidently do very well for themselves. His home is on [?Cloudhead]. His sister was coming to these parts for a visit. Richard seems very lively & pleased with things. As you told me not to tell you anything about the difficulties with F. C. B. I did not do so. The suspicions of Stoke on Trent are well founded, but they will do well not to put their oars in. I am doing all that can be done, & I am losing no time over it. [But the thing must necessarily be slow when F. C. B. is perfectly well aware that no legal proceedings will be taken. Moreover it would be useless to drive him too far. The bare fact is that every cent realised of the mater's estate up to June 30 1916 has been appropriated—disappeared. Of course his attempted justifications are absurd, as he well knows. This result could not have been achieved without the most gross deception of myself throughout. I have done whatever an executor could do, short of declining, 10 months ago, to let him act any further as solicitor. But at that date I had not suspected the lengths to which he would go in ingenious deceit. You had perhaps better not say anything about this, from the point marked above.

Our loves,

Yours, A.B.

102. Captain Mason: not otherwise known. The *Journals* mistakenly identify him as A. E. W. Mason, the author, who was also a friend of Bennett's.

ELDIN / MS / 103
(*To Septimus Bennett*)

Comarques
29 Augt 1916

My dear Sep,

Many thanks. I think there is no doubt but that you will get your holiday. I should urgently advise you not to take any drugs except under the advice of a doctor. If you do you will certainly regret it. The Boots stuff is of course a drug. Drugs don't create energy; they only draw it out of the reserve more quickly. This is obvious. Foods create energy. Advice as to diet is what you want.

Need I say that I am fully expecting, sooner or later, a crash on Frank's part? The last family crash cost me £3,500. The next won't. Alice Longson is going to be married to a son of Malkin, flint miller. As I keep an eye on this family, out of regard for Uncle's blindness, I have sent her a present. The ineffable Willie has now got a post as assistant Tax-surveyor, & regards his future as bright. The letter which this youth sent me when I took financial charge of Uncle's eye operation is the most priceless epistolary document I ever saw. I will show it to you one day. Yet I think he means well. What with dentist & insomnia (not due to dentist) I am rather slack now. I do water colours. We are pleased with Richard. There is something in him. But for sarcasm he takes the first prize in the whole family.

Thine, A.B.

103. The last family crash was presumably Frank Beardmore's. He founded the firm of Frank Beardmore & Co. at the Sutherland Pottery, Fenton, where in 1901 he produced his famous Sutherland Art Ware. Septimus designed for him. He was a gentle, emotional man, and carried a copy of *The Tempest* with him that he recited from when deeply moved. His firm crashed in 1913. Bennett contributed £500 towards redeeming the furniture of the house and giving it to Fanny Gertrude.

Alice Longson (b. 1884), another daughter of Bennett's uncle John, married William Malkin. Willie: unidentified; possibly William (b. 1891), son of another John Longson, joiner, at Fenton.

ELDIN / MS / 104
(*To Septimus Bennett*)

Comarques
23 Sept 1916

My dear Sep,

I have sent some blue to Maud. Rather worn but wearable. Your takings seem to be on the upgrade. I have been semi-idle for some time, & water colouring—going out with a fine painter of the name of Wright, and improving myself. But at the end of the month I begin a novel. We have sent Richard to Oundle School, & it is a good one. I think he will be all right in every way. Anyhow it's an experiment. Marguerite is in London. We may have a flat there. Marguerite wants one, & I shall have to be in London somewhat as my new novel is about London & I don't seem to know anything about London. Rather awkward. We have a convalescent wounded officer here, recouping. Aged 21. When he came he said (quite a stranger to us): 'I know you're very intellectual, Mr. Bennett, & I want to explain to you that I have no brains.'

Thine, A.B.

104. John Wright (1857–1933).
The Roll-Call: begun on 16 October 1916 and finished the following 30 April.

ELDIN / MS / 105
(*To Septimus Bennett*)

Comarques
3 Oct 1916

My dear Sep,

Thanks. The nearest we have been to a Zep raid is that our own shrapnel fell within 2,000 yards of the house. Zeps are both seen & heard here, but they would only drop bombs on us by mistake. From my experience of being under fire at the front, I can imagine that you have had all you want & a bit over. A young officer here went home to Streatham for 4 days leave, & during the night found himself dropped in bed through the second floor into the bathroom on the first floor. Unhurt, but obviously suffering from shock. I have just spent 5 days at Corfe Castle painting with a watercolourist named John Wright. Very good man. I have made progress. In fact you will be surprised. The mater affair is still hung up, waiting for counsel's opinion which is to settle the dispute on a point of law between Frank & me. When this comes along I shall send a formal report to all of you, and the trouble will begin. Richard is at Oundle School, & has run $2\frac{1}{2}$ miles in 17 minutes. Also he makes munitions there. It is a wonderful school & a ditto headmaster. We went to inspect & I was impressed. I begin a new novel.

Thine, A.B.

ELDIN / MS / 106
(*To Septimus Bennett*)

Comarques
15 Oct 1916

My dear Sep,
    Your accounts are colossal. You ought to be chief accountant at Vickers'. And if you had less brains you would make a marvellous private secretary. Your wages are evidently on the upgrade. However, I agree with you that you oughtn't to work so hard. It won't ultimately be good for the war, as you may knock up. And the money anyhow, under the circ., is not worth it. The shell total is prodigious. The story about abandoning God for you is A1. I shall use it. You will infallibly see that story in print soon. I return the ledger. Frame it. Insure it against accident. Anyhow keep it. Nothing can beat it as a civilian memento of the war. Yes, Frank's casual irresponsibility is prodigious. I fear he will have nothing to show after the war. I am still waiting to finish up the mater's estate. But the delay now is apparently partly due to the dearth of barristers caused by the war. I am now in full work again. My London novel is begun. I have to visit munitions factories for the Ministry of Munitions—not to inspect them & put them right, but to describe them for the British & neutral press. I go to Nottingham next Friday I think. The press-publicity of the Ministry of Munitions is now in the hands of Sir Hedley le Bas, who did all the recruiting advertising. I know him pretty well, & when he demands the sacred pen of the novelist, it is imposs. to refuse. Also I think I am about to undertake a special short weekly article for the *New Statesman*. I haven't yet broken it to

Marguerite, as she is so strongly against my doing extra work while on a long novel. Also I haven't broken to her that I have bought a magnificent hospital picture by young Nevinson. Women don't understand the true economy of helping artists while investing your money in property that is bound to go up. Unfortunately while I was keeping a masterly silence, the Leicester Gallery people told the *Daily Mirror*, & as the whole army reads the *Daily Mirror* every officer who comes into the house says: 'I see you've been buying pictures.' Etc. Lively time for my diplomatic skill in equivoque. However, I am emerging well.

Richard seems to be all right. I spent two hours on a monotype this morning & spoilt it through insufficient ink on the plate.

Thine, A.B.

106. Septimus's story appeared in the *New Statesman* on 2 December 1916. It was reprinted as an item in *Things That Have Interested Me* in 1921:

The Appeal to Providence

The air raid of Monday reminds me of an incident in the last air raid over the Midlands. A man, whom I will call Mr. Bigsby, was staying in a house inhabited by five women. In the noise and excitement one of the women dropped on to her knees on the hearth-rug and began to pray. She appealed to Providence, with great apparent sincerity, for some time, and then she suddenly jumped up, crying: 'Oh, dear! This is no good. I'm going to fetch Mr. Bigsby!' and ran out of the room.

Bennett began his anonymous 'Observations' in the *New Statesman* on 28 October, and continued them until 19 April 1919. He was on the board of the journal, and contributed the column gratis. Several of the columns in the latter part of 1916 concerned munitions. The *Daily News* articles were in abeyance from April 1916 until January 1917.

Sir Hedley le Bas (1868–1926), the publisher.

C. R. W. Nevinson (1889–1946).

KEELE / MS / 107
(*To Marguerite Soulié Bennett*)   [Royal Thames Yacht Club]
                                                [80, Piccadilly]
                                                26 Oct 1916

My dear Marguerite,

I had better recall certain facts to your mind. You begin by saying that you are furious with me because I have taken a room at this club. I am determined to stop this at once. Do not think I am vexed. But I will not have any more scenes about my room here. I have already had one too many, & one that I shall not immediately forget.

You always said you wanted a flat in London, but a small one with a kitchen, & that it would cost little. I said I would give you £100 a year for that. I will, *but I will not give more*. I think the idea of having a flat in London during the war can be criticised, but I am quite willing to give way. I have for some time past often told you that I should have to spend more time in London on account of my novel. Trying to combine the two things, I found a furnished flat that might do. You certainly could not find a better at the price. It was central, & no servants are required. So far as I am concerned a flat that is not central & that depends on one's own servants is absolutely out of the question. You did not care for the flat. You not only said that you did not want *that* flat, but that you did not want *any* flat, & that you could not leave the officers. Quite right. I did not mind at all. I then found that I had difficulty in being sure of a room at the club. I took a room definitely, where I can keep all sorts of things that are necessary to my work, & it is cheap. I didn't take it for fun, but for business. It was necessary for me, and necessary *at once*. I can't postpone a decision for weeks. Every week lost is a week lost. My novel has got to go on. I have already quite enough difficulty with my novel, without extraneous difficulties. You can call it a bedroom, or a bureau, or anything you like, but I have got to have it. And you have no right whatever to be furious about it, & I will not stand your being furious about it. You have always said you wanted a small, cheap flat, without servants. Have it, by all means. I shall only be too pleased for you to be pleased. Wherever it is, I can always come to see you in it. If it is not central, & if it is difficult to get to or from & there is trouble with servants, that is your affair. I repeat: do not imagine that I am vexed. I am not. But I am not going to have any more observations about my room at this club, & I hope you will understand.

Thine, A.B.

Unless you hear from me I shall *arrive* at 5 p.m. Friday.

ELDIN / MS / 108
(*To Septimus Bennett*)

Comarques
4th Dec 1916

My dear Sep,

I now have four letters from you unanswered. I have had much physical derangement, ending with congestion of the liver, which has stopped my own (fiction) work for over a week. I hope to resume tomorrow. The Lord Mayor asked me to lunch for last Thursday but at the last I was obliged not to go. The Frank affair will be very difficult. But since I wrote my formal letter I have come round to think with you that legal proceedings *ought* to be taken, & I have told him so. Of course legal proceedings, if they went far, would mean his being struck off the rolls & losing his livelihood and his reputation entirely. However, it is quite simple for him to prevent them. Florence has resources, & she will have more later on. If these are not to be used, the inference is that Florence & her family prefer him to be struck off the rolls. This I doubt! Nothing will ultimately prevent Frank from coming to smash except a constant supply of outside money. I have found him about £1,000 myself in the past, & I am not going to find any more. £700 of this I simply gave him. It is a bit thick that afterwards he should treat me as the correspondence shows he has treated me. Still, I have never been able to feel much resentment against Frank. Emily threatens legal proceedings of her own. But as the bulk of her income is a free gift from me, I flatter myself I can keep her in order.

I hope you will be able to find some one else in the works who can 'see' things from your angle. It is important for you. Your work is very monotonous, but it has this advantage—that the responsibility is definitely limited & is not immense. I wish sometimes I could say the same. A very large part of my time is cut to pieces by affairs which really do not concern me & from which I derive no benefit whatever. I cannot say that I am hard up, though my income has greatly decreased, & the income tax is simply inconceivable. On 1st January I have to pay about £4,000 for income tax & super tax. I shall get a few hundreds returned, but it will still be nearly half of my actual income. These figures are calculated to stagger the stoutest heart. Do not transmit them to anybody else.

The Admiralty have returned my yacht. They didn't want to pay anything for repairs. This really annoyed me, as I lent them the yacht free of charge. I threatened to have a question asked in the House of Commons about the treatment of yacht-owners. They eventually licked my boots. There is too much of this in governmental departments. Marguerite has now got a small & humble flat in London.

Yours, A.B.

P.S. I enclose a form for you to sign.

A.B.

Copy. In consideration of moneys paid to me by him I hereby transfer to my brother Arnold Bennett all my interest in the debt of £525 owing by him to the estate of Sarah Ann Bennett deceased and I renounce in his favour all claims in regard to it. Dated Dec. 5th 1916.

108. Marguerite's flat was 6 Thackeray Mansions, 52 Oxford Street.

KEELE / MS / 109
(*To Marguerite Soulié Bennett*)

Comarques
mercredi
27–12–16

Infanta cara,

J'espère que tu auras une bonne journée très réussie. J'ai trouvé mon billet sur la table de la salle à manger. Merci. Je te conseille de réflechir un poco avant de flanquer ton argent dans un abonnement pour Arno. Tu n'as pas encore la moindre idée si ça va réussir ou non. Par hasard j'ai vu ce matin Ethel qui montait un plateau au deuxième. J'enquête. Richard au lit.

'Comment, tu es souffrant?'

'Non, je me porte très bien.'

'Pourquoi donc es-tu au lit?'

'C'est tante qui m'a dit hier soir de rester au lit aujourd'hui à cause d'un commencement de rhume.'

Pourtant hier soir la dernière chose que tu m'as dit à moi c'était qu'aujourd'hui Richard pourrait aller jouer avec Phyllis. Je ne dis rien sur l'idée de mettre un enfant au lit à cause

d'un commencement de rhume: ni sur l'idée de condamner un
enfant à une journée de lit sans se donner la peine de s'informer
le matin si c'est nécessaire. Mais je pourrais dire quelquechose
sur l'idée enfantine de dire une chose à Richard et une autre
chose à moi. Naturellement puisqu'il fait très beau, et puisque
Richard se porte très bien, je lui ai donné la permission de se
lever quand il veut.

Je travaille, mais je ne sais pas si mon travail est bien.

Je te bise.

Ton N.

109. [I hope you will have a very good and successful day. I found my ticket on the
dining room table. Thank you. I advise you to think *un poco* before throwing your money
away on a subscription for Arno. You have no idea yet whether or not it will be a
success. This morning I happened to see Ethel taking a tray up to the second floor. I
made enquiries. Richard was in bed.

'What, are you ill?'

'No, I'm very well.'

'Then why are you in bed?'

'Yesterday evening, aunt told me to stay in bed today because I'm starting a cold.'

But the last thing you said to me yesterday evening was that Richard could go and
play with Phyllis today. I make no comment on the idea of putting a child to bed
because he is starting a cold; nor on the idea of condemning a child to a day in bed
without taking the trouble to find out in the morning whether it's necessary. But I could
well have something to say about the childish idea of telling Richard one thing and me
another. Naturally, as the weather is fine and Richard is perfectly all right, I told him he
could get up when he wanted to. I am working, but I do not know whether my work is
any good. I kiss you.]

ELDIN / MS / 110
(*To Septimus Bennett*)

Comarques
1st Jan 1917

My dear Sep,

Thank you for yours. It was a good letter. I have begun the
N. Y. with a violent colic, & feel very feeble. Also with a visit to
the dentists. So that I am not yet recovered. Richard also is
denting. The dentist says his teeth are *very* bad—naturally.
Happily they have not been neglected as ours were, & as his pa
has always neglected his own. By the way, if I have much more
trouble with Frank I shall simply put the matter into the hands
of another solicitor, with carte blanche. The amount of time I
have to give in order to cope with Frank's inexpressible &

continual slackness is really ridiculous. You will do quite right to go and live in the country after the war. The Potteries *is* a horrible place to live in, & it is a good thing you have perceived it acutely. Of course you won't be able to move during the war. I quite expect that after the war you will be able to resume your position in the Pots. The same causes that operated before will operate again. But times will be hard—that is certain; even if they aren't special hard for the first year or two, they will be hard later on. Personally I shall not have a good year this year. But 1918 ought to be a pretty good one for me. You will let me gaze upon your marvellous bookkeeping & tell me the amount you need to balance the ledger & it will be forthcoming. I have heard twice from the Barlows. They seem very cheerful, but Auntie Sarah's reference to the raid was indicative enough. As a fact, I scarcely knew there *had* been a raid in the Potteries. I have never heard anything of the damage done—except to Auntie Sarah's nerves.

We are getting on all right with Richard. But he is very raw material on the surface. Marguerite's efforts to make him take part in the conversation at table are excrutiatingly funny. One of her chief points is that he is absolutely obedient, when the thing to be done is defined. When you merely instruct him to talk he merely doesn't. He is by nature idle—that is certain. He gets on excellently with young women. It is of course lamentable that you have to be away from your children. But it is better that it should be now than 8 years later, that's all.

I expect to be fully recovered from my influenza in about a year.

Yours, A.B.

110. Sarah Barlow, Enoch Bennett's sister, was married to Samuel Barlow (d. 1924). Bennett describes them in 'The Making of Me'.

She was a tall, slim, auburn-haired, refined, and yet forceful woman, who had clear and personal ideas about books. She quarrelled with her fiancé, a plumber and an organist and a 'cellist, and while living within a mile of him, never spoke to him for a dozen years or so. They then met again, married, and were perfectly happy ever after.... Their sitting room was behind the plumber's shop. The furniture of it was never altered.

Septimus's children were born in 1908 (Ruth) and 1910 (John).

KEELE / MS / 111
(*To Marguerite Soulié Bennett*)

Royal Thames Yacht Club
25-1-17

My lonely girl,

J'ai regretté d'être forcé de te laisser toute seule cet ap. Il faut que tu apprennes te servir de Londres. Tu as des amis — et des amis qui seraient enchantés de passer la soirée avec toi quand je suis pris, mais toujours faut-il faire les arrangements d'avance. Tu savais vendredi dernier que je serais pris les soirées de mard., merc., et jeud. cette semaine. Fallait t'arranger. Si tu laisses les arrangements jusqu'au soir même tu seras toujours fichue parce que Londres ne vit pas comme ça. La semaine dernière j'ai passé 3 soirées sur 4 avec toi. Mais ça ne pourrait toujours se passer comme ça. FROID DE LOUP à l'impériale de l'omnibus.

Je te bise tendrement.

Nouche

111. [I was sorry to have to leave you all by yourself this aft. You must learn to make use of London. You have friends—friends who would be delighted to spend an evening with you when I am engaged, but you must always make the arrangements in advance. You knew last Friday that I would be engaged on Tues., Wed., and Thurs. evenings this week. You should have made arrangements. If you leave the arrangements until the last moment, you will always be done for, because London life is not like that. Last week I spent 3 evenings out of 4 with you, but it can't always be like that. *Cold as the grave* on the outside of the bus. I kiss you tenderly.]

KEELE / MS / 112
(*To Marguerite Soulié Bennett*)

Comarques
vendredi
26-1-17

Ma chérie enfant,

C'est parfait. Je comprends tes idées, et je les partage. Je ne releverai rien de ce que tu as dit. Je dînerai avec toi mercredi soir. J'avais un autre rendezvous, mais je peux le changer (chez Rickards). Le fait est que je me plais toujours avec toi seule, et je ne m'embête pas. Ce matin j'ai failli d'envoyer mon train au diable et venir te voir. Mais je suis trop pris pour me permettre de tels caprices.

Il faut maintenant que je te dise quelquechose de ma part.

Nous nous voyons *beaucoup plus* que la plupart des époux. Nous ne pouvons pas toujours nous voir, quand nous nous voyons, seuls. Il faut souvent qu'il y a du monde. Or, quand il y a du monde tu n'es pas toujours la même femme. C'est peut-être la nervosité, c'est peut-être inconscient, mais c'est ainsi. Quand il y a du monde, c'est comme si tu avais une seule idée dans la tête — de me discuter ou de me critiquer. Tu ne le soupçonnes pas, au moins je l'espère. Des phrases comme,

> Ne l'écoutez pas
> Quel type.
> Tu es extraordinaire.
> Si j'étais libre....
> Tu es....
> Comment peux-tu dire...?
> Rubbish!

sortent continuellement de ta bouche. Je ne saurais pas dire à quel point je trouve ça assommant. Et de plus en plus. Je veux dire ces deux idées — que je suis l'être le plus bizarre qui ait jamais existé, et que tu es une femme esclave, l'une aussi fausse que l'autre. Je t'assure que des fois quand je suis dans le monde et tu n'es pas là je me dis: Je regrette qu'elle n'est pas là, mais au moins on ne relèverai pas tout ce que je dis. Je t'assure que le soir que j'ai amené Ross, par exemple, tu ne m'as pas dit *un seul mot* agréable, mais beaucoup de désagréables. Et tu ne le soupçonnes pas. Aussi, pour le monde tu es extrêmement difficile. Ross, par exemple, a enchanté Mrs. Wheeler. C'est un homme exquis, causeur très brillant, très estimé, très recherché, aussi patriote que n'importe qui; mais parce que sa conversation était moins crûment chauviniste que la plupart des conversations d'officiers etc. auxquelles nous assistons, il ne t'a pas plue. Pourtant la plupart de tout ce qu'il a dit — ce sont les lieux communs des gens cultivés. Je sais très bien que les conversations sur la littérature et la politique anglaises sont très difficiles pour toi, mais une femme comme toi sait toujours s'en tirer si elle veut. Je pourrais amener toutes sortes de personnes chez toi, et elles ne seraient que trop contentes de venir, mais je crains toujours t'embêter. Madame Vandervelde, par ex., chez qui j'ai dîné mercredi. C'est une femme cosmopolitaine et brillante, épouse d'un ministre belge. Mais dieu sait si tu ne la détesterais pas. C'est vrai qu'elle n'est pas la perfection. Son flat est froid comme un parc en hiver. Si tu l'invitais pour le thé, elle volerait vers toi.

Je te dis comme tu me dis: Ne relève pas ce que je t'ai dit. Je comprends très bien tes idées. C'est tout ce qu'il faut. Je suis même passablement flatté. Tout ce que je te dis dans cette lettre je te le dis amoureusement.

Tu ne seras jamais heureuse à Londres si tu ne trouves pas quelquechose à faire, et quelquechose de sérieux. C'est impossible. Du reste le spectacle d'une femme qui va toutes les semaines à Londres exclusivement pour son plaisir n'est pas très joli à l'heure qu'il est, surtout quand cette femme est toi qui as fait tant pour des officiers et des soldats. Je te bise et je t'aime.

[A.B.]

P.S. Je n'ai jamais trouvé l'occasion de te dire que ce mot 'rubbish,' dont tu te sers de plus en plus *n'est pas bien.* Tu l'as très innocemment pris de Tertia. Ça peut aller dans Waterloo Road. Dans notre monde c'est [?].

112. [Perfect. I understand and share your ideas. I won't argue with anything you said. I will dine with you on Wednesday evening. I had another engagement, but I can change it (at Rickards'). The fact is that I am always happy and never bored alone with you. This morning I nearly consigned my train to hell and came to see you. But I am too busy to be able to allow myself such whims.

Now I have something that I must say to you. We see each other much more than most husbands and wives. We cannot always see each other alone, when we see each other. Often other people have to be there. Now when other people are there, you are often not the same woman. Perhaps it is nervousness, perhaps it's unconscious, but it is so. When other people are there, you appear to have only one idea in your head—to argue with me or criticize me. You don't realize that you are doing it—at least I hope you don't. Phrases such as

> Don't listen to him
> What a fellow
> You are extraordinary
> If I were free . . .
> You are . . .
> How can you say . . . ?
> Rubbish!

come out of your mouth all the time. I can't express how tedious I find it. More and more. I mean these two themes—that I am the most extraordinary person who has ever lived and that you are an enslaved wife—each as false as the other. I can tell you that sometimes when I am in company and you are not there, I say to myself: I am sorry she isn't here but at least no one will pick on everything I say. I can tell you that the evening I brought Ross, for example, you did not say *one single* pleasant word to me, but a lot of unpleasant ones. And you don't know you are doing it. In addition, you are extremely difficult about your social life. For example, Ross charmed Mrs Wheeler. He is an exquisite man, a very brilliant conversationalist, very highly regarded, very much sought after, as patriotic as the next man; but because his conversation was less crudely chauvinist than that of most of the officers etc. that we hear, you did not like him. But most of the things he said were the commonplaces of cultivated people. I am well aware that conversations about English literature and politics are very difficult for you, but a woman like you can always make out all right if she wants to. I could bring all sorts of people to visit you, and they would be only too pleased to come, but I am always afraid of boring you. For ex., Mrs Vandervelde, at whose house I dined on Wednesday. She is a brilliant, cosmopolitan woman, married to a Belgian Minister. But God knows whether you might not take a dislike to her. Of course she is not perfection. Her flat is as cold as a park in winter. If you invited her to tea, she would come flying to you.

I say to you what you say to me: don't pick on everything I say. I understand your ideas very well. They are all we need. I am even quite flattered. Everything I tell you in this letter is said lovingly.

You will never be happy in London unless you find something to do, something serious. Otherwise it's impossible. Anyway a woman who goes to London every week solely for her own pleasure does not make a very pretty sight at the present time, particularly when the woman is you, who has done so much for officers and soldiers. I kiss you and I love you. . . . PS. I have never found an opportunity to tell you that this word 'rubbish' which you use more and more often *is not good*. You picked it up innocently from Tertia. It goes down all right in Waterloo Road. In our world, it is [?].]

For letters to Robert Ross (1869–1918), Oscar Wilde's defender, see Vols. II and III. For letters to Gwladys Wheeler see Vol. III. She had theatre interests, and directed Dorothy Cheston Bennett in *Byron* in 1929 (see pp. 554–5).

Dr Jeanne Vandervelde, wife of Emile Vandervelde (d. 1938), Belgian minister of state.

ELDIN / MS / 113
(*To Septimus Bennett*)

Comarques
28–1–17

My dear Sep,

I have your Thatched House letter. I expect you will soon speed up. In fact I have no doubt you will. I had the crucial interview with Frank on Tuesday. He came up to London to see me. He is ruined. Happily, owing to the dearth of men, he will probably be able to get a situation. His practice will be closed down as quickly as possible. He has behaved with the most astounding casualness & indifference. For some time past the working expenses of his business have exceeded the *gross* receipts therefrom by at least £3 a week. I should say that for years the gross receipts have never even equalled the expenses. As he has kept on spending money just the same he has obviously had to get the money from somewhere. The result of course was inevitable. Yet in the matter of providing a statement & clearing things up he is now showing exactly the same slackness as he has shown in everything else. However, I have now begun to bully him. He himself saw that he was in danger of prison. It was rather an understatement than otherwise. I regard all this as chiefly due to drink. There is one thing that cannot be made too clear to everyone. Namely, that the idea that he impoverished himself & the business in order to keep the mater is quite incorrect. I have gone into the accounts myself, & his payments to the mater averaged 14/8^d a week; which cannot be called excessive. Florence herself had no idea of this. I am very sorry for her. At least £1,700 has absolutely disappeared: probably much more, but I know of sums amounting to that.

A friend of mine, Lieut. Samuels, [?] Camp, Sheffield, is now in your neighbourhood. Architect, writer; peculiar, interesting, & very agreeably gloomy. I gave him your address & said he might write you in case sometime you had a Sunday free. You might drop him a line if you think fit. Aged about 30.

Yours, A.B.

113. Lieut. Samuels is not otherwise known.
The portion of the letter from 'for some time' to 'due to drink' and from 'at least £1,700' to 'amounting to that' is marked private.

ELDIN / MS / 114
(*To Septimus Bennett*)

Comarques
12th Feby 1917

My dear Sep,

We regret this finger accident, & hope to hear that the said limb is going on all right. I should say that if the accident doesn't affect you, you will ultimately beat the 'star' man. You should certainly not put more into war loan than you can afford. You already have no margin, and nothing in the way of reserve. A great deal of half-truth has to be talked about war-loan in order to fit the subject for the ear of the masses. The bigger the loan is the better it will be for the government, but the government could carry on the war for years, by means of treasury bills, without any war loan at all in the ordinary sense of the term. A big war loan looks well, it may save a little in interest, it keeps people from wasting the amount which they have put into the loan and therefore prevents a waste of corresponding labour to that extent, it is a symbol of national perseverance. But it is by no means necessary to the prosecution of the war, & people who run undue risks in order to subscribe to it are making a mistake from both the national point of view and their own. However, war loan can always be resold. I have taken £300 of it. I couldn't take more, having regard to my liabilities known & unknown. I now see that Frank's affair will ultimately cost me a further £700 at least, which I think is a bit thick. The alternatives to this forking-out would be either Frank going to prison, or being utterly disgraced in a bankruptcy examination, *or* the disappearance of the whole of the remains of Florence's means. Anyhow I should have to pay. Frank's affairs will not bear public examination. Hence certain creditors must be kept out of the bankruptcy. The sole reason why Frank did not furnish the statement which D'Arcy & I specially met in London to discuss was idleness & negligence & slackness. This is difficult to believe, but it is so. It appears that D'Arcy has probably got him the offer of a situation as solicitor's managing clerk in Manchester. I am fairly sure I can get him a temporary situation in the office of the Public Trustee—in fact it has already been almost offered. Both these things are before Frank. It remains to be seen how he will handle them. Nobody can handle them for him. Let us know about finger.

Yours, A.B.

As to liquidation & 2/- in £ of F. W. B's estate, I haven't heard of any defalcation there. If there is one, it is yet another concealment of Frank's. But I doubt the tale.

A.B.

114. F.W.B.: Francis William Beardmore.

KEELE / MS / 115
(*To Marguerite Soulié Bennett*)

Royal Thames Yacht Club
15th Feby 1917

My dear Marguerite,

I have your letter. I shall continue to maintain that you ought not to have given the order without first consulting me, & that I had the right to protest. I did protest, & I do protest, but that is not to say I am angry. You yourself said in your letter that you knew it would make me angry. Yet you did it. Comment is needless. The matter concerns me just as much as it does you. It humiliates me deeply. Supposing that an officer came to us to dinner, and said: 'I am staying in a house where they have central heating, but when they go to London they take the heat off!' what would you say? You would be furious, once more, & talk as you always do about the way soldiers are treated; and you would be right! As for the economic side, that cannot be disputed. Neither wood nor coke in the grates will heat those rooms, & whatever is used will cost more than the central heating. The coal question is very serious, and so is the money question. Of course if, having no money, you still go and buy things at bazaars, that is your affair.

I cannot, save very exceptionally, lunch with you when I am in London. I do not come to London for pleasure. It is absolutely necessary for my articles & my work that I should see a great deal of men of affairs, politicans, etc., & I can only see them at lunch time. I work all the time; I have a great deal to do; I have a large number of anxieties of all sorts. All my lunches are for the purposes of my work, & they are very valuable to me. In fact they are essential. Evenings are quite different. I usually *do* dine with you, each week. I have spent three evenings with you de suite. I could have spent two evenings with you this week, but you are engaged. I am not in the least blaming you for being engaged. You asked me to dine with you tonight. But you did not ask yourself what I should do after dinner. Was I to go back & work, or was I to go to bed? You surely did not expect me to go and see that desolating play of Knoblock's *again*. You surely must realise the awful, bad effect of such plays on an artist. Or don't you?

I shall not come to see you this morning. I cannot do it. You are always saying: 'Je ne peux rien dire.' Etc etc. But when anybody else says anything, even if it is only in reply to you, you get angry. You say it is irritating for you to control yourself. Of course it is. It is irritating for everybody to control himself. Nevertheless self-control is essential in any regular & organised society. In this particular difference between us the point is quite plain. You have a perfectly free hand to do exactly as you like in matters which affect only you. Everybody knows that you are as free as any wife, and infinitely more free than the vast majority. But you are not free to do as you like in matters which concern both of us without at least first consulting me. This I insist on. It is a principle which I practise myself, and I shall insist on it, whatever happens. I have had to insist on it before. I should never do such a thing to you; and you are not going to do it to me. You deliberately did a thing which you quite expected would annoy me. It was a thing which concerned me, and which of course must humiliate me before our guests. (It could not have made any difference to you as you were coming to London. It merely cost more money, while leaving the house uncomfortable!) What is that but a deliberate challenge to me, a défi. You say you know me. If you do, you know that I am the man to take up a challenge. I could quite understand that in giving the order you had not fully realised what you were doing. But your letter this morning put a different light on the matter, and it is not agreeable.

Yours, A.B.

115. Knoblock's play was perhaps *A Government Office*, produced early in the month at the Comedy Theatre, with Charles Hawtrey and Gladys Cooper. During the War Knoblock wrote a number of pieces that were produced briefly in aid of charities and the war effort generally. Another sketch, *A War Committee*, was put on at the Queen's Theatre at the end of January.

KEELE / MS / 116
(*To Marguerite Soulié Bennett*)

Comarques
28 Feby 1917

Infanta carissima,
Thy letter received. I wrote 2 articles yesterday. I dined with H. G. & Rebecca West at Victoria, & went to bed at 10.30.

Goodish night. Today,—novel. Lunch with editor of *Statesman*. Dinner with Shufflebotham (type médecin expert des 5 villes). Je passerai demain jeudi vers 7.30 au plus tard. We will dine either in or out as you wish. If you closed up Comarques you would soon have me ill. Apart from that, I fear you do not realise that I cannot carry on my work without my books & without an office, & that to close Comarques would cause me the most grave inconvenience—quite apart from my health. However, we needn't trouble about that, as Comarques will not, I imagine, be closed as long as I can afford to keep it open.

10.30 a.m. J'ai déjà fait une heure de trav.

Ton mari te bise.

[A.B.]

116. Rebecca West (1892–1983) was known to Bennett chiefly via H. G. Wells. For other references to her see Vol. I.

Clifford Sharp (1883–1935) was editor of the *New Statesman* from 1913 to 1931.

Dr Frank Shufflebotham (d. 1932) was Bennett's personal physician for a while and also a friend.

ELDIN / MS / 117
(*To Septimus Bennett*)

Royal Thames Yacht Club
4th Mch 1917

My dear Sep,

I've been too busy to write, in a burst of fecundity over my novel. When in London I get up early to write letters. It is not so easy at home, as before breakfast I discuss God, man, & woman with Marguerite. Tertia & Marguerite junior are coming for the next weekend. Mr. Canoodle Canoodle is *not* coming. I suppose he keeps the house. Frank's engagement as managing clerk to a first-class firm in Rochdale is now settled, subject to his clearing up his own practice. This will be very difficult without a bankruptcy, & if he bankrupts he loses his certificate & can't practice as a solicitor. I seem to glimpse through the end of a telescope that it will cost me money. However D'Arcy will see that it is done as cheaply as poss. D'Arcy is really very clever in negotiations. He has great tact & ingenuity, and a soft voice. It is in hearing D'Arcy that you perceive that F. C. B. was no good whatever at that kind of thing. In his new place, if he gets it, he will only have to do conveyancing & that sort of thing. I said to D'Arcy that I would find no more money for Frank. He said: 'Well you can't see him starve. If he bankrupts he will starve. At any rate you'll have him on your hands permanently. The question is, which procedure will cost you least.' I said that in my opinion I shall at any rate have him on my hands permanently. I don't think he will keep that place for long. I shall be extremely surprised & pleased if he does. He has absolutely forgotten what hard & continuous work is & I think he is now getting incapable of it. Also he has no sense of responsibility & is very careless & dilatory even when he does work. Further, he still drinks & will probably drink more. What people can't see is that Frank's state cannot be cured by any good resolution that Frank is capable of making.

I now salute thee & depart to breakfast.

Yours, A.B.

117. Marguerite junior: Margaret Kennerley.
Mr Canoodle Canoodle: W.W.K.

STOKE / MS / 118
(*To Florence Bennett*)

Comarques
19th Mch 1917

My dear Flo-flo,
Thanks for yours. I told Frank at once, some weeks ago, that he would have trouble in selling the books advantageously. It will be a great bore moving to Rochdale, but then you seem to have a morbid taste for the joy of removals! The situation seems to be a pretty good one, & I doubt not that Frank can cope with it. But after comparative leisure & absence of real concentrated work for so many years, he will probably find the change very exhausting. In fact I am sure he will, especially at first. In the end I should say that it will do him an immense amount of good. I suppose I may without offence breathe a few plain words in your ear at this juncture when candour may be valuable. In my opinion Frank has two dangers in front of him. The first is due to his irresponsibility, which is rather extreme. He probably honestly believes that he has an average sense of responsibility. This, however, is not the general view of his

friends who know him best. And I should suppose that the
Rochdale firm will not stand much irresponsibility. The second
danger is of course due to alcohol. Nothing could give me more
relief than to hear that Frank had definitely & really parted
company with alcohol. Unless he does, my confidence in the
future will always be limited. I think this is about all I have to
say, except that you may count on our active sympathy in this
trying affair.

Our loves,

Yours, A.B.

118. When Frank Bennett died in 1938 the causes of death given in the *Evening
Standard* were heart muscle failure, hypostatic pneumonia, and delirium tremens.

KEELE / MS / 119
(*To Marguerite Soulié Bennett*)

Comarques
3–4–17

Chérie enfant,

I hope you will not come home & say that you have bought
those small tables for tea-time. I have not the slightest intention
of spending any money at all on useless luxuries till after the
war. Of course you may say that you will pay for them yourself,
although you have only 30/- in the world. You are certainly
very clever in making money go a long way. Eleven weeks ago
you said you had only £3. Immediately afterwards you bought
a Sèvres vase costing 2 guineas & a mirror costing about the
same, & a lot of other things at a bazaar, & you have kept on
buying things ever since and paid your expenses for eleven
weeks in London—all out of £3. This is marvellous! It is
magical! I could not do it myself—I admit that! But still, do not
go and buy those tables. It is contrary to the Government's
imploring request to do so. And what is more, I absolutely
object to your buying any furniture for this house (apart from
your rooms) which I strongly dislike. I should never dream of
bringing in furniture to which you had in advance strongly
objected. And I expect you to act in the same way. It is true that
you do things regularly in the house to which I strongly object,
but then I spoil you. You now say constantly that you spoil me.
In fact the remark is becoming one of your habits. But you

know quite well that you do not spoil me. I think there is
something very funny in the spectacle of a group of women
whose lives are largely devoted to pleasure and repose sitting
round a fire and agreeing that a man who lives the life I do is
spoilt. You must see the humour of it yourself. However, I don't
mind spoiling you to a certain extent. I rather like it. But there
are limits. And a woman who brings furniture of which I
disapprove into this stylistic house, after I have objected, will
exceed those limits.

Je suis maintenant éreinté. Ici on existe et on travaille.
Amuse-toi bien.

Je te bise,

Nouche

Tell Rich I have just received his papers.

119. In the margin against the sentence about the women of leisure, Bennett has
written, 'You can tell ole Glad this.'

KEELE / MS / 120
(*To Marguerite Soulié Bennett*)

Royal Thames Yacht Club
12–4–17

Infanta carissima,

Je suppose que Lockyer est devenu fou. Je t'envoie une copie
de la lettre que je viens de lui écrire. Je l'aurais mis
immédiatement à la porte, mais s'il part nous serons joliment
fichus pour l'électricité. Aucune femme ne peut faire marcher
ça, et c'est défendu d'embaucher les hommes ayant moins que
60 ans. Toutefois, si Lockyer ne s'incline pas carrément et
immédiatement, nous serons forcés de supporter les
incommodités de son départ. Je ne pense pas que tu as compris
mon attitude vers Lockyer. Lockyer est un 'homme' de premier
ordre, avec un cerveau rare dans sa classe. Il sait son métier, —
et plusieurs autres! Il n'a pas besoin d'être surveillé. Il aime son
métier, et il travaille admirablement. Pour le travail et
l'honnêteté j'ai la plus complète confiance dans lui, et je sais
que je ne me trompe pas. Dans le temps je suis sûr qu'il n'a pas
bien compris des choses que tu lui a dites. Il y avait des
malentendus. Mais il a toujours parlé de vous avec le plus

grand respect, et j'inculque à tous les employés le même respect pour toi. Jamais je ne supporterais d'un employé qu'un ordre de toi soit désobéi, s'il y avait moyen de t'obéir. Pour moi ça va sans dire. Le contraire me semble inconcevable.

J'ai vu Webbo et Swinnio hier soir. Rickards déjeune avec moi. Ce soir je dîne avec un vieillard et deux femmes. Je suis invité.

Je te bise.

[A.B.]

Demain 5 heures à Thorpe avec old Glad.

120. [I suppose Lockyer has gone mad. I am sending you a copy of the letter I have just written him. I would have dismissed him immediately, but if he goes, we'll be in a fine spot for electricity. A woman couldn't make the thing work and hiring men aged less than 60 is prohibited. Still, if Lockyer does not give way fully and immediately, we will have to put up with the inconveniences of his departure. I don't think you have understood my attitude to Lockyer. Lockyer is a first class 'man', with an unusual brain for someone of his class. He knows his job and several others too. He doesn't need supervision. He likes his job and he works admirably well. As far as his work and honesty are concerned, I have complete confidence in him and I know I am not mistaken. In the past, I am sure he has not properly understood some of the things that you have said to him. There have been misunderstandings. But he has always spoken of you with the greatest respect, and I instil the same concept of respect for you into all the servants. I will never permit a servant not to obey an order from you, if there is any way that it can be obeyed. In my view, that goes without saying. The opposite would be unthinkable.

I saw Webbo and Swinnio yesterday evening. Rickards is having lunch with me. This evening, I am dining with an old man and two women. I am the guest. I kiss you.... Arriving Thorpe tomorrow, 5 o'clock, with old Glad.]

Bennett's letter to Lockyer, printed in Vol. III, reads: 'I understand that Mrs. Bennett asked you for some keys and that you refused to give them to her. If you cannot see that this kind of thing is absolutely inexcusable you must be mad.'

Webbo: apparently Alexander Webster. See Vol. II for other references to him.

Swinnio: Frank Swinnerton.

STOKE / MS / 121
(*To Septimus Bennett*)

Royal Thames Yacht Club
14–6–17

My dear Sep,

I heard from my secretary that the mount has safely arrived, but I haven't seen it yet, as I am in town. You seem to be doing pretty well. I doubt whether I can do with any smaller mounts, as my watercolours are almost all of one size. I will send you one soon, for yourself, as you would like one. Your instructions as to 3-ply etc. shall be carried out. It is about time that you sent me a bill, I should think. I am not doing much work now, myself. If I obeyed Marguerite I should do none at all for a time. She was in the air raid at Liverpool St. yesterday. The train came into the station at the exact moment, & the end of the train was bombed. Yet, although Marguerite was towards the end of the train she saw nothing of the bombing. Anna, the maid, who was in the carriage in front of her, saw 'smoke by the side of the train' before she ran. I have been examining them both this morning. They heard no glass breaking, no cries of wounded; nothing except the explosions, of which there were four. People took refuge in an underground urinal, very roomy. Anna says she can't remember anything between the time she saw the smoke behind her, & the time she ran across Marguerite in or near the urinal. This morning I saw the remains of a Boche aeroplane being motored up Piccadilly. Last night I was told by the captain of H.M.S. Hardy, who was told by another man, who was told by the Secretary of the First Sea Lord, that 3 planes had been brought down. I was at Richmond at the time, painting purple trees. Aeroplanes were practising overhead all the time. Richmond Park is the great flying ground. Nothing to do with raid. Balloons were floating over Piccadilly eastward at 1:30. Nothing to do with raid either. I had a Turkish bath yesterday afternoon with Frank Shufflebotham & Masterman. Shuffle (of Newcastle) is a very nice chap, & very brainy. I expect you know him. He is the great poison-gas expert in this country, & is paying a visit to the Front to see his hellish devices in operation on Saturday. I never had a T. bath before. I am rather depressed at the moment as some people in U.S.A. who owe me £3,500 for a serial won't pay up, and legal actions are in the air. Pity about your kids. But many others are the same. *I* have none of these worries.

Our loves,

Yours, A.B.

121. Anna was a maid at Thackeray Mansions.

For a letter and other references to C. F. G. Masterman (1873–1927) see Vols. I and III. He was a literary and political figure, and in 1917 was Director of Wellington House (propaganda).

In his *Journals* a few weeks later in 1917 Bennett wrote: 'Frank Shufflebotham . . . said that up to now £100,000,000 had been spent on gas, of which a large portion had been spent on experiments on animals such as guinea pigs.'

For Bennett's quarrel with the Munsey Syndicate in America, see Vol. I.

KEELE / MS / 122
(*To Marguerite Soulié Bennett*)   [Royal Thames Yacht Club]
                                                            Wednesday
                                                            20–6–17

Respected Madam,

I have written two articles today, and am very well. As it is evident that nothing agrees with me like work, I will now write a third article, my subject being Programmes for dances. In my opinion it is a very serious mistake not to have programmes for dances. Everybody expects to have a programme, especially when the dance has to be paid for, and everybody is disappointed if there is no programme. Of course if you say to people 'Don't you think it is a good idea not to have programmes?' people are forced to reply 'Yes', just as they would be forced to reply 'Yes' if you said to them: 'Don't you think I am beautiful?' or 'Don't you think my flat is beautiful?' But I imagine that if you said to them: 'Do you or do you not prefer to have programmes?' nearly everybody would reply: 'I prefer to have programmes.' I am also quite sure that many people will be staggered at the absence of programmes. The idea of informality and chance is very agreeable for the first dance or two, but not afterwards. Certain people wish to make arrangements to dance with certain other people, and they cannot do so unless each has a programme. The consequence is that many charming young ladies are left without partners, whereas they would have had partners if they had had programmes. This happened last time, as I frequently observed for myself while you were upstairs. *You* of course, and other ladies of powerful individuality, will always have partners, but not all ladies have powerful individualities. I will go further and say that last time the music was sometimes playing without a single couple dancing, all because there were no programmes.

I am well aware that all this has nothing to do with me, and that you will do exactly what you like, and that I ought not to interfere. But I am not interfering. I am only writing one of my bright readable articles, so as to express my opinion (to which I am entitled) that not to have programmes will be a very serious mistake and that 19 people out of twenty will agree with me in their hearts, whatever they may say tremblingly before you. SARDONYX.

I saw Johnnie Atkins today. He sends you his congratulations on your escape, and his admiration for your presence of mind. I *may* come home by the last train on Friday. But, whatever train I come by, I will *walk* from the station, unless I wire to the contrary.

I am, respected madam,

Dutifully yours, N.

122. 'Sardonyx' was the name under which Bennett wrote his pieces for the *New Statesman*.

KEELE / MS / 123
(*To Marguerite Soulié Bennett*)

Comarques
4 July 1917

My dear Marguerite,

You have no right whatever to say I am sick of you. You take a great deal too much on yourself. And if I behaved to you as you behave to me there would be dreadful scenes. If now and then I am obliged to object, that does not mean I am sick of you. It simply means that I am not the man to let things go too far. You are constantly saying that you are allowed to do nothing either in the house or in the garden, and that I alone am the boss. Yet you must know that this is ridiculous. I am supposed to look after the garden, but trees are dying in the garden because you won't let a tree be cut down—and everyone knows this, and remarks on it. Two years ago you shut the folding doors of the drawing-room in defiance of my wishes, and they remained shut ever since until the other day you suddenly discovered that the doors were much better open and you opened them. You completely altered the furniture of the small drawing-room, also in defiance of my wishes. I am not complaining of these things, I am stating them. *You* complain that I give orders to the servants against you. It is not true. But you give orders to the servants against me. I gave orders about blinds & locking up—and in every household that I know matters which concern police and burglars are directed by the husband—you completely changed those orders without consulting me. I allowed it to be so. But when you forgot to shut windows, as you were bound to do, and I told the servants to shut them, you said that I had humiliated you. This sort of thing is absurd. What about you humiliating me? For a very long time the servants have had orders to bring Fifi & Raton to your room, & Rex and Peggy to mine. Suppose that *without saying a word to you*, I gave orders that Raton was not to be taken to your room but put somewhere else. You would be absolutely furious. Yet you think it quite natural that *without consulting me* you should give an order about Rex. Again, I do not complain; I state. You have imagination: exercise it. I agree to you giving a charity ball. I detest balls myself, but I am quite willing to agree to it to please you, and you on your part say that the house shall be put straight immediately afterwards. What happens? *Without consulting me*, you entirely change the disposition of two rooms and the hall—the most important part of the house. Supposing that, *without consulting you*, I went and changed the look of the house—you would think I had gone mad and you would be extremely angry. If you ask me whether really I don't like the new arrangement, my answer is that I certainly do not. It is very bad and banal artistically, and it is impossible for the piano. There is only one safe place for the piano, & that is where it was. A piano is not a table; it is a very delicate instrument. I know that you did not know this, but you know now I have told you. I never make any changes in this house without consulting you, if they affect you, and I must have the same treatment from you. I never give orders in this house, if they affect you, without consulting you, and I must have the same treatment from you. I quite understand that with your headache (which 70 minutes conversation with Jessie cannot have improved), and with the absence of a servant, it may be difficult for you to change the furniture at once, but I rely on it being done *entirely* when I come back. Unless both doors are kept closed the piano ought not to remain where it is at all; it has already been there much too long, but I will agree to the piano risking its life a little longer. I am sorry that you should have to receive this letter on your wedding day; but you should have chosen your dates differently. Do not imagine that I am sick of you, even for an hour. But at intervals you oblige me to explain to you that there are certain things I will not stand. My feelings toward you will never change, and I suppose you know what they are.

Ton mari vieillard qui te bise,

Nouche

123. Fifi and Raton, Rex and Peggy: dogs; Raton was a pekinese, Rex a dachshund. In *Arnold Bennett* Marguerite writes:
I felt that there was no possible way for me to learn through my own experience the best place in a room for a picture or a piece of furniture. Like a naughty child, I would rebel at times, and would change the position of the furniture, secretly thinking it might even improve the room. But alas! every time I tried such a daring experiment I had to admit to myself that the place first chosen by Arnold Bennett was the only possible place.
Jessie: possibly the daughter of Dr Farrar.

KEELE / MS / 124   Charlton Arms Hotel
(*To Marguerite Soulié Bennett*)   Luford Bridge,
                                         Ludlow
                                         Saturday
                                         7–7–17

Infanta Carissima,

The beds are rather hard, but I had a good night. Slight dyspepsia, owing to cider. I have done my first water-colour. The hotel is on the high bank of the river, et on peut entendre nuit et jour le bruit de l'eau. Il y a deux barrages tout près. Ce matin j'ai fait ma première aquarelle — du château, une ruine. C'est le pays de M. Marriott. Il a fait des tableaux terribles de Ludlow Castle. La nourriture est bonne. Nous sommes servi par une jeune personne qui a l'air d'avoir 16 ans. Mais en verité elle a 22; elle est mariée (à un soldat) et elle a un enfant, que je caresse toutes les heures. Elle est bien. Excellente salle de bain (Geyser) j'ai pris mon bain chaud à 6.45 ce matin. Tu t'embêterais ici je pense parce que il n'y a rien à faire. Mais avec Wright je me plais beaucoup. C'est un type tranquillisant. Il a énormément lu, etc. Et il a des idées. Il y a un autre peintre dans l'hôtel. C'est un idiot, je pense. Il est ici depuis un mois. Cette semaine il est arrivé une américaine (peintre) de Paris. Ils font des excursions ensemble; ils mangent ensemble (salon particulier). Wright dit qu'il ne la pense pas la maîtresse du peintre. Je lui dis: 'Jamais vous ne feriez pas croire ça à une française.' Pourtant me dit-il, je ne pense pas qu'elle est sa maîtresse. Pour moi je ne les ai pas encore assez vu pour juger. Avec ces américaines, c'est toujours possible qu'elle ne l'est pas. Je l'ai vue en peignoir ce matin. En tout cas elle n'est pas vierge. La pauvre fille a peut-être 39 ans (non, 35) et elle est passablement laide. Temps superbe. J'ai reçu une lettre de Jane Wells ce matin remplie de louanges de Richard et du roman de Swinnerton. Swin m'a écrit. J'espère que tu passeras une bonne fin de semaine. Je compte réintégrer Londres jeudi. On pourrait dîner ensemble jeudi soir. Il faut je pense que je vois le Galsworthy. Ça commence à 8.35.

> Je te bise tendrement.
>
> Nouche

Autre aquarelle cet après-midi.

124. [And the sound of water can be heard night and day. There are two dams just near. This morning I did my first water-colour—of the castle, a ruin. Mr Marriott comes from round here. He has done some terrible pictures of Ludlow Castle. The food is good. We are served by a young person who looks 16 but is really 22. She is married (to a soldier) and has a daughter, whom I often fondle. She is nice. An excellent bathroom (with a geyser). I had a hot bath at 6.45 this morning. You would be bored here, I think, because there is nothing to do. But I am having a good time with Wright. He is a very calming chap. He has read a tremendous amount etc. and he has ideas. There is another painter in the hotel. He is a fool, I think. He has been here for a month. An American woman (painter) arrived here from Paris this week. They go on excursions together; they eat together (in a private room). Wright says he doesn't think she is the painter's mistress. I said to him: 'You would never make a Frenchwoman believe that.' But, he said to me, I don't think she is his mistress. I haven't seen them enough to be able to tell. With these American women, it is always possible that she isn't. I saw her in a dressing-gown this morning. She is not a virgin in any case. The poor girl could be 39 (no, 35) and is fairly ugly. The weather is marvellous. I had a letter from Jane Wells this morning full of praise of Richard and Swinnerton's novel. Swin has written to me. I hope you will have a good weekend. I am expecting to be back in London on Thursday. We could dine together on Thursday evening. I think I will have to see the Galsworthy. It begins at 8.35. I kiss you tenderly.... Another water-colour this afternoon.]

Bennett went to Ludlow on the 6th to have a few days of painting.

Swinnerton's novel was *Nocturne*, published in July.

Galsworthy's play was *The Foundations*, playing at the Royalty.

KEELE / MS / 125
(*To Marguerite Soulié Bennett*)

Ludlow
11th July 1917

Mon enfant chérie,

I was very sorry indeed to receive your first letter of the 9th, as it shows you must be very gloomy, & I do not like you to be gloomy. But you are probably looking in the wrong place for the explanation of your unhappiness. There is nothing in my letter of the 4th to explain it. It is true that we had a difference of opinion, but I wrote you a quite polite and decent letter about it, and if you showed it to any third person, that third person would smile at the idea of taking it tragically. Differences of opinion there are bound to be, and no one knows better than you that certain things will infallibly lead to trouble. Your situation is in every way better than that of the majority of women. You have a husband who loves you, & who has tried for ten years to please you (just as you have tried to please him). You have far more freedom, far more admiration, far more change, and far more pleasure, than the majority of women of our class or of any class. And also far more money. You are envied by nearly everyone. It is not the fact that artists do not need a companion. They do. You are far more of a companion to me, and see far more of me, than the wives of the majority of businessmen. If you could be the wife of a businessman for a time you would soon see! These are not matters to be argued about. They are indisputable facts. The cause of your gloom is not that you have had a difficulty with me. I am quite sure that, though I am by no means an angel, I treat you much better than most husbands treat their wives. (You often admit this yourself.) And I think that you treat me better than most wives treat their husbands. The cause of your gloom lies beyond all this. I remember indeed that *a fortnight ago* I saw a letter from Gwladys in the drawing room of your flat, from which it was clear that you had written to her that you were very sad; she said that she was sad too. And so on. The cause of your gloom lies in your temperament (not the French sense of the word, but [?]). You are of a melancholy and disillusioned disposition. This is not in the least your fault, & you are not in the least to be blamed for it. The trouble is that *you expect too much from life*. You would never get what you expect from life, even if you had married an archangel. You often say that you have lost nearly all your illusions; & one would think that your life with me had been a terrible tragedy. Of course it has not. All this springs from your instinctive attitude toward life. You cannot help it. You probably do not know that you have such an attitude, but there it is, all the same. And of course as the years pass it is likely to be more pronounced. It is a great misfortune. Nobody but yourself can fight against it. But *you can* fight against it, and I hope that you will do so. In fact I feel sure that your commonsense will lead you to do so. Otherwise old age is likely to be rather disagreeable. This world may be a very bad world, and men may be very bad animals. But the world is as it is, and men are as they are. And you should remember constantly that you are far better off than most women. You might also remember the good qualities of the man you have married. I need not catalogue them, because in 10 years you have doubtless perceived them for yourself.

I have Vernon's address, but not here. I told you long ago that Miss Nerney had not got it. I shall *leave Liverpool St.* at 4.59 on Friday with Swinnerton, & I hope that you will then be more cheerful. I leave Ludlow at 10 tomorrow morning.

Je te bise bien,

Nouche

KEELE / MS / 126
(*To Marguerite Soulié Bennett*)   Royal Thames Yacht Club
                                          Wednesday
                                          18th July 1917

Mon enfant chérie,

I went with Webster last night to *Le Mariage de Figaro*. *It was divine*. You must go with me Thursday next week. Webster paid for the seats last night. I was so tired that I preferred to leave at the end of the 2nd act (10.50 p.m.!) rather than see the 3rd act and be completely exhausted. I did not sleep at all well. It is raining.

I did not expect to say anything more to you about the Rochdale affair, but I have received the enclosed letter from Frank & of course you must see it. (Frank has just telephoned to me. He is in London on business for his firm, but I have not seen him. He may come to the club, but I have very little time to spare.) I think Frank's letter expresses their ideas very well and with conspicuous moderation. It is impossible to disagree with it. Certainly there is nothing that humiliates a provincial family more than for a relative to stay in a hotel in the town in which it lives. But this is not the most important part of the question. The most important part of the question is that in the case of the adoption of a child whose parents are still living the greatest tact is always necessary, and the greatest tact will naturally be exercised by the most intelligent of the parties concerned. As I have not seen your letters to Florence or her letters to you I do not know what passed between you, or how much absence of tact Florence showed. All I know is that Florence has said that she would prefer you to come at some other time. It is extremely difficult for me to believe that you would insist on going at a time when you had been asked not to go. The fact that you would stay at a hotel does not improve the situation at all. It makes it worse. You are not going to Rochdale to walk about Rochdale by yourself. You are going to see Richard & Richard's family. Either you will take Richard away from his family to spend time with you, which would be monstrous & which Florence would much resent, or you will see Richard & his family together. Richard's family do not want this, and if you were in Florence's place, if you were poor, and Florence, rich, had adopted a child of yours and insisted on coming to your town when the child came, I know what *your* attitude would be. You would be furious. You would say: 'Comment! Je n'ai pas vu mon gamin depuis un an, et maintenant elle ne peut pas me laisser tranquille avec mon gamin — elle, la tante riche qui fait la pluie et le beau temps, et qui s'impose parce que on n'ose pas la contrarier! Elle manque du tacte celle-là!' That is what *you* would say. I am quite sure that Florence would be delighted to have you at Rochdale some other time; but if you go while Richard is there you will humiliate the family, you will greatly distress me, and of course you will spoil the boy's holiday. You will also damage your reputation for tact with the whole of my family, because it is absolutely certain that no member of my family would approve. Worst of all, you would not do yourself any good with the boy, who is a very acute judge of things, and would infallibly in his own mind decide against you. I daresay you have some good reasons for going to Rochdale just now, but I don't know what they are as you have never stated them. They cannot be as strong as the reasons for not going. You have simply said that you intended to go, and that nothing should stop you from going. There is, however, one thing that may stop you from going, & that is your own good sense. You will naturally decide for yourself. You are a free woman and you have your own money. I shall say nothing more about the matter. I have only said this because Frank's letter obliges me to do so.

Pour demain soir, je t'attends sans faute. La pièce commence à 8.15. Donc, il faut dîner avec de la vitesse.

Je te bise bien,

Ton Nouche

126. Marguerite wrote to Florence in June to express dissatisfaction at the way the adoption was proceeding. When Richard came on his two-week visit to Rochdale (his first in ten months) Florence and Frank must impress upon him that he must regard Marguerite as his true mother, and in general they should aim to distance themselves from him. Florence's conciliatory reply did not satisfy Marguerite, and apparently in a jealous fit she decided to go to Rochdale while Richard was there. Bennett forced her to abandon the notion, but she then wrote to Florence to say that had she come she certainly would not have stayed with them and that she thought it rude of Florence to object to her coming. She saw that it would have to be laid down that Richard would write less to his parents.

ELDIN / MS / 127
(*To Septimus Bennett*)

Royal Thames Yacht Club
25–7–17

My dear Sep,

One guinea will be quite all right. I see no reason why you shouldn't get hold of what mounts you can. They are always useful—at any rate to me. I will send you a cheque when I get home. In any case I should not supply mounts. You seem to be doing pretty well just now. And I think it is better that you should earn £6 in $5\frac{1}{2}$ days than £8 in 7 days. In fact I am sure it is. By the way the British army is *now* using more shells per hour than it has ever used before. I wish you could go to the seaside instead of to Burslem for your holiday. I shall stay at home for mine, but then I am close to the sea. I spent last night with T.

Hardy at J. M. Barrie's. He is quite changed since he took his 2nd wife, & is much brighter. He is very simple and A1, in spite of great age. His wife is about ½ his age—was his secretary, I think—a most excellent creature. There were only us four to dinner, but about 10.30 Barrie routed both Shaw & the Wellses out of their bedrooms by 'phone, & they came along. Barrie has a large flat on the 5th floor of Adelphi Terrace, with the most marvellous view of the river I ever saw. It has large windows at different angles, & catches the river at the bend, so that you can see it all from London Bridge to Lambeth Bridge. I am going to paint the same at the first opp. (Not the whole of it.) As I consider Hardy the equal of the Greeks, I was much impressed by yesterday evening, & I naturally have a headache this morn, but I don't care.

Yours, A.B.

127. In his *Journals* on the 25th Bennett wrote:
    At dusk we viewed the view and the searchlights. Hardy, standing outside one of the windows, had to put a handkerchief on his head. I sneezed. Soon after Shaw and the Wellses came Hardy seemed to curl up. He had travelled to town that day and was evidently fatigued. He became quite silent. I then departed and told Barrie that Hardy ought to go to bed. He agreed. The spectacle of Wells and G. B. S. talking about the war, in their comparative youth, in front of this aged, fatigued and silent man—incomparably their superior as a creative artist—was very striking.
    For other references to Barrie (1860–1937), Hardy (1840–1928), and Shaw (1856–1950) see the other volumes. For letters to Shaw see Vol. III. Florence Dugdale (1881–1937) became Hardy's second wife in 1914.

KEELE / MS / 128
(*To Marguerite Soulié Bennett*)

Comarques
29–7–17

My dear Marguerite,

I appreciate the spirit of your letter. At the same time, you also must know certain things.

I do not want 'orages', & do all I can to prevent them. I wrote you a perfectly polite & kind letter. I said there might be arguments on your side, & I recognised the excellence of your motives. The matter, however, is not one for argument.

It is not the fact that I concealed from you my objection to children. On the contrary I stated it clearly, and at first you agreed heartily. Then you changed. I did not change. I finally gave way to you, against my judgement, and you wrote back most clearly declining the offer. I was very glad. These are the facts and they cannot be disputed.

It is not the fact that I object to children because of my work. Far from that. I have never stated my reason, because I hate to state it. Nevertheless you ought to be clever enough to see it. My reason is that my father died of softening of the brain and was always slightly queer in the head; and that two members of your family are abnormal mentally. These things are apt to jump a generation. This reason, which I have never before mentioned to anyone, *and which I absolutely decline to discuss,* seems to me a good one.

It is unquestionable that you have helped me very much with my work. However, the meaning of my letter was quite plain, and must not be twisted.

You said a considerable number of extremely unjust things to me this morning. All I ask is that you won't repeat them. When you are calm you know them to be unjust. It is monstrous that you should say that you are only my married mistress. It is equally monstrous that you should say that I always say 'No' to everything you ask. The truth is that I almost always say Yes. When I say No in a matter which deeply concerns me, you are so startled that you feel insulted. This is not right. It certainly is not fair. Do you suppose that you do any good, whenever I happen not to be able to agree with you, by pouring out a torrent of fantastically unjust and baseless accusations? Do you suppose it improves my opinion of you? It is bad enough that you should say these things when we are alone; but that you should make such a remark as you did make at lunch today in the presence of Mrs. Tracy, apropos of Mrs. Turbague, is utterly inexcusable. As a fact, if I said to you one tenth of the things you think yourself entitled to say to me, you would walk straight out of the house. You really must learn to control yourself better. You could show my letter of yesterday to anybody, and nobody would agree that it deserved the treatment which you gave it. It was a perfectly amiable letter, full of consideration for you, and I would not care who saw it. I resent extremely the way in which you received it.

I fully realise that your intentions are excellent. I only wish you would realise how extraordinarily unjust and abusive you are to me. I hope you will. Nobody can be more exquise than you when you like. Like you, I am quite ready to forget all this difficulty today, et je te bise bien.

Ton Nouche

128. See p. 62 for Bennett's suggestion that he and Marguerite have children. See also the Introduction, p. xxx. The Beardmores in their edition of the correspondence say that they laid the present letter before Marguerite's nephew Etienne Lombrail, a notary and the executor of her estate. Lombrail denied there was any known example of mental abnormality in the family. In the early twenties Bennett said that Marguerite's mother was 'the slightest bit cracked' and he feared that Marguerite might be too. Somewhat later he said that Marguerite was 'demented'. See pp. 315 and 414. On abnormality within the Bennett family see pp. 5–6.

Kathleen Tracy, wife of Louis Tracy (1863–1928), author and journalist.

Mrs Turbague: unidentified.

ELDIN / MS / 129
(*To Septimus Bennett*)

Comarques
31 Augt 1917

My dear Sep,

I have had lumbago severely twice, but it affected the use of my arms, not my legs. I could not put on my coat for 3 days, though I could walk about. I expect by this time your attack is over. It must have been a most damnable muisance. My holiday ends today at midnight. I have just had a request to furnish another serial to *Harper's*, by the end of the year! I shan't & can't do it. I shall be busy on a novel entirely unfit for a serial, seeing that it intimately describes the life of a prostitute. I don't see that in *Harper's*. The weather is still rotten & has interfered not merely with the war & the harvest, but also with my tennis & watercolours. I have made decided progress with monotypes. In fact I have done one very good one & two fair ones. Also I have at last finished overlooking Mary in the production of an illuminated alphabet of her own composing about her mother. 'I love my mother with A because she is' etc. Mary could find nothing for X except 'extraordinary', but your witty nephew said: 'I love my mother with X because she is an unknown quantity.' And this has been included in the alphabet. Mary has certain indications of artistic gifts. It seems now as if Richard was going to be a chemical engineer in the grand manner. It is less banal than being an electrical engineer or anything of that sort; it combines chemistry & engineering, & he is interested in both of them. I have just had another dust-up with Frank. Russell's bill was entered in the estate accounts as paid. Only it was not paid, & never would have been if Nurse Grey hadn't written to me. I have got the money out of him. Don't say anything about this—unless Nurse Grey has herself told you. Marguerite sends you her respectful lumbar sympathies.

Yours, A.B.

129. Bennett wrote *The Pretty Lady* from 24 May 1917 to 28 January 1918. It outraged certain people. See Vols. I and III.
Mary: Mary Kennerley.
Dr Russell.

KEELE / MS / 130
(*To Marguerite Soulié Bennett*)

Comarques
9–9–17

Dear Marguerite,

I shall be much obliged if you will at once change your order to the servants not to ring the gong until you are ready. I am ready to put up with your continuous lack of promptitude because I know you can't help it. But I am not ready to put up with you making everybody else late. In any house where I live the meals must be served promptly, not at the moment when a lady who is always late chooses to come downstairs.

Having given the order, the least you could have done was to tell me about it. These tricks are insupportable.

Yours, A.B.

KEELE / MS / 131
(*To Marguerite Soulié Bennett*)

Comarques
17–9–17

Mon enfant,

In order to oblige you I don't mind paying for *the alteration* of your will (which will be quite simple), but I do not think that it would be at all 'fair' that I should pay for a document to which I strongly objected, which was made in defiance of me, and which has caused me a large amount of discomfort and worry.

You say that you have the right to express a wish. That may or may not be so. But it is absolutely certain that you have not the right to desire the boy, in a formal and solemn document, to do a public act which you know must cause me intense pain and annoyance. That was an outrage. It is true I should have done all I could to stop the act. But that is not the point. The point is your attitude to me. No self-respecting husband would stand such a thing. You will never have any trouble with me so long as you do not defy my feelings *in matters which concern me as much as they concern you.* To do so is to make married life impossible; and it can never end in anything but trouble. You have proved this again and again. You sometimes do things to which I object, but when they affect only yourself I never say anything. When they affect me also, I protest. You say that my name is yours. It may be so, but it remains at least as much my property as yours. You cannot properly ask a third person to do something with property which belongs also to another unless you first obtain the consent of that other person. In married life if a course of conduct is suggested which affects both parties, the consent of both parties must be obtained to it. Otherwise no action should take place. If one insists on defying the other in a mutual matter, he or she must accept the risks and the resulting friction.

I know how much it has cost you to give up an impossible position, and the fact that the position was impossible will not lessen your annoyance at all. I don't wish therefore to say anything beyond what it is absolutely necessary to say. This is not, as you think, a 'victory' for me. It is a victory for your commonsense over your impulsiveness. Far from enjoying such victories, I regret the necessity for them, and they make me just as unhappy as they do you.

If as you say your point in taking Richard no longer exists, it is a pity that you did not say before we took him that your only object was to get him to alter his name to mine. We should then have cleared that matter up at once. But you never mentioned it to me in any form. You first mentioned it to a solicitor, and told me afterwards. I should never have agreed to it at any time, however, as it would be exactly contrary to my principles.

No one knows better than you that you don't always have to give in.

When you have had your will altered, by means of a short codicil, tell the solicitors to send the bill to me. Je viendrai demain soir, mardi, vers 6.30, en tout cas avant 7h.

Je te bise et je t'aime,

Nouche

131. Marguerite wanted to have Richard's name changed, presumably either to Richard Arnold Bennett or to Arnold Bennett.

KEELE / MS / 132   c/o Dr. F. Shufflebotham
(*To Marguerite Soulié Bennett*)   21, London Road
                                   Newcastle-Under-Lyme
                                   dimanche
                                   21–10–17

Mon enfant chérie,

J'ai reçu ta bienvenue lettre ce matin. J'étais persuadé que tu aurais des histoires. J'espère que tu n'as pas payé la semaine de la patronne. Tu aurais dû faire venir la police. Enfin tout ça c'est de l'expérience pour toi. Moral: ne vas jamais dans les private-hôtels. Nous avons eu un raid vendredi soir. Les Zepps sont arrivés assez près — 20 kilomètres je pense. À Londres, pas de canons; rien; les Zepps étaient très haut, et un d'eux a lancé une bombe sur Piccadilly en face Swan & Edgar; plusieurs personnes tuées, une vingtaine de blessés. Tous les carreaux cassés, naturellement, et un trou dans la chaussée aussi grand qu'une chambre. C'est heureux que nous n'y étions pas. La semaine a été passablement mauvaise pour les alliés, et l'affaire de la mer du nord est une sale affaire. J'ai eu mal à la tête toute la journée d'hier. Je pense que c'était le changement de climat, puisque j'ai bien mangé toute la journée. Il y a eu des invités ici. Les hommes très forts, habiles, riches, intellectuels; les femmes assez province. Je me suis amusé. Nous nous comprenons, Madame S. et moi. Elle et lui ne s'entendent pas. C'est une femme bizarre, *très* laide, sans aucune espèce de charme. Mais elle aime la faïence et les vieilleries et elle aime aussi étudier les gens. Nous sommes très bien ensemble. Le docteur, lui, pense (je pense) que toutes les femmes sont dépourvues d'intelligence vraie. La maison est confortable, et le maître en est rempli de charme. L'enfant (six ans) est amusant. J'ai vu les Barlows, Maud, les enfants, Mrs. Beardmore, Joan, et Edward Beardmore. Aujourd'hui je vais chez Sissie ce matin, et nous irons, le docteur et moi, en auto chez les Mason (23 k.) cet ap.

Enfin ma chère Margot (Auguste)....

Je te bise tendrement. Je n'ai pas mal à la tête to-day, mais je ne me sens pas très fort.

Nouche

132. [I received a welcome letter from you this morning. I was sure you would have trouble. I hope you didn't pay the landlady for the week. You should have called the police. Anyway it's all experience for you. The moral is never go to private hotels. There was a raid on Friday evening. The Zepps came quite near—to 20 kilometres I think. No firing in London—nothing; the Zepps were very high, and one of them dropped a bomb on Piccadilly, opposite Swan and Edgar; several people killed, about twenty wounded. All the windows broken of course and a hole in the pavement as big as a room. It's lucky for us we weren't there. This has been a pretty bad week for the allies and the North Sea business was rotten. I had a headache all day yesterday. I think it was the change of climate because I ate well all day. There have been guests here. The men were very tough, cunning, rich, and intellectual; the women rather provincial. I enjoyed myself. Madame S and I understand each other. They do not get on together as a couple. She is a strange woman, *very* ugly, with no charm of any kind. But she loves pottery and old things and she also loves studying people. We get on very well together. As for the doctor, (I think) he thinks that all women are lacking in any real intelligence. The house is comfortable and its master is full of charm. The child (of six) is amusing. I have seen the Barlows, Maud, the children, Mrs Beardmore, Joan, and Edward Beardmore. Today I am going to Sissie's in the morning and the doctor and I will go by car to the Masons (23 k) in the aft.

Finally my dear Margot (Auguste).... I kiss you tenderly. I have no headache *today* but I am not feeling very strong.]

Bennett was in the Midlands for a few days, staying with Shufflebotham and his wife Ellen Mary.

In the preceding week the Germans seized control of the Gulf of Riga, with heavy Russian naval losses.

Auguste: unknown.

KEELE / MS / 133   St. Aidan's
(*To Marguerite Soulié Bennett*)   Merrion
                                          Co. Dublin
                                          vendredi
                                          26–10–17

Mon enfant chérie,

Mer très agitée hier, mais je me portais très bien. Nous avions seulement 30 minutes de retard en arrivant. Les officiers et les soldats sont forcés de porter des ceintures de sauvetage à bord; ils ont l'air très ridicules, avec leurs éperons et les ceintures énormes! Il y avait un auto pour nous transporter chez M. O'Connor le ministre de justice. Ce sont des gens charmants et *qui jacassent*. Deux fils, un de 20 ans officier, et l'autre de 17 ans étudiant. Deux filles au boarding school. Madame est petite et souriante sans aucun chic. Monsieur est causeur, orateur, très droit, très souriant, très passionné, et full of jokes. La maison est assez grande. J'ai une vaste chambre, assez mal agencée mais bien. La salle de bain est grande, mais mal agencée aussi, étant donné que l'eau prend 19 heures (à peu près) pour couler. En somme je suis très bien ici, à cause du climat et à cause du charme des gens simples et habiles. Hier nous avions: le deuxième secrétaire du viceroi, un vieux amusant, le chef de police de Dublin, et le chef de police de tout le reste d'Irlande. Des gens très intéressants et sincères. J'ai pris force notes. J'ai demander la permission de me coucher at 11h 30m. Le chef de police de Dublin est resté jusqu'à une heure du matin. C'est un homme énorme, autrefois 'champion amateur boxer' of the world — jamais vaincu — donc, adoré par ses hommes. Dîner assez compliqué, 3 vins, je ne sais pas combien de plats. Un dîner d'hommes — Madame n'y étais pas. Elle aurait été seule parmi 6 hommes. Encore une fois j'ai bu du champagne. Ça ne peut pas continuer! J'ai assez bien dormi, et ce matin (glorieux — la mer en face) je me porte comme un rêve. Ce qui prouve, après les grandes fatigues du voyage et de la soirée d'hier, que ma santé doit être énormément mieux.

Sur celui-ci, je te quitte, dans l'espoir que tu ne t'embêtes pas trop à Comarques — la maison ancestrale.

Je te bise tendrement.

Nouche

Il est presque certain que je ne rentrerai pas avant samedi. Dans ce cas je resterais à Londres jusqu'à mercredi en huit.

133. [A very rough sea yesterday, but I felt fine. We arrived only 30 minutes late. The officers and soldiers have to wear life belts on board; they looked quite ridiculous, with their spurs and these huge belts! A car was waiting to take us to the house of Mr O'Connor, the Minister of Justice. These are charming people and *they chatter*. Two sons, one of 20, an officer, the other of 17, a student. Two daughters at boarding school. Madame is little and smiling, with no elegance of any kind. Monsieur is a conversation-alist, an orator, very upright, very smiling, very ardent and full of jokes. The house is quite big. I have a huge bedroom, not very well equipped, but nice. The bathroom is big, but badly equipped as well, seeing as the water takes 19 hours (about) to run. All in

all I am very well off here, because of the climate and the charm of unpretentious and clever people. Yesterday we had: the second secretary of the viceroy, an amusing old man, the head of the Dublin police and the head of police of all the rest of Ireland. Very interesting and sincere people. I took a lot of notes. At 11.30 I asked if I could go to bed. The Dublin police chief stayed till one in the morning. He is an enormous man, a former champion amateur boxer' of the world—never beaten—therefore adored by his men. The dinner was fairly complicated, 3 wines and I don't know how many dishes. A men's dinner—Madame was not there. She would have been the only woman with 6 men. I drank champagne again. This can't go on! I slept quite well and this morning (glorious, with the sea opposite), I am feeling wonderfully well. Which, after the great fatigue of the journey and yesterday evening, proves my health must be enormously much better.

Upon which, I leave you, in the hope that you are not too bored in Comarques—the ancestral home. I kiss you tenderly.... I will almost certainly not be home before Saturday, in which case I will stay in London until Wednesday week.]

Bennett went to Ireland for nine days at the request of the General Officer Commanding, Ireland, Intelligence Department. James O'Connor (1872–1931) was Attorney-General of Ireland from 1916 to 1918. For other references to him see Vol. III. Bennett wrote three articles on Irish affairs, published in the *Daily News* on 8, 12, and 15 November 1917.

KEELE / MS / 134
(*To Marguerite Soulié Bennett*)

St. Aidan's
samedi
27–10–17

Mon enfant chérie,

Encore un grand dîner hier soir. 3 vins. champagne. C'était un dîner des hommes de la loi, avec un professeur et moi. Infiniment amusant. Tous les Irlandais parlent politique tout le temps. La politique c'est le 'bridge' et le golf d'Irlande. Hier j'ai déjeuné avec Sir Bryan Mahon, le commander-in-chief d'Irlande. Type simple et bon, très ingénu. Chose étonnante pour, par exemple, un Français. Une grande réunion de 'rebels' s'est passée dans l'hôtel de ville hier et avant hier. C'est une conspiration ouverte contre le gouvernement. Et on le permet. Vraiment, il n'y a que les anglais pour être tolérants. 2,000 'rebels' dans l'hôtel de ville. L'entrée a été strictement défendu aux anglais et surtout aux écrivains anglais. Mais je peux exercer des influences énormes et quand j'ai donné une parole de ne pas dire dans des chroniques que j'y étais, le rebel-leader — de Valera — m'a donné un laissez-passer devant lequel tout le monde a baissé la tête. La réunion était complètement idiote — à mon avis, enfantine. On couve tout de même une autre rebellion! Toutefois la dernière rebellion a mis le centre de

Dublin en ruines — un peu comme Ypres était quand je l'ai vu
il y a deux ans.

Je rêve la politique irlandaise.

Je révasse la politique irlandaise.

Je la mange je la bois. Je suis fatigué, mais je me porte bien.

Je te bise tendrement.

Nouche

134. [Another big dinner yesterday evening. Three wines and champagne. It was a
dinner for lawyers, and one professor and me. The greatest fun. All the Irish talk
politics all the time. Politics are Ireland's bridge and golf. I had lunch yesterday with
Sir Bryan Mahon, the Commander-in-chief of Ireland. A good, straightforward chap
very unsophisticated. Here's something a Frenchman, for example, would find
amazing: a big 'rebel' meeting was held in the townhall yesterday and the day before. It
is an open conspiracy against the government. And it is allowed. There really is no
people as tolerant as the English. 2,000 rebels in the townhall. Entry was strictly
forbidden to the English, particularly to English writers. But I can exert tremendous
influence and when I gave my word not to say I had been there in my articles, the rebel-
leader—de Valera—gave me a pass to which everyone bowed. The meeting was utterly
idiotic—childish in my view. For all that they are plotting another rebellion! Still, the
last one laid the centre of Dublin in ruins—rather like Ypres when I saw it two years
ago.

I dream about Irish politics. I daydream about Irish politics. I eat and drink Irish
politics. I am tired but well. I kiss you tenderly.]

Sir Bryan Mahon (1862–1930), later a senator of the Irish Free State.
Eamon de Valera (1882–1975), later prime minister of Ireland.

KEELE / MS / 135
(*To Marguerite Soulié Bennett*)   St. Aidan's
                                                    vendredi
                                                    2–11–17

Mon enfant chérie,

J'ai reçu avec plaisir hier soir ta lettre de mercredi soir, écrite
seule dans le flat. C'est embêtant que tu sois seule dans le flat,
mais on ne peut pas avoir les plaisirs de la société sans les
ennuis de la société. Tu vois sans doute que la guerre va être
encore plus longue. Ce qui veut dire que je serai de plus en plus
pris. Tu conviendras que je passe déjà la grande plupart de mes
soirées avec toi, à Londres. Je ne pense pas pouvoir faire
davantage, parce que les journées sont tout-aff autre chose. En
tout cas je serai au flat mardi soir, et si tu veux j'y coucherai.
J'aime beaucoup y coucher, à la condition seulement que je n'ai
pas grand'chose à faire le lendemain. Il est impossible que tu

sois aveugle au fait que je me plais toujours quand je suis avec toi dans la tranquillité. Seulement pour mardi soir, je ne sais pas si je vais pouvoir apporter mes choses de nuit. Sans doute je peux m'arranger, ou tu peux m'arranger. J'espère que tu as toutes tes choses à Londres. J'ai toujours regretté que tu n'as pas acheté cette espèce de machin noir que nous avons vu dans un magasin près de Queens Hall l'après-midi que nous avons visité le flat de Michaelis. Je trouve que dernièrement il te manque un peu des 'nouveautés nocturnes.' Aujourd'hui je suis éreinté. Hier j'ai été à Belfast, et ça m'a fini. J'ai mal à la tête. Heureusement je n'ai pas grand'chose à faire cet ap. Mais ce matin je suis très pris. I leave tomorrow morning Saturday by the boat at 8.40. Je coucherai au club jusqu'à mardi. Je te bise bien.

Nouche

Remember me respectfully to Richard.

N'ai pas relu cette lettre.

135. [Yesterday evening I received with pleasure the letter you wrote on Wednesday evening, when you were alone in the flat. It is worrying that you are alone in the flat, but one cannot have society's pleasures without society's anxieties. No doubt you realize that the war will be even longer. This means that I will be more and more engaged. You will agree that I already spend the great majority of my evenings with you, in London. I do not think I can do more, because the days are quite another matter. Anyway, I will be at the flat on Tuesday evening and if you like I will sleep there. I very much like sleeping there, but only on condition that I have not got much to do the next day. You cannot possibly be blind to the fact that I am always happy when I am in peace with you. But on Tuesday evening, I do not know whether I will be able to bring my night things. No doubt I can manage it somehow, or you can manage it for me. I hope you have all your things in London. I have always been sorry that you did not buy that sort of black thing which we saw in a shop near Queens Hall the afternoon we went to Michaelis's flat. You have not had enough 'night-time novelties' recently, I find. I am exhausted today. I was in Belfast yesterday and it finished me off. I have a headache. Luckily I have not got much to do this aft. But I am very busy this morning.... I will sleep at the club until Tuesday. I give you a good kiss.]

Lieutenant Grant Michaelis was an Australian soldier who had stayed at Comarques in 1914. In *My Arnold Bennett* Marguerite writes:
General Fitzgerald, head of the staff at Frinton-on-Sea, called on us with his aide-de-camp, Lieutenant Trotter.... Lieutenant Trotter informed us that a detachment of engineers had arrived at Thorpe in the morning, that the men were billetted in the village and that there was one young officer who was rich and used to comfort who had to be satisfied with a room in a stuffy small cottage....
I looked at Arnold as though to say, 'Let us ask him to stay here with us ... plenty of room.'
Arnold understood, and I ventured to say, 'He might like to stay with us better?'

'That would be very kind,' said the general.

'Not at all.'

'When do you think you could have him, Mr. Bennett?'

'Whenever he likes.' ...

When our visitors had departed I said to Arnold, 'I am so happy, Arnold; you do not mind that officer coming?'

'Why should I mind? Besides, it will give you something to do.'

Michaelis stayed with the Bennetts for eight months. Later he went to the Front and was killed.

ELDIN / MS / 136
(*To Septimus Bennett*)

Royal Thames Yacht Club
6–11–17

My dear Sep,

Yes I meant war-work, but I had forgotten that you are not yet over age, & that there might be risks in attempting a transfer. With regard to the new works at Shelton, you might at any rate ask the boss. To get back would be an immense advantage to you in every way, & not less to Maud & the infants. But of course the chances of success are small. Still, you might ask. I agree with you that you could not have helped better in the war than you have done. I wish *I* could say as much; but when I see important propaganda work handled badly that everyone knows I could handle with unequalled adroitness I regret the stupidity of departments. I have just been doing some propaganda work in Ireland. They come to me when they want something really difficult, but it doesn't occur to them to ask for half of my whole time gratis. I think I have seen everybody in Ireland who counts, & I crossed on Saturday nearly dead with fatigue & listening to Irish talkers. I have just been offered £1,000 to go and describe the American fleet in English waters, for an American magazine syndicate. I could well do with £1,000, but I refused it as I cannot stand this popular reporting work, & fiddling about with admirals on flagships, etc. It does no earthly good for the war — all that they really want is some sentimental Kiplingisms with my signature attached. The military situation is now [?very] serious. I should suggest to you to get the *Manchester Guardian* on Saturdays, if you can. The military article by 'A Student of

War' is unequalled in all the Allied Press. We go home on Friday. I have much Irish stuff to write before then.

Yours, A.B.

136. Septimus was interested in a transfer to work in Shelton, Stoke-on-Trent.

Harold Sidebotham (1872–1940) was the student of war. He wrote leaders for the *Manchester Guardian* for twenty-two years, and later became Scrutator of the *Sunday Times*.

ELDIN / MS / 137
(*To Septimus Bennett*)

Comarques
18–11–17

My dear Sep,

Well, you have anticipated great woe at regular intervals for a year or two now, & it hasn't come off yet, & I see by your letter of Sunday that it is even receding further again. Also I doubt whether the whole country *will* be on strike next week. But certainly the A. S. E. men have had, & still have a considerable grievance against men like you. It is marvellous to me how they have stood it. You must have a rather weird notion of things if you think I could write the 'Student of War' articles in the *M.G.* This man *is* a student of war, and also a born strategist. His name is Sidebotham, & he lives in Manchester. He has refused various offers to come to London, where he could make an even greater name than he has. But he won't come, simply because his hobby is to mess about Manchester & suburban bars and sample barmaids. He will go miles to see a well-made or peculiar barmaid, & will also take his friends miles to see one. And so on. His domestic existence (married) is very sloppy, I imagine. I have sat up till 2 a.m. with him at the Manchester Press Club, he drinking & me not. In fact it is all highly remarkable. I am still having my weekly Turkish bath, and am constantly meeting acquaintances there. This house is now under a new arrangement—closed 3 days a week—it saves money. Lillah McCarthy, who divorced Granville Barker last week but one, is here for the weekend. She does not conceal the fact that she is still in love with him. She is a simple minded creature. She thinks I haven't suspected that she has invited

herself here simply to get a play out of me. We hope the family is
all well.

Loves,

Yours, A.B.

I shall send dry point tomorrow. Not up to much.

137. ASE: Amalgamated Society of Engineers. See p. 148.
Bennett presently wrote *Judith* for Lillah McCarthy (1875–1960). For letters and
other references to her see the other volumes. H. Granville Barker (1877–1946)
produced *The Great Adventure*. For other references to him see Vols. I and II.

KEELE / MS / 138
(*To Marguerite Soulié Bennett*)

Comarques
10–1–18

Mon enfant,

You are continually talking to me about the propriety of
closing this house and living in London, and saying that no one
can 'adapt' himself better than I can. I do not seem, after
explaining several times a week for a year, to have succeeded in
making my position clear. I will now make a final attempt to do
so.

My existence is utterly different now from what it was when
we lived in hotels—anywhere. I never wrote articles 'd'actu-
alité' then, and I had a small correspondence. Now I have an
immensely larger correspondence, and I write two articles a
week which cannot be written without a large apparatus of
books, papers, and letters. I spend four nights each week here,
and by leaving to the end of the weeks the greater part of my
correspondence and my research, I can manage very well; but I
only do it by careful organisation, & I only do it because it is
necessary for me to be in London for my work. If this house
were closed, I should have to take Miss Nerney to London, and
I should have to rent and furnish an office for her in London,
and I should have to transport to London all my office
apparatus, all my files and papers, and a large number of
books, and even then I should work under much greater
difficulties than I do here. Miss Nerney could not work at my
club, nor could she work at the flat. There is no reason why I

should undergo all this disastrous inconvenience, and I shall not do so. I do not suppose there will be any difficulty about keeping this place open and the flat open also; but if there *is* any difficulty it is London and not Comarques that will have to be closed. It is much easier to get food and much easier to get servants, here than in London. I cannot continue to be menaced every few days by this idea of going to live in London. I simply will not do it, and rather than do it I would live here alone.

Now about *your* work. I did not say anything about your returning here on Saturday evenings instead of Friday evenings, because you had arranged it without consulting me. It was therefore useless for me to say anything. However, I greatly object to it. Then, within less than a week of telling me that, you suggest that you should spend still another night in London, so that you would only have one complete day here—namely Sunday. And if I did not protest you would do this. And what is this work? According to you, it is work that 'any fool could do', that Mrs. Dumas formerly did without assistance, and that is at most 12 hours a week. For this, if I did not protest, domestic life at Comarques would be reduced to a mere farce. What do you suppose Mrs. Dumas would say if some one suggested to her that she should be absent from her own home except from Saturday evening to Monday afternoon in order to do 12 hours work that 'any fool could do'? And what do you suppose her husband would say? You would never have dreamed of taking on such work if it had not been in *London* and given you an opportunity of staying longer in *London*. If you really want to do war work, as I believe you do, you can quite well get work on Tuesdays, Wednesdays, Thursdays, & Fridays, if you try. I know that you prefer to be in London. Well, you have got a flat in London and you have three days in London. You ask for my opinion. You have it. You are, as always, free to do what you like. And I only give you my opinion because you ask for it. In any case please do not talk any more about closing this house. This idea is always putting me off my work, & stopping me from sleeping, and my work is quite difficult & complicated enough without that.

Je te bise,

A.B.

138. Winifred Nerney estimated that in these years Bennett wrote twenty letters a day.

Marguerite worked at a YMCA canteen near Victoria Station. She was proposing to work there on three days of the week for four hours each day.

ELDIN / MS / 139
(*To Septimus Bennett*)

Comarques
21–1–18

My dear Sep,

I've had no time to answer your letter before. I am now on the last week of my novel, and really in full blast. The publishers have seen the first half of it and are deeply struck by it. In fact they call it 'tremendous'. It is usually a bad sign when publishers are knocked flat by a novel. Still, this publisher is a writer himself. It is a pity you have had such a bad start. It is true, in a way, that Sheffield *could* lose the war. So could ten other cities, as well as a hundred departments. But in practice these things don't happen. The war is rather like an operatic performance ill-rehearsed. It ought by rights to come to a dead stop through some horrible blunder or ill-will. But it never does. Except in one of my novels, I doubt if any operatic performance ever did come to a stop through stage inefficiency. I spent last Friday with Richmond the managing partner of Weir's, one of the largest munition firms on the Clyde; and he said that on the Clyde the labour situation had never been so good since the war began. In fact he was quite cheerful. However, he didn't know anything special about Sheffield. Personally, I should say Coventry was a more dangerous place than Sheff. After all, it is the people who don't hear too much detail, but who hear only a certain amount of detail about all parts of the situation, who can best judge what is what. Some of the best judges in Glasgow said that Glasgow would fail to produce the desired 10 millions for her tank. I said she wouldn't fail. Not that I wish to boast. There was marvellously awful weather in London last week. Olive (Ledward that was) & Marguerite & Captain Mason went to see *Sleeping Partners*, with Seymour Hicks in it on Tuesday last. I have never cared for Hicks, but the play was most funny & improper and he was simply great in it. Through various circs I had to go round and make his acquaintance. I thought I could never stand that man, but I liked him. He is lunching with me & E. V. Lucas on Wednesday. What I want to say was that when we came out of the theatre there was 3 ins. of slush on the streets & snow driving in every direction. No taxis of course. Women, equally of course, in satin shoes. I had the snow shoes that Uncle John B. gave to the pater in the year 1880. I paddled Marguerite back to the flat. Mason, I trust, got Olive into a bus. As a war widow Olive is perfectly delightful. She is now in colours & good spirits again, and jolly good-looking too. I have now finished touching-up the last of the eight full-page coloured illustrations that I have done for Johnnie Atkins's book on the Thames barge. [?] book. Price 10/6, on account of my drawings. You won't like them. I give ½ day a week to art. On Wednesday I go back to dry-points. I see Lanteri is dead. Spielmann did quite a good obituary of him in *The Times*. I have written 7,000 or 8,000 words in 3 days. Exhausted.

Loves,

Yours, A.B.

The enclosed is certainly Harold Hales. The *Near East* is a magazine published in Tokyo. Strange! Please return it.

139. *The Pretty Lady* was issued by Cassell on 28 March 1918. Newman Flower (1879–1964), author of several musical biographies, headed the firm. For letters to him and other references see Vols. I and III.

In *The City of Pleasure* a band concert is interrupted, and in *Sacred and Profane Love* a two-handed playing of *Tristan* at the piano is interrupted, but neither because of stage inefficiency.

The Ledwards were a Burslem family related to the Kennerleys. Olive (later Mrs Olive Glendinning) was the widow of Guy Nossiter. For another reference to her see Vol. III.

Seymour Hicks (1871–1949) adapted *Sleeping Partners* from the French of Sacha Guitry.

E. V. Lucas (1868–1938), author and publisher, was a friend of Bennett's for many years. He was on the staff of Methuens, and eventually became chairman. For letters and other references to him see the other volumes.

Uncle John Bennett (b. 1841) was Enoch Bennett's brother. Bennett describes him in 'The Making of Me':

The elder son was a pottery-painter. The Potteries being too small for him, he went to London, to a cottage in Lambeth. He exhibited a pottery-painting in his parlour window. Sir Henry Doulton, strolling that way, saw it, and engaged the artist for his Lambeth works.

Then, Doulton's being too small for him, my uncle migrated to America, where he succeeded and made money. . . . He had a powerful, stimulating, and unconventional individuality. Full of more or less original ideas, he talked like an artist, and was one;

but lack of education fatally vitiated his modes of thought, and his taste was, I fear, deplorable.

Atkins' book, *A Floating Home*, with eight water-colour illustrations by Bennett, was published by Chatto & Windus in 1918.

Professor Edouard Lanteri, of the Royal College of Art, taught sculpture to Septimus there. M. H. Spielmann (1858–1948) journalist and author, wrote on the fine arts.

Harold Hales (d. 1942) was the original Denry of *The Card*.

STOKE / MS / 140
(*To Septimus Bennett*)

Comarques
10–3–18

My dear Sep,

I send a new dry point & also a reproduction of a water colour. I expect you won't like them. I will send you a copy of my new novel. You won't be able to put it down once you've begun it: this goes without saying. You remember I told you long ago they were overdoing the shell business. Anything may happen. I am now on a Committee (consisting of Masterman, Lord Rothermere, & me) which has charge of seeing that the whole war business is recorded in paint & sculpture. Great larks. I defend the artists, & they need it, though Masterman is quite all right. Beaverbrook put me on this Committee. It means much extra work of course. Beaver allows us £20,000 to begin with. He is a terrific hustler, & knows as much about art as Grandpa Longson. Still he buys all my books & has them bound specially. I have arranged with Eadie & Vedrenne for my new play—political, very sarcastic & funny. To be produced at the Haymarket. I haven't begun to write it yet, & it has to be finished by 31 May. Next weekend we go to stay with the Headmaster of Oundle—a jolly chap. One of the hero-worshipping house masters has already announced his intention of meeting us at the station—whether with a band or not is not yet known. The raid on Thursday night got us all out of bed. It nearly killed Northcliffe, who was staying with his mother at Totteridge. Totteridge suffered severely. You probably know that it is a northern suburb. Maida Vale also got it. I have now got an absolutely satisfactory fountain pen. Watermans gave it to me. I have six f.p.s in use, & this one is easily first. We have just bought 3 mirrors, a Regency sofa, & some odd [?], for £6–

5–6 at Clacton. The mirrors (1 vast) were fixed yesterday. I seriously reckon that the stuff would cost £50 at least in London.

Our loves,

Yours, A.B.

140. *The Pretty Lady* was published on 28 March, and sold better than any of Bennett's earlier novels.

The new play: *The Title.*

Lord Rothermere (1868–1940), owner of the *Daily Mirror*, was air minister in 1917–8. For letters to him see Vol. III. Lord Beaverbrook (1879–1964) owned the *Daily Express*. He headed the Ministry of Information. For letters and other references to him see Vols. I and III.

ELDIN / MS / 141
(*To Septimus Bennett*)

Royal Thames Yacht Club
18–3–18

My dear Sep,

Thanks for yours of the 13th. I may tell you (what Maud doesn't know) that there is *no* chance of him getting a partnership. I had already sounded that matter, through D'Arcy, & have seen a letter from the firm to D'Arcy in which the partnership is absolutely ruled out, as they have young relatives coming in. It is characteristic of the amiable F. C. B. that I should learn casually through you that he is expecting a rise in a month's time. About a month ago I was pressing him for interest, which is 15 months overdue, & his reply was that he was about to apply for a rise. Since then, not a word. And yet I had been upbraiding him for his carelessness about keeping me informed. There is now going to be a breach between us so far as any practical help from me in future is concerned. I have been trying to get some decent security for the money which he diverted from the estate. I insisted on having a charge on the policies which I alone am keeping alive by paying the premiums. I have been unable to get this charge—one of D'Arcy's mistakes, I fear,—D'Arcy cannot or will not see that more is involved in this affair than mere business cleverness. I still maintain that if the beneficiaries had cut up rough, Florence would have made any sacrifice to find the whole sum missing. D'Arcy seeks to persuade me that sooner than fork out another penny she would have permitted bankruptcy proceedings, which would have involved at best a frightful scandal & removal from the rolls & loss of situation, and at worst a criminal prosecution. But he cannot persuade me that it would have 'paid' Florence to lose Frank's salary of £250 a year, rather than find £500. I maintain that F & F have merely taken advantage of the beneficiaries' unwillingness to be nasty. I told them what would happen if the security I asked for was not given. It will happen. In the first place, I shall pay no more premiums on the policies, which will have to be surrendered. After waiting a week or two for possible developments, I shall send a letter to the beneficiaries explaining the situation. This breach with Frank is to me exceedingly painful, but I have to draw the line somewhere. During the last ten years he has received from me nothing but cash & forebearance, & I have received from him nothing but negligence and the most gross and deliberate deceit. The which I regard as a bit thick.

We have just spent the weekend at Oundle, as guests of the Headmaster thereof. Sanderson is a great chap, & I thoroughly enjoyed the affair. The organ in the big hall being out of order, they turned on the Kreutzer Sonata for us on Sunday evening— just that & nothing more!—and the piano part was played by the mathematical master! An excellent performance. We came away this morning.

I shall be extremely interested to see the 1915 diary. Tomorrow I begin my political play. I shall shortly send you another dry-point, my best. Corfe Castle, from one of my water colours.

Probably a raid night.

Yours, A.B.

A holiday won't harm you.

141. Septimus kept a journal of his years in Sheffield. It is in four bound volumes: '1915. On Munitions', '1916. Shells', '1917. More Shells', '1918. Still More Shells'. In 1918 he notes that in all his life he has met three people with the name Septimus. The girls he works with call him Mr Bennett, Old Bennett, Father, Arthur (his middle name), and Benny.

ELDIN / MS / 142
(*To Septimus Bennett*)

Comarques
30th April 1918

My dear Sep,

I'm sorry I had no time to reply to your previous letter. I got the second one this morning, & am answering it at once. Just off to London. There can be no question at all—you must stay where you are for the present. At best the difficulty of getting you moved, while keeping you out of the army, would be extreme. It might be less difficult if all the influential people were not so busy. But they are. Moreover you could not well be moved without the goodwill & consent of Vickers. At the same time I see no particular reason for you to worry. The works is bound to settle down again soon. Until it does, the situation cannot be usefully surveyed. You have always acted for the best upon the information which you possessed at the moment. Nobody can do more. I wish I could say $\frac{1}{2}$ as much for Frank & one or two others. I shall send you some more money this week, & it will reach you probably on Monday. Nothing else can be done at present. I now think that plans should be made on the supposition that things will get tighter & tighter & that the war will last for *quite* another 18 months. It mayn't; but it far more probably will. All depends on the U.S. army. Unless our sea communications break down, the U.S.A. will have transported 2,000,000 men into France, at least, by April 1919. They are now bringing 30,000 a week, & there are $\frac{1}{2}$ million, & over, in France, but of course only comparatively a few trained. They are all fed from America. This business should end the war during 1919. If our sea communications *do* break down, then the war will be ended at once—& in favour of Germany. (I don't suppose for a moment they will.) So that anyhow, in my opinion, the war is bound to end not later than next year. Still, it mayn't end till near the end of next year. I am infernally busy. I am just taking up the directorship of British Propaganda for France—an immense job, as to which I know practically nothing. Today I shall learn what my staff is. In addition I am the most active member of the British War Memorials Committee—an affair crammed with detail & I must earn my living by journalism. I shall drop all other work. I get no pay for government work. Still in addition, by a gigantic & totally mad effort, I am finishing a play in the middle of all this. I have done 2 acts. I contracted to deliver the play by May 31st, before I guessed that I should have nearly all my time taken up by government work. I could of course on that plea get out of the contract, but I don't want to get out of it. If necessary I am going to have a 'political chill' next week in order to finish the play, & the government will have to believe that I am in bed.

Our loves,

Yours, A.B.

142. For other details about Bennett's work for the Ministry of Information see Vols. I and III.

BENNETT / MS / 143
(*To Septimus Bennett*)

Royal Thames Yacht Club
12–5–18

My dear Sep,

I am returning your diary. I have read a good deal of it, but not all, because I simply have not had time. I have just taken on a new job at the Ministry of Information. It is gigantic. It is also in a thorough mess, & I have more than all I can do. Happily I have the nucleus of a good staff. You will understand that for me to go back to an office after over 20 years of freedom is a bit thick. However, I enjoy the work, and although it is much more tie-ing than creative literature, it is vastly less exhausting. I can't get rid of the idea that in merely seeing people & telling them what to do I am really not working at all! The diary as a whole is good, & the pictures greatly help it. The observation is often rather too general, & not particularised enough, either as regards what you see, what you hear, or what you feel. But the thing is decidedly superior to the average. I daresay you are unconsciously trying to make the record too serious. If I were you I should have it half-bound. Send it to Bagguley, tell him what you want—or leave it to him/ & tell him to charge the item to my account. It will get more interesting every year. It is a pity that, as regards the pages consisting solely of your own writing, you don't give more consideration to the margins. They are not considered.

I came home on Saturday afternoon & return early tomorrow. And all this damned Sunday I have to work at clearing up things.

Our loves,

Yours, A.B.

P. S. Your finance I shall doubtless hear of in due course, as it goes on.

P. S. The account is all right.

A.B.

143. George Thomas Bagguley (1860–1950) of Newcastle-under-Lyme bound books and manuscripts of Bennett's for many years. For letters to him see Vols. II and III.

ELDIN / MS / 144
(*To Septimus Bennett*)

Royal Thames Yacht Club
22–5–18

My dear Sep,

Yours undated, written from Thatched House. Further in reply thereto. I scarcely have any time to write my own letters. In fact I have to do them in fragments. I don't want to compare your day with mine, because I admit mine is infinitely more amusing than yours. But I gravely doubt whether yours is more exhausting, & though I would sooner have neuralgia than sciatica, there isn't much in it. I don't suppose for a moment that my existence will get easier as my department gets better organised. It won't, in fact. In London my day begins at 6.45. By 9 a.m. when I go down to breakfast I have cleared off most of my private correspondence & odd writings & have done something to arrange my ideas for article. Do you know that I now write 3 articles one week and two the next, & that in order to do this I only rob the Ministry of 2 hours of my full office time? Believe me, sir, this means some organisation. *Lloyds* articles began last Sunday. I forgot to tell you, or perhaps I did tell you. My business at the Ministry consists of controlling a staff there, feeding it with ideas, placating other departments, seeing strangers who desire to prove to me that I don't know the

A. B. C. of propaganda, seeing the two people above me, that is to say, the director of propaganda in general (Sir Roderick Jones, owner & manager of Reuters) and the Minister, Lord Beaverbrook (whose letters I sometimes draft for him), controlling officials & committees in Paris, Bordeaux, Lyons, Toulouse, Marseilles, St. Etienne, discussing the reports of my private agents (c. e. spies) in France. Well, that's some of it. I am rather pleased with myself. After being in the Ministry only 3 days I wrote a report on the existing state of the French section with my ideas for its reform. This report has moved my 2 superiors to enthusiasm. In fact Beaverbrook said it was the only really comprehensive report he had seen since the Ministry came into being. I have of course a great pull, because in the Report I can make them laugh while keeping to official phrases. They roar with laughter while reading it. But my great difficulty is getting extra men for my staff. Beaverbrook says: 'Go to Fleet St. & choose the men you want, & I'll guarantee to get 'em for you if they're under 51. I'll bomb 'em out.' He is a terrific man, little. Really interested in no form of propaganda except cinematographs. It is now 9 am & I must descend & face my private correspondence of this day's arrival, which I beg respectfully to remind you comes from all over the world.

I hope everything is all right at wum.

Our loves,

Yours, A.B.

144. Sir Roderick Jones (1877–1962).

KEELE / MS / 145
(*To Marguerite Soulié Bennett*)

Comarques
26–5–18

Mon enfant chérie,

Une douce mélancholie règne sur ces parages. But it is very beautiful & tranquillising. Et même seul, j'aime être ici, après Londres. I was sitting in the garden yesterday afternoon, after my arrival, when Mr. Matthews came with a gun & a friend of his came with a gun, and we shot rooks. As soon as they left it began to rain. Everything was in pretty good order; flowers on my dressing table & in my study, etc. It seems the A.S.C. had taken some of your chairs (apparently by getting in through the window of the hut), & had brought back the wrong ones. A bit thick! These have to be changed. Old Wicks said she had enough meat without using my meat-card. I wish to God she knew how to cook. She was most charming & obliging with me, but her dinners will kill me. Boiled potatoes, the same old soup, no sauce. I swear Stannard would have had a sauce to the fish. I get sauces everywhere else. There was enough fat on the meat dish to fry potatoes for a regiment. She had an excellent quality of meat (steak) but she had quite spoilt it. Hard as leather. I don't know how she grills her steaks, but she gives them a peculiar sickly taste. I have often noticed it. I ate part of mine but couldn't finish it. It gave me mal au cœur. There is no doubt this excellent & kind creature ought to be on the land & not in a kitchen. Of course I didn't say anything to her—she was so anxious to oblige. In spite of what you say I still can't see how the housekeeping can continue to cost £30 a month, especially as that includes nothing for vegetables, nothing for drinks, & nothing for wages. The amiable cook must be wasting money somewhere. I now have to take all my meals in London in clubs & restaurants, & I am in London nearly all the time, so that my food is costing me a very great deal more, & I get no advantage. I have had another request from another government department to reprint one of my articles. This makes three in a month! Not bad. The sale of the *P.L.* has now passed 20,000. I haven't heard anything further about prosecutions etc. Mr. Hogg can't come today, but he is coming next week. I may go up to Matthews for tea. My foot is better. I have now to correct the typescript of Act III of play. I feel strangely idle. You now know the Masons, & I bet you like them. I do hope you'll have decent weather. Here it looks like rain soon. I shall depart to London by the early train tomorrow. The dogs are all right.

Je te bise tendrement,

Nouche

P.S. I hope you will reconsider your decision not to go & see the people at Burslem. You will give a great deal of pain if you don't. *Maud, the Barlows, & old Mrs. Beardmore* ought to be seen.

It will be strange if you cannot spare an afternoon from your pleasures to do this. You are always asking for war-work. This is war-work.

145. The Reverend H. G. S. Matthews was a neighbour.
ASC: Army Service Corps.
Hogg: unidentified; Stannard: the housekeeper.
On the threatened attempt to ban sales of *The Pretty Lady* see Vols. I and III.

ELDIN / MS / 146   Ministry of Information
(*To Septimus Bennett*)   Norfolk Street
                                   Strand W.C.2
                                   10–6–18

My dear Sep,
   I haven't been able to reply till now, & now I haven't your letter before me, & can't remember whether there was anything that needed answering. I have left Marguerite at home today. She has had a very bad throat. Since she took a flat in London her health has slowly deteriorated; but she is not able to see any connection between the two things. The Ledward women have now installed themselves at Comarques for the summer & autumn. It is a much better arrangement than leaving the house to a servant or so for 5 days a week. We had a quite full house this weekend, 2 men & 2 Ledwards. A third Ledward & infant arrive today. I had neuralgia all the weekend, & still have it. Insufficiency of beef. It is now arranged that Marguerite will go to Harrogate at the end of the month, for a cure. I am gradually getting my official work organised. His Majesty the Minister told me today that I was doing the job 'brilliantly'. In this he was rather mistaken. In case you hear the rumour that a submarine came up under the propellers of the Olympia & was smashed to pieces, I may tell you that it is quite true. I had lunch today with Beaverbrook & a Canadian chaplain about 6ft 6ins high. Beaverbrook gave the chaplain a copy of *The Pretty Lady* & the chaplain, quite ignorant of its contents, promised to read it in bed tonight. This is a fair sample of one of Beaverbrook's jokes. My article in *Lloyd's* yesterday has met with great 'acceptance'. But doing these articles every week is a great strain. I have the slightest idea

what the next one is to be about, and so it goes on. This is all for today.

Thine, A.B.

146. Marguerite had some sort of foot trouble as well as a bad throat. The Ledwards: Mrs Ledward and her daughters Enid and Olive.

KEELE / MS / 147
(*To Marguerite Soulié Bennett*)

Ministry of Information
11–6–18

Mon enfant chérie,

J'ai reçu ta lettre. I think it is a great pity that you are not staying at Thorpe this week. You have undoubtedly been very unwell, & everyone says how ill you look. To come to London to a flat without a servant when you might stay at home at Thorpe must strike everybody else as a very queer thing to do. However, it is your affair. Of course you cannot hope to have the same health in London as you have at Thorpe. Your health has steadily gone down since you came to London. I recognise that this is not a reason for staying away from London altogether; but the fact must be faced all the same. Again, it is your affair. The international situation is extremely serious. Preparations are being made to evacuate Paris. This is *most strictly private* between you & me. I know I can rely on you not to say anything. I am exceedingly busy therefore, and I hope that you will not keep on saying that you never see me in London. It is not fair to say so. I much prefer an evening at the flat to any other evening, and you are aware that last week, for instance, I spent every possible evening with you. As I always do. A certain amount of reasonableness is necessary in these matters. I know that your attitude is very flattering to me, but it also worries me. It does just happen that this week I have official engagements every night, but such an occurence is rare. Indeed it has never happened before. Anyhow I can't help it. And when I remember the condition of men at the front & of wives who do not see their husbands for 6 months or a year at a time, I imagine that we can both survive this inconvenience. I hope

you will find some friends for the evenings this week, & will not
be too lonely. Téléphone-moi.

Je te bise bien.

A.B. Nouche

KEELE / MS / 148
(*To Marguerite Soulié Bennett*)

Royal Thames Yacht Club
18–7–18

My dear Marguerite,

Two of our gardeners have already died in the war, defending *us*. Lockyer is now going into the army. It would not have
been difficult for me to keep him out of the army. But I didn't
want to keep him out, and he didn't want to be kept out. He is
quite as patriotic as either you or me. He is under 45, and a
Grade 1 man, and he will almost certainly go out to the front,
where he will risk his life, defending *us*. If he is killed, of course
we shan't have him back. But if he is not killed he will come
back. *I have already told him, of course*, that the situation will be
kept for him, and by God I will keep my word, no matter what
the consequences are. Make no mistake. There would never
have been any question of his leaving the situation if he had not
to go into the army. Well, he goes into the army, he leaves his
home and his family, he risks his life, and according to you his
reward is to be that I shall say to him: 'Of course you can't come
back. The recompense of doing your duty is that you will lose
your situation, and you will have to leave your house, and the
village where you have lived so many years.' (For there is no
other situation that would do for him in Thorpe.) Am I going to
say this to him? I am not! I have said to Lockyer as I have said
to every man who has left us to go into the army: 'The place will
be open to you whenever you want to return.' It is a little
enough thing.

I am not going to commit an infamy. And if you understood
me as you say you do, if you realised the depth of my feelings on
such matters, you would never suggest such a monstrous thing.
I never interfere with you in the house, and I beg you not to
interfere with me in the garden. I have found a woman-
gardener solely to please you; but the situation is going to be

kept open for Lockyer, if he lives. You have no right whatever to say to me: 'I am—not—going to have—Lockyer—back.' I warn you in the most solemn way that there will be the most serious trouble if you reopen this question.

Yours, A.

KEELE / MS / 149
(*To Marguerite Soulié Bennett*)

Comarques
6–8–18

Mon enfant,

You have quite spoilt my holiday by running away. That you should deliberately arrange to be away at all was bad enough, especially as there was no reason for it, but that you should impulsively decide to go away and stay away is a bit too thick. Your excuse that you cannot talk to me without irritating me is ridiculous. On the other hand if you make impossible proposals to me you must not expect me to agree to them. Our present arrangement of living in London may not be ideal, but it was due to the war, and it suited you well enough at one time. It now happens to suit my work better than anything else could. I have an immense amount of work to do, and I can only get through it by the most careful organisation. At the club I have no household worries of any kind. I am excellently served. I have no servant troubles; no food troubles; no coal troubles. Everything is done for me. I am perfectly quiet. The whole of my work is directly connected with the war. I get up at 6.30 4 days a week to do it, and I *do* do it, but only just. I shall certainly not change my way of life until either my work stops or the war stops. I shall certainly not put myself to the bother & expense of taking a larger flat, & seeing to the furniture, & running all the risks in connection with servants, lighting, coal, etc. that people will have to run this winter in London. No fear! Why should I? Because mysterious people say that we are separated. The idea is childish. I fully admit that the arrangement is not ideal from the conjugal point of view. But there is certainly no hardship. Every free evening I spend with you. And I would certainly sooner spend an evening alone with you than in any other way. I am here every weekend. And if you go away while I am here I can't help that. The sacrifice we make is very small, and even if it were larger we ought still make it without grumbling. Anyhow I have got my duties to do, and I must arrange things so that I can do them. I shall not agree for a moment to any other flat being taken. You are always saying that you wish you could help me more. This is very nice of you. You can help me a great deal more by not complaining, by remembering what has to be done on account of the war, and by not making impossible suggestions, and by being cheerful. You would be much happier if you had regular work to do, and I hope you will get some. You can't possibly be happy as you are.

Je te bise,

N.

I write this in bed.

KEELE / MS / 150
(*To Marguerite Soulié Bennett*)

Comarques
7–8–18

Mon enfant,

I daresay that what you say about Richard is quite true. His manners will never be, and could not possibly be, equal to John Howe's. As for his mother, she is behaving as I expected she would, and as nearly all mothers would. Women don't reason about these matters. They know what they want, & they get as much of it as they can, and they have no conscience in the affair at all. As regards legal adoption, I told you when we took Richard that there is *no such thing* as legal adoption in England. There is in almost all other countries, but not in England. Nothing that we could do legally would bind either Richard or us in the slightest degree. Our hold on Richard will depend solely on the way we treat him.

Comarques is now 'having a rest'. I spent the whole of yesterday from breakfast to dinner entirely alone. As a number of important things have been sent on to me from the Ministry I have to work today. Also an article to write. I am very short of

sleep. I hope you are amusing yourselves. I shall arrive on
Friday before 7.50 at the flat.

Je te bise,

Nouche

150. John Howe: unidentified.

Until the Adoption of Children Act in 1926, parents could not surrender their
responsibility to their children.

In the summer of 1918 there was further correspondence between Marguerite and
Florence, with Marguerite still aiming to diminish the hold of Florence and Frank upon
Richard. She wanted Florence to write to him once a month rather than once a week.

ELDIN / MS / 151
(*To Septimus Bennett*)

Royal Thames Yacht Club
24–8–18

My dear Sep,

I'm writing this on office-time while waiting for Miss Nerney
to finish my letters. The financial prospects for you don't seem
to be very brilliant at present. I wish you could get something
else where you could live with the fam. You have been away
from your fam. quite long enough. So have I, though I see mine
thrice a week at least. I certainly don't see enough of Richard in
the holidays. Florence is not behaving quite right in the
Richard affair. She does everything to keep him attached to his
natural family. It is natural, but not right. Marguerite, having
exchanged letters with Flo-Flo, now wants me to butt in also. I
doubt if I shall. I foretold all these difficulties to Marguerite at
the start. It seems probable now that I shall abandon the
French propaganda and be put at the head of all British cabling
and wireless. I have long maintained that I ought to have this
job & that I could produce an official world-wireless the like of
which never was seen. As an opportunity for displaying the
reality of style wireless messages to the world are unequalled, *I*
think. I have done a great deal to set French propaganda on its
legs, & my last feat is to get a special grant of £100,000 out of the
Treasury for it. It annoys me not to have the spending of this. I
am also arranging to get the Earl of Lytton as my chief
representative in Paris. I shall lose the glory of this too. A hard

world. I haven't had a proper night's rest for three weeks. But after being ill last weekend I am now very well considering.

                                                                Yours, A.B.

151. Victor Alexander Lytton, 2nd Earl of Lytton (1876–1947), was British Commissioner for Propaganda in France in 1918.

KEELE / MS / 152
(*To Marguerite Soulié Bennett*)

                                                    Royal Thames Yacht Club
                                                    27–8–18

Mon enfant chérie,

Yesterday I had some of the *worst neuralgia I ever had in my life.* It got worse. Nevertheless I had to stay at the office. I was not well enough to go to Marian Vaughan's, & telegraphed her that I would go tonight. My neuralgia is better today, but I have spent very little time at the office. Rest has done me good. I have heard from the Doctor. He says that the only thing you have is bronchial catarrh, which will soon be cured. But he advises me to take another flat for you. *Although* the letter is such that you might have dictated it for him to sign, and bears every evidence of a conspiracy, & *although* I shall be put to a great deal of inconvenience & *although* I am somewhat surprised that you cannot accomplish the small sacrifice which the present state of affairs involves,—I believe in following the advice of a doctor when once he has been consulted. We shall therefore have a new flat. It will be necessary for you to find it. I think that it will be necessary to have a 'service' flat, where you will have no responsibility for either servants, heating, or lighting. If you have to see to servants etc., you will have more worry than ever, and so shall I. And I cannot stand it. This flat must be central, as near to parks and to clubs as possible. I shall want two rooms in it, one bedroom, at the back—I don't mind how small—and a room to work in, which *must* be a good room. You can put your own furniture into the rest of the flat, but I must see to my 2 rooms myself entirely. Your furniture is all right for you, & I don't want to say anything against it; but it is entirely against my notions of furniture, which notions are quite different from yours. This flat will not be at all cheap. That can't be helped. It will be much cheaper in the end, so far as my work etc. is concerned, to spend a few hundred a year extra & get what is really comfortable, than to save a few hundred and be worried all the time. You had better get Gwladys W. to help you to look for it. You will certainly need a woman to come in daily & do all sorts of things in the flat for you & me. In fact, a maid. No 'flat service' will do all that we need. I once saw with you a flat near the Queen's Hall, occupied by the Australians (I forget their names). That sort of a flat would do if it was unfurnished and in a different position. I wish you wouldn't say to people that your present flat only cost me £100, besides the rent. It cost me over £300. I have all the accounts. So there can be no argument about it. Vedrenne has written me again about the play. He is very gloomy about it. Lloyd's do not want any more of my articles after Sept. 8. They have done better than I expected. I counted only for 3 months. They have lasted for four months.

You had better ask Gwladys W. for dinner one night next week, & we will go to the Russian Ballet at the Coliseum. Settle it at once & let me know the night.

Je te bise bien,

Nouche

152. *The Title* opened on 20 July and ran for 285 nights.

KEELE / MS / 153
(*To Marguerite Soulié Bennett*)

Comarques
2–9–18

My dear Marguerite,

I want you most clearly to understand that I will not have these scenes before other people. *I will not have them.* Make no mistake. You have made violent scenes with me before other people in the past. I need not recall them. Last Sunday at lunch you had an outburst in front of Mrs. Ledward, about the terrible existence I forced you to lead. Last night you had a worse outburst in front of Mrs. Ledward & her daughter. Do you imagine that I am going to permit our most intimate relations to be discussed in that way before other people? Do you imagine it does any good? Do you imagine it does anything but the gravest harm? Do you reflect how awkward & unpleasant it is for the Ledwards? Do you remember what *you* would think of any other woman who behaved in a similar way? These things must stop, and they must stop absolutely. *I shall not submit any more to these monstrous and abominable humiliations.* I have tried various ways of stopping them, without success. I now tell you that it will be impossible for me to live with a woman who behaves in this way. If these things continue, I shall look after you in every way, but I certainly shall not live with you. Many husbands would let the matter drag on indefinitely, until it got quite out of control. I shall not. I will not have it. Exercise your imagination, and think how you would feel if *I* behaved as *you* behaved last night. The thing is utterly inexcusable, and I hope therefore that I shall receive some expression of regret from you. I know of course that you *do* regret what you did.

Even if all that you said was true there would be no excuse for these scenes. But what you said gave an entirely wrong impression of the facts. It was completely unjust. I never accused you of deceiving me, & I never have done. I said that I felt you were trying to get the better of me (about coming here for weekends). The exact words I used were 'Je sens que tu as l'idée de me rouler.' Moreover I was perfectly polite. And what else should I feel but that? When it was a question of taking all kinds of food to London you never found any difficulty. But now that it may be a question of bringing meat (only) here *from* London, the difficulty is suddenly enormous. You have arranged for people to sleep in the house; you have Stannard. But because it is a question of coming here *from* London, mysterious difficulties suddenly rise up. That was why I said that I felt you meant to get the better of me. Perhaps I was wrong, but I had good ground for thinking so.

You say that you cannot talk to me when we are alone. This is nonsense. Our talks go on perfectly smoothly, so long as I agree instantly to everything you suggest. But immediately I don't agree, then, according to you, I become 'impossible'. This has occurred again & again. However, I do not want to discuss these points. I merely want to say, in the clearest way, that I am not going to have any more scenes in public. The future depends on yourself. You are always saying how strong I am. Don't force me to use my strength.

Yours, A.B.

CAMBRIDGE / MS / 154
(*To Richard Bennett*)

Royal Thames Yacht Club
14–10–18

My dear Rich,

Yours of yesterday has reached me. The general plan is this: that you leave school when you're just under or just over 18— preferably over, & that you then go to Cambridge, & that during at least your first year at Cambridge you still continue your *general* education, without specialising. When you are 20 or nearly so, you can begin specialising. You see that up to now it has been impossible to formulate any plan as the war was so uncertain. The war is now practically over, & we can begin. As regards after-University, I suppose it is understood clearly between us that you want to go in for chemical engineering. This is about as far as we have got yet, or can get, I think. I doubt whether Captain Mason's place would be quite import- ant enough for your vast potentialities! Of course you compre- hend that the planning of your career is not to be a series of instructions laid down by me, but an equal collaboration between you and me. I should not dream of doing more than offering you advice. And refusal of my advice would not make the slightest difference between us. Such is my notion. My duties here, broadly, consist in keeping the public opinion of all countries in the world (except enemy) as favourable as poss. to Great Britain. This is done by means of wireless, cables, articles, books, agents, and inviting foreigners to England, & sending Britons abroad. The organisation is vast. I am the head of it. I will consider your b.p.

Thy distracted uncle,

A.B.

The new war situation involves me in a whole series of new activities.

154. At the end of September Bennett became head of the Ministry of Information, with authority directly under Beaverbrook. He wrote to his agent, Pinker: 'I cannot understand it, & don't like it. But I was not the man to refuse.'

ELDIN / MS / 155
(*To Septimus Bennett*)

Royal Thames Yacht Club
10–11–18

My dear Sep,

A line to tell you that you had better be finding out how you stand for leaving Vickers. If the war doesn't end today it will probably end tomorrow. And as soon as the armistice is signed I see no reason why you should not give notice and depart. Whatever money you may need to resume existence & business in the Potteries will be immediately at your disposal, as and when required. Don't send me any more specimens of diary at the moment, as I am living in a whirl of varied activities which leaves me no leisure for the consideration of arts & crafts.

Yours, A.B.

155. The letter is dated 11–10–18 by Bennett.

KEELE / MS / 156
(*To Marguerite Soulié Bennett*)

Bath Spa Hotel
Bath
31–12–18

My dear Marguerite,

As this affair may be serious I had better say again in writing what I said in writing in the summer. I write so that there can be no misunderstanding.

First, I should tell you that until I got Miss Nerney's card yesterday morning I had no idea that Lockyer had returned or would be able to return soon. Before he went to the Front you accepted his presence, & there is no doubt that if he had not gone to the Front you would not have questioned his staying. When he went off to risk his life in the army you wanted me to take advantage of this fact to dismiss him. I positively refused to do so. In the meantime he has done nothing but his duty; he has had no relations with you; he is exactly the same man as you accepted before; but you now want me, as a recompense for doing his duty and going through all the discomforts and dangers of a soldier's life at the Front, to deprive him of his job, which would mean his leaving Thorpe and breaking up his home! You often remind me about patriotism, but philosophers in all ages have noticed that the people who talk most about patriotism are the least anxious to practise it.

You inform me that, unless I treat Lockyer in this infamous way which you demand, you will refuse to do your domestic duties. That is to say, you will think of neither me nor Richard—not to mention Lockyer—but only of yourself. In the summer I wrote you that although I would not dismiss Lockyer at once after his return, I would (much against my wish and judgement) let him go later on, when things were settled down, if you found another suitable man. But this does not satisfy you. Nothing will satisfy you except Lockyer's instant dismissal, even though there is no one to take his place. Very well. I once more absolutely refuse to dismiss him. No decent man would do it. Every decent man throughout the country has made it a point of honour to keep jobs open for men returning from the Front, and I am not going to behave in a disgraceful manner to satisfy the caprice of anybody in this world. I am quite ready to accept the consequences of behaving properly to a returned soldier. The *immediate* consequences will be extremely inconvenient to myself as I shall have to go to Thorpe anyhow, at any rate for the present, and manage as best I can alone. But I am not thinking of the immediate consequences,—I am thinking of all the consequences. I shall never give way any further. If my wife, aged 40, chooses too often to behave like a girl of 14, I shall have to act accordingly. We shall see.

Yours, A.B.

156. Bennett was in Bath from about 23 December to 5 January.

ELDIN / MS / 157
(*To Septimus Bennett*)

Comarques
16–2–19

My dear Sep,

Kind regards to the girl assistant. I think you have little reason to complain yet. It is a great point to have already more work than you can do, even if the profit is small. You certainly didn't hope for it. In your place I should cultivate the novelty business as much as poss., because it makes you more independent & less replaceable. I think that on the whole you are to be congratulated. I am glad you think well of *The Roll Call*. (You ought never to judge by reviews.) You know I wrote it 2 years ago, long before *The Pretty Lady*. I always said the *P.L.*, though more brilliant, was inferior to it. The most sound people are very impressed by the *R.C.* and I am thereby much pleased. The *Sentinel* review was not at all bad. The book is selling well. My Biblical play is now well on the way to production. I think Granville Bantock will do the music. Charles Ricketts will do the scenery & costumes. Nothing further from *The Title* could be imagined. I also see some chance of *Don Juan* being produced. The Tube strike gave a blow to *The Title* from which it will almost certainly not recover. I expect it will disappear on March 15th. The flat has *not* materialised. Marguerite in the end would not have the Cavendish Sq. flat, & I think she was right. It was so 'flatly'. The flat in Berkeley St that we are temporarily in is also damnably flatly. Two of the rooms are in eternal darkness. One of these is the dining-room. (See next week's *New Statesman*.) Yet this is a very classy flat indeed & costs £12 a week. However, we have seen a flat (opposite St. George's Hanover Sq) which I will take if I can get it. It is a great flat. Top floor of an old house. Spacious & light rooms. A tradition behind it. Formerly occupied by the Earl of Shrewsbury. I am now negotiating for it. If I get it (which is doubtful, as I do not mean to be done in the eye) you will witness what I call a flat, believe me! We have just driven over to Brightlingsea in the rain, with 3 friends, & had 3 punctures en route. A great & inspiring excursion. I have sciatica. As you know what sciatica is I will not expatiate on it.

Loves to all,

Yours, A.B.

157. Septimus returned to his studio in the Old Post Office Buildings, Hanley, on 1 January 1919. Bennett lent up to £500 to get him started.

Reviews of *The Roll-Call* were mixed. The *Staffordshire Sentinel* thought that aside from *The Old Wives' Tale* it was Bennett's best work.

Bennett wrote *Judith* in January 1919. It opened at the Kingsway Theatre on 30 April, and failed.

Granville Bantock (1868–1946) was Professor of Music at the University of Birmingham from 1908 to 1934.

Charles Ricketts (1866–1931), painter, sculptor, and engraver.

:LDIN / MS / 158
To Septimus Bennett)

Comarques
12–4–19

My dear Sep,

I see nothing unsatisfactory in your business at all. Surely you did not expect to re-establish the thing completely in three months, did you? My impression is that you will do very well if you stick to it. In fact I have confidence. Do not forget by the way that the interest on the capital should be paid every six months. We shall then know where we are. We have just been through a most wearing weekend at Eastbourne for the production of *Judith*. It was a great success, & I think it will be ditto in London. Indeed this is a world-play & contains a rôle to appeal to star-actresses of all nationalities. Scenery & costumes by Ricketts. Music by Bantock. Both good. Dance arranged by ballet-master of Russian ballet. But the charm of the play is the nudity of Lillah MacCarthy when she assassinates Holofernes (after kissing him) in the tent. Upwards, from a line drawn round the body one inch above the clitoris the lady is absolutely nude except for a black velvet band (4 in. wide) round the body hiding the breasts, & a ditto going down perpendicularly therefrom & hiding the navel. The manager of the theatre had some fear of a prosecution. I asked him if he had seen *Chu Chin Chow*. However, I think Lillah beats anything in *Chu Chin Chow*. Marguerite wanted the skirt (which by the way does not hide the legs) a little higher—not for decency, but for beauty. But Ricketts did not agree with her. I wonder what Aunties Bourne & Sarah would say could they have seen this affair. Lillah is very fine indeed in the part.

Loves, A.B.

158. *Chu Chin Chow*: revue-spectacle that had run throughout the War.

KEELE / MS / 159
(*To Marguerite Soulié Bennett*)

St. Aidan'
30–8–19

My dear Child,

I received your long letter this morning. We must keep an ey
on Richard. I think I shall send him a telegram about it. W
had a tremendous day yesterday. Journalism & politics in th
morning. Race-course in the afternoon. Theatre (Irish plays) a
night. I went to bed exhausted, but slept 6½ hours without
break, & am all right today. This morning we go to see pictures
This afternoon more racing. Tonight, repose. The Irish rac
course is very Parisian in appearance, & there are heaps of well
known English people in the train of the Viceroy. Nevertheles
the big officials are always followed about & protected b
detectives. The English still hold Ireland only by force of arms
& beneath all the gaiety, luxury, honest justice, order, etc etc
there is always this feeling. The Irish theatre was packed & th
atmosphere dreadful. The plays mediocre, but vastly mor
interesting than West End plays. The audience is quite dif
ferent—more vivacious, critical, & appreciative. But among
the Irish audience there were last night many Englis
aristocrats over for the Horse Show, and you could see a
Englishwoman half naked sitting next to an Irishwoman with
hat on & furs round her neck. We lunched yesterday with th
Sous-secrétaire d'Irlande at his official residence, with his wif
& daughters. All the official residences are in a most beautifu
park (Phoenix Park) and close to the race course.

You do not say anything as to your health, sauf que t
surnages. Est-ce assez? Please address all future letters to th
Midland Adelphi Hotel, Liverpool. Et je te respectueusemen
bise.

[A.B.

---

159. Bennett was in Dublin for several days at the end of the month. He was visitin
James O'Connor (see above, pp. 204–5) and Thomas Bodkin, a barrister and late
Director of the National Gallery of Ireland. For letters to Bodkin, see Vol. III.

Bennett went on to Liverpool for rehearsals of *Sacred and Profane Love*, which opened
the Playhouse Theatre on 15 September.

KEELE / MS / 160
(To Marguerite Soulié Bennett)   Midland Adelphi Hotel
                                                    Liverpool
                                                    1–9–19

My sweet Child,

I have just got here after a terrible journey on a packed steamer in pouring rain. My trunk is lost. But I expect it will turn up soon. Also I have just got your telegram about Richard & your letter & his letter. It is a great pity he should be so naughty & sarcastic. I have written to him, firmly. Send him home if you like: but in your place I should not send him. Otherwise he will think he has won the game. I enclose his letter to me for you to read, & also my reply to him. Please hand him this reply. Of course a tremendous lot of patience is necessary with these youths of 17. That is the nuisance.

I am very glad you are not going to France. It would have been a great mistake for you to go. I think you are mistaken about the garden accounts. Ask Miss Nerney. I feel sure I have paid for June, if not for July. August of course I have not paid for as it is only just over. Tell Miss Nerney to send me the total; then you won't have to trouble. I ought to have these accounts every month promptly. I always pay them immediately I get them. There is never any delay.

I have already seen 3 people I know in this hotel. I shan't go out tonight. I am too exhausted. Owing to my trunk being missing I am obliged to sit in damp boots, hour after hour.

We went motoring yesterday amid superb scenery. It was very good weather.

I am exhausted.

                    Je te bise bien.

                                        [A.B.]

160. The crisis with Richard began when Marguerite refused to let him drive the car. Later the same day he received the telegram from Bennett mentioned in the preceding letter. It merely concerned Richard's piano lessons, but he refused to show it to Marguerite. At dinner, with other boys present, there were further difficulties, and Marguerite ordered Richard to leave the room (her version) or go to his bedroom (his version). He stayed in his bedroom that evening and all the next day. She sent him two notes demanding apology. He then wrote a note to her, saying, 'I was never really fond of you, I am sorry to say, but later I began to like you better. Even now, however, when Uncle is away I feel bound by your presence. When Uncle is here I always feel more free; and I always enjoy a holiday when I am here with Uncle as well. When Uncle is away I feel unhappy and not free.'

KEELE / MS / 161
(*To Marguerite Soulié Bennett*)   Midland Adelphi Hotel
                                                    Tuesday
                                                    2–9–19

Mon enfant chérie,

I was too preoccupied last night to reply properly to your letter & telegram, & I am glad I did not write any more as your letter received this morning makes the matter clearer. I have not telegraphed as it would be impossible to express oneself in a telegram on this complicated matter. On the whole I still think that it would have been better to keep Richard at home than to send him to Rochdale, simply because he will think he has won the battle. Which he has not. Of course he has a very powerful individuality, but on the other hand he is generally liked. If I were you I should not attach too much importance to the episode. You *are* attaching too much importance to it. It will pass and be forgotten. Richard is quite wrong in saying that I let him drive the car when he chose. Of course I would let him drive the car back from the station; but I have never let him go out with the boys alone, & I only let him go out with the car at all on the condition that Leslie sat by his side & that Madame Bion was there. I should certainly hesitate to let 3 youths go out alone in the car. Let him wait till he is over 18. He is also quite wrong in saying that it was not agreed that he should have only a fortnight at home each year. It was so agreed. In any case we have taken on this responsibility of Richard, and we must carry it through, though it will be difficult. And the fact that Richard would have been treated 100 times more strictly if he had remained with his parents than he is by us will not make him any easier to deal with. In my telegram to Richard I merely asked him to keep a daily record of the time he spent at the piano. Nothing else.

Mr. Charles has at last got a good Victorian sideboard for us. I haven't seen it, but I have seen a drawing of it. It is low enough to allow the big mirror to stand on the top of it.

I sleep well & I am well, though I spent 9 hours yesterday in wet boots and socks. But I am very worried about you, et je t'envoie mes affectueuses sympathies, et je te bise tendrement.

                                                    Nouche

P.S. I enclose cheque for £12 for next Saturday, & cheque for
£25 on account of garden.

161. Leslie; Mr Charles: unidentified.

STOKE / MS / 162
(*To Frank Bennett*)

Midland Adelphi Hotel
2–9–19

My dear Frank,
    I have just received a copy of the letter Margurerite has
written to Florence. Do not be misled by Marguerite's English.
Anyone might be justified in thinking that Marguerite wanted
to wash her hands of Richard. Nothing of the kind. Our
responsibilities remain & will remain, to the full, in every way.
As to the shindy, I cannot judge as I have only received
fragmentary accounts. All I know is that Marguerite has been
& is ill. She still has had to be inoculated every week. I am tied
up here with rehearsals till the 16th. If Richard could come
back for the final weekend before he goes to school I think it
would be a good thing.

Yours, A.B.

CAMBRIDGE / MS / 163
(*To Richard Bennett*)

Midland Adelphi Hotel
4–9–19

My dear Rich,
    I am glad to have your letter. And if it can be arranged I
should like you to come to the first night. But you must
remember that you will have to meet Auntie, & that you have
wounded her feelings terribly. As to your complaint to me, it is
true that you are older than you were, but you are by no means
grown-up & you are still a school boy. It certainly is not for you
to decide exactly at what point you are to be treated as grown
up. Your complaint is a complaint made by all youths. Your
father will agree with me that he & I had less liberty at 20 or 21
than you have already. In the matter of driving the motor-car

alone with Robert & Roger, you were wrong in thinking that I should have agreed to it. I certainly should not. Moreover you cannot constitute me a court of appeal from Auntie. When I am away she has both the full responsibility and the full power. This is essential. Again, you probably have not realised how ill Auntie has been & how her illness has reacted on her nervous system. Auntie has a quite different temperament from yours and mine. This does not mean that hers is better or worse than ours. It is merely different, and very different. She sees things in a different way. She has different methods. You have sense enough of your own to perceive this, & to act accordingly. On the main point you were wrong. You were rude & you were obstinate. That you behaved as you did under a sense of injustice I can quite see, but that is not an adequate excuse. There are certain things that you owe to Auntie on account of her position as your adopted mother and on account of her age. These things are the very basis of family life and they cannot be ignored without disastrous consequences. Among them is a cheerful and respectful acquiescence when argument has failed to win a case for your view. At the worst you will soon be unquestionably grown up. You will, I suppose, admit that Auntie has looked after you with the most extreme conscientiousness throughout your life with us. I hope you will write to Auntie some expression of your regret and ask her to consider the affair as wiped out and forgotten. You will not like doing this, but you will be well advised to do it, as the proceedings of the next few days may have vital consequences.

Your disturbed uncle,

A.B.

163. Robert: Robert Bion. Roger: unidentified.

KEELE / MS / 164
(*To Marguerite Soulié Bennett*)

Midland Adelphi Hotel
5‒9‒19

Mon enfant chérie,

I am very glad you are somewhat better. I got your second letter yesterday afternoon, in which you say I understand, but can't feel, your situation. This is a mistake. Believe me people can't write books & plays like mine without feeling as well as understanding. I fully appreciate your situation. All I say is that *nothing* can relieve us of the responsibility we have undertaken in regard to Richard. We accepted certain grave risks & we cannot refuse our responsibility simply because these risks seem to have turned out badly. You say Richard does not like you. He does. But even if he does not, ces choses ne se commandent pas. You could not possibly have said to Frank & Florence at the start: 'I take Richard, but if he does not love me I shall throw him over again.' Many mothers are much *less* liked by their sons than you are by Richard. And the responsibility of parents, once undertaken, only ends with death. However, I need not insist, as I am sure you understand. I am now better. But life in Liverpool is very tedious at times. I think the play will be all right. Basil Dean returns to work today after his illness. You will like Iris Hoey. At least I think so. On ne sait jamais. Please telegraph me *at once* what day you are coming. It is difficult to get bedrooms, & I must try to get one for you close to my own.

> Je te bise bien,
>
> > Nouchly

164. Basil Dean (1888–1971) produced *Sacred and Profane Love*. For a letter and other references to him and to the play see Vols. I and III. Iris Hooey (1885–1979) played the leading role.

CAMBRIDGE / MS / 165
(*To Richard Bennett*)

> Midland Adelphi Hotel
> 11–9–19

My dear Rich,

Thanks for your letter. It is a great pity that you did not acknowledge my letter at once. You ought always to acknowledge letters at once—especially important ones. Here have I been waiting exactly a week without knowing what was occurring. You do not, I think, take this matter seriously enough. There is no doubt that Auntie is still extremely upset, & I am convinced that it would be a great mistake for you to come here for the first night. I have already more than enough on my shoulders without having the anxiety of presiding over a meeting between you and Auntie amid all the nerves of a first night. If I had heard earlier from you I might have been able to prepare the ground; but it is too late now. Moreover Auntie has written me expressly asking me to leave your affair alone until after the first night. We will see you at Comarques at the end of the week. We shall return to London on Tuesday. I suggest that you might send Auntie a box of chocolates; address it to 12B George St. Hanover Sq W.1. & see that it is not late.

The rehearsals are very trying.

Your exhausted uncle,

A.B.

CAMBRIDGE / MS / 166
(*To Richard Bennett*)

Midland Adelphi Hotel
15–9–19

My dear Rich,

Having discussed your affair with Auntie, I discover that it is very much more serious than I had thought, & I do not see that any good can come of your returning to Comarques these holidays. You had better therefore go direct from Rochdale to school, by the shortest way. I am sorry, but it is impossible not to blame you in the matter.

I understand that you began your letter of apology to Auntie by saying that I had asked you to write it!! You really ought to have had more sense than to do this.

I enclose cheque for £3. Send me in due course an account for the £6. 10/- you have now had.

On Tuesday I shall be in London & on Thursday at Thorpe.

Your very much upset Uncle,

A.B.

I have written to your father.

ꝏEELE / MS / 167
(To Marguerite Soulié Bennett)   12ᴮ, George Street
                                            Hanover Square W.1.
                                            17–9–19

Mon enfant chérie,

After what you said about Richard I wrote to him & his father & told them that he could not possibly come to Comarques. I think I had better send you at once the letters I have just received from them. I did not ask in any way for Richard's own account of the affair (Nor, by the way, did I suggest to him that he should send you a birthday present.). I of course do not know how far Richard's account is correct. But if it is true that you sent him to bed you were only asking for trouble. To send a boy within a month or two of 18 to bed in the presence of other boys was bound to lead to trouble. Any youth who did not strongly resent it would be a weak kind of creature. In Richard's place I should most strongly have resented it, and so would you. I had not the slightest idea that you had sent him to bed. You gave me no hint of it. When I tell you he is a boy, you say 'No; he is a man.' Well, men are not sent to bed as a punishment. I should like to see the letters that passed between you. After that I shall say nothing more about it. If you have decided I shall of course accept your decision & do the best I can under the circumstances. But you will never persuade anybody on this earth that it is a right and a just thing to separate eternally from a boy of nearly 18 because of any rude and bitter things he may have said or written after having been publicly sent to bed. You may have been perfectly right to send him to bed—I wasn't there and I can't judge—but you are not right in resenting permanently his resentment after this humiliation. Anything that he said or wrote ought to be forgotten, under the circumstances. Let me repeat that I am not going to question your decision. The boy will never come to Comarques again unless he comes with your full consent as our adopted son. You may count on that.

                    Je te bise,

                                            Nouche

167. Bennett and Marguerite moved into the flat at 12ᴮ, George Street at the beginning of July 1919.

CAMBRIDGE / MS / 168
(*To Richard Bennett*)

Thorpe-le-Soken
19–9–19

My dear Rich,

I have now read the letters which passed between you & Auntie. I see nothing in hers to justify yours, & it is a great pity that you did not take the advice which was twice offered to you not to insist on her reading it. I quite understand your point of view. But there are several things in your letter which cannot be justified as statements of truth. As to the holidays for instance. Your parents relinquished all claim on you; & you agreed, after what adoption meant had been fully explained to you. Your relation to your mother & father necessarily became that of a nephew, & the question of holidays was one absolutely within our discretion. I consider that a fortnight a year at Rochdale was ample, & this arrangement was most distinctly made. You say you were unhappy. Of course you were. Everybody expected you to be unhappy at first. You were certainly not more unhappy than your parents were. Adoption is a very big thing. But you did not go into it blindly. Nor did any of us. It necessarily entails serious sacrifices. No pressure of any kind was, so far as I know, put upon you. If you had objected, the matter would naturally have been dropped. That you could not realise all that adoption implied at 15 I understand; but 3 years later you ought to be able to understand it, & certainly in a very delicate crisis between you & Auntie, you ought not to bring it up again.

I telegraphed to you about the piano solely because my experience of you had been that you had to be constantly reminded of it.

Then what you say about the car is utterly incorrect. I have never let you go out in the car without somebody older than yourself to keep an eye on things. You must remember the way I insisted on Leslie overlooking you when you drove to Little Holland. There is no exception to this except that once I let you drive the car back from the station alone. I only did that because I saw no alternative. On this matter you completely misled Auntie, & I have an idea that the car business was the real origin of the trouble.

However, the only really important part of your letter is the phrase 'I was never really fond of you I'm sorry to say, but later I began to like you better; etc.' You ought to have had more sense than to write a thing like this to Auntie, who was not born in the Midlands. I appreciate that you wrote the letter in a kind of cold anger caused by a sense of injustice & that too much importance must not be attached to it. But the fact remains that Auntie has been most *terribly wounded*, & she cannot get over it. Her condition is dreadful. I myself can make allowances, but the fact about Auntie still remains. She always resented your continual sarcastic attitude (which probably you yourself do not notice much), & she has always thought it out of place in a schoolboy toward herself. In this she was right. I hope you will have a good term at school, & I have no doubt that you will work well.

Love to all,
Your distressed uncle,

A.B.

ELDIN / MS / 169
(*To Septimus Bennett*)

12ᴮ, George Street
25–9–19

My dear Sep,
   Thanks for yours. I am no judge of sculpture. These photos seem to me to be photos of good things; but of course they are very old fashioned in conception. I suppose that won't harm them. I should certainly see what can be done with Fielding. There is no doubt in my mind that you can find something that will pay you. Of course you would soon make your way in America. That is certain. And the fact that you are my brother would open all doors to you, as I am a much greater swell there than here. It would not do for you to take out the family at first. Still, no monetary inducement would induce *me* to live permanently anywhere outside England.
   I can't usefully say anything further until I have heard from you re Fielding.

Loves,

Yours, A.B.

CAMBRIDGE / MS / 170
(*To Richard Bennett*)

[Comarques]
14–10–19

My dear Rich,

Referring to the first part of your letter, I cannot give any answers at present, except of course that as far as I am concerned you will be just as well looked after as if nothing had occurred between you & Auntie. As regards Auntie it is not your *behaviour* that is worrying her. It is your deliberate written statement that you never liked her. It is of course not your fault that you never liked her. But it is your fault that you deliberately told her so, & insisted on doing so. The least you could have done, for your own sake, was to hide this lamentable fact. (Unless of course you wanted to break with her.) I should never feel as violently as she does, but I can understand her feeling. It was *her* plan, not mine, to take you over & give you the best possible start. She was always thinking of you & worrying about you (perhaps too much—but if so it was a good fault) & then she suddenly learns that you never liked her. Of course she says to herself: 'What's the use of going on? How can I do anything for a boy who deliberately says he never has liked me? There would always be that between us, & I can't stand it.' That is Auntie's nature, & it is not uncommon at all. You may think that this is a very big thing to spring from such a little thing as a phrase in a letter. But most big things do spring from very little things. How it will end I don't know. Auntie's attitude may change. She of course fully recognises that, as you have been taken on, you must be thoroughly well looked after till you are well planted on your own feet, & she has no desire whatever to put any obstacle in the way of this. We shall see how things are toward the end of the term. I have told Miss Nerney to see to your birth certificate. She will send it.

I asked you for the date of your birthdate, but you haven't sent it. Miss Nerney is not here & I don't know where the birth certificate is. Auntie & Stannard have just gone by the 8.23 to the flat. Miss Nerney & I both go by the 10.8. I shall have the furnace lighted here at the end of the week.

A good thing you did not swim the river.
>Love,
>>Your Turkish bath'd uncle,
>>>A.B.

I return here on Friday.

170. On 24 September Marguerite wrote to Richard, 'I want you to know that I forgive you for not liking me—but at the same time I want to inform you that I can no longer consider you as my adopted son.' Richard wrote at least four letters of apology to her, but she was unmoved. His last letter was written on 8 October. In it he withdrew his assertion that he did not like her and said that he had written it in anger. He acknowledged the impossibility of transferring his affections entirely from his natural home to his adopted home. She replied on the 9th that this was the letter he should have written earlier, but now it was too late.

CAMBRIDGE / MS / 171
(*To Richard Bennett*)

>Leixoes
>[Portugal]
>7–II–20

My dear Richard,

We arrived here yesterday from Havre, & ought to have left last night, but shan't leave till 2 p.m. today, getting to Lisbon tomorrow, Sabbath, morn. Mr. Swin & I & a Brazilian gent motored into Oporto yesterday. It is about 6 miles up the river Douro, but big ships can't go up the Douro, or even into it at all. So this port has been built, just north of the mouth. Oporto is a great place, on about 40 hills, with towers on the top thereof. The principal street is certainly steeper than the Sytch. About 200,000 inh. The life of a car here must be about as long as that of a horse at the Front. The roads are simply appalling—even in fine dry weather as now. I never thought such roads existed—at any rate near a big city. It takes 2 men to do one man's work in Portugal. Thus we had 2 chauffeurs, No. 2's sole duty was to wind up when necessary. We had a Fiat, very noisy. The name of Oporto ought to be Inefficienza. Still it is very amusing. We had a perfectly smooth passage through the bay of Biscay, with bright moonlight nights, etc. Today we loaded up a lot of steerage passengers, & about a million barrels of wine. The monetary system here is continuously funny. Three of us had a magnificent lunch at a great restaurant called the Crystal Palace. It cost fifteen thousand, three hundred reis.

Still, after paying for it, I had money left, as the equivalent in
English is £1.1.10 about. We saw rings in jewellers marked
million reis. The value of the Portuguese dollar (scudo) (1,000
reis or milreis) has fallen owing to the war from 4/- English to
1/7d. English. Very advantageous for us, but it makes the
Portuguese very cross. The whole place is limp and slack. Two
hours after we had arrived here yesterday we were talking to the
agent, & a telegram was brought to him. He said: 'It may
interest you to know that this telegram informs me that your
ship has left Havre.' It had taken 2½ days. Some wires take a
week. I had to wire to Lisbon from Havre, so I sent a wireless
from the Bay of Bisk. 26 words, £1.1/6. The wireless operators
have shown me all their Marconi House and got me to sign a
copy of *The Roll Call*. The wireless system was explained to me
at great length, mais je n'y ai rien compris. Je t'embrasse.

Your neuralgic uncle,

A.B.

Ship's notepaper not on tap at the moment.

171. On 29 January Bennett and Frank Swinnerton went for a month's holiday to
Portugal. According to Swinnerton in his memoir the holiday came about when he and
Edward Knoblock were having lunch together, and Knoblock said, 'Arnold's very ill.
She gives him no peace. If you don't get him away from her for a complete rest, he'll
die.' Swinnerton thereupon arranged a leave from work for himself and persuaded
Bennett to arrange a holiday together. Marguerite then came to Swinnerton 'in a state
of furious anger' because Bennett was taking Swinnerton's advice but not hers: she
herself had been trying to persuade him to take a holiday. In *The Georgian Literary Scene*
Swinnerton writes:

> I went with him . . . on the understanding that as a holiday was necessary to save his
> health he was to do no work at all; but on the third day following our arrival at Mont
> Estoril he confessed that he had written six hundred words before breakfast. When I
> said, 'Oh, no; that's not what you're here for', he answered: 'I know. I had to.'

The Sytch is the valley between Burslem and Brownhills on the old Liverpool Road
(now Westport Road). The word sytch has several meanings—brook, ditch, gutter,
ravine, boggy spring.

KEELE / MS / 172
(*To Marguerite Soulié Bennett*)

Hôtel d'Italie
Mont Estoril
11–2–20

Mon enfant chérie,

   J'ai été extrêmement content de recevoir ta première lettre
hier soir à la dernière heure. 11 days since I had news of you.

You might have been ill, dying, or dead. However, tu existes toujours. As regards the last remarks in the said letter, I do not les prendre en mal. Je sais qu'il faut absolument des fois que tu dises ces choses désobligeantes et inexactes. C'est plus fort que toi. You know perfectly well that I undertook this voyage solely at your request, & to please you. You know also that you yourself insisted that you must not go with me. Lastly you know perfectly well that when *you* announce your intention of going away alone, I do not indulge in remarks & observations. The contrary. I am well pleased with Swinnerton, but it is not my intention to thank him for coming with me. The whole responsibility of the expedition is mine, & I make all the arrangements & take all the trouble. I have taught him quite a lot. We are being absolutely idle. We drove out yesterday afternoon for about 2 hours, & we went a short walk in the morning. The East wind prevents me from doing any painting. I was hoping that it would disappear today; but it is still blowing. There are one or two interesting people in this hotel. But the women are terriblement ficelées. C'est fantastique les laideurs que je suis forcé de contempler. Une seule femme chic. C'est une française, avec un petit garçon de 7 ans (et un mari). You will shortly be going to Leicester for another séance. (Sais-tu que tu écris toujours 'scéance' pour 'séance' et 'Beaudelaire' pour 'Baudelaire'? Moi je n'attache pas la moindre importance à l'orthographe, mais si tu écris à tes correspondants français on serait capable d'en rigoler un peu.) I do not doubt that this séance will be a considerable success. I am not surprised that there were very few people at the Verlaine musical séance. Sans le nom que tu illustres tant, tu n'aurais jamais beaucoup de monde à tes séances. Ce n'est pas question de talent ni même de génie. Il n'existe pas un vrai 'public' pour ces choses étrangères. After all, the celebrity of a name does not go very far. There is a well-known man here, qui a fait des merveilles d'organisation du 'shipping' dans la guerre, et qui est extrêmement intelligent, who thought that I was 'either a painter or a sculptor'. Anyway he was quite sure that he had heard my name. I hope that you will be able to do something for M. Legros. On ne peut pas faire trop pour ces gens. Sur ces entrefaites je te respectueusement bise.

Nouche

The ship by which we return has been delayed in Brazil, and we cannot possibly arrive in London before March 4th.

Accident de voyage.

172. [But the women are appallingly dressed. What amazing ugliness I am forced to contemplate. Only one elegant woman—a Frenchwoman, with a little boy of 7 (and a husband). You will shortly be going to Leicester for another séance. (Do you realise that you always spell séance 'scéance' and Baudelaire 'Beaudelaire'? Personally, I don't regard spelling as at all important but if you write to your French correspondents, they might get a laugh out of it. . . .) Without the name which you render so illustrious, you would never have many people at your performances. Talent, or even genius, are not involved. There is not a real 'public' for these foreign things. . . . There is a well-known man here who made a marvellous job of organising 'shipping' during the war. . . . One cannot do too much for these people. At this juncture I kiss you respectfully.]

After the war Marguerite began to give poetry recitals, and later in 1920 the Anglo-French Poetry Society was formed in part to help her. Bennett was president, and Marguerite, Edith Sitwell, and Helen Rootham were the managing committee. According to the Beardmores Marguerite sent out a leaflet in which she said that 'she had been trained by professors from the Conservatoire and the Comédie Française, and had worked under M. Lugne-Poë at the Théâtre de l'Oeuvre'. In June 1921 Lytton Strachey described one of the Society's evenings at the Bennetts in a letter to Dora Carrington.

He was not there, but *she* was—oh my eye, what a woman! . . . There was an address (very poor) on Rimbaud etc. by an imbecile Frog; then Edith Sitwell appeared, her nose longer than an anteater's, and read some of her absurd stuff; then Eliot—very sad and seedy—it made one weep; finally Mrs. Arnold Bennett recited, with waving arms and chanting voice, Baudelaire and Verlaine till everyone was ready to vomit.

Very likely the Frenchman was René Pierre Legros (1890–1963). He was born in Rennes and studied at the lycée and university there. He also studied at Edinburgh University and at Balliol College. He was at Balliol in 1913–14 and again in 1919, and took a first in modern languages (French). From August 1914 he served in the French army, as staff interpreter, liaison officer with the 13th Hussars, instructor in aerial gunnery. From 1919 to 1932 he was lecturer in French at London University, teaching first at the Bedford College for Women. He became reader in 1932. The Beardmores describe him as 'shortish, with a small moustache, and dark deep eyes'. Frank Swinnerton says he was unimpressive.

KEELE / MS / 173
(*To Marguerite Soulié Bennett*)

Grand Hôtel d'Italie
Sunday
15–2–20

Mon enfant chérie,

Ces anglais sont épatants. N'importe où ils se trouvent il leur faut leur messe à eux. Dans une chambre souterraine de l'hôtel ils ont installé un harmonium que j'entends en ce moment. J'ai eçu ta lettre du 6 hier soir, dans laquelle tu dis que je te comprends mieux que n'importe qui et que tu auras toujours un âme d'enfant. Ceci est exact. Je ne te voudrais pas autrement que tu l'es. Pourtant, quoique tu dises que tu as souffert, je te dis que tu n'as pas souffert plus que les autres — et peut-être moins. Tu auras toujours l'illusion de souffrir spécialement. Notre sort a certainement été au dessus de tes espérances, et des miennes. Tu as plus d'intérêt, plus de vanité dans ta vie, plus de luxe, plus d'argent, plus de liberté, plus d'amour que la grande plupart des femmes mariées. Toujours je me rappellerai la scène quand tu m'as dit que tu exigerais les droits ordinaires d'une femme anglaise mariée. Juste ciel! Regarde autour de toi, et réflechisse. La chose la plus précieuse, après l'affection, est la liberté d'action. Compare la tienne avec celle des autres. Même moi, si je m'accordais la liberté que tu prends — si par exemple je prenais l'habitude de venir en aide des jeunes filles solitaires et ingénues qui avaient appartenues aux corps de femmes dans la guerre — quelle histoire surviendrait. Étant très exceptionelle, avec des idées exceptionellement larges, et estimant que tout individu devrait avoir son indépendance, j'approuve tout ça. Aussi te fais-tu l'illusion que les femmes d'artistes sont nécessairement plus solitaires et délaissées que les autres. Inexacte. Les femmes des grands hommes d'affaires et des politiciens sont beaucoup plus à plaindre. Toi et moi, nous nous voyons énormément plus que la plupart des ménages de notre niveau. Ce voyage m'a rendu le goût du voyage. Je voudrais voyager davantage, et avec toi — pourvu que tu ne sois pas trop fantasque aux arrivées et aux départs des grands terminus. Aurais-je jamais l'idée, moi, de faire ce voyage sans toi, si tu ne l'avais pas exigé? Ce qui est embêtant pour le voyage, c'est d'avoir deux établissements délaissés. Ça m'embête. Ça rend la vie trop compliquée. Aussi est-il trop coûteux. Si on n'as pas trop d'établissements, c'est aussi bon marché de voyager que de rester chez soi. J'estime que Comarques, avec les intérêts sur le capitale qu'il vaut, nous coûte au moins £1200 par an, c'est à dire, si nous l'habitons pendant six mois, à raison de £50 par semaine. Ce climat est délicieux. On peut sortir le soir sans pardessus. On peut prendre un bain avec la fenêtre grand ouverte. J'ai fait deux aquarelles, très dégoûtantes. Nous nous portons bien, mais la

nuit dernière j'ai mal dormi. Je n'ai pas encore eu des nouvelle
sur la date du départ du bateau. Hier il a plu un tout petit poco
Le baromètre tombe. L'hôtel est bondé pour le carnival. Mai
les anglais ne sont pas très carnavalesque. Je n'ai pas encore ét
au casino, qui est pourtant à deux pas. J'écris cette lettre dans le
jardin. Un orchestre orphéonique vient de jouer G. Save the K
Je n'ai pas bougé. C'était trop infecte. Le train porte des fleur
au devant de la machine et *un serpentin derrière le fourgon*
Tordant! M. Swin. te respectueusement salue. Je te
respectueusement et tendrement salue.

Nouch

173. [The English are amazing. Wherever they are, they have to have their ow
religious service. They have installed a harmonium in an underground room in th
hotel and I can hear it now. Yesterday evening I received your letter of the 6th, in whic
you say that I understand you better than anyone and that you will always have th
soul of a child. This is true. I would not want you any different from how you are. Bu
although you say that you have suffered, I would say that you have not suffered an
more than other people—perhaps less. You always have the illusion that you suffe
especially. Our fate has undoubtedly been above your expectations, and above min
You have more interests, more vanity in your life, more luxury, more money, mor
freedom and more love than the great majority of married women. I will alway
remember the scene when you told me that you would demand the ordinary rights of
married English woman. Good heavens! Look around you and think. The mos
precious thing, after affection, is freedom of action. Compare yours with that of othe
people. What quarrels there would be if even I allowed myself the freedom that yo
take—for example, if I adopted the habit of going to the help of lonely and unsophisti
cated young girls, who had belonged to the women's corps during the war. As I am ver
unusual, and have unusually broad-minded ideas, and as I think that every individua
should have his independence, I approve of all that. So you are under the impressio
that artists' wives are of necessity more lonely and neglected than others. Incorrect
The wives of important businessmen and politicians are much more to be pitied. We se
each other, you and I, a great deal more than most couples of our class. This journe
has given me back my taste for travel. I would like to travel more, with you, provide
you are not too unpredictable during arrivals and departures from main terminuses
Would I have ever had the idea of going on this journey without you, if you had no
insisted? What bothers me about travelling is having two unused establishments. I
does bother me. It makes life too complicated. And it is too expensive. If we didn't hav
too many establishments, it would be as cheap to travel as to stay at home. By m
calculations, Comarques, including interest on its capital value, costs us at least £120
per year, that is, £50 a week if we only live in it for six months. The climate here is lovely
You can go out in the evening without a coat. You can have a bath with the windo
wide open. I have done two watercolours, quite awful. We are well, but I slept badl
last night. I have still had no news of the date of departure of the boat. It rained a tin
bit yesterday. The barometer is falling. The hotel is packed with people for the carnival
But the English are not very carnival-minded. I have not been to the casino yet
although it is only two steps away. I am writing this letter in the garden. A chora
orchestra has just played G Save the K. I didn't move. It was too revolting. Trains her
have flowers in front of the engine and *a paper streamer behind the guard's van.* Hilarious! M
Swin sends you his respects. I send you respects and tenderness.]

KEELE / MS / 174
(*To Marguerite Soulié Bennett*) Hôtel d'Italie
Tuesday
17–2–20

Mon enfant chérie,

This is the day after the ball, & it is pouring with rain. It has rained heavily all night, & the glass is still going down. Needless to say that the ugliest, stiffest women in the hotel alone put themselves into fancy-dress for this ball. Elles avaient l'air totalement ridicule. From the young women's point of view the dance was a failure because there were scarcely any dancing Englishmen, & the girls did not know the Portuguese young men. Everyone said that this would happen, & it did happen. However, I am glad, et extraordinairement fier, to say that in the management of old women I did something that no one believed could be done. Madame Bartholomew, wife of the celebrated Scotch geographer, has exceedingly narrow Scotch ideas,—so has her husband. She had never been in a casino before. Her daughters had never been to the continent before. She absolutely refused to go from the ball-room to the salle des jeux, or to let her young daughters go. She began talking about *The Pretty Lady*, which it appears has shocked all Scotland terribly. She was very plain; but not so plain as I was. After half an hour I took her & her daughters up to the salle des jeux. I gave both her daughters money out of my winnings, I taught them to play before her eyes. They won, paid me back my money, & went home with over £1 each, winnings. The daughters were simply staggered that I had been able to persuade the mother to allow it. It was the most astounding thing that had ever happened to them. But I had not even tried to persuade the mother. I had simply slanged this dignified dame. I had told her that English hypocrisy was bad enough, but that Scotch hypocrisy was far worse; & that the illegitimate birth-rate was much higher in Scotland than in England, & that all she & her friends said about *The Pretty Lady* was not only disgraceful but puerile. (Mr. Swin, observing us from far off, thought we were going to have a row. Not at all.) I then told her that I was going to take her daughters upstairs to play. She said: 'Shall I come too?' I said: 'By all means.' This affair was a tremendous lark. We left about 1 o'clock, as there was so little

dancing to see. I did another water colour yesterday morning. I
am still eating those sweets which you gave us at Euston. The
chocolate is all gone, but I eat 2 of the other sweets every day, en
pensant à toi, et il en reste assez pour encore une semaine. We
meant to go to Lisbon tomorrow, but if it doesn't clear up we
shan't. Mr. Swin & I are both reading Balzac. He has written a
long letter to Jane Wells. Also to Hughie. Je n'ai pas encore
reçu un seul mot sur Leicester. Aujourd'hui dernier jour du
carnaval. Ça sera triste à Lisbon. I am very well. Hommages de
M. Swin.

Je te bise bien mon tout enfant,

Nouche

174. Janet Bartholomew (née Macdonald) and John George Bartholomew (1860–
1920), celebrated for *'The Times' Survey Atlas of the World*. He was in Portugal for his
health, and died there.

Hughie: Hugh Walpole (1884–1941), the novelist. For letters and other references to
him see the other volumes.

KEELE / MS / 175
(*To Marguerite Soulié Bennett*)   Hôtel d'Italie
                                                    Thursday
                                                    19–2–20

Mon enfant chérie,

J'ai reçu ce matin ta lettre du 10, avec la nouvelle de la folie
de Mdlle. Ferré.

Tu dis:

'Tu me manques.'

Je dis:

'Tu me manques.'

Tu dis:

'Si je n'ai pas une lettre journellement ça me manque
beaucoup.'

Je dis:

'Si je n'ai pas une lettre journellement ça me manque
BEAUCOUP.'

C'est triste, l'histoire de Mdlle. Ferré. Ça ne me surprend pas
énormément. Elle était trop contenue. Excellente fille, mais
terriblement rentrée. Chez les vieilles filles ça tourne assez
souvent à la folie. M. Legros t'a très sagement conseillé.

J'aurais dit exactement la même chose. Tu as bien fait de prendre Kathleen avec toi. Je suis de l'avis du monsieur français qui t'a dit que tu es un génie manqué à la scène française. Pourtant, tout ça admis, si tu avais eu la vraie vocation, *rien* ne t'aurait empêché de te faire actrice. Tu n'es ni plus ni moins heureuse. Actrice, tu aurais eu de grandes compensations, mais aussi des ennuis terribles, et une vieillesse infiniment plus triste que la tienne ne sera.

I have now painted 5 water colours. Ça va un peu mieux. Nous avons eu mauvais temps, même très mauvais, mais avec des couchers de soleil merveilleux. À l'heure qu'il est le temps se remet, le baromètre monte, et ce matin est magnifique. Madame Jayne, et un écrivain anglais qui habite le Portugal, Edgar Prestage, viennent à déjeuner de Lisbon. Je pense, mais je ne suis pas sûr, que je connaissais Prestage il y a 27 ans. Je me porte admirablement, tout en rêvant beaucoup la nuit. Ce système de portes entre les chambres est assommant, mais j'ai des voisins très convenables, qui lisent tard dans la nuit, mais qui ne soufflent mot. C'est un monsieur de 40 ans avec une femme de 30. De la partie sont sa sœur à lui et sa sœur à elle. Ils sont toujours bien entassés les uns sur les autres, et je l'appelle lui, 'the man with 3 wives'. Nous faisons des promenades en voitures, des lectures, et des discussions. Le soir j'ai pris l'habitude de jouer du whist avec des gens des deux sexes de mon âge. Le bal costumé était le plus noir des jours, mais infiniment divertissant pour moi. M. Swin. se porte aussi très bien, et s'amuse autant que moi. Il est particulièrement rosse avec toutes les femmes et toutes les jeunes filles. Pourtant il les fait rire — peut-être un peu jaunâtre. M. Loraine m'écrit pour demander une pièce.

Sur ces entrefaites, ma carissime infanta, je te doucement et gentiment bise.

Nouche

Nous pensons quitter ces parages environ jeudi proche, le 25, pour passer 2 ou 3 jours à Lisbon. Tu adresses mal tes lettres. J'espère qu'elles arrivent toutes.

175. [This morning I received your letter of the 10th, with the news of Mlle Ferre's madness.
You say: 'I miss you.']

I say: 'I miss you.'

You say: 'If I don't get a letter every day, I miss it very much.'

I say: 'If I don't get a letter every day, I miss it very much.'

The story of Mlle Ferre is sad. It does not greatly surprise me. She was too reserved. An excellent girl, but terribly closed in on herself. With old maids, that can often lead on to madness. M Legros gave you very good advice. I would have said exactly the same thing. You did well to take Kathleen with you. I share the opinion of the Frenchman who told you that you are a genius who has disappointed the French theatre. Granted; nevertheless, if you had really had a vocation, *nothing* would have stopped you from becoming an actress. You are neither more nor less happy. You would have had great rewards as an actress, but terrible worries as well and your old age would be infinitely sadder.

I have now painted 5 watercolours. These have come off a little better. We have had bad weather, even very bad, but with marvellous sunsets. The weather is now improving, the barometer is rising and this morning is beautiful. Madame Jayne, and Edgar Prestage, an English writer who lives in Portugal, are coming to lunch from Lisbon. I think I used to know Prestage 27 years ago, but I am not sure. I am in excellent health, and I dream a lot at night. This system of doors between the bedrooms is very annoying, but I have very proper neighbours, who read until late into the night but never breathe a word. They are a man of 40 with a wife of 30. His sister and her sister are of the party. They are always all in a crowd together and I call him 'the man with 3 wives'. We go for car trips, we read and talk. In the evenings, I play whist with people of my age of both sexes. The fancy dress ball took place on the blackest day, but I found it tremendously entertaining. Mr Swin is also very well and is enjoying himself as much as I am. He is very harsh with all women and young girls. Still he makes them laugh—though perhaps not wholeheartedly. Mr Loraine has written to me asking for a play.

At this juncture, my most beloved infanta, I kiss you gently and nicely.... We are thinking of leaving these regions around next Thursday the 25th, to spend 2 or 3 days in Lisbon. You address your letters badly. I hope they all arrive.]

Mlle Ferre; Kathleen; Madame Jayne: unidentified.

Edgar Prestage (1869–1951); he was a press officer attached to the British Legation in Lisbon during the latter part of the War.

Robert Loraine (1876–1935), the actor-manager.

KEELE / MS / 176
(*To Marguerite Soulié Bennett*)

Comarques
1–4–20

My sweet child,

.A further complication has now arisen in regard to Richard. I thought, & he thought, that his O.T.C. camp near Eastbourne would be the last fortnight of his holidays. It now appears that it will end five days before the holidays end. I am not going to send him back all the way to Rochdale for those 5 days. He will spend the Thursday to Tuesday here with me. I know that you object to this, but I strongly maintain that you are wrong. I did not argue the point with you when it was mentioned before, because you were not in a condition to argue. Your feelings are still so strong about Richard that you cannot. I can see no reason whatever why Richard should be prevented from spending some days in his uncle's home merely because his auntie is not there. And I most particularly do not want him to come & stay when you *are* there, until you feel able to treat him ordinarily. You say you cannot yet do this. I can understand that quite well. But the social atmosphere, if you & he were together, and you could not treat him ordinarily & insisted on ignoring him and leaving him to me, would be rather more than I am prepared to stand. That is why, after what you told me, I instructed him not to come to the flat. I hope that you will have no difficulty in exercising your imagination & putting yourself in my place in this affair. I never wanted to adopt Richard. I knew the dangers of it, & I told you of them. I said that he was too old to adopt. However, you wanted it very much, and quite against my judgement I yielded in this most important thing. (Moi qui ne cède jamais, à ce qu'il paraît.) Exactly what I feared has happened as usual. The difficulties were too great. Still, you had what you wanted. You knew the boy's character—how sensitive and how obstinate he is; & you knew the character of his parents. By the way, the behaviour of his parents is no fault of the boy's. Of course I blame the boy very severely for his letter to you. More than anything he was an *ass* to write it. I quite understand that he wounded your amour-propre in a way from which you cannot recover. On the other hand it is certain that the boy would never have done this idiotic & shameful thing if he had not been most deeply hurt in *his* amour-propre. There is always an explanation of things, even if there is not an excuse. You did your duty to the boy in the fullest & most conscientious manner. Neither he nor anybody will deny that. But in my opinion it was imprudent of you to treat him like a child while expecting him to behave like a man. It was certainly imprudent of you to denigrer son home, as you often did. Often have I seen his face show resentment of that. And I have *never* known you speak of the Five Towns (ce malheureux district, auquel nous devons notre situation) without disdain. However, all this is beside the point. The point is that at your urgent request, I undertook a most solemn responsibility in regard to that infernal youth. You have renounced your responsibility. That is your affair. Certainly I do not blame you. But I have not renounced mine, and cannot. I took that boy out of his own atmosphere and gave him a promise of a new and much larger life. That promise I shall fulfil until he can stand firmly on his own feet. It is far from being a question of paying money. At best the business will be exceedingly difficult for me; but you can do a lot to make it easier. I don't want you to see him. In fact I prefer you not to see him at present. But I want to be left free, & I want you to think a little less of your amour-propre and a little more of the great difficulty of the situation which I am in *owing solely to my desire to please you*. Richard will be here from 22nd to 27th April.

It is raining hard—naturally. I am not doing anything except bricoler et surveiller the estate. Je te tendrement bise.

Nouche

KEELE / MS / 177
(*To Marguerite Soulié Bennett*)

Comarques
jeudi
8–4–20

Mon enfant chérie,

Merci beaucoup de ta dépêche de Toulouse qui est arrivée hier après-midi vers 4 heures. J'ai reçu ta lettre du 5 seulement ce matin; ce qui prouve que les postes sont assez désorganisées. Mais pas autant que les Postes Portugaises. J'ai reçu ce matin, de Mont Estoril, la lettre que tu m'y as adressée avec les nouvelles de la première de *John Ferguson*! Chic! Il pleut terriblement. Mais je n'en suis pas fâché parce que je me suis offert un nouveau caoutchouc des plus épatants, et ce matin j'ai pu l'étrenner. Très réussi. Les journées sont longues, mais bien remplies. Je travaille. Je lis. Je me promène. Je ne me couche pas avant minuit moins le quart, et quand je me couche ma seule idée est de me lever le lendemain. Beaverbrook nous a invité pour la fin de semaine. Je savais que si je restais coi ce type ferait les avances. Par l'intermédiaire de Blumenfeld, directeur de l'Express, il m'a fait dire que je l'avais complètement abandonné (deserted him). J'ai envoyé par le même

intermédiaire un message des plus raides. Ces millionaires
pensent toujours que tout le monde est comme le monde trop
empressé qui les entoure. Pourtant il m'est très sympathique,
Max. Il a les défauts de ses qualités — et de son argent. Aussi,
j'aurai besoin de lui bientôt pour mon prochain roman. Il me
sera indispensable pour ça. Toutefois j'ai naturellement refusé
son invitation. Je le verrai un jour à Londres. Il est très
chatouilleux. Ça lui fait du bien que je le traite comme le
premier venu. Et pourquoi pas, enfin? Tes observations sur les
Cinq Villes — je ne les déteste pas du tout. J'y suis accoutumé,
et du reste j'ai mes idées bien arrêtées sur les 5 T. Je les ai, pour
une fois, mentionnées, pour expliquer certaines choses. C'est
très vrai que tu attaches peu d'importance aux choses que tu
dis, mais tu attaches une énorme importance aux choses quand
on les dit à toi. Tu as horreur des chatouilleux, mais tu es très
très chatouilleuse toi-même. La preuve!... Percy arrive demain.
Samedi et dimanche — deux journées de peinture. Je crains
que cette lettre n'arrive pas à Toulouse avant ton départ. Donc
je l'adresserai chez Hélène. Continue de t'amuser bien avec
tes cousins. Et n'oublie pas de transmettre à ta mère toute
l'affection que j'ai pour l'être qui t'a mise au monde.

Je te bise bien.

Nouche

177. [Thank you very much for your telegram from Toulouse, which arrived
yesterday afternoon at about 4 o'clock. Your letter of the 5th only arrived this morning;
this proves that the posts are fairly disorganized. But not as much as the Portuguese
posts. This morning I received from Mont Estoril the letter you sent me there, with
news of the première of *John Ferguson*! Great! The rain is terrible. But I don't mind
because I have given myself a most beautiful new waterproof, and I christened it this
morning. A great success. The days are long but very full. I work. I read. I walk. I do
not go to bed before a quarter to twelve midnight, and when I go to bed, my only
thought is of getting up the next day. Beaverbrook has invited us for the weekend. I
knew that if I kept quiet the chap would make overtures to me. He told me through
Blumenfeld, the editor of the *Express*, that I had quite deserted him. I sent him a very
stiff message through the same intermediary. These millionaires always think that
everyone is the same as the over-eager crowd around them. But I find Max very
congenial. He has the faults of his qualities—and of his money. And I will need him
soon for my next novel. He will be indispensable to me for it. All the same, of course I
refused his invitation. I will see him in London one day. He is very touchy. It will do
him good for me to treat him as just anybody. After all, why shouldn't I? I by no means
hate your observations on the Five Towns. I am used to them and besides, I have my
own very clearly formed ideas on the 5 T. I have mentioned them for once to explain
various things. It is very true that you grant little importance to the things you say, but
you give tremendous importance to things other people say to you. You can't bear
touchy people, but you are very, very touchy yourself. The proof! ... Percy is arriving

tomorrow. Saturday and Sunday will be two days of painting. I am afraid this letter will
not reach Toulouse before you leave. So I will send it to Hélène's. Go on enjoying
yourself with your cousins. And don't forget to give your mother all the affection that I
feel for the person who brought you into the world. With a good kiss.]

John Ferguson: play by St John Ervine.
    The novel had to do with the career and death of Beaverbrook's father, and journal
entries of 1919–20 record conversations with Beaverbrook about him. The novel was
never written, but the material on the father's death was incorporated in Part II of *Lord
Raingo*, written in 1926.
    R. D. Blumenfeld (1864–1948) edited Beaverbrook's *Daily Express*. For letters to him
see Vol. III.
    Percy: Percy Jowett (1882–1955), painter, husband of Enid Ledward; later Principal
of the Royal College of Art.

KEELE / MS / 178
(*To Marguerite Soulié Bennett*)

Comarques
9–4–20

Mon enfant chérie,

J'espère que tu achèteras quelquechose de chic dans le genre
lingerie intime, pour me récompenser de ton absence un peu. Je
n'attends pas de lettre de toi aujourd'hui puisque tu es plus loin
& que les lettres prendront encore plus longtemps pour arriver.
Je n'ai pas eu une seule lettre intéressante aujourd'hui. Cet
après-midi j'entame mon troisième acte, moment sérieux,
parce que tout dépend du troisième. Percy arrive à 7 h. Samedi
et dimanche, rien que la peinture. Lundi, continuation de
l'acte. Je suis sorti ce matin, et je viens d'entrer, trempé pour
les pieds, mais autrement sec — grâce à mon caoutchouc
mirifique. Dans mon soi-disant cerveau je t'ai picturée avec tes
deux preux chevaliers faisant la roue dans les rues les plus
selectes de Toulouse. Tu as probablement créé une certaine
sensation. Ici, tout marche — même M. Canham. Ingram a
toujours froid, bien qu'il fasse beaucoup trop doux et la maison
soit trop chaude.

Je te chaleureusement bise.

Ton Nouche

178. [I hope you will buy something elegant in the way of intimate underclothing as
some measure of reward to me for your absence. I am not expecting a letter from you
today because you are further away and letters will take even longer to arrive. I have
not had one single interesting letter today. This afternoon I am starting on my third act,
an important moment, as everything depends on the third act. Percy is arriving at 7

o'clock. Saturday and Sunday will be entirely devoted to painting. On Monday I will continue the act. I went out this morning and have just come in, with my feet soaked but otherwise dry—thanks to my wonderful mackintosh. You are pictured in my so-called brain with your two gallant knights strutting down the most select streets of Toulouse. You must have made quite a sensation. Everything continues here—even Mr Canham. Ingram is always cold, although it is much too mild and the house is too hot. I kiss you passionately.]

Bennett wrote *The Bright Island* between January and April 1920. It was produced for two nights by the Stage Society in 1925.

Ingram: unidentified.

KEELE / MS / 179
(*To Marguerite Soulié Bennett*)

Comarques
23–4–20

Mon enfant chérie,

Veuilles me télégraphier, ici, dimanche ou lundi (au plus tard) le jour de ton arrivée à Londres. J'ai des arrangements à faire. C'est deux sombres tableaux que tu traces (avec une certaine maîtrise) des God. et des Martin. (Enfin tu commences à écrire ce que j'appelle des *lettres*.) Je conçois bien que Madame Martin n'a pas l'air d'une épouse. Elle ne peut pas l'être. Quand on pense que toute la tragédie de Martin trouve son origine dans une très petite chose. Tu l'as vu dans son lit et presque muet, parce que il s'est trouvé une nuit, il y a peut-être 30 ans, dans le lit d'une grue à Dundee (Écosse). So that's that. C'est une démonstration effrayante du fait que les plus minuscules causes puissent avoir les plus énormes effets. Je conçois aussi que Madame Martin a l'air d'attendre. Ça doit être assez dur pour elle. Mais ça ne peut pas durer longtemps, et les choses se sont assez bien arrangées pour tous les deux. Stannard vient de me dire qu'elle connaît une cook housekeeper de ses amies, dont les maîtres s'en vont aux États Unis pour quelque temps, que c'est une excellente femme, et qu'elle pense que la dite femme pourrait venir au flat en attendant que tu trouves une autre. Elle écrit à la cook housekeeper aujourd'hui, et je lui ai dit d'arranger ça pour vendredi prochain si c'est possible. J'aurai la réponse bientôt.

Richard est ici.

Je serai au flat mardi soir. Je dîne avec Tayler et nous irons voir *As You Like It*.

Tu ne m'as rien dit sur la fin de semaine de Max. J'ai donc décidé que tu iras avec moi. Tu t'embêteras peut-être, mais dans le service de l'art du roman. Nous irons en auto. Plus commode. Une heure seulement.

Il fait toujours un temps infecte.

Je dors mal. Mais je ne suis nullement 'éreinté'. La chronique portugaise est presque finie. J'avais fais *les notes* en voyage, et aussi j'avais écrit la tierce partie de la chronique. Je dors rottenly.

Ta lettre de dimanche, tu peux l'adresser ici. *Après* dimanche s'adresser au flat.

La nouvelle pièce de Barrie au Haymarket a l'air d'être un assez gros succès. Ce qui m'embête dedans c'est qu'il y a une île dedans. Mais Barrie même n'est pas le premier avec son île. Brighouse avait une île. Il y a peu d'île dans Barrie. Dans ma pièce il n'y a qu'île.

Sur ces entrefaites je te tendrement bise ma grosse, partout, dans ta nouvelle lingerie.

Nouche

La recette de *S.P.* à New York en 'Holy Week' dépassait 10,000 dollars. Pas mal.

A.B.

179. [Please send a telegram here on Sunday or Monday (at the latest), to tell me the day of your arrival in London. I have some arrangements to make. What gloomy pictures you paint (with some skill) of the Gods and the Martins. (At last you are beginning to write what I call a letter.) I can well imagine that Madame Martin does not seem like a wife. She cannot be one. To think that Martin's whole tragedy grew out of a very little thing. You saw him in bed and almost speechless because one night, perhaps 30 years ago, he happened to get into the bed of a whore in Dundee (Scotland). So that's that. It is a most frightening illustration of the fact that the smallest causes can have the most enormous effects. I can also imagine that Madame Martin looks as if she is waiting for something. It must be very hard for her. But it can't last long and things have worked out there quite well for both of them. Stannard has just told me that she knows a cook housekeeper whose employers are going to New York for some time, that she is an excellent woman, and that she thinks she could come to the flat until you can find someone else. She is writing to the cook housekeeper today and I have told her to arrange it for next Friday if possible. I will have the answer soon.

Richard is here.

I will be in the flat on Tuesday evening. I will dine with Tayler and we will go to see *As You Like It*.

You have not said anything about the weekend with Max. So I have decided that you will come with me. Perhaps you will be bored but in the service of the art of the novel. We will go by car. More convenient. Only an hour.

The weather is still awful.

I am sleeping badly. But I am not at all 'exhausted'. The Portuguese article is almost finished. I had taken notes during the journey and had also written a draft of the article. I am sleeping *rottenly*.

You can send your Sunday's letter here. After Sunday, send letters to the flat.

Barrie's new play at the Haymarket seems to be quite a success. What annoys me is that there is an island in it. But even Barrie is not the first with his island. Brighouse had an island. There is not much about the island in the Barrie. In my play, there is only the island.

At this juncture, I kiss you tenderly, my fat one, all over, in your new underwear.... The takings from *S.P.* in New York during Holy Week were over 10,000 dollars. Not bad.]

Alistair (Duff) Tayler (d. 1935) was a good friend of Bennett's. In 1918 Tayler, Bennett, and Nigel Playfair formed a company to run the Lyric Theatre, Hammersmith. For other references to Tayler see Vols. I and III.

'Some Impressions of Portugal' appeared in *Harper's* in January 1922, and was reprinted in *Things That Have Interested Me, Second Series*, 1923.

J. M. Barrie's play was *Mary Rose*. Harold Brighouse (1882–1958).

Sacred and Profane Love was a commercial success in America. Bennett received royalties from it of £1,453, £1,300, and £600 in March, April, and May 1920.

CAMBRIDGE / MS / 180
(*To Richard Bennett*)

12^B, George Street
3–5–20

My dear Rich,

I congratulate you on being made a school prefect. You had better order evening dress from the local artist, also 2 shirts, I should think. The old ones would certainly be too short in the sleeves if not elsewhere. You can remind me at the end of the month about that 6/6 you paid for the bicycle carriage. I gave the moon a miss. I have just returned from a weekend at Lord Beaverbrook. Auntie couldn't go, as she came back from Paris speechless with a cold & had to retire to bed. She is now recovered. I don't quite understand why the Marquis has put you in an ordinary class, & you had better let me know at once if there is anything I can do.

I was not wholly satisfied with you during the few days we spent together. It is not so much that I object to your being idle, unkempt, untidy, & dirty—though the time is coming when you ought to be getting rid of these boyish defects. It is that I object to your extraordinary self-centredness & most marked self-conceit: which show themselves throughout in your general behaviour. You ought to think more of what other people are feeling & thinking, & to remember that if you enjoy the advantages of living in a community you also owe certain things to the community. Your indifference to others is really astounding; & your manners are also most regrettable. On leaving the Wells's the other day you quite refrained from thanking Mrs. Wells for her hospitality, & held yourself just as if it was you who had conferred a favour. This of course is the act of a lout. I am ready to make allowances for the fact that, going to Rochdale with all the prestige of a big public school & as the winner of a scholarship at Clare, you are likely to be spoilt, and you assuredly are spoilt. But while I make allowances I must at the same time tell you how matters stand in my estimation.

Your watchful uncle,

A.B.

180. The Marquis: title given by Bennett and Wells to Sanderson of Oundle.

CAMBRIDGE / MS / 181
(*To Richard Bennett*)

Comarques
18–5–20

My dear Rich,

My remarks to you seem to have lost their effect. Why are you more often than not late with your letters? There is no reason for it except that odious indifference & slackness, which will certainly do you harm later on if you do not deal with it. As regards the dress-coat, I don't know whether you mean coat or dinner-jacket. I presume the latter. If so, a roll collar is correct. My latest dress-coat is in London & I can't remember whether it has a roll collar or not, but I should think not.

I have no sparklet syphon & never had one.

As a blazer usually has no shape at all after it has been worn five minutes, & as the worst blazer is by the tradition of centuries always considered to be the most chic, I should say that it doesn't matter 2^d where you have the O.O. blazer made. But wherever you have it made, have it made large enough.

I take very little stock in these military field days. In fact I object to them. It seems to me that the combined wisdom of the heads of public schools might devise something better than a silly imitation of war, which in itself is the most criminally silly institution now surviving amid humanity. If either you loyal infants or the heads had spent a year or two in the trenches you wouldn't be so keen on attacking towns. I am sure that H. G. Wells could invent a better method of spending a day of sport and physical and intelligent rivalry in the open air.

I see no reason why you should not go to Cambridge on the bike—except one reason,—namely, that the frame does not get back in time.

To Mrs. McM. I will write. We are just off to London, that is to say, after breakfast. We had some tennis on Saturday, but I shone only very sporadically, the foul east wind having upset my liver completely. 70% of Sunday I spent in bed. But yesterday I began to write a short story, the first I have tried for 7 or 8 years.

There is no reason why you should not pass the little go easily. If you don't you will be in a nice mess.

Love,
Your departing uncle,

A.B.

CAMBRIDGE / MS / 182
(*To Richard Bennett*)

Comarques
26–5–20

My dear Rich,

Thanksletter. Explanation amounts to nothing. The thing is to have a regular time & stick to it. It doesn't matter what time the letter arrives so long as it arrives regularly. I always write to you immediately on receipt of yours. Your letters now generally arrive on Tuesday afternoon. If this is to continue you had better address them for the present to the flat. But I do not see how circumstances have altered with you. The bell, the wakening, the changed hours in summer, were surely ever thus. However, the thing is to be regular. We have had a most magnificent Whitsuntide. Tennis each day & a tennis party yesterday afternoon. People staying here: Jane Duncan, her fiancé Maurice Marston, & Pierre Legros—reported to be the only Frenchman who ever got into Balliol. He is about 30 now & much knocked about in the nerves by the war. I drove the company to Clacton on Saturday morning, & in turning a corner at bottom of a hill found that the foot brake did not act at all. The excellent Fred must have put it on too sharply & simply stripped it. Since then I have been driving on the hand brake alone, ticklish; but I have let no one else drive. I hear of a very good car—the A.K.S. or some such name—friction drive, been on the market 5 or 6 years, but now much improved. £400 new. If I was buying a car I would buy that one, but as we shan't use a car after October, & as the present one is in perfect order (bar brake) I see no point in buying a new one, especially as I want a yacht. There is a horrible slump in theatres. I don't see why the Ford shouldn't last for years. I have not the slightest expectancy of arriving in your city before Saturday; but it will finally depend on the Wellses. Two guests gone; last one goes at 7 a.m. tomorrow. We go on the 10 train.

Love,
Your holidaying uncle,

A.B.

182. Jane Duncan; Maurice Marston: unidentified.

Fred Harvey, butler and also chauffeur, was Bennett's most trusted servant of later years. When Bennett went away on trips he usually wrote postcards to Harvey and to other employees.

KEELE / MS / 183
(*To Marguerite Soulié Bennett*)

South Western Hotel
Southampton
6–8–20

Mon enfant chérie,

J'ai bien reçu ta lettre ce matin. Le *Wanderer* est un bateau qui me va, mais il faudrait modifier les cloisons des cabines et installer la lumière électrique. On a demandé £3,000. J'ai offert £2,500. On a dit que c'était impossible, mais à 9.30 hier soir on a accepté! Naturellement je ne prendrai le bateau qu'après examination détaillée par un expert ('survey'). Il y a deux canots et *un troisième grand canot à moteur*. J'espère que le 'survey' sera satisfaisant. C'est possible que nous passerons la fin de la semaine chez Knoblock. Je compte rentrer lundi soir. Pour M. Legros, il faut que tu fasses comme tu voudras. Quand tu m'as dit que tu avais invité Legros pour six semaines, j'étais assez surpris. Six semaines c'est un période bien long. Je n'ai absolument rien contre Legros, qui est toujours agréable et poli. Ses compliments sont, pour moi, exagérés, mais j'y suis accoutumé. Je conçois que sa présence serait excellente pour les enfants, et pour lui-même aussi, mais il va de soi que notre maison n'existe pas principalement pour l'éducation des jeunes. Bien ni pour la rétablissement des jeunes officiers. Je te présente seulement mes idées, et je ne serais nullement froissé si tu décides de retenir Legros. En attendant j'ai l'énorme préoccupation de l'éducation de mon neveu et mon fils adopté. Rien ne m'a tracassé, ni me tracasse, comme cette affaire, qui deviendra toujours plus difficile. Il aura six mois (en tout) de Cambridge et six mois (en tout) de vacances chaque année. (La théorie de l'éducation universitaire est que les étudiants travaillent et digèrent pendant six mois chez eux ce qu'ils ont appris au Collège pendant les autres six mois.) Laisser Richard pendant six mois à Rochdale sera de ruiner son éducation, sans compter qu'en le faisant je manquerais à un devoir solennel que j'ai solennellement accepté. Jamais de ma vie je ne me suis trouvé dans une situation si assommante. Jamais je ne me reveille la nuit sans y penser. Il faut que je passe quelque temps avec Richard avant la rentrée des classes. Je suppose que je serai forcé de faire un voyage. Sans doute je suis assez habile pour trouver une solution, mais je ne la vois pas.

Je te bise tendrement, mon enf. ch.

Nouche

We leave this hotel Saturday morning, tomorrow.

183. [Your letter arrived safely this morning. The *Wanderer* is a boat which suits me, but the partitions of the cabins would have to be altered and electric light installed. The asking price was £3,000. I offered £2,500. I was told that was impossible but at 9.30 yesterday evening, it was accepted. Of course I will not take the boat without a detailed examination by an expert ('survey'). There are two dinghies and a *third big motor dinghey*. I hope the survey will be satisfactory. We may spend the weekend at Knoblock's. I intend to return home on Monday evening. About M Legros, you must do as you please. When you told me that you had invited Legros for six weeks, I was quite surprised. Six weeks is a very long time. I have absolutely nothing against Legros, who is always very pleasant and polite. I feel he overdoes his compliments, but I am used to them. I can see that his presence would be an excellent thing for the children and also for himself but it goes without saying that the principal function of our house is not the upbringing of the young nor the recovery of young officers. I am only telling you my ideas and I will be in no way offended if you decide to keep Legros. Meanwhile my tremendous concern is the education of my nephew and adopted son. This question has

worried me and still does worry me more than any other and it will become even more difficult. He will have (a total of) six months in Cambridge and (a total of) six months' vacation every year. (The theory of university education is that students spend six months at home studying and digesting what they have learned at college during the other six months.) Leaving Richard at Rochdale for six months would amount to ruining his education. Quite apart from the fact that in doing so I would be failing in a solemn duty which I solemnly undertook. Never in my life have I been in such a bothersome situation. Never do I wake in the night without thinking about it. I must spend some time with Richard before term starts. I suppose this means I'll have to travel. No doubt I am clever enough to find a solution, but I can't see it. I kiss you tenderly, my darl. ch.]

CAMBRIDGE / MS / 184
(*To Richard Bennett*)

Comarques
10–8–20

My dear Rich,

I have just received your letter. I am glad to hear about the prizes, & the cup will no doubt be useful at meals; but the accident & the apprehension by a policeman were grave mistakes. If you are summoned, your father will be able to advise you. I don't know that it would be absolutely necessary for you to attend. You must have been expeding the seed limit pretty considerably, I should imagine. I returned from Cowes & Brighton yesterday afternoon; I saw several of the finest yachts in the world, costing from £35,000 to £150,000. Reluctantly declining these, I at last bought the 'Wanderer' (subject to survey), which belonged to the late Sir Hubert Parry, head of the R. C. of Music. She is 75 ft over all, & 17.5 beam, & her saloon is a foot wider than the large drawing-room here. I am going to install electric light. She has a Thorneycroft engine. She also has 3 boats, including an 18 ft. motor launch, with an American engine about the size of a peanut. I hope that you will sail in her next year. I am no more forward with my arrangements for the present autumn than I was before, as I can't get any exact information about my theatrical productions. I much regret to say that it will be inadvisable for you to come here at present. Auntie has never got over your letter to her. I said before I saw it that this letter must be a masterpiece of ineptitude, and when I read it I was deeply confirmed in this view. The situation is very difficult; you two brought it about between you, & the entirely innocent uncle has all the resulting bother. If I can be free, which is not yet by any means sure, I will take you to Scotland before term begins, & incidentally we can see some of the biggest works on the Clyde, which may be useful later on. In the meantime, if your parents have no objection you had better stay on with them, paying your proper share of everything. To go to Southampton etc, Mr. Sullivan & I hired a Rolls Royce; it costs no more than any other car; for comfort I don't reckon it is equal to either a Cadillac or a Lanchester.

Love,
Your blameless uncle,

A.B.

KENNERLEY / MS / 185
(*To Tertia Kennerley*)

Comarques
19–8–'20

My dear Tertia,

Thank you. You did very well to take a taxi & it was not too dear. But be it known to you that a big Rolls Royce, resembling Solomon's Temple with Solomon on the box, can be hired for £7.7/- per day. We are indeed summering here, & the house is very French. There are 5 French people in it at the moment. I have been & am undergoing a long course of microbes for pyorrhoea, & I have been stuffed with neuralgia and rheumatism. Nevertheless I have written a play since July 1st, & bought an 88 ton yacht (subject to survey). And I have played much tennis—too much. Marguerite is preparing for a reciting tour. I am greatly preoccupied and tracassé with the Richard question. I fear it is all over between Aunt & nephew. In my absence she deeply humiliated him in the presence of 'company', & the next day he administered such a shock to her as I don't think she will ever get over. The affair was all over before I heard of it. He was an ass, but he was very angry and resentful. Apologies seem to cut no ice. The really amazing thing is that I never wanted to adopt the kid, and that I foresaw and foretold the kind of thing that would occur & that did occur. Still, having solemnly adopted the boy, I can't, because he has been an angry ass, throw him over, much as it would ease me to do so. Nor can I discharge my responsibility merely by signing cheques. It would be a mere waste of cheques. I think I shall take him for a tour in Scotland before inducting him into Cambridge. Though still damnably 5-Towny, he is all right, & I can manage him all right. But to do so without a home-base is rather on the difficult side. He has done excellently at school, & the Headmaster says he is a great organiser. One of the causes of the trouble was that Aunt and parents were always mutually inimical. Aunt had a grievance there; but Richard is passionately attached to his original home. Strange. His parents went under the remarkable delusion, horridly foretold by me, that they could abandon their offspring & still keep him.

I have four finished, unproduced plays—& no idea when any of them will be produced. I am just starting to write an original film. There is trouble awaiting me there.

I think that something will soon have to be done as regards the money which I hold in trust for you. It has been remarkably fruitful. The original £500 stands at £800, & in the last 20 years (I suppose it is about 20) you have had about £2,000 in interest, whereas if we had only got £1,000 in interest & the capital had not increased, we should have had nothing to complain about. Thanks to the first rate advice which I could always get in the city, it was not so difficult during the war to work the changing investments so as to get, in one way or another, about 12% regular. But the markets are greatly changed now, and adventures are much more dangerous. I scarcely care to run the risks now. To my mind it would be best to put the money into fixed-interest-bearing securities repayable in a few years' time at a higher price than they now cost. In this way the capital would increase with certainty though the rate of interest in the meantime would be decreased. Also I prefer that the investments should be entirely separated from mine, and that you should know and approve of any change made from time to time in the investments, if any change *is* made. The only sound alternative to this is investment in trustee securities, which can be got to yield about 7%. You needn't reply to this at once. I am ready to continue the old arrangement up to the end of the year.

I have seen the Lanchester's eldest child, & it was a dreadful spectacle. As for Mrs. Lanch. she is intelligent and an excellent talker, but she leaves me cold. Rickards is getting better, & I hope in about a year to be rid of the dreadful nuisance that this young man's financial affairs have been to me for 15 months past.

Our loves,
Yours,

A.B.

185. Bennett wrote *The Love Match* in July 1920. It opened at the Strand Theatre on 21 March 1922 and ran for just a month. The other as yet unproduced plays were *Don Juan*, *The Bright Island*, and *Body and Soul*. *Body and Soul* opened at the Euston Theatre of Varieties (renamed The Regent for the occasion) on 11 September 1922, and was a failure. The other two plays never had commercial productions.

Bennett did not buy the *Wanderer* but bought instead the ketch *Hayden* from Lord Alastair Leveson-Gower.

The film story was *The Wedding Dress*. It was never produced. Bennett's difficulties over the story with Jesse Lasky, the film producer, are described in Vol. III.

E. A. Rickards died of tuberculous meningitis on 29 August 1920.

CAMBRIDGE / MS / 186
(*To Richard Bennett*)

[Scotland]
27–9–20

REPORT
Upon The Social Tactics of Richard Bennett of C. C. C.

At breakfast he replied to an enquiry as to his health as though the question was perfectly normal and proper: but as he responded with no similar enquiry, it is presumed that he considered enquiries about anybody else's health to be an unnecessary and futile formality.

On a remark being made he gave no sign that he had heard it, thus indicating in his opinion the absurdity of the old theory that if only for politeness a remark ought to evoke some kind of response. On the remark being repeated he kindly gave way and condescendingly conformed to the absurd theory.

He made no conversation whatever, thus indicating his opinion that if one party had planned and paid for the holiday, he on his side was doing enough in providing the honour of his company.

He attended well to the mechanical details of the transport

from Glasgow to Inverness, making very few slips and still fewer remarks.

The journey from Glasgow to Inverness comprises some of the most beautiful & historic scenery in Scotland. He made no remark on it whatever from 10 am to 2.30 pm although he had previously been informed, and he had agreed, that it was advisable & polite not only to feel interest but to show it.

At 12 o'clock he said that the train was made up of different sorts of carriages.

At 2.30 he said that the train leaked.

These were his sole voluntary remarks throughout the journey.

For three days, from lunch Wednesday to lunch Saturday, I consistently attempted beginnings of conversations, with no appreciable results. I then decided that I would for the future behave to Mr. Richard Bennett as he behaved to me. Thus very many hours passed in absolute silence, while he was continually seeing new and interesting phenomena. At noon today I decided to try again, and by immense efforts got some information about his plans for Cambridge. The process resembled prising a piece of concrete out of a road with a lever. I then, with admirable perseverance, asked him how he had done in the exam. for the higher certificate. He replied: 'All right' & said no more until I did further heavy prising. The conversation then expired.

The luncheon baskets awaited us, & I had said that we would eat at 1 o'clock. Mr. R. B. said nothing for 150 minutes from noon. At the 90th minute he began to look interestedly at the baskets; but he could not act contrary to his principles. It would have been against his conscience to make some polite remark about the time, or the lunch, or about the possibility of Uncle being hungry. No hollow politeness, no initiative, at any cost! He preferred to go hungry. He did go hungry. But he amply demonstrated that in his opinion all the initiative, all the politeness, all the silly froth of social intercourse, ought to, and must, come from one side—not his side. He was providing his august presence, and that ought to suffice. At 2.45, sturdy as ever in his crusade for the total abolition of polite intercourse, he was suddenly relieved of 10/-, to pay for the lunch which he had spoilt. Nevertheless his principles had survived intact, and his celebrated imitation of a stupid and ill-mannered lout had been carried through to perfection. The paying for the lunch gravely unsettled him, & his magnificent silence grew more silent than ever. We arrived at Inverness at 4.45, & he is in a position to say that he has accomplished the world-renowned passage through the Highlands to Inverness without showing the slightest interest in it or the slightest curiosity about it.

At Inverness he once more attended to mechanical details with efficiency, and then fell back on his grand old principle of confining his contribution to the amenities of the tour to his mere physical presence.

Marks: for mechanics 90%.
  ,,   ,, socialics 15%.

A.B.

SUPPL. REPORT
Evening Prep.

Marked abandonment of the sublime principle, and acquiescence in the traditions of civilised society.
Marks 75%.

A.B.

186. Bennett and Richard went to Scotland for two weeks on about 22 September.

CAMBRIDGE / MS / 187
(*To Richard Bennett*)

12^B, George Street
9–11–20

My dear Rich,

Well, it is incontestable that you are a pitiable organiser. You had better admit yourself beaten & we will alter the day for me to receive your letters from Monday to Tuesday. Remember that this is a defeat. Otherwise your letter is better & contains more informative news than any of yours received by me for a long time. I understand about your evenings being overfull, but efforts must be made. These efforts are part of what is called LIFE. Perhaps your increased knowledge of histology will enable you to explain to me how a high frequency electric current passed into my gums by contact with a glass tube forces a certain drug into their histos & at the same time spurs the said histos to greater cellular activity. Because I'm hanged if I can see it. All I understand, comprehend & feel, is the disagreeableness of the treatment. I am glad you are reading newspapers. I recently made a detailed criticism of the *Cambridge Review* for the editor thereof. But how an undergrad can find time to edit a weekly at all is a puzzle to me. It cannot of course be efficiently edited, as the job is a whole time job. There is no good Sunday paper, but on the whole the *Sunday Times* 'has it' over the *Observer*. Among dailies the best paper for general news is *The Times*, for foreign news the *Morning Post*, and for editorial opinions the *Westminster Gazette*—not counting the *M. Guardian*. You don't say anything about what you are reading in the way of books. For 4 days I have been struck down with acute neuralgia & am only just returning to life today. I have the following horses in my chariot;—

a. 2 different dental treatments every other day at the dentist's.

b. a treatment which I have to do myself every day.

c. one long novel.

d. a short story—several.

e. a film.

f. rehearsals of *Milestones*.

g. my usual correspondence & business.

I much doubt whether you can beat this.

Auntie goes to Scotland next Tuesday for about 14 days.

Love,

Your defiant uncle,

A.B.

187. Bennett also gave the *Cambridge Review* four very brief pieces of writing. They were published with the title 'Souvenirs of France' in the issue of 22 October 1920.

The novel was *Mr. Prohack*, begun on 11 October 1920. The several short stories were gathered into the collection *Elsie and the Child*, 1924. For further detail on them see Vol. I.

Milestones was revived at the Royalty Theatre on 20 November, with Dennis Eadie, Haidée Wright, Violet Graham, and Hubert Harben.

KEELE / MS / 188
(*To Marguerite Soulié Bennett*)

12^B, George Street
18–11–20

Mon enf. chérie,

J'attendais une dépêche avec les nouvelles de ton récital. J'ai reçu ta lettre ce matin. Merci. J'ai mieux dormi. J'ai brillament travaillé hier après mon film. Dentist. Meeting. Soir je me suis couché à 8.30. J'étais si fatigué. Que veux tu? Ce matin je continue mon film. Cet après-midi répétition générale de *Milestones*. Ce soir dîner au Club avec Bertie. Demain je vais avec Reeves-Smith inspecter un établissement à la campagne pour les soldats réformés. Je soupçonne qu'il me demandera une chronique, mais je ne marche pas. Mardi soir je donne un dîner ici. Dimanche j'irai à la campagne voir M. Clutton Brock, critique d'art du *Times*. Swinnerton rentre demain. J'espère le voir dimanche soir. J'ai invité M. Legros à la première. J'ai donné deux fauteuils à Tertia, et deux à Olive. C'est tout. J'aurai une loge avec Bertie et Legros. Ce n'est pas une vraie première et je m'en fiche.

Or, j'espère que tu as eu un vrai succès hier. Je ne doute pas. Même chose pour demain. Quelle vie tout de même. Enfin tu l'as voulue. Je te bise tendrement.

Nouche

188. [I was expecting a telegram with news of your recital. I received your letter this morning. Thank you. I have slept better. I did some brilliant work on my film yesterday. Dentist. Meeting. In the evening I went to bed at 8.30. I was so tired. What else could I do? This morning I am going on with my film. Dress rehearsal of *Milestones* this afternoon. Dinner at the club with Bertie this evening. Tomorrow I am going with Reeves-Smith to look round an establishment in the country for discharged soldiers. I suspect that he will ask me for an article but I won't co-operate. On Tuesday evening I am giving a dinner here. On Sunday I will go to the country to see Mr Clutton Brock, the art critic of *The Times*. Swinnerton returns tomorrow. I hope to see him on Sunday evening. I have invited M Legros to the first night. I have given two seats to Tertia and two to Olive. That's all. I will have a box with Bertie and Legros. It isn't a real first night and I don't care.

Well, I hope you were a real success yesterday. I am sure you were. Same for tomorrow. But what a life. Still it's what you wanted. I kiss you tenderly.]

Bertie: Herbert Sullivan.
George Reeves-Smith (d. 1941) was managing director of the Savoy group of hotels. For a letter to him and other references see Vol. III.
Arthur Clutton-Brock (1868–1924).
In *Arnold Bennett* Marguerite writes:
Soon after the war I made a tour in Scotland, reciting chiefly the works of Charles

Baudelaire. My husband went to the station with me.... I expressed the pleasure I
felt at the mere thought of reciting Baudelaire's poems. My husband, who is one of
my admirers, said, 'Do you realise that you have undertaken to do the most
astounding thing? It requires nerve! Not even Baudelaire could have foreseen that
his poems would be recited in Scotland!' The remark stimulated me. It helped me in
my work.... Critics have said that if I had been on the stage I should have become a
great actress....

KEELE / MS / 189
(*To Marguerite Soulié Bennett*)

12^B, George Street
20–11–20

My poor sweet child,

I was desolated to get your letter from Edinburgh this
morning, & to learn that you hadn't received any letters. Your
programme given to me said 'Princes Street Station Hotel
Edinburgh'. There are 2 station-hotels in Princes Street, & I of
course assumed that you would stay at the North British, which
was the one originally mentioned & the one where we had
already stayed & where I always stay. However, I telegraphed
you this morning where the letters were. I need not tell you that
I have written to you every day. Among letters forwarded is one
in the handwriting of Mrs. Wheeler. I wrote my first letter to
Glasgow Central Station Hotel. You ought to have had it. The
others I sent to Edinburgh. I expect that your recital yesterday
gave you more satisfaction and that your mood is now less
gloomy. Of course all this professional travelling & staying in
hotels & seeing strangers is awful. But it is the price artists have
to pay when they travel professionally. For 2 hours of triumph
they pay 22 hours of boredom, discomfort, & depression. I can
tell you one thing,—it will be much worse in America.
However, it is all experience for you, & it is part of the career, &
I have no doubt that you will survive it brilliantly.

I am better this morning. I slept 6 hours without a break.
The dress-rehearsal last night was a great success, in fact very
great,—except the song-singing, which was rotten. Professional critics & managers shed tears, & wiped their noses to
hide their emotion. Etc. St. John Ervine was there for the
Observer (all the Sunday paper critics go on Friday instead of
Saturday), and he sat next to me & there is no doubt that he

was profoundly impressed. I took a rug & a hot water bottle with me but the theatre was warmed. I have decided on the electrical apparatus for the yacht. I was too ill yesterday to go with Reeves-Smith into the country. Did I tell you? I am now just off to the dentists.

> Je te bise et je te donne du courage.
>
> Nouche

189. America: Marguerite had the notion of going there to give recitals, and thought it would be useful to take Legros along as an assistant. Bennett persuaded her to abandon the thought. She did go to America in 1923, but it is not known whether she recited there.

St John Ervine (1883–1971), dramatist, novelist, and journalist. 'What a fine play *Milestones* is!' he said in his review on Sunday. He thought it was as pertinent to 1920 as it had been to 1912.

KEELE / MS / 190
(*To Marguerite Soulié Bennett*)

> 12^B, George Street
> 31–12–20

My dear child,

Read this letter with calmness. I write it because you alone, of all the people I have known, will not permit me to finish my sentences. I know that you are so impulsive that you cannot help it; but the fact remains. Also I will not have any scenes with you. There will be no more scenes between you and me. This is one of my periodical sermons and is very well meant.

You spent 1 hour 25 minutes last night in telling Canoodle-Canoodle that 'no-one has a right to interfere with the artist', & that you needed help and encouragement, & that I was a stone-wall, and that it was a great shame. You said this about 20 times, until I pointed out that I had done everything to help you. You then stopped. The whole tirade was a deliberate attack on me, & I much object to it. Do not say, as usual: 'Nous ne nous comprendrons jamais.' The comprehension is perfect. It is merely a question of justice and truth. I *have* helped and encouraged your reciting in every way. I *have* thoroughly understood your point of view, and sympathised with it, and said so again & again. I have also again and again paid you for your recitals. When I said positively that I thought it would be a very grave mistake to take Legros to America I also said that you were free to act as you liked. You then insisted that *I* should ask Legros to go. This I shall never do. But I am not 'interfering with the artist'. I am giving the artist a free hand. The artist is trying to interfere with me.

This is the sort of thing I get after I have done everything possible to help & encourage you. Pardon me if I suggest that in the future I shall pay for no more recitals. And I shall begin to help and encourage you again in your work when you have expressed regret for the entirely unjust attack of last night. Not before.

I must also give you a hint that you treat me generally with increasing rudeness. On Wednesday, though I was in for lunch, you went out for lunch without saying a word to me, & when you came back you made no reference of any kind to your absence. I do *not* say that because I am in for lunch you must be in for lunch. Certainly not. I do *not* say that you ought always to tell me where you have been for lunch. Certainly not. You are perfectly entitled to go where you like and to tell me, or not tell me, as you prefer. But you are not entitled, and no one is entitled—least of all the mistress of the house, to absent yourself from meals without a word of warning before, or a word of explanation afterwards. To do so is extremely rude, and it is rude whether you are ill or whether you are well. Two days before that, in the morning, someone rushed into my study to get the key of the brandy because Madame was unwell. I came shortly afterwards to see how you were. You had gone out. You returned towards 7 o'clock. You were out the whole day, but you never offered a word as to your absence. It has happened to me, this autumn, to have tea by myself here *every day for a whole week*. And only on one day did you give the slightest hint as to where you had been. I say again that you are entitled to this silence, & this mystery, and these absences. But a certain moderation & discretion is advisable in these matters. Whereas I tell you everything that I do, you do not tell me as often as once a fortnight what you do. Once or twice some months ago I asked you, but the replies I received were so evasive and so 'hargneux' that I did not ask any more. This behaviour is unwise. About once a fortnight you say casually that you have been to Legros' flat, but that is all. You like to pretend that I am jealous of Legros. It flatters you to think so.

But it is not true. I am incapable of being jealous, probably because I should regard a woman capable of doing anything deserving jealousy as not worth being jealous about. My behaviour to Legros has always been extremely cordial and nice. No fault can be found with it. You know this. He knows it. No man who was jealous could treat Legros as I treat him. So far as I am concerned you are absolutely free to go and see any men you like in their own garçonnière, and to leave me alone while you do it if necessary. Few husbands would say this. No French husband would say it. Even the admirable Georges would not say it. But I say it. You yourself would be ferociously sarcastic about any other woman who does as you do, and you would call her husband a fool. But my ideas are fairly broad. I am rather fond of you, & I have no doubts of you. At the same time, perfect freedom should not lead you into exaggeration. And above all it should not lead you into being constantly rude to your husband by neglecting the elementary politeness which is due to him.

As regards presents, do you not agree that present-giving should be not a duty but a pleasure? To give to one whose behaviour is constantly wounding is not a very keen pleasure. I think that when you have realised what is due to me, and acted accordingly, you will not go short of presents. All sensible people must regret to hear you say, as you often do: *'I am determined to think only of myself & to do exactly what I like.'* They regret it, because it sounds so very queer from a student of Marcus Aurelius, and because such a line of conduct always has led, and always will lead, to unhappiness. You are in danger of making a fool of yourself with your husband. Don't do it. Your husband is worth caring for & worth treating properly. He is also very strong and very clever and his affection will not lead him into excusing too much. I can excuse a lot on the ground of ill-health & nerves; and I do. But not all. And do not make the mistake of thinking you are a femme incomprise. You aren't, at any rate by me.

Ton mari

190. Canoodle-Canoodle: W. W. Kennerley, who had come to discuss Tertia's investments (see above p. 270). Georges: Georges Bion, Marguerite's uncle, husband of Hélène.

CAMBRIDGE / MS / 191
(*To Richard Bennett*)

12ᴮ, George Street
3–1–21

My dear Rich,

A feeble letter, but ∂ I don't seem to be hearing much about your work & I have serious doubts whether the reason you don't mention it is that it is not worth mentioning. The yacht work is proceeding. I hear that 8 joiners are on board: which rather frightens me. She ought anyhow to be ready for sea some time in April. I wrote 2,800 words of my novel yesterday, Sunday. This ought to give *you* something to think about. The New Year's Eve dinner at the Savoy was the noisiest, vulgarest, costliest thing of the sort I ever had anything to do with. I had scarcely imagined that there were so many people in London with so much money & so little taste. However, I got all the material I wanted, & I had 2 gifted young creatures to dance with. Home at 1:30. Enfeebled the next day. *The Beggar's Opera* people are having a ball on Friday week, at which I shall be. This piece has just been produced in New York, under our auspices, with apparently great success. Nigel Playfair went over to do it. *Milestones* is not doing very brilliantly. The literary editor of the *Daily Express* is coming to see me today about some articles (short). Auntie is not going to the Riviera yet. She got the Ford up to London by Fred, but he skidded on wet tramlines near Islington & broke the near back wheel completely to smash. So that there is delay in her outings. Fred had a shock. I had told him that driving in winter in the trammy suburbs was dangerous. He now knows it. He nearly killed a few people.

Love,
Your productive uncle,

A.B.

191. ∂ appears in several letters and seems to mean yes/agreed.

The Savoy Hotel appears under the guise of the Grand Babylon Hotel in *Mr. Prohack.* Several years later it became the setting for *Imperial Palace.*

The Beggar's Opera, adapted by Bennett, was put on with great success at the Lyric Hammersmith, opening on 5 June 1920. It ran for three years. Nigel Playfair (1874–1934) was the effective head of the Lyric Hammersmith. He produced *The Beggar's Opera* in New York at the Greenwich Village Theatre, 17 January 1921. For other information about him and the Lyric Hammersmith see Vols. I and III.

The *Daily Express* published six articles by Bennett on theatre from 26 January to 2 March 1921.

KEELE / MS / 192
(*To Marguerite Soulié Bennett*)

12ᴮ, George Street
5–1–21

My dear child,

Je te remercie de ta lettre, que j'apprécie. I am glad that you see my point of view, & I was also glad to hear you say that, en vieillissant, je devenais plus gentil. You speak of differences of temperament, but the matters which I complained of had nothing to do with differences of temperament. They are matters of ordinary politeness, justice, and discretion: which qualities are equally obligatory upon all temperaments, if organised society is to continue to be possible.

You cannot possibly be more free in the future than you have been in the past but as you wish me to say that I agree to your having Wednesday evening in each week free & entirely to yourself, & also to your taking 3 holidays a year without me, I say that I agree to the same with pleasure & goodwill.

Je te bise bien.

Ton mari

KEELE / MS / 193
(*To Marguerite Soulié Bennett*)

12ᴮ, George Street
4–4–21

Mon enf. ch.,

Enfin j'ai reçu une lettre de toi. Et, comme trop souvent, je suis entouré de mystères! I don't think you & Legros understand how I look at the affair. You imagine that I take it much more seriously than I do. But I will enlighten you. What startles me, even to the point of making me laugh, is Legros' lack of savoir vivre. Legros can be a most charming man & a most agreeable companion, but his social clumsiness is astounding. And this is by no means the first instance of it. I have always treated Legros with the very greatest courtesy, and also with the very greatest hospitality (a hospitality, by the way, which he never attempts to return, apparently on the ground of poverty, though he can find the money to wander up & down Italy with a lady!). Further I have always treated him with the greatest intimacy and candour. Yet, though I see him constantly, he never says a word about going away for a holiday until the eve of his departure, when he comes in, without notice, and announces that he is going to Brittany to see his mother. Within about a week of this he is taking his mistress to meet my wife in an obscure town in central Italy; and I am supposed to believe that this meeting in Frascati, or Rome or elsewhere, is a mere accident, arranged on the spur of the moment!! Let him exercise his imagination, if he has any, and conceive how he would have felt had he been in my place. He would assuredly have been intensely annoyed. And it was an immense social clumsiness on his part not to have foreseen that I should be annoyed. This social clumsiness is strange in a Frenchman, that mirror of good manners! I strongly resent his secrecy and want of *franchise*. I regard it as a very bad return for my constant good nature towards him. Even he must surely see that if I am to be treated in this way the relations between us cannot continue on the old footing. And it is absolutely certain that unless I receive some explanation & apology direct from him. our relations will *not* continue on the old footing. And you can tell him frankly that I say so. And what is more, if I do not hear from him, he will hear from me; he will receive a letter such as he will not soon forget. After all, some commonsense & some decency must be brought into this affair, & I shall bring them Count on me, my child.

As for you, I think you might have telegraphed me of your change of place. Here I am writing day after day to San Remo—letters which you will almost certainly not get. To have telegraphed would have been easy, & I should not have been without news for 5 days. And I do wish you wouldn't keep on saying that you see so little of me. You know very well that you see far more of me than 9 wives out of ten see of their husbands As for Richard, my views remain the same. All I ask you to do is not to make yourself unpleasant and so to make my task ever more difficult than it would be. Your outburst at your last breakfast here was an inexcusable outrage.

We will now leave these matters.

I had neuralgia & dispepsia for a week & couldn't do a stroke of work. It went off on Saturday. Yesterday I did a very good day's work, & today a fair day. I danced 3 times last week, & I shall dance 3 times this week. Captain Mason went to see Olive at Mentone, without asking permission. Another sad instance of social clumsiness! She was furious. She came to lunch with me today & told me all about it. Not only did he go to Mentone, but he insisted on coming home with them and slept a night at their house! Quelle couche!! The industrial situation in England is exceedingly grave; has never been so grave before. I don't know how it will end. But it will end somehow. I have become rather friendly with Marjorie Gordon, a young musical comedy actress. But it is improbable that she will bring a young man with her to meet me in Timbuctoo by accident. Ma pauvre enfant, j'adore ta couche, et je te bise bien.

Nouche

Esperons qu'au dernier moment la maîtresse du pauvre Legros n'a pas été empêchée de l'accompagner en Italie! Tu seras bien aimable de ma la décrire quand tu la verras. Elle m'intrigue.

N.

193. [Let us hope that nothing happened at the last moment to stop poor Legros's mistress going to Italy with him! Please be so kind as to describe her to me when you see her. She fascinates me.]

Marguerite left London on 23 March to go for a holiday to Italy and France. At about the same time Legros left to go to France. Marguerite's announced destination was San Remo, but she went to Frascati. Legros joined her there by or before 4 April.

Bennett took up dancing in 1920, apparently recommended for his health by Shufflebotham. He had his first dancing lesson on 18 March, and on 29 October he danced in public for the first time. He described the occasion in the *Journals*.

Friday night, Olive, Marguerite, Legros and I went to the Hammersmith Palais de Dance.... There was no ordeal about it. I even danced with M., who knows less about dancing than I do. Intense respectability of the whole place.

An article on dancing appears in *Things That Have Interested Me, Second Series*, 1923.

In the first months of 1921 a general strike was in prospect. On 15 April, 'Black Friday', the transport and railway workers called off their strike before it began, and the miners were left isolated. They held out until 1 July.

Marjorie Gordon (b. 1896). She had recently appeared in *The Witch of Edmonton* at the Lyric Hammersmith.

KEELE / MS / 194
(*To Marguerite Soulié Bennett*)

12^B, George Street
6–4–21

Mon enf. ch.,

Your second letter from Frascati arrived today. It took 5 days to come. Your description of the town & district is very good, in your best style. As for me, my health is now very much better. Probably because of dancing. I went with Olive, Tennyson Jesse and Captain Harwood (her amant, I suppose) to the Grafton last night & left at 1 a.m. Slept very well. Tonight I am dining with Swinnerton & his friend Dorothea Cobden-Sanderson. Mrs. St. John Ervine was to have been there also, but she was taken ill last night & can't come. She was to have come with me afterwards to the Waltz competition at the Grafton. So I have telephoned to Lorna Lewis & got her to come instead. On Friday, after Clark's concert, he & his sister & Mrs. Lovat Fraser are going to dance. Tomorrow I am going to see the yacht. Although I am very busy my work is not moving fast enough. It still gets more & more in arrear. The play business also gets more & more complicated. McKinnel came to see me yesterday. It seems pretty sure that we shall get Gladys Cooper for *The Love Match*. My life is exceedingly complex.

Although your letter is very interesting so far as it goes, it does not go very far. I notice that you give me no further information about how it has happened that Legros & his mistress are meeting you in Rome or in Frascati. The old policy of secrecy is apparently being followed. In my last letter I referred to Legros, but you know that you also are to blame about this affair. Supposing that *I* had been seeing Mary or Diana nearly every day for many months. Supposing that *you* had complained several times, not about the meetings, but about the fact that as a rule I did not tell you where I was. Supposing that *I* insisted on having a free night a week, and that every such night I spent with Mary or Diana. Supposing that *I* had demanded a long holiday alone, & that again & again I had insisted that I must be *alone* on my holiday. Supposing that on the night before my departure Mary or Diana had called & I had said to her, in front of you, having previously said nothing at all to you: 'I am expecting you to meet me in Italy', and that afterwards I had still said not a word to you of my plans, though it was obvious that Mary or Diana & I had been discussing plans at length, & that I had gone off, still without saying a word.

What would *you* have thought?

You would have thought either that I deliberately intended to annoy or insult you; or, alternatively, that I was a perfect fool. I should be a fool because I had not the imagination to foresee that you would be annoyed or hurt by my secretive conduct, or to foresee that you would be forced to write letters to me about it which would interfere both with the pleasure of my holiday & the efficiency of your work while I was away.

Well, that is the case.

Mon enfant, you often call yourself a child & a fool. Your action proves that you are not far wrong in doing so. It is inevitable that I should treat you according to your action. I most certainly shall not tolerate such action. No husband who was not an idiot would tolerate it. Unless I receive not only full apologies from Legros, but also an expression of regret from you, my relations with Legros will be completely changed, & if you take any more holidays 'alone' you will pay for them yourself. No wife could be more free than you are. I give you far more freedom than I allow myself. But there is one freedom I will not give you, c.a.d., the freedom to behave improperly towards me. I don't object to your meeting anybody anywhere. You may be indiscreet—you are—but when I have warned you I say no more. What I object to is being kept in the dark & treated as if I did not exist.

Do not imagine that I am taking this affair tragically, or that I have ceased to be absurdly fond of you. No! The end of the world has not yet come. I merely mean that you have treated me with gross rudeness & lack of consideration. You have acted as if I did not count. My intention is to show you that I do count. In the words of Moliere, 'Tu l'as voulu, Georges Dandin.'

I forgot to tell you that the hospital is so busy that Fred can't have his operation till the 14th & he will only have it then because he told the doctor that he was in the service of Arnold Bennett. Le quel te bise bien.   Nouche

194. F. Tennyson Jesse (1888–1958), novelist and playwright, was known to Bennett in the Ministry of Information during the War. She married H. M. Harwood in 1918; she wrote several plays with him.

Dorothea Cobden-Sanderson: unidentified.

Lorna Lewis: reported in the *Journals* for December 1920 to be twenty years old and Welsh.

Edward Clark, conductor, gave a concert on 8 April at the Queen's Hall, of music by Bax and Stravinsky, and a second concert on the 20th, of music by Bliss and Vaughan Williams. Years later he became head of the International Society for Contemporary Music. His sister Stella was connected with the Anglo-French Poetry Society.

Grace Lovat Fraser: wife of Lovat Fraser (1871–1926), who was now redecorating Bennett's new yacht.

Norman McKinnel (1870–1932), actor and manager, took an option on *The Love Match*, which Bennett wrote in July 1920. He presently sold his option to Frank Vernon. Gladys Cooper (1889–1971) did not do the play, and Kyrle Bellow took her place.

'Mary or Diana': one woman or another. In a surviving draft of the letter, Bennett began with 'Olive or' and presumably thought better of seeming to refer to Olive Ledward Nossiter. Diana would presumably have referred more harmlessly to Lady Diana Cooper (b. 1892). She had served as the model for Queenie Paulle in *The Pretty Lady*.

KEELE / MS / 195
(*To Marguerite Soulié Bennett*)

12^B, George Street
8–4–21

[no salutation]

What a good prophet I am! I told you I thought L. would arrive alone. I am expecting letters from both of you, in the sense that I asked for.

N.

KEELE / MS / 196
(*To Marguerite Soulié Bennett*)

12^B, George Street
9–4–21

Mon enf. ch.,

I have your letter in which you tell me about Legros coming alone, as of course I knew he would.

The whole letter shows that you felt you were doing something that you knew I should gravely disapprove of. And if you have acted for the best your best is very poor. All your reasons are perfectly absurd. But the worst thing is that you should have discussed your projects with various people, and said nothing whatever to me. The first & only thing I heard of the matter was a question put to Legros in my presence. Not a word to me personally. If you have any commonsense at all you must realise that this sort of conduct must inevitably lead to trouble.

Either Legros is an absolute fool, or he has behaved scandalously.

I telegraphed you as follows this morning:—

'I think you should ask Legros to leave immediately and cable me that he has left. Love, Arnold.'

I am now waiting to hear from both of you. I have shown the greatest patience in this affair. If I do not get satisfactory letters you may believe me that the trouble *will* be serious. Don't say afterwards that I haven't warned you.

Clark's first concert last night was a great success.

Je te bise.

[A.B.]

KEELE / MS / 197
(*To Marguerite Soulié Bennett*)

12ᴮ, George Street
13–4–21

Mon enf. ch.,

Merci de ta dépêche reçue ce matin. I do not understand why my telegram should take 4 days to reach you, & if you will keep it I will have enquiries made. Such delay is inexcusable. We now know how this affair stands, and although I do not mean to take it too seriously, I am bound to take notice of it. Having taken notice of it, I shall forget it.

You insisted to me many times that it was necessary for you to be absolutely alone on your holiday. You didn't want anybody at all.

But you were discussing plans for meeting Legros in Italy. Of them I knew nothing until the last moment, & then only the slightest hint of them by a question put by you to Legros, who answered in an evasive and self-conscious manner and immediately left the house.

There can be no doubt that the thing was deliberately concealed from me.

Before Legros joined you, you knew from my letters that I

strongly objected to it. Nevertheless you did not stop him from joining you.

The excuses which you make in every letter are merely silly. You knew that you were doing something which I objected to, and which was wrong, & which you would condemn without pity in another woman.

All I have to say is that I have no intention of providing you with money to spend continental holidays with Legros, my simple child, and that for one year from the present date I shall pay for no more holidays for you. So far as you are concerned I now forget the affair, though it has caused me a great deal of pain; and you may rely upon me not to let it influence my relations with my sweet child.

The case of Legros is different. Legros has behaved very rudely to me. With every intention of holidaying with my wife in Italy, he tells me that he is going to stay with his mother, & he tells me nothing else. I have always treated him, for your sake, with the greatest friendliness & intimacy. It was his business to talk to me of his plans, quite apart from anything that you might or might not have told me. To do so was the merest elementary politeness. Not to do so was proof of an intention to conceal. You and he may say what you like about his attitude to you, but the fact remains that he has left not only his mother but his mistress in order to be with you. I will not tolerate his behaviour to me. I absolutely refuse to do so. I insist that he shall write and apologise to me in the fullest possible manner. If he does so—and I quite expect that at a word from you he will—I shall forget what has passed & our relations will be exactly as before—for after all I am inclined to think that he has been merely silly & lacking in imagination, like you. If he does not, our relations will cease entirely, and when he comes into this house I shall go out. The matter will be solely in his hands.

If you think my attitude is wrong, find out what Georges Bion thinks; but tell him the whole of the facts. You are very friendly with him, you have confidence in him, he adores you, & he is a member of your family. If he disagrees with my conduct in the affair I will make every apology. I want to be fair.

Let me now turn to other things. The menace of the strike is exceedingly serious, & I am afraid that the railways will stop. If they do, *anything* may happen.

My work is going along, but not satisfactorily & much too slowly.

The yacht is getting done. I went down there with Fraser last week. We were delighted.

The Love Match was *very nearly* put into rehearsal last week. Gladys Cooper agreed to play the part, but the next day she withdrew. So it is postponed; & a good thing too. The business at theatres is awful.

Eadie very nearly bought *Body & Soul*. He likes it extremely. I think Vaughan stopped him from buying it. Anyhow he is going to let the theatre.

Clark & sister & Olive all came here on Sunday night after dinner, & we all played duets.

I saw Jane West on Monday night. She is going back to America the day after tomorrow. Last night Marjorie Gordon (who is to play at the Lyric Theatre Phoenix affair soon) dined with me at the Criterion. Lady Beaverbrook & her perfectly charming young sister were there. I have been 3 times to the Grafton with Olive, the Clarks, Mrs. Lovat Fraser, Lorna Lewis, Tennyson Jesse & her lover. I stay up too late, & I am worried, but I am *well*. Dr. Rosenbach, the big American book dealer, tried hard to buy the MS. of *The Old Wives' Tale*. He would have given £1,000 for it. I told him I was too afraid of you to sell it! He offered £250 for *The Pretty Lady* & didn't get that either. In fact he got no MS.—to my regret. He is willing to take all my drawings, & is most anxious to have an exhibition of them in New York. He says they will sell for from £30 to £50 apiece easily. I have agreed to this.

Je te bise bien, mon ingénue femme.

[A.B.]

197. Jane West: unidentified.
Dr A. S. W. Rosenbach (1876–1952) met Bennett in America in 1911.

KEELE / MS / 198
(*To Marguerite Soulié Bennett*)

12^B, George Street
14-4-21

Mon enf. ch.,

Thanks for your letter of the 10th, which arrived at the same time as Legros'. I am glad to see that it contains no attempt to justify that policy of secrecy towards me which cannot possibly be justified. It is this policy of secrecy of which I chiefly complain. I do not approve of certain things that you do in regard to Legros. I consider them highly indiscreet, to say no more; but, having warned you about them, and expressed my disapproval, I leave the matter at that. You are of course infatuated, quite innocently, with Legros. Such an infatuation might happen to anyone, & you cannot be blamed for it. The one thing for me to do is to treat it benevolently and understandingly and indulgently, & this I think I have always done. But I am bound to express my views, to do the little I can to influence you, and to take care that I myself am treated with consideration.

I cannot conceive any self-respecting husband doing less than I have done. Nor can I conceive any husband giving a wife more freedom, or being less exigeant about her behaviour, than I do and am. Nobody can say that I am difficile about your doings. You know this better than anybody.

My letter to you was not written for Legros to see, as you well knew, and you were very wrong to show it to him.

As for you saying that I object to hearing of anything that is not positively decided—that is merely silly. You are perfectly well aware that all I object to is leaving *my own plans* vague. As an explanation of your policy of secrecy this is about the feeblest excuse you ever invented.

I have written to Legros. As he will only be at Florence for a few days my letter might miss him; so I enclose it with this for you to forward to him.

This matter is now ended.

It seems likely that the big strike will occur tomorrow. If it does, you will not be able to return till it is over. Fred has had his operation, & has come through it very well. He is now in bed.

I am going to a grand ball tonight with Olive. This will be the last festivity before the strike.

Je te bise,

N.

ELDIN / MS / 199
(*To Septimus Bennett*)

12ᴮ, George Street
22–4–21

My dear Sep,

This is all a very great pity. I enclose you a cheque for £30 to keep you out of immediate danger. You will be able to understand that, relatively, the financial situation is just as stringent here as it is in the Potteries. It is worse in one respect, namely that authors' remuneration has not increased at all since 1914. In fact it has in practice diminished. Securities are unsaleable except at a heavy loss & money can only be borrowed at a high rate of interest. (Which reminds me that you have neither paid my interest lately nor said a word about it.) Of course I still make a lot of money, but my life is so arranged that I spend a lot. Nor can my dispositions be altered at short notice. It was most unfortunate that I bought my new yacht just before the slump began. If I had expected any slump I shouldn't have bought the damned thing. But there she is, & I have no intention of laying her up unless I am absolutely compelled to. Further, I have a number of calls upon me similar to yours. If yours were the only call, or even the most urgent one, it would be very different.

I want to say something to you as regards yourself—not at all in the way of criticism, but in the way of realism. You are undoubtedly a great and steady worker. Of course the war (in which your record was A1) upset you, as it upset millions, but you were 36 or more when the war began. Up to that time you had had capital on various occasions, but I don't think that you made any marked mercantile success or even did more than just live. The war has now been over 2½ years. You started again with more capital which is now, I gather, all gone. Yet during most of that period trade was booming in the Potteries. It was not booming in your particular branch, but as a whole it was, &

a lot of people were making a lot of money. I am very glad now that I did not supply that £100 a couple of months ago, as it would in all probability have been lost. Your situation now is that you want money, not for new enterprises, but to keep you going from day to day. This of course is no commercial proposition at all. In one way it is a good thing that in the last resort you can rely on me, but in another way it is a very bad thing indeed. I am not blaming you; I think that you have done the very best you could; but I want to give my opinion that your faculties, admirable in themselves, do not seem to me to point to a successful independent commercial career. You are 43, I think, & despite the war one ought now to be able to come to some definite conclusion on this point. I think that you would be better off and much happier in a salaried position of trust & that it might be well for you to look out for this. You ask me if I can suggest anything for you. I can't. Nor do I see any opening for you in London, & I doubt whether after all these years you would be suited to London. You *might* be, but I doubt it. I am now nearly 54 & I have been trying to help all manner of people for the last 30 years, & my experience is that you can't really help people except by direct technical instruction in a subject which both the helper & the helped are keen on and fitted for. True, I have kept people out of prison; but this is exceptional! This letter will at first make you gloomy, but I think that ultimately it may contribute to your peace of mind.

Yours, A. B.

KEELE / MS / 200
(*To Marguerite Soulié Bennett*)

[? Yacht Marie Marguerite]
4–6–21

My dear M.,

You said this morning that I was an utterly selfish man. If you think this, you are certainly the only person on earth who does so. What is much more serious, you said that while pretending to help you in your enterprises, I was always determined to spoil them and that in secret I did what I could to prevent you from succeeding in them.

You were thinking specially that I was stopping Baxter &

Newnes from using your articles. This suspicion is both monstrous and idiotic. I should only be too pleased to see your articles in print, & I have little doubt that they will appear. As I have told you more than once, I said to both Baxter & Newnes that I hoped they would be able to use the articles; and as both of them have good reason for wanting to keep on good terms with me, I expect that what I said will influence them. I have also told you again & again that delays in publication are quite usual. I have myself experienced hundreds of them. But you will not believe me. You prefer to think that I am secretly plotting against you.

Unless you are incredibly stupid you ought to be aware that you have no more loyal supporter than your husband. In all your enterprises I have *never* failed to help you as well as I could, and there is no foundation for any belief to the contrary.

What you said this morning is horrible. Nothing could be more wounding. Supposing that I said savagely to you that you were an utterly selfish wife and that while pretending to help me you did everything you could in secret to work against me! How would you feel? Yet if I said that I should not be more shockingly untrue than you were this morning.

If you say these things in momentary irritation about matters with which I have nothing to do you ought to be ashamed of such cruel words and such lack of self-control. There is no more to be said. If on the other hand these things are your considered and deliberate opinions, then something must be done. Love is obviously impossible in such conditions. You have often talked of a separation. I have never talked of it. But I now talk of it. Two people cannot decently live together when one thinks the other is always secretly and disloyally working against her while pretending to help her. At least I can't. And I won't. Something will have to be arranged.

A.B.

200. Bennett named his yacht the *Marie Marguerite*. She sailed with a crew of eight. During the summer of 1921 he sailed in her off the coasts of England and Europe.

Baxter and Newnes: presumably Beverley Baxter (1891–1964), director of the *Daily Express*, and Frank Newnes (1876–1955) of Newnes-Pearson. The Newnes-Pearson *Strand Magazine* had recently contracted with Bennett to publish a series of articles on 'How to Make the Best of Life'. Marguerite published at least one article at this time, 'Why Poetry Has No Public', *Sunday Express*, 26 June 1921. In 1924 the *Daily Express* published her articles on Bennett. See pp. 436–7.

CAMBRIDGE / MS / 201
(*To Richard Bennett*)

Yacht Marie Marguerite
13–6–21

Mon cher,

Your first act will be to put on rubber shoes.

You will occupy the port-cabin, so that you will not have to change when Mr. Atkins comes aboard on Friday. Ernest (the steward) will show you all the lockers and shelves & things in this cabin.

Your friend will occupy the large after cabin, which Mr. Atkins will occupy on Friday.

I expect to join the ship at Southampton on Friday evening between 9 & 10. Mr. Atkins will probably arrive before me. If so, do the honours.

Edgar, the engineer, will show you the engines.

If you feel like being ill, open the medicine tin case in the after locker in the saloon. You will see some 'Mothersill'. Take one of each coloured powder, in the little tube all complete. Only take one dose (2 powders) with a swallow of water. Lie down for 30 minutes. It will infallibly put you right.

Remember that the Captain (Joseph Major) is the absolute autocrat of the ship, and treat him as a social equal.

William Bishop, the cook, is the greatest individuality on board, & will appreciate chats about meals & cooking. You can go & see him in the galley.

The part of the deck forward of the mainmast is supposed to be exclusive to the crew save on special occasions.

There are 2 decklights with Chinese lanterns which you can use at night (one or both) if you choose. Ask the engineer for them. The light in the deckhouse turns on just under the top curve of the bannister.

I think this is all.

Love,
Your regretfully departing uncle,

A.B.

P.S. There are bells everywhere. Ring for the steward. Don't go & look for him. The ship should sail Tuesday morning sometime.

A.B.

201. Richard sailed with Bennett for two weeks.

Ernest had been in Bennett's employ early in the War and had been conscripted. Bennett helped to support his wife while he was away.

Edgar: Edgar Gentry.

KEELE / MS / 202
(*To Marguerite Soulié Bennett*)

12ᴮ, George Street
17–6–21

My dear Marguerite,

I have already told you the following things several times.

1. My plans are definite only for 3 weeks from today.

2. *Nothing else is arranged.*

3. I am going to Carantec if the Godebskis are there; but the date cannot be fixed till I hear from them.

4. I am quite prepared to go to Ostende or to Dinard & meet you there with the yacht in September. *I have said this again & again.* I think you would enjoy Dinard most; but I don't care which. I never said to Olive that I should not go to Ostende. I said it was not sure, & I only said that because when I suggested that she should come you maintained a most significant silence. I wanted to prepare her for not going. It is obvious that if you are on the yacht I shall not ask anybody to whom you object. You are perfectly well aware that I shall be delighted to have you on the yacht.

As to the motor car, of course I regret that I cannot buy a new one now. But I ask you to remember that you have got one that is in perfect working order.

I have *always* told you all my plans; *which is a great deal more than you can say*. This has always been so.

It will not be possible for you to have Legros at Comarques unless there is a third person always staying in the house—at least with my consent.

I cannot discuss these matters with you now. You say to me that you are 'furieuse' & that I treat you 'like a servant' & then you ask me to discuss things with you in a friendly manner. The idea is impossible. I will write you fully from the yacht.

Yours, A.B.

KEELE / MS / 203
(*To Marguerite Soulié Bennett*)   [Yacht Marie Marguerite]
                                          Bembridge
                                          20–6–21

Mon enf.,

I continue the letter I wrote on Friday. And I shall now speak plainly. If your behaviour to me does not fundamentally alter, my behaviour to you will fundamentally alter. I will remind you of one or two instances of your recent behaviour. I should have thought that the inexcusable Italian episode, which you never even attempted to defend, because you could not, would have taught you a lesson. But it seems not. You have been worse than ever. You said to me that I was always secretly working against you, that I had you fast in a cage, that I was determined you should fail in everything, and that in particular I was preventing, in secret, the publication of your articles because Legros had helped you to write them. You were exceedingly rude, disagreeable, and violent. All that you said was totally untrue. It was the contrary of the truth. There was absolutely no excuse for it. Two days later, when you were obliged to realise the monstrous injustice of your accusations you tried to justify yourself by saying that I had written you a letter in which I had said that I intended to break the friendship between you and Legros. This again was the contrary of the truth. And why you should tell me such a silly untruth I cannot imagine. If I wanted to separate you and Legros I should simply breathe one word to the University Authorities that I objected to his attitude towards you, and Legros, professor to young ladies, would be asked to resign, and he would never get another situation in England because he would not get a certificate of character from Bedford College. And that would be the end of Legros in England. Happily I am all in favour of the friendship between you and Legros, provided the conventions are strictly observed.

Not satisfied with your previous accusations you said a few days later that you suspected me of regularly committing adultery at a certain period of the war. Even if you have such disgusting suspicions you should not speak them without some cause. What would you say if I suddenly told you that I suspected you of regularly sleeping with another man?

There are a large number of persons like you who say whatever comes into their heads without exercising their imaginations sufficiently to realise how hurt and angry they would be if other people said similar things to them.

Further you are constantly saying to others in my presence that you never see me, and that the only opportunity you have of discussing private domestic matters with me is in the presence of strangers. This has become one of your cliché phrases. It is absolutely untrue. You see much more of me than most wives see of their husbands, and you have ample opportunity of discussing everything with me. If you do not see more of me the fault is your own. Who insisted, violently, on having a month's absence from me three times a year and one night every week, because she saw too much of me and needed relief from my 'powerful personality'? Was it you, or am I dreaming? Your constant statement that you never see me and have no chance to talk to me is extremely offensive.

Further, I maintain that you deliberately neglect me; and yet I should have thought that my friendly attitude towards your relations with Legros (which no French husband and jolly few English husbands would permit) would have caused you to take special care not to neglect me. But no! I am left day after day to have tea alone. I am only working, it seems, so I do not matter. You go out for the whole afternoon, sometimes for the whole day; you return in time for dinner. You say not a word as to where you have been. You make no enquiry as to where I have been. Indeed often, far from being agreeable, you are positively disagreeable on returning home. Once when I told you that you might at least be in sometimes for tea, or let me know that you would not be in, you replied ferociously: 'Je ne suis pas esclave.' And when I said that you might be polite you replied: 'Polie? Tu es mon mari.' Still, you did improve—for a short time. You are now worse than ever. And nearly all your movements are a mystery. And yet you are continually saying to other people that I never tell you anything! At any rate I tell you far more than you tell me, & I always have done. You always know where I am or have been. I seldom know where you have been. True, tu n'es pas esclave! True, je suis seulement ton mari!

I repeat that you are constantly making the most mon-

strously untrue accusations against me, and that you constantly neglect me.

Marriage is a *mutual* contract, and the wife's part is a great deal
more than mere housekeeping. The wife, who has no financial
responsibilities, should supply agreeableness and attention and
charm. You will say that it is sometimes difficult to do so. Of
course it is. The worst mégère on earth can be charming and
attentive when everything goes smoothly. *I* don't say to you at
the end of a week: 'I have had great difficulties. I shall not fulfil
my part of the contract and there is no money for you.'

For a husband, where is the point of being married to a wife
who is always unjustly accusing him in the most offensive
manner, and who neglects him? She keeps house for him, but he
could get forty housekeepers.

I tell you plainly that I am profoundly dissatisfied with your
neglectful attitude to me and profoundly resentful of your
infamous and false accusations. You will always grumble; you
will always pose as a martyr; you cannot help that; you are of a
melancholy, suspicious and jealous disposition, and I am very
sorry for you, and quite prepared to accept the natural consequences of it. But the other things I will not stand. They are
quite different. They must be altered, or my whole attitude to
you will be altered. No one can be more charming, agreeable,
and attentive than you, if you choose. You had better think
about it. All the generosity is not going to be on one side. If you
cannot behave to me as I behave to you there will be a notable
change, my child. I tell you quite candidly. I shall at once cease
to do all sorts of nice things that I now do. Why should I keep
both your father and your mother, except for the reason that it
pleases me to be agreeable to you? There are two men in your
family perfectly capable of looking after your parents, or at least
of helping to do so, and if I were in their place I should be
ashamed to allow a relation by marriage to undertake the whole
charge of both parents. (And please note that I *do* keep both
your parents. I used to pay for your mother separately until you
asked me to add the sum to your private allowance; but I still
pay, all the same.) Why should I give you the very large
allowance of £700 a year—(I should like to know another
author's wife who gets as much!)—except for the reason that I
like to please you. There is no other reason why I should give

you any regular allowance at all. Few husbands do. There is no reason why I should increase the London housekeeping money by £2 a week for your personal expenses except that I like to please you. There is no reason why I should not insist on housekeeping accounts, or should allow you so much as £13 for a week like last week, except that it is a pleasure to me to be agreeable to you. There is no other reason why I should help you in your Poetry Society. There is no other reason why I should tolerate your very close friendship with Legros. (For you would never tolerate a similar friendship on my side—oh-la-la!) Happily for you, it has always given me pleasure to be agreeable to you.

I could give other examples, but perhaps I have given enough.

I have no greater pleasure than to give you pleasure; but unless your behaviour completely alters, that pleasure will cease. Let there be no mistake. You know my feelings towards you. It depends entirely on yourself whether they remain constant or whether they change. Is this plain? I hope it is. I don't ask for any arguments. As a fact it is impossible to argue with you, because you at once make a scene, call me bad names, & then express surprise that I cannot 'discuter en ami'!! I have had more than enough of arguments. And I don't want any apologies or any regrets. All I want is a complete change. I have feared for years that I should have to write this letter. You now have it. The decision rests with you. You can either keep me as a generous and loving friend, or you can have me as a husband who will do nothing for you that he is not obliged to do.

If you decide to keep me as a friend you have only to write me that you will join me on the yacht in September. I shall be delighted. Nothing will please me more. And I will see that the yacht remains in port all the time.

Don't answer this letter impulsively. If I have brought accusations against you remember that they are nothing to the accusations which you are always bringing against me, and remember also that my accusations are based on facts that cannot be denied.

Much depends on your answer.

Your still loving husband,

A.B.

P.S. I am now at Bembridge, Isle of Wight. We have been to Portsmouth & Southsea. Weather good. On Friday I shall send to the Post Office Southampton for letters. Any letters should be posted not later than 5 p.m. Thursday. Otherwise I shan't get them. Address: A. Bennett, Yacht Marie Marguerite, Poste Restante Southampton.

KEELE / MS / 204   Yacht Marie Marguerite
(*To Marguerite Soulié Bennett*)   Dartmouth
                                      28–6–21

Mon enf. ch.,

I received 3 letters from you this morning, though apparently there were none at the Post Office when I went last night. I return the article. This is all right, except for several mistakes in English. When Newnes says that he does not publish much stuff dealing with superstition etc. he is only making an excuse, and it is not true. Some of the famous things in the *Strand* have dealt with subjects similar to yours. The difficulty with yours is that everything depends on the events narrated. There is no characterisation, or dramatic power, or emotional interest; because you have depended on the subject itself. Now the subject and the plot, so far as the plot goes, are among the very oldest in popular fiction. Hundreds of stories extremely similar to this one have been written—and published. Hundreds & hundreds! There is no originality in it, and no scope in it for you to show what you can do. I should think the best thing to do would be to send it to that ladies' monthly which once published one or two articles of yours. I forget the name. They might like to have something signed by you. You will probably not agree with my judgement of the story now; but you will agree with it later on. Also, there are many mistakes of English in it, & constructions such as English people would not use, and a number of typewriting errors. I return the story, and Newnes's letter. I am sure that you can do very much better than this with a subject that suits you & that has some originality in it. There are 4 big yachts in this harbour. Two of them started out this morning, but both had to return on account of the violent weather. We went *up* the river Dart in the launch to an old town called Totnes, & there were biggish waves even on the enclosed river, & we got wet with spray. I hope to be able to leave tomorrow, however, for Salcombe. I don't want to invite Olive with the Keebles. I want her to come to Dinard, unless you have any objections. Moreover, she told me she couldn't come in August. I haven't yet heard from Keeble. I don't know yet what I shall do about Miss Gordon. As regards Comarques all I want is enough food to keep me free of neuralgia. If I don't get my usual quantity, neuralgia is absolutely certain to arrive. I am glad you are better. Tonight is your 2nd A.F.P.S. I trust it will be a great success. Everybody is enjoying this trip enormously. Richard t'envoie le bonjour.

Je te bise tendrement.

Nouche

204. The Keebles: Frederick (1870–1952), Professor of Botany at Magdalen College, and Lillah McCarthy, recently married to him. For a letter to Keeble see Vol. III.

KEELE / MS / 205
(*To Marguerite Soulié Bennett*)

Yacht Marie Marguerite
5–7–21

Mon enf. ch.,

Nous voilà en pleine mer, en route pour Plymouth. Richard est parti hier matin, et Usher est arrivé hier soir. Temps toujours superbe, trop superbe. Le vent, très léger, est mauvais. Mer plate. J'ai eu un chill mais je me suis remis totalement. J'ai presque fini une nouvelle. Ida m'écrit qu'ils ne seront pas à Carantec, mais au Touquet. Je t'envoie la lettre. Le malheur est que (je pense) ce yacht tire trop d'eau pour le petit port du Touquet. En tout cas c'est près de Brest. Je suis passablement embêté parce que je ne peux pas toucher de l'argent. On me doit des sommes considérables aux États Unis, mais la galette n'arrive pas. Aussi n'ai-je eu aucune espèce de nouvelle sur le film. Un peu fort, ça. Pinker s'en occupe maintenant. Il me tarde de réintégrer le lit conjugal. Je rêve à peu près tous les soirs, et dans ces rêves l'enf. ch. fait toutes les choses que je lui demande, et surtout quand elle sait que je l'attends elle garde exprès pour moi son petit p-p-, avec lequel elle baptise pour

mon plaisir sa délicate lingerie intime. Enfin un tas de bêtises e
de folies. C'est fatigant des fois.

Le docteur Rivers est exquis, mais d'une apparence peu
charmeur. Il est modeste et son savoir m'émerveille. Aussi, i
est Master of Arts M.A., Master of Medicine M.D., Doctor o
Laws L.L.D., Doctor of Science D.SC., Fellow of the Roya
Society F.R.S., Fellow of the Royal College of Physicians
F.R.C.P., President of the Anthropological Institute, President
of the Folk Lore Society; et je ne sais pas quoi d'autre.

Il dit que Atkins est le plus charmant homme qu'il ait jamais
rencontré. Je te bise bien.

Nouche

Address Friday Southampton

205. [Here we are in the open sea, on our way to Plymouth. Richard left yesterday
morning and Usher arrived yesterday evening. The weather is still wonderful—too
wonderful. This very light wind is bad. A smooth sea. I have had a chill but am
completely recovered. I have almost finished a short story. Ida writes to say that they
will not be in Carantec but Le Touquet. I am sending you her letter. The trouble is that
(I think) this yacht draws too much water for the little port of Le Touquet. Anyway it is
near Brest. I am fairly irritated because I cannot draw out any money. I am owed
considerable sums in the United States, but the cash hasn't arrived. Nor have I had any
news of any kind about the film. A bit much. Pinker is seeing to it now. I am longing to
return to the conjugal bed. I dream almost every night, and in my dreams the darl. ch.
does everything I ask her, and particularly when she knows I am waiting for her she
keeps especially for me little p-p-, with which she baptises for my pleasure her delicate
intimate underwear. A whole lot of silliness and nonsense anyway. It is tiring
sometimes.

    Doctor Rivers is delightful, though hardly charming to look at. He is unassuming
and his knowledge amazes me....]

    Usher: identified elsewhere only as Captain Usher.

    W. H. R. Rivers died the following year, and Bennett wrote some recollections of him
in the *New Statesman* on 17 June. It is reprinted in *Things That Have Interested Me, Second
Series*, 1923.

KEELE / MS / 206
(*To Marguerite Soulié Bennett*)   [Yacht Marie Marguerite]
                                                  [Southampton]
                                                  23–7–21

My child,
    I have your letter.
    If it is mean to refuse to pay for what Legros has paid for,
then I am mean.

If it is mean to insist that money paid for board & lodging shall go into the housekeeping money, then I am mean.

If it is mean to refuse to let you make a profit, at my expense, out of the visit of your friend, then I am mean.

You told me that Legros would pay for his board, & I assumed that you spoke the truth. In any case I do not think that Legros is the man to make you personal presents of money.

You are perfectly well aware that far from being mean, I have always been very generous to you, both morally and materially. Unfortunately your judgement is disturbed by your infatuation for Legros, which is getting you into trouble. Let me recall some facts of the past week.

On the first four nights of my short stay, Friday, Saturday, Sunday, & Monday, you chose to spend the evenings with Legros instead of me. It is true that on the first night I was asked if I would go for a walk. I said I preferred not to, and you left me. On the other three nights you completely ignored me; asked me nothing; walked straight out, took Legros away from me, & disappeared for two hours with him & Miss L'Hermite. On the fourth night, Monday, you returned through the garden arm in arm with Legros, Miss L'Hermite walking discreetly a few paces in front. You were utterly absorbed in each other, so much so that you did not even see Wolfe & myself sitting close by as you passed. Legros enters the house and without hesitation shuts the door. Bang goes the door! Krrrk goes the key in the lock! And I have to knock for admittance. 'I thought you were in' says Legros. Not the fact. He didn't think, nor ask, nor look, though I was approaching the door as he banged it. With one of his grand, possessive gestures he acted by instinct, absorbed, & banged the door. Of course he didn't do it on purpose. He would have cut his hand off sooner than do it. But what a symbolic act! And it could never have occurred had you not been so infatuated that you didn't dream you were grossly neglecting me.

Rather alarmed by my demeanour after this, you were most attentive the next morning, most charming. Would I go and bathe? If not, would I like you to stay at home with me? Things are improving, I thought. I thought I should have the pleasure of your society in the evening. I was mistaken. You said: 'I am going to be by myself.' And you walked about the garden by yourself, no doubt doing urgent work.

On the Wednesday night, after my visit to London, you asked me into your boudoir, & we did get some chat—until Legros, wondering what on earth husband & wife could be doing, came and disturbed us.

On Thursday afternoon I had to work and was therefore unworthy of attention. When you told Legros you would take him to bathe, he did suggest that you might stay for tea. But no. You said sharply: 'Do you want to bathe or not, Pierrot?' Pierrot said that he did. 'Well then, we shall go at once. Arnold can have his tea with Wolfe.' And you went off at the very moment tea was served, though you knew the importance I attach to tea. You had plenty of time. The tea would not have delayed you 15 minutes. You had 3 hours. But no! You could not wait. You must get away with Legros. After 3 hours of Legros you return to dinner, a little late. At 7.45 you go out again. I am talking to Legros in the garden. You take him off. You & he take a few hesitating turns at the pond, and then you disappear, infatuated. So infatuated that you see nothing extraordinary in the proceeding. I wait 3/4's of an hour. I then go in. This is my last night. Astounded that I am hurt, you actually try to discuss the matter before everyone! Then finally you have the pleasing cheek to get angry because I refuse to pay over again for what Legros has already paid for. Legros absolutely absorbs you. Even at the table in front of everyone you cannot help telling him that you 'almost love' him. Of course everybody notices your infatuation, & there must be a good deal of talk about it. But you don't see it. You don't ever see, except by short glimpses, soon past, that you grossly neglect me in favour of Legros. It is certain that Wolfe has been much impressed by it, and as for Robert he does not quite succeed even in keeping it out of his conversation.

But *you* cannot see it. You think that I am mad. You say it is all perfectly innocent. I know it is all perfectly innocent. But it is amazingly stupid, amazingly indiscreet, amazingly rude to me and amazingly ridiculous. Neither you nor Legros seem to have any savoir vivre. Even for your own sakes it would have been advantageous to be polite and attentive to the old gentleman during his short stay. What is worse you seem to have no imagination—not even enough imagination to imagine how *you* would feel if I was living at Comarques with two women & you came for a few days & I and one of the women ignored you as you & Legros ignored me, or to imagine how Legros would feel if he were the husband & I the 'almost-lover'.

Nor have you the sense to take the warnings which I have already given you. The next time I have any complaint to make, I shall proceed to action. I shall deal direct with Legros, and also I shall put the whole matter before Georges Bion, in the hope that he may advise you. You need advice. And you have no one here except Legros, who is extraordinarily stupid in important things. Legros of course, though amiable enough, is only what the English call your 'tame cat'.

You understand: I shall not warn you any more. The future, and Legros' future, depend on your commonsense and on your self-control. I am perfectly willing for the friendship between you & Legros to continue, and to do what I can to help it and to make it agreeable and correct in the eyes of the world. But only on the condition that I am treated absolutely properly, and with the utmost attention, and that you & Legros do not make yourselves ridiculous when I am there.

I am still rather doubtful whether you have a proper conception of your duties as a wife. I was somewhat disturbed by your casual remark that you could easily go to Paris at the end of September as the servants could look after the flat. In my opinion the flat will need the attention of the mistress at that time. Many details necessitating the attention of the mistress will certainly arise in settling in for the winter. Moreover, you have either to get a new servant or to train one of the servants you already have; for the service at Comarques and the *vie simple*, though all right for a summer in the country, will not do for London. I see no reason why you should go to Paris to buy hats just at the moment when my work is beginning and I have need of attention. I do not know whether you had any idea of meeting Legros in Paris. Perhaps not. But if you had, please note that I absolutely object to it. You see Legros almost daily in London during most of the year; you spend most of the summer with him at Thorpe. If you insist also on meeting him on the Continent there will be trouble. This is positive. If you cannot control your infatuation, I must help you to control it.

Please don't waste time in saying that all you did at Comarques this week was for my benefit, & that I understand nothing; or that you will commit suicide; or that I ought to separate from you. You won't commit suicide, and I have not the least intention of separating from you. Why? Because I am fond of you. Your greatest fault is your lack of self-control when your feelings are aroused. I do not blame you for your infatuation. You cannot help it. It has happened to millions of women. But you do not realise how dangerous it is, nor how Legros is exploiting you. Happily for both you & me, I am master of the situation. I shall remain so. And I hope you will not compel me to prove that I am master of the situation in any unpleasant ways. I much prefer to prove it pleasantly.

Je te bise,

A.B.

P.S. If you reply to this letter do not do so in a hurry. You are apt to be very rude when you write in a hurry. Think it over. Read the letter again, and also read again the previous letter that I wrote you when you last made a great scene. It will pay you handsomely to control yourself.

206. Edward Wolfe, the artist (b. 1896), was painting Marguerite's portrait. His portrait of Bennett is reproduced as the Frontispiece of Marguerite's little book *Arnold Bennett*, published in 1925. Wolfe and Legros were friends. Miss L'Hermite was a friend of Wolfe's.
Robert: probably Robert Bion.

KEELE / MS / 207
(*To Marguerite Soulié Bennett*)   Yacht Marie Marguerite
                                          4th Augt 1921

My child,
    Thanks for your letter of the 1st received yesterday after-noon. I am very glad that you have not attempted any answer to the complaints which I made; because there was none. In reply, you merely make complaints against me, which is natural. However, if my behaviour can be changed to suit you, I am only too willing to change it. I have not asked you to 'court' me. I hate being courted by women, and I know something about that! All I asked was that you should not

neglect me. As regards courting you, I assume that you do not expect me to compete with Legros for your society!

It is a striking example of your methods, to refer to my sexual habits. You always expect that you should be judged by a different standard from anybody else. What about *your* sexual habits? You didn't learn anything from me. In the same way you constantly accuse me of egotism. It doesn't occur to you that your own egotism is intense. Only your intense egotism prevented you from foreseeing that the way you have treated me, in connection with Legros, was absolutely certain to exasperate me in a high degree. When you accuse me of egotism I laugh. When I accuse you of egotism your face is covered with an ugly scowl and you are furious.

All these are details. The point is that I have always treated you with both material & moral generosity. And particularly so in regard to your friendship with Legros. If this generosity is to continue I am determined that you shall treat me with the greatest consideration and attention. I should have thought that the least you could do, in return for my benevolent attitude toward the Legros affair—an attitude of which not one husband in a thousand would be capable—would be to take particular care that I should not suffer. You yourself would never treat me with similar generosity in similar circumstances. You couldn't do it. Also I am determined that your arrangements with Legros shall not be hidden from me until they are definitely decided. I will not always be confronted with the fait accompli. And also I absolutely decline to agree to your spending holidays with Legros on the continent. You see quite enough of him in England. You may think that I am insisting too much; but I am anxious that there should be no possibility of misunderstanding on these points between us. It is very little that I am asking—and it is much less than most husbands would demand and enforce—but what I am asking I am asking, and if you cannot or will not agree to it then I shall have no alternative but to change my attitude fundamentally. You know that I am very fond of you—nothing but my fondness for you has led me to treat you as benevolently as I have—and I am exceedingly anxious that everything should go smoothly and that you should be as happy as I can make you. I have no fear of losing your respect—not the slightest. Or my own self-respect.

You will receive all the money you need in ample time
whether I am in Brittany or not.
                    Je te bise,

                                                    N

P.S. I haven't heard from the Godebskis at all. Lillah, Keeble
& Olive all absolutely adore yachting. Lillah is much nicer on a
yacht than at rehearsals. In fact she is exceedingly nice and
agreeable. Her husband rules her absolutely and teases her all
the time. They send you their loves. These people leave on
Monday & Shuffle and Tayler come; but I don't know where
we shall go. *Up to Monday night my address will be Southampton.*

KEELE / MS / 208
(*To Marguerite Soulié Bennett*)   Yacht Marie Marguerite
                                             Cowes
                                             6–8–21
My wife,
    As you object to the word 'child' I will no longer use it.
    I have never treated you as an irresponsible child. On the
contrary I have always agreed to your having a very large and
free share of responsibility in our mutual existence—much
larger than that of most wives.
    If you mean that I must not mention your parents to other
people, of course I should not dream of doing so, & I never have
done—except in a favourable sense. I have often told people
that I like your mother. If you mean that I must not mention
them to you, of course I must mention them to you. It would be
rather queer if I, who provide for both your parents, should be
forbidden to mention the matter to you! I have always been
very sympathetic to all the members of your family, & I have
always done my best to help them—at your request. And I have
been glad to do so.
    Naturally I expect you to keep our house as my wife. I am
very fond of you, & I know that you are very fond of me, and my
one desire is that everything should go smoothly. Anything that
I can do I shall be very willing to do. But anyone would think
from your letters that in protesting, again and again, against
your continued unsatisfactory treatment of me, I had committed

ted some crime & that I was to blame, while you were a victim!

This is not so. That I have had just cause for complaint is unquestionable. I am bound to complain; I am bound to protest, and to point out that if proper treatment is refused on one side it will be refused on the other. The matter depends entirely on your good sense, and as I have confidence in your good sense I hope it will end happily. I have explained myself perfectly clearly, and there is no use in me saying any more. No one knows better than you my affection for you, and my generosity in all matters where generosity is right. As for your duties as a wife, there is no need for me to tell them to you. You know them perfectly well.

Your husband,

A.

I will wire the next address. It may be Trouville. It will depend on the weather, which up to now is awful. The guests all send their greetings.

STOKE / MS / 209
(*To Margaret Beardmore*)

Yacht Marie Marguerite
Ostende
19–9–21

My dear Margot,

I was very glad to get your very interesting letter. Auntie also read it with much pleasure. While you are striving more or less hard in a new career, we are being perfectly idle here in the yacht, which is better than any hotel or even sitting rooms with 6 chairs & a green teapot. You will doubtless soon lose that feeling of 'beastly superiority'. At least I hope so. The differences between human beings are not so sharp as to justify such feelings for any length of time. You were quite right to want *not* to be a school teacher. It suits some people, of course, but it wouldn't suit you. Keep an account of every penny—and read through the accounts *at intervals*. I have kept an account of every penny for 33 years, but as I seldom have the heart to examine the appalling record, I doubt if the result is fully worth the trouble. Save some money, and keep sole control of it. Be as interested as you can in your clothes, both those that people see

& those that people don't see, and in your general appearance
and all that. Beware of anybody, man or woman, who disdains
these things. Do not avoid the society of men. The tendency of
serious professional women, like yourself, is to do so. A disastrous error, which always ends by making such women
'peculiar'. You will undoubtedly have a very interesting time,
& I think it is excellent that you are by the sea. But I wish the
town was larger. The larger the town the more interesting the
time. Small towns are never fully alive. In the year 1889 I began
as you did (but I was 21), and I didn't have 2 rooms; only one.
And I didn't earn £100 but £65. Also there was no bathroom. I
attach little importance to the absence of bathroom. The
ingenious can always achieve cleanliness without too much
trouble. I was forgetting that the most important thing of all is
to eat well. Women on their own scarcely ever do. All right, I
won't send you any money. I might lend you a book or two
when I get home without giving offence perhaps. I should like
to see some of Cedric's productions. I take little notice of
precosity, but *if* he means to use a pen I expect I could save him
a certain amount of trouble.

I suppose that you are now having a rather easier time than
you had in London. In fact Whitehaven is the first reward of
London. So that you *can* read. Well, do read. I always read in
bed at night till I'm too sleepy to read any more—which isn't
long. I suppose you never read your uncle's book on *Literary
Taste*. Nevertheless it is not an absolutely worthless book.
Auntie will be here till Saturday, & I shall sail home (Thorpe)
in the yacht on Sunday, and return to George Street on Oct 1st
for the winter. I have been cruising for over four months. Quelle
vie! Much love from us both. Let me know if I can be of any
service to you. People write to me for *advice* every day; but I will
put you in the reserved seats.

Your affectionate uncle,

A.B.

209. Margaret Beardmore (1901–76) was the daughter of Fanny Gertrude and
Frank Beardmore. She trained at Chelsea College *c.*1918–21 and then went to the
Whitehaven School, a mixed school, to be games and physical training mistress.

George Cedric Beardmore (1908–74) was Margaret's youngest brother. The family
lived in Glasgow for at least a couple of years in the early twenties and possibly before;
they returned to Stoke-on-Trent in 1923. George Cedric was educated at Glasgow High
School and also at Wolstanton Grammar School.

Bennett's first position in London, in 1889, was as a shorthand clerk in the law offices of Le Brasseur & Oakley. His first address was 197 Coldharbour Lane, SW.

Literary Taste was published in 1909. It is a guide to the forming of taste.

KEELE / MS / 210

(*To Marguerite Soulié Bennett*)

12ᴮ, George Street
1–10–21

[no salutation]

You have put me in a very difficult situation, & I don't know what do to. But there is one thing that is quite clear, & I have no hesitation as to it whatever.

You make a certain demand from me.

In reply I say: 'If I consent, either I shall have to sell the yacht, or we cannot continue to live in two houses.'

These are the exact words I used.

Immediately you make a scene. You say that I intend to sell Comarques.

You call me Crapule, Crapule, Crapule.

You say further that unless I agree to your demand without any conditions you will 'me mener une vie de chien,' etc. etc.

I have no hesitation whatever in telling you clearly that unless you offer me your excuses for this scene, I shall have no further negotiations with you. My only reply to such conduct will be and must be: 'Fais.'

If you apologise we can continue. If you feel that this is impossible I shall quite understand.

A.B.

210. In Bennett's hand on the envelope of this letter is written: 'Je retournerai à 7 heures. Je ne peux pas rester pour le thé. Ne déchire pas cette lettre sans le lire. C'est grave.'

KEELE / MS / 211

(*To Marguerite Soulié Bennett*)   12ᴮ, George Street
[*c.* 7 October 1921]

[no salutation]

I have written a statement of our financial situation for you, and made you a very handsome offer. You refuse even to read it. Very well. If you change your mind, let me know.

A.B.

keele / MS / 212
(*To Marguerite Soulié Bennett*)   12ᴮ, George Street
                                                     9–10–21

Dear Marguerite,

Please do not twist my words. What I said was that if you refused to read my statement everything was finished between us as regards this affair. I simply decline to carry on any further negotiation. Under no circumstances shall I give way about this. But I certainly should not be so ridiculous as to suggest a separation because you refuse to read my statement.

You frequently, however, talk of a separation. You seem really to want it. If so you must go to your solicitor, who will communicate with me. Separations are complex legal things. I think I should be acting unfairly in continuing to object to a separation if you want it.

The statement which you refuse to read contains a very handsome offer, but it is not an acceptance of your demand. I assume therefore that I must not give it to you for a third time. If you decide to read it you will find it in the middle drawer of my desk.

On Monday I will give you the cheque for Courbevoie. I promised to keep your father, & I do not wish to put you in an awkward position by refusing suddenly to continue. This payment, however, is the last I shall make for your father unless some agreement is come to between us.

I shall have to consult books at the Club Library this morning for my *Strand* articles. I shall not be in for lunch. This afternoon I go to the Sharpes. I shall be in for dinner tonight. As you know, tomorrow night I have to dine with Loraine.

                                                     Yours, A.B.

212. On the *Strand* articles see p. 293 n.

berg / MS / 213
(*To George Cedric Beardmore*)   12ᴮ, George Street
                                                     11–10–21

My dear Cedric,

I am glad to hear from you, as Margot had told me about your intentions. I return the essay. It is good, & I thank heaven that it is not precocious. I have marked one or two small slips of mere writing and spelling. We shall see what you do in the way of writing during the next year. This present specimen is rather short as material for judging what you can do. To be an ordinary journalist is very hard work, & badly paid. But if you can be a journalist after the style of your aged uncle I dare say you might find it agreeable enough. Remember me to your mother, father, & everybody.

Your aff unc, Arnold

CAMBRIDGE / MS / 214
(*To Richard Bennett*) 12^B, George Street
13–10–21

My dear Richard,

You doubtless thought it odd that I referred not to your birthday. The simple fact is I quite forgot all about it—in the midst of my worries. I got one worry a little off my chest by an hour's interview with your Auntie Emily yesterday. The situation of your Uncle Sep is most serious; I don't know what to do about it. I tell you of course in confidence. I have other troubles still graver; & this morning I heard that Auntie Sarah Barlow is dying! Still, I do wish you many happy returns on your birthday, & you might let me know what you would like for a cadeau. I cannot give my mind to it. It must not cost a lot.

Love,
Your agitated uncle,

A.B.

214. Emily's current lodgers had left. For some years up to this time Bennett gave her £100 a year.
Septimus was drinking excessively.
Sarah Barlow lived until 1924.

KEELE / MS / 215
(*To Marguerite Soulié Bennett*) 12^B, George Street
[21 October 1921]

[no salutation]

I want you to understand that if you are going to this concert I am not going.

A.B.

215. The concert was by Cedric Sharpe, on the 25th. On 30 October Bennett wrote in the *Journals*:

> I left the yacht on Oct. 1st, and came here. I had kept the log regularly. But here owing to conjugal worries, I could not possibly keep the journal. On Tuesday 18th inst I consulted Braby [solicitor] as to the marital situation. I determined that nothing should be done until after M.'s recital at Lady Swaythling's on 19th inst. This was the last evening I spent with her. Braby sent for her on the Thursday. She wrote him on Thursday night confirming her desire for a separation. Yet on Friday she asked me to take her to a concert! I told Braby about this, and he wrote suggesting that she should go and live somewhere else.
>
> On Saturday morning 22nd inst. I went to the Tate Gallery so as to be out of the house. When I returned she had gone, but I did not know this until the next day!

KENNERLEY / MS / 216
(*To Tertia Kennerley*)

12ᴮ, George Street
23–10–21

My dear Tertia,

A great calamity has occurred in this household. I am obliged to arrange for a separation from Marguerite on account of her relations with Legros, whom she absolutely refuses to give up, & with whom she is certainly very much in love. 47–31. She has several times suggested a separation, and at last, after witnessing their manifestations of passion in my presence, after an episode in Italy where they met (after hoodwinking me as to their intentions until the meeting had taken place), and after certain occurrences at Comarques, I was obliged to take advice, both legal & from friends. I then learnt to my astonishment that I was being regarded by various people as a mari complaisant! The actual rupture occurred through Marguerite insisting on me giving her £1,500 a year for her own private use—doubtless so that she might have more money to spend on Legros. She was seldom getting less than £1,000 a year from me for her own private use, but that was not enough! The unfortunate creature has simply been carried away. Legros is undoubtedly a scoundrel, but she can't see it & I hear that no one has been able to make her see it. When the inevitable row occurs there, she will realise (what she now utterly fails to realise) that she has made a most ghastly future for herself. She ingenuously dreams of a career as a French reciter in London. It is pathetic. She has enjoyed enormous prestige, and resents always that she enjoys it as my wife, and she thinks she can continue it apart from me. One of the worst aspects of the affair is that as of course I must see to her financial independence—I am giving her £2,000 a year free to tax; she wanted £4,000!— she will have money to spend on Legros. She is, I am told by our mutual solicitor, convinced that at the last moment I shall ask her to stay! Whereas my fear is that at the last moment, or later, she will ask me to let her stay. The only thing that worries me is the tragedy that she is making for herself. Her increasingly terrible temper is bound in the end to triumph over Legros' love of her money. Not that Legros is not genuinely fond of her—I think he is, at present. Precisely the same thing happened to her mother, who is the slightest bit cracked, & I fear that Marguerite is too. Various persons have tried to make her see reason. No success. Even her own people, papa & mama Bion, have each written to her to protest against her relations with Legros & to warn her of the consequences. I should not have heard of these letters, but they so infuriated her that she was obliged to talk to someone about them, & she came & talked to me, though our relations were then practically broken off! I am most acutely distressed by the fact that Marguerite is behaving with the most tragic idiocy and that nobody can stop her. Otherwise, if I thought she was going to be happier, I should be only too pleased at the change, though of course nothing can end my responsibility for her material welfare. (In this latter view my friends scarcely agree with me.) I think I must come down tomorrow Monday night, after dinner, about 8.15. If it won't suit let W.W. telephone me.

Yours, A.B.

STOKE / TS / 217
(*To Frank Bennett*)
Private

12^B, George Street
24th October 1921

My dear Frank,

I am obliged to arrange a separation from Marguerite on account of her relations with a certain Monsieur Legros, a Frenchman. I hear that she told someone she once consulted you about me and that you advised her to commence an action for alimony or something. Knowing the wildness of her statements, I hesitated to believe this, but I should be very much

obliged if you would let me have your version of the affair. I
may tell you that she has never had any real grievance against
me at all.

Yours, A.B

KEELE / MS / 218
(*To Marguerite Soulié Bennett*)   12ᴮ, George Street
                                                25–10–21

My dear Marguerite,

I appreciate the friendly tone of your letter.

I do not think that Braby has made any confusion. My offer,
which you first accepted and then declined, is perfectly clear:—

£2,000 a year provided that it is not more than one quarter of
my net income.

If in any year the sum paid to you should be less than £2,000,
and if in a subsequent year my net income should exceed
£8,000, then the balance not previously received by you to be
made up accordingly.

£5,000 capital at my death, if I die before you, & the income
for your life of two thirds of my estate after this £5,000 has been
paid.

If you accept this offer please tell Braby at once. He must
deal with the matter, not I.

If you decline it, it will be withdrawn entirely and you must
take your own course.

I wish you to understand that I cannot possibly undertake to
pay you £2,000 a year whether my income falls or not.

I think it would be an excellent thing for you to go and live on
the continent. Let me advise you that what you want more than
anything else is repose.

It would be very unwise for you and me to meet at present.

I am full of sympathy for you; so is everybody.

Yours, A.B.

218. Percy Braby (1867–1924), of the firm Braby and Waller.

KENNERLEY / MS / 219
(To Tertia Kennerley)   12^B, George Street
10—11—21

My dear Tertia,

I heard from Jim Bennett today asking me if I could put up Aunt Mary during her stay in London. I see myself doing it! I've replied grumbling at them all for not warning me earlier of the peregrinations. I'm going away to the Mediterranean to Bertie Sullivan's yacht before the end of the month, & for Aunt-Mary purposes I have ante-dated this departure. Jim says he is also asking you to put up A.M. To be on the safe side I have said that Putney would be very difficult for a woman with business in Camberwell & other parts & suggesting an hotel in central London.

The separation is going along all right. Marguerite has chosen most of the furniture she would like from me, & other things. But the draft of the deed has not yet been approved by her solicitors. I now perceive that this change is an enormous relief to me. I am very well looked after here. M. says she has nearly got a maisonnette, somewhere, I don't know where, & hopes I will go & see her in it. I suppose I shall have to, but I don't want to.

That great psychological expert Swinnerton dined with her at her club the other day, & talked with her for 3 hours with extreme candour. He is a great friend of hers, but a much greater one of mine. He gives me his impression that he is inclined to think that there has not been adultery between these too. Not that I attach much importance to the mere fact. I only tell you in fairness because I told you that personally I was convinced there had been.

For income tax purposes I was looking through my journal this morning, & I came across an early encounter with your Mary. She sat on my knee and put her finger up my nose and withdrew it & said: 'There's nothing up *your* nose, anyway.'

Yours, A.B.

219. Jim Bennett: James Booth Bennett, cousin (b. 1870).
Aunt Mary: Mary Bennett (b. 1871), daughter of John Bennett (Enoch's brother), who went out to America.

KEELE / MS / 220
(*To Marguerite Soulié Bennett*)   12ᴮ, George Street
                                                    14–11–21

Dear Marguerite,

   Thanks for your letter of Sunday. I hope you will soon be better. Which means that I hope you will establish yourself definitely as soon as possible. I appreciate your offer, but I do not wish anything to interfere with your settling into your new home. *Some* things you may be able to do without for a time, but I will see that you have all *essentials* immediately they are needed. I would much sooner not let the house, or this flat, than delay your installation.

                                                    Yours, A.B.

P.S.   Sorry about the maisonnette.

   220. Bennett wrote in his *Journals* on 23 November: 'On this day the two parts of the deed of separation between my wife and myself were formally exchanged by our solicitors and the matter is complete.'
   In his memoir Frank Swinnerton recalls that in the final days of the break-up Marguerite and Bennett came to him separately to discuss the matter. Marguerite made no mention of Legros but was concerned only to describe her sufferings at the hands of a stingy and self-centred man. She was now determined to leave him. Bennett 'was very much disturbed, saying more than once "I married her for life" '. Swinnerton visited Bennett on the last day or two that Marguerite was in the house. She remained in her rooms, and Bennett said to him the only unkind thing Swinnerton ever heard him say about her: 'To think of that poor middle-aged fool, sitting there, thinking ... all sorts of things!' Bennett never again mentioned her to him.
   On 22 December Bennett wrote to Winifred Nerney:
      As I sent coloured cards to the servants I don't quite want to send ditto to you; but I want to wish you the best wishes & to thank you very much for the extremely sympathetic & valuable help which you have given to me during recent events. I have greatly appreciated it. I dare say that my manner is often rather curt, but no doubt after all these years you understand that my feelings towards you are not precisely cold.

ELDIN / MS / 221
(*To May Beardmore Marsden*)   Yacht Amaryllis
                                                   Cannes
                                                   17–12–21

My dear May,

   You will receive literature at Xmas, but I can't inscribe it. Sorry. I am out here on Bertie Sullivan's yacht, & working at a tremendous rate, also living a life of pleasure in gorgeous weather. To write 1,000 words & dance afternoon & evening & go out to dinner is some achievement for a day of 16 hours. It is very difficult to worry me here, & my secretary, Miss Nerney, is the most devoted dragon of defence. She guards me from London. Everything is now arranged between Marguerite & me, but there is bound to be trouble later on, when at last she comes round to the general estimate of the character of her youthful friend, Monsieur Legros. Well, I did everything to keep the fat out of the fire, & I have several times been told that I did a great deal too much. But in the end I was compelled to force her to choose absolutely between Legros and me. As she was and is madly infatuated with this person, she decided that a handsome income from me and the society of Legros discreetly enjoyed would be the ideal solution for her. Nobody has succeeded in making her see that she is constructing a tragedy for herself. What has happened to her is a misfortune that might happen to almost any woman or man, & I think that some of my friends are too hard on her. At the same time I am inexpressibly relieved to be independent again—that is, relatively independent—though worried by the mess that Marguerite is making of the last third of her life.

Best wishes to you, Joan, grandma, Ed' Harry & all.

Yours, A.B.

221. Bennett sailed with Sullivan during December and January.

KENNERLEY / MS / 222
(*To Mary Kennerley*)

Yacht Amaryllis
Monte Carlo
1–1–22

Ma chère Mary,

On me dit que tu as été surmenée. Un peu de surménage est bien, mais trop en est idiot. Tâche donc de ne te surmener qu'un tout petit peu. Nous avons à bord deux Irlandais, deux Anglais, un Français, une Belge, et sept Italiens. Tous parlent français pire les uns que les autres — sauf ton excellent oncle, qui est plus ou moins forcé de corriger tout le monde. (Et encore ton oncle ne le parle que très médiocrement.) Les orangers et les citronniers sont merveilleux de beaux fruits. La mer est bleue comme Reckitts et le ciel bleu comme Cambridge. Mais

un matin il a gêlé, à la stupéfaction des populations! Il y a peu
de yachts. L'Amaryllis est le seul dans ce port, sauf celui de son
Altesse Sérène, le prince de Monaco — gros bateau de 1,200
tonnes et très laid. Le notre a 109 tonnes. Un rien! Il faut
absolument que bientôt tu fasses un petit voyage dans mon
yacht à moi, lequel est passablement chic. Mais si tu es malade
je te jette tout de suite pardessus bord. C'est ça que je fais avec
tous mes passagers qui ont le mauvais goût d'être malade d'une
certaine façon....je n'insiste pas! Je connais Miss Long, c.à.d.
que je l'ai rencontrée deux fois, et elle m'est particulièrement
sympathique. Elle a promis de venir me voir. Quand elle
viendra je lui demanderai si tu es une étudiante vraiment
sérieuse. Je te souhaite bonne année, et, ma foi, je t'embrasse.

Ton affectueux oncle, A.B.

222. [I am told that you are overtired. A bit of overtiredness is a good thing, but too
much is silly. So try only to overtire yourself a little bit. We have on board two
Irishmen, two Englishmen, one Frenchman, a Belgian woman and seven Italians.
Each one speaks French worse than the other—except for your excellent uncle, who is
more or less compelled to correct everybody. (And even your uncle does not speak it
any too well.) The orange and lemon trees are marvellous with beautiful fruit. The sea
is blue like Reckitts, the sky is blue like Cambridge. But there was a frost one morning,
to everybody's amazement. There are not many yachts. The Amaryllis is the only one
in this port, except for that of his Serene Highness, the prince of Monaco—a big, 1,200
ton boat and very ugly. Our boat is 109 tons—a trifle. You absolutely must have a little
trip soon on my own boat, which is fairly elegant. But if you are ill, I will throw you
straight overboard. That is what I do with all my passengers who have the bad taste to
be ill in a certain way. . . . I will say no more. I know Miss Long, that is I have met her
twice, and I find her extremely congenial. She has promised to come and see me. When
she comes, I will ask her whether you are a really serious student. With best wishes for
the near year and, yes indeed, a kiss.]

Reckitts: name of a commercial bleach.
Kathleen Long, the pianist (1896–1968). She studied with Bennett's friend Herbert
Sharpe, and she taught piano to both Mary and Margaret Kennerley.

KENNERLEY / MS / 223
(*To Margaret Kennerley*)

Yacht Amaryllis
Monte Carlo
1–1–22

Ma petite brune,
    Tu sais, il va falloir que tu m'écrives une toute petite lettre
gentille en français. Je suis sur que tu peux. Et s'il y a des fautes
dedans, 'ne t'en fais pas', ce qui veut dire: 'don't worry about

that.' Je sais que tu es entêtée, et les gens entêtés arrivent toujours. Donc, si vraiment tu désires parler et écrire bien le français, tu y arriveras. Ce raisonnement est-il clair? J'ai donné beaucoup de cadeaux de Noël. J'ai reçu beaucoup de vœux, mais pas l'ombre d'un cadeau. Les vœux sont agréables: mais j'aime mieux les cadeaux. Et toi? Je suppose que tu as été comblée de cadeaux. C'est exprès que j'ai fait cette lettre un peu difficile, pour t'ennuyer! Ma lettre à ta sœur est plus facile à comprendre, parce que la pauvre vieille est bien fatiguée.

Je t'embrasse bien,

Ton oncle, A.B.

223. [You will have to write me a nice little letter in French, you know. I am sure you can. And if there are mistakes in it, 'ne t'en fais pas', which means: 'don't worry about that'. I know you are determined, and determined people always succeed. So if you really want to speak and write French well, you will succeed. Is this reasoning clear? I gave a lot of Christmas presents. I received a great many best wishes, but not the ghost of a present. Best wishes are pleasing; but I prefer presents. What about you? I suppose you were overwhelmed with presents. I am writing this rather difficult letter on purpose to vex you! My letter to your sister is much easier to understand, because the poor old lady is very tired.]

KENNERLEY / MS / 224
(*To Tertia Kennerley*)

Yacht Amaryllis
Monte Carlo
1–1–22

My dear Tertia,

I was glad to have your letter. Can you imagine going out on Xmas Eve without an overcoat? I gave a great party at Cannes Casino on that night. It ended at 3 a.m. It said in the paper that the party was given by Mr. & Mrs. A.B. We were to have had another party last night, but it fell through, owing to the defection of young women with previous engagements. I danced daily, & twice daily often, until we came here—last Tuesday—where I found all the people I knew were bachelors (confirmed) & gamblers. So that it has taken me some days, by various introductions, to find partners suitable to me. I met the chief one this morning on the Casino Terrace—aged 29, très chic—and she said she was just going to church & wouldn't I go, & before I knew where I was she was telling me that once you had grasped the fact that the English are the descendants of the 10 lost tribes the whole Bible became perfectly clear; also that the 2nd Coming of our Lord was expected to occur in 1935, & that all the great dates in history, including this last, are to be found inscribed in a secret place beneath the Great Pyramid. Was I happy? If not, why not? Her husband & she had been very happy since they found the truth, etc. However, I kept out of church, but not easily. The whole conversation was like a dream, too perfect to be true. Bertie Sullivan is a confirmed gambler. I have joined the 2 private gambling halls, run by the Casino; but I never play & have lost all desire to play. Winston Churchill was playing mightily last night. I asked him if he had won, & he said he hadn't. His mother-in-law lives here & plays twice daily and tries to cheat the whole time. The curious thing is that she looks almost exactly like his late lamented mother. Well, I think Churchill is a very great man, but spends 50% of his time in being a super fool. We have on board Chartres Biron, the destroyer of Bottomley. He is 57, a fine tennis player, a fine talker, very handsome, rather a dandy and as mean as Ephraim Tellwright. Bertie is very generous, but not an organiser nor an anti-muddler. We are lying here beyond our time because he has muddled the engines, the engineer, & the electricity. Happily his housekeeper, a Belgian aged 60, once a cook, now our companion at all fêtes, a wonderful individuality, and the favourite servant of the late Arthur S., who left her £1,000. She has saved £9,000 in addition, gambles frequently, & seldom loses. She runs the household part of the ship very well. The Italian cook consistently gives us the best regular cooking I ever had. Do not imagine I am idling. On the contrary, I have written over 1/2 a novel in less than 3 weeks, & shall finish the thing by the end of this month. With regard to Marguerite, her pen, like her tongue, runs away with her. She has already quarrelled by letter with Pauline Smith, whom she used to admire more than any other woman. Most of the people to whom she writes writes to me & tell me. The mischief is that often what she says bears no recognisable relation to the truth whatever. Meantime she loses no occasion to write to me, good wishes, assurances of affection, readiness to come at once if I am ill, etc. I wrote her a formal 3 lines in reply to her Xmas greeting & she answered that the mere sight of my handwriting did her good. My impression is that she wants to return, but you can't be sure. Bertie sends you his best wishes & respex. I commend myself to William & you.

Yours, A.B.

224. Winston Churchill (1874–1965), later portrayed by Bennett as Tom Hogarth in *Lord Raingo*.

Chartres Biron (1863–1940), Chief Magistrate of Bow Street.

Horatio Bottomley (1863–1933), journalist and member of parliament. He was convicted of fraudulent conversion in 1922.

Ephraim Tellwright: the father in *Anna of the Five Towns*.

Bennett began writing *Lilian* on 4 December 1921 and finished on 24 January.

CAMBRIDGE / MS / 225
(*To Richard Bennett*)

12^B, George Street
9–2–22

My dear Rich,

I arrived last night, 3 1/2 hours late, after 1 1/2 days in trains & steamer. Much exhausted this morn. I had quite enough worries & harassments on coming home, but the worst by far of all this morning: my agent, J. B. Pinker, died suddenly in New York last night. Apart from the fact that he was a very old friend of mine, he had the whole of my affairs in his hands, & I very much doubt whether Eric, his son, has the brains, or the sort of brain, to carry on the business successfully. Also there is *no* other really good agent in England. The difference between a good & a bad agent might mean a difference of thousands a year to me. I am just off to Eastbourne now, with Mr. Tayler, to see the play. I am positively informed that the leading lady is appalling. Another considerable worry here. I have had a bad throat for a fortnight, and today I am really taking it in hand. Sprays etc. Your letter is interesting. I saw pictures of bumping at Cambridge in the *Westminster Gazette* today, but no Clare therein. I am glad to hear that the work is keeping steady.

Love,
Your much agitated uncle,

A.B.

225. For letters to Eric Pinker (b. 1891) see Vol. I.

The Love Match, with Kyrle Bellow and Arthur Bourchier, opened at Folkestone on 30 January and went on to Eastbourne. It opened in London on 21 March.

STOKE / MS / 226
(*To Margaret Beardmore*)

12ᴮ, George Street
26–2–22

Dear Margaret,

Whether I have heard from you since your letter of 29th Nov., and whether I have replied to the said letter, I am now too old to remember. Did I or did I not send you a book? Do you or do you not ask for more? What have you been reading? Have I or have I not already invited you to come on my yacht some time during the summer? How are you? How am I? Anyhow I am back in London & have been for 17 days, which period has been chiefly spent on rearranging this flat to suit the altered circumstances of existence. Some of the furniture from Comarque is here, & some has gone to Auntie. I've just been to Eastbourne to see one of my plays (and was not made enthusiastic thereby), & tomorrow I'm going to Liverpool to see another. After my return I hope to do a little work. I am informed by removers that the books which my secretary & I have just arranged weigh 5 tons. Probably an exaggeration. I went to Auntie Tertia's the other night (going again tonight), and found Mary & Marguerite delighting their parents by their skill in water-colours and in piano-playing and in housekeeping. A justifiable delight, but I do wish their mother could dress them differently. As I am just now having plays produced, I am cast much into the theatrical world, which means dancing & late nights. I adore dancing, but hate anything after 12.15 a.m. except bed. Dancest thou? Richard is coming here for the last fortnight in March. He is working fairly hard, as I have promised him an extra year (fourth) at Cambridge if he takes his first tripos at the end of 2 years. I doubt if he will. He has become a mighty oarsman before the Lord. I trust you are going on all right.

Your aff unc, A.B.

226. *Body and Soul*, which Bennett wrote in the summer and autumn of 1919, opened at the Liverpool Playhouse on 15 February.

BERG / TS / 227
(*To Dorothy Cheston*)

12^B, George Street
27th March 1922

Dear Miss Dorothy Cheston,

If you are not going to the Boatrace will you come and have tea on Saturday next at 4.30? If you are going to the Boatrace, will you make it Sunday?

The entrance to this abode is in Maddox Street—round the corner westwards from George Street.

Yours sincerely, Arnold Bennett

227. For Dorothy Cheston's background see the Introduction, pp. xxxi–xxxv. She was playing one of the two female leads in *Body and Soul* in Liverpool. The review of the play in the *Liverpool Post* on 17 February praised the other lead, Viola Lyel, for her 'infectious enthusiasm and fine sense of comedy' and said that 'Miss Dorothy Cheston ... had not quite that assured strength, but it was a very intelligent performance, with much clever touching in of detail'.

BERG / TS / 228
(*To Dorothy Cheston*)

12^B, George Street
11th April 1922

Dear Miss Cheston,

Many thanks for your letter. I shall count on hearing from you immediately you come to London, and I hope that we may then foregather. I can assure you that Playfair, however he may put it to you, is at least as 'definite' as I am in the affair. I fully sympathise with your feelings. I will, however, express my feelings more fully when I see you.

Yours sincerely, Arnold Bennett

228. Dorothy was hoping to play in *Body and Soul* in London, but did not. Instead she appeared in *The Torch*, which opened at the Apollo on 12 September, the day after *Body and Soul* opened. Playfair produced *Body and Soul* in both Liverpool and London.

KEELE / MS / 229
(*To Marguerite Soulié Bennett*)

12^B, George Street

13–4–22

Dear Marguerite,

I am glad that people are sympathetic towards you. This is what I wish & what I have tried to bring about. But please do not trouble to repeat to me the silly scandal & the unjust things that your friends tell you about me. I hear lots of things about what you do & what you say about me, but I should not think of repeating them to you.

Believe me, silence is the best course.

Nothing that you or I can do will stop any persons from talking, or stop some persons from spitefully lying.

As to Helen Rootham, all I know is that you and she had a tremendous row, in which it is quite possible that things were said that were misunderstood. I have never used either to her or to anyone else, any phrase resembling the phrase you quote. I did once, before our separation, in writing to *you*, refer to Legros as a '*tame* cat'. This is a perfectly ordinary & perfectly correct phrase, which must have been used by many of our friends about Legros. It is the first phrase which would spring to the mind. 'Tom-cat' is a very different and a very offensive phrase, and I do not for a moment believe that Helen Rootham used it.

I hope I shall not have to tell you any more that I do everything possible to preserve your dignity. I have never said anything about you that I should not care for you to hear. I answer your letter in some detail simply because I desire to be courteous to you, & not because I think it is wise to do so. I am sure that such correspondence is ill-advised. Let me therefore, with great respect, suggest that we do not continue it.

My health is excellent; my play is a failure.

Remember me to all your people kindly.

Yours, A.B.

229. Helen Rootham was governess and later companion to Edith Sitwell. She sang and wrote. She and Marguerite had been active together in the Caledonian Market during the War, and she was later on the managing committee of the Anglo-French Poetry Society.

STOKE / MS / 230
(*To Margaret Beardmore*)

12^B, George Street
26–4–22

My dear Margaret,

In haste.

You will want for the yacht *warm* things, even in the height of summer. The exterior garments should be white or as near white as possible. You must have white shoes with indiarubber soles. None other is allowed on my decks.

You might also need one evening frock, as you never know what will happen on a yacht. I have given several dances on mine.

It is not my intention that this holiday should cost you anything at all. Hence any clothes you buy for the yacht I will pay for; also your travelling expenses to and from the yacht, wherever she is & wherever you are.

Respex to all,

Your aff unc, A.B.

KEELE / MS / 231
(*To Marguerite Soulié Bennett*)

12^B, George Street
3–5–22

In reply to your letter I shall be happy to oblige you with £3,000, after the sale of Comarques. (Comarques is not sold, and I have *no* money to spare until it is sold. But it will soon be put up to auction—aux enchères.)

Of course I can only let you have this money if proper legal arrangements are made. The interest on £3,000 at 6 per cent (the lowest percentage at which money can now be borrowed) is £80. If I give you the money I shall be losing this interest, which I do not propose to do. It will therefore be necessary for the interest on whatever sums you receive from me to be deducted quarterly from your allowance. Otherwise I should be giving you a house rent-free in addition to your allowance. Of course, if I die before you, you could receive at once the balance of the £5,000, and no further interest would be payable.

If you consult your solicitor you will find that the arrangement I suggest is quite fair and proper.

Personally I should not have advised you to buy a house anywhere. But I have no doubt you will act under the advice of Georges, in which I have the greatest confidence.

The tea service shall be sent to you, & the trunk taken away.

You have also taken away a large valise which I bought for myself when I went to Portugal. I don't want to inconvenience you, but if you could let me have it I should be glad.

Yours, A.B.

KEELE / MS / 232
(*To Marguerite Soulié Bennett*)

12^B, George Street
11th May 1922

Dear Marguerite,

Thanks for your letter of yesterday. You are totally mistaken about my dealings with Stannard.

It was certainly convenient for me to have Stannard, but I could have done perfectly well without her. And before I went away last autumn I specially sent for her, and paid her expenses, in order to make it perfectly clear to her that I was very anxious for her to go into your service. She will confirm this if you ask her.

When you moved your furniture from Thorpe and from here, and I had to move my furniture here, Stannard agreed with me that there was nothing for her to do at Comarques.

As I heard nothing about you taking her, I wrote to her on the 21st February:—'*If you are not going to Mrs. Bennett* I should be glad to have you here.'

On February 24th Stannard replied thanking me but saying that she had arranged to go into your service.

I naturally assumed that you were in touch with her and knew the facts.

I paid Stannard up to March 1st, the same wages as she always had.

I think I understand the angle from which you see things; and I have the friendliest feelings towards you; but I remain of the opinion that it is rather too soon yet for us to see each other.

Yours, A.B.

232. Marguerite was again occupying her flat at Thackeray Mansions.

STOKE / MS / 233
(*To Margaret Beardmore*)

Yacht Marie Marguerite
17–6–22

My sweet niece,

No. I am informed by my confidential secretary, who files all my correspondence, that you never did give the date of your return to business. You said you weren't sure. I didn't ask you for the date of your entry into freedom, because I knew it and had it before me.

I don't know exactly who else will be on the yacht; but I know that your cousin Mary Kennerley will. It is imposs. for me to say at present where we shall go, but we will go as far as we can; and as early in August as possible. You know, niece, that my life is very complex; I have many professional interests, which I can only imperfectly control, so that it is extremely difficult for me to plan exactly in advance a mere holiday. The fact is, I *never* have a holiday complete. At present I am toiling deeply with Edward Knoblock in a joint play. (We are at Southampton today.)

I took the precaution of *not* going to see the film of *Sac. & Prof.* I divined that I could not 'stand' it. At the same time I have to live & keep yachts going, & your advice to break with films is not practicable. You must remember that the cinema is a new art, & must be given time to learn. To adopt a superior attitude toward it would be very wrong, and even very harmful. This quite apart from the aforesaid fact that I have to live!

Your aff unc, A.B.

233. Bennett sailed off the English coast during the summer.
Knoblock and Bennett wrote *London Life* from April to June 1922.
The film *Sacred and Profane Love* was produced in 1921 by Famous Players Lasky.

CAMBRIDGE / MS / 234
(*To Richard Bennett*)

Yacht Marie Marguerite
5–7–22

My dear Rich,

Thank you for yours of the 2nd. I said: 'I assume.' You didn't confirm. I then *asked*. You now answer. That is just all right about the 4th year. The difficulty was that I wasn't sure if only a 3rd class entitled you to a degree or whatever it is. Even now I don't understand about 'honours'. How have you got honours? I am glad your mind is steady about your career.

Come to the yacht any time you like. On the 15th two women are coming, whom you don't know. Mrs. Collinson Morley and Miss Forster. And on the 27th Sir Denison & Lady Ross (he is head of the School of Oriental Studies) & Harriet Cohen (pianist). The place will be rather full. What are you doing in August? I should have *preferred* you to work now & come with Margaret Beardmore & Mary Kennerley & me to Carantec to see the Godebskis. Leaving England August 4th or 5th. But perhaps you mean to stay on board all the time. I wish you could decide exactly, & when, about the component parts of your vacation. I am all for prearranged programmes.

It is absolutely certain that 5 people will not have daily baths (morning) on this yacht!

This is the 25th successive day of gales and rain.

Write at once to Thorpe please.

Love,
Your play-finished uncle,

A.B.

P.S. I was nearly forgetting to say that you haven't made yourself at all clear as to your alternative plans for education during the next 2 years. So that I cannot judge between them. In fact you have explained them very imperfectly, if not badly. Hence you must choose for yourself, and when I have the felicity of seeing you I will judge, & if necessary suggest alternatives.

A.B.

234. Mrs Collinson Morley: Rose Morley, hostess, patron of pianists. Miss Forster: unidentified. The *Journals*, 1924, refer briefly to an Evelyn Forster.
Sir Denison Ross (1871–1940) and Lady Ross (d. 1940).
For letters to Harriet (Tania) Cohen, the pianist (d. 1967), see Vol. III.

STOKE / MS / 235
(*To Margaret Beardmore*)

12ᴮ, George Street
9–9–22

My sweet Margot,

This is about the only chance I shall have of acknowledging your letter of one week ago. I am submerged in rehearsals. I was rehearsing till 1 a.m. this morn & the 2nd dress rehearsal occurs at 5 p.m. today & the final D.R. at 2 p.m. tomorrow. I have had 17 hours sleep in 5 nights, but about 35 hours in bed. As for Uncle Sep I am informed that with him things are decidedly looking up, as with Uncle Edward's driving. Not that the latter will ever be able to drive properly. He will not. The electric light is now in perfect order on the yacht, but I haven't heard that the launch is yet in order. I told them to wire me the instant it was. I return to Southampton with Mr. Tayler, Dr. Shuff, and the author of *Nocturne* on Tuesday morning, after my first night, & I shall be a broken man, believe me. I've heard from Mary the sage & industrious. I hope you will be wicked and happy until I see you next. I now have decided to leave this flat *at* Xmas, & get another if I can; if not, store les meubles.

My best respex to all,
Your [?] aff unc,

A.B.

235. *Nocturne*: Swinnerton's novel, published 1917.

CAMBRIDGE / MS / 236
(*To Richard Bennett*)

12ᴮ, George Street
11–9–22

My dear Richard,

Thanks for your letter which staggered me this morning by arriving promptly. I am in a great state of nervous exhaustion, owing largely to the fact that the landlords have not handed over in time the theatre as a working concern. The switchboard will not be complete till 5 this afternoon, and no 'lighting rehearsal' has yet been held at all! And you know—no doubt you don't know—how complicated and tricky what is called the 'lighting plot' is, and how essential it is that the lighting should be timed with absolute exactness. Such is theatrical life. The theatre has faults; the chief of which is that it is too big. It is enormous. Still—a great sensation, seeing the name 'Regent' in vast gilt letters over the super-card's theatre! We are now engaged in educating cabmen.

'Regent Theatre, please.... Good God. You don't mean to say you don't know the Regent Theatre!'

But Ian Hay came to the dress rehearsal yesterday, & he told me that his dialogue with the taxi driver was as follows:

Hay. Euston Theatre of Varieties, please.

Driver. You mean the Regent Theatre, sir.

Accidents apart, I leave with Swinnerton & Tayler for S'ampton tomorrow morn, Tuesday. Dr. Shuff was to have come but has wired he can't 'on account of illness'. Very mysterious. I am concerned about that man.

Miss Forster was here yesterday & enquired after you.

Tania was here a week ago & enquired after you. My address will be here, but I am going to Dieppe. I have decided to leave this flat at Xmas, & the landlords agree.

> Love,
> Your fatigued uncle,
>
> A.B.

236. 'The Regent': the name of Denry Machin's theatre in *The Regent*, 1913, sequel to *The Card*.

Ian Hay: dramatist and novelist (1876–1952).

Tania: Harriet Cohen.

KEELE / MS / 237
(*To Marguerite Soulié Bennett*)

12ᴮ, George Street
25–9–22

Dear Marguerite,

Thanks for your letter of today. I have just come home.

In May last you wrote me that you were thinking of buying a house in France, and you asked whether, if you did buy a house, I could let you have £2,000 or £3,000. I replied that in order to be agreeable to you I would let you have £2,000 or £3,000 to buy the house, on the condition that interest on it at 6% was deducted from your allowance.

This is exactly what occurred. To let you have the money would have been very inconvenient to me, & I only promised it in order to help you to buy a house in France.

You are receiving an ample income from me, & I must ask you to be content with it. As regards 'risks', they are no greater than if we were still living together. In fact they are less. As regards your parents, your family is by no means poor. If you choose to support both of them entirely, that is a matter which concerns you only. It is nice of you to do it, but there is no obligation on your part to do it. If you died before them you may be quite sure that I should do what was proper in helping your family to keep them in comfort. I know that I need not tell you this, because you are perfectly well aware of it. If Georges or any other member of your family doubts my generosity in the matter of money I shall be happy to place before him or them all my account books for the last ten years. They can then judge for themselves.

I want you to understand that although my feelings towards you are very friendly, I cannot increase my responsibilities towards you unless in case of the gravest necessity.

I have written to Georges as you wish.

I am sending you the inscribed copy of *Body & Soul*.

Yours, A.B.

CAMBRIDGE / MS / 238
(*To Richard Bennett*)

12ᴮ, George Street
25–9–22

My dear Rich,

We sailed direct from Newhaven to Brightlingsea. 33½ hours. Headwind all the way, & the captain called the sea 'very nasty'. He said 9 out of 10 yachts wouldn't have faced it! Miss Nerney spent the whole cruise in bed. We & Fred came to town at 2.30 this day. I am exhausted & dyspeptic & have many people to see, but otherwise I am very well & cheerful.

You haven't done the right thing in mentioning a car for a birthday present. I am entirely against it. What would you do with it when you leave the Univ. & have to keep yourself? No, my boy, a car would offend my conscience even more than my pocket, which is saying a great deal. It is infelicitous for you that you happen to reach your majority at a very bad time for the country, for finance, and for me. You must put up with it. Kindly ascertain the approximate cost of such a set of golf-clubs & such a camera as would suit you. I will then see if I can manage the two. I know nothing whatever of either of these mysterious branches of knowledge.

I have given orders as to the gramoph.

Lord Justice O'Connor is now coming in to see me about Irish business, so must regretfully close.

Love,
Your involved uncle,

A.B.

KEELE / MS / 239
(*To Marguerite Soulié Bennett*)

12^B, George Street
27–9–22

Dear Marguerite,

Thanks for your letter of yesterday in which you explain your motives.

You say at the end that no English gentleman would treat his mistress as I treated you. I do not agree. On the contrary I think I treated you very handsomely, and I have not yet met anyone who disagrees with me. However, there is no more to be said, and we had better leave the matter.

Yours, A.B.

CAMBRIDGE / MS / 240
(*To Richard Bennett*)

12^B, George Street
30–10–22

My dear Rich,

Thanks for your letter, which arrived punctually. I shall be very interested to see your digs. It will be quite all right about the Christmas Vac, but I don't yet know how I personally shall be situated. I've seen a house on Sloane St which just *might* do. It's too large. You would have a bedroom & large bathroom of your own. What frightens me is the question of my liability for repairs at the end of the lease. I hope you gave my love to Claude, Pat, & their mother yesterday. Dr. Shufflebotham has been & gone. He is in a *very grave condition* of nerves & delusions. At 2 a.m. on Saturday morning he roused Fred, which roused me, to inform us—he was quite wide awake, & had been for a long time—that there was a woman in the corner by the window, & also that a lot of cinema people were trying to take a film of him—quietly without disturbing him, but he could hear & see them all right. This sort of thing at 2 a.m. is extremely upsetting to the host. His doctor, Dr. Griffin, wanted him to go to a nursing home at once, but he wouldn't. He went off to Newcastle in charge of his unwilling sister, Mrs. Moody, to see his patients. Every patient he sees is bound to think that Shuffle has gone, or is going, off his head. The trouble originates in the goings-on of his separated wife, but whiskey (consequent on this) is having a great deal to do with it. Treat all this as most strictly private. I had a day by myself yesterday (till 8.30) reading & playing the pf., & greatly enjoyed it. I then went out to dinner & dance & greatly enjoyed that too. My novel is going on excellently. The fly in the ointment is that this sort of weather always gives me neuralgia. Mr. Sullivan wants me to go again in his yacht this winter (Spain). He is putting in new engines. I don't know yet whether I shall go. Mr. Tayler came home on the 6th proximo. I haven't heard anything about your work lately.

> Love,
> Your lasting uncle,
>
> A.B.

240. Claude, Pat: unidentified.
  Dr Ernest Griffin (d. 1936) was Bennett's physician in the 1920s. He trained in London and began practice there in 1902.
  Bennett began writing *Riceyman Steps* on 10 October.

BERG / MS / 241
(*To Dorothy Cheston*)

12ᴮ, George Street
1–11–22

Dear Miss Dorothy Cheston,
    I promised to let you know when I returned to London. I have been back a month, & I am beginning a new month with

righteousness & satisfaction by letting you know. If you have
nothing more important on Sunday night next, let me offer you
food and drink in a Sabbatic manner. Will you telephone?
(Mayfair 1532)

Yours sincerely, Arnold Bennett

BERG / MS / 242
(*To Dorothy Cheston*)

12ᴮ, George Street
3–11–22

Dear Miss Cheston,
    Many thanks. I am glad you can come here on Sunday, as I
wanted to see you in order to make sure that you had not at the
back of your mind an idea that I had failed you in certain ways,
and Sunday is the only free evening I have for some time. God
forbid that you should dress 'sabbatically'! I only meant by that
word that there would be merely a coldish sort of a supper. It is
not a party, but only a tête-à-tête.
            8 o'clock
                    Yours sincerely, Arnold Bennett

CAMBRIDGE / MS / 243
(*To Richard Bennett*)

12ᴮ, George Street
6–11–22

My dear Rich,
    This cannot possibly last! Your letter arrived by first post for
the 2nd week in succession! At least, I assume it did. Anyhow it
was here when I rang for my letters at 11.30. Under my new
regime I see no letters in the morning till my creative work is
done. Thanks. I have now finished the first part of my novel—I
don't know the title yet—20,000 words. I may be wrong to be
pleased with it, but somehow I am. On Saturday I took Tania
to Clerkenwell & showed her what a romantic & curious place
Clerkenwell is, & where my hero & heroines lived. The chief

heroine is a char-woman. I don't usually work on Sundays now, but I did yesterday, desiring to finish. The whole day alone; but in the evening Dorothy Cheston, one of my histrionic interpreters, to dinner. Also I have to work today, correcting proofs & so on; so I shall take my Sunday tomorrow, Tuesday. I saw a house in Nash Terrace on Saturday that might do—Regent's Park, a few doors off where your Auntie Maud's sister lives (ça ne me sourit pas)—& it would do only it is too small to hold my furniture. The question is, shall I sell furniture, or take a house to shelter furniture rather than me? I have news that Dr. Shuff has turned over a new leaf & is somewhat better; but I doubt the reality of the improvement. Anyhow he is coming up here again tomorrow, & both Fred & I are anticipating his *nights* with some apprehension. I see you are once more fretting because the whole University has not been organised to suit your particular case. I wrote something rather good about this somewhere lately—I forget where. I wonder at the Election excitement at Cambridge. Up to now practically all the electioneering I have come across is of the most puerile description, & Bonar Law's most puerile of all. Fancy saying: 'The country is in a hades of a mess. Therefore we will do nothing.' As for liberals, their one idea is to 'down' Ll. G. at any cost. Also puerile. And Labour, though it has a programme, has no men worth a d—. I have been generally unwell, but highly creative. Today I have an enormously enlarged liver which fills the whole of my frame.

> Love,
> Your bursting uncle,
>   A.B.

243. The setting of *Riceyman Steps* is King's Cross Road at the steps leading up to Granville Square. Bennett was acquainted with the district from his early years in London. He and a fellow clerk at Le Brasseur & Oakley used to go there to buy second-hand books. See pp. 482–3.

Bonar Law (1858–1923), prime minister 1922–3; David Lloyd George (1863–1945), prime minister 1916–22.

BERG / MS / 244
(*To Dorothy Cheston*)

12^B, George Street
13–11–22

Dear Miss Cheston,

I am glad you can come on Sunday 8.30. If you go into Claridges by the restaurant entrance, the ladies cloakroom is on your left & I shall be in the main hall at the end of the same passage. If you go in by the main entrance, the ladies cloakroom is on your right up the passage. But the first object you will see will be me.

The Savoy on such nights as Saturday is
APPALLING
I went to New Year's Eve Dinner there 1920–21, & it was one of the most dreadful spectacles I have ever witnessed.

Yours sincerely, Arnold Bennett

CAMBRIDGE / MS / 245
(*To Richard Bennett*)

12^B, George Street
28–11–22

My dear Rich,

Thanks for your letter, which arrived yesterday evening (too late for me to answer it) instead of in the morning. I must say I can't see anything of a 'newspaper stunt' nature in our simple and too brief visit. Nor can I think of anything I said to cause amusement in the breast of Hickson. I thought we were all most sedate. There was one thing I noticed which rather disconcerted me. Namely, that in one day you had 2 beers in addition to my champagne. I do not like this. I think you are making a great mistake. Most men 'up' do not drink 2 beers a day; many of them could not afford it. To drink anything at lunch is a grave mistake. You have got to remember that there is a decided tendency to alcoholism in our family. You of course think that any reference to alcoholism in this connection is extremely far-fetched. Well, nobody knows whether it is or not. A minor point is that any alcohol will prejudice you in working for exams. I am by no means against alcohol. I should privately prefer you not to have more than about one drink a week because your character is not yet fully formed & you are still very susceptible to the influences of habit. But I should not dream of exercising pressure to get you to reduce yourself to one drink a week. If I objected to alcohol, I should not offer you champagne. But I certainly think you shouldn't have more than one drink a day. And never under any circumstances spirits. I've just had the spectacle of Dr. Shuff here, taking his solemn oath to me that to save himself he would abstain completely, & within an hour creeping out to get a drink, & thinking that he could deceive me. He couldn't deceive even Fred. This is pathetic, tragic. But it is what drinking too often leads to. No victim of alcohol ever suspects that he is a victim of alcohol until it is too late. Dr. Shuff would laugh at the suggestion. Nevertheless he is a ruined man unless he can find in himself the force to stop completely. I have now definitely taken 75 Cadogan Sq. I've seen Tania twice since she was at Cambridge; I dined, with several other people, at her house on Sunday, but not a word have I heard as to Cambridge, & I quite forgot to ask her. Please give me a somewhat detailed estimate of your probable financial needs.

Love,
Your wide awake uncle,

A.B.

245. Hickson: unidentified.

STOKE / MS / 246
(*To Margaret Beardmore*)

12^B, George Street
1—12—22

My sweet niece,

See how well I am beginning a new month!

My health is in the main very good, with slight stumbles. I have entered upon a new way of life and work. I do all my serious toil first i.e. I put on my jaeger suit (which you must have seen), & I do nothing else. I do not shave, wash, clean teeth, bathe, dress or anything! By 11:30 (3 1/2 hours) my serious toil is accomplished, and I am free for oddments for the rest of the day. I can do more like this, & easier, & better. True,

I am not really dressed till 12:30. Note well, that I see no correspondence nor receive any messages till the work is done.

After much searching and disappointment I have taken a house No. 75 Cadogan Sq. It is not so central as this but it is the best I could get. There were no flats that would suit me. It is a large house, & I am subletting the top floor (4 small rooms) to my secretary Miss Nerney & her mother. It is an immense advantage to have your secretary on the spot. There are 2 staircases. I shall still have 3 floors & a basement to myself. I shall leave here at or about Xmas. But Xmas itself I shall spend with the Wellses, after all. I am *not* leaving England at Xmas. I expect to leave later on, to join Mr. Sullivan's yacht at Lisbon: but Mr. Sullivan being Irish & a yacht being a yacht, I cannot be sure. In my new house there will be a bedroom and a separate bathroom for you. Lastly, I have begun a new novel of a marvellous excellence, & indeed it is nearly half done.

I had heard nothing of your family. I'm glad Alan has not gone to Galapagos. However he has now begun to wander & will probably continue to wander for many years. Not a bad thing, I think! It is a pity you bought *Lilian* as I should have sent it to you. I've just re-read *Dead Souls* myself. It is terrific. I first read it 30 years ago. You must read the rest of Gogol as it comes out. The superannuation dodge is very trying, especially as they won't probably return the payment to you when you leave; and 1/ in the £1 is a consideration. I cannot of course send you any money until you have lifted off the curse which a year or so ago you laid on any man who should dare to do so. Fred is all right. He nearly blew himself up with the geyser the other night, & me with a big party here too! Mr. Tayler's name is spelled with an E. Otherwise he's all right, but he's been ill with rheumatism. The yacht is laid up: that's all I know. 'Cherrio' is not English.

Your most aff & loving unc, A.B.

246. Alan Beardmore (1899–1977) became a pilot in the RFC/RAF during the War, but he did not see action. In 1922 he planned a treasure hunt to the Galapagos but wound up instead in West Africa. He made his career as a commercial traveller for the Michelin Tyre Company.

BERG / MS / 247
(*To Dorothy Cheston*)

12ᴮ, George Street
15–12–22

Dear Lady,

I couldn't explain to you on the phone this morning that I have had charge of the respondent in the recent divorce case (Shufflebotham v. Shufflebotham—a scandalous miscarriage of justice), he staying in my house all the time. Also I have had charge of an American guest lying ill with 2 nurses at the Savoy, & for whom I am responsible to his wife & child. Also that I have been helping someone else to move into a new abode; also that I have had all the negotiations & worry of preparing to leave here, selling my fixtures & buying other fixtures, & 10,000 matters. Also that in my spare time I am writing a long novel. All which leads to the statement that, as I have to go out to dinner tonight, I could not possibly 'go on' afterwards. *I am too worn out.* I hope to be recovered tomorrow. I should have loved to come. I might have one night to suit you next week; I should much like another dance; but I don't know yet. It depends on God & the devil. I will write or wire you, & if you don't hear you will know that I am in a sad way.

Thanks ever so much for asking me.

Ever yours sincerely, Arnold Bennett

247. The Shufflebotham case was in the courts for two years, with charges of adultery on both sides. Mrs Shufflebotham won a decree nisi in 1922.

STOKE / TS / 248
(*To Margaret Beardmore*)

75, Cadogan Square
S.W.I.
4th January 1923

My sweet niece,

(Why do you spell it neice?) I am very glad to have your letter. I feel much better, but am not yet cured, so I am still dictating letters which I ought to write with my own hand. I had nothing but very plain food at Christmas, and very little of that, and I had neither turkey nor Christmas pudding. Not that I minded about that in the least.

I should not say that Housman is superior to Hodgson, but I should say that he is decidedly superior to R. Brooke, who is an over-praised poet. I am no longer very keen on Meredith. I much prefer Hardy. Yes, I did go to the first night of *Polly*, and I ought not to have gone, as it gave me a set-back, being out at night. The affair is the most prodigious success, but as a show it is not equal to the *B.O.*

I have every expectation of being in London at your half term, and you can occupy space in this house. But the space will not be a flat. It was at the house in Sloane Street and the house in Rutland Gate that you would have had a flat. You will however, have a bedroom and bathroom of your own. I shall be delighted to have you. You can also go to *Polly*. *Polly* will not be the death of the *B.O.* In fact since *Polly* was produced the 'business' of the *B.O.* has most decidedly increased.

This is about all for the present, except that I regret your boredom.

Love to all,

Your constant aff unc, A.B

248. Bennett moved into 75 Cadogan Square, 'my rather noble thing in houses', in December 1922.

Polly: sequel to *The Beggar's Opera*, adapted by Clifford Bax, with music by Frederic Austin, was playing at the Kingway Theatre.

BERG / MS / 249
(*To Dorothy Cheston*)

75, Cadogan Square
7–1–23

Dear Dorothy Cheston,

I've been asked to take a dancing partner to a private dance at the Savoy Hotel on Wednesday 17th inst. Can I take you? The dance is given by Richmond Temple, who is, among other things, the chief publicity agent of the Savoy group of hotels. I can answer for him, as he is a friend of mine, but I can't answer for the other guests, as I know nothing of them!

Yours, Arnold B

249. For letters to Richmond Temple see Vol. III.

BERG / MS / 250
(*To Dorothy Cheston*)

75, Cadogan Square
17–1–23

My dear lady,

I much regret to say that owing to the state of my chest, I cannot permit myself to go out tonight, & I have so informed our host. I hope, however, that you will nevertheless do me the kindness to dine *here* as soon after 8 as possible & spend the evening with me. I shall look forward to it.

Yours, Arnold Bennett

BERG / MS / 251
(*To Dorothy Cheston*)

75, Cadogan Square
25–1–23

My dear Dorothea,

Many thanks for your letter (although it contains no form of address at the beginning). I am in your hands as regards Saturday, but unless you have undisclosed reasons for the plan, I don't really think much of it. You will have to eat, & you mustn't eat too late. You cannot get as good a meal at any restaurant near here as you would get in this house. It is important that we should both eat well & comfortably. Therefore I think it would be better to eat here. You can name your own time, & if you are behind with your packing (which God forbid) I will escort you back to 21 Ch. St. when you ordain. And there is no reason why you should dress up more than you want. Just send me a p.c. If you should arrive a bit late it won't matter, as I will arrange for a meal that will not spoil through the effluxion of time.

R.U.R. Private.

It now seems more probable that we shall control this production ourselves. I have discussed the matter with Tayler (who is my ally on the Board) & he thoroughly agrees with me that in the circumstances you ought to have a fair trial as Helen if you want it. I have therefore written to Playfair in this sense, & indicated to him that he had better not tell me that he has already decided on someone else. I feel sure that for certain reasons he will be against you, but if Tayler & I agree, after hearing you, that you ought to have the part, Playfair will have all he can do to throw you over. Be it understood that in casting he officially has the last word. Be it further understood that if I don't appreciate your reading of the part I shall crudely say so.

Yours, Arnold B.

251. 21 Church Street: where Dorothy had rooms.
Bennett, Playfair, and Tayler were negotiating to produce Karl Čapek's play *R.U.R.*

BERG / MS / 252
(*To Dorothy Cheston*)

75, Cadogan Square
31–1–23

My dear Dorothea,
(Better get used to beginning your letters to me with my name!) If I were you I should not send the letter yet. I return it to you, for the present. The phrase at the beginning of the 2nd paragraph will want altering. What I told you was that *I* would see that you had a trial—not quite the same thing. When I last saw you I hadn't heard from him at all. Since then some animated correspondence has passed between us. He is entirely against giving you a trial; but he will have to give way, as Tayler is on my side completely & we can outvote him. I don't quite see what purpose your letter to him would serve. You will judge better when you see the correspondence. I shall see him tomorrow—& I bet he won't say a word. I am very glad the first night was good & comprised a success for you. I wrote you today that I should arrive at Brighton station on Thursday at noon. I didn't get your letter until tonight.

Ever yours, Arnold B.

252. Dorothy began a provincial tour in Sudermann's *Magda* in January, playing Magda's aunt.

BERG / MS / 253
(*To Dorothy Cheston*)

75, Cadogan Square
6–II–23

My dear Dorothea,

He says he will give you 'the fullest consideration', & that you have 'personality & ability', & that he would like to talk the matter over with me. So I have asked him & his wife to lunch. So that's that for the present.

Many thanks for your letter. Your skirt was certainly *not* hanging crooked when I saw it. I am terrific on skirts, & notorious even. I let you depart alone with regret. In fact it seemed to me a disgusting thing for me to do. Mais que voulez-vous? (I think that if you send a tour-card to Robert you might send one to me.) My life is so full, too full, but happily less full than it was 18 months ago. I ought to do nothing but write my novel, but I am doing 50 things besides. A woman of 45, rich & used to every luxury, came to me last night & told me she was absolutely ruined. (A big shareholder in Cox's Bank & under the transfer the shareholders don't get a cent. Evidently the Bank was only *just* saved by Lloyds from a colossal smash.) She wept terribly. I had to take her & her affairs in hand. Would she listen to reason? No. I telephoned my friend Sir Chartres Biron, the beak, to come at once & reinforce me. He came at once—in a jaeger bedroom suit! He reinforced me. We knocked sense into the unhappy creature. I thought that nothing except you could drag me out of my novel. This did. Yet I would sacrifice almost everything to the novel in the way of honour, duty, etc. But when it is done I shall return to the path of virtue. So do let me hear more about life on tour, & that you are still happy & well.

Yours, A.B.

253. Robert: Robert Loraine.
Violet (Mrs Ralph) Hammersley (1878–1964), hostess and art patron, whom Bennett described elsewhere as having 'a devil of a lot of money'.

CAMBRIDGE / MS / 254
(*To Richard Bennett*)

75, Cadogan Square
12–2–23

My dear Rich,

Thanks for yours of yesterday which arrived promptly. Look here, don't you give away any of your knowledge about Cox's! This matter is still greatly worrying me. Not that it affects me in the slightest, personally. You will have a copy of *Things* shortly. Also the address of Frank Mason which you asked for. I had a great time in the Potteries. Sundry hours with Wilcox Edge in the train! He is a very interesting old man, & the Potteries is too much obsessed by his failings. The Mayor wore his 2 ton chain. I sat on his right. I saw all sorts of people who knew me & whom I didn't know, & whom I admirably pretended to know. Edward Beardmore, May Marsden, & one of the anniversary Wood girls attended. Dr. Shuff placed himself & his car at my disposal the whole afternoon. I arrived at 2.20 & left at 6.39 & got home without a headache, & the next 3 days did vast quantities of my novel. Yesterday I reposed, & had the Robert-Loraines to lunch, Dorothy Cheston to tea, and a musical supper party. At this party Arnold Bax & Eugene Goossens sat down to the piano & improvised, without a preliminary word to each other, a Spanish tango which lasted a quarter of an hour — to which Tania danced. It was full of new tunes, & there was never the slightest hitch, discord, or fumbling. How they do it I know not. But in that line it was the most marvellous thing I ever heard. Bed at 1.45. Today I am writing the preface to *Don Juan*. The house is not yet finished, but progress continues. Let me know about your visit & friends & dates, please. Uncle Sep is probably coming up soon for a week. I had much speech with him & Auntie Maud. Your uncle S. is decidedly better.

Love,

Your greatly creative uncle,

A.B

254. *Things That Have Interested Me, Second Series*, a collection of essays and sketches was published on 8 February.

Frank Mason: unidentified.

On the 12th a General Trades Exhibition was opened in the Potteries. A band concert followed the opening ceremony. Later a banquet was held in honour of Wilcox Edge (b. 1844), businessman and former mayor.

Arnold Bax (1883–1953), the composer, and Eugene Goossens (d. 1962), the conductor and composer.

Don Juan de Marana was published in a limited edition by Werner Laurie in October 1923.

BERG / MS / 255
(*To Dorothy Cheston*)

75, Cadogan Square
13–2–23

My dearest Dorothea,

The thought of you going off by yourself into the deadly Euston hotel was obnoxious to me on Sunday night, & still more so the thought of your return solitary to industrial Lancashire. I haven't heard anything from Robert, but I'm going to have tea with Winnie Loraine on Saturday—not before. I daresay I shall get some news at our directors' meeting tomorrow afternoon. I am not at all hopeful about the matter & I trust that you aren't either. If the thing fails, there is plenty of life left yet. I was very tired on Monday morn, & didn't do much work. Still, yesterday & today I have written the preface to my *Don Juan*, & prepared the last part of my novel, of which I can now see the end. A month, at most, ought to finish it. Last night I spent alone, to see what it felt like. I scarcely ever have an evening alone. Well, although I had a very light dinner, it gave me indigestion. Instead of reading studiously I dozed in my chair in the small drawing-room. Thank God I'm dining out tonight, Weds., Thurs., Fri., Sat. & Sunday. At least on Friday I have a party—here, & I wish that you were to be among it. Harriet Cohen said to me yesterday that when I wrote to you I was to tell you that she liked you very much. I said: 'How do you know I'm going to write to her?' She said: 'Well, *if* you write to her.' There is no doubt you have made a considerable impression on that child of nature. She desires to see you again soon. I really do think that that improvisation of Bax & Goossens at the piano was one of the most miraculous things I ever witnessed. I can't get over it. And I think they were pretty well impressed by it themselves!

I now look forward with hope & anxiety to your next visit. I hope that Wellfield House has reached your expectations.

Ever yours devotedly, A.B.

BERG / MS / 256
(*To Dorothy Cheston*)

75, Cadogan Square
18–2–23

My dearest Dorothy,

I looked out for a letter from you yesterday morning, but did not see it. However it turned up later. My rule of working life is never to look at my correspondence till my fiction for the day is done. My secretary, unaware of my secret intention to break this rule, had taken all my private letters at 8 a.m. according to *her* rule (of which I was ignorant), and put them in a drawer. It is astonishing to me that that excellent woman knows which of my letters are private & which aren't; but she does, & never makes a mistake. I was disturbed to discover, in the midst of your long and good letter, that you were 'counting' on *R.U.R.*, & so I had the more distress in sending you the telegram yesterday. I knew *nothing* when I wrote you before, except Loraine's temperament. I gave him 4 extra days, &, needless to say, at the end of the 4 days, he had made no communication of any sort to the Lyric. He might at least have sent word that he couldn't proceed. He was busy telephoning me on Friday, but I wouldn't see him without Horne being there. I made an appointment for him & Horne to meet me here. Horne came but Loraine didn't. Nor did Mrs. Loraine know where he was! The usual thing. Yesterday I went to have tea with Mrs. L's 6-months old baby, & incidentally saw Robert, who evidently had nothing whatever of a definite nature. The play was then in the hands of Dean. Dean of course may refuse our terms, in which case I suppose that Loraine can have another try. Loraine told me that Nigel was suggesting to Dean for Helen someone named Ruth Taylor; which fact disposes of Nigel's objection to you that you had not had sufficient experience of 'leads'. I wonder what experience of 'leads' Ruth has had. It is a queer world. Loraine again spoke interestedly of you & he is still expecting you next Sunday! Why he should expect you next Sunday, seeing that he has almost no hope of getting the play, I cannot imagine. The only reason is that he is Loraine. *Professionally*, I can see only one purpose in your coming up,— namely that you will so engrave yourself on Loraine's mind that he will seriously think of you for other productions. For *un*professional reasons I want greatly to know if you are coming up. There is no night-train from Blackburn after 9.55, but I suppose you could catch that. The Sunday train leaves at 8.40 a.m. & gets in at 4.40 p.m. There are plenty of down trains on Monday. Assuming that with your adventurous & valorous spirit you *do* come, I want to know whether you want me to have a party here in the evening or not. And all this essential information I not only want, but want immediately. I know you are frightfully disgusted with the Loraine affair, & I wish I could say something to *vous remonter*; but I can't. It would be no use me putting you before Dean because some time ago I was obliged to admonish him rather severely about his business methods, & I don't think he has got over it or ever will. You might, however, get Loraine to put you before Dean, if you choose. But I feel perfectly sure that Dean has his own plans.

I'll bear the other Dorothy in mind. *Very* difficult, her case! All this week I've been working and playing hard—been in scenes of gaiety every night & heard much music—my novel is rapidly proceeding to its end, thank God. I had a most urgent invitation to be Beaverbrook's guest on the Mauretania which is beginning this week a special cruise through the Mediterranean to the Holy Land. He had evidentally decided to *make* me go. But of course I refused. He came to dinner on Friday very gloomy about it all. Gertrude Jennings & Marjorie Gordon were here & both of them ragged him terrifically about things in general. Did him good. Now I wonder what sort of rooms you will get in Blackburn, whether you are eating, whether you are on the verge of suicide, whether your 'head is bloody but unbowed', & most particularly whether you are coming to London.

Ever your devoted A.B.

256. A. P. Horne was business manager of the Lyric, Hammersmith.
    Basil Dean (1888–1971) was currently managing director of the St Martin's Theatre. For a letter to him see Vol. III.
    Ruth Taylor appeared in several plays in London in the 1920s, most notably as Mrs Fainall in Playfair's production of *The Way of the World* in 1924 at the Lyric, Hammersmith.
    Gertrude Jennings (d. 1958), playwright.

BERG / MS / 257
(*To Dorothy Cheston*)

75, Cadogan Square
27–2–23

My dearest Dorothea,

I hope you are all right at Halifax, after the exciting evening here—if it *was* exciting for you. I think we both explained ourselves very well. Nor did I feel at all depressed. Nor did you But while your mind is divided, mine isn't. However, you needn't fear that I shall make any attempt, direct or indirect, to swing your mind either one way or the other. In the circum stances I do not think that would be a justifiable course for me to take.

I've read 'Polly's' work, and the longest piece in it, 'An open cage', a short story, is in my opinion really very remarkable. It is jejune, naive, clumsy; but it is highly original & quite beautiful. I was quite enchanted by its charm. But I shall wan to see more of her work before I solemnly advise her to continue with seriousness. 'An open cage' more than bears out all that you said of her.

Last night I was at a musical party at Harriet's. Crowds of people. I didn't get to bed till 1 a.m. But I have worked well today. Whereas yesterday I couldn't do a stroke till 6 p.m when I wrote a little article for Cassell's new weekly *Men Women, & Books*. I have a dinner party here tonight. And I mee N.P. again tomorrow, after which I may have something more to report to you about *R.U.R.*

Ever your devoted A.B

257. Polly: a New York friend of Dorothy's.

The article for *Cassell's Weekly* appeared as 'Is the Novel Decaying?' on 28 March 1923. In it Bennett remarked of Virginia Woolf's recently published *Jacob's Room*, 'I have seldom read a cleverer book ... but the characters do not vitally survive in the mind because the author has been obsessed by details of originality and cleverness.' Presently Virginia Woolf responded with her famous essay, 'Mr. Bennett and Mrs Brown', in which she argued that Bennett himself did not know how to create characters.

STOKE / MS / 258
(*To Margaret Beardmore*)

75, Cadogan Square
27–2–23

My sweet niece,

If I were you, in my own mind I should regard that young man with respect. After all, he had some taste. But perhaps you do, & the tone of your writing is a mere mask.

I do implore you not to get up in yourself any general prejudice against Jews as a race, merely because you have happened to come across some unpleasant ones. And I think that the word 'beastly', though permissible enough in the impulsiveness of conversation, scarcely looks well when written, unless of course it is used in its proper sense, which is not the sense in which you use it. I may mention again that I know a considerable number of excellent Jews, & I have not noticed that gentiles are superior to them. The anti-semite prejudice is the sure mark of a narrow mind.

I should *very much* like you to come to London for a few days. But Easter itself is not at all a good time to come to London, which is then full of holiday persons & not its usual self, & most of the shops are closed & Sundayish, & most of the entertainments too full. The week after Easter would be better. How long are your holidays? I can't bind myself down to a date at present, as I shall probably go to Paris & I don't yet know just when. It will be after my book is finished, & I expect to finish the said book in a fortnight or so. I might postpone Paris until after you've been here.

As regards *Lilian* I didn't hope you would like either it or her. I would sooner have your opinion about the book in 20 years time, though, if I exist at all, I shall be very antique then. And you won't be in your first youth either. I think that you want a considerable amount of experience of life in order to judge *Lilian* justly. Some people never would like it. Your Auntie Tertia didn't like it in the least; in fact I think she detested it; and yet she has had experience of life, and in general is an A1 judge of literature. However, I can't help all that. I am glad to say that many people are extraordinarily enthusiastic about this booklet.

You had better keep on reading Hardy; but I doubt if you'll

care for *The Well Beloved.* Try *The Woodlanders* or *The Mayor of Casterbridge.* These are the two best.

This house is now nearly finished, but not quite. I don't suppose it ever will be quite. H. G. Wells & wife & some others are coming to dine in it tonight. The house will then be judged. I think you will like the place. I am settled down. I go to bed pretty regularly at 12.30 & begin work at 8 a.m. My health is much better, as everyone remarks. And that's all for the moment about me.

I hope that your father will soon be settled down in a new post. As for Alan, my hopes of him are but slight. What your mother needs is repose.

Through subscribing to a fund for Viennese children I got 3 little Viennese handkerchiefs, which I enclose for your use.

Your aff unc, expectant, A.B.

258. *Lilian* was published on 19 October 1922. It was a slight work, written in response to Swinnerton's *Coquette*, and was generally deplored by the critics. The review in the *Spectator* thought it was so bad that it must be by a young man named Bennett Arnold, who might improve with years. The heroine is a typist who marries well.

Frank Beardmore and his family returned to Stoke-on-Trent in 1923 after some years in Glasgow.

BERG / MS / 259
(*To Dorothy Cheston*)

75, Cadogan Square
8–3–23

My dearest Dorothea,

I smile at the notion that in the midst of finishing my novel I shan't have time to write to you. However, you didn't mean it.

In reply to your wire I wired you yesterday at eventide that nothing decisive had occurred about *R.U.R.* but that Dean would almost certainly get it. I should have wired you in any case at the same hour. Not having heard of your new address, I sent the telegram to Peter Street. (Touching the new address I have been unable to decipher it with certainty. Ditto my secretary. I hope I've got it about right.) The delay in *R.U.R.* has been due to Dean's absorption in the production of *The Great Broxopp.* We have got an extension of our option on the play, so that we are no longer in the same feverish haste for a production.

I expect I needn't say that my attitude would have been very different during your recent visit had I not been acting on the assumption that your situation rendered it permissible. I entirely agree that people can learn more of each other on a holiday together than at vast numbers of dinners à deux. I will endeavour to organise that holiday as soon as I know your dates, & I shall look forward to it with intense interest. I beg to inform Dorothea that there are probably very few persons on earth with a keener sense than mine of the immense difficulty of understanding another human being. I have made a living out of my alleged faculty in that direction for many years; but I have no pretensions at all to being able to do it. And I get more diffident in the attempt every year. Did you write 'Rome' as a place for the holiday, or have I failed to read the word? Travelling continuously you couldn't travel to Rome in less than 44 hours, & it is one of the most difficult cities in Europe to get accommodation in at the present time. So I am told. Later on, beginning June, my yacht is the place for another holiday. We can always stay in calm water.

My novel is nearly done. Monday it ought to be finished. I'm doing nothing at it today. Too tired! I went to Lady Londonderry's Dance last night & met half the divorced, unattached and semi-attached women in London & got home at 2.30 this morn. But I am very well. In fact my health is so good that it alarms me. I'm so glad you've got decent rooms at last.

Your letters cannot be too long.

Ever your devoted A.B.

259. Dorothy's Peter Street address was presumably a temporary one after she left 21 Church Street. Her new address is unknown except for the number 284. By March 1924 she was at 21ᴬ Sloane Street.

The Great Broxopp, A. A. Milne's play, was on at the St Martin's Theatre.

Lady Londonderry (1879–1959).

BERG / MS / 260
(*To Dorothy Cheston*)

75, Cadogan Square
11–3–23

My dearest Dorothea,

Thank you for yours of the 9th. I hope you *haven't* fallen ill. Of course personally I should prefer you to return to London. You certainly needn't think about Mrs. Pat calling you ungrateful, or that you sticking to her will make any difference to your chances with her later on. If she wants you she'll ask for you, & if she doesn't she won't. And if she calls you ungrateful she'll be merely silly. You owe her nothing whatever in the way of an obligation. If you have learnt from her it's because you've been clever enough to learn. I've been further reflecting, re you, that as I have been very kind to Vedrenne's most cherished son Leslie and given him help that he couldn't have got anywhere else, I could properly put you on to Vedrenne, which I will do. I have also written to Hicks by this post about you. I am told that Leslie Faber is positively going into management in September, & as I know him very well I will deal with him too. I think on the whole you would do well-ish to give notice, & one reason why is that I feel you'll feel you haven't done right if you don't give notice. The Russell case is quite clear. The baby is John's all right. But I think she asked for trouble, & I don't think she is being hunted because John's possessive sense was outraged, though it was—and justifiably. If John had carried on as she did she would have probably made a considerable fuss. But John is a fool to keep on bringing the action again & again; & his father & mother are strange people to bleat about being ruined by the action which they themselves strongly instigated. The whole thing is rotten. I may go to Paris for Easter, with Rosenbach (New York), the biggest antiquarian bookseller in the world. I should see some things with him that I want to see, and I shall probably do quite a respectable deal with him about my own water-colours. But if I go it will only be for a few days. I'd go again if useful after Easter. I haven't heard from your Polly yet. I've written all but the last chapter of my novel, & I'm rather undecided as to the form of that. But I'm in a general state of indecision, especially as to my programme of movements; which indecision is based on the aunt in *Magda* & is not

her fault in any way. In fact I don't know where I am, highly
unusual for me. You surely don't want to stay at the Lutetia,
left bank and all! I can tell you of much more suitable places
than that. The food used to be magnif at the Lutetia. I had an
antique 'pavillon' near there & often dined in the hotel-
restaurant. I saw *Advertising April* on Wednesday. Anything
more awful than the play, or than Sybil in it, could scarcely be
imagined. I wanted to leave at end of the 1st act. Tayler agreed
to leave at the end of the 2nd, & regretted much that he hadn't
agreed earlier. I like writing to you, even though I can say
nothing worth saying.

Ever your devoted A.B.

I took up my water-colour painting again this morning, fired by
Rosenbach, with whom I spent last night at Ciro's!

260. Mrs Patrick Campbell (1865–1940) played Magda and directed the production. For other references to her see Vols. I and III.

Leslie Vedrenne (b. 1899) published half a dozen books in the years 1924–8. One of
the books, *This Generation*, has for epigraph a passage from Bennett's *The Author's Craft*:
'Not the charity which signs cheques, but the more precious charity which puts itself to
the trouble of understanding.'

Leslie Faber (1879–1929) directed and starred in the revival of *The Great Adventure* in
1924.

In the Russell case the wife, Christabel Hulme-Russell, had refused conjugal rights
to the husband, John Russell, and had argued in court that one's separate soul should
be cultivated. She was adjudged to have committed adultery with an unknown man
instead of the named correspondent, but the child she bore was not adjudged to be
bastard.

Advertising April was running at the Criterion. Sybil Thorndike (1882–1976) was in it.
She was soon to have her great success in *St Joan*.

BERG / MS / 261
(*To Dorothy Cheston*)
Hotel Majestic
Paris
24–3–23

My dearest Dorothea,

We couldn't get into any other hotel, & this is at the Arc de
Triomphe, & the Champs Elysées is 125 miles long. As Dr.
Rosenbach is leaving for Rome on Tuesday morning, I shall
leave this hotel then too, & find something more central. Now
that I am on the spot I can exercise more influence than from
London. Not that there is anything wrong with this hotel except

its uncentrality. Dr. Rosenbach is a great mover before the Lord. We had to go to a music-hall last night after our journey! There is a great row going on here about nude women on the stage. We saw them all right, a sight I've only seen once before. I shan't know what is *really* going on in Paris till this afternoon, when I take tea with some of my friends who are in the movement, totally. The weather here is just as bad as in London. Last night was vile in the extreme. I've only brought one book to read: the Bible. I usually travel with it, & for good miscellaneous browsing I don't know anything to beat it. I haven't heard anything more about *R.U.R.*. Horne & Playfair think Dean is certain to take it: but I am not at all sure— because I know Dean's business manager, Clift, who is a perfect devil about terms. So you will be all over London tomorrow, but I shan't see you. I shall be all over Paris, & I'm going to the races. In fact this holiday will about ruin my health, which has of late been so marvellously good. I have received & refused about 40 invitations for Easter or round about Easter, which it would have done me more good to accept, but I was determined to come to Paris, & I've come, & after Easter I shall come again. I do hope you're all right.

Ever your devoted A.B.

261.　Bennett went to Paris for a few days in late March.
Ernest Paul Clift (1881–1963), manager and dramatist.

BERG / MS / 262
(*To Dorothy Cheston*)

Hotel Majestic
27–3–23

My dearest Dorothea,

I got your welcome letter yesterday afternoon. I had written to you on Sunday at the Park Theatre Eastbourne. I hope you will get the epistle. The chief thing here is the weather which is like full summer & most marvellous. You drive in the Bois at night! I have formed the habit of going to bed at 2 a.m. I will get a hotel for you all right when the time comes. It has been very difficult to get rooms at all just now, owing to the Horse Show & the imminence of Easter, but there will be no trouble after Easter. The paper *Vogue* is in my hands, & it has a special 'service de voyageurs'. It has even placed an office with secretary at my disposal free of charge. There is nothing like asking the right people to lunch! Half England is here. I shall not be able to come to Eastbourne as I shall not return to England till Sunday night. I have too many engagements— what with friends, publishers & authors & my private affairs. My friend Rosenbach has gone to Rome this morning, & I have changed my apartment, smaller, but still very magnificent. It is in the most exclusive 'annexe' of the hotel on the other side of the street, & is inhabited by people like fashionable cocottes, Earl Beatty, & so on including Mrs. Nash. I must say I don't quite see you & Mrs. Pat on the Pier at Eastbourne. It is an excellent thing that you get on with her so well. Where shall you come when you come to London? I have to tell you that it will probably be necessary for me to postpone by a day or a couple of days my next visit to Paris. I met Ravel on Sunday night. He is a friend of mine & he is coming to London for a concert on 14th April (Saturday), & I must give a dinner for him after the concert (which is in the afternoon at Queen's Hall). No one can be invited to this dinner who does not either speak fluent French or play Ravel's work extremely well! I could come to Paris on the 15th Sunday, not a bad day for travelling. I trust you are in A1 physical & spiritual health.

Ever your devoted Arnold B.

262. Earl Beatty (1871–1936), first sea lord, 1919–27.
Mrs Nash: unidentified.

BERG / MS / 263
(*To Dorothy Cheston*)

Cherkley
Leatherhead
Surrey
29–4–23

My dearest girl,

I wonder how you are passing your solitudenous Sunday. We had a good talk on Friday, & perhaps tomorrow night we will have another of a different sort. As this house is a regular repository of rumour & I know the inhabitants thereof very intimately I heard quite a lot about myself as I am in the eyes of the world. It appears that I am the lover of several young women, but nobody seems to suspect you yourself at all! I maintained my usual calm, & did not *too* strenuously deny any of the rumours! Je me demande if I shall ever be of any use to you. I hope so, though my answers to your questions may often disconcert you. They all asked me why I was in such high spirits. Yet I was not aware of showing any high spirits. I played tennis yesterday afternoon. Today it has rained until the afternoon. I don't know what they are doing now. I've just had my sleep. I've been in the very centre of the crisis as to the failure of the Prime Minister. He was here yesterday, & he is here again today; & his son & son-in-law came down to see Beaverbrook at a quarter past midnight last night & left at 2 a.m., & are here again today also. Nothing is settled. The P.M. is very frank about himself, even to me, though I don't know him at all well, & Beaverbrook confides with great gusto in me when he & I are alone. After hours & hours of talk, nothing whatever is settled. But I expect that by tonight the immediate course of British politics will be settled by the arguments & persuasions of the P.M.'s one bosom friend, Max.

Well, I will see you tomorrow at 8.30. In the meantime I will think of you. You are very soothing & stimulating & precious. C'est déjà quelque chose n'est ce pas?

C'est un baiser.

Ever your constant A.B.

263. Cherkley: Max Beaverbrook's home.

Bonar Law had cancer of the throat, and died in the autumn. The crisis concerned his successor as leader of the Conservative party. The choice seemed to lie between Stanley Baldwin and Lord Curzon, neither of whom was satisfactory to Law, who resigned in May without naming anyone.

C'est un baiser—beginning with this letter, Bennett characteristically embellished his letters to Dorothy with kisses, hearts, and other decorations of his initials.

BERG / MS / 264
(*To Dorothy Cheston*)   Yacht Marie Marguerite
                                          Southampton
                                          5–6–23

My dearest girl,

Have my thoughts followed you like a benediction? Even if they haven't, you were delicious on the bateau, except when you were naughty about lying down after M'sill—and even then ... Well! I was most gloomy last night, and read 2 acts of

The Sea-Gull. I reserve my views about this play; but I may respectfully state at once that I don't think any British audience would understand the first two acts. It is a technique far more subtle than Ibsen's. Do you understand me, not only about the play, but generally? I rather think you do. In which case je suis tranquille. I've heard from Anthony. He suggests next Sunday; but I don't want him on Sunday now, as you are to leave on Sunday evening. So, as he said he could come any day, I wired him suggesting Monday instead. He would be gravely in the way on Sunday. The Godebskis are *most enthusiastic* about your coming. General chorus of exultation and laudation. A splendid manifestation of real appreciation. They boarded the yacht this morn at 7.15. Fresh as paint. Slept excellently on the steamer, ravished with everything they saw. I seem to think that I *will* get you to come to Poole on Friday, & we will sail to Cowes on Saturday & here on Sunday; or something like that. The weather is fair, after too early sunshine, but terribly cold. Seeing the awful conditions of your first yachting trip, & the fact that it *was* your first yachting trip, I say you came through it fine, with first-class honours. I wrote 500 words of my article before breakfast. I have 1,000,000 things to say to you, but they are too vague, subtle, implicit, elusive to be written. I can only look at them & throw in a spoken word now & then to elucidate. I hope the new servant is 'shaping' & that you are as content as any human being ought to be at your early time of life. Et je t'embrasse bien et tendrement, within all my famous reserve.

A.

P.S. D.V. we sail to Poole tomorrow, Wednesday.

264. Bennett sailed off the English and European coast during June, July, and August.

Anthony Ellis (1873–1944), manager and critic, was proposing a theatrical enterprise involving Bennett and Dorothy and some other people. One of his intentions was to produce *Don Juan de Marana*, and Bennett expected that Dorothy would obtain a role in it. The play was not produced, and the whole enterprise came to nothing.

Bennett wrote a few articles for the *Adelphi* at this time. He may also have begun writing the series of ten articles for the *Royal Magazine* that began to appear in November.

BERG / MS / 265   Yacht Marie Marguerite
(*To Dorothy Cheston*)   Poole
                                         Thursday
                                         7–6–23

My dearest girl,

I got 3 letters from you this morn, 2 in 1 envelope & 1 in 1 envelope. These letters are exceedingly interesting. It is true that in the matter of the sea you desolate me; but that can't be helped. If you don't enjoy the sea you don't. Les sentiments ne se commandent pas, surtout les sentiments maritimes. I shall now change my plans. I shall leave here tomorrow Friday morning & stop the night probably at Cowes & get to Southampton during the Saturday morning. Will you please take the 4.30 on Saturday afternoon, & I will meet you at the gare at 6.2. This is a great train. I cannot willingly consent to you coming down merely for the day. That would be too awful for me. After this week I shall have to think of taking the Godebskis somewhere that *is* somewhere, as they came for the sea. We had a magnificent voyage yesterday, arriving at 9 p.m. I'm frightfully busy on my article, & think only of you & it. Now Pauline Smith has just come.

If you wire me you can't come till Sunday I shall drop down dead.

> In haste,
> Your constant loving
>
> A.B.

BERG / MS / 266
(*To Dorothy Cheston*)   Yacht Marie Marguerite
                                         Poole
                                         7–6–23

My dearest girl,

I had no time to write to you today, except formally, plus ou moins. It is certainly very sagacious of you to give me your real ideas and predilections instead of hiding them. Surtout 'la belle franchise'. You see there are 2 sorts of women. Those with a career of their own, & those whose career is to complete somebody else's career. The latter do *not* want what you want from the male, and please don't judge them by yourself, for you are utterly different, except at certain moments. Your career is as much your main preoccupation as mine is mine. And rightly so. Believe me, I understand all that quite well. You are extremely independent, & you are bound to be egotistic. Also rightly so. All artists are. Further you are very original, & disturbingly intelligent. I am not intelligent in the way you are; don't pretend to be; don't want to be. I'm instinctive & never have any desire to analyse myself. My job is to analyse other people. But I have a highly-unusually-developed faculty of putting myself in another person's place, so that it is fairly easy for me (1) to avoid upsetting them and (2) to do things which will please them. And I can actively sympathise with nearly anybody. I seldom take a real dislike to a person; more often I pretend to take a dislike. I have never been able to be jealous or envious. I know I am apt to be exacting & even ruthless when anything threatens the efficiency of my working organism. For twenty five years & more I have kept whole communities quiet or moving on tip-toe for an hour a day because my afternoon sleep is essential to my productive machine. I am a terrible stickler for punctuality, & one of the greatest proofs of regard I can give is to remain calm & benevolent when unpunctuality deranges my programme. (That is the sort of egoist I am.) Yet I know that my punctuality is exaggerated to the point of being almost a neurosis. I should like to know more of that German play. I have read *The Sea Gull.* It is good, but far inferior (I think) to *The Cherry Orchard.* There are too many prominent women in it; the interest is too diffused, & the heroine not salient enough. I don't seem to see it on any English stage. Have you ever read Becque's *La Parisienne?* That is one of the great modern plays. Have you read Edmond Sée's *L'Indiscret?* Very fine. I tell you you are a strange union of artistic curiosity & feminine tenderness. These 2 things do not often go together. I was exceedingly intrigued by your brain when I first met you, & I am still more intrigued by it now. Well, I was then determined to know you ... and you see now! Is not this to my credit? I kiss you very lovingly,

A.B.

I attend you at Southampton at 6 o'clock on Saturday without fail.

A.B.

266. Henri Becque (1837–99); Edmond Sée (1875–1959).

BERG / MS / 267
(*To Dorothy Cheston*)   Yacht Marie Marguerite
       Guernsey
       17–6–23

My dearest girl,

Sunday noon. The whole yacht is clean & bleached and glittering, & some of the crew lying in Sunday idleness on the deck. It rolls slightly in the swell that runs all the way round the island from the west. The sun shines, rather feebly, but it shines. The wind is in the N.E. The whole sea glitters. Through the harbour mouth can be seen Herm, Sark, and Jethou in the distance. A 500 ton steam yacht is lying near us—a yacht notorious for the drunken nights of its owner. Little sailing boats keep coming in & out. The Godebskis are at mass. I have read the *Observer*, Osbert Sitwell, Balzac, & had one of my brief morning snoozes after my 6 a.m. rising. Blue suit, black tie, white handkerchief: the chic of severity. Your cabin is empty, and as usual when empty is employed as a writing-room by all the guests. Mr. Prohack is feeding on my damask cheek. He ought not to be doing so, the day being Sunday; but he is. After a week's serious cerebration I have come to perceive that almost 6/7ths of the novel has to be cut away from the tale if the tale is to be a play. Also I have definitely reduced the 4 acts to 3. I have got Act I & II into fair constructional order, but not Act III at all yet. All the customary despairs, disgusts, exasperations, exhaustions, & futilities are being experienced by this highly practiced writer, just as if he had not written some 23 plays & didn't thoroughly know the rigours of the preliminary process of shaping a play. I see that you are destined to be the daughter in the piece; the secretary is not important enough. It seems to me to be a great waste of a portion of eternity that you are not here this day, so that I might enjoy the spectacle of your physical and mental and spiritual being. I am so much more capable of appreciating it than any of the Shute's. (I hope you have done some useful business with the Colonel.) I well understand how you *burn* to be at work. It must be frightful not to be able to prevent oneself from being prevented from working. (I have very rarely been in that impasse, & never except through illness.) One of the advantages of being a novelist is that I can live your life in my mind from hour to hour.

Oh yes, I can follow your sensations from end to end of the day rather well, you know. I am now waiting for a telegram from you to say whether or not we are to meet next weekend; as upon it will depend my movements. I regret to say that my movements also depend on the weather, and too much so. I'm not sure yet whether I shall go to Dartmouth on Tuesday if I am to pick you up in Southampton on Saturday. I may be running it too fine by doing so. I can already see you joining the yacht again, in the evening, & the dinner & the games & then the other people going to bed, and then the beginning of the real evening, & the passings to & fro between 2 rooms, and the changes of dress and of mood, and the intimacies & confidences, and the ingrained Englishness, so strange & exotic to me, & I can feel the softness. Yes, well. Intentionally there is nothing, or little, practical in this letter, except the most practical matter of all. You have a secret idea that you care for me more than I care for you. This idea is wrong. It makes me smile—my indulgent smile that slightly exasperates you at times. You are a wonderful woman, full of delicious danger to mankind. I embrace you, enfold you, wrap you up in me.

A.

267. For letters and other references to Osbert Sitwell (1892–1969) see Vols. I and III.

Bennett wrote and rewrote *Mr Prohack* with Edward Knoblock. He worked on it during the summer of 1923, the autumn of 1924, early 1925, and October 1927.

The Shutes: unidentified.

KEELE / MS / 268
(*To Marguerite Soulié Bennett*)

Yacht Marie Marguerite
25–6–23

My dear Marguerite,

Thanks for your letter. I was just posting the enclosed when it arrived. I am sorry to hear of Raton's death, & I know it must be a cause of great sorrow to you. I do not know what your cousin means by me having 'peur' of you. I always think of you in the friendliest way, and I wish you to be happy, but I do not consider that any good would be done by me calling to see you or you calling to see me. We shall be friendliest apart. Please read this as it is written, in a perfectly kindly way.

Yours, A.B.

BERG / MS / 269   Yacht Marie Marguerite
(*To Dorothy Cheston*)   Southampton
                                  Tuesday
                                  26–6–23

My dearest girl,

As soon as I left you I felt the cloud of neuralgia advancing slowly upon me. I was not mistaken. It advanced. It is somewhat better this morning. I do hope you have had the sleep you need. I wrote another 1,000 words of Prohack yesterday afternoon, despite neuralgia. At 10.25 the Godebskis, gloomy, wistful, and grateful, faded away in the launch. Still, I did buck Cepa up with a beef-steak-and-kidney pudding, which he absolutely adored. Soon after you departed Middleton Murry wired that he is coming to lunch with me today. Severe squalls yesterday afternoon. Flat calm last night. Flat calm this morning, with the addition of fine persistent rain, I did my exercises in the fine rain. And it is 8.30 a.m. And I hope to write another scene today. I think I have now recovered from the all-night séance. I expect I did not express myself very cleverly then. 2 a.m. is not an advantageous time for delicacy in self-expression. But it doesn't really matter so long as you see that the relation between husband & wife is very different from that between lover and mistress, and that ours must inevitably be the latter—and it is much better that it should be the latter. Each has its advantages & disadvantages, but nobody can have everything. Our relation, while just as close in one way, in several ways in fact, is decidedly freer in others. It involves fewer duties & fewer rights, especially in the smaller things of life. This is the price of liberty. It is part of the price which everyone has to pay for a career. The woman without a career can identify herself completely with the man who has a career. And she does so. She gives a tremendous lot and receives, generally, complete protection (which never does go & can't go with complete liberty). The relation is not fundamentally different, but it is different in rather important matters. Some women expect to be perfectly free and perfectly protected, which is not only impossible in one way but impossible in every way. It is contrary to all natural laws. As for you, with your highly unusual put-yourself-in-his-place imagination (the finest kind of imagination—the imagination of which Mary Grey showed something when she expressed the engineer's feelings in the launch), I of course do not count you among them. The merely financial aspect of the matter does not loom large to me. In postponing any action in regard to it I thought I was consulting your feelings. And I do not agree with your position that I ought not to expect you to make any suggestions in regard to it, and that I ought to find out for myself. No! To my mind this is not quite right. You know that I want to help you in every possible way. (If you had only the hundredth part of the perception which you actually possess you would still be deeply aware of my feelings for you. If you doubt them there is nothing more to be said. It isn't your fault, nor mine either.) I am older than you; I have more material resources and more experience, etc. I want nothing in return for anything I can do, except your love and kindness. I do not want dominion, such as I should be bound morally to exercise over a wife whose existence was solely attached to mine. If you asked my advice & I gave it and you ignored it, I should not be in the least resentful or hurt. I should expect you to use the same freedom as I use myself. I cannot do more than this. (By the way as soon as I get to Weymouth I will make a beginning in the matter of your finances. I can't do it here.) You actually expect more from life than I do. And quite right. But there are some things you mustn't expect. You keep on saying that you hate the secretiveness of our relations. It is no use doing so. The thing is inevitable. It is possibly a disadvantage, but as a disadvantage it has to be weighed against the advantages. Similarly with the impossibility of being continuously or very frequently together. These are unchangeable facts which have to be faced. We cannot have everything or nearly everything, I think we do have more than most people. I for instance should have to go a long way before I met another woman who combined in her soul and person the qualities which you have. I have not met them in one individual before. But I wish you could make up your mind about yourself and about me. It is decidedly disturbing to be told that one is a stranger, that you don't know whether in coming to me you are being guided by Satan or by heaven, that I forget you when you are not there, that you count after a yacht, and that I regard you only as an agreeable mistress—that is, toy. How disturbing it is you can judge by exercising that put-yourself-in-his-place imagination of yours, and conceiving what you would feel if I announced to *you* that in coming to you I wasn't sure whether Satan or heaven was guiding me, or that you only came to me for what you could get out of me, etc., etc. I nearly always know my own mind. I seldom have any doubts as to what I ought to do or as to what my feelings are on any subject. I know my instinct is to expect others to have the same certainty, & I know that I ought not to do so. I have always been told that I expect too much from others. I dare say I do. Mais que veux-tu? I don't expect anything at all from anyone to whom I am not profoundly attached. Je t'aime tendrement.

A.

269. For letters to John Middleton Murry (1889–1957) see Vol. III. He was currently editing the *Adelphi*.

Mary Grey (d. 1974), singer, actress, costumier. In 1925 she had her great success as Madame Ranefsky in *The Cherry Orchard* at the Lyric Hammersmith.

BERG / MS / 270
(*To Dorothy Cheston*)   Yacht Marie Marguerite
                                                Swanage
                                                5 p.m. 27-6-23

My dearest girl,

A fog this morning, which delayed us by 2 hours in starting! The sun could be seen yellow climbing up behind it, but would not pierce it. So that we missed half the tide. Then, after a flat calm, a strong headwind! So that we have only got to Swanage, and shall not get to Weymouth till tomorrow about lunch time: when I shall have letters & write letters. Anyhow we shall be at Torquay on Friday night sometime, & unless you hear from me to the contrary in the meantime you will please travel to Torquay by the noon train, & I will meet you at the station, on Saturday. I seemed to do nothing yesterday but answer the letters of an enormous mail, and think about the play. No

riting. I wrote a little scene this morn, en route, but am not
uite content with it, & shall probably write it again. One more
:ene & the act will be finished. I had neuralgia all today. It is
st going off. Due, I think, to not eating enough. Also I have
een *tracassé* by the ideas for a *conte libertin*, which I have had in
y head for 3 years. Unpublishable of course, but I have
lways wanted to emulate the great writers, such as Balzac,
Iirabeau, de Musset, and Dumas, who produced strange and
xciting stories in this kind. How art thou? Possibly there is a
:tter waiting for me from you at Weymouth—and I am not
ere. Je t'embrasse comme je t'aime.

A.

ERG / MS / 271
To Dorothy Cheston)

Yacht Marie Marguerite
Weymouth
28–6–23

Iy dearest girl,
    I have your letter of Tuesday night. I'm sorry I didn't
nderstand about Satan & his opposite. Above all I like you to
e honest & fully candid, & therefore I admire your letter. I
oubt if I've made myself clear as to my conception of what our
elations can and cannot be. You appear to think—though you
on't say—that I imply something in them derogatory to you.
'his of course is not so. Far from it. You are the only woman in
y heart. If I were free & you were willing I should undoubt-
dly become your legal husband; but you, as a woman with a
areer, as an artist, would still, in the sense that I mean, remain
ir more a mistress than a wife. In my opinion it is almost
npossible for two people with separate ambitions, to be as
1uch husband and wife as lover and mistress. The relationship
 and must be different—no matter how much each tries to give
f himself or herself. Of this I am profoundly convinced. And I
m quite sure that if I, for instance, began demánding from you
ll that a husband usually does demand from a woman who is
irst and foremost a wife, you would revolt as an artist, and you
vould be right to do so. I am surprised that this attitude of mine
urprises you, for it is at the root of all my work dealing with
exual relations, and, instead of weakening, it has strengthened

with time. Quite apart from all this, one fact is utterly clear
Our relations have to be secret. If this secrecy grates on you
nerves more than you can stand, what is to be done? I do no
want to rush you into anything, and I have never done so. If you
prefer that we should be only friends, let us be only friends. Bu
being only friends does not to my mind mean allowing our
selves every liberty except the embrace. Such a state of affair
imposes far too great a strain on *my* nerves. And yet I suppos
you realise the power of your physical attractiveness. I hop
most ardently that you will not decide that we are to be only
friends. If you do so decide I shall very strictly respect the
decision. I am gradually getting a notion of *your* idiosyncracy
My idiosyncracy (or part of it) is that my relations with you
have to be, physically, either one thing or the other. We are
both sensual—thank God. I can cut the flesh right out, but
cannot healthily indulge in half measures.

To be honest, I do not yet clearly see what the trouble is al
about.

I ought to have received a communication from my banker
here today; for some incomprehensible reason it hasn't come
so I can't send a communication of a similar nature to you. Ye
I am a day late here. We got here at 3 p.m.; and shall leave for
Torquay at 11 p.m. tonight, so as to be sure of being there in
time for me to meet you & Irene W. on Saturday afternoon. I've
finished the 1st act, but shall probably write some of it again.

Yours, A

271. Irene W.: presumably a mistake for Beatrice W.; see next letter.

BERG / MS / 272
(*To Dorothy Cheston*)   Yacht Marie Marguerite
                                          Torquay
                                          29–6–23

My dearest girl,
    This is my second letter today. I received yours after I had
sent the first one ashore. I much prefer you to come in advance
of B.W. How odd that you should have been told that I was
divorced! I don't know how these stories spring up. If I had
been through the divorce court, such is modern publicity that
the thing would have been a front page item in every daily in

England and America! I do not agree with you that complete
freedom is compatible with complete protection. To my mind
the two are mutually exclusive. However, I think that the great
pending argument about marriage v. liaison is merely a question of words. Certainly I am prepared, and always have been,
to give you as much protection as can possibly go with freedom.
I am also prepared to give you as much confidence (confiden-
tiality—I mean) as I could give to any legal wife. What I am not
prepared to do is to make the liaison public, or other than
secret. I am not prepared to go into the divorce court (nor do I
think that whatever I did my wife would agree to a divorce; she
still has a sort of hope—utterly delusive—that she may join me
again). I was entirely innocent in the trouble that separated us,
& I do not propose under any circumstances to bring obloquy
on my own head if I can help it. Nor, financially, could I treat
you on the same footing as I legally bound myself (out of an
absurd generosity) to treat her, without reorganising my whole
existence. But I am prepared, & only too anxious, to protect
you from any financial worries so that you can pursue your own
straight path without having to turn off it in order to live well
and at ease. I don't think I can say any more. In fact I know I
can't. I do not at present see where the trouble lies. In
particular I do not see why you repeat again & again that you
are determined that your life shall not consist of a succession of
lovers. I perceive no point in that. A marriage, either in theory
or in practice, is no more permanent nor impermanent than a
liaison.

Bertie Sullivan is here in his schooner. I am dining with him
& wife tonight. The weather is heavenly. If it keeps so you will
love this little holiday—I hope! Till tomorrow.

Yours, A.

272. Beatrice Wilson (Mrs Norman V. Norman, d. 1943), actress. She played at the
Liverpool Repertory Theatre in 1922, and perhaps knew Dorothy there. In later years
she taught at R.A.D.A.

BERG / MS / 273
(*To Dorothy Cheston*)   Yacht Marie Marguerite
                                          Thursday
                                          5th July 1923

My dearest girl,

When I returned from the station yesterday afternoon, on foot, hoping you would have a pleasant journey untroubled by psychological analysis, I saw standing on the quay overlooking my yacht a middle-aged woman, well-dressed, & very plump. She smiled nervously at me & addressed me. It was Emily Phillpotts (wife of Eden ditto). I hadn't seen her for 16 or 17 years (since the estrangement between Eden & me, which I once recounted to you). 'I knew I should meet you again sometime', she said. Having seen the arrival of the yacht in the paper, she had come down to inspect the same. She was still very nervous, wouldn't even come on board, although continually exclaiming, 'I *am* so glad to see you.' However after half an hours talk on the quay she agreed to come to dinner, just her & me. Eden & daughter were away. She is a disappointed but cheerful woman. She had meant her daughter to be a brilliant social success, & her daughter is an advanced feminist, boots without heels, any rags, won't spend more than £20 a year on her clothes, disdains men, & has just written a novel, which Heinemann is to publish. Her son is a ne'er do well, a painter, made an ass of himself in the war, won't work (can't work, I expect) & has to be kept. Eden is more hypochondriacal than ever, & hasn't been out of Devonshire for years. Her brother-in-law died a morphinomaniac. And so on. Emily & I resumed our friendship just as if 16 years had not passed. At ten o'clock the yacht was taken out into the bay, & I brought her ashore in the launch, & she went home by tram. Why? They have heaps of money. We left Torbay at 6.30 this morn. Perfect weather. Except that the wind was dead wrong & had been all day. Towards 4 o'clock we discerned the Amaryllis overtaking us. She got into Portland long before us, & we are now just entering Portland harbour. It has been a marvellous day. I have read a lot of André Gide's *Dostoievsky*, which he sent me, & was pleased to find that great panjandrum of modern French criticism referred therein to some opinion of mine about Dostoievsky expressed many years ago. I shall go and see Bertie and Elena

onight if it is not too late. Good night, my douce enfant. I hope
rou are in form. I have had neuralgia all day, but only slightly.
Much sleeping.

Friday 6–7–23   5 p.m.

Another gorgeous day. But still the same rotten East wind,
right in our teeth. Nevertheless this East wind is quite *warm*.
Sunshine magnif. Various yachts. I saw Bertie & Co last night.
They've asked me to dinner tonight at the South Western
Hotel, Southampton—if I get there in time. We left Portland at
5.25 a.m. & are now in the Solent, pushing up against both
wind & tide. The Amaryllis left Portland at 7 a.m. & passed us
n the middle of the morning. The weather is astounding.
Plenty of yachts. Also we've passed 2 liners going to S. & N.
America respectively. I have reflected at intervals on the play,
out my neuralgia has not yet got right out of the door. It is on
the doorstep, though. I suppose I shall have recurrent
neuralgia to the end of my life. With regard to Ostende I am
making what arrangement I can for silent mornings, but the
swabbing will have to be done, & we shall all have to call upon
God to help us to take the rough with the smooth,
equanimously. On late nights I will strive to arrange for no
swabbing, but swabbing will be the *rule*. I shall be greatly
surprised if you do not somewhat enjoy Ostende. Yes, I was
very pleased with B. Wilson. I may tell you also, from information received last night on board the Amaryllis, that the
Sullivans were extremely taken with yourself. They particu-
arly remarked on your voice.

A.

Je te bise tendrement. (There is a word you perhaps don't
know.)

P.S. I expect to be at Southampton about 7.30.

273. The quarrel between Bennett and Phillpotts seems to have concerned financial
aspects of their collaboration on *The Statue* in 1907–8. See Vol. I. In a letter to Dorothy
of 18–8–23 (unpublished here) Bennett says, 'I've received a wonderful letter from
Eden Phillpotts, in which I appear as the only friend he ever loved.'
    Adelaide's novel was *The Friend*, published in November. She became a distinguished
author. In 1976 she published her memoirs, *Reverie*, under her married name of Ross.
She recounts there the reunion of her family with Bennett, and presents a more
sympathetic view of her brother's career.
    Elena: Herbert Sullivan's wife.

BERG / MS / 274
(*To Dorothy Cheston*)   Yacht Marie Marguerit∢
                                          Ostende
                                          30–7–23   5 p.m.

My dearest girl,
    I am now longing for a telegram from you describing you⒭
voyage. I fear that in places it was jolly rough. I had quite ⒜
good deal in my mind to say to you in this letter, but you were s∢
tender & charming before you left that I shall suppress most o∢
it. There are, however, one or two things which even at the risᛕ
of being tedious, I must say. One of them is that I utterly resis⒯
your repeated cavillings at my 'growing habits' of this that &
the other. Sometime since you showed a very considerabl∢
nerve in beginning late at night to 'scold' me about my 'growing
habit' of self-will. You apparently did this to justify certain self
willed acts on your own part—acts which you yourself frankl⒴
admitted to be deliberate and calculated. As for the alleged
instances of *my* self-will you failed to produce one. You said yo⒰
would later on, but you never did. Then my 'growing habit' o∢
'scolding'. I never scold, and am notoriously *not* a complainer⒭
My criticisms generally take the form of silence. I have *neve*⒭
criticized you until you asked for my opinion or until I had to d∢
so in order to defend myself against *your* criticisms. ('Thi⒮
animal is wicked; he defends himself when attacked.' [Volt
aire]) I am extremely appreciative of your fine qualities, & you⒭
tenderness & your capacity for loving; but this appreciatio⒩
does not in the least blind me to your self-willedness, and you⒭
profound & unconscious egotism, and your disposition t∢
grumble and to regard yourself as specially the victim of fate. ⒤
put this plainly as I think it plainly—but not more plainly tha⒩
many of your remarks upon myself. Lastly about the mone⒴
question. The trouble here is this. You quite properly wan⒯
money, & ought to have it, & it would be absurd for you not t∢
have it. But what you really want is to have money withou⒯
having to receive it. You think there is something humiliatin⒢
to yourself in receiving money. Of course there is no such thing⒭
And you *can't* have money without receiving it. You ma⒴
consider this very unjust, but it is a fact. You can't have an∢
not-have. You are asking for the impossible. After rebuffin⒢
every attempt of mine to give you money, you pointed out to m

hat I had not attended to this financial question, which you bsolutely declined to discuss. I sent you £100 to go on with. Today you told me that you had not expected I should give it ou in such a way, 'rubbing it in'. What in God's name did you mean? There is only one way of transferring money to you, & hat is by bank-notes. You surely do not suppose that I am going to compromise both of us by sending cheques to your bank when my secretary keeps all my accounts of banking ransactions, which are also minutely seen by my income-tax xpert! The letter which accompanied the bank notes was a perfectly proper and very nice letter, and I cannot imagine vhat on earth you found to object to in it. Then you say that you ad expected that 'this matter would settle itself, as it does between husband & wife'. Good God, my dear innocent, what a implicity is yours! This matter *never* settles itself. How could it? Someone has to settle it. As you won't have anything to do with t, I must settle it. I propose to give you £50 a month, & I will personally hand you the £50 for August when next I see you, & hope that in so doing, I shall not have the misfortune to vound or insult you. There is implicit in all your general ttitude that strange assumption, so common in popular fiction, that in 'giving herself' to a man a woman is conferring a avour on a man. It is not so. Or rather I should say that if love s present each confers an equal favour on the other. Nor does he woman 'give herself' any more than the man 'gives himelf'. Obviously! These phrases have only to be examined in rder to fall into dust. Nor does a woman desire love less than a nan. Every experienced man or woman is aware of this. Beware, my dear girl, of the habit of mind of those inferior and mbittered thinkers, of both sexes, who are constantly begining sentences with 'Men are' or 'Women are' and ending them vith something disadvantageous to the other sex. Not one in a housand of such phrases is true or even half true, and the vast najority of them are merely the expression of an individual rievance. And beware of the fatal example of those terrible and uthless charming women who after trailing for hours in their rivacies issue forth with an expression on their lovely faces vhich is the equivalent of: 'You ought to be jolly thankful that I ondescend to exist and be here at all.' Such women are the aughing-stock of all sensible persons. Beware of inveighing against the 'sex-cruelty' of men, which is no worse & no bette[r] than the sex-cruelty of women. I am not accusing you. I am simply pointing out dangers to you. And if you are the woman [I] take you to be—with your extraordinary and admirable facult[y] of seeing a point of view different from your own when it is fairl[y] stated to you—you will read what I write in the affectionate & forebearing spirit in which it is written. And you will not resen[t] it. For you will know that though you have got yourself into th[e] clutches of an uncompromising realist with a startling faculty o[f] detachment, that realist is profoundly in love with you an[d] admires you as well as anybody on this planet could, and ha[s] done & will do everything in his power to prove this. I have jus[t] had a wire from Tania from Aviemore, Scotland: 'Gillet[t] probably coming. Writing. Tania.' I presume she is at th[e] Station Hotel. As I shall almost certainly not get her letter [I] have wired her to write to London. I suppose you couldn'[t] telephone to her. Perhaps she isn't at the Station Hotel (whicl[h] is the best hotel in Scotland), but I think she is. If she is, sh[e] would certainly be in the hotel at 7.30 p.m. By the way, I tol[d] Miss Nerney to telephone to Swinnerton & find out if by an[y] chance he could after all come during Cowes week. If he can— lo! another complication. Will you mind telephoning to her an[d] finding out what has happened. Massingham, I see from th[e] *New Statesman*, is in Bavaria, or recently was. Now my belove[d] creature, je te bise bien tendrement.

A

P.S. The Captain has no hope of starting tomorrow Tuesday

274. Captain Eric Gillett: described by Harriet Cohen as 'my cricketting friend'.
H. W. Massingham (1860–1924) was editor of the *Nation* from 1907 to 1923.

BERG / MS / 275
(*To Dorothy Cheston*)
Yacht Marie Marguerit[e]
Ostende
10 a.m.   31–7–23

My dearest girl,

I have about a million things to do, but I must write to yo[u] first—'commune', as for some reason or other they call it. [I] hope you are sleeping well this morning & that you won't b[e] lonely. After a long talk with my skipper & my ex-skipper last night about weather & yachts, I took a sleeping draught in some hot brandy & water, & have had a night—not equal to your average night, but a wonderful night for me. I must have slept about seven hours, with three wakings-up. It is only when I have had a decent night that I fully appreciate the inordinate nuisance of having bad nights. Insomnia is a *great* curse, & I have lived under it for 35 years now. Quelle vie! I was delighted to have your cable last night. It is marked as leaving Dover at 7.30. It was delivered on board at 8.10. Not bad. But surely the ship must have been late. You don't say how your organs behaved—you only mention the behaviour of the ship—and hence I fear that they did not behave very well, and am sorry. I may tell you that there is no hope of starting today, but we *might* start very early tomorrow. The glass has gone much lower and is steady, and the wind is high & still in the west. So that I shall have no address yet. I'm not going to bother my head any more about the man for Cowes. I shall leave it to God, & take a rest from worrying about the felicity of other people—except yours. The amount of time I spend in helping other people in their affairs is ridiculous. Hang Tania! It isn't my fault. Do you know why I haven't bought you a ring? Because I haven't been able to find one. But I shall. I won't give you any example of the ordinary 'article de commerce'. I've been looking for a ring for months. This reminds me of a useful saying of Sir Fred Keeble to me on this yacht once (Professor of Botany at Oxford, & Lillah's spouse): 'success generally lags ten years behind the work which procures it.' And this reminds me that I often think how exasperating it must be for you not to have work. Still we are both doing all we can. And I confidently look forward to you having a great personal success in a play written by me—or in default by somebody else. Do you know the life-story of Henri Balaille, the famous (but impermanent) dramatist? He was a chemist (not pharmacist, but scientific). He fell in love with Berthe Badz, an actress of very considerable gifts who seemed doomed to tour the provinces for ever. He asked her what she wanted & she replied: 'To be a star in Paris.' This astonishing second-rate brilliant man turned to writing plays for her, & in a few years he did, by his plays, make her a star in Paris. It pains me to say that I have heard that she did not treat him well. On account of you I shall write more plays than I otherwise should. Indeed I was at the beginning of this year very near leaving the stage. Well, I like being intimate with you on both the physical & the intellectual planes. With most people an equal intimacy on both planes is not possible. I loved Sunday morning last; and also sharing your long guerilla warfare with shopkeepers on Sunday afternoon. I was just as tired as you were, but not a bit bored. This and our two excursions by car into the country were the best days I have had for years. My thoughts are now veering towards work again—a little. It is perhaps a good thing to have lost all touch with work for 10 days. I never knew it happen to me before. I must work—for both of us. I must go to bed reasonably and get sleep—for both of us. I must keep as young as I can—for both of us. And I *know* that for the preservation of youth and of industry in either man or woman, early hours, temperance, and general regularity are the sine qua non. How many people do I know, of both sexes, who in their too-ripe middle age are cursing the fact that in youth they drew over-drafts on the bank of energy and health! I remember a bookseller-printer in the terrible town of Burslem, Joseph Dawson, one of my most intimate friends. When he died at 66 or so, I ceased to go to the Five Towns except for funerals or the bankruptcies of my relatives. He was as young at 60 as I was at 40. I remember once when I made some sarcastic remark to him about Tennyson's *Idylls of the King*, tears came into his eyes. 'Don't say such a thing! Don't say such a thing!' he protested. The book had meant so much to him. He was 63 then. Fancy a man of 63 being so young that he could be so moved about a book! I shall never forget this incident, which seemed to me to be very beautiful. I shall use it sometime. I spent hours every day in that fellow's shop, and when he had to have all his teeth out at once, he insisted that I, and not his wife, should go with him to the dentists. And I remember how the teeth as the dentist snatched them out one after the other with astounding rapidity, flew all over the room. He was a J.P. & I would go and sit on the Bench with him. Well, it occurs to me that I have had vast numbers of friends to whom I owe much. I'll tell you something else. I do not really like seeing you dance with other men. I should be very annoyed if you didn't dance with other men, but I have that feeling. Never had it before! Percy told me

hat Olive, sister of Percy's wife and my once-dancing partner,
never dances with anyone but her husband now, because he
cannot bear it. She is a fool. She would have been perfect if she
hadn't been a fool, & I have often told her so. That he cannot
bear it shows how lamentably weak he is. Au revoir, mon douce
enfant. Je t'étreins.

A.B.

No address for you to write to yet.

275. Henri Balaille (1872–1922) began writing for Berthe Badz in 1894.
   Olive Ledward Nossiter: now Mrs Alexander Glendinning.

BERG / MS / 276
(*To Dorothy Cheston*)

Yacht Marie Marguerite
Ostende
1–8–23

My dearest girl,
    Another hopeless dawn. It blew *like hades* all night. Little
sleep. The wind dropped and veered to S.W. for a few hours
yesterday afternoon, & a S.W. wind would suit us, but it went
back early in the evening & blew worse than ever. This
morning is absolutely lovely, but that thrice-curst wind is still
blowing hard. Nor do I see any immediate chance of a change.
And yet I can't give an address here, & can't hear from you and
know about you. For if the wind did change we should fly off at
the next tide. I was most melancholy yesterday evening. I
couldn't read, so I went off to examine the Kursaal, and
assisted at part of a perfectly rotten concert. I got aboard at
10.30. Well, I was most melancholy. And still am, rather. I
realise more & more what a fantastic nuisance my insomnia
is—not only to me. How can one be loving & make love and be
vivacious and diverting when one is worn out physically with
lack of sleep? No answer. However, I'll leave this topic, as it
must be a great bore. But I tremble for next week. I've heard
from Tania, she still gives no address. She wires definitely that
she is bringing Captain Gillett on the 7th. So that's settled, & I
hope he'll be all right. I expect he will. I wish I could think who
he is. I can't. Now about that date—the 7th, which is Tuesday.
I doubt whether they'll be able to come earlier. Another thing, I

doubt whether the ship itself will be ready earlier. It might take
us a full 3 days to reach Southampton in this godless weather, &
we assuredly shan't start till tomorrow & might not start then
There are now six yachts held up here all waiting to start for
England. And I heard yesterday that the 11 yachts held up a
Ramsgate reached Dover with much difficulty & are now, with
others, held up at Dover. I wanted to paint & can't. It poured
here yesterday afternoon. I wanted to work & can't. I've only
collected about 1½ ideas out of 100 I want. There's one thing I
have done. I bought a ring. I do not say it is *the* Ring. But it is
certainly *a* ring—sapphire and brilliants. It is classic in style, &
thank heaven not a brand new one. I spent some hours
yesterday in examining the jewellers' shops of this city, and am
now in a position to say that I know a bit about them. I say this
you are worth buying a ring for, and this is no understatement
And I say this: you are worth writing a play for, & this is no
understatement either. I wonder what you are doing in
London, & I do hope you aren't having lonely evenings—
unless you want them. *I* never want them. I suppose that when
I have got a bit more used to the notion that you are attached to
me I shall begin to work again. Not before. As things are I seem
to spend about 75 per cent of my time in chasing your image
round & round in my so-called brain. Yes, I *do*. When you
charge me with being 'calm'—what I think is that it is a jolly
good thing for both of us that I am what you call 'calm'. When
you see me un-calm you had better look both ways at once for a
dug-out. It is a highly perilous thing for a man like me to be in
love. Still, I can't help it. Je t'embrasse bien, & whether you
will call this letter northern or southern in latitude I'm damned
if I know.

A.B

BERG / MS / 277   Yacht Marie Marguerite
(*To Dorothy Cheston*)   Southampton
                              Tuesday night
                              14–8–23

My dearest girl,
    'Yes.'
    And more. It is no doubt because you are gradually being

unfolded to me through my understanding better the idiom in which you express yourself. I do not mean only speech idiom, but every sort of idiom of manifestation of your being. Time is needed to learn such idiom. I can now discount your exaggerations of demeanour, allow for your diminishings, and translate some of your mutenesses into articulateness. All this is very difficult to explain even at all, & I am not really *trying* to explain it. But I know what I mean. The general result is that a juster appreciation of what you are about in the act of being alive prevents or lessens those disturbances which were caused by the violent differences between your idiom & mine. I knew I was all right with you at the start. That was an instinct, which precedes reasoning processes, which processes are very much slower, more suspicious, more exacting—and rightly so. (I have seldom written worse, but no matter.)

We have to be serious. I know that I can be of service to you and you to me. Now I am dissatisfied about the break in my work. Considering what I have been through these last few weeks in the way of emotional excitement, the break has really been very slight, and inevitable. But still it disturbs me. Work must be resumed, and at once. My peace of mind depends on it as much as on anything. I shall not be happy till it is in full swing again, & if I am not reasonably happy you will be upset, secretly worried. People cannot love satisfactorily whose consciences are not clear. I was an idiot to begin that play when I did. I had not the sense to refuse to yield to habit. On the other hand I have to urge *you* not to be deflected from *your* course by side issues & transient temptations. If you keep on as you are doing you are *bound* to get a job. Never be discouraged. There are many who have waited far longer than you have waited. (I did.) Try to organise your existence, especially in regard to study and finance. In the matter of dress you can safely rest on your laurels for a bit. I picture you making your disclosures to Daisy. That matter can only move slowly. The utmost caution is advisable. For me also. I have to think how I am going to account, in *my* domestic world, for my absences. I tell you another thing I should like, namely, to come to your abode sometimes for my afternoon snooze. I would snooze with you in the bedroom. I should love it. The afternoon is the leisured time for tenderness. Then I should stay to dinner, or we should go out for dinner, & neither sleep nor work would be interfered with. If they are interfered with there cannot be full satisfaction. I promise you to work only six days a week & not to work anyhow more than four afternoons a week and six mornings. And your work is quite equally important.

There were times when you were simply wonderful on the yacht. I like that nightcap idea immensely. I think you can understand anything. As I came back from the station, I encountered the enclosed oriental silver plaque necklace. It only wants a bit of black velvet to clasp it at the back. I think it is Turkish, about 50 or 60 years old. The evening is marvellously beautiful. If I am not gloomy at your absence it is because I am filled up with my resolve to work & to make *you* succeed. I hope you're not feeling forlorn & lonely in August hot London.

Je te bise tendrement,

A.B.

277. Daisy: Dorothy's maid.

BERG / MS / 278   Yacht Marie Marguerite
(*To Dorothy Cheston*)   Poole
                                    Sunday
                                    19–8–23

My dearest girl,

A curious fellow, that fellow Arthur Arnold Burnett. Himself he only calls 'Arthur', but his friends call him both 'Arthur' & 'Arnold'. His mother always marked his linen A.A.B. until she died, & then at last he was able to have his own way & have only the 2 initials, which he likes because they are the first of the alphabet. It was when he was in New York that some experts there pointed out to him that he had a great natural gift for really high-class advertising. He might have had lucrative posts there, but he would not leave his family, which is entirely dependent on him. He got a lucrative post in England—Southampton & London—and would have plenty of money to spend were it not for the aforesaid family, which treats him very tyrannically, & with whom his secretly married wife is not at all on good terms. The poor chap is a very bad sleeper, & the constant travelling between Southampton & London does him no good. Under an appearance of wonderful calm, he is in reality a highly nervous subject & has to be treated (as a contrast with the treatment by his family, to which he is most absurdly devoted) with great care & consideration. As a consequence of his nerves & his work he is at times subject to dyspepsia & cannot eat everything he sees. What precisely are the circumstances which make it advisable for his marriage to be kept secret I have not yet heard. The whole thing is a strange romance. He is exceedingly fond of music & might have been a professional musician had he chosen & had he been free of his nuisance of a family. He hates society, but is interested in the stage. That was how he met his wife, as once, to oblige a friend, he did some marvellous theatrical advertising.

There are lots more details, but I will not weary you.

As for the ring for that lady, I don't see how I can possibly get it on the present cruise. But you might get it, as your taste is very reliable & as her finger has exactly the same circumference as yours, & I could reimburse you later. I am sure she would approve of your taste.

Let me talk of ourselves a little for a change. I sailed up to Poole this early afternoon. A fine wind. The voyage took only an hour. I am expecting my secretary & my literary disciple tomorrow. The glass has risen, but the rain has fallen & is falling, & no one sees any immediate hope of better weather. Most deplorable. There is a chance of me being able to let the yacht for September. By the way that curious fellow Burnett told me he should positively come up to town on the 31st & should stay with his wife for one night before rejoining his family. He is absurdly fussy about the quality of his bed, it seems. Sometimes it is not convenient for his wife to receive him. In that case he doesn't stay late. A meek person, I imagine. Now I meant to talk about ourselves & here I am talking about that fellow again. He was very communicative last night—for him. He said that his new passion was a mere quicksand unless based on comradeship. (It appears that he is a great friend & pal of his wife's.) Rather good this, I thought.

Je t'embrasse tendrement.

A.B.

278. Twice in the *Journals* in 1927 Bennett mentions working on a 'private novel about Arthur'. No manuscript of the work is known. Also unknown is whether it is

connected to the *conte libertin* mentioned on p. 367 or the pornographic novel mentioned on p. 523.

BERG / MS / 279   Yacht Marie Marguerite
(*To Dorothy Cheston*)   Poole
                                         Monday 7.30 p.m.
                                         20–8–23

My dearest girl,

No! Your letters are not too long. And you are entitled to express yourself freely; it is up to the receiver to interpret justly, as you say. The generalisation about women in my book is honestly the fruit of my long experience, & it coincides with the general masculine view. I cannot honestly say that I have noticed much this trait in you. There must of course be exceptions; that is why I continually saved myself with the 'seldom'.

No! Since you ask me I do *not* want to go to Wells. I should have to meet a perfect stranger & get used to her & trim my sails & so on. Whereas I have been steadily looking forward to spiritual repose with you *alone*, which I shall certainly need. Also I had decided to go to my own house to sleep on Sept 1st. There is immense virtue in the first of a month. I have a vast amount of work in hand & in my head, & this work must be done. And before it can be attacked I shall have a certain amount of organising to do in my own house & at least a full day in clearing up with Miss Nerney the arrears of 3 months' non-urgent things. These must be disposed of before I can get to work. I never do any good unless I make a programme & adhere to it. When I get back I shall have 13 short stories, 5 long articles, a play, and a novel all definitely demanding to be done. Believe me, this is a great deal. I can make the acquaintance of Frieda later. I do not like cross-country travelling, nor picnicking in farm houses, nor strange surroundings, when my head is bursting with work, & responsibilities, & you, and a very changed existence with its new experiences. Nay more, I don't like them at any time. And I am always in mortal fear of that phrase a 'few days' when it is a question of my programme. I trust you to realise the way my brain works at my age as I try to realise the way your brain works at yours. My brain is bound to be more rigid than yours. The convolutions of it are fixed. The convolutions of yours are not. Am I clear?

I got your letter one minute after I had posted my last to you! 6 p.m.

The Harrods purchases sound inviting. But you won't expect me to sleep much the first night, because it is absolutely certain that I shan't. I should much like you to buy me a pajama suit that suits you. The size known as 42 is a shade big, but allows for shrinkage. 41 would be better. They are *not* cheap, these things. I'm expecting Miss Nerney every minute. Now I do want you imaginatively to understand that I shall be seriously undone if I do not start on what lies before me on the 1st of the month. This doesn't in the least mean that I shall not see you. I shall want to see you, & shall work better, incidentally, for seeing you, but my machinery, the mechanics of my work, must not be deranged. The mere thought of upsetting it sets every nerve in my body on edge. So that's that. I love you & kiss you in all manner of places.

A.B.

279. *Our Women*, published in 1920, offers any number of generalizations about women to which Dorothy might have taken objection. See the Introduction, p. xxxvii.

Some of the stories that Bennett wrote at this time appeared in the collection *Elsie and the Child* in 1924. He was working on the *Royal Magazine* articles (see pp. 403, 404) and the play, *Mr. Prohack*. The next novel was *Lord Raingo*, which he did not begin writing until 13 May 1925.

Frieda: unidentified.

BERG / MS / 280   Yacht Marie Marguerite
(*To Dorothy Cheston*)   Poole
                                    8.30 a.m. Tuesday
                                    21 Augt 1923

My dearest girl,

I am just breathless from my exercises, & my hand shakes. I put the enclosed letter in an envelope last night, & have torn it open this morning (waste: 1½d) as I thought 2 might go in the same envelope. Do you know, what I worry about a lot is the exasperation which you must suffer in not getting a part. The one remedy is the remedy you are applying,—work. Still I have an idea amounting almost to a conviction that you will get a part soon. I did *not* have a good night last night. Although I have plenty of things on my mind I really think the insomnia was due to having eaten a little of a savoury which I had had prepared for Duff—anchovies in it. *The weather is frightful.* We cannot move. The South cone is flying at the harbour office for a gale. This is the 6th day of hard contrary wind. Well, I have never been able to get up any enthusiasm for motor cars. I think a good car is a really beautiful object & that its mechanism is most laudable. But at its best I regard it as merely a mechanical device for getting from one spot on the earth's surface to another. I think also it is on the whole the best of such devices. Some country motoring is highly agreeable, but for me all motoring within 30 miles of London is chiefly an affliction, especially with the growing number of amateur drivers that there are spread-eagling about. (Permit me respectfully to say that I drove cars for 8 years & never touched a thing.) I never cared for driving. Still many admirable persons seem to enjoy it all right. I notice, my sweet child, that you are still preoccupied with my 'pedestal'. Believe me I am intimately acquainted with a considerable number of people of considerable importance, & I have never observed that *on that account* their intimate friends stick them on a pedestal. Rather the reverse. (Strangers & mere acquaintances of course unavoidably do so.) If men & women are on pedestals the reason lies not in their achievements but in their masterful or difficult characters. There are tens of thousands of ordinary men & women who in their own homes live permanently on a pedestal, far more so than the majority of really important people. I know that *my* intimate friends don't keep me on a pedestal, because, for one reason, they are well aware that I hate it. All I ask for is the common politeness which is due to *any*body, even from an intimate. I am invariably polite myself until I perceive that the only way to obtain such politeness is to withhold it from the offender. Then I am apt to let go. It is the one method, in my experience. Turning the other cheek, to which I have given an extensive trial, never succeeds. I think that as a rule Saturdays would be the best night, for both of us. Any other would probably interfere with our work, & nothing is more likely than such interferences to militate against smoothness. Of course it can't always be Saturday, as I might have to weekend or you might. Though God knoweth I do little such. This sleeping out is an immense enterprise for me, with my habits; but I see no alternative & I doubt not that the results will be excellent. My party here is now complete, & I have already begun to instruct Pauline in the way she should go.

My dearest child, I embrace you closely & ardently.

A.B.

280. Duff: Alistair Tayler.

BERG / MS / 281   Yacht Marie Marguerite
(*To Dorothy Cheston*)   Poole
                              Wednesday
                              22–8–23

My dearest girl,

I thank thee. The silken thing arrived this morning & is very beautiful. I shall wear it as a muffler. It is too thick for a waistband, as it will not go through the belt attachments in the trousers. To do this it would have to be cut in two. But it is a fine thing. The Thermos has not yet arrived. I suppose it will during the day. I am not so anxious about it now, as I am sleeping very well. I often wake up, but I must have had 7 hours in all last night—rather too much, I felt, as it gave me a slight headache. Thank heaven I'm working every day. I have an *immense* amount to do, & my work is of course the bed rock foundation of my existence & of our joint existence. I have not made myself clear to you about my work. I can work in any place, *if I stay in it*, but I cannot possibly divide my work between two places. It is out of the question. I have to have a complete apparatus for a very delicate, complicated, & exhausting business. I have to have a relatively fixed environment. And I cannot shift it about every few days. I only work in the yacht because I stay in it. Smoothness and routine are essential to me; & the absence of them would merely ruin the work & drive me into a state of nerves which you would be the first to regret. I am getting rather worried about this, & I want you to realise it. I never had the least intention of working in your abode. I might meditate there occasionally, but no more. I am a tremendous worker, & my habits *cannot* at this stage of my life be altered without disastrous consequences. My feelings on this are intense. I cannot yet say how things will turn out about weekends. As I look at the matter at present, a weekend means a serious upset of my Mondays. You don't suppose that I can leave you on Monday mornings, after all the excitations of being with you, and go straight to my work! Because I cannot. In the ordinary way all my weekend mail has been dealt with before 9 o'clock on Monday mornings, & then I am free for *work*. I never count anything as work except creative writing. However, I certainly do not expect you to grasp, without some experience of it, the sort of dynamo that you are attached to. You will grasp it bit by bit, I am sure. My notion was to leave you on Sunday night. However, we cannot decide all this now, either one way or the other. In order to judge the matter fairly, you have only to think what your attitude would be if you were playing, and anyone were to suggest enjoyments which would impair your artistic efficiency. Many stage artists do constantly indulge in pleasures which impair their efficiency, but you wouldn't be one of them. Unquestionably our relationship, though it has obvious advantages, has also disadvantages, and the disadvantages have to be fairly faced. Three pints cannot be poured out of a quart pot. About that important day Friday 31st., I expect to come up from some such place as Torquay on that day, & I shall have had considerable work in fixing up everything for leaving the yacht—and still more if I succeed in letting it—in addition to 4 hours in the train. Hence I shall not be in quite the first freshness of morning. *I* was rather hoping for a thrilling repast at 284. However it is *your* birthday, not mine, & if you *prefer* to dine out we will dine at the Hyde Park Hotel, which is one of the best restaurants in London, and near to. We cannot have a spectacular dinner, as I shall have no evening dress. If I can catch the 12.10 I shall arrive chez toi soon after 4. If I only catch the 2.25 I should arrive about 7.15. This will depend on circs. I may not even get to Torquay at all. The weather is still ghastly, and at this moment—noon—more impossible than ever. It is fine about the piano. I have heard from the Wigmore people & have dictated a letter in reply. I doubt whether your Woolworth idea for the temporary ring is a sound one. You had much better buy a plain gold ring. These are the most respectable! For myself I move in such circles that I have never seen anything else on a woman's hand. Anything else seems to me highly untraditional. Pauline Smith, need I say, is once again laid up with neuralgia! What a life she has! Duff Tayler leaves tomorrow. Miss Nerney as usual is unfailingly cheerful, smiling, and even-tempered; and ready to do anything. I see your point about leaving on Saturday morning & will stay till Sunday anyhow. Do not imagine that I do not realise & appreciate the fullness of your desire to make things smooth & for the best. I utterly do. But I have to tell you the facts for you to start on, or from. Several times you have said & written to me: 'You will have trouble with me.' *If* I had to say anything similar to you, it would be: 'You will have trouble with my work.' Je te bise tendrement, et je te bise encore, plus tendrement.

A.B.

P.S. I certainly have the most perfect confidence in you about arranging beds & bedrooms comfortably, but I don't want you to do too much. I am not much reassured about your back, which disquiets me. You are probably over-exerting yourself in some way. God knoweth.

By the way, how shall I turn on the light without emerging from bed? Pardon. You have no doubt thought of this detail.

A.B.

BERG / MS / 282
(*To Dorothy Cheston*)

Yacht Marie Marguerite
Poole
Wednesday
22–8–23

My dearest girl,
Although it is only 5½ hours since I wrote to you, & in fact now only 6 o'clock or less, you are to imagine that it is in the middle of the night & I am unable to sleep and you & I are having a soothing chat about things in general & about nothing,—the sort of chat that only people like you & me *can* have. I have undoubtedly allowed myself to be worried today, though I was positively resolved to write 600 words of my article and *have* written them at last. To begin with the weather has been fantastically dreadful. It blew one of the big passenger steamers on to a sand bank at the mouth of this harbour yesterday; and today the gale is decidedly worse. Miss Nerney

& Duff went ashore after lunch to transact business, in the launch, & during the voyage back they were *soaked* by spray, & Edgar & the other fat man were tossed about like corks. Yet this spot is in a comparatively narrow channel & at least a mile from the harbour mouth, & the harbour mouth is at least 4 miles from the open sea. So you may guess what the open sea *is* like. Round this ship the water is white all over with spray blown off the tops of waves. The ship doesn't roll, but it shakes with the blows of the wind. All this is exceedingly annoying, as it is absolutely certain we can't leave even tomorrow. Secondly I am exercised all the time about the mystery of your back. I thought you ought to see a doctor about that. Thirdly, Pauline Smith has been completely laid aside today by her neuralgia (due to an ear affliction), with pain so acute that she couldn't open her eyes! She is now rather convalescent again. Fourthly I am doing articles while I want to do short stories; but they have to be done. Fifthly I have been disturbing myself about the mere mechanics of our immediate future. I know quite well that they will settle themselves & that our combined wisdom will prevail, & yet I continually reflect upon them, because, I suppose, I am convinced that brain-work employed upon even the minorest details of these problems will certainly save trouble later on. The course is not without perils, but then, as I have so ably and so often said, life without risk is death. I've heard from Anthony today. He still wants to talk to me about my film rights—while professing that he agrees with my principles & that he does *not* want the Company to get something for nothing. He returns to town immediately, full of resolves to get the thing through & make it hum. I hope he will. I should very much like to meet Mrs. Cochran & see what sort of a woman she is. For this reason, I was positively assured that she personally assisted at the notorious orgies between C.B. and the dreadful Dolly Sisters, than whom I have never seen more coarse creatures on the stage. My sweet child, there are strange people on earth. I am *sick* of this cruise. I *long* to be at 284, which I now regard as a haven from all manner of weather. Nevertheless I can't and won't arrive before the 31st. I will see the affair through, & meanwhile drug myself with a moderate dosage of work. By the way, interesting temperamental people seldom spell correctly. George Moore is one of the world's worst spellers & one of the world's best writers. Your spelling has much originality, which pleases me. But I beg you ma belle, not to plunge into excess. Niece is not neice. I draw the line there.

Still, the power of my love is not impaired, nor my embrace weakened. I kiss thee, my sweet girl.

A.B.

282. Edgar: Edgar Gentry.
Anthony: Anthony Ellis.
Mrs Evelyn Cochran, wife of Charles Cochran (1873–1951), the theatrical manager and producer. The Dolly sisters were a famous variety team of the day.
George Moore (1852–1933). For letters to him see Vols. II and III.

BERG / MS / 283   Yacht Marie Marguerite
(*To Dorothy Cheston*)   Poole
                              Friday
                              24–8–23

My dearest girl,

Thanks for your letter. I note what you say about your midnight letter. I will say no more about it except that to write it was excusable, but to post it was not. At your age & with your experience you should have had more savoir vivre than to post it. I fear that with your unconscious egotism you did not reflect what an enormous upset this act, due immediately to your coming home tired from golf, would make in my mind. You sent it off without even waiting for my reply (which came by return of post) to your mandate about weekends. I know that you unfortunately cannot help at intervals going off at the deep end in this way. I remember that you have several times told me that I should have 'a lot of trouble' with you. I do not resent it. I do not grudge the 'trouble'. But this will not prevent me from putting my point of view before you with the same fullness & the same plain-spokenness as you have been using to me.

I entirely and most actively differ from your general argument that I seek to impose my will on yours. You need not send my letters back to me. I know what was in them. But when you see me you can show the alleged offending passages to me, & I warn you that you will receive an exceedingly lively defence of them, & in particular against the charge that they justified your 'indignation'. The fact is that I have continually acquiesced in your imposing *your* will on *me*. Who arranged the whole plan for 284? It was not my plan. It was yours. You produced it and laid it down, & I agreed to all the main points. You issued the mandate & I accepted it. But when I dissent in one detail you are up in arms instantly with talk about mandates and you dash off 'All is over'. And I do wish once again, my child, that you would not indulge in that novelette note of 'the man's game'. It 'makes the judicious grieve'. Suppose that I began about the woman's game, what a fuss there would be! I fully agree with your estimate of what you wrote, but did not send, about 'a cockney Saturday night'. You seem to think that your inward life is different from, and finer than, other people's. It isn't. You remind me of those ladies who say in earnest tones: 'I cannot bear to see animals suffer.' (Ten to one they are wearing an Osprey plume.) As if to indicate that they are not like others, are superior in sensitiveness to others, as though others can bear quite easily to see animals suffer. You say that anything less than a whole-hearted sort of thing is so difficult for one. It is no more difficult for you than it is for me or for 10,000 people. You say that I like 'being agreed with'. I like being agreed with just as much as you like being agreed with, and not more. You explain that after you have thought the best of me there remain certain 'bitternesses' in your mind, and that you hide them. Precisely the same is true of me towards you. No person's mind can be fully exposed, and to expose it fully is one of the very worst sins against the social virtues. Any conceivable society would break up under such a strain. We all have secret thoughts & there is no special merit whatever in hiding them. I could say with precisely the same justification and sincerity as you make a similar statement to me: 'As a rule I silence these revolts & you receive my second thoughts, which are not a bit submissive really, but are dictated by a sense that since women wish to play the game they do, men must play up to it if they wish to preserve the least trace of peace & happiness. One can always find a ghastly tongue in one's cheek.' Everyone has these special qualities. To me your impatience at the slightest difference of view was new because I had never met its equal before. Etc. And I might also say to you: 'Most people in my position wouldn't dream of making trouble. They would say, I will give what is needed—take what is given—keep my emo-

tions out of the whole thing—*and take my emotional life where &
when I can get it.*' But supposing I did. I wonder what in God's
name you would say.

I doubt whether even yet you have sufficiently reflected
about my work. The bulk of my work, & the most important of
it, has always been done in the mornings. And it will always
have to be so. For me to lose the morning is to lose the day. It
has always been astounding to me that people—especially
artists themselves—*will* instinctively think that a creative artist's work can be shifted about & done at any time. If I had been
the head of a big commercial enterprise & had to be at a certain
place at certain times, or if I had been a successful barrister &
had to be at my chambers at 8.30 a.m. to read my briefs (as
many do), you would have accepted my hours without the
faintest murmur. But because I am a creative artist—with work
far more exacting, exhausting & delicate than those other
important male individuals, it is assumed that hours don't
matter, really, to me. I should very much like to know what
Wells, Conrad, or Galsworthy would say if a suggestion was
made to them to change their hours. I should very much like
you to hear the asperity of their remarks on the matter.
Considering that I have done & shall do everything in my
power to help *you* in *your* work, I rely upon you in due time to do
the same service to me & not to try to make me feel like a
criminal in the proper execution of my duty. There is another
point. I have recently very considerably increased my financial
obligations, and I have been deeply glad to do so. But the extra
money will not make itself; it will have to be made.

Lastly, I honestly don't know a man less 'Eastern' in his
attitude to women than myself. Unless all my sociological
books are grossly insincere you must be well aware of this fact.
If not to agree wholly with every mandate issued to me is
Eastern, then I am Eastern, I admit. But you will have to be
Queen Elizabeth or Catherine the greatest.

That is all on the subject of your recent outburst. I beg you
not to imagine that I am nursing secret resentments & grudges.
I am incapable of such things. I am merely answering you in
your own idiom, as I am perfectly entitled to answer you; and
as, indeed, I am bound to answer you. Please take my words as
I take yours.

I shall be delighted to take you to dine at the Savoy (though to my mind it leaves far more than most alleged first-class restaurants to be desired), but this cannot happen on Saturday Sept 1st, for the reason I have already given you,—I shall not have my evening clothes at hand. When I have, which will be on the Monday, I will take you there with the greatest pleasure to our first dinner.

The weather here is super-appalling. Yesterday there was a gale accompanied by many hours of soaking, driving rain. Today is little better. It is highly improbable that we shall be able to leave tomorrow. Still I am working. I could not work yesterday, but I am working today, with the remains of a neuralgia from yesterday. I do hope, my dearest, that you have seen the doctor and are taking his advice. I shouldn't myself have thought that golf was much good for a disturbed back, but perhaps it is.

And now the rock embraces thee tenderly,

A.B.

BERG / MS / 284   Yacht Marie Marguerite
(*To Dorothy Cheston*)   Poole
                             Monday
                             27–8–23

My dearest girl,

Many thanks for Saturday-Sunday letter. We are still here! Gale still blowing! Still quite impossible to move! No present prospect of improvement. I've finished the last article I shall do on board. This, with the weather, makes me think of coming to town on Wednesday, to you. The yacht *may* be able to move then towards Torquay. If so, Pauline S. & Miss Nerney will go in it. But I can see no advantage in *me* taking a day, or two days, rough sail in order to go further away from you. So I have told them I may depart on Wednesday. I slept rather better last night, but have a powerful neuralgia. I'm very glad you've seen Dr. Griffin. I think he is a good man. One of the funniest things I ever heard was àpropos of him. He was off Ecuador (or Uruguay) in a ship, & the President sent for him urgently. The President had syphilis, which Griffin cured. As a reward the President invested him with the *Order of the Redeemer—of the 2nd class.* Griffin also was the man referred to in my *Things*, who was given up for dead & after coming back received a bill for 'Memorial Service (full Choral) 7 guineas' (or some such sum). I laughed aloud when I read one part of your letter, where you say: 'We can't very well arrive at harmonious conclusions if we didn't *both* say what we feel is essential to the making of harmony.' Most true. I have never shown the slightest objection to you saying it; but when *I* said it, you wrote to bust up the whole thing. I have no 'accumulations' against you. I think you are extremely self-centred & egotistical, & that you often do not *sufficiently* reflect upon the effect which your acts & plans will have on other people. Also that you have a marked sex-bias; also that you have the 'grievance' illusion & the 'personal bad-luck' illusion. Also that you have a noticeable tendency towards hysteria. But don't think these things trouble me. They don't. *If* they in fact exist, you can't help them and I allow for them. Moreover I take people as they are, as wholes, recognising the absurdity of trying to chop pieces off them or add pieces on to them. Considered as a whole character & mortal frame, I beg to say that I regard you as the goods. I have now sufficiently humoured your wish.

I think. Well, I'm looking forward to seeing you *in* the room. There is a prom conc. We might go to on Thursday, if I arrive on Wednesday. I desire thee to understand that though there is a probability of me coming Wednesday, it is not certain yet. I will however wire you definitely one way or the other tomorrow, Tuesday. I fear Wednesday will be rushing you, mais que veux-tu.

It is now pouring with rain.

We shall certainly be here till Wednesday morning, as the laundry won't be back till Tuesday night.

Ma belle créature, je te bise très tendrement et j'attends avec impatience notre petite lune de miel, tout en esperant que tu seras en bonne santé et bien disposée. (No, you don't know what the last 2 words mean. They mean 'in the humour for' a thing.)

A.B.

27–8–23   3.30 P.M.
P.S. I said to myself, 'I won't fasten the envelope, as there may

be something to add.' And there was. Your 6,000,000 telegram came. This is all right. The weather is worse than ever. *Terrific* squalls. I have now *decided* that I shall come on Wednesday. And you may count on me arriving some time between 2 and 4.30, for tea, unless I wire to the contrary. I don't know yet what train I shall come by, and if I did I wouldn't tell you, lest you might have the beautiful but mistaken idea of meeting me at Waterloo. Strange as it may appear, I should not desire you to meet me at Waterloo or anywhere. I want to see you first in your drawing-room as the chatelaine thereof & not in the row and hurlyburly of stations or elsewhere. It might be well for us to go out for dinner. You have been too lonely, & have been eating practically all your meals at Daisy's hands, which must have been rather trying. But don't let's eat out Friday night.

Just had to let more chain out on the anchors, which were dragging under the fearsome wind pressure. Miss Nerney has already begun to pack up books and things. I'm not going to leave any *valuable* books here for Colonel Elwes's military young family to spoil.

I hope your back is continuing to get better & that your menstrual indisposition is proceeding normally.

My neuralgia is a shade better, but then I had a bottle of stout for lunch. I was much too neuralgic to do my exercises this morning.

Your letter this morning gave me the greatest pleasure, though I *did* laugh at a bit of it.

Je te re-bise tout ce délicieux corps.

284. *Things That Have Interested Me, Second Series, 1923.*
Colonel Elwes and his family were to rent the *Marie Marguerite* from Bennett.

KENNERLEY / MS / 285
(*To Tertia Kennerley*)

75, Cadogan Square
3-9-23

My dear Tertia,
    Many thanks. I hasten to tell you that just before your letter I got one from Ida—Jean—Mimi, in which were fine appreci-ations of yourself. Ida indeed said that you are 'the nicest woman I know'. Enough. I presume. You are right as to the

relative value of the members of the family. Ida is easily first. Mimi is the next; she suffers from lack of marriage, & from hard work & hard play. I note all you say about Marguerite. It must have been very trying indeed for you, especially as about 50% to 75% of what she says in these moods is not only untrue, but has no basis of any kind; it is not even truth twisted out of all shape. Yet I think she believes it at the moment, no matter what it may be. She is not responsible—exactly like her mother—& must be regarded accordingly. I hope she will continue to see you, as your influence is bound to be good. She is evidently very unhappy, & I wish I could do something for her. I hope Legros will not desert her—& as long as she gets £2,000 a year from me I don't think he will. Not only jealousy is at the root of the trouble. Suspiciousness is also in it. She lives in an atmosphere of suspiciousness, always did. This talk about the workhouse etc. is merely the fruit of a desire to get some substantial capital sum out of me. She is always trying to do it, and always failing of course. Apparently she can't or won't realise that she runs no more risk now than she would have run had she remained with me. Indeed, less, as I have bound myself to bequeath to her 3/4s of my goods; and also as she has unfettered use of £2,000 a year, & can & certainly does save. To me & to others she now & then expresses a deep devotion to my welfare; yet she causes endless trouble to my income tax agents by refusing to sign papers which must be signed by her. And this although out of sheer silly good will I pay her super-tax, which I am under no obligation to pay. We 'correspond' only in this sense: that she loses no opportunity of writing to me, usually to get something, & that I reply as briefly & politely as possible. On my birthday she sent down a note of good wishes. So I suppose I must do the same, though it will mean another letter from her. She has made two serious attempts to get me to call on her, but I have tactfully refused, as the notion seems to me to be merely equivalent to a demand to ignite a powder barrel. If she sees you again & mentions this you might give her your views. Having had enough of the violence of S.W. gales I have put myself ashore & let the yacht for 3 weeks to a simple-minded Colonel's wife.

Love to all,

Yours, A.B.

285. Tertia and the girls were holidaying at Carantec, and Marguerite visited them there.

CAMBRIDGE / MS / 286
(*To Richard Bennett*)

75, Cadogan Square
7–9–23

My dear Rich,

Thanks for yours of the 4th. Our correspondence seems to be getting decidedly mixed up. I now know no longer when I write to you nor when you write to me. Regularity has vanished: which is most regrettable.

No, you did not say 'post-prox'. And if you had said 'post-prox' the phrase would have been inexcusable. Civilised people do not employ such singular diction.

How much will it cost you to fly from Manch. to London?

I got letters from you criticising Margaret & letters from Margaret criticising you. I expect you are both at fault. I know that her manners sometimes leave something to be desired (don't tell her I said so, of course), & I suspect (she does not say) that she regards you as rather conceited. She also has an immense opinion of herself. However, I am doing the best I can for both of you, & I hope all will be well. There is some genuine stuff in Margaret, & she made an extraordinarily favourable impression on my friends when she spent a few days here earlier in the year.

Tania played the enormous Symphonic Variations (piano & orch.) of Bax last night at the Promenade Concert, and had a very rousing reception indeed: which she well deserved. She & her band came here afterwards—Dorothy Cheston, A. Bax, Bacharach, Stephanie (surname unknown), Tania's younger sister, Efga Myers, husband ditto, & a Dane I've never seen before. The girls stole every rose I had in the house, & left after midnight with their cavaliers. Still, I am in great form for work today.

Harold Hales (the original of 'The Card') is coming to tea today. I need not say he asked himself. He would. He is now home from the East & is writing short stories. He writes really rather well.

Middlemen v. producer. Middlemen make more money, sometimes: but for an interesting life, I say producer every time. It depends what you want. To do something worth doing, or to be a parasite on the producers.

Your education must be completed, job waiting or no job waiting. I don't see you undergoing a 5 year apprenticeship beginning at the age of 23.

Love,

Your reflective uncle,

A.B.

286. Margaret: Margaret Beardmore.

Alfred Bacharach, editor of *Lives of the Great Composers*, scientist and chemist by profession; Stephanie: unidentified; Olga Cohen, also a musician; Efga Myers, an actress who had appeared on the London stage since 1911.

BERG / MS / 287

(*To Dorothy Cheston*)

75, Cadogan Square

5–x–23

My dearest girl,

Well, I had 1½ hours sleep again last night, despite every effort and precaution. I have now put my play definitely aside, as I cannot even keep my thoughts on it; & pressing contracts will force me to leave it now for 2 or 3 months. Which is very disturbing & disappointing—quite apart from the loss of time, time being money. Not that I am worrying about that. But I am still worrying about something else. When you asked me last night, in an interval of 30 seconds or so while Richard hunted taxis, if I was worrying and I said I wasn't, I've no doubt you comprehended that I only gave that answer because I specially wanted not to raise electricity just then. I am still worrying because you have assured me (& I appreciate the compliment) that you will not disobey the doctor's advice *when you are with me*—only when I am not there. The doctor's advice was that you were to confine yourself to 'a little wine'. I simply can't talk easily when I am in a state of nerves—and my condition can always be judged by the ease or difficulty with which I talk—and so I thought I would write to you. I know that I am putting you in a difficult position by continuing this subject, and I fully admit that you have taken all that I have said magnificently and with the most adorable goodwill and the nicest affectionate disposition to consider my feelings. Therefore I hesitate the more to continue about it. But I know that the last thing you would wish would be for me to conceal my thoughts from you. Hence I am writing, & I think you will bear with me patiently, as before. Anyhow, the mere fact that I can think about this one subject for a whole week & more, to the exclusion of all else, is some proof of the place which you hold in my heart, isn't it?

I absolutely believe all you tell me about your habits in the past, & I know roughly what your present habits are. I admit that I was a little startled when you told me about double whiskies, and solitary drinks, and 'no one to care'. But I am convinced that you have never taken alcohol immoderately, even to a slight degree. Nor have I ever suggested such a thing. Nor was my letter to the doctor primarily about alcohol. It was to let him know that I did not think the results of his treatment entirely successful (I was responsible for recommending him to you); the alcohol question was only a part, & not the main part, of the letter.

What I do think is, first, that you have a natural predisposition to *like* alcohol, and second that you make far too little of the dangers of alcohol, and third that you do not realise what the physiological effects of alcohol are. That is all.

I want to make one or two general remarks about these matters.

The people to whom alcohol is the most dangerous are the gifted, the finely-organised, the highly emotional—*not* ordinary plain persons. You can begin with Coleridge and Lamb. And you can go on to Maurice Baring, E. V. Lucas, George Mair, Maire O'Neill, Dion Calthrop, Marjorie Gordon, Cissie Loftus, etc. etc. When I first met Cissie Loftus she was divine in every way. She took to drink little by little. Then to drugs. She is now supposed to have been 'saved' (I hope she has) by Eva Moore. Eva Moore knew the business. Her husband, Harry Esmond, drank himself to death. Nobody is exempt from the risks of alcohol. Everybody thinks himself exempt. There never yet was an alcoholic subject who was not convinced, until it was too late, that he could drop the habit quite easily whenever he chose, and that he drank less than most people. There never yet was an alcoholic subject who could not always find a good reason for having a drink. To take alcohol is like keeping a tiger-cub in the house as a pet. The cub is delightful and charming for a long time. But keep him too long & one day he will growl without warning and maul you & perhaps kill you. I am certainly not suggesting for you an alcoholic future. Far from it. But I am suggesting that you are specially exposed to the risks of alcohol. Youth, genius & beauty are no protection whatever against them. I fear that *I* should have become alcoholic, like my two brothers; I was saved from it by the fact that alcohol always gave me the most infernal indigestion and sick-headaches. (Not that I am claiming either youth, genius, or beauty!)

In nearly every case of alcoholism, the thing is begun through taking alcohol as a remedy for tiredness. Alcohol is not a remedy for tiredness, or rather it is only a temporary remedy. It always leaves you worse than before. It is a scientific fact that nobody can dispute, that alcohol impairs all the physical and mental faculties. It may be useful in special crises, *is* useful; and it is less dangerous to the old, whose appetites are sobered by age. But as a bulwark against any continuous or ordinary strain, it is utterly deceitful & in the highest degree perilous. Most alcohol is merely a stimulant—like any other stimulating drug. Beer, stout, and red wine are a food as well as a stimulant. (And food also is a stimulant in itself.) When fatigued, what the body wants is chiefly *nourishment*. The nourishment itself will stimulate. Hot milk, hot milk-and-water, bovril, marmite, are all infinitely more efficacious against fatigue than alcohol. All alcoholic subjects are convinced that they do not 'like' and cannot take, when fatigued, anything but alcohol. It is an illusion. You now understand why I was so incensed against Donald's midnight drinking of champagne because he was tired.

People who live an open-air life can withstand lots of alcohol for a long time. Those who live an enclosed life (vitiated air of theatres and dressing-rooms) cannot.

You are about to undergo a tremendous strain—12 performances a week—fifty hours a week at least in a theatre. You will unquestionably feel drawn to alcohol for relief.

You are not the first person who has called me a fanatic about alcohol. Plenty of people have. The last one was Dr. Frank

Shufflebotham, an intimate friend of Griffin's & of mine. He
called me a fanatic for years. He called me 'unbalanced', & far
worse names. The last I heard of him, a few weeks ago, was that
Griffin had had to go down to the Five Towns to treat him again
for delirium tremens. And I shall not soon forget him having
D.T.'s in the middle of the night in my flat, & Fred & me
listening to his impassioned assertions that some film people
were crowding in a corner of the bedroom & taking a film of
him.

You know that I adore you; that I am completely wrapped
up in you; & that I would do anything to ensure your complete
success in life—the sort of really brilliant success which you
deserve. I am not making any accusation against your beloved
self. There is no charge to bring. But I should feel constantly
unhappy, and guilty, if I did not put before you in the plainest
possible way my view of the whole matter. You have aspired to
what ought to be my 'trust' in you. There can be no question of
trust. You are not a unique human being, saved by some special
destiny from the risks that all of us have to run. You are subject
to those risks, & more subject to them than most people.
Nothing can move me from this position, and no doctor will try
to deny it.

If I urged you to become a total abstainer I would accept this
charge of being a fanatic. But I do not. I know the good
qualities of alcohol as well as anybody. And I was saying
twenty years before you that there must be *something* in an
institution which had triumphed for thousands of years. I still
say so. But the bad side of alcohol certainly far exceeds the good
side.

I am making no attack on your 'sturdy independence'. I am
telling you my views, which are the views of all people of
experience. I quite understand your objection to binding
yourself by any hard-and-fast rules, though you would bind
yourself fast enough to rules if you thought it was a question of
your complexion or if you were liable to tuberculosis, for
instance. I will agree that you are not 'that kind of person',
though I must tell you that a healthy objection to hard-and-fast
rules is also a characteristic of the advanced alcoholic! I would
not now urge you to bind yourself to hard-and-fast rules. But if
you are to break wise rules, I would far sooner you broke them

when I was present than when I was not present, provided I concurred in the breakage, as I sometimes would. I have had the most terrible and tragic worry for nine years, and my forebodings of woe all turned out true. (Not that I regret it now.) You can only stop me from worrying in one way, & that is by saying that you will never take anything containing any form of spirits except when I am present. Don't tell me I have no *right* to suggest this. I do not claim any right. Certainly not. And if my peace of mind & my work are to be interfered with I shall put it down to my excessive concern for you. I shall not blame you. But it will be impossible for me to prevent some of the consequences of my state of mind from disagreeably affecting yourself. That will be a misfortune, springing from my perhaps undue regard for the longest possible continuance of your beauty and the fullest exploitation of your gifts.

Now I daresay I have been clumsy here & there in this letter. But it is the best I can do in present circumstances, & it had to be done somehow. Neuralgia has at last supervened, & I don't feel in the least tired (a symptom of prolonged insomnia), though I know I *am*.

Je t'aime,

A.B.

P.S. I shall arrive at 1 o'clock tomorrow Saturday. I sent the books by Richard today.

A.B.

P.P.S. You might read this letter twice.

A.B.

287. Maurice Baring (1874–1945), author; on George Mair and Maire O'Neill see pp. 54–5 and 60; Dion Calthrop (1878–1937), artist and author; Cissie Loftus (1876–1949), mime and actress; Eva Moore (1870–1955), actress, who starred in *The Title*; Harry Esmond (1869–1922), actor and author; E. V. Lucas, see p. 213. For letters to Maurice Baring, see Vol. III.

Dorothy took the role of Viola in *Twelfth Night* at very short notice. It opened at the Kingsway Theatre on 5 November 1925. Donald Calthrop was the producer.

Bennett's worry concerned his brother Septimus.

CAMBRIDGE / MS / 288
(*To Richard Bennett*)

75, Cadogan Square
16–x–23

My dear Rich,

I am very annoyed with you. I got your letter tonight, & it is the first word I have heard from you since you left nine days ago. You speak of a short note. What short note? I have had no note from you. You may not think it, but I am absolutely determined to hear from you every Monday morning without fail, regularly. And if I do not you will come up against a side of me with which you are still very imperfectly acquainted. I don't want to say too much, & I hope you will bring your intelligence to bear on the matter. All this repeated vague talk about not having time serves merely to make me angry. I ought to have heard from you on your arrival, & it was because I did not that you did not hear from me on your birthday. Your birthday is now a wash-out.

I purposely took the sound box away, as I did not wish to leave the gramophone usable on the yacht while the yacht was let to a family with young children. I will ask Miss Nerney to see to it.

Your annoyed uncle,

A.B.

STOKE / MS / 289
(*To Margaret Beardmore*)

75, Cadogan Square
28–x–23

My sweet niece,

Well, yes, it is a long time since I wrote to you. But the interval has not been as long as one or two of the intervals which *you* have been responsible for in our correspondence. I agree with you that next year you should change your situation, geographical & otherwise. It is a great mistake to remain very long in one place unless the place holds out good opportunities for rising to a really high position. I further agree with you as to the immorality of bazaars. I have preached against them for many years. I go further & object to all the various social devices for raising money. The other day I was implored to take tickets for a grand fashionable ball (3 guineas each) at Grosvenor House (Duke of Westminster's town house) in aid of some excellent charitable work. I declined & I suggested to the dame who supplicated me that it would be much better if all the dancers gave up the dance & gave 3 guineas apiece direct to the charity together with all the money they would have spent (clothes etc.) in order to go to the ball.

2nd Well. The novel is out, & you will receive a copy of it about the same time as this letter. It has been, on the whole, magnificently received by the press up to date. And the best people say it is inferior to nothing else that I have written, & some say it is superior to all else! So that I am rather glad. At $56\frac{1}{2}$ there is life in the old uncle yet.

I have not yet finished my play. It is all done except $\frac{1}{2}$ the last act. And today I have had to put it definitely aside for a time in order to do an urgent short story & an urgent article. The first of my new series of articles appears in the just out *Royal Magazine*. You will see my name blazing in red on the forehead of the cover of the same. I shall soon be having some plays produced. *What the Public Wants* is now having a short run at Hampstead. *The Great Adventure* is going to be revived, at the Haymarket after *The Importance of Being Earnest*; & 2 other plays are ripening for production. Further, I am very well, thanks to the attentions of a Swedish masseur, who comes to see me every morning. Sandow was good, but the Scandinavian is 50 times better. He says that he is absolutely sure that shortly he will be making me sleep regularly six hours at a stretch: which has never happened to me before, 3 hours being my best. If he does this, I shall be in such a condition that I will fight the whole world.

Your father was in town last week, but I had no leisure to see him, & the first day I was free he departed. Such is life.

I have noted everything in your two letters.

Your ancient aff unc embraces you,

A.B.

289. *Riceyman Steps* was published on 25 October 1923. It won the James Tait Black prize for the best novel of the year. The curious name of the hero, 'Earlforward', was, said Bennett some years later, 'concocted out of the telephone book by combining two names'.

The unfinished play: *Mr. Prohack*.

The articles in the *Royal Magazine* were on 'the pleasures of life'—friendship, travelling, and the like.

What the Public Wants opened at the Everyman Theatre on 19 October.

The Great Adventure was revived on 5 June 1924 at the Haymarket Theatre, with Leslie Faber and Hilda Trevellyan in the leading roles.

Two other plays: production of *London Life* was in prospect at Drury Lane; Bennett still had hopes of *Don Juan de Marana* being produced.

The Swede was named Fjellstedt. Eugen Sandow (b. 1867) came to England in 1889. He performed great feats of strength; he was author of the 'Sandow exercises'.

BERG / MS / 290
(*To Dorothy Cheston*)

75, Cadogan Square
5–XI–23

My dearly beloved child,

You have now come victoriously through a great ordeal; you have put yourself on a quite new plane, & you have given real satisfaction to at least one person—meaning me. You have every reason to be uplifted. I want you to realise this, and to get at once out of that mood of complaining which has been growing on you for a long time. I say this to you because I am intensely desirous for you to make the very best of your life. It simply is not the fact that you are a creature pursued by heaven's anger. You have simply given way to an unfortunate habit of complaint. You want the earth, but you can't have it. Try to make what you can of your slice, and be cheerful. You have said that I am a sad man, but I certainly am ten times more cheerful than you've been for at least four months. This mood, also, tempts you to hand out the feminine 'rough stuff' to an extent which I consider to be excessive, & my fear is that if you continue with it you may one day be highly disconcerted by a return volley of rough stuff. You have said that I am a patient man. Well, I am. I know that you make amends *with the most exquisite charm.* I know you are beautiful, gifted, extremely intelligent, a splendid companion, an A1 brain, an artist, etc. etc. But your complaining groweth in the land, & your rough stuff waxeth. I don't think you appreciate this, because I'm absolutely sure that you are filled up to the brim with a desire to play the game of life properly. And it isn't so much the rough stuff that I object to—because I can protect myself when I feel inclined to—but the effect of your mood of complaining on yourself. Enough!

I congratulate you on having done so well against spirits & cocktails, though I was a bit humiliated to find that at the dress-rehearsal you shared the honours of whiskey-drinking with Moxon, a lady who drinks & who has been publicly seen drunk. I wish you had had the strength to follow my advice & Griffin's advice. I wish even that you would do what you certainly might & only take alcohol once or twice a week. But I know you cannot reach to that. You have absolutely persuaded yourself, quite falsely of course, that you cannot get through a day without alcohol, & there it is! You have a marked natural tendency to enjoy the stuff, & the taste has *got* you to that extent, & you *couldn't* leave it off. But I think you might confine yourself to alcohol once a day. Good God, my dearest girl, need I tell you that I only say these things because I am bound up in you, & because, well, you know, though I can't run to passionate kisses when I have completely exhausted myself in your service.

I hope the 2nd night will pass off well, & that the notices this morning did not make you too furious. I shall come as near 2.45 tomorrow as Mrs. Eadie will let me. Let us then have a little of that domesticity which you say you don't get (though when you have a chance of it your first thought is Claridge's). I will try to prove by such kisses as I am capable of what the bedrock of my feeling is for you. I may have to go down to Torquay for 3 days middle of next week. E. Phillpotts is getting very restive. But I should be back on the Friday & should propose to sleep chez-toi Friday & Saturday nights. Believe me, dear madam, I am all for domesticity, perhaps more than you are. If you want to sup at Ciro's this week, it ought to be either Thursday or Friday. I say this because you complain that all your pleasures are within the house. I can't say I've noticed this. Do you feel 'bottled up' as you did on the yacht? Be cheerful & resigned to your terrible fate, I beseech thee, my enchantress. And this is a barbed, passionate kiss from the rock.

A.B.

Fairbrother, and Frank Cellier—but did not mention Dorothy. Donald Calthrop wa
the producer.

May Eadie, wife of Dennis Eadie, actor-manager.

Phillpotts and Bennett were perhaps planning renewed collaboration. In 1925 the
wrote a comic opera, *The Bandits*, that was never produced.

CAMBRIDGE / MS / 291
(*To RichardBennett*)

75, Cadogan Squar
12–11–23

My dear Rich,

Thanks for your space-saving letter. Please tell me about th
following items in your account

motorcycle exes	5.19.0
Misc.	5.7.0
Gramophone	4.6.6
Munsey watch	3.11.0

I'm sorry about the over-training. But gales would explai
anything in these days. What I am chiefly interested in now i
not the rowing, but the exam, as to which I should like to hea
something more detailed. I've just come back from Beaver
brook's, where I wrote 3,900 words of a story from Saturday ev
to Monday morning, & where I had the advantage or dis
advantage of consorting with Austen Chamberlain, Birken
head, Churchill, & Ll. G. not to mention Lord Wargrave, Si
Edward Hulton (now retired) & Evelyn Fitzgerald (engaged t
Helen Drury). The 4 first-mentioned politicians are a self
seeking crowd who were plotting & conspiring against the gov
under the benign influences of Max. I never heard principles o
the welfare of the country mentioned. Churchill had too muc
to drink last night & was quarrelsome with Birkenhead, &
Birkenhead is now no more a habitual tippler. Ll. G. & Auste
quite sober & restrained. On the whole a pitiable spectacle, &
not in the least reassuring. And see 'em all squinting askance a
me when they said anything to judge what effect they wer
making on me & fearing my fountain pen. Still, I had a grea
lark. 'Arnold', said Max to me this morning, while I sat in hi
bathroom as he laved his limbs, 'you've seen hell with the li
off.' Well, I had. I have a big dinner here tonight of theatrica
personages connected with the Lyric to hear John Drinkwate

read the libretto of his new *Burns* opera. Uncle Edward Beardmore came to lunch with me last Wednesday. He is certainly a
very wise, sound, and nice fellow, & we got on A1. I got all the
news, good and bad, about the Potteries. Chiefly bad. It is still a
hotbed of alcoholism. Tomorrow I'm going down to Torquay
to spend 3 days with E. Phillpotts and fam. But I shall work
there. I am in immense form for work. Mr. & Mrs. Sullivan &
Eliz Lewis dined on Friday, & sent messages to you. Dorothy
was very pleased with your wire. It was hung up in her dressing
room with 2 strings of telegrams.

> I salute thee.
> Love,
> Your productive uncle,
>
> A.B.

P.S. I'll send a cheque tomorrow.

291. Austen Chamberlain (1863–1937), soon to be foreign secretary in the new
Conservative government; Lord Birkenhead (F. E. Smith, 1874–1930), secretary for
India in the new government; Lord Wargrave (1862–1936), barrister and member of
Parliament; Edward Hulton (1869–1925), newspaper proprietor; Evelyn Fitzgerald (d.
1946), businessman, married to Helen, née Drury. In 1926 Bennett had an amusing
public quarrel with Birkenhead over the use of political figures in *Lord Raingo*. The
exchanges are given in full in *Arnold Bennett, the Critical Heritage*. See also Vol. III.

John Drinkwater (1882–1937). The Lyric Hammersmith did not do the *Burns* opera.
Earlier in 1923 they produced his play *Robert E. Lee*. For letters to him see Vols. II and
III.

Elizabeth Lewis, daughter of Sir George Lewis (1868–1927).

BERG / MS / 292
(*To Dorothy Cheston*)

Eltham
Torquay
14–XI–23

My dearest girl,
The Drinkwater reading-of-play kept me up till 1.30 on
Monday night. None of the fellows would go after the reading
was done. Most annoying. Libretto rather good & promising,
but too long. Drinkwater is conceited. I think he thinks he is
really a first-rate artist. I only had 3 hours sleep. But I slept a lot
in the train coming down. However, I had neuralgia, somewhat
acutely, which made me sick when I came to bed. I was all right
this morning, save for faint traces of neuralgia & pimples all

over my forehead as the result of the pain. Very soothing &
placid here, though father & mother & son & daughter are all
of the most nervous disposition. The son is definitely queer in
the head. The daughter came to meet me in the awful weather
at the station. The mother I take out shopping & we get a little
flirtatious, being of about the same age. Papa Phillpotts I yarn
at great lengths with. Yes, they are all excessively sensitive.
Weather frightful yesterday, beautiful today. I have a large
bedroom, with a prize view over Torbay. I didn't say much
about your mention of Madame Behuke on Monday, because I
didn't feel like talking then about far-away matters, but I may
now tell you that I appreciated your speaking to me of the
matter. Few people would. My wife never did. I am naturally
very touchy about it. I have met pupils of Madame Behuke
(who only took the business up because she was the widow of
her husband) who were just as uncured as me. I know her
system. I think I know all the systems. I have lived with
professors of curing, had them to live with me, and travelled
with them. Any treatment will do you a certain amount of good
for a time, because the affection is extremely responsive to
hetero-suggestion. But none that I have ever heard of will act
when it is really needed. I used to discuss this matter with the
late W. H. R. Rivers, one of the greatest specialists in nervous
affections. He could never suggest anything better than to
forget the trouble & leave it alone. As he stammered himself, he
would be likely to know all there was to be known. Also he was a
very intimate friend of mine, & a really great man. The
affection is due to a defect of the brain, which gives contradictory orders simultaneously when disturbed in a certain way.
My experience makes me think that if I had nothing to do for a
year & gave my whole time to the matter I would produce a
marked improvement, but whether it would last I doubt. I have
even tried hypnotism. I have not tried osteopathy. But I know
& had much correspondence with a man who did, & he told me
that the results were absolutely nil. Why the subject is not more
generally studied than it is by experts I have never understood,
for the affection is very widespread (among males—it is very
rare among females) & the nervous strain of it is of course
continuous and severe—very severe. The said strain is too
much for many sufferers and they retire to the completest

privacy that they can arrange for. It is always a marvel to me
that I, with my acute general sensitiveness, have risen above
his *enormous* handicap and am even, in spite of it, recognised as
a great 'persuader' of people.

I hope you are steadily pursuing the matter of your stage-
clothes, being very firm & pertinacious about it. I think that if
you don't see him, you should write to Donald—as briefly as
possible. I've only seen one criticism of the *Dream* (*Times*). And
he flat. My enchanting child, you have something to do. You
have great interests in life. So have I. Let us thank God for it.
The day after tomorrow I shall see you. Meanwhile my soul
loves & my fancy embraces you.

A.B.

292. Madame Behuke: not otherwise known.
A Midsummer Night's Dream played in matinée at the Kingsway Theatre, where
Twelfth Night was running. Donald Calthrop (1884–1940) produced both.

ERG / MS / 293
To Dorothy Cheston)

Eltham
Torquay
15–XI–23

My dearest child,
This mutual eagerness to understand is fine, & the
divergences of view, if startling, are interesting.

  1. I know well that (alcohol) 'this is a hopeless case', as you
playfully say. I admit that you have done something in the
matter. But you are a slave to the habit, daily. And if at any
evening I said: "Let's have no alcohol tonight", you would
suffer tortures. So there it is.

  2. Complaints & grievances. Of course if you don't feel them
as complaints & grievances, then they aren't. But they *are* what
I or anybody else are accustomed to *call* c. and g. The
dictionary wants altering. You need not defend your stating all
these matters. I have already agreed that it is right & necessary
that they should be discussed. The point is at what length. You
are wrong in your defence of your piling up of detail. The only
judge of the effect of this is the listener. You cannot keep to the
point. You are always at something else before one thing is
finished. Your super abundant detail, instead of making a true

picture, only confuses and even exasperates. It is proper for you to know this.

I want you to ask my advice whenever you feel you'need it.

3. I don't think A. Ellis will be worse than anybody else. I would certainly sooner have him than Dean. I would prefer Donald, but then Donald would want to play Don Juan! All the big managements have refused the play.

4. Love & work. I quite agree & understand. But I had not gathered your intention the other afternoon. No love certainly; but if no love then no bed, no propinquity. This sort of frustration would merely ruin my nerves. In this matter I am different from you. I can work at my best after making love. I never said I left at your convenience. I said your monologue ceased at your convenience.

5. Our joint lives are not any more shaped by my work than by yours. But much less by mine than by yours. I have frequently abandoned my work for yours. I have never asked you to abandon yours for mine. From the moment when you got a job you were utterly absorbed in your work. You will not 'soon' make your roots in work. They are already fixed in work, & I should think have been for years. You are far more absorbed in your work than I am in mine, &, I should imagine, would make greater sacrifices for it. I *absolutely* fail to understand what you mean by saying that I never attempt to live near the roots of happiness. I think I am a much happier being than you are, & that I enjoy the business of *being* much more, & more continuously than you do. It occurs to me that you mistake the sobriety natural to my years for gloom; because it has not the *abandon* of *your* years. *I very much want you to explain to me what you mean by the statement that I 'also cut you off from the roots of happiness'.* If you mean by 'the most important thing' to you, me spending several days in your home consecutively, I should like you to show me how this is to be done. It would have been done this weekend only for an excursion which was planned solely for your pleasure. You always want—I don't say it is a bad thing— more than life can possibly give you. And you carry away a very inaccurate notion of the past. As for instance when you said more than once that your sole pleasures were indoors, whereas the fact was that I had had you out twelve times for pleasure in 3 weeks. There can be nothing whatever in your—not com-

plaints, then, say 'repinings' unless they imply that I ought to sacrifice my work to yours. Nothing! It would be just as reasonable for me to ask you to give up your evenings of work as it would be for you to ask me to give up my mornings of work, as I should be obliged to do if I stayed several nights consecutively with you. You don't get up early, and can't; you have to eat early. You have to rest in the afternoon when you aren't working, and you have to work every night. And yet you have the nerve to say that our joint lives are conditioned by my work! You know that I let my work slide for 3 weeks more or less in order to help yours, & that I had to makè up the time as best I could, & yet you have the nerve to reiterate that I haven't stayed with you from 5.30 to 7, the very time when I could squeeze in a bit of my neglected & postponed work!! My girl, you have still got something to learn about give and take. It is not agreeable to me to tell you this, but I must. There is no alternative. The conditions of our joint working lives are difficult, as I always said they would be; & they would be impossible unless the most scrupulous mutual comprehension, fairness, and forbearance were practised. And you ought, further, to realise that these absences from each other are quite as trying a nuisance to me as to you. When we can go away together we shall have some continuous time together, but not till then.

I am absolutely determined for both our sakes to maintain the outward conventions to the utmost possible degree. And I am absolutely determined, also for both our sakes, that our work shall not be sacrificed. You do not understand my work. At the back of your mind is the idea that I could give up an occasional morning, without any material difference to my work. This alone shows that you do not understand the 'wholeness' of my work, & that it is not a series of separate séances but a whole. That my work has to be & can be sacrificed to other things I have shown, & I do not deny. But that it should be sacrificed to a domestic scheme would be wrong: it would be fatal, as the same thing would be in your work. (Not that *you* would ever dream of doing it.) We are both immense workers. In most women love is and ought to be the basis of their existence. (In men it seldom is, & never ought to be; if it is, disaster is bound to ensue.) In you, work *is* the basis

of existence. For you are masculine just as I am feminine. We
have to accept the consequences of the facts—and be thankful
that they *are* the facts; for such facts mean the durability of
happy relations. You cannot pour three pints into a quart pot.
Get this into your golden-thatched head. You pride yourself on
facing facts. Face this: the basis of my life is mornings, which
debars more than one late night a week. The basis of yours is
evenings & afternoons. Therefore dalliance *must* be infrequent.
Don't try to get away from it by vague talk about being cut off
from the roots of happiness: talk which is just about as
convincing as the statement that 28 is a good healthy number in
a street. You are not cut off from the roots of happiness. You
merely have discontent. Discontent may be 'divine'—it probably is; but you have it.

   I am having a fine restful time here. My health today is
perfect. I shall arrive at Paddington at 3.55 tomorrow, & shall
be with you at about 4.15, D.V. The news about your flat is
great.

Your A.B.

BERG / MS / 294
(*To Dorothy Cheston*)

75, Cadogan Square
15–XII–23

My dearest girl,
   In the past you have twice told me that I should have a 'lot of
trouble' with you. I have had it. I now tell you, plainly, that you
are going to have a lot of trouble with me. I mean that I will no
longer stand the way in which you go on with me. I do not mean
that I want to 'break off', as you usually say when I complain. I
have not the slightest desire or intention of breaking off. But I
have every intention that you shall change your manners. I
insist on it, & I will have it. It is merely *me*. And we shall soon
see whether or not I can insist effectively. This letter makes no
pretence to be a complete survey of your character. It merely
deals with one or two points which are not fundamental in it but
to which I strongly object. Your morbid indulgence in self-pity
is becoming *terrible*, and you must check it, and at once. It will

ruin your life if you don't. It won't ruin mine because I shan't
let it. About your interminable complaining recitals of trifling
& quite ordinary domestic worries I have often remarked
critically. They still go on. And you must needs go back to
worries which are quite over, & run through them again! You
will say that you have been ill. True; but whether you are ill or
well these things go endlessly on. And you're nearly better now.
Far worse than your wearying talk about domestic trifles is
your general attitude that you are the most unfortunate of
God's creatures. You aren't. You are comparatively very
fortunate. You seem determined to indulge your morbid craving for self-pity at my expense. I am not going to have it. Last
night you gradually became an 'outcast'. This kind of talk, to
me, is silly, offensive, ill-mannered, and grossly egotistic. I am
not going to have it. What are the facts? You always knew that I
should be fast with Richard at Xmas. You wrote to me that I
might regard it as settled that you would spend Xmas at
Haslemere with your mother. (No consulting *my* desires, or
even pretending to consult them.) You then told me that you
would be at your mother's flat for Xmas. You then told me that
both these projects were obviously ridiculous & impossible.
You then spoke of Paris, Dieppe, & arriving at Southsea after
dark, & so on. I attached no importance to these wild suggestions as they were merely absurd & not worth a moment's
discussion. You have only 3 days; you proposed to spend one
day in repose & two in travelling, & those two Sunday and
Xmas Day! My suggestions you turn down, & then upbraid me
because I can't solve an impossible problem—for all the world
like a spoilt girl who on coming out of a theatre on a wet night
slangs a man because he can't create a taxi. And then you are
an 'outcast'. If you can't see that this kind of self-indulgence is
odious & intolerable, I am now telling you plainly that it is. You
protest you are not blaming me. Of course you are blaming me.
I now tell you that I am not going to spend a night away from
home if Richard is here. The most I will do is to come down for
the day if the place is within reasonable distance. Again, when
you can't think of anything else to say on the subject, you begin
afresh thus (with awful disquieting energy): 'And now I've got
to look for a flat, & furnish it. It simply means that if you give
your existence to another you have to do everything for your*self*

in the end.' These are your words. Another instance of the grossest bad manners & injustice, merely to minister to this morbid craving. You don't have to do everything for yourself, & you well know it. Among other things which you don't have to do for yourself is to earn the larger part of your income. I *do* You don't like this kind of retort, of course. Don't ask for it then. You are obliged to live separately from me, as every actress ought who is not married to an actor. You have your separate establishment. You have an ample income to run it on. I have never taken, & never will take, responsibility for the mechanics of your establishment. You have got to run it yourself, as other people do. I am always ready to advise if my advice is asked, but beyond this I won't go. Another point. You have begun hinting about divorce. Don't do it. You came into your present situation fully informed. I told you that I did not consider my wife responsible for her actions, in other words, that she was somewhat demented; I told you I would have nothing to do with a divorce; I told you about my finances. My intentions & views are unchanged. The other day I had to tell Muriel Atkins, who was well-meaningly but stupidly trying to bring about a reconciliation between my wife & me, that she put me in mind of a baby playing with a razor. I tell you the same. My wife is & always was eaten up with jealousy in a very acute form. She had *no* chance to be jealous of my relations with women, & she wasn't. But she had the illusion that every woman I met fell in love with me; she was openly jealous of my prestige (what she called my 'gloire') while always using it for her own purposes; and she was wonderfully jealous of my men-friends. If I were to suggest to her a friendly divorce, the chances are 100 to 1 that she would reject it, but at the same time her ferocious jealousy would be aroused & she would raise hell. My youngest sister, who is one of the best-balanced women I know, told me not long since that she thought that if my wife met me in one of her 'moods', my life would not be safe. I can well believe it. (My sister tries to keep on good terms with my wife, & does so.) My advice to you is to let sleeping dogs lie. No 'reasonable arrangement' can be made with my wife, because the poor thing cannot be reasonable. As for you, you have no grievance. You have been deceived in no detail. Like me, you have got to accept it & make the best of it. I am still absolutely determined that the conventions shall be observed, & most especially in relation to my own family, & I shall most strongly resent any [?] or suggestion on your part against this.

There is no compromise in this letter. There is not meant to be any compromise. I think I have been spoiling you. You had better face the facts—all of them, & make a most serious & sustained effort to treat me properly & yourself properly.

Your rock,

A.B.

P.S. You want as usual the impossible. You want all the protection of a domestic woman who has no other career. And you want the freedom of a woman with a public career. (All this trouble about going away for 3 days at Xmas originates in your anxiety about your career.) You can't have both, either from me or anybody else.

A.B.

294. Dorothy had a septic throat and was out of *Twelfth Night* for several nights.
Like Muriel Atkins, Marie Belloc Lowndes tried to reconcile Bennett and Marguerite. She was one of the few mutual friends who took Marguerite's side in the separation. In the 1940s she wrote of her effort:

> I wrote to him, at her request, and begged him to reconsider his determination that they should have no more to do with one another. I reminded him, not at her suggestion, of how she had nursed him through three serious illnesses, and I added that but for her unselfish devotion during their early married life, he could never have written the books that made him famous.... He sent me an angry letter, informing me of what had been his principal grievance against her.

STOKE / MS / 295
(*To Margaret Beardmore*)

75, Cadogan Square
15–II–24

My sweet niece,

I was glad to have your letter. I have been nearly as busy as you, & far too busy for my aged hand to write to you as it ought. I have had a little rheumatism, but very little. Massage will usually put it right, if it is done by an expert Swede—not otherwise. But Miss H's attack must be highly acute. I suppose that is why she asks me of this, that, & the other. I have not read my complete works lately, so I can't remember whether I have ever written anything that I should now regret. Certainly I could write *Friendship & Happiness* now in the same vein as before. A still better article on the same subject is the Sermon on the Mount. I hope she will soon be relieved, & anyhow she has my benediction & sympathies. If you have no desire to write journalistically, don't try. I doubt if you would care for the Colonies, but I should certainly advise you to go forth & try one of them—for a time. Don't worry about being a doctor or a nurse. You are too old to take up these things now. You can't go on for a second career now, though your g'father Bennett *did* become a solicitor at the age of about 35. Some feat! Harold Spender I know. I can describe him to you in two words: he is a perfect ass. He never ceases being an ass, he is an ass & a conceited ass the whole time. If he wakes up at 3 a.m. he is an ass even then. Don't confuse him with his brother J. A. Spender, who is 1st rate. All 3 brothers are journalists. Hugh is another ass, but less of an ass than Harold—but only a tiny bit less. I am not sure whether I am enthusiastic about girl-guides, though probably I prefer them to boy-scouts. I cannot conceive how any bigwig who permits boys to go about in those ridiculous uniforms can be other than a nincompoop & incapable of organising a really good thing.

I have just finished a beautiful long short-story about Elsie (of the *Steps*) & Miss Nerney says it is 'a fair treat'. I know. I wrote it in a month & am now nearly dead, though in the best of health. I'm going into the country tomorrow for 2 days. I then return to write my last article of *The Royal*, thank God!

The new show at the Lyric, Congreve's *Way of the World*, nearly as indecent as *The Beggar's Opera*, is a *prodigious success*, & the theatre is packed nightly. But the snow today will put some of 'em off, I apprehend. However, nearly all the seats are booked & paid for, so I don't really care. I hope you are not crushed beneath the burdens of your daily existence.

Your antique aff unc,

A.B.

---

295. *Friendship and Happiness*—a later title for *The Feast of St. Friend*, published 1911, one of Bennett's pocket philosophies.

Harold Spender (1864–1926), author and journalist; J. A. Spender (1862–1942), editor of the *Westminster Gazette* for many years; Hugh Spender (1873–1930), author and journalist.

'Elsie and the Child', the title story of the collection of stories published in 1924, told another tale of the third major character in *Riceyman Steps*.

The Way of the World opened on 7 February 1924 at the Lyric Hammersmith, with Edith Evans as Millamant and Robert Loraine as Mirabell. Bennett wrote in his *Journals* that Edith Evans 'gave the finest comedy performance I have ever seen on the stage'.

CAMBRIDGE / MS / 296
(*To Richard Bennett*)

75, Cadogan Square
25–II–24

My dear Rich,

Thanks. Yes. Your work seems to be too much in the background. What I think about your prospects is as follows. I doubt if you have a very special bent towards any *branch* of applied science, & that is why I encouraged you to browse for qualifications here & there instead of going in a straight line. Of course I attach little importance to general qualifications, but they serve a certain purpose—classifically labels etc. I think that, unless you make an ass of yourself, which seems to me improbable, you will succeed in whatever branch presents itself to you, provided of course you don't yield to constitutional idleness. I think you will be able to manage *people*, & from an educational point of view therefore I do not regret all this Captain of the Boats business—in fact I applaud it as highly educational in addition to being amusing. But if I were you I would cut out balls entirely for the present. I have not much hope of *Kate*, which I go to see tonight. It is a batch of old English tunes strung together on a story which I fear is very feeble, being the product of 3 amateurs, 2 of them aged. I fear the stage will be too full, & that the production will cost a great deal too much ever to pay. But there are some good artists: Ranalow and Marjorie Gordon. *The Way of the World* is a most prodigious & startling success. Nobody can be more surprised than I am. I went to the 1st of the Shaw plays in the 1st cycle, but had to sleep. It was terrible. I think this is the general opinion. I wouldn't go to any more. And I doubt if I shall go to *Joan of Arc*; but perhaps I shall. I took D. Cheston & Duff Tayler to a great musical party at Tania's last Wednesday. Tania had a temperature of 101, & defied her doctor, who came at 11.30 to send her to bed. I left then, so I don't know if he succeeded. She is playing at a concert in conjunction with Beatrice Harrison

tomorrow night. I shall be present. I have recently made the
acquaintance of Armstrong Gibbs, one of your Cambridge
professional nuts in the musical line. He is a delightful red-
haired youth, & it is possible that he may do something for the
Lyric. He professes at the R. Coll of Music. I have been
somewhat cast down by overwork, but I have got over it. I
resume overwork tomorrow. That's me.

Love,
Your renascent uncle,

A.B.

296. *Kate*, described as a 'fantastic ballad opera', was produced by Donald
Calthrop. Frederick Ranalow (1873–1953), singer, actor, teacher, played Captain
Macheath in the Lyric's *Beggar's Opera*.
   Back to Methusalah opened at the Royal Court Theatre on 18 February. In the *Journals*
the next day Bennett describes falling asleep during it and having to be wakened on
account of his snoring.
   Beatrice Harrison (b. 1892), the cellist.
   Armstrong Gibbs (1889–1960), professor at the Royal College of Music from 1920 to
1939.

BERG / MS / 297
(*To Dorothy Cheston*)

75, Cadogan Square
3–III–24

Sweet madam & darling,

   Well, anyway you had a lovely day for your journey. Grave
news! Grave news! I have now had 18 hours total sleep in 3
nights, & I felt so well this morning that the desire to work
entirely left me, & I have done no work all day. My masseur
assures me I shall get 6 hours *unbroken* per night, soon. If that is
so, I shall never work again. A pity! I have arranged with the
masseur to see you at 10.15 in the mornings, beginning on
Monday next. Also I have got that rare thing, a small papier
mâché tray, for you; quite unusual in style. £2.7.6. Harold Scott
has written to me, urgently. They have found a studio, with
stage, in Kensington. They can get £100 from his bank,
repayable weekly, if I will be guarantor. I see no reason why I
shouldn't be, if it will help them. He wants to see me & I have
telephoned him an appointment. Goossens lunched with me.
He wants me to compress *Judith* into a 50 or 60 minute one-act
opera—in prose. It is a good scheme. I have promised to do it,

in my own time. Eden Phillpotts wants me to rewrite a grand
spectacular Byzantine play which he has written. I am now
reading it. It is certainly a play. This is perhaps enough for the
present, especially as I haven't written a line of my story today,
& it is now 5.15; and Tania is coming to dine here. She swears
she will & must leave at 10 P.M. in order to go to bed. She at
any rate has some good resolutions, & is seeing the folly of
persistent late hours; but she will only keep it up till she feels
just a *little* bit better. Oh, well, one can't be wise for other
people. At least *I* can't, although Reeves-Smith the head of the
Savoy once said to me that I had such a devilish talent for
persuading that I was a public danger because I could persuade anybody of anything. Oh, child, why saidst thou that you
felt that you & I generally parted in the evenings with a cloud
between us? Another proof of your imaginative powers regarding other people. Except Dolly Wilson, I think I know none of
your friends or mine about whom you have not at one time or
another imagined a vain thing unfavourable to yourself,—& a
thing which has ultimately proved to be quite baseless.
However, I like myself in my new role of 'the cantankerous
husband'. This of course ought to upset me, but it amuses me. I
fancy it extremely. Be it known to you that I unalterably regard
myself as one of the most patient of men, & one of the least
prone to criticism—unless of course it is asked for. H. G. Wells
once gave me a wonderful written certificate to that effect. I
really must show you that letter, for its general interest. Also, I
lahhhff at the spectacle of *you* dreading what *I* shall grumble at
next, & *me* wondering what *you* will complain of next. Of course
when in your role of a spoiled woman you let yourself go too far
you are bound to get told off with a certain smartness; but in my
role of a patient man I let this happen but very rarely. Still,
when it happens it *does* happen. I think on the whole your mind
is the most interesting feminine mind I have yet met; in analysis
you are as interesting as you are [blank] when your conversation assumes the detailed narrative form of complaints. I will
give you a tip: Never, in conversational narrative, recount
dialogue, unless it is of surpassing dramatic quality. And don't
expect me to go careening about after taxis unless I am asked.
This is not my line—save for old & infirm ladies. If you can't
walk 200 yards on a wet pavement without danger of grave

illness, tell me, & stay in, & I will get the said taxi. I suppose
there are few men who would really look after a woman
(beloved, that is) better than I do; but I have my own code
which is not in the least the code of the young man who take
mere ornaments to Ciro's of a night. You say you have neve
been used to thinking of 'those things' for yourself. How, with
all your single existence & your travelling, you have continued
to live so long without thinking of them, I do not conceive. Bu
anyhow you had better begin to accustom yourself to thinking
of them, & not in future reserve your animadversions till the
incidents are over. You said on Saturday that we had been ou
very little of late. But I find that in the last week I spent between
£12 & £13 on our four evenings, & I think we had better go a bi
slow, as all these things count in the financial situation, which
needs attention in small things. Of the £1,200 odd which I have
paid to you or for you since June last I have provided £600 by
selling securities and not out of income. This is a mere piece o
information, to which you are entitled by reason of you
fundamental commonsense. It is nothing else. And if you try to
read anything more into it, I can heartily promise you that you
will be as much smacked as kissed when I meet you on
Thursday night. By the way don't get the idea that I am
keeping accounts of everything I pay for you. This £1,200
consists solely of cash or cheques paid to you and the cost of one
or two presents. Nor do I in any way whatever regret it. But it
will be well for us in our weekly expenditure to keep an eye on
the financial situation as a whole. I thought Ciro's last night
was extremely interesting. You said it was sad. So it was. Bu
very interesting. I now warmly kiss & embrace thee.

A.B

297. Harold Scott (1891–1964) and Elsa Lanchester gave cabaret performances in
their studio in Kensington.

Bennett wrote the libretto of *Judith* on 16–17 August 1924. It was produced at Covent
Garden on 25 June 1929.

Phillpotts's 'opera' was *A Comedy Royal*, privately printed in 1925, which he drew
from his book *Eudocia*, 1921. Bennett had no hand in the dramatization.

Dolly Wilson: presumably Beatrice Wilson.

ᴮᴇʀɢ / MS / 298

(*To Dorothy Cheston*)

75, Cadogan Square
5–ɪᴠ–24

My sweet darling,

Thanks for your epistle this morning. It shall be done as you suggest about Harold Scott, who is coming to see me at 6.15 on Thursday, this being the only time I can manage for the boy. I see that there is a row in the Drury Lane camp, & that the contract for B.D.'s management has never been signed! The imbecility of these people is wondrous,—in this case the imbecility of giving publicity to a thing as accomplished before it was accomplished! But the mania among most theatrical persons for personal advertisement is pathetic; it is not what I call sinful, but wistfully farcical. By the way, my adored infant, you would do better for yourself (I think) if when you entered into argument with me you would remember the sort of man you were arguing with; you *could*, if you knew how, make your arguments much better than they are. I think I must, Dorothea willing & D.V., show you. When you start on the 'perfect man' tack and the 'celebrity' tack, of course I know where you are & where I am. You are merely hard up for an argument. I think it is a bit 'Odettish' of you so often to refer to my celebrity. My celebrity is not my fault, & I have never done anything whatever to encourage it. On the contrary. I certainly never trade on it. Permit me to breathe into your tender ear that I have walked further on wet pavements with far more celebrated women than you. Nor do I take much stock in your contention that you are always hurrying for my sake & to please me. I venture to think that I do far more things to please you (though unlike yourself I do not continually praise myself for the practice) than you do to please me. And I will tell you one and an important one:—the foundation of my own life is punctuality. I regard non-punctuality as bad manners. I don't expect you to be punctual; I know you are now incapable of it, save under great stress. On the other hand I don't expect to be told, when you are late, that it is my fault that you are hurrying. I spend hours every week in waiting for you at appointments which you have yourself fixed, & I get an expression of regret from you about once a month. On Sunday last you specially asked that we should leave at 7.45. You were ready at 8.7. And then naturally you are cantankerous. But, my ingenious creature, you can't 'put it over'. Further, I am not going to keep taxis waiting for you. Nor am I going to rush out & get taxis & then come back & tell you that madame's carriage is waiting; nor am I going to wait on pavements till Madame happens to *be* ready. If this sort of thing has to be done, it will have to be done by servants & not by the perfect man. But if madame expresses a wish for a taxi, and is ready for a taxi, I can get one as amiably, if perhaps not as efficiently, as the cavaliers of Juliette Clifford or the girl in green. If you have been hitherto so sheltered from the rough world and are so innocent, or so haughty, that you can't say when you want a taxi or anything else fetched, then I shall respectfully ask you to take the consequences. Your argument that, if I can't divine & fulfil wishes of yours which you don't express, your opinion of me will fall, I shall support that with the most disconcerting fortitude. And I must regretfully tell you that in that case your opinion of me will not fall anything like so low as mine of you. I don't in the least mind you playing the spoilt beautiful woman, but when this performance entails complaints against me you can absolutely rely on getting your answer. I am quite sure there is no 'Swann' about me, and I hope there is no 'Odette de Crecy' about you. (And before you refer me to the behaviour of Swann, let me suggest that you read *Swann in Love* to the end. It will give you something to think about. For it is one of the most ruthless and just attacks on woman that I ever read.) And Tania, my blonde tyrant, broke no engagement with me. She told me beforehand that she must leave at 10, & I asked her on that understanding. I needn't tell you that when it came to the point she wouldn't go! She stayed till 10.40, and only left then because I put her out of the room. Well, I wrote 1,200 words yesterday, & had my dinner party last night. Marjorie Madan was confined to bed & couldn't come. I telephoned to Ethel & Nancy & told them the facts plainly & asked whether one of them would fill the gap. Nancy at once said that *one* of them would, but she didn't know which. Ethel filled the gap. It pains me to say that, by too hot water, Fred has cracked my eighth champagne glass. I must now either confine my parties to six, or buy some new glasses. You are hereby invited to meet the

Snagges on Monday night. I asked the Sinclair Lewises, but they are away, and Duff, who *will* be away. And now I don't know whom else to ask, as Lady Snagge is a hunting, doggy, maternal woman, & knows & cares nought of the subjects which interest most of my friends. I suppose & hope that you & Charles divided the triumph between you last night. God! I have had now 5 consecutive nights of fair sleep, though far from unbroken. I expect to break into the sanctity of your castle on Thursday night between 11 & 11.30, and I am (in my perfect and celebrated way) intensely looking forward to holding the blond tyrant & all of her soft & tender & exquisite contours in my cantankerous arms. Je te bise bien.

A.B.

298. B.D.: Basil Dean became co-manager of the Drury Lane Theatre in 1924. Juliette Clifford: unidentified.

Marjorie Madan (née Noble), wife of Geoffrey Madan (see Vol. III).

Ethel Sands: a wealthy American woman who with her friend Nan Hudson had homes in Lowndes Place and in Newington.

Lady Snagge (née Inez Lubbock), wife of Sir Harold (1872–1949), who had been with Bennett in the Ministry of Information.

Sinclair Lewis (1884–1951), perhaps the most famous American author of the middle 1920s, married at the time to Grace Livingston Hegger.

Charles: unidentified.

BERG / MS / 299
(*To Dorothy Cheston*)   Grand Hotel Madrid
                                          Sevilla
                                          17–4–24

My dearest girl,
    Your 2 Algiers letters reached me this morning, & I was delighted with both of them (though not with the spelling, which approaches the criminal). You did the salary business very well I think. I have known old Watson for 25 years & he is always the same. I had a cable from Faber this morn saying that Dean wanted Aylmer & Faber wanted Aylmer & that Aylmer would take my decision. Being a man of sagacity, I cabled refusing to decide. They must wrangle it out themselves. I should like Aylmer in both plays! All right! I will now regard you as perfection. Still, you have something to learn about the various mysteries of love-making. I must perfect you in those, with what you call my corporeal body, & the S. of France will

be ideal for it. It is not yet certain that you will use your return ticket, infant ? I don't know how long the Mayers will stay at Biarritz, & the last thing I desire is that you & I should get onto the Paris train in which they are; or meet them in Paris. If therefore we *do* go home via Paris, we shall go straight through Paris, & there will be millions of English on the train! That is certain, & I don't like it. You have had *some* invitations for Easter. And now, my poor sweet dear, you are eastering all alone, & reflecting and excogitating—no doubt in full wisdom. And rightly indulging your 'home-sickness'. Well, I spend about ½ my time in thinking about you—especially in bed & when I am walking alone. And I imagine you in all sorts of responsive & acquiescent states, & in all sorts of states of attire, and abandoning yourself to all those pleasures which you really desire but which something in you inhibits you from appearing to desire. I must now rush off to lunch. Great moral battle with Max this morning in the adjacent Square, which he was crossing. 'Max', I cried. 'What is it?' he cried. 'I must speak to you', said I, and stood still. He was dying to say: 'Come here then.' But he didn't. He retraced his steps & came to me. Extraordinary fellow. It was an event in his life, & he thought he was doing something *marvellous* in coming back to me.

Well, I tenderly embrace my perfect girl.

A.B.

P.S. Dot, I haven't heard from you from St. J. de L. yet. Shows what the posts are.

299. Bennett was in Spain during April with Lord Beaverbrook.

Horace Watson (1867–1934) presently took over the management of the Haymarket Theatre.

Basil Dean wanted Felix Aylmer (1889–1979) for *London Life*, but got Henry Ainley. Leslie Faber got himself for the revival of *The Great Adventure*.

The Mayers: Robert Mayer (1879–1985), the musical impressario, and his wife Dorothy (née Moulton).

CAMBRIDGE / TS / 300
(*To Richard Bennett*)

> 75, Cadogan Square
> 19th May 1924

My dear Rich,

Please excuse typewriting. Knoblock has fallen ill and is in bed in the country, so that I have more work than ever. I quite understand, now, about Wembley. I shall be glad to have further news about appointments as soon as possible. Perhaps you have heard that your Auntie Sissie has had a breakdown, and has to stay in bed for an indefinite period. I asked her to stay here with a nurse, and Tertia asked her to Putney; but she has, most unwisely, refused both propositions. I am writing this while eating my breakfast, which is very bad for the breakfast and also for me. Happily I am pretty well. Yesterday Tania, Dorothy and I went down to the Atkinses for the day.

> Love,
> Your respectful uncle,
>
> A.B.

300. Wembley: possibly refers to the Beardmores, who moved there at about this time. Frank became a London representative for firms in the Potteries.

KENNERLEY / TS / 301
(*To Mary Kennerley*)

> 75, Cadogan Square
> 6th June 1924

My dear Mary,

Oh, so it was your birthday on Tuesday, was it? And you are 17? Well, I ought to have remembered your birthday, but I did not. However, I now wish you the best, which I hope is not more than you deserve. You will find a present for yourself one day arriving, but I do not know when. I am most fearfully exhausted with my recent labours, and I have still two more heavy nights before me. Kindly tell your mamma, thanking her for her letter, that if *London Life* is a success more money can be made out of it than out of any other theatre in London. Immense as the expenses are, the margin for profit is also immense. The intervals for scene changing are awful, but they are being shortened and will soon be normal or nearly so. Last night the play ended at 11:23. I was there last night, and though I think that the play is being and will be vulgarised in performance by the bigness of the theatre, and though I have no desire to see it again, I think it has an excellent chance of success, and also of changing somewhat the awful traditions of Drury Lane, which was what it set out to do.

This letter is typewritten because I am nearly dead.

Your aff unc,

A.B.

301. *London Life* opened at Drury Lane on 3 June and was immediately seen to be a failure. It was withdrawn early in July. Bennett's aim was to provide a spectacle with more substance than the usual Drury Lane play, but the critics saw no difference.

BERG / MS / 302   Yacht Marie Marguerite
(*To Dorothy Cheston*)   between Weymouth & Poole
                                   10.45 a.m.
                                   21–6–24

My sweetest child,

Your sage & sensational & welcome letter, duly received at Weymouth this morning, was as exciting as one of my serials used to be.

1. You will certainly do well *not* to motor down to Portsmouth. If you did you would spend over 6 hours in the car & would be exhausted. The train is far better, and about a quarter of the price, & far less fatiguing. There are 2 routes to Portsmouth. You should *come* by the one from Waterloo 9.50, arriving P. Harbour 11.54, as you suggest; but should *return* by the one to Victoria, leaving 4.45 & arriving 6.50. These are the best trains, & if you leave the return later you may be in a fix for your night's work. (Don't, therefore, take a return ticket.)

2. The B's dinner. If I were you I should certainly write to Lady B as you suggest. They are evidently intending to be nice and friendly towards you: which is good. I'm sure Gladys will be delighted for you to come in later. You can be there *before* 10.30.

3. Ellis has a nerve. I return his letter. Are the directors also going to work manually? If physical effort such as washing-up puts you all askew, what about painting? I should have thought

designing things & planning decorations would be more in your line.

4. Hurlinghams. I haven't the rules here, but I fancy that the giving of vouchers by absent members is now forbidden. When the member is present himself he has 2 free vouchers for ladies for every day, and he can introduce males at about 10/- per noddle.

5. 'Benefit of the doubt.' Yes, that's all right. But these plans can only be discussed in advance in principle. To the principle I agree of course. But supposing you are working? You have chosen a hell of a profession and I—apart from the fact that it involves the hardest work there is—have chosen a heaven of a profession. (But neither of us chose.) I may say that I don't think you are a bit more sensitive to environment than other artists. And if you are going to call last winter 'horrible', what words would you have left for anything really disastrous? It's a question of vocabulary, I suppose, as I have before said. Nor do I think that you suffer more than other people. It is merely that your boiling point is lower—that is, you boil over at a less heat—of either pain or pleasure .... Yes, in reply to your postscript 'hope', I think you understand all right, if you put your mind to understanding. Well, I had a great day on my yacht yesterday. Left Torquay at 5.37 a.m. *No* wind till noon; so that we missed the tide at Portland Bill, & had to steam & sail hard for 2 hours without moving—against a $5\frac{1}{2}$ knot ($6\frac{1}{4}$ land miles per hour) spring ebb-tide! We dropped anchor outside Weymouth harbour at 6 p.m. One thing I like about yachting is the extraordinary apparent length of the day. My thoughts all day are under my own control, & I have time to sleep, moon about, read a lot, and also work a lot. Yesterday was a heavenly day. I thought for about 6 hours about you, & yet wrote 1,200 words of a short story, and read a lot in 3 different books, and read a whole volume of my journal (with a view to my 'reminiscences'). Also the weather was heavenly. It is *now* heavenly (11 a.m.). We are nearing St. Albans Head, and I am 'below' thinking about you and writing to you. Are you aware that I 'like' giving in to you, & I should give in a lot more, only I know that to do so would be a very bad thing, in the end, for both of us. Unless you have great insight you cannot *feel* my feelings for you. The fact that I put work and 'right' living

(according to my lights) before anything else, does not in the least impair the strength & sincerity of my emotions towards you. I can get at least as much pleasure from being with you as you can from being with me, but never would I sacrifice my notion of justice and right to that pleasure. I have my feelings on the curb; you have yours on the snaffle. A rough simile, crude & unsatisfactory; but it will serve. I fully admit that your special qualities of beauty, charm, tenderness, and satisfying-ness to the eye and ear, would not *go* with curb-riding, & I don't expect them to, but *my* qualities can *only* go with curb-riding. I shall be at Poole tonight and shall stay Sunday there, and shall send for Pauline Smith to come down & see me tomorrow if her damned mother's alleged ill-health will let her. Well, I have done something there, anyhow, with my much-criticised will-power! I have saved that woman's mental life for her. She is 41 or 42; her back is crooked; she has a violently red nose due to indigestion; she is unwell $\frac{1}{2}$ the time; she is very dowdy; she is tyrannised over by her people; she is (she says) a worse sleeper than I am. Yet she now likes life, because she has found herself as a writer. *I* have made her a writer. *I* have brought out her talent. It took me 15 years to do it, & from her I got nothing but discouragement. However, I *knew* she *could* write, & I swore I would make her, and I have done, and I have changed her whole existence. So that's that. And I get nothing out of it except the contemplation of her first-rate work, on reading which I say: 'That's *me*, that is!' I should like you to wire me at Poole early on Monday morning that Portsmouth for Wednesday is a fixture. I will meet the train. Send Colletty out at once with the wire. Whether the matinée is off or on, the fixture can stand. I have just heard from Atkins. He & Muriel will join the yacht on the 8th July. Is this letter longer than yours, my sweet darling? Anyhow, I now kiss you, everywhere.

A.B

P.S. I haven't heard from Ellis in reply to mine.

A.B

302. Bennett sailed off the English and French coasts during much of the summer.
Dorothy was playing Honoria in the revival of *The Great Adventure*, which opened at the Haymarket Theatre on 5 June.
Gladys Beaverbrook (d. 1927).
Hurlingham: the reference is presumably to the London club, though Bennett is not known to have been a member.

Bennett wrote several short stories at this time, 'The Toreador' on 11–17 June and The Umbrella' on 25–9 June. The present story may be 'Death, Fire and Life'. These and other stories were gathered into the collection *The Woman Who Stole Everything* in 1927.

Reminiscences: Bennett did not publish extracts from his journals at this time; he did so in the *Criterion* in 1927–8.

Colletty: Dorothy's maid.

BERG / MS / 303   Yacht Marie Marguerite
(*To Dorothy Cheston*)   St. Peter Port
                            Guernsey
                            Sunday
                            [19–7–24]

My sweetest girl,

There is no post out of here between 8 a.m. on Saturday & 8 a.m. on Monday! Yes, thanks I got your nice wire at Falmouth, just before leaving. As regards your Thursday's letter, I think I must now bear in mind 2 pieces of advice which you gave me (1) 'You always take me too seriously, A.B.' (2) 'When I am wayward or naughty you ought to talk to me kindly *but firmly*.' All right. In this Thursday's letter you say 'If things are talked over for mutual decision I try to ensure the best decision for the *other* chap, but if it is settled without my being consulted I look out for my own interests.' Now if ever anything was 'talked over', in the whole history of human controversy, my movements in August were 'talked over'. They were also written over. Nothing could possibly have been clearer, both in speech and in writing, than the arrangement we came to that I should spend the first week in August in town, and should be back again in town in time for a week beginning before your birthday. Again & again was this stated & agreed. Yet you are now talking about my being 'so reserved', dash you! When Ellis wrote & telephoned asking urgently to see me about a production it was of course clear that I *might* have to be in town all August. And in view of this I told you that I should try to let the yacht, to which you replied that of course I should have no difficulty in letting the yacht, to which I replied that it was not so sure as all that. In order not to risk a loss *if* there was a production, I determined to let the yacht in any case, if possible, whether Ellis produced or didn't produce. I thought it was unwise to leave letting the yacht until after Ellis had come to a decision. Ellis is now off, and the August arrangement stands as it originally was—unless some agent *does* let the yacht in the meantime, in which case I shall let the yacht go, and stay in town. *No* decision has been come to about September.

Immediately I heard that my principal chance of a let was off I wrote & told you.

I only heard from Ellis yesterday afternoon, after I had posted my letter to you, that he would not produce. And I am losing no time in telling you of his decision.

So you will oblige me, my sweet child, by saying no more about my 'reserve' etc. etc. In my opinion I am appreciably less reserved than you are.

I enclose Ellis's letter. On the back of it is a copy of my reply. Please give this back to me in due course. I haven't another address yet.

In reply to your second point, I have already told you, more than once, that, though I can of course manage, I am 'hard up'. I quite appreciate your desire to be economical. But as I have often told you I cannot possibly advise you on details of expenditure, because you don't keep accounts & I don't know how you stand. When you spoke of the Ospaval dress, *after* ordering it, I said that I couldn't advise you about spending 45 *guineas* (not £42 as you wrote) on one dress. I said the same as to the £28 expenditure which you said you feared was extravagant. I gave you *general* advice, which I give you again now. You seem generally to think *first*: 'Ought I to have such & such a thing?' You will never, never keep your finances straight until you learn to think *first*: 'Have I the money to pay for such-and-such a thing?' This is the basis of all sound finance, & I cannot too strongly insist upon it. You know what your regular fixed income is, apart from windfalls. (By the way, it is not £80 a month as you say, but £70 a month). I cannot recall what the £66 debt is. Is it something in America? In my last Doran accounts there was one item which I paid for you, through him, in U.S.A. But I forget what it was. You said you had received over £80 lately from *R.U.R.* & that a further cheque had come or was coming. Why don't you pay the £66 out of this? As to 'small bills', of course they are always coming along, the same for you as for everybody. You asked me to tell you just what I think, and I have told you. I will only add this: Assuming that you have spent the £80 odd, or are keeping it for liabilities incurred before you got it, what should you have done if you hadn't received it? Is it possible that the receipt of the £80 encouraged you to spend more? If so, you are but human, like all of us. We must remember that I shall have the Owensmith bill to pay, in addition to the £730 which you have already had for installation. The theatrical situation is decidedly disappointing and troublesome. I didn't count on making money out of these 2 plays, but I did count on getting enough to recoup me for the loss of time in rehearsals. This I shall certainly by no means do. If I had written short stories instead of attending rehearsals I should have earned at least £1,600. It is as certain as anything can be that I shan't make even £1,000 out of the 2 plays together. So that the result to me is a heavy loss. Last Monday the *G.A.* receipts were under £100, & on Tuesday they were £133. I do not see how this play can run very much longer. But, my child, do not be gloomy about these finances of mine. I know that I can count upon you to be reasonable in your expenditure. And I *do* want you to have a good time. I should hate you not to have a good time. I think on the whole you *do* have a good time. As regards that £66, if it weighs on your mind, it must be settled, & I will discuss this with you. I trust I haven't taken you too seriously, or been too firm, or not kind enough. No more now to tell you about our voyage. It took $28\frac{1}{2}$ hours from Falmouth here. We reached here at 2.50 yesterday afternoon, in heavenly weather. But we had a very noisy night. The wind fell, and the storm of Thursday had left a heavy rolling swell, so that the main boom 'chucked' most of the night—not enough wind to keep the sail steady—and as the boom weighs about $\frac{1}{2}$ a ton, the row and the shaking were considerable. Heavy rain in the night. The men are going to church. I expect to leave here on Wednesday morning (? for where), so don't write here after receiving this. My sweet pet, je te bise bien.

I am in excellent health.

A.B.

P.S. Have I told you that the McClure scheme for a weekly article is off? They wouldn't pay more than £3,000.

A.B.

303. The McClure Newspaper Syndicate in America wanted a weekly article for a year. They had paid Wells double the sum. Further details are in Vol. III.

KEELE / MS / 304
(*To Marguerite Soulié Bennett*)   Yacht Marie Marguerite
                                          (Southampton)
                                          28–7–24

Dear Marguerite,

Thank you for your letter, which I got on Saturday night at Ryde. I need not tell you that I should like to do everything possible for your happiness; but I am convinced that neither of us would be any happier if you returned to me. You doubtless think you would, but I feel sure that you would not. The old difficulties would very soon begin again, & I am not prepared to face them again. It is too soon. The past is still too fresh in my mind. You have your own friends. You have Robert. You are a very clever woman; you have plenty of intellectual resources, and plenty of enterprise. When I last saw you I thought you looked extraordinarily young, vigorous, & beautiful. You have already created an existence for yourself, and if you set your mind to it you can go on creating it more & more. I suggest that you should continue to work. This is unquestionably the best thing for you. It is not for me to advise you, but if I could advise you I should urge you to go to France for a bit, and see your own people, who are all very nice.

I am glad you enjoyed the King's party.

                              With best wishes,
                                   Yours sincerely, Arnold B.

BERG / MS / 305
(*To Dorothy Cheston*)   Yacht Marie Marguerite
                                          Boulogne
                                          23–8–24

My dearest girl,

Years since I heard from you. This is a line to say that I am still existing. Weather appalling!! Gale! Raging sea!! Thunderstorms!!! Lightning!!! Very heavy rain!!!!! We meant to leave yesterday. Imposs. We meant to leave today. Imposs. We *mean* to leave tomorrow, Sunday. Of course while waiting we enjoy ourselves. Freddie works all morning every morning. He is a great worker. I don't seem to be able to work. My neuralgia is constantly returning in feeble doses. Nothing—but something. I can't go on with my reminiscences because the journals were returned from Southampton to London, & I was not going to trust them to the French post & custom-house. No! So there I am. I wired Miss Nerney this morn, when I wired you, to wire if anything really urgent. She immediately wired that the Crown Solicitor was going to put me in court for £515 balance of super tax if it isn't paid by Wednesday next. I've sent him £300 to quieten him. I haven't paid *any* income tax yet, because the amount hasn't yet been formally settled between the authorities & Till. But when the demand *does* come in I shall have to weigh in, from somewhere. I suppose it will be about £2,000. To my intense annoyance a call of 5/- per share has been made on my 800 Cyprus Asbestos Co. shares—10/- paid up. This means £200 to be found—also from somewhere. And I must placate Owensmith for you. I hope you've got the money for the piano out of Duff. I look like having a lively time, financially, on my return home.

The Keebles have read my story 'Elsie & the Child' & their rich & genuine enthusiasm for the same has greatly pleased me. It is in the September *Storyteller*. But how it can please the ordinary readers of the said *Storyteller* I cannot conceive. I suppose that sometime I *shall* feel like writing something else decent, but I don't at present. I trust that *you* are writing in my stead. Somebody must. It is now becoming necessary for me to see you. There is nothing new in the fact that I am always thinking of you, because always I always am thinking of you. But of course as the days go on I think of you more & more in your bedroom & in your various chemises de nuit or even not in them. A sign! A sign!

My sweet blonde child, I kiss thee well.

A.B.

P.S. I see in *The Times* that Ellis has had the damned cheek to put *Don Juan* among his productions!

P.P.S. Our destination from here we can't yet tell. It might be

Dover, or it might even be the Colne. Depends on wind & weather.

A.B.

CAMBRIDGE / MS / 306
(*To Richard Bennett*)

75, Cadogan Square
8–9–24

My dear Rich,

Though your letter is very well written, I doubt if you are quite covering yourself with glory in this Rochdale affair. At any rate you have all your time to yourself, & the surest way of antidoting the dreadful ennui of a place like Rochdale for a man like you, is to use the time programmatically & methodically. Why don't you lay out a plan of reading? You might at least begin it. There are plenty of books around you. This is a temporary difficulty which you have to meet, & you won't meet it satisfactorily if you resign yourself to idleness. That you are idle by temperament is no doubt true, but you might do something against that. I fear you won't be able to come here for some time—I mean to sleep. Your Auntie Sissie is coming here shortly with Nurse Hilda Theaker. Auntie S. has been at Auntie Tertia's for some time. She goes down to Stoke for a bit today. She oughtn't to go, but she is going, being very set in her own ideas. On her return she will install herself here, & the nurse in the next bedroom to hers. She has had a *very serious* breakdown & I do not see that she is any better than 5 weeks ago. She cannot believe that she is as ill as she is, & her one notion is to go back home & resume her labours on behalf of the commonwealth. I have told her that she can have 2 bedrooms & the small drawing-room & the nurse, & all the excursions, theatres, etc she wants but that I must be allowed to continue to lead my own simple little life, seeing her & taking her out when I can. I hope it will be all right. *The Great Adventure* is doing far better than ever: but there is a risk that, on a/c of previous contracts (which Harrison was fully entitled to make when the receipts of the *G.A.* fell below the agreed level, of it being taken off or transferred. As, however, Harrison is at the present time making himself £350 a week clear out of it, I doubt if he will really meddle with it! I was at the 100th pfce. Faber & D. Cheston had greatly improved. Auntie Marguerite & Robert were there (not through my intermediance). I spoke to Robert. I have got him a place in the Midland Bank.

Love,

Your now-settled-down uncle,

A.B.

306. Frederick Harrison (d. 1926) ran the Haymarket Theatre for many years. *The Great Adventure* came off in October.

On 2 July 1924 Bennett wrote to Georges Bion that through friends (Beaverbrook and possibly Harold Snagge) he had got a job for Robert. On 6 October he wrote to Beaverbrook to ask if Beaverbrook would talk to Richard, who 'is thoroughly qualified as a chemical engineer', about prospects in Canada for young men.

CAMBRIDGE / MS / 307
(*To Richard Bennett*)

75, Cadogan Square
16–9–24

My dear Rich,

Yes. I knew something was afoot when no letter came. I enclose a cheque for £20. Why are the accounts 'service'? You must now accustom yourself to the ways of the world, & remember that you will be able, when you have secured a job, to spend what you earn & not more. This will be something of a change for you, but your affair will be to improve it as quickly as poss., & in the meantime it is an absolutely necessary discipline—self-discipline I mean. Don't imagine yourself hardly done-by. There was an uncle of yours named Arnold who lived on 25/- a week at your age & bought books. Say that 25/- then was worth 50/- now. Add a £1 for your more expensive tastes, & you will see what you really need. I don't know that I can do anything for Hickson. You see I don't *know* him; I don't know his character, & I never recommend or suggest people whom I don't know. Surely he must be acquainted with people of some influence. I am now working very hard. I toil on a new play in the mornings & on a volume of literary reminiscences in the afternoons. I go out nearly every night. J. B. Atkins & D. Cheston are coming here tomorrow night, & Robert Bion is dining with me at the Reform on Thursday. I was at Auntie Tertia's last night, & met Ernest Hales (brother of 'the Card') there; he is much superior to his brother. In fact I had quite an evening. I heard from Auntie Emily this morn from Seaford. Some weeks ago at 9.30 pm she was stopped by 2 thieves in the Boltons & robbed of all she had. A distressing experience! It upset her, & no wonder. I don't yet know when exactly Auntie Sissie is coming here, but anyhow not till next week.

Love,
Your exemplary uncle,

A.B.

307. Hickson: unidentified; mentioned also p. 338.

The new play was *Flora* (original title *Dance Club*), written between September and November.

CAMBRIDGE / MS / 308
(*To Richard Bennett*)

75, Cadogan Square
29–9–24

My dear Rich,

Extreme haste. I am in fullest work with my play, & have many other things on my mind. I have to break up my morning by going & chatting with your Auntie Sissie in bed. She seems better. Nurse Hilda Theaker is all right. Things are going smoothly for the present. The specialist is to be seen tomorrow, Tuesday, at noon. Beaverbrook rang me up on Friday to tell me that your Auntie Marguerite had written a little book about me, biographical; & that a literary agent had offered the serial rights to the *Express*. I told him he might as well publish it, because if he didn't someone else would, & I would prefer it to be published by a friend who could keep an eye on it. He has read it & says it's all praise. It may be; but the taste shown in her doing it at all is really deplorable. It is revolting. She wanted to make it a condition that I should be told nothing about it, but of course he wouldn't agree to that. I did not tell you before, but some weeks ago your Auntie wrote to me & confessed that she had been entirely in the wrong, & badly advised, & had made a mistake, & begged me to take her back again. Of course I refused, but soothingly, as I don't want her to lose her head completely. She saw your uncle F. W. B. yesterday & told him that the book was her 'reply' to my refusal. It couldn't be, because it must have been finished, or nearly, before she wrote to me. However, there you are.

I am working very well, but not without neuralgia.

> Love,
> Your employed uncle,
>> A.B.

P.S. When you come to London where shall you stay? Not here. No room.

308. Marguerite's articles began appearing in the *Daily Express* on 24 November. They were published in book form under the title *Arnold Bennett* in 1925.

BERG / TS / 309
(*To George Cedric Beardmore*)

> 75, Cadogan Square
> 3rd November 1924

Dear Cedric,

I return your book of verse and prose. I have kept it a long time, but I have had no time to read it until just lately. I made a few notes as I read, and I enclose them. The mischief with you, as with most writers, is that you get tired of a composition before you have finished it. We need not give too much attention to these verses, etc. because it is certain that in a short time you will have adopted a new style. I sent you the books because I felt sure that you must be unacquainted with modern poetry. Hodgson's 'Song of Honour' and 'The Bull' are supposed to be two of the finest modern poems. Unhappily Hodgson, though a friend of mine, is an idle man and has not done any work for a long time—no doubt because he has had nothing to say. His chief interest is dogs.

> Your affectionate uncle,
>> A.B.

P.S. Send me some of your new poems, will you?

>> A.B.

16 November 1924

BERG / MS / 310
(*To Dorothy Cheston*)

75, Cadogan Square
16–11–24

My dearest girl,

Thanks for your azure card-let, I got it Saturday night at 6.30. Rather good. I'd posted my letter. My child, trunks are always going wrong—because owners of trunks after locking them, don't unlock them to see if they will unlock. However, hotels are quite used to this phenomenon. It is an axiom of the life of pleasure & repose that *all* hotel bedrooms are next either to service staircase or a lift. This fact is notorious. So long as you're happy it's all right. Work is going along tremendously. After a day on *Dance Club* I worked for 1½ hours with Knob on *Prohack*. Then to dine with Temple, who gave us the most amazing account of the *politics* & publicity of a great group of hotels. My opinion of him went up very high. Then he said he wanted to consult me about his love affair—whether *she* would ultimately have him (widow with £5,000 a year, younger than him; millionaire father) & whether father would come round. Well, I advised him till 12.5, while Knoblock paced the foyer (Savoy) waiting. He read me portions of a letter of hers. I said: 'That's no good to me. Read me the end.' So he bravely read me the end, all about 'love' & 'darling' & 'ever'. Whereupon I could judge. Home 12.20. Asleep 12.45. Tea at 7.45 this morn. Work at once. I shall work all day. Dine with Duff at Garrick at 6.50. *Guilty Souls* by Bob Nichols at 8. And so on. Health good. Thinking about nothing but you—and sometimes work. This is all for the day. I now embrace thee fondly, & wish thee much artistic delirium in Flo-flo.

Bise, A.B.

Health fine.

310. For letters to Robert Nichols (1893–1944), the poet, see Vol. III.
Flo-flo: Florence, Italy. Dorothy went to Italy with Muriel Atkins after *The Great Adventure* finished its run. Bennett joined her there in the middle of December.

BERG / MS / 311
(*To Dorothy Cheston*)

75, Cadogan Square
19–11–24

My adored child,

I am expecting a letter from you this afternoon. I think it ought to arrive by about then—I mean the first Italian letter, containing the first reactions to the first attack of Italy on your sensitive organism. I saw *The Show Off* with sister, & it is exceeding good. Excellently acted. In fact, what I call an evening. The Granville Barkers were there. Also Marie Tempest. Marie asked me to dinner. She said: 'Is there anyone you'd like to bring with you?' I always did say that Marie was the goods. Very decent of her. I was obliged to reply with one of my benevolent NO's. I got a lot of invitations that day. I met D. Moulton at Tania's concert. I had refused 2 of her invitations. $\frac{1}{2}$ way through the concert she came & sat beside me. She said: 'If I give you a choice of dates for dinner, will you come?' Difficult! Difficult! Then Mrs. Morley asked me. Then Ethel gave me a choice of dates. Willie Rothenstein asked me to supper. (I refused). Somebody else, but can't recall whom. I'm going to Diaghileff's ballet Friday next week. But with whom? This day London is full of me. Buses & God knows what else. 'My husband by Mrs. A.B.' The first instalment, highly conventionalised, is harmless. It reads rather like the opening of a *Daily Mirror* serial—with the addition of a few true things showing Latin perception. One error of fact. To wit, that she got up early to make my morning tea for me. I don't think! But it is more about her than about me. Agreeable evening last night at Festing Jones's. Two youths there: one the art critic of the *Nation*—Angus Davidson. He had that day heard of Brockhurst! 'Do you know anything of Brockhurst's work?' he asked me. 'Yes,' I replied, 'I bought his portrait of his father about 7 years ago.' Silence. Girl, what sort of a time are you having? I may tell you I think one of the loveliest of the 120 churches in Flo-flo is S. Lorenzo. Then Santa Croce. I have an illustrated journal of Florence in my archives. It is not much of a joke working all the time. I feel I should like to be idle with you for a while. But you would tire of it long before I did. You would be bored sooner. Yes. How trying it must be for you to be constantly with a gent who won't think of thirteen things at once! Well, it is a fine thing you *have* a mind. Most people haven't. I enjoy watching your mind most when my own mind is free: which it seldom is. I enjoy watching your body whether my mind is free or not. It unbends the mind and therein fulfills a high purpose. I don't say your body is superior to your mind, because I don't think it is. Your mind is a most pleasing organic circus, and would be still more so if there were 124 hours in every day instead of 24. I wonder if you will like my pyjamas. My first theatre article appeared in the *Standard* Tuesday night. They are taking advantage of the boom! I won't write any more now, except x x x x x x x to burn you in sensitive places.

Your devoted
A.B.

311. *The Show-Off*, George Kelly's most famous play, was finishing its run at the Queen's Theatre.
  Granville Barker married Helen Huntington Gates in 1918.
  On Marie Tempest see p. 59.
  Dorothy Moulton: Mrs Robert Mayer.
  Mrs Collinson Morley.
  Ethel Sands.
  Sir William Rothenstein (1872–1945) was Principal of the Royal College of Art. For letters to him see Vol. III.
  Henry Festing Jones (1851–1928), authority on Samuel Butler.
  Angus Davidson: (b. 1898), later secretary of the London Artists Association.
  Gerald Brockhurst (d. 1978), portrait painter, RA 1937.
  Bennett's *Florentine Journal*, with drawings by him, was published in 1967. Excerpts appeared in the *Criterion* in 1927 and 1928.
  Three articles on theatre appeared in the *Evening Standard* on 18 and 25 November and 2 December 1924.

BERG / MS / 312
(*To Dorothy Cheston*)

75, Cadogan Square
20–11–24

My dearest girl-let,

Your twin letters of the 16th & 17th—one blonde the other brunette—arrived by the last post yesterday, Wednesday. So that apparently the course of post is a full 2 days. Well, I hope you will revise your first impression of Florence. After I had been there 2 months it seemed to me that I was only just beginning to perceive it. Anyhow it contains the very finest work of M. Angelo, Donatello, & Botticelli, to mention 3. I care little for the cathedral; but see the doors of the baptising shop adjacent. I only stopped at Pisa a few hours, & liked it not. But then I didn't see it in the twilight. With a companion of your hypercritical talents I fear that Muriel may have rather a rough time. Of course she is terrible in her leave-it-to-God-&-other-people policy. She doesn't mean it [?]. You see now one reason why the Atkinses are where they are. Slackness—combined with continual complaining bursts of the vast amount of 'chores' they have to do. That is Muriel all over. I was talking to Lucas about Johnnie the other night. He said: 'Johnnie & I are the greatest friends, & I think he is the most charming man I know. But in all our friendship he has *never once* made the slightest move to see me. *I* have always had to suggest a meeting.' To which I said: 'I have had exactly the same experience.' And it is so. Johnnie has come through life on his charm, & on his native journalistic ability, and left other people to help him. He has never helped himself—I doubt if he has even tried to. Don't stay in Florence on my account, my sweet child. But I think it is the most interesting town in Italy except Venice. Jane Wells (with the Swinnertons & Duff) was here last night. She told me H.G. had written her about breakfasting in the open air at 7.30 a.m. & so on, & wearing glasses against the sun. He is somewhere behind Grasse—I doubt not with his new lady, or *a* new lady. Mary Swinnerton came through last night excellently well. She had got a new frock, evidently, for the occasion. Quite simple. She has beautiful & small feet, good ankles & calves etc. And good hands. Swinnerton was in the greatest form. I proceeded well with *Dance Club* yesterday despite a not-too-good night on Tuesday–Wednesday. Last night I slept over 6 hours, & am in terrific form this morning. It is now 8.15 a.m. We have had some lovely weather here, but it broke up on Tuesday at eventide & poured with rain & grew warmer. This morning is dark with mist. My sister leaves this house at 1.45 tomorrow, Friday. That's something. I dine with de Bear tonight; probably Robert Bion (wife's nephew) tomorrow; Sybil Colefax Saturday; Sunday Tania dines with me. Monday I take Adelaide Phillpotts to the 300. Tuesday I have a dinner here. At the weekend I shall be alone, except at evenings, & shall work all the time. Believe me, if I keep well, some work will be done. I now tenderly embrace thee, my chores-doer, nymph, sylph, seductress, dangerous-fair.

Ton A.B.

312. Mary Swinnerton (née Bennett), Swinnerton's second wife, married to him this year.

Archie de Bear (1889–1970), theatrical manager.

Sybil Colefax, a great giver of parties, was the wife of Sir Arthur Colefax (see below, pp. 495, 497).

BERG / MS / 313
(*To Dorothy Cheston*)   75, Cadogan Square
                                            Thursday
                                            27–11–24

My dearest girl,

Your pencil & pen letter, partly written on Monday at the Astora of Pavia reached me this Thursday morning. The following is an extract from it.

'If you don't like my letters in pencil you can always refuse to read them darling.'

However, it is something to know that I count among your 'intimates'.

If your pen will only write a short sentence without refilling, it must be gravely indisposed. I think fountain pens are very hard & cruel to women, for they are always indisposed to women.

I am now in a state of much desperation. Perhaps I oughtn't to have finished *Dance Club*. (Still, it *is* finished.) Anyhow the reaction after writing it has been too much for me. Two bad nights; last night awful; depression, indigestion; the usual phenomena after a 'work'. But *Prohack* tortures me all the time. I worked hard at it yesterday & nearly all that I did was no good. I hoped for better today; and lo! in the night from 2.50 onwards I watch the hours go by; get up, smoke, drink, do exercises at intervals. No sleep; and I watch also the hope of a day's work gradually destroyed. I fear I cannot work today. I had a few dozes between 7 and 8 this morn. And every day is precious. I feel harried to death in a triangle of which the sides are fulfilling my engagement to Knoblock, fulfilling my engagement to you, and my financial worry. I don't at this moment see how I can finish *Prohack* and leave here on the 14th. But perhaps I may be more hopeful later on. I don't know. I hate keeping my promise to go down to Torquay Saturday–Monday, though it may do me good, and it will certainly lead to some perhaps profitable business. Every hour of the day-time is precious or seems so, & I have cut out all social things from all afternoons. People who *must* see me have to come to lunch and leave at 2 p.m. When you wrote from Certosa you hadn't had my appeal about chores. My sweet pet, do have some mercy on me. If you knew how in my present state the prospect of going out shopping to buy a cushion for you devastates me, choosing it, & choosing it wrong, and having it sent off & all that when I ought to be either at work or in bed! Surely it would be at least as easy for *you* to go out and buy one in Florence, where you can get anything. Have you even tried? Please do. I feel sometimes just as if I should go off my head, & I remember that at exactly my present age my father's brain gave way. I will bring dictionary & rug. You suggest me coming to Florence now. Well, I don't know. A few days ago you were reproaching me for not realising your difficulties as a 'dishonest woman'. Now you suggest acute dangerousness. To my mind it would be nothing better than sheer lunacy for us to stay together in Florence, where I should unquestionably be recognised all the time, & where I have various friends & acquaintances; you also. I have always been strongly against large towns. Your own original notion, to which I agreed, was a small place. But I can see that you feel you will not be able to stand my unadulterated companionship for a month. I have felt this for some weeks. *I* don't know what to do. It is perhaps to the good that you do *not* feel you cannot live without me. All this is doubtless very lugubrious and sinister, overlaying as it does the tenderness of my feelings for you and of yours for me. But I *know* that I am getting near the end of my mental & physical resources. I have had a terrible autumn, & I daresay I am perhaps not quite so much of a philosopher as I think myself, or am thought to be. I must say I think my wife's stuff passes the limit. Obviously it is written with the most intense malice. And anyone who could be misled by it, even not knowing me, must be a perfect fool. When you say 'how you would have disliked me', after reading it, if you had not known me, I hope you do yourself an injustice. Even your strong sex-bias could not have carried you so far. When I think of the enormous amount of trouble I took to give that lady a career as a reciter; how I listened to her practising for hours, & formed a society for her, & arranged tours for her & God knows what, & how by herself she did, & could have done, nothing—all to the detriment of my own work—I smile as I read her. Well, I must smile. Poor thing; I fear she is intensely unhappy in her ferocious egotism. Today's instalment is comic-monstrous. Jane Wells was darkly furious when she mentioned the matter to me on Tuesday night. That amiable ass, Hamilton Fyfe, editor of the *Daily Herald,* wrote me yesterday to break to me the sad news that the rumour was abroad that she had written the stuff in collusion with me! I daresay it *is* abroad, but the people who put it abroad or accept it are not worth troubling about. They would believe anything. I shall now after all try to do a little work; but I have to shave, bathe, & dress first. It is 10.50. Forgive my gloom, my sweet girl. Je te bise bien.

A.B.

313. Bennett's income fell in the middle twenties. In 1925 it was £6,800 after deducting professional expenses but before income tax deductions. 1923 was also not a good year. In 1928 and again in 1929 he earned at least £8,000.

Hamilton Fyfe (1869–1951), journalist.

BERG / MS / 314
(*To Dorothy Cheston*)

75, Cadogan Square
2–12–24

My dearest girl,

It is of course rather distressing that you should have a tendency to be sympathetically 'angered and roused' by my wife's articles, because it shows how *willing* you are to believe, & how easily you can be hoodwinked. At the end of those articles Miss Nerney burst out to me, without me having mentioned them to her: 'I do think Mrs. Bennett's articles are disgraceful! Disgraceful!!' She was quite passionate; which happens to her rarely. But then she knew a lot of the facts. You don't, my child. I have never said a great deal about my wife to you, nor about her articles, because I really scorned the whole subject; but I think I will tell you a few things now. She was a very beautiful woman, & I never knew any woman who could exercise more charm & tenderness—when it suited her to do. At first she was rather at sea. She had mixed only with fashionable dressmakers (whom she despised), theatrical people, amateur novelists and amateur painters. When she encountered a professional she was amazed. She certainly resented the rules by the observance of which alone anything worthy can be achieved. She had her sham artists who would call on her every day, & spend hours with her. She scorned business men, & never comprehended that a serious artist must have the seriousness of habit of a business man. She was eager enough to enjoy the fruits of my work, oh yes!; but she imagined in her silly way that somehow I ought to be able to do it while arranging my life *chiefly* around her. She did at last reconcile herself into permitting me to work in the only way possible for serious work; but in thus reconciling herself she regarded herself as the most marvellous & accommodating of women. This of course came from mere ignorance of what life is & from lack of early training. She was very frank, sometimes, and openly said to me that she was jealous of my work, and still more jealous of what she called my 'gloire'. She said it with intense bitterness. As a fact she did not *really* consider my work, or my health. She desired ducks & I procured her a fine assortment of ducks. She kept them on the lakelet at the end of the front lawn. They woke me daily at 4, 4.30, 5, for months, & she wouldn't move them. However, one morning when they woke me I went into her room, & woke *her*. She moved them to a more distant pond the same day. This is one sample of many. On the other hand I never neglected her. I always had meals with her, even afternoon tea, if she was in. I devoted every evening to her. Until she fell in love with the young adventurer, Legros, I never spent one evening in 12 years apart from her, when she was herself free, save for war purposes, and I only spent one evening alone with another woman (a friend of hers, not mine), and she was furious about this, though I was alone in London war-working, and she was in Essex enjoying herself with a choice selection of officers. She constantly left *me* alone. She wanted to write, and I gave an immense amount of time to trying to teach her to write (but she couldn't). She wanted to have a career as a reciter, & I successfully organised that career for her; she practically killed it later, by quarrelling with all the people associated with her in it. She had a fantastic temper, & she didn't care a curse where she let it break out; it might just as easily be on a railway carriage or in the street as at home, & just as easily at table with guests present as in our bedrooms. Like all untidy and unpunctual and inefficient people she *resented* order & punctuality and efficiency, just as she resented the results which they brought. She was incapable of seeing that to be habitually late is gross and selfish rudeness. She was intensely self-centred. She loved me tremendously, & this enabled the affair to go on pretty well; but of course when she fell in love with the youth, and violently, there was nothing to be done. She had no longer any motive for behaving decently. I feel sorry for her, but not for the reason that you feel sorry for her. I feel sorry for her because she was and is utterly self-centred. Exceedingly few self-centred people can be happy. I always feel sorry for self-centred people, whoever they are. Even for Nigel Playfair. I remember once at a Lyric Board meeting when I was stating your case apropos of something which I have now forgotten, N.P. burst out: 'But it *isn't* so; and Dorothy Cheston is a hysterical woman!' It was a genuine cry of suffering. He was obviously miserable. Duff & I looked at each other. My wife's articles are a mass of false suggestion and entirely unscrupulous. For instance she expresses how grieved she was when I went away in the yacht & left her behind. Good God! She had decided to go and visit her relatives in the Midi. She did not want me to go, because she was snobbishly ashamed of them. I said I would go off in the yacht. And she was perfectly agreeable, until I asked another man to join me. Then she made a great fuss, for she was dying to go off with 2 men. She never learnt the complete uselessness of making a fuss with me in certain circumstances. The funniest thing in her articles is the statement that she made my early tea for me. To anyone familiar with the ways of the household this is side-splitting. She never made my early tea for me. But I often used to get her early food for her—she didn't drink early tea. The whole series from beginning to end presents a clever, lying & grossly misleading picture of our relations. Towards the close of our relations she constantly threatened to leave me. The poor thing was absolutely stunned when at last, after terrible scenes, I took her at her word & told our mutual solicitor to arrange the separation. I now give her £2,000 a year & pay taxes on it, and she goes about saying that she is so poor that she cannot afford new dresses! She is very mean, in money, & must be saving at *least* £1,000 a year. I used to pay the whole of the maintenance of her father & her mother, and, when her sister became consumptive, of her sister. I found ½ the money to start her brother in business (in which he brilliantly succeeded—thanks to his wife). But she always made it appear that the benefits came from her & not from me at all.

On the 25th July this year she wrote to me: 'I suffer continually through being away from you. How disordered must my mind have been, how evilly influenced and how misguided I must have been, to separate from you, my husband, the just and kind and generous being that you are, the only man I have really loved and respected, & with whom I have passed the most wonderful 14 years of my life. I have paid heavily for the faults I committed. You know my nature & the circumstances. You are generous and kind. I put myself in your hands.... Have pity on me. Life is impossible without you. Take me back if it is possible. And if you have created for yourself another affection I will respect it. But take me back; protect me; I love you.' I was of course foolishly but profoundly touched by this letter, but equally of course I had to turn the suggestion down. I did this with the utmost gentleness. Shortly after this she approached my brother-in-law, Frank Beardmore. She got him to her flat (he said 'Never again'), and she went several times to see him at Wembley. She said 'I asked Arnold to take me back. He has refused. Very well. I am now writing my answer. And there will be more when that is done.' The answer was the *Express* articles. She uses from F.B. material as to my early life for those articles!

All the above facts are within the knowledge of various people, and cannot be disputed.

I remain of the opinion still that my wife would stick at *nothing* to injure me. Others are of this opinion.

She is constantly asking me to do things for her. Even while the articles were appearing she wrote and asked me to grant her a favour! Which I granted. But I am not in the least blind to the strong probability that one day my absurd kindness & decency & thoughtfulness to and for the martyred sex will cause me some considerable misfortune. I know now that I treated my wife all wrong from beginning to end. She was incapable of appreciating magnanimity.

Je te bise tendrement.

A.B.

P.S. Do not agilely leap to the conclusion that I am implying, in the above, that I was a perfect husband. No! All I say is that M. had no more to complain of than the average *happily married* wife: less than Muriel, for instance, has to complain of in Johnnie, & far less than I had to complain of in M.

A.B.

BERG / MS / 315
(*To Dorothy Cheston*)

75, Cadogan Square
7–12–24

My sweet doe,
    Said Knoblock seeing a pencil sketch on my study mantelpiece, said: 'This is very nice. Is it by a young lady?' I said: 'It is.' Knoblock was here for dinner last night, & we worked on Act III for 3 hours. I was already, before then, fairly exhausted, having finished Act II in the morning, & begun an article for the *Sunday Pictorial* in the afternoon! I think Knoblock is not doing very well in this play. He is conscientiously doing his best, but his best is very feeble. His dialogue has to be seen to be believed. He is not supposed, I admit, to take much care over the dialogue, but even so its badness is amazing. His forte is of course construction. When I read his draft of Act III yesterday afternoon, I was staggered by its ineptitude; I almost despaired. I almost said: 'Look here, A.B., you have never had any luck with this play; you'd better abandon it.' But when Knob arrived for dinner he began by saying that my finished Act II was fine,—he'd just had it to read. This gave me some glimmering of hope! He at once admitted that he had been quite at sea with Act III, & felt it to be wrong all the time. By about 11.30 p.m. *I* had reconstructed Act III—a terrible time.

He is to draft it again & deliver it to me on Monday night. And I shall have rewritten it, bar accidents, by Friday night. I have arranged with him to do nothing with the play till I return, when we shall calmly consider it in a true perspective. I shall do the same with *The Dance Club*.

This modification of programme leaves me with an unexpected free day—today—which I most seriously needed, for my health. So I have almost nothing to do but write to my beloved. I announced that I should return to bed after breakfast & I did. I am reading a *really* original & exotic book: *Goha the Fool*. I shall bring this for you to read. It is about life in Cairo, & apparently by 2 Egyptians. In regard to oriental domestic life it is evidently & most convincingly the goods. In fact I have never read anything like it. Gerard de Nerval's *Femmes du Caire*, though fine, is not to be named with it. Unfortunately, for me in my present circumstances, it is sexually of a very exciting nature. Still it sends my thoughts to you & round you & over & in you. You don't yet know me—& are deceived by the shell of the nut. I am feeling excessively lonely, despite a certain amount of female companionship at a meal now & then. I had a slow and luxurious bath, in a warm bath-room. Everything perfect. Yes I thought all the time, 'I am told I am a child. Someone ought to be here to bath me.' At this hour next Sunday I shall be in the train, scrunching & vibrating toward the someone.

Note. I had Edward Hutton to lunch yesterday. I gave him an hour, and he took exactly 60 minutes. For 2 months, since he invoked my aid (me being a perfect stranger to him!) in settling up a dispute with Methuens, his publishers, I have been striving to settle that dispute—so much so that Methuens in the end took to writing to me & not to him at all! I think it is now settled. The point, however, is that Edward Hutton is the first living English authority on Italy. He knows simply everything in it, every village. He told me he had twice walked from end to end of Italy and back (four journeys) and numberless times across the peninsula in various parts thereof. So I got some information from him. I said I was going to Ravenna. He said: 'You can't go to Ravenna in December.' I said: 'But I *am* going.' He said: 'I hope you won't. If you do, you'll regret it. You'll almost certainly be ill there. It is the coldest city in Italy. It is built on a marsh & the fogs are terrible.' He said he thought it was perhaps the most interesting town in Italy except Rome; but unvisitable in winter. I transmit to you the information, for what it is worth.

Did I tell you that at the Lewis's dinner party, Birkenhead, the obstinate fool, insisted on playing bridge for highish stakes, opposite to Scatters Wilson, who is one of the finest players in London! He lost £44 in one hour. He jumped up; his wife saw him jump up (she was playing mahjongh); she jumped up; they departed; he was furious. I was just going at the same time. A few minutes earlier while I was talking engagingly with Lady Hogg, and Lady Wilson, Douglas Hogg (attorney-general) came up behind his wife & said: 'Dear, we must go.' She gave a start, & went instantly. At my party on Thursday I was talking with Mrs. Maxwell, when *she* suddenly jumped up. 'What's the matter?' I said. She said 'Willie wants to go.' Willie was standing up! Nobody could be more benevolent than Willie. I love him. These three striking examples inevitably made me reflect upon my own excellences of absolutely, acquiescent, yieldingness, non-tyrannicalness, etc, etc.

I dine with the Reeves-Smiths tonight; they are giving a dinner-party at Claridges. No idea who is to be there. I *may* have company (female) for lunch, but it is not yet sure.

My sweet doe, je te caresse et je te bise tendrement et formidablement. Sleep better.

A.B.

315. The *Sunday Pictorial* published several articles by Bennett on miscellaneous topics in 1925.

Goha the Fool, by Gogol.

Gerard de Nerval (1808–55), symbolist author.

Edward Hutton (1875–1969), author of many books on Italy and England.

Sir George (1868–1927), solicitor, and Lady Marie Lewis.

Sir Matthew (Scatters) Wilson (1875–1958), soldier and politician; Lady Barbara Wilson (d. 1943).

Sir Douglas (1872–1950) and Lady Hogg. He was attorney-general to the Prince of Wales 1920–2.

W.B. (d. 1948) and Sydney Maxwell. He published *Spinster of this Parish* in 1922.

BERG / MS / 316
(*To Dorothy Cheston*)

75, Cadogan Square
Monday 10 a.m.
8th Dec 1924

My sweetest pet,

2 letters from you this morning, 1 Wednesday, & 1 Friday. Grazie. I am very sorry you have been laid up with fainting pains. I trust it is all over now. As for me, as the result probably of draughts in a taxi, I had a *fantastic* neuralgia last night 2–5 a.m. It is only ½ over. I wish you had told me earlier about keeping your letters. I never keep your letters, & I have always asked you not to keep mine. Such letters are the equivalent of highly inflammable material & very dangerous. However, I will guard what henceforth comes & bring it all to you. You needn't reproach yourself about not keeping a journal. I have only too often found that when a 'work' gets thoroughly going, a journal is dropped. I still find this. It has to be. As Goethe said, everything withers away in the vicinity of a 'work'. I fear, my sweet child, you were not clear over the dictionaries. As I haven't the letters I will not affirm anything—except that you distinctly asked me to bring the English Dict. *with me*. I certainly understood you to mean an Ital–Engl. dictionary to be *sent*. My train arrives at Genoa at 11.45 a.m. on Monday. I always said I should leave on the Sunday, & by God's grace I shall. My tickets have arrived. Lucas's remark about the unbearableness of people who are always right & always punctual runs through all literature. It is in the letters of Cicero, & it is also in the moral works of A.B. in various places. The converse is equally true, that people who are never right & never punctual are unbearable. Speaking personally for a moment, I can assure you that my faculty for being in the right is often *most annoying* to me, & I would much sooner be oftener in the wrong. I agree the Italians are charming, but they only understand a small part of life. Their happy-go-lucky methods have had the result of the most appalling trouble several times in every century since Rome fell. Happy-go-luckiness is bound to end in a mess. It recently resulted, in Italy, in people pouring castor-oil into other people who disagreed with them, shaving their head & painting the tricolour on the craniums in indelible paint, murdering them etc. & in wholesale bribery and terror-

ism. Much of this is still going on. Witness the recent proved scandals in Bologna. Hutton tells me that nearly all the English in Italy are in favour of Fascism. They would be. English colonies abroad are ever the same, a festering mass of reactionary political opinions. (Aldous isn't pro-fascist, nor is Reggie Turner, delightful fellow, Reggie; I felt sure you would like him; I knew he would be hospitable; I have been hospitable to him in a perfectly wholesale manner). To return. Mark my unbearably right words. There will be another upset in Italy in 2 years & perhaps in a year. Mussolini is bound to fall. Then quite possibly the people who had castor-oil poured into them will pour castor-oil into the original pourers. Similar events will happen in Spain.

I shall greatly look forward to reading your story, but as I told you I do *not* want to read it in MS. To do so would be as unfair to me as to you. You must have worked pretty hard. Upon which I congratulate you, as also upon your letters. You seem to think I object to some of your letters. Not at all. I like you to be frank. But when I differ from your views I say so. Doubtless this is wrong of me. But I do it.

Latest from my wife: I got a letter from her this morning asking me to let her reproduce the first page of the MS of *The Old Wives' Tale* as a front piece to her book! Marvellous! This is the first time she has ever mentioned the book in her letters to me. I have received large numbers of condolences from strangers & friends about that book.

No wire from you is necessary.

I cannot work this morning; but D.V. I shall finish my *S. Pictorial* article this afternoon. I proceed with play tomorrow. Four of *Harper's Magazine* people are dining here tonight. Miss Cohen honoured me with her company at lunch yesterday. She was (comparatively) humble. The Reeves-Smiths gave a big dinner last night. Not wildly amusing. Some dancing, but I could only dance once owing to neuralgia. Except one golfing & bridging girl, nobody under 45 or 50 was present. I was in bed at 11.45.

I now earnestly salute thee, with many & varied caresses, my sweetest.

                                                                    A.B.

316. Aldous Huxley (1894–1963), the novelist.
Reginald Turner (?1869–1938), author and wit.

BERG / MS / 317
(*To Dorothy Cheston*)   75, Cadogan Square
Friday 12.30
23–1–25

My sweetest writer,

Your letter of Sunday (ink) must have been delayed. It only reached me this morn. With it came your other letter (pencil), which regrettably was not dated; but I suppose it was Tuesday, as I received your letter dated Monday on Wednesday night. Most confusing. And I still am not sure if you've had my letter written in the train to Paris. I certainly got your wire giving address, on Friday afternoon; but by that hour I had written you twice.

It is essential that you should sleep. If it means moving to another hotel, move. If it means spending more, spend.

I should very much like you to go to Siena.

I am already looking forward to another holiday with thee.

I feel in thy letters, & show in mine, a much deeper & sounder intimacy. All right, that.

There is something in what you say about Miss & Mrs. But—in my opinion—not so much as you think or imagine. When I reflect upon the number of misses I know who are certainly not troubled by this subtle difference of acceptance of the world, & some of whom would be very cross if they were forced to call themselves 'Mrs.'. . . . No! Very little in it.

Fred's wife was delivered at 6 p.m. only yesterday. Baby weighed $7\frac{1}{4}$ lb. and was 22 inches long! Think of it.

Yes, it would be a good plan for me to write fragments to you at odd minutes, as I am assuredly very absorbed in & preoccupied by *Prohack*. However, today I have finished my morning's work on it (good), and have 30 minutes to spare. I lunch at home as much as possible; it saves time, & secures better afternoon sleep. Believe me, I am really not working too hard, & I have divided the end of the play into $\frac{1}{2}$ day sections smaller than I *could* do if I tried. Nevertheless all my existence just now has to fit itself to the play. I had a bad night last night. The optimistic Fjellstedt advised me to begin to eat things that of old did not agree with me, as he wished me to accustom my improved stomach to all manner of experiences. Well, I had Brie cheese at lunch yesterday. . . . This morning he said he thought I had been too previous with the experiments. I am gathering material for my Lord Rhondda novel, though I haven't yet been able to see Tommy Horder about it. I dined with Walter Roch last night at the Reform & got from him the whole history of Rhondda, so far as he knows it—and he was one of Rhondda's most intimate friends, also his adviser in various scrapes (for Rhondda was a bit of a crank). Would you believe it, Roch said that the dramatic aspect of the suicide-mistress part of the story had never struck him until the night he dined with Max and me at my George Street flat and heard us—and especially Max—expatiate upon it. Strange, how people can't see things for themselves. Yet Roch was in the very heart of the affair. I got a lot of stuff. I've been exercising my imagination upon you, as usual. This proposed separate room of yours. I see you going to it. I don't see how you could get to it before 11.45 or begin to work in it before noon. Then lunch at 1 or 1.30. I see you confronted with new, added domestic difficulties in that room, of which you don't like the furniture and which has to be cleaned and heated anyhow. You arrive & find imperfections & have to adjust yourself to the atmosphere etc. *Then* to begin to work. I see clearly that the chances of finding a *quiet* room, when you rent only one, are exceedingly small, because of other people on the same floor. Then if you're there at night. I see further complications & atmospheres of suspicion in me being there. And I see us leaving there & going home with you and then going home myself. Further I see you returning to your flat, say in the afternoon, & finding all sorts of things going wrong there because you haven't been on the spot. Such are some of the things my imagination sees. By the way, they are still knocking next door! I think I have never told you that the bedroom of 2 servants is over my study, and that I am almost daily subjected to the sort of noises that afflict you. But I have trained myself to ignore, almost, all noises outside the room in which I work. In my opinion you might easily fall into a worse situation than your back-rooms. After all, the people upstairs *are* out most of the day, & the noises when they *are* there are not in my opinion abnormal. You have the *tremendous* advantage of no other pianos in the building. Even a house is not safe as regards to a piano. Mrs. Hammersley is being driven out of her house in St. Leonard's Terrace by the next-door piano. Of course your front-room is noisy. But I always maintained that it would be unbearable, with music & traffic, & you maintained it wouldn't. And you never told me, till I saw the place for myself & you had decided to take it, that the kitchen opened into the parlour. However ...! My sweetest fawn, how is your story? I agree it isn't in short-story form proper. As regards finance, the situation is unquestionably grave; but I am not unduly worrying about it. Sometimes I don't think about it for a day at a time. I'm too busy to think of it. As regards Paris hotel, you won't get anything better than your last one. All the Rue de Rivoli hotels are the same. You might try the Hotel de l'Univers et de Portugal, rue Croix-des-Petits-Champs (near Palais Royal), but it will be very English. My sweetest child I immerse you in kisses & love.

A.B.

I haven't had time to read this through. It is 1 oclock.

317. Fred Harvey's wife Milly.
Fjellstedt: see pp. 403–4.
   Lord Rhondda (1856–1918), politician and businessman, provided in his life the plot of *Lord Raingo*, which Bennett was now actively preparing to write. He was involved with a prostitute, who committed suicide. Thomas Horder (1871–1955), physician to royalty. Walter Roch (1880–1965), member of parliament, barrister, and journalist.
   On Mrs Hammersley see p. 345.

BERG / MS / 318
(*To Dorothy Cheston*)

75, Cadogan Square
Saturday 8.15 a.m.
24–1–25

My sweetest fawn,

   I got 3 letters from you yesterday, Friday, those of Sunday, Tuesday & Wednesday. Yes. Yes. Yes, my pet, my thought coincides with yours that we have come much closer to each other. Yes. Yes. But of course, I am very slow in coming near to anybody. So I think are you. Also intimacy follows, often slowly, and never precedes, lovemaking. I now beg respectfully to announce to you that I am definitely decided not to come to Paris. I can't conscientiously do it; anyhow, I was always very doubtful about it, as you know. It would be bound to cost £20, 4 days time at least, and an upset in my creative work. I can't afford any of these, & ought not to. I've had one immense holiday, & can't take another now. Moreover my work makes it absolutely imposs, believe me. I told you something yesterday about Paris hotels. But you can consult a Paris guide, surely, at Vessemes. If not, buy one. As regards London, the Belgravia might do all right; but I'll cause enquiries to be made about that hotel near your place in Sloane St. I can't go myself—too dangerous & dubious. I think I'll get Ethel to call them. I don't in the least mind about Ouida and about Muriel. I often think of Muriel as 'that woman' myself,—have done for years. Ouida could not possibly understand her—she is a profound & complex study. I have had a bad night—I should say largely due to Tertia's mince-tarts—des flatuosités fantastiques, but I feel quite in form for work. Ethel S. & Nan Hudson gave a dinner last night, at which I was present, & sat next to the other Hilda Trevelyan (painter), a person who exists. I left at 11.15— the first to go. As the play draws to a close, I think more & more of the novel; but 2 stories & an article have to be done between the play & the novel. I am having another dinner on Tuesday night (Max and Roch) to the end of getting further material for the novel. Your attitude toward *your* work is absolutely correct. For you it is *the most important thing*; nothing must come in front of it; & physical conditions enabling you to do it properly *must* be obtained. Do you realise what importance *I* attach to you doing this story fully & completely—whatever its quality may turn out to be? There is a very brainy review by John Franklin, of Aldous's novel in today's *Statesman*. Extract therefrom: 'Calamy (hero) will make no progress until it dawns within him that a path excluding women from humanity is no path. The problem is vital, & his capacious brain (really Aldous's) knows less about it than does Mr. Arnold Bennett's little finger.' I am posting you the latest bit about ME. I hope it will reach thee. And now I become an atmosphere surrounding thee, a tonic, a rock, for thee. Yes. Au revoir. Sleep well. I don't—but shall. And I sharply & softly embrace thee,

Your A.B. Little

318. Ouida: Marie Louise de la Ramée (1839–1908), whose popular novels were among the earliest works Bennett reviewed in the nineties.

Hilda Trevelyan: landscape painter active 1908–28, and Hilda Trevelyan (1880–1959), actress, who played in *The Great Adventure* in 1924.

John Franklin: unidentified; reviewed *Those Barren Leaves*.

BERG / MS / 319
(*To Dorothy Cheston*) 75, Cadogan Square
Monday 8.30 a.m.
26–1–25

My sweetest sweetlet,

Before I forget, Knoblock took away those Florentine fancy papers from here the day after I returned, & left them in a bus, & has never seen them since. I don't know what he wrote to Mrs. Bartlett. I always forget to ask him, but I will try to remember next time.... I am following your advice about writing bits of letters at intervals.... Knob was here for lunch yesterday & was much struck by the scenes I had written in the last act of *Prohack*. And so he ought to be. His own contributions to this play have been terribly feeble. Still, it can't be helped. At any rate he has been a useful critic of all that I had done before.... I've nearly finished reading *A Passage to India*. It is a bit uneven, but most of it is simply magnificent.... My 'attack' (stomach & intestinal) is now over. I only got up for lunch yesterday (Sunday) & I slept about 2 hours off & on in the afternoon. I arose at 7 for supper to which came Tertia and spouse & Olive Glendinning (one of my oldest friends, & cousin of Tertia's husband) and spouse. I played duets with Tertia. I played duets with Olive; & Tertia played duets with Olive; and all was very agreeable. They left at 11. On Friday I had taken asamatic chalk with opium for my attack. This spoils my sleep with inane & apparently continuous dreams.... I was rather shocked on Saturday to read in the *New Statesman* a letter from John Rothenstein saying he was preparing a catalogue of the drawings of his 'late father'. William Rothenstein must have died & been reported on one of the days when we did not get *The Times*. He was an old friend of mine, & one of the last things I did before going away for my holiday with you was to refuse an invitation to supper at his house. Young John is also a friend of mine. William was principal of the Royal College of Art, a bad artist with good ideas about teaching art. I have written to his widow. She is a nice woman, who always used to boast that she never read a book.

10.15 p.m.

Just got your 2 letters (Thursday & Friday). I had to wire

you that Paris is *quite* imposs. for me. I had already written to you to that effect. I regret it; but it is so. I was always nearly sure that it would be imposs. but I didn't care to give you a decisive negative in Naples, as you would have replied (perhaps rightly) 'Why be so positive in advance?' I am drowned in work, and behind with everything. Fortunately I am in excellent health (Saturday's crisis now over). I am on the last scenes of the play, & utterly absorbed in them (Knob is no good at them). The mischief is that when I am in full blast, creatively, I either *am*—or I am not. No ordinary business thing can put me out of my stride. For instance I am desperately worried about money, but that never upsets my work in the slightest degree! Strange! But in any matter where my affections are engaged, I am at the mercy of the same. My head was bursting with my final scenes at breakfast. I read your letters, & my head was at once empty of the play. It is nobody's fault but it is a damned nuisance. I shan't get the ideas back until I have posted this & telegraphed you. I hate to telegraph you I can't come. I also hate the idea of you being weeks in London in a hotel; for I am sure it will be exceedingly unpleasant for both of us, & is a great mistake. You had much better stay away till within a week or so of your flat being available. Look here my sweetest girl, *don't ask me to go about looking for hotels for you.* Plenty of things I can do for you, but not that sort of thing. Moreover, it would be very unwise. My phiz is a damned sight too well known. I have asked Ethel to enquire at Sloane St. hotel. I have always said I would not mix up Miss Nerney in our affairs. It is not fair to her. You had much better stay at Belgravia on arrival & from there choose a hotel yourself. Food at Goring is fair. My sweet child I kiss you well. Am frightfully busy.

A.B.

319. *A Passage to India*, E. M. Forster's novel, was published in 1924.

For a letter to John Rothenstein (b. 1901), later director of the Tate Gallery, see Vol. III.

BERG / MS / 320
(*To Dorothy Cheston*)

75, Cadogan Square
6.15 p.m. Tuesday
27 Jan 1925

My sweetest girl,

In my letter this morning I didn't tell you that, *failing* to sleep
(like you), I got up (like you) & proceeded with work—at 5
a.m. I finished the play at 12.45. Miss Nerney thinks it's A1. So
do I. I now have a headache. (But I don't care.) Muriel wrote
me this morning asking me to get a place in a chorus for a friend
of hers who is young & charming & has a child aged 4, and is
thrown on the world. She also asked me to suggest an evening to
dine with them. Now today I had my business lunch with
Lucas. And here is the sort of woman that Muriel *can* be when
she likes. She invited Lucas twice to invite her to a meal, &
twice he put her off. The third time he yielded & asked her. She
then told him that I had told her (1) that he drank heavily, (2)
that he was a dangerous man, (3) that she ought to have
nothing to do with him. I said to him, 'It is true that I told her
that you drank too much, but 2 & 3 are absolutely untrue.' (1)
rather upset him, but I stick to it. (I think it may influence his
future potations.) He said: 'Isn't this sort of thing between men
only? Ought it even to be mentioned to women?' Rather funny,
I thought. But I agreed handsomely with him that I ought
never to have said a word about it to Muriel. Of course Muriel's
behaviour was simply an outrage. She must have known that
she was making a situation of the gravest difficulty between
Lucas & me. (And mind you, I only told her what I did tell her,
at first, because she had asked me whether E.V.L. was 'still
drinking'.) Happily Lucas, as I have often said, is a man of
profound sense. So am I. And we came out of the situation
intact. He began by saying: 'Arnold, I've got something serious
to say to you. But I'll only say it on the condition that you'll
never dig it up again.' When he had told me, I simply couldn't
speak. And he stroked my hand. He said afterwards: 'Why *do*
we have anything to do with that damned woman?' And he
answered this by saying: 'Because of Johnnie, I suppose.' Later
he said that the secret of Johnnie's general attitude toward life
was mere callousness,—he just went blandly on, & never really
troubled about anybody or anything. There is something in

this. Well, I think both E.V.L. & I have emerged from a very trying ordeal with some credit. He said to me: 'I'd sooner anybody had said it than you, because everybody believes in you & your judgement. It's like God saying it.' But what I *did* like about his demeanour was his stroking my hand.

Thursday 10:15

Great haste! Great haste. One of my teeth has come out (false) & I have to go out to the dentist. 45 minutes out of an already full programme! So that I have to hurry. I didn't hear from you this morning. But I heard from her cousin in Paris that my wife is ill in a nursing home in San Remo! An 'urticaire'. I can't think of the English word for 'urticaire'; but it is a very severe rash that swells up the whole body. 'Urtica' is the Latin for nettle; but 'urticaire' is not nettle rash. Cousin Hélène says she knows that this illness is due to Marguerite's sorrow at being alone, etc. But I know it isn't. She had a very severe urticaire about 12 years ago at the Berkeley Hotel. Hélène says she will go down to San Remo if my wife isn't better. But I gather that she *is* better. And I am well aware that the gravity of the illness would lose nothing at the feverish pen of Hélène, who would give her head to see Marguerite with me again. It is astounding that I cannot genuinely convince any of these women that nothing would ever induce me to take Marguerite back. A friend of ours (chiefly mine) wrote me from Paris the other day that Marguerite had been 3 times to see him & was all the time hinting that he might effect a reconciliation. But he knew better. C'est touchant. All morning I shall be with Knobbo going through the last act of *Prohack*. All afternoon with Komisarjevsky going through the scheme of production of *Bright Island*! I dine with Duff tonight. I'll give him your message. How's the work? I got *tons* of stuff for my novel from Max & Roch last night. My sweetest girl, I kiss you well & tenderly & think always of you.

Little

In Harvey & Nichols I saw a very remarkable (what looked to me like) night-dress, black, *extremely* transparent, with no sides to it, practically. It was in a window with lots of other

nightdresses, chemises, etc. etc. And if it isn't a nightgown I
don't know what it is.

L.

320. Bennett wrote *The Bright Island* between January and April 1920, and revised it
in 1923. Theodore Komisarjevsky (1882–1954) produced it for the Stage Society in two
performances at the Aldwych Theatre on 15 and 16 February 1925.

BERG / MS / 321
(*To Dorothy Cheston*)

75, Cadogan Square
29–I–25

My sweetest darling,

   Your Sunday's & Monday's letters. How I sympathise with
you in the insomnia scourge! What solaces me is your keenness
throughout on your work. This is fine. I can always tell the state
of your nerves by the tidiness or otherwise of your writing. Paris
seems a very long distance away—another world; but I should
have loved to come. However, we must try to turn London into
Paris. Though play is all finished I am just as busy, what with
conferences with Komisarjevsky, arrangements at the Lyric
(which is in difficulties), overdue articles, short stories, &
conferences about selling *Prohack*. I shall be rather surprised if
Prohack isn't sold fairly easily. But as for *The Dance Club*—I
tremble to re-read it. Of course my greatest work-preoccupa-
tion by far is the terrific new novel. I have obtained tons more
stuff for it & shall get still more next week. The bigness & the
richness of the theme frightens me. I shall get the real inside
story from Max shortly. Need I say that he knew the lady very
well, & dined with her alone! He told me a lot on Tuesday, but
wouldn't tell me everything while Roch was there. Your
solutions of the suicide mystery are very good, and show that
you have that very important faculty in a novelist—invention.
Soon—too soon—I shall be drowned in that novel. This morn I
must go & look at some big shops, to get ideas for my article on
shops for the *Sunday Pictorial*. All the garments, from frocks to
chemises de nuit etc., will make me think of you. So I don't
mind. It is now 15 days since I left you—or you left me. It seems
longer. Well, we are both exceedingly busy & short of sleep; so
that is some compensation, but only a little. I doubt if you

understand me. Yes, you do. Yes, you do. I often kiss you & do all sorts of things to you & throw you down brutally on beds & things—& you don't know it. I have a dinner tonight—one of those affairs to which people come in order to be in the swim, as you say—you know how formal and stiff I am & how I love tedium. Marie Tempest is coming. Another formal & stiff creature—I don't think.

By the way Cadogan Hotel:—

 Lovely suites at back £2/2/

 Bedroom with bath at back 17/6 (Private bathrooms not
  always to be had)

 Without 12/6

 Back bedrooms on court 10/6

 A front room with bow window 15/6.

Ethel got me all this. She likes the hotel. She is coming tonight—still another stiff creature.

Beloved infant, infanta, wife, sleepless one, nervous one, adorable one, je te bise tendrement.

Little

321. The article on shops appeared in the *Sunday Pictorial* on 15 February.

BERG / MS / 322
(*To Dorothy Cheston*)

[75, Cadogan Square]
8 a.m.
31 Jan 1925

My sweetest girl,

No letter from you yesterday. God knows when you are going to Paris, & whether this will reach you. At first I thought it was useless to write, but afterwards it struck me that you were giving up Paris, or only going there for a day or two. *I* don't know. I wrote nearly all my *Sunday Pictorial* article yesterday afternoon & shall finish it this morning (D.V.). P. Smith is staying with Tertia & is coming this afternoon to have her novel doctored etc. I feel frightfully busy. Rehearsals of *B. Island* have begun, but I am not attending them till Monday. Tania called me up last night just as I was setting off to Grand Theatre with Duff. She returned from Paris on Thursday afternoon & wanted to come here last night *after* the theatre with the Dane (I forget his name), but I wouldn't have it. She goes to play at Norwich today; leaves Norwich at 7:15 Sunday morning; plays at the People's Palace at 2 p.m. Sunday, and plays at the Music Club at 9 p.m. I am going with her to the Music Club. Some life. Well, she is killing herself. Well, the Grand Theatre! A large audience. A feeling of vitality in the place. Shaw has taken a machine-made play of Trebitsch's, left the heavy 1st act, and then worked out the development on realistic and witty lines in the 2nd & 3rd acts. *The thing is simply masterly*, & contains a *lot* of the finest scenes that Shaw ever wrote. Duff & I were carried off our feet. So were other people—in fact most people. I should say that Violet Vanbrugh, Leslie Frith, and Nancy Price have all put money into the venture. And it is astonishing how good scenes make good, or at least tolerable, actors. If anyone had told me that Leslie Frith, who is nobody at all, could adequately sustain a leading part through 2 acts, I could not have believed it. Nancy is good. This play is certainly a commercial proposition. It is first rate work, & it is bound to fill theatres. A good sign for the future. The conventional insincere plays are failing & the others are succeeding. If Ellis (his production is quite decent, if old-fashioned) had begun with this play & followed it with *Don Juan*, or vice versa, he would have made a name for his theatre. Whether it was the exhilaration of this play, or from some other cause—I simply could not sleep. I slept from 2.30 to 5.15 & that was all. Still, I feel perfectly well. I trust that your sleeping is better, & that your work is proceeding well. You are a naughty child, but never mind. Je te bise bien.

Little

322. Pauline Smith's novel was *The Beadle*, published in 1926.
   Shaw adapted a play by Siegfried Trebitsch (1869–1936) as *Jitta's Atonement*. Trebitsch himself was Shaw's translator into German. Violet Vanbrugh (1867–1942), Leslie Frith (1889–1961), and Nancy Price (1880–1970) starred in the production. Nancy Price played in the stage adaptation of Bennett's novel *Helen with the High Hand* many years earlier.

BERG / MS / 323
(*To Dorothy Cheston*)   75, Cadogan Square
                                          10 a.m.
                                          2–2–25

My sweetest sweet,

Your volume of letters (Monday, Tuesday, Wednesday, etc) arrived this morning. I had not heard of you since Thursday. I am very glad that the story is so rapidly proceeding. Perhaps by this time it is finished. But is it *finished* in the real sense? I mean, is it ready to go to the typewriters. I don't see any advantage in troubling Ethel S. again. The best course is for you to go to a hotel provisionally, & then see other hotels for yourself. Nobody else can settle it for you, & perhaps you wouldn't like what somebody else does like. Ethel S. certainly liked the Cadogan, & I should say, myself, that it is a far higher-class place than the Goring. Food at Goring not good, I think. I can only judge by the look of the hall, the demeanour of the servants, & the appearance of the clients. No use discussing further about the comparative advantages of hotel life. All I say is that I shall be very agreeably surprised if it works out well. (Note, I shall try to make it work out well.) For one thing, whether you have a suite or not, if you receive very frequent visits, especially at eventide, from the same man, you will undoubtedly become the subject of remark & *perhaps* of protest from the landlord. (This depends on the hotel.) The man will be also the subject of remark, & his identity will be known within 24 hours.... Here I am discussing it again! I very much question whether you diagnose correctly the previous situation at number 21A. I doubt if the *causes* of trouble were either servants or physical conditions of environment. The ideal servant does not exist. You are exceedingly difficult to please in regard to servants, or in regard to most other things. I was staggered that Sunday morning when you had the row with Colletty, telling her she must either apologise for her intolerable insolence or leave entirely,—I mean I was staggered when I heard the reason, in the taxi. Viz, that she had said she came on Sundays solely to oblige you. She was obviously annoyed & strained at the stitching, as to which, knowing her brain-feebleness, you ought to have given her full instructions at the start. Believe me, my child, that employers constantly support

far worse things than this from servants. And as regards
evenings, the servant didn't trouble you then because she
wasn't there, and also, for most of the period, you had to be out
every evening. As regards noises (apart from street noises) I
don't think you will find a quieter place. You *may*, but it is very
improbable. I undertake to say that you were less disturbed
than I am. I don't think I've ever yet told you that every
morning at 7 a.m. there is a fine awakening noise (15 minutes of
it) in the next room to mine (in No. 77). And my servants, &
Miss N., never seem to settle down at night till midnight or so. I
don't know what you mean by restraining yourself, not giving
yourself, because of the conditions. The conditions in that
respect will most probably always be the same. And they are
the same, nearly always, for the vast majority of married people
too. The v.m. of m.p. only want children at *very* rare intervals,
perhaps once in 3 or 4 years; and the rest of the time they have
to employ one device or another to avoid them. We have
employed every known device. There is no doubt that you are
excessively difficile. You can't help it, & you have all my
sympathies, but the fact remains.... No, in my opinion the
previous trouble at 21A & other places sprang from the spirit in
which you originally came to me. I am absolutely sure it did.
That spirit was bound to lead to trouble. This trouble was
exacerbated by the struggle between us over the yacht. And it
was brought to a head when you had the singular idea of
suggesting to me that you should take a second lover. Physically, I have not yet got over this. It needs an extraordinarily
broad-minded and understanding man to get over it at all. I
refuse absolutely to disguise or gloss over my opinion of it. The
improvement in our relations (which began only at Naples)
was in my view due to 2 causes. First the working in your mind
of something that Mrs. [?Watkins] said to you. 2nd. My sudden
determination never to let you seriously irritate me, after the
cocktail scenes at Genoa & others just after that. I saw the *folly*
of allowing myself to be concerned in your welfare up to the
point of serious irritation. I also saw that to be irritated in any
marked degree was unworthy of me and a gross failure in the
management of intercourse. I saw that by nature you were 50
times more irritable & difficile than me, and that it was part of
my job to allow for that. That you are sometimes wilfully

naughty is of course undeniable—and you don't deny it. Your instinct to think the worst of another, as in the case of my cable to you, is also undeniable. You do it about everyone. I may say that my attitude toward you has never altered. I have always sincerely thought of *your* welfare & happiness; I am always thinking of *you*; and I have always tried to oblige you, except when I could not conscientiously do so. As to this my conscience is clear. I know that my patience, though great, has often fallen short of requirements. I also eagerly admit that of late you have made a tremendous effort, on all sorts of occasions, to keep our relations in an ideal state—and you have succeeded.

Some of your observations, my sweetest girl, are so *naïve* as to be *touchant*; they moisten my eyes.

As regards Komisarjevsky, I have only seen 1 production of his, and it was good. Whatever he was in the past, I have noticed one thing about him at our 2 interviews,—his steady gaze at me. So that he must have altered. I have little hope of the *B.I.* production, as there is no time for rehearsals. I finished my article on Saturday, and have another to do at once. And I must do a story at once. Last night I took Tania to a restaurant which I *hadn't* frequented for 30 years. Afterwards she took me to Music Circle, where she played. At 11.15 I insisted on leaving. But it was very good. I had a good night on Saturday, but last night only about 3 hours (de fantastique flatuosités).

Milly's child is a girl. They are both here, temporarily, and all is going well with them.

I expect I have forgotten about a million things I ought to have mentioned.

Je te bise tendrement, ma Dorothée chérie.

Little

Rothenstein is *not* dead. It was an inadvertence of the *New Statesman*. His wife has been snowed under with condolences by post!!

323. The few known reviews of *The Bright Island* were very mixed, ranging from delight to boredom.
Milly: Fred Harvey's wife.

BERG / MS / 324
(*To Dorothy Cheston*)

75, Cadogan Square
11–2–25

Fairest girl,

Your two letters—last night & this morning, enchanted me. I laugh silently at the thought of your thinking that I don't understand you. I am most deeply aware that my 'strong' letters are not appetising. The point is that they are inevitable. I never write a strong letter till I get one from you. But all the time I'm writing one I am cherishing you, O fairest. And when you are naughty, & I know you are naughty, & you know I know you are naughty, I am still cherishing you. Constancy is my strong suit. You might get smacked one day, you do occasionally get thrown down and crushed between my arms, & my eyes burn into yours at close quarters,—nevertheless constancy is my strong suit. I mentioned your name today to Miss Nerney for the first time for ages, & said you were coming over, but I hoped not today. She said the weather *was* a pity, & how she *knew* you hated a rough sea. Then said the Damsel: 'Would you like me to have some flowers sent to her room?' Rather nice of her. As regards the day of your arrival, you have never *fixed* a date, but you have suggested at one time or other, *every* day this week except Tuesday & Friday. I *had* to wire you this morning. The night was terrible. One of Owensmith's men went onto the roof to secure a cauk that was noisy; but he could not stay there to do it—the wind was so cyclonic! I slept better because I stuffed up my ears. I rushed into my study early to look at the barometer. Falling. And (4 p.m.) *it is still falling*. I have now given up all hope of Alan Trotter (Harlequin—a long & important part). Why do such men become actors? He has not even a voice; and of talent, not a trace! However, I don't care. I must now close this. Doll Mass & E. V. Lucas were here last night. Lucas would *not* drink! At most he had ½ glass of wine—no port, no brandy, no whiskey. It was touching & pathetic. Perhaps he went home & drank there. My sweetest dangerous face, do you see my eyes gazing at you? I kiss yours, & hurt you in the vise known to the world as my arms. (But perhaps you'll be gone before this arrives.) I wired you at 11 a.m.

There is *no* sign of improvement in the weather. Are *you* better, even if the weather isn't?

Splendid about Mimi. I bet you they will implore me to go to the wedding.

Bise, Little

P.S. I have a bad cold. Usual rehearsal cold.

324. Alan Trotter: dancer and actor. Others of the cast of *The Bright Island* included Felix Aylmer as the Captain, Frederick Lloyd and Isabel Jeans as James and Susan Maddox, Arthur Pusey as Pierrot, and Dorothy Hulmes-Gore as Columbine.

Dorothy Massingham (1889–1933), actress and playwright, daughter of H. W. Massingham. She played in *Abraham Lincoln* at the Lyric Hammersmith in 1919.

Mimi Godebski married André Blaque-Belair.

CAMBRIDGE / MS / 325
(*To Richard Bennett*)

75, Cadogan Square
23–2–25

My dear Sir & Rich,

I have been ill all week (? flu). 3 days in bed. Only out of the house 3 times in 7 days. No work whatever. But I am now better, I resume work today. I wish you would give some descriptions of the men in power who say these bright things to you. Then I could judge better what they are worth—I mean the things. It occurred to me for a moment that to say to a young tyro: 'Look out for a job that you can do better & oust the present holder', might be a 'common form' at Sunlight, a cliché, a regular proceeding. However, I am inclined to think that it is not. What gave me to suspect was that 2 of them should say it. Evidently there is scope for you there, & that in my opinion is the main thing. Also there is what I call staff-fluidity. Owing to *Kismet* Knoblock has been invisible for a week, & will be. You & 'Bunny' are quite wrong about at any rate part of Knoblock's house. The dining-room is awfully clever, but inexcusable. It is a fake & an ugly fake. The upper floors are much better. In fact very good. But would you care to live in a museum? That is what I ask myself about all Knoblock's houses & flats that I have seen. They are wonderful, often beautiful, always complete to the door-furniture; but are they homes? Still, I admit he is rather marvellous. My work is gravely in arrears & I am earning nothing, & very poor. When shall I owe you money? I took D. Cheston to the 1st night of *Hamlet*, which was one of the greatest stage-functions for years past. (I liked the show much, in the main). We were all there. The Asquiths & I had the chief show in the newspapers next day. In fact in some papers the A's & I were the only people important enough to mention. But I must say I was startled to see the *Evening Standard* calling my hair white. Is it? I suppose as usual you are reading nothing. If only you *read*, that would be a great bond between the Russells & you. Walter Russell is just about the greatest reader (of modern stuff) I ever met. I must now close, the portion of my time allotted to your rising self being exhausted. I am glad you enjoyed the weekend. I doubt if I did.

> Love,
> Your recuperant uncle,

> A.B.

325. Richard began work at Lever Brothers Ltd, Port Sunlight, in November 1924.
Kismet: Knoblock's great success of 1911, revived in April. The house referred to was probably Beach House, Worthing.
Bunny: unidentified.
Hamlet: John Barrymore's production.
Herbert Henry Asquith (1852–1928), long-time leader of the Liberal party.
Walter Russell: unidentified.

STOKE / MS / 326
(*To Margaret Beardmore*)

> 75, Cadogan Square
> 5–3–25

My sweet niece,

This is about the 1st moment I've had to reply to your letter. Some people have recently left from lunch, & more are coming in for tea, & then I have to go to the theatre tonight (Sunday). I arrived home from Naples, Rome, & Paris on Jan 15, & have been hard at it ever since with one interval for flu and another interval for going to Brighton to recoup (very short). I am now recouped. Personally, I don't think it's such an awfully good thing (for you) going to live at home. In addition to the house being too small, you will certainly have a trying time. I hear from Cedric that your mother is the picture of health. She may be the picture of it, but she isn't health, especially in the matter of nerves. Of course, *I* maintain that what your mother most needs is firm handling. Will she get it? I doubt. I have a sort of vague idea that, literarily speaking, there may be something in Cedric. He is young, & I much mistrust precocity; but I question if he is really precocious. Anyhow if there *is* anything in him I will see that it comes out. He couldn't have chosen a better uncle for that particular purpose. Nor am I much smitten with the notion of you living in the Potteries at all. Hence I hope that after a proper interval you will move on to something else and something better. I missed seeing Alan while your mother was here. The only times when he could arrange to come up from Eastbourne I had to be out. I was very busy just then, & I am very busy just now. I agree with you that Herzen Vol III is not as good as I & II. But there are jolly passages in it. Have you read *The Constant Nymph*? If not you must read it, as it is A1. The author, Margaret Kennedy, was among those who came for lunch today. She is a shy and caustic-clever woman of, say, 38. It is the best novel by a new author that I have read for years. I'm re-writing a play, about a lady who runs a dance-club. I'd finished it once, & thought it was good; but 3 expert friends who have read it say that it won't do at all as it is; so I am humbly and charmingly writing it again. I smile; but it is a great bore, re-writing is! When shall you come to London?

Love,
Your aff uncl,

A.B.

326. With her mother's illness, Margaret Beardmore returned to Stoke-on-Trent, and until her marriage she was assistant organizer of physical training for the city. During World War II she was games mistress at Brownhills High School for Girls in Tunstall.

The fourth volume of *My Past and Thoughts*, by Alexander Herzen (1812–70), was being published in English.

The Constant Nymph was published in 1924. For a letter to Margaret Kennedy (1896–1967) see Vol. III.

CAMBRIDGE / MS / 327
(*To Richard Bennett*)

75, Cadogan Square
6–4–25

My dear Rich,

Yesterday's is one of the most interesting letters I have received from you. Strange you couldn't find the 'Cave of Harmony'!

In the private & semi-private reports, I should advise you to be careful of the phraseology. Unless you are a great master of phrase you will always get more weight by a mild phrase than by a strong one; moderation is a quality much appreciated in this country. In today's *Daily Express*, where I have flamboyantly started a controversy in the grand manner about decadent plays, you will find an example to the contrary, but it is exceptional, & moreover the work of an expert—ahem! You may be interested to know that this affair is a plant devised by me, at Edgar Selwyn's request, to boom *Dancing Mothers*, which is very ricketty. The *Daily Express* does not know this. It may further interest you to know, with reference to the *D. E's* leading article, that on Friday the editor of the *D. E.* expressed personally to me views entirely contrary to the views in the leading article today! Doubtless the leading article was done so in order to promote a fracas. Yes, I can well understand your antipathy to regular routine, especially at early hours. Still, this is a fine thing for you, or for anyone. You will perceive the benefit of it later on. I seem to see bright hopes for you at Sunlight. I have been illish. I was taking some French pills (full of thyroid, pituitary & suprarenal etc) to the end of reducing my embonpoint. After 15 or 17 days I began to perspire & to puff—more & more. And I could feel my heart twittering around. So I sent for the doctor. He told me to stop the pills instantly, & forbade all dancing & other physical efforts for ten days. I had been positively assured that the pills were perfectly harmless. I don't see that they have reduced me, either. So that the whole thing is a bit of a sell. Moral, don't (at my age) take strange drugs without consulting a doctor. These pills were earnestly recommended to me by Mrs. Somerset Maugham. She is dining here tonight together with husband, Viola Tree,

Max Beerbohm, etc. She will hear from me on the subject! I am
still far from normal.

Love,

Your infected uncle,

A.B.

327. The Cave of Harmony: Elsa Lanchester's theatre on Gower Street.

'Is Real Life Worse Than the Stage?' appeared on the front page of the *Express*.
Bennett defended Lonsdale's *Spring Cleaning*. Coward's *The Vortex*, and Selwyn's and
Edmund Goulding's *Dancing Mothers* against the charge that they show us the cesspool
of life. He did not suppose that an unchaste mother and a son who takes drugs (*The
Vortex*) are unheard of in real life. Perhaps people who criticized these plays would like
to criticize *Hamlet* on the same grounds. The leader admired Bennett's logic, but
nevertheless thought that one character in *Spring Cleaning* was an insult to the audience.
One just does not meet such immoral people in one's daily life. On the 13th Bennett
replied to the leader, saying that he thought that plays of today held the mirror up to
nature about as well as plays ever had. He supposed that contemporary drama was not
of the highest quality for the reason that theatre managers had to please the public in
order to survive and the public wanted superficial drama.

Viola Tree (1884–1938) starred in *Body and Soul* and presently became a friend of
Bennett and Dorothy.

<table>
<tr><td>BERG / MS / 328
(To Dorothy Cheston)</td><td>Yacht Marie Marguerite
Southampton
6.45 a.m.
17–8–25</td></tr>
</table>

My darling child,

So tired I couldn't keep awake last night. I was in bed by
about 10.10. I must have slept 6½. Anyhow I was having my tea
at 6 a.m. feeling that I had had ENOUGH sleep. I then went on
deck to do my exercises. Marvellous! The sun just rising
through the mist—as clear reddish amber as a stone on a ring
which *you haven't* got on your finger. Yachts all round. There
was scarcely a yacht in the water yesterday afternoon. But as
evening progressed they one after another crept in, like girls in
white frocks returning with an air of innocence from some
secret & distant rendezvous. There are 2 Belgian canal-yachts
which give a foreign air to the water. Prior met us at the station,
intensely delighted to get us back, radiating his satisfaction. All
the crew delighted too. Yacht in order. I have resolved to do *no*
work for several days. A strange feeling—vast stretches of time;
empty! I now discover that generally speaking I keep my brain
always working, arranging or planning *some* work. I never even

walk from my house to yours without having some definite cerebration to do on the way. I think a slight & slender holiday may do me good. Anyhow I am exceeding well this morn. Of course it is nice being quite alone. But also, equally of course, it is *not* nice. What I wish (impossible) is that you should *love* yachting, like, e.g. Dolly does. That would be the ideal. I repeat, imposs. You do not like it. Naturally, as usual, *a great deal* of my cerebration is spent upon yourself. I live again certain moments. When you lay back on the sofa on Saturday night, & I kissed you a long time, you were exquisite. Also when you said goodbye to me Sunday afternoon, & said in your appealing voice: 'We *are* near, aren't we?'—well you were exquisite.

I hope you are enjoying yourself & working, & not worrying too much about Mary. You *must* let all sorts of things go by, with her. Everyone has to do so in such cases. I don't see how you can *reproach* her for not seeing to the button on your shoe. You can only ask her to do it. It is first of all *your* business to keep an eye on your clothes. She is the servant & she has 2 floors to see to, & it is enough for her. She never set out to be a lady's maid, & she never will be one. That's how I look at the affair. I shall wire you, fair one, either tonight or tomorrow morning what our next destination is. The weather here is marvellous, but no wind.

I will now see you as you were on Saturday night, & Sunday afternoon as you were, & as you were many other times, and permit myself to kiss you. Yes we are near, nearer, nearest, dearest.

A.B.

P.S. I forgot to bring the key of my private drawer here, & *the MS. of my novel*!!!!!!! Miss N. will have to hand it to Sep this afternoon at Waterloo.

A.B.

328. Bennett went sailing for the last two weeks in August.
Prior (d. 1928): the new captain of the *Marie Marguerite*.

BERG / MS / 329
(*To Dorothy Cheston*)   Yacht Marie Marguerite
                                          2.30 p.m.
                                          21–8–25

My sweet girl,

I have lunched & slept, and we are now approaching Ostende. We left Newhaven at 9.30 yesterday, Thursday, morning, & had a quiet night at sea. The wind was contrary the whole time. At first, all day yesterday in fact, the sun shone & it was lovely. Same sun this morning; but it hid itself & we have had some rain. The sky is not very overcast. We shall not stay in Ostende long; in fact we may leave on Sunday again, if we go to Bruges tomorrow. I did no work up to yesterday, but yesterday evening I began thinking about my novel again, also about short stories. My health is eccellentissimo. Sep is still very quiet, but he is improving. I do not think he is awfully interesting, but one can't be sure. Anyhow he reads very little. I wonder if your rehearsals have begun. I see that on Wednesday Tania had an encore. I am still thinking of you & reading *Anna Karenina*, which is so much superior to any novel I could write. Isn't it disgusting? Isn't it discouraging? Lillah & Sep are dying to see Ostende, which they have never seen. I've told them it's most romantic; which it is. The crew is lowering the sails preparatory to entering the harbour. All is excitement. I alone am down below, writing unto thee. Well, I trust you are all right. I often want to see you when I'm alone in here, & think how badly I treat you, & how hard I am, & how I comprends rien. That 'M. of Mag' is really wonderful. For several days I have had enough sleep—despite 2 nites at sea. Now my sweetest infant, I kiss you well, in various places, & I hope you are not in pain, yes I do.

Little

329. Septimus came on the cruise for his health. It was not known at the time that he had consumption.

Dorothy was rehearsing Pirandello's *And That's the Truth* (*Right You Are*), which Playfair was producing at the Lyric Hammersmith.

M. of Mag: milk of magnesia.

BERG / MS / 330
(*To Dorothy Cheston*)

Yacht Marie Marguerite
Saturday 5.30 p.m.
22–8–25

My sweetest Dot,

I wrote you this morning, & wired you. But as I have since received 2 excellent letters from you I write you again. Shan't post till tomorrow. I'm impressed at the length of your part. I've heard from N.P. saying he had no idea at all that my name had been put into the lease as a surety. I think you are right about Tania. By the way if you want seats for the 1st night of *Prisoners of War*, telephone to Duff. He will give you them. He said I could have seats for friends. He is the chairman of the company that runs *Prisoners of War*. He may not yet be back from Sweden. I think you are quite right about Tania. Your macintosh is here. You must have left it at Dartmouth. I have been wearing it. It is too small, but I can just get it on. My own is worn out. But yours is a far better one than mine ever was. You are certainly underpaid in 'Pirandello'. The weather is bad, with intervals of sun, but very heavy showers. Re dining room. I cannot visualise the effect of colours from descriptions thereof. But you have been so successful on the lower floor that I have very little doubt about your success on the upper. I hereby authorise you to spend as a beginning £25 on the foundations of this room. I will give it you when I see you. (I am longing to see you.) Freddie took us all to Bruges today in a car. We had, as usual, a magnif lunch at the Panier d'Or. It was followed by a great thunder-and-rain storm. I still enjoy Bruges very much. We got back at 3.45. More rain. Lillah has gone out to get her hair washed & Freddie to be masseured; and Sep I think has gone out alone. Sep is fitting in all right. But he is very taciturn, except when he & Freddie are ragging one another. Of course, he is provincial, but he 'comes through'. He has been worn down (& worn out) by existence; & has lost his resiliency & his capacity for enthusiasm. But he has good taste, au fond, and is improving in various ways. Your letters seem quite cheerful, & I hope they accurately express your mood. I suppose you feel that I am always thinking about you. You ought to, if you are really 'psychic'. I don't yet know what my next address will be. Haven't got full information about naviga-

tion & depths of canals etc; so I don't know where the ship *can*
go.

Sunday morning 6.30
[A few lines unreadable.] No doubt I am very bizarre; but I
am as I am. And your power over me is startling, perturbing
sometimes. I suppose that my desire is about six times, or more,
as frequent as yours. Perhaps that is natural. Anyhow it can't
be helped. Incidentally it shows how much my health has
improved. This acting of yours is splendid for your career, & for
your career I am very joyful about it. But it will be immensely
uncheerful for yours devotedly. [A few lines unreadable.] The
English-speaking sailor who was to have come yesterday to
guide us in Holland did not come. I know not what will happen.
I shall cable at the earliest poss. moment. Je te bise
formidablement.

Little Mr. Dot.

330. *Prisoners of War*, by J. R. Ackerley, opened at the Playhouse Theatre on 31
August. Playfair produced it.

The unreadable lines in the letter were made so by Dorothy by inking over Bennett's
writing with india ink, probably in 1934 when she prepared her memoir with its
selection of letters.

BERG / MS / 331   Yacht Marie Marguerite
(*To Dorothy Cheston*)   Dordrecht
                                    Friday 7 a.m.
                                    28–8–25

My darling Dot,
The situation must & will be handled with the greatest
possible love and commonsense. [Several lines unreadable.]
The event has happened & we shall tackle all the sequel not
only cheerfully but gaily. So far as *I* am concerned I adore the
idea of your having a child by me. And if you adore it too that
aspect of it is all right. What disturbs me is the extreme
difficulty of the father, who will be in his 60th year, doing his
full duty by the child. When that child is ten I shall be seventy. I
daresay I shall be in great vigour; but I shall be seventy. The
economic aspect also troubles me. You see, the bulk of my
possessions, under our separation deed, goes to my wife, &
nothing can alter this. Of course I shall take every means to put

as much as possible of my possessions into other hands as opportunity offers. I shall have to work harder, but I doubt whether that will cause me much discomfort. We shall have to be more careful, in fact much more. The whole balance of life will be altered. Before, & during, & immediately after, *you* will of course have the great bulk of the burden moral & physical— indeed almost all of it. But afterwards the main economic responsibility will be *mine*, & it will always be there. I must tell you that if I am to be six months out of England my novel will have to be abandoned. I can just manage with a month or two out of England; but I cannot remain indefinitely away from my sources of reference, & especially from Max. The novel is not going well. These things having been said I must also tell you that I have a curious feeling of elation, of response to a challenge from destiny. I love you more (which I should not have thought possible). I desire intensely to embrace you and inspire you to accomplish well what lies before you. And I shall be more masterful. The yacht will reach Rotterdam tonight, and will set forth for the Hook of Holland & England on Saturday. I have the Rosses and Knoblock coming on Tuesday, & I do not want to put them off, & must not unless absolutely necessary to do so, which it in all probability won't be if you continue rehearsing. But I shall come up to London for one night. If I could sleep at your place I should; but I will warn the parlourmaid at 75. You might get Griffin to call in the evening or for dinner. It might be Monday or Tuesday: depends on the weather. I am expecting a wire from you at Rotterdam this afternoon. If I don't get it I shall go right on & wire on my arrival at the white cliffs of O.E. And now I kiss you, mother, & more so than ever.

Little

331. Dorothy telegraphed to Bennett that she was pregnant. He telegraphed in return, 'Very Sorry. Very glad. Shall catch boat Hook of Holland, be with you tomorrow.'
Again the unreadable lines were made so by Dorothy.

BERG / MS / 332   Yacht Marie Marguerite
(*To Dorothy Cheston*)   Rotterdam
                                   Saturday 6.35 a.m.
                                   29–8–25

My darling Dot,

This is the 2nd night I have lain awake various hours thinking about you, & feeling somehow the life grow within you (for after all, as you say, I am very feminine). I am well, not depressed at all, but very much on the alert; and I hope you are. Curious, while at Middelburg we were extremely struck by the beauty of the native women's costume. So much so that I bought a complete one for you. It is high waisted. I was also much struck by the lovely effect of it on young women with child. Of course this was before I had the least idea of your condition. It makes them look like 15th & 16th cent. madonnas. There is of course not the slightest attempt to disguise the condition, indeed the dress accentuates it, & renders it extraordinarily beautiful. The contrast between these women, & the young landlady of the café, where we had tea one day, who wore an ordinary costume designed to hide her pregnancy (without the least success in doing so) was really remarkably in favour of the former. I was glad to have your wire, & I think an operation will not be necessary. I have always had a strong objection to operations. Many doctors simply love them. However in any case we must be guided by the best advice. I leave here today at noon. The weather is good, and I *may* get up to London on *Monday*. I am exceedingly anxious to see you. I think it will be better for me to sleep at home. I should return to the yacht on the following day with the Rosses & Knoblock. (This affair has necessitated a lot of cabling.) The Keebles & I went over to the Hague yesterday to see some diplomats at the Palace of Peace, and had a very interesting time. The Hague is a fine town, finer than I thought the last time I was there. Not that I care about the Hague being a fine town. What I care about is you being a fine woman.

I kiss you most tenderly.

                                                      Little

P.S. Of course I shall wire the moment I reach England. If you have an engagement for Monday night, don't break it, unless you want to, if I come then. I can see you in the morning. I think you have an engagement for Tuesday night (*Prisoners of War*). I told Duff to send you seats. And Monday is your birthday!

Little

332. On 1 September Bennett wrote to Winifred Nerney from Cadogan Square:
I have never mentioned to you the subject of my relations with Dorothy Cheston, because I felt that if I did so, formally, I might put you in a rather delicate position. I thought it was better that you should have no formal knowledge of them from me; and my reserve was in no way due to any lack of confidence in your discretion and your loyalty, which to my mind have always been unsurpassable and for which I could not be too grateful. Happily Miss Cheston has been received by my principal friends exactly as if she was my wife, which she ought to be and would be if circumstances permitted, but on the other hand of course we have observed all the external conventions. The situation is now going to be complicated by the fact that there is a strong probability of Miss Cheston becoming a mother. I tell you this because I prefer to be open with you in so important a matter, and not because it will make any difference at all to the external conventions of my life here. I detest concealing things from you, as I think you have deserved better from me than that.

CAMBRIDGE / MS / 333
(*To Richard Bennett*)

75, Cadogan Square
8–9–25

My dear Rich,

Thanks for your letter of yesterday. Look here, I will tell you something—namely the reason why I came home so soon. You will, I know, treat the news with all due wisdom, benevolence, and discretion. You are the first member of the family to hear of it. You cannot have failed to notice the closeness of the relations between Dorothy and me. It is indeed known to most of my friends here, who usually invite us together. The present point is that in April next Dorothy expects to become a mother. This should not be, but it will be. As the ideas of this age are very different from those of the past, I have every expectation that everything will be alright, so long as all the external conventions are observed, as they have been up to now. I may tell you that your aunt M. will not agree to a divorce, which does not in the least surprise me. Of course the two separate ménages (Dorothy's & mine) will continue just as before. Dorothy is somewhat alarmed, but much more delighted. Mr. Tayler cannot contain his joy. I don't want to suggest anything to you that you don't feel like doing. If you *do* feel like doing it, send

Dorothy a nice note. But if you don't that will be perfectly all right. I've been without Miss Nerney for 8 days. Thank God she returns tonight. I've been without Fred ditto. God knows when he will return. The yacht has been held up at Flushing (with various other yachts) by the gale. He is on board. I've been without a parlourmaid ditto. She returns tomorrow.

I've written to John Macleay, although it would have been more regular for me to send the introduction to you & for you to present it. However...

I am very busy,

Love,
Your expectant uncle,

A.B.

Dorothy will play in the Pirandello for about 6 weeks.

A.B.

333. On 2 September Bennett wrote to Georges Bion to sound him out on the possibility of divorce.

John MacCleay (1870–1955) was editor of the *Liverpool Post*. Richard had hopes of doing some journalistic writing.

Bennett wrote to H. G. Wells on the 9th:

And now I have to tell you that my Dorothy is to become a mother. Rather a startler for the undersigned! She is alarmed & delighted at the discovery. Friends have the air of being ecstatic with joy. I perceive that I have a new & violent interest in life. The only flaw in the situation is that it was not deliberately brought about.

KENNERLEY / MS / 334
(*To Tertia Kennerley*)

75, Cadogan Square
14–9–25

Dear Tertia,

Thanks for p.c. By this time you will be able to judge Sep for yourself—whatever you may think of him, he is immensely better than a month ago. At Southampton station his appearance shocked me. He had no appetite, but a big cough. I think he is very nice—perhaps nicer than ever. He was beloved in the yacht by everyone. Sissie too is wonderfully better. She says she will stand for the County Council. She sleeps 6 hours, & is very bright. But she still complains of her heart. I had something to tell you, & didn't mean to write it. But as Sissie was up here I couldn't very well not tell her, & as I can't come down before Saturday, when probably you won't be alone, I must write you. (I think I shall give Emily a miss.) I was summoned home a fortnight ago by the news of the probability that Dorothy Cheston (of whom you must have heard) would become a mother. (A slip.) Startling. I found her excited & delighted. One or two of her friends also. The 2 or 3 of my friends whom I have told are equally delighted. The discovery was made after the rehearsals of the Pirandello had begun. As the event won't be till April, she will play for the present, under doctor's advice. By the way I have had nothing whatever to do with putting her into this play. She knew Playfair before me. In fact I knew her through him, as he cast her for the lead in *Body & Soul* at Liverpool, where I sat next to her at a supper. I find also that I am credited with putting her into Donald Calthrop's Shakespeare at the Kingsway & with financing Calthrop. This is absolutely untrue. I had nothing whatever to do with it, nor did I furnish Calthrop with 1d. I did suggest her to Harrison for *The Great Adv.*, & he was delighted with her. She is 34, daughter of Chester Cheston the architect (dead), & brother of Cheston the painter. Her mother is a rich woman of 70, who lives in hotels. When I speak of my age, her reply is that her father was just over my age when she was born. She is as tall as I am, and a hefty wench. I see all the drawbacks of the matter; but am getting rather excited and pleased too. Socially there will be little difficulty as my friends have greatly taken to her & generally ask us together. Sissie met her several times & likes her very much. Georges Bion tells me that in his opinion Marguerite will never agree to a divorce; but this remains to be seen—later on. The Phillpottses are enchanted. I think I needn't tell you any more now.

If Mary cares to go with me to hear Harriet Cohen play the 1st Beethoven concerto on Friday I will take her, & put her on to a 22 home. The concert ends about 10. Queens Hall. She might send me a p.c. by return. Eat here about 6.45. I'm sorry the U.S.A. scheme is drooping.

Yours, A.B.

On Thursday doubtless William will say when you will be at home.

334. On Dorothy's family, see the Introduction, pp. xxxi–xxxii.

CAMBRIDGE / MS / 335
(*To Richard Bennett*)

75, Cadogan Square
22–9–25

My dear Rich,

Thanks for yours of yesterday. I suppose you have now given up writing on Sundays. I quite understand about the atmosphere of P.S. Of course you must not on any account go to live there. There is no reason why you should not know lots of people in Liverpool. I'll speak to Dorothy about the office; she knows all sorts there. You might go and see Armstrong at the Playhouse Theatre. I suspect you know him, but if you don't you have only to mention my name. Go and see a play. Show an interest in his work. Ask to meet 1 or 2 of the artists, and there you are. Ought you not to belong to the Sandon Club? I don't think the University Club would be much use in the evenings. Besides, there are no women there. You 'must have women— they unbend the mind'. Of course also you have to 'stick it'. That is part of the business. I felt very much like you feel now when I first came to London. Only I'd no social relations whatever, & couldn't get any for a long time—except one clerk in the office, a fellow named Eland, who had a passion for bibliography; which meant a great deal to me. *You* can undoubtedly know plenty of people in Liverpool. I expect Macleay is away. He will be certain to reply.

I much doubt the chances of *And that's the truth*. The play suffers from lack of variety in the plot; also from bad production. The receipts so far are not good. But the 1st night was all right. I see that I was wearing 'a huge buttonhole' & smoking 'an enormous cigar'. I was smoking a small cigar and wore no buttonhole of any sort. Last night I went with the Eadies to the 1st night of *Taffy* at the Royalty. It was dreadful. My boredom was mountainous. However I had a good lark at the dinner at their house before the play. They're coming here a week today to *lunch*, as Dorothy can't dine. She is giving an A1 performance at the Lyric, & the nervous strain of 1st night & dress rehearsals is over.

Love,
Your resourceful uncle,

A.B.

335. William Armstrong (1882–1952) was at this time a director at the Liverpool Playhouse. He was mounting a production of *What the Public Wants*.

John Eland was a fellow clerk at Le Brasseur & Oakley. Bennett describes him in *The Truth About an Author*:

He could chatter in idiomatic French like a house on fire, and he knew the British Museum Reading Room from its centre to its periphery. He first taught me to regard a book not as an instrument for obtaining information or emotion, but as a book, printed at such a place in such a year by so-and-so, bound by so-and-so, and carrying colophons, registers, water-marks, and fautes d'impression. He was acquainted, I think, with every second-hand bookstall in the metropolis; and on Saturday afternoons we visited most of them. We lived for bargains and rarities. We made it a point of honour to buy one book every day....

Bennett himself issued two catalogues of books entitled *A Century of Books for Bibliophiles*, the first in 1891, the second probably in 1892.

And That's The Truth opened on 17 September, with Nancy Price and Claude Rains. Dorothy played Signora Sirelli.

Taffy, by Caradoc Evans, was playing at the Royalty Theatre.

KENNERLEY / MS / 336
(*To Tertia Kennerley*)

75, Cadogan Square
9–10–25

My dear Tertia,

Thanks for your letter. You will be relieved to know that I have never been so contented & excited as I now am. I've seen to your seats for tonight. Dorothy is well indeed & most pleased with things. Supposing you met her at the first night of the next Lyric piece? (As you like. I don't think.) I don't think Emily ought to be annoyed. My letter was most sweet, & not at all final. She hasn't even had the courtesy to answer it yet. Today I get a request from Sissie to write her election address for her (City Council)! I have damn well refused. I am tremendously busy. Going down to Brighton on Monday to meet Mamma Cheston.

I am glad to say that all my friends are very (what E. Phillpotts would call) 'sporting' about my affair.

Yours, A.B.

KENNERLEY / MS / 337
(*To Tertia Kennerley*)

> 75, Cadogan Square
> 13–10–25

Dear Tertia,

I trust you are only pretending when you imply that D. Cheston would not be much interested & keen to meet you and W.W.K. I had never before suggested it because, well, dash it, there is a certain delicacy in these matters. Tu me comprends. I hope you & W.W. will come to dine here. I suppose Wednesday 21st *might* suit all parties? I haven't a night till then, except this Saturday, & that is not quite sure. Mamma Cheston is a great infirm old lark, striving to be very serious etc, but easily made to giggle. I offered her a most magnif. lunch—& then Harry Preston wouldn't let me pay for it! Emily is rather naughty. I wish you could see the letter I spent on her. It began 'My dear Em. I do *not* want to disoblige you.' I then gave her my arguments against an absolutely deaf person being brought just to look at me. I told her I was looked at a great deal too much. And I concluded: 'If you have any other arguments in reserve, push them up to the front.' To which she has not deigned to reply.

> Your aff elder brother,
>
> A.B.

P.S. I gather that Sissie is a bit hurt at my not composing her blasted election address. But she is swallowing the affront.

CAMBRIDGE / MS / 338
(*To Richard Bennett*)

> 75, Cadogan Square
> 10–11–25

My dear Rich,

Thanks for yours, which arrived by f.p. yesterday. I seemed to be too busy yesterday to answer it. And during parts of the day I forgot it. The chief evidence which you have yet produced in support of your theory of a real decline in P.S. is the character of the hard soap maker. That alone is enough. You should keep your eyes open for 'fresh woods & pastures new', but of course you will. You are right about the need of an article on Armistice Day. I would have written one, only I've been far too absorbed in my novelette to deal with any side shows. It cannot, however, be doubted that the appeal for solemnity on this occasion has had a very decided effect on public opinion. I think that when you get your next rise in salary you might consider the question of owning a small car. Your young, tender life seems to me to be incomplete without some contrivance for moving you about from one part of the earth's surface to another. Not that I have the least intention of giving you a car—even the cheapest! Such an act would be contrary to my principles in dealing with you. But I could lend you some money towards buying a small car if you agreed to pay me back by instalments. I was driven in a small car, called I think 'Lynx', on Sunday from Brighton to Amberley & back. It was a polar day, with a wind that tried to blow the car over when the speed exceeded 30 m.p.h., abeam the wind. It seemed a goodish car. There were 4 up. Dorothy & I went to look at a cottage at Amberley which she desires to inhabit with her offspring for 6 weeks in May & June. I liked the cottage. I don't think there is much secret about Dorothy's secret, & I don't see why there should be—in our world (though I doubt Rochdale yet). Anyhow Dorothy makes no effort to keep the secret secret. Rather the contrary. She is immensely proud (privately) at the prospect of having a child by the illustrious undersigned. Other women say to her: 'My dear, how I envy you!' Que veux-tu qu'elle dise alors? I beg to announce to you that all the political part of my novel *Lord Raingo* is now finished. Beaverbrook has vetted it, & is thrilled thereby—most enthusiastic. Says it is the finest thing he has read for years. In 400 pp. he has found only one small slip. I am tremendously uplifted by this verdict, & am forced to the conclusion that a man who can get the atmosphere & effects of the most private meetings of Cabinet ministers etc., with all their chicane etc., & with all the Downing Street stuff, solely from hearsay & occasionally meeting the said Cabinet Ministers, is no ordinary fellow. I trust you agree. When I got B's verdict yesterday, & saw Dorothy afterwards & she approached me, I said: 'Stand away. You don't know who I am.' The fact is I don't know myself.

I think what you need is a travelling job for a few years.
                              Love,
                    Your healthy uncle,

                                                           A.B.

338. Mrs Stratton's House (today Boxwood Cottage), Amberley, West Sussex.

CAMBRIDGE / MS / 339
(*To Richard Bennett*)

                                              75, Cadogan Square
                                              25–11–25

My dear Rich,
    My previous letter was written before the post came. This is a
most important matter—indeed of the very highest importance, & I hope (& believe) it will be all right. I have a certain
faith in your commonsense. My only objection, so far, to the
affair is that it takes my thoughts off my novel—not a grave
objection. You should tell Rochdale, I think; but please yourself. She is very young. Not that that really matters. What will
the 'perquisites' cost? I should like to see this Stella, but I don't
perceive how I can till next spring. I trust you have disabused,
or will disabuse, the Lisles of any idea they may have that you
are an heir. Because you aren't. And for your sake I'm glad you
aren't. You have all my benedictions. I will say more when I
know more. On the 15th I shall be in Paris, seeing the
Godebskis, who are in a state of considerable excitement &
ecstasy over Dorothy. I'll tell Dorothy.
                              Love,
                    Your guardian uncle,

                                                           A.B.

339. Estelle Mary Lisle (b. 1904). Her family came from Wolverhampton. Her
father was Joseph Lisle, motor-car manufacturer. Her mother was Bessie Ferret Lisle
(née Babbage).

CAMBRIDGE / MS / 340
(*To Richard Bennett*)
Hôtel Russie
Rome
5–2–26

My dear Rich,

   Thanks for yours of 1st. It arrived a day late. It now appears that your Uncle Sep is worse, and from what I can gather from the doctor's (consumption expert) letter to me & his letters to Auntie Maud, there is very little hope of saving him. The doctor says he has a highly nervous & worrying temperament, which prevents him from taking things easily. He needs food, but cannot assimilate it. His weight is under 7 stone! I don't know whether Rochdale has been informed of this affair; but if it hasn't you might transmit the latest news thither. I have arranged for a special consultation this week, but I don't think it will do any good. In fact I only did it so as to soothe Auntie Maud. The mischief with this family is that it hasn't a cent. However, Auntie Maud has 2 well-off brothers-in-law, who are helpful, and me. You see, whatever happened I couldn't go to England now. It would be impossible for me to leave Dorothy, or for her to travel except in slow stages, & there is no place for her to *be* in England, as she has let her flat till June. We shall in all probability move on to Pisa–Genoa–Mentone, leaving here on the 14th, Sunday week. So that your next letter—I mean the one you write just before you receive this one, or on the day of the reception thereof, should be the last one to this address. You shall know the next address in due course. I'm glad you took Stella to Rochdale. If you want to be at 75 Cadog at Easter weekend I see no reason why you should not be. In all probab. I shall be there myself. Anyhow I shall be close to. I am now thinking of another novel! I wrote a *Sunday Pictorial* article yesterday. Health good. Dorothy in great form. But I sleep not well. We had the Sullivans to dinner last night, & we dine with them tomorrow night. I suppose you are over-spending again.

Love,
Your apprehensive uncle,
A.B.

340. Bennett and Dorothy left England on 14 December to go to Italy and France for three months.

   Bennett finished writing *Lord Raingo* on 26 January 1926, and began writing *The Strange Vanguard* on 8 February.

STOKE / MS / 341
(*To Stella Lisle*)

Winter Palace
25–2–26

My dear Stella,

I hear Richard wants you to come to London for something or other. I shall be delighted if your mother & you will consent to your staying at 75 Cadogan Square. Richard can stay somewhere else. I am a stiff upholder of the conventions. If you come, put yourself in the hands of my secretary, Miss Nerney, who really *will* look after you. I may be in town, or I may not be, myself; but in any case I have no expectation of being at No. 75. If I'm in London I shall of course see you. In fact, you might ask me to dinner at 75. I am exceedingly anxious to know you. Your photograph was most alluring and exciting.

Your sincere and benevolent and anxious-to-be-affectionate future uncle,

Arnold Bennett

KENNERLEY / MS / 342
(*To Tertia Kennerley*)

Winter Palace
1–3–26

My dear Tertia,

I've sent your tragedy to William. I must say I hadn't realised the loneliness. He said, & Maud also said, that everybody was very kind to him & he was the pet of the place, & I imagined he was seeing people constantly. I suppose you couldn't get his room changed to a room with a view: and I expect you'll say something to Ash about the meals, & him not being wakened when a meal is brought in. Your being there is the best thing that has happened to him. Dorothy thinks that he ought to be told why I can't come over. Do you? If so, will you tell him, or shall I? I doubt if it would interest him much at this stage. A complication has arisen. I find I can't get seats on the luxe trains for a journey of less than 500 kilometres (300 miles). We meant to break the journey at Marseilles first. Now I've taken a double berth on the luxe to Lyon. It is $11\frac{1}{2}$ hours, but I hope it will be better than $6\frac{1}{2}$ hours in an ordinary train, with no space to lie down and no privacy. I expect to be at the Grand Nouvel Hôtel, Lyon, on Sunday night next & to stay for 2 nights. For 4 hours or so in a train, Dorothy is all right; but after that she is apt to get very restless. We only came so far from London because the doctor encouraged it. Myself, I didn't much believe in it. She's very well & walks a couple of miles a day; but she's getting a bit ample. Harriet Cohen, who is with Spahlinger at Nice, is coming over tomorrow. Harriet got hold of Spahlinger through Dr. Leonard Hall, & I suppose she proceeded to fascinate him. All I know is that Spahlinger treatment is at present unobtainable. Harriet is not better. But she interrupted the treatment in order to go to London & give God knows how many concerts & have a great time. We see a good sprinkling of people. Had lunch with the Beaverbrooks on Saturday. Lady B. is a very fine woman, & Dorothy much cottons to her. The weather is superb. Went to the theatre last night. I told Dorothy she would be fantastically bored. She was quite ready to leave after the 1st act. We left therefore. Rather difficult to get her to bed. However, she slept 9 hours night before last. She has a weight frequently on her stomach & her heart then beats enough to incommode her. Otherwise the pink is her condition. I suppose it would be difficult to write to Sep about himself without upsetting him in some way or other. I've been in communication with D'Arcy about his affairs, & am assured they can't be in better order than they are, & that a will is quite unnecessary. I say nothing about Maud ..., but she ought to be aware that finance doesn't stand in the way of anything being done. I repeat I'm awfully glad you're on the spot.

What's this knitting.

Loves,

Yours, A.B.

P.S. Don't address anything here after Wednesday.

342. Septimus was in a nursing home in Wales.
M. Spahlinger was the head of a tuberculosis clinic in Geneva. Dr Leonard Hall is not otherwise known.

KENNERLEY / MS / 343
(*To Margaret Kennerley*)

75, Cadogan Sq
8–4–26

My dear sweet Margaret,

It was topping of you to send the flowers, and the flowers are topping, & I have examined them all. None got lost on the way, and all are flourishing, & they look tophole, & I am much obliged. It is now, I regret to say, 43 years since I passed your Matric, but of course I needn't point out that it was far harder then; in fact the Matric *was* the Matric in those dear dead days. I say, what is this about Masefield and De la Mare? De la Mare is the real goods; but are you still thinking up Putney Hill that my gloomy and bass-voiced friend John is a genuine poet? Because he isn't. As for choirs, when I have heard certain choirs screech & growl, I should have been *glad* to be deaf. But no doubt your choirs were dulcet-toned. Your activities in their variety and vastness frighten me. I don't know how you can get through them all at once. I couldn't. But then I am younger than you (really). That's why I know more about Masefield than you. Only the young can see through a hollow-solid. I Eastered in London, working, not-sleeping, and ambulating in Parks. I went to a film & was bored, & to a play and was bored. I hope that the new piece at the Lyric-Ham will not bore me. You might tell Pop & Mop that I have no news for them as this letter goes to press. I think you are entitled to lose 3 balls per diem, id est, trois balles, but not more. Love to all. And much thanks for your most agreeable letter.

Your aff unc,

A.B.

343. Margaret Kennerley did the General Schools examination in 1926. She read classics at Somerville, but after the first term she became ill and was told she should not return for a full year. She returned earlier and suffered a nervous breakdown and had to withdraw. For some years she worked in a bookshop, and later she trained and taught dyslexic children and started a centre for them in Bognor Regis.

John Masefield (1878–1967) became poet laureate in 1930. Walter De la Mare (1873–1956).

The new piece at the Lyric Hammersmith was A. P. Herbert's and Nigel Playfair's great success *Riverside Nights*.

CAMBRIDGE / MS / 344
(*To Richard Bennett*)

75, Cadogan Square
12–4–26

My dear Rich,

Thanks for yours of yesterday. The *New Statesman* seems to be lying low about the future of Levers. Anyhow it isn't prophesizing. Personally I think that, financially, the thing is now being better managed. Yes, 4 days enforced idleness is terrible. Yes, I will give formal intimation to Rochdale. I don't follow your reference in 'Last week's paper caused a certain amount of doubt. . . .' What is this? Your cold which you can't throw off indicates that you are run down. Dorothy went into the Nursing Home (27 Welbeck Street, W.1.) on Saturday evening; but as she couldn't sleep no operations were begun yesterday, & she emerged again for lunch, tea & dinner. Last night she slept 5 hours, there, & I presume that operations have now begun. I am going up & see her at noon. Then I have to attend a lunch of the *Cosmopolitan Magazine* at the Ritz. Auntie Maud is coming up to town tomorrow, & I must see her about Uncle Sep's affairs. . . . Dorothy is still very well indeed; but she hates Homes & despises nurses, so I expect that the passage will not be uniformly smooth.

You can have Paul Whiteman; I heard him & his once at the Kitcat Club. Once was enough. Still, as an acrobatic performance, the thing can be amusing for ten minutes—especially the simultaneous pianos. After that it becomes a deathly nuisance. I reckon he is the best advertised man on earth at this present. £1,000 he gets for his 2 shows in each provincial town. What do I know about Minton-ware used at Cambridge? Anything? True, I have no memory. I returned to this house at 10.30 last night. It exhibits the most marvellous illustrations of spring-cleaning that I ever saw. I am informed that the operation took 6 weeks. I slept well, but with a headache throughout. Inexplicable. I attended the first night of *Riverside Nights*, Saturday, & was loudly cheered as I entered my box. Never happened to me in any theatre before. I think it must have been due to the publication of the fact that I never made anything out of the Lyric Hammersmith. Everybody thought I was making a fortune out of it, instead of being inspired, as I was, by a pure motive to advance the London stage! (Which I have done!) People couldn't believe in the pure motive business. The show is uneven. The best of it is simply marvellous; but there are three poor, dull, flat items, & one of these takes about 1/2 an hour! A bit thick. Need I say that the trouble arises through Playfair refusing to act on my advice? I told him what would happen if he didn't. It has happened. He cannot learn. Still, the show as a whole is very remarkable. You may be hearing from me in a day or two.

Love,
Your palpitating uncle,

A.B.

344. Paul Whiteman (1891–1967), the American band conductor.

CAMBRIDGE / MS / 345
(*To Richard Bennett*)   75, Cadogan Square
                                          13–4–26

Girl. (Virginia) 7.50 am. This day. All excellent. Dorothy was much pleased with your letter. A big child.

A.B.

STOKE / MS / 346
(*To Frank Bennett*)
                                          75, Cadogan Square
                                          13–4–26
My dear Frank,
    Official. Failing to get a divorce agreement from Marguerite, I am now in unofficial conjugal relations with one Dorothy Bennett (her own name): a daughter was born of this union at 7.30 a.m. this day, and all is going well. One can never foresee what your morning post will contain.

Yours, A.B.

Dorothy is recognised by all friends as my wife.

346. Dorothy took the name Bennett by deed poll in the preceding December or earlier.

KENNERLEY / MS / 347
(*To Tertia Kennerley*)

75, Cadogan Square
16–4–26

My dear Tertia,

It is most regrettable about Mrs. Peggotty. It is arranged for Miss Nerney & Mamma. I've told her 8.55 at Vic. She hasn't fixed the day yet. Dorothy & Co. are going on all right, & the Co. is becoming daily less repulsive, though I am told that from the first she was surpassingly beautiful. She had to be pulled out at last. Dorothy is recovering strength, despite the vastness of the bed and her own celebrated 'narrow pelvis'. The Matron (& proprietor) of the home, said it was a good thing the infant was induced, as it would have amounted to a 10lb child if it had stayed at home till the fullness of time. Dorothy's room is too full of flowers and telegrams. As she is allowed to see no one but mother & husband in the first week, and as mother is aged & at Brighton, I have to do a full share of shuttle work between here & 27 Welbeck Street. Maud came for lunch today. She began by breaking down. Trying! Trying! Still, she came through all right. 2½ hours of her. But it was much better on the whole than I had feared.

I have given official notice to Rochdale. Frank's letter in reply was characteristic & Florence's exceedingly nice. I also gave official notice to Emily, & from her reply, much inspired by 'complexes', I gather that she is furious at not having been told earlier. Indeed her letter is a masterpiece of its kind. She calls the matter 'your last affaire'. I thought of replying & pointing out to her that I hadn't had an 'affaire' (what an Emilian word!) for over 18 years. However, I shan't reply. Remember me to Flo-flo.

It was wonderful of you to write at all. Love to all.

Yours, A.B.

347. Several days after writing this letter, Bennett was at the Royal Academy. 'Henry Ainley came up, and in a hard clear voice said: "Arnold, how is your daughter?" I said: "I needn't tell you she's the finest kid ever born." He said: "Yes, I've got several of them myself."' (*Journals*, 30 April).

Flo-flo: Florence Hazell, wife of Stanley Hazell, a friend of Bennett's from the 1890s. For letters to the Hazells see Vol. II. Tertia was visiting the Hazells.

ELDIN / MS / 348
(*To May Beardmore Marsden*)

75, Cadogan Square
19–4–26

My dear May,

I was very glad to have your letter. Maud's visit was all right. She began by crying, but she soon laughed. Both symptoms were those of slight hysteria of course. I think she has come through very well, & she is certainly far from being a fool. She has been very nice about my daughter, Virginia Mary. So has everyone. In fact the attitude of my friends in this perhaps startling affair has been marvellous. Dorothy's room in the Nursing Home is like a flower show & visits paid to her have to be arranged like an American programme. The one exception has been the excellent Emily. I had already got into trouble with Emily through objecting to her bringing a totally deaf person merely to look at me. I am looked at a great deal too much. William K tried to soothe her but without much success. I told her of the daughter on her birthday. She is furious, simply because she hadn't been told earlier. But I wonder what the hell it has to do with her. I never hear from her except when she wants something from me. In her letter she speaks of my 'latest affaire'. How Emilian! At first I thought I'd answer it. At second & third I thought I wouldn't. The grievance I think is that she heard of the prospects from others—at some dinner party, from 'two men'. Well, all is going well. Miss Nerney, my secretary, has just come from the home with the news that the kid is 'simply beautiful', & that the other babies in the home are like monkeys compared to it. (This, I may say, is Dorothy's opinion. Strange!) D'Arcy asked me to go down to the Felon's Dinner, but I wouldn't. No. No more of those dinners in the Potteries. I had one, & I shall never forget it. Everybody was most friendly, but the alcoholic aspect of the Festival—no I couldna' abide it. Russell would have been better with a few less dinners. When he came to see me 5 years ago, I positively was shocked by the change in him. Still, same as you, I'm very fond of him. Respex to Edward. I wish he would come & see me again. I greatly enjoyed his last visit, except that he told me he drank 2 whiskies every night.

Thine, A.B.

348. Dr John Russell.

BERG / MS / 349
(*To Dorothy Cheston Bennett*)

75, Cadogan Square
19–5–26

My dear girl,

I do not resent you giving me your ideas about me & about your life. I am thoroughly accustomed to hearing the phrase, 'If only I had a husband who', etc. (A phrase you have never heard from me.) I accept it. What I do strongly resent is being wakened up in order to hear it. The excuse that you 'never see' me & have no chance to speak to me is of course too absurd for serious discussion. You are a *tremendous* talker, & if you don't talk about what is important the fault is not mine. You knew that I had had a long bout of neuralgia, that I have been in acute pain for days, and was still in pain, and that I had had two atrocious nights & was terribly short of sleep; nevertheless you deliberately came downstairs & woke me, well knowing that you would ruin my night & my next day's work & probably bring on a relapse of the neuralgia. The explanation of course is that you are visited by an overwhelming impulse to free your mind, & you yield to it. Normal husbands would naturally accept this treatment quite gracefully, but I, being abnormal & so abnormal that people on seeing me thank God they are not me,—regard it as most cruel & callous, and I strongly resent it. This has to be said.

I now take much less notice of what you say than you may imagine, for I am gradually learning the lesson which you yourself inculcated, namely, not to take you too seriously. I have no hope of pleasing you for more than a few hours at a time, or of ridding you of the notion that fate has got a down on you. I yield to you in every possible way: I do what I can, & I can't do more.

But nothing that you have said has startled me so much as your outpouring last night since you announced, 18 months ago, that you thought you were entitled to have two lovers at once. No doubt normal husbands, such as Angus Roberts, Jim Eve, and Arthur Colefax, would regard it as quite proper for you to have two men at once, and to leave our baby in my charge while you lived freely alone and came along daily to enjoy the child when your freedom permitted. But I am abnormal.

It is undeniable that I am 24 years older than you in years. We can't alter this. The objection should have been weighed rather earlier in the proceedings. But you yourself are not quite a young girl, and you weren't quite a young girl when I first met you. Moreover you are, & have always been, free to frequent younger society. I have encouraged you to do so. Again & again, you have said that you wanted to alter the whole of our joint life, and again & again I have asked you to explain how. You have never even begun to explain how—in the slightest degree.

You asked me my opinion on certain points last night. I repeat them.

You will never make a monetarily-profitable name as an actress. Because you despise the profession & aren't really interested in it, not because you can't act. You will always be able to act, & with real distinction.

You will never make money in business, because you have not got a head for money, nor regular habits.

You may occasionally make a little money by selling a play. I think you are a good judge of a play, & also that, with a vast deal more experience, you would produce a play *well*. I do not think you would ever successfully manage a theatre, even if you got one to manage. I know very much more about managing a theatre than you do, and this is my firm opinion.

Fourthly, those who have to be kept, or mainly kept, cannot possibly be independent. This is a truth which will always come out on top. No wife could possibly have more freedom of action than you have.

I do not suppose for a moment that you would wish to throw over the grave responsibilities which you have taken up. But if you did, you would only have to tell me plainly. I should know how to act. Only it will not do for you to play fast and loose with me; to insist on one course one day, and then on an entirely opposite course the next week.

I was the more startled by what you said last night because I had thought that you were succeeding very well in your new surroundings, and I had told you so. In fact, remarkably well. Our friends also have, I think, done remarkably well. But it won't do to play fast and loose with them any more than with me. A mistaken step now might do irreparable harm.

A.B. Esquire

349. Angus Roberts, Jim Eve: unidentified. Arthur Colefax (d. 1936), patent lawyer.

Dorothy was at the nursing home in Welbeck Street until 9 May. She and Virginia then came to 75 Cadogan Square. More than two months later, though, on 22 July, Bennett recorded in the *Journals*: 'This day Dorothy came "definitely" to live here, and slept in her own bedroom next to mine. Most of her furniture was also moved in.'

KEELE / MS / 350
(*To Marguerite Soulié Bennett*)

75, Cadogan Square
20–v–26

Dear Marguerite,

Some months ago I wrote to Georges to ask him what he thought your ideas were about the future. (No doubt he told you.) I told him that if you were ready to divorce me, I would furnish the necessary evidence. He replied that in his opinion you would certainly not agree to a divorce.

When I was talking to Ida Godebski some weeks ago, she told me that you had expressed the same decision to her, but more strongly.

As you know, I have formed a new affection. But you may not know that a child has been born of the union.

Having regard to this child, I should like to know whether you still hold to your decision, or whether you would now agree to a divorce.

I hope you are well. Best wishes.

Yours, A.B.

CAMBRIDGE / MS / 351
(*To Richard Bennett*)

Amberley
Sussex
30–6–26

My dear Rich,

Thanks for yours of Monday, which reached me only this day. I don't see how the fact that you spend £1 a week in travel will enable you to buy a motor-car. But no doubt you do. I will give you a sailing-dinghy. The last sailing dinghy I had—33 years ago or more—was made specially for me at Gillingham, Kent, & delivered at Chelsea in a barge. It cost £4-15/-

inclusive. One day when I was living at the Marriotts, I happened to be at the front-door, & a shabby man came up the steps and asked me if I was me. Whereupon he gave me a paper, which was a county court summons for £4-15/-. The slope which you mention is not mine at all; but Captain Macheath's. I have pleasure in giving you and Stella the green, flowered bedroom suite. It was on the edge of being put up for auction. You don't say anything as to your new work at P. S. What kind of work is it that enables you to sleep for 70 minutes of an afternoon? I have a terrible idea that I shall soon have to buy a motor-car myself, though I haven't the slightest personal desire for one, & I find hiring both simpler & cheaper. Is Parkgate on the same side of the river as P. S.? I should have thought you would save money by getting a motor-bicycle then. I should like to hear more of your health, though Griffin much reassured me, I must say. Still I want to know how it goes on. Dorothy's hay-fever is not yet over; but she seldom gives it a chance to die. The family is still in marvellous form. I shall return to London on 13th July, & D. & Co, with Fred to expedite them, on 14th. I've had more than enough of packing & directing journeys this last winter & spring to last me for many years to come. Emily formerly cook, henceforth nurse, arrives this afternoon. The weather is heavenly. I now have less than 10,000 words of my new novel to do. I have been in terrific form for work, though still insomniac. Mr. Hornibrook's abdominal exercises are undoubtedly working good within me. They take only a very short time per day. Auntie Tertia & Co arrive at Aldwick (12 miles from here) tomorrow for 3 months, & we shall go over to see them on Saturday afternoon.

With loves,
Your work-devouring uncle,

A.B.

351. At the end of May Bennett and Dorothy went to stay in Amberley for seven weeks. On 8 July Bennett wrote in the *Journals*:

I finished *The Vanguard* today at 4.15, having written 5500 words of it in two days. I began the work on 8th February in Rome; it was very seriously interrupted by the birth of Virginia, and I wrote the 10 or 12,000 words of it all over afresh, and I'm glad I did it. I wrote the last two-thirds of it here in Amberley in 44 days. I have never worked more easily than during the last six weeks.

Frederick Arthur Hornibrook (b. *c.* 1879) was author of *The Culture of The Abdomen*, a very popular work at the time.

CAMBRIDGE / MS / 352
(*To Richard Bennett*)

75, Cadogan Square
26–7–26

My dear Rich,

Yours dated 24th only arrived this morning. Believe me, you & Stella are deserving of all sympathy, & you have all mine. Her idea that I have any objection to her is of course merely one result of her nervous strain, & is not worth discussing. I have no objection of any kind to Stella, & I feel sure that she would make an excellent wife for you. I have little doubt that your mother thinks the same. If you married now, or soon, it *might* turn out all right: but the probabilities are in my opinion against this. And I cannot alter my view just because you would like me to alter it—you understand that, naturally. I think it would be a great mistake for Stella & you to marry at present. Your mother thinks so too. She wrote me a letter full of sense. If Stella wants to go home, she must of course go. In fact her wanting to go is in my opinion a sufficient reason for her going. I can't say any more, except that if your affections & hers are secure, there is nothing to worry about. Everything is a great nuisance, I know, & it would be strange if you were not very depressed, mais que veux-tu? Dorothy, having gone to 'The Retreat Winchelsea', came back therefrom on Sunday. It seems the house is so noisy (char-a-bancs etc) as to be uninhabitable. So we are taking rooms at the Royal Victoria Hotel, St. Leonards-on-Sea, Sussex, & shall for the present sleep there. Babe & nurse can sleep at the Retreat, because they have a room at the back. The present arrangement is not stable. Dorothy returns to Winchelsea this morning, & I shall go on Thursday. Tomorrow I'm going down to see Mrs. Wells at Easton—returning Thursday.

Keep going, my boy,
Loves,
Your philosopher uncle,

A.B.

352. Easton Glebe was the Wells home in Essex.

CAMBRIDGE / MS / 353
(*To Richard Bennett*)

> 75, Cadogan Square
> 4–8–26

My dear Rich,

I return the letter from father & daughter. These family affairs are very distressing & exasperating & you have all my sympathies. So has Stella. Papa is evidently very cross. I should judge that though he is obstinate, he is not really very strong. This I gather from bits of his letter. Of course, to be candid, as I must be, I think that you *are* rather inclined to make critical remarks of the sort that might upset some people. Clearly you have upset him, & this shows that, however excellent your intentions, you have not been wholly successful in tact.

I will now give you some advice.

On no account allow your private affairs to interfere with your course of work. This should never be done. It would involve the loss of the respect of everyone—including Stella herself. Every man who has sacrificed the latter to the former has been despised. If Stella can't or won't go, go without her. And if she prefers to break off the match, well, that can't be helped. I like Stella very much, but she is extremely young, & cannot be expected to be entirely uninfluenced by her parents. Your suggestion that she could come here in a helpful capacity would not work, I think. It would certainly, in view of what you say about their attitude to Dorothy, annoy her parents excessively.

For the present, maintain a policy of masterly inactivity, as regards the domestic trouble. Do not judge the future by the present. Things will calm down. I am all in favour of Stella doing 'something useful'. Her present existence must be very unsatisfactory to her. Exercise more tact. Tact is not a major characteristic of our family. Your three aunts & your father are all deficient in it, & the lack has caused them all lots of trouble, again & again. There is too much moral self-sufficiency in our family. You doubtless feel old, but are in truth very young. Older people have struggled on so far without your moral help, & they will be able to continue to do so. Please take this in the right spirit, for I think it may be valuable to you. Even if you have never made a critical remark at Fordhouses, it cannot be disputed that you have not succeeded there as a guest.

This may be their fault, but I doubt if it is wholly their fault.

The answers to your questions are short.

1. Immediate future. You ought most positively to proceed with the Brunner Mond affair instantly.

2. 1 years time. I don't think that Stella ought to go out with you.

3. 2 years time. You will know better then where you are. You don't know now how things will be, & you can't make a definite plan. The plan will depend on yours & Stella's feelings in 2 years time, or say 18 months time. You probably won't stomach this letter very well, but it is all right.

The infant is in great health. Dorothy has slight pleurisy, & is neither better nor worse. She now has a nurse.

Love,

Your very watchful & interested uncle,

A.B.

353. Brunner Mond, the chemical firm, whose former head was J. T. Brunner (1842–1919). Under the direction of Sir Alfred Mond (1868–1930) it became Imperial Chemical Industries.

KENNERLEY / MS / 354
(*To Tertia Kennerley*)

75, Cadogan Square
13–8–26

My dear Tertia,

Many thanks. Good heavens! You could have knocked me down with a feather. I thought I'd told you about her coming here. A good thing she did come. It would have been much more complicated her being ill at the flat! She is much relieved at being here. The babe is in great form. Dorothy gradually declined at Amberley. I loved the landscapes but had *no* use for the climate. She had hay fever, which is a grave thing, &, while obviously fatigued by it, she would go on working at a scenario. Nurse & I said daily that she would be ill, & by heaven she has been! She got up this afternoon for the 1st time in 17 days, & dressed, but did not leave the bedroom floor. It's fine you having such a fine time. Saw the Galsworthy play last night. No good. My first evening out in 17 days or 20 days!

Love,

Yours, A.B.

354. In the third sentence Bennett draws a feather instead of writing the word. Galsworthy's play was *Escape*, at the Ambassadors Theatre.

CAMBRIDGE / MS / 355
(*To Richard Bennett*)

75, Cadogan Square
14–9–26

My dear Rich,

Thanks for your letter received today. Yes, it seems a great piece of wisdom to appoint your statistical officer. I fear there is very little to be said about the same. Nor is there anything to be said about Stella. I gathered pretty well what sort of a lady Mrs. Lisle was when Stella told me that she was scarcely ever left alone at the piano—always being called off to do things. Your allowance will no doubt be attended to. I got back yesterday at 4 p.m., after a night spent in a first-class carriage with 3 other people—two women & a man. One of the women, by pure chance, I knew; and the man knew me. His agent in India happened to be H. K. Hales. In fact everybody seemed to know me. I was walking along platforms at Milan when a wagon-lits employé whom I had appointed to meet me called out loudly from a distance 'Mr. Bennett? Mr. Bennett?' and a man whom I knew not, just in front of me, called out in reply: 'Mr. Bennett is behind.' This morning when I came downstairs I found a telegram from Dorothy alleging 'decided return pleurisy' & announcing that she would return at once. But I fancy this 'return' is due mainly to nerves, and that all it means is that she much dislikes being alone. I don't know yet exactly what will happen; but I have sent her a discouraging cable. I couldn't get a sleeping berth to myself; I might have got 1/2 a double berth, but I much prefer being free in a 1st class compartment to being cooped up with a complete stranger for a night. I had been in the house 5 minutes when Max began ringing me up. I went with him & Mrs. Norton last night to *Blackbirds* at the Pavilion. It is a marvellous show, and evidently a great success. I had 3 hours sleep in the railway carriage Sunday night, but I'm very well. I have now lost 1 stone 2 lbs, & am down to 11 1/2 stone, which is my proper weight, according to the tables. The *Raingo* boom is just beginning. Max has spent £5,000 on posters, he says; they start to appear today. It appears that many people think that Raingo & his love affair are taken from Max's own life. This tickles him immensely. Rhondda of course is the original, but I never knew Rhondda personally, nor his wife nor his lady-love. I only knew his daughter; who will doubtless be a bit cross, though there is nothing offensive in the least to the man's memory in the book. Pauline Smith is coming up today for 2 days. I have an appointment with Barry Jackson about the Phillpotts–Bennett–Austin comic opera on Thursday night. I'm supposed to be going to Max's for the weekend and to Torquay on Tuesday. My trunk has not arrived, & God knows where it can be. It's insured, but it contains correspondence and my diary (at least 65,000 words), which I should hate to lose. The weather is fine, but it seems very chilly after the heats of Venice. Love to Stella.

Love,

Your struggling uncle,

A.B.

355. On 31 August Bennett and Dorothy went to Italy for two weeks. Dorothy remained there a few days longer.

Mrs Jean Norton (d. 1945), wife of Richard Norton, Lord Grantley. She was Beaverbrook's companion for some years.

Blackbirds was a revue, by Lew Leslie, with fifty black artists.

The posters for *Lord Raingo* had Bennett's picture on them, and were described by him to Harriet Cohen as 'horribly revolting'. Serial publication of the novel began in Beaverbrook's *Evening Standard* on 20 September.

Barry Jackson (1879–1961) ran the Court Theatre at this time. Nothing came of the comic opera, *The Bandits* (also called *Vallombrosa*). Frederic Austin (1872–1952) had composed music for the Lyric Hammersmith production of *The Way of the World*.

CAMBRIDGE / MS / 356
(*To Richard Bennett*)

75, Cadogan Square
4–10–26

Sweet Sir,

Thank you.

Well, the Lisle family & its caprices must be put up with. I suppose. But they are very annoying. There are, however, far more annoying things on earth. The worst piece of news I have received lately was from your father, who has received notice to leave his situation at the end of the year. How he is to get another situation, at his age, I cannot imagine. I hope he will, but if he does it will probably be by a fluke. His three sons all have a responsibility towards their parents, & yours is the chief responsibility. Your father has to leave in order to make way for sons of one of the partners. It is quite natural, but not less calamitous for that. I have written to D'Arcy Ellis about it, & I have also seen your Auntie Tertia about it; or rather she called to see me. The position is grave.

The verdict on Dorothy is satisfactory. There is no *active* tubercle. We all have *passive* tubercles. At the X-ray performance last Monday, I saw Dorothy's heart beating all by itself, & also the faint darkening of the plasma on the right, where some liquid still remains. It was rather sensational. Dorothy will be all right in a few months if she takes care of herself (not that any woman ever does) & doesn't get another pleurisy. I am told that another pleurisy would be a highly serious matter. I am now $\frac{1}{2}$ way through *Clissold* II, & think on the whole it is better than the first. I seem to be mainly occupied in reading my friends' books. Osbert Sitwell's novel accusingly awaits my attention. Mr. Thomas Bodkin spent most of yesterday with us; but you don't know him. Anyhow he is Irish & a great picture expert. We went to the Tate. Dorothy departed early to bed. She now has a cold, & it spoils her nights: which is very troublesome. Today I'm going to have a private performance of a German *Faust* film for which I've been asked to write the English titles. Great dispute as to price; but they have given in. There seems now to be some chance of *Riceyman Steps* being produced, by Leon M. Lion: but only at matinees to start with. The new Haymarket play is (deservedly) a complete frost.

> Loves,
> Your resilient uncle,

> A.B.

356. *The World of William Clissold*, the new novel by Wells. Sitwell's novel was *Before the Bombardment*.

For letters to Thomas Bodkin (1881–1961) see Vol. III.

Faust, with subtitles by Bennett, had its first public showing on 2 January 1927.

Riceyman Steps, dramatized by Michael Morton, was produced at the Ambassadors Theatre on 25 and 29 November 1926. Leon M. Lion (1879–1947) played Henry Earlforward.

The Haymarket play was A. P. Herbert's *The White Witch*.

CAMBRIDGE / MS / 357
(*To Richard Bennett*)

> 75, Cadogan Square
> 18–10–26

My dear Rich,

Thanks for your letter, which arrived by first post. With regard to Selfridge, it depends when you are likely to come up. If I were you I shouldn't come immediately. And of course in the circs Selfridge is not likely to pay your expenses. In fact it couldn't possibly be suggested to him. I should let 2 or 3 weeks pass. By the way you won't be able to sleep here. I suppose you will sleep in the train! Lucky to be able to do so. I can't. It is a great pity about Fordhouses & a darned nuisance also; but these frictions are probably far more common than you think they are. The best policy is to say & do as little as possible in the matter. Your auntie Tertia called to see me on Saturday morning (in the midst of my work) about your father. She showed me a letter from your mother, which was really full of the right spirit. Your auntie Emily was in for tea the same afternoon. Hadn't seen her for years. Quite a day of aunties! She also had heard from your mother, but she hadn't got the letter with her. Auntie Emily also is going through evil times. The College of Science printed their list of rooms for students wrong, & put her price at £3 instead of 30/-. Result: she hasn't had a single application from prospective boarders. This is perhaps a graver immediate trouble than any of yours. I congratulate you on your prestidigitation with lamp. Quelle histoire, tout de même! Dorothy is seeking to have a French lesson every day. She is much better; but doesn't sleep enough. I fear we have a heavy fortnight before us of sociableness. Your Auntie Sissie comes on Wednesday. We have a late party at the Lewis's on Tuesday—to meet Arthur Rubenstein again & doubtless to hear him play. When he starts to play he usually finishes about 4 am. I am praying for the best. We had a party here on Friday, but I got them all away by 11.35. Colefaxes, Herberts, Osbert, & Eliz Lewis. H. G. Wells & wife & others are coming this Thursday. Another *late* party Tuesday week, & we are having a party on Wednesday week to meet André Maurois. Still, a lot of work is being done. I had 2 walks yesterday, went for a motor drive to Epsom Downs with family,

went to evensong at Westminster Cathedral, and wrote 1,900
words. Dorothy has written a story.

Loves,

Your continuing uncle,

A.B

357. Gordon Selfridge (d. 1947), of department store fame. He once wanted Bennett
to write some advertising for him, to which Bennett's name would be signed. Bennett
declined with regret, saying that he himself had no objection but he did not think the
public was yet prepared for that sort of thing.
   Arthur Rubinstein (b. 1887).
   A. P. Herbert (1890–1971), barrister, prolific author, wit.
   André Maurois (1885–1967), the author, had some notion of doing a French
adaptation of *Milestones*. Bennett describes him at the party as showing 'extraordinary
charm'.

CAMBRIDGE / MS / 358
(*To Richard Bennett*)

75, Cadogan Square
25–10–26

My dear Rich,

Grazie! Yes, it is deplorable about the Lisle situation, but I
think it will right itself. In the meantime Stella will do well,
perhaps, not to put any wild talk into practice. And if she does
'buzz off' the last place she ought to buzz off to is your place.
However, she won't buzz off. So that is all right. As regards
Selfridge I think that you ought now write to him & ask him for
an appointment stating whose nephew you are & referring to
his letter to me, & saying that you are coming up from
Liverpool on other business, & that therefore if he could fix an
appointment after such & such an hour, it would be a convenience to you. I enclose his letter again for you to refer to. I
return the 'class' documents. Yes, I have seen this sort of thing
before. Think naught of it. I think that you are quite right to
return to Liverpool for the winter. Why are you so unwise as to
pay money to see a thing like *Lash*. You must have known it was
superlatively tedious & preposterous. True it is that I at
present experience more festivities etc. than you do. But then
you see I paid for my festivities during a long course of years.
When I had attained your degree of maturity I worked in an
office 9.45 to 6 (stealing an hour or so in middle of day to go to

British Museum), and I worked, chiefly on bibliography &
articles, at night. I scarcely ever went to a party, never to a
restaurant, except ABCs for lunch, never to a dance. And so on,
& so on, in the usual style of ageing gentlemen of 59 1/2. Still,
look at the matter justly! Dorothy & I dined at the Savoy last
night & danced a bit. Had a great party here on Thursday—
Wellses, Nicholses etc. We go to Galsworthys tonight, theatre
& Colefaxes tomorrow night, & we have an André Maurois
party here on Wednesday. Dorothy is an invalid, practically!
Today I am going to the inauguratory lunch given by Austin
Reed for his new premises—just for fun. I'm in an intermediate
period just now—not writing, but preparing stuff for my
'critical introduction' to the edition de luxe of the works of Eden
Phillpotts. Rather a grind, but not (what I call) work.

> Loves,
> Your observant uncle,

> A.B.

358. *The Lash*, by Cyril Campion, author of *Ask Beccles*.
Austin Reed (1873–1954), founder of the clothing firm.

CAMBRIDGE / MS / 359
(*To Richard Bennett*)

> 75, Cadogan Square
> 20–12–26

My dear Rich,
    Thanks for yours of yesterday, which arrived punctually.
Not very cheerful. I don't see anything much to say about Stella
at present. But I should certainly see father-in-law if he called.
However, I don't think he would call. It would be a great
mistake for Stella to abandon her home in the present circumstances. It would be better for her to raise hell within the home.
I hope the new job for your father will be fixed up. Difficult to
discuss this matter fully with you. The only fundamental thing
is that expenditure must be within income—whatever the latter
is. I can see no point in helping Rochdale financially, & I
certainly do not want to do so. I gave a great deal of help in the
past; but as far as I can judge it did little but harm. I said in
the most solemn manner that I would never do it again, & I
have a most strong desire not to go back on my word. This does

not mean that I don't very much sympathise with your father. I do.

Now on Thursday night Dorothy & I have to go to the first night of *Liliom*. So that we probably shan't see you, even if you call here. Send word if you are coming for breakfast on Friday. About 9 or 9.15 if you *do* come. 2 seats have been got for *Blackbirds* Monday afternoon. They are not good seats, but they are the best that could be got. As regards Friday night, this can be left open; there will be no difficulty in getting into any theatre. As regards Monday night, we can decide nothing. The big successes & most others will be impossible. Dorothy is going into the matter. Great trouble here with the nursemaid, who has gone, & Virginia is now temporarily in charge of a hospital nurse. This means that we cannot leave on 29th as originally arranged; which is most exasperating & complicated, as all tickets & rooms had been obtained. However, I am impressed that God reigns.

> Loves,
> Your sturdy uncle,
>
> A.B.

359. *Liliom*, by Ferenc Molnar, with Fay Compton and Ivor Novello, playing at the Duke of York's.

BERG / MS / 360
(*To George Cedric Beardmore*)

> 75, Cadogan Square
> 16–I–27

My dear Cedric,

You will do well to send me your stuff to read. If it is short I will read it before I go. If long, while I am away. I shall be glad to help you in every possible way. When I know what you are doing, I will advise you what to do in future.

I may tell you that I also have received severe criticisms from Auntie Tertia, & within the last few years too. In fact, at least once she has been so disgusted with my work that she would not say anything about it at all. Her remarks are always rigorous, but they are kindly & well worth thinking over. I know Edith Shackleton. She is a bright creature, but I have never seen anything of hers that, for me, has any interest at all beyond the merely journalistic.

Love to all,
Your aff unc,

A.B.

360. Edith Shackleton Heald (d. 1976), drama critic and leader writer for the *Evening Standard*.

BERG / MS / 361
(*To George Cedric Beardmore*)

75, Cadogan Square
18–1–27

My dear Cedric,

I think there is something in this. A sort of passion for things. But I don't know what the sketches are supposed to be. Are they parts of a whole, or quite separate? In any case *I think you have something to say*. So that is all right. You have to go on. The 1st sketch is the best & the last the worst. They all have points, though. The writing needs much improvement & much more care than you have yet been able to give to it. You might read carefully through everything, so that you won't miss any of the points I have pencilled. I have by no means marked all the errors I saw. I want to know the books you have been reading with pleasure during the last 2 or 3 years. Some one has been influencing you, of course. I seem to see Dickens here & there. Of course you *must* be influenced, *ought* to be influenced. But I wonder if you have been reading good modern books. Your method strikes me as a bit old fashioned in places. Could you write a 2,000 word sketch or story? Or if you have one finished would you send it to me? I'd like to see if you can hold the interest, & keep up the intellectual strain, over 2,000 words.

Send me some more, anyway.

I should call your style 'uncouth' and negligent & a bit 'perky'. But these defects, if they exist, are trifles & will soon pass.

Your aff unc,

A.B.

P.S. I return the sketches.

A.B.

KENNERLEY / MS / 362   Hotel Savoy
(*To Tertia Kennerley*)   Cortina d'Ampezzo
                                        Belluno
                                        Italy
                                        3–II–27

My dear Tertia,

Thanks. Your letter is a masterly & terrible document. Anyway I've sent Florence a cheque for £20—from us both. Yes, I do admire Florence. I never knew that Florence lost £2,000 in B & B. She may have lost it privately with Frank. One of the things that finally decided me that I must finish up with F.C.B. was the fact that he had stuffed Florence up with a tale of having paid over to the mater sums which he would have been able to pay over to Florence if I had borne my share. I was able to prove to Florence that Frank's net payments to the mater had averaged 14/5d. a week during the entire period between his taking the business & her death. Florence was wise enough to make no reply to my letter, which was very long; but it would have been interesting to know what were her remarks to Frank. I don't see how Frank can be helped, really. If I did, I would help him & be damned to him. Richard says that the Rochdale budget will balance in normal circumstances. If you could convey to Florence that if some money is needed to help her into a situation I could find it, perhaps you will do so. I haven't said anything to her myself. I should have thought that a boarding house would be more in her line, & perhaps more remunerative. I doubt if Emily has committed suicide. She has just come into £36 from the Revenue—returned income-tax. She may be spending some of it somewhere. I wouldn't blame her. Well I can get on with F.W.B. In fact I like him; he is full of sense, to my mind; but I am so damned used to talking literature & art & theatres & music that conversation with him is not too marvellously easy. I think I've only seen Alan once—many years ago. I'm keeping an eye on Cedric. He is developing slowly. Some stuff of his I saw about a month ago is very crude & mannered, but I have a suspicion that there may be something in him. If there is, I will get it out of him. He certainly likes my criticisms, harsh as they have to be. . . . In this district, l'ennemi—c'est la constipation et l'insomnie. Otherwise I greatly like it. I am now skating again—after 18 years. Dorothy is both skating and skiing; and she adores it. The Aldous Huxleys, who have a house here, are excellent companions. Also the Crown Prince has just arrived this moment, complete with bands and popular applause, to stay in the hotel. We expect to leave here on 16th for Milan, Nice, and Paris. Back in London about March 3rd. Fine daily accounts of Virginia. The wench now crawls to the bookcase & pulls out all the books she can. Dorothy is always saying: 'That heavenly child!' Insomnia at least permits me to get up early & do some work. In fact I do a day's work before Dorothy is dressed, usually. All is snow. The balls in the hotel are wonderful. The bulk of the clientèle is Italian, and Italian women (of style) are quite as beautiful as English, and darker, with sidelong glances, and immensely more chic.

Loves,
Yours respectfully,

A.B.

P.S. I'm not happy about the chit Mary doing all that sewing for naught. I must talk to her.

362. Bennett and Dorothy left England on 20 January to go to France, Austria, and Italy for seven weeks.
  B & B: Bennett & Baddeley, Frank's firm, and Enoch's before him.
  F.W.B.: Frank Beardmore.

CAMBRIDGE / MS / 363
(*To Richard Bennett*)

75, Cadogan Square
21–III–27

My dear Rich,
  Thank you. I had a letter this morning from your father about a scheme for him to take a practice in London. He is coming to London to look into it, & I shall see him, of course. But the scheme does not appeal to me at all. I do not think for a moment that, after all these years in the provinces, he would be able to hold together any sort of a London practice, & I do not think he realises this in the least. However, apparently the scheme came from D'Arcy Ellis, to whom I have written. Dorothy is now in bed with a nurse in charge of her. She had an operation under ether yesterday for haemorrhoids & all is very

well, but she will be where she is for about a week. We struggled to buy a car, or rather to decide definitely on one, before she had to take to her bed. I like a Delancey Belleville that we saw, but Dorothy didn't—said it was too clumsy, so we pass it up. I may say that under advice we are buying a 2nd hand car. We have now settled on a Rolls Royce. It is 1921, but went through R R works for reconditioning only 2 months ago, & is now in perfect order. Except the all-weather top which has to be thoroughly reconditioned, & this is part of the bargain. Total price £650. We should have had a Fiat cabriolet. It suited us in every way: but in these Fiats there is no room for a 6 foot driver such as Atkinson (whom we are pinching from Smiths) is. In fact I maintain there is no room for any driver. You dissuaded me from Sunbeams, but the whole body of expert opinion & of users here is dead against you. I should have got one, but there wasn't one with either an all-weather or a Cabriolet body. Or rather there *was* one but I arrived at the garage just after the thing had been sold to someone who could run quicker. The MM will almost certainly *not* be fitted out this year. In fact I shall sell her. Otto Kahn is not 20, but 56 or 57, with snow white hair. Very busy!

Loves,
Your nursing & everything else uncle,
A.B.

363. Atkinson became Bennett's chauffeur.
Otto Kahn (1867–1934), American banker.

BERG / MS / 364
(*To George Cedric Beardmore*)

75, Cadogan Square
21st March 1927

My dear Cedric,

Thanks for your letter. Send me *one* of my corrections that you cannot understand, and I will try to explain it further. These corrections from the point of view of good writing are rather important. What books, if any, have you on the subject of English composition? What dictionary have you? Have you got Roget's *Thesaurus of English Words and Phrases*? I see I must look after you in detail.

Yes, write a short story, but do try to make it readable by the ordinary public. Of course before you can really hope to find a market for your work you will have to acquire a little more skill in it. I think you have the essential stuff somewhere within you.

Your aff unc,

A.B.

CAMBRIDGE / MS / 365
(*To Richard Bennett*)

75, Cadogan Square
11–IV–27

My dear Rich,

Thanks for yours of yesterday, received first post—for a change—today. Well, as I keep on repeating, it is a pity about Stella. These people have got across each other, & the matter is now I suppose entirely separated from reason. I wonder what kind of a 'fight'. You look like having quite an interesting Easter. Well, it will all be experience for you. I had a p.c. from your father with the Bury announcement. I have never been able to see eye to eye with your father as to methods of conducting business; an instance occurred between us the other day. But I am inclined to think that his methods may be well suited to a solicitor's office, & I hope that the job may be permanent. Strictly between ourselves, solicitors' offices are grossly unbusinesslike organisms; you may take this from me, who know. I sail from Victoria on Good Friday at 9 a.m. and am supposed to reach Rome at 8 p.m. on Saturday, & Syracuse (Sicily) Monday evening. The sailing of the yacht 'Flying Cloud' from Syracuse has been altered to Friday 22nd (why, I don't know). Kahn & Ko will be dancing about Sicily & I shall probably meet them at Taormina, to pass the time. I have not been sleeping well, owing to late & exciting evenings; but my health is such that I have been able to do an immense amount of work. I have 2 or 3 articles to do by Thursday, but that is all. I've written 2 short stories in the last 10 days. I've been studying Einstein's R_____y. I've read Bertrand Russell, & J.W.N. Sullivan, & Montmorency thereon. It is very interesting, & nearly as incomprehensible as it is interesting. I am going to write about it in the *E.S.* I may say that I disagree with Einstein's theory of curved space. There cannot, to my simple mind, be curved space. I also disagree with him when he says that there is no such thing as universal cosmic time. However _____! No mistake, he has a *mighty* brain. So have his disciples. The R. R. car will probably not be ready for Easter. So the vendors are to lend Dorothy a 20 Austin for her excursions. She's going to Avebury for Easter. She is extraordinarily keen on 'remains' of primitive man. It appears that Avebury has the oldest in Europe. I never knew. Virginia has a slightly blotched face. Teething? Diet? But she is very well. The Messmore Kendalls were here for tea yesterday, & Dorothy Massingham for lunch. At 6.30 'Tubby' 'blew' in, & stayed ½ an hour. [?Taciturn] but agreeable. The Maugham party was a great success. As soon as she saw me Marie Tempest kissed me on both cheeks, & Tallulah Bankhead wanted to emulate her, but I calmed her. Only Maugham & wife were a bit gloomy. *He* always is. I hear the play is rotten. I always say that Fay Compton would kill any play that wasn't vixen-proof. Crowds & crowds at the party.

> Loves,
> Your eastering uncle,

> A.B.

365.   Bennett sailed in the Mediterranean on the *Flying Cloud*, the Duke of Westminster's yacht, with Otto Kahn and others. Rudolph Kommer (d. 1942) was a German theatre and film man associated with Max Reinhardt.

Bennett's article 'Einstein for the Tired Business Man' appeared on 21 April 1927. It was one of the 'Books and Persons' series that he did weekly for the *Evening Standard* from November 1926 until his death. It reviewed *The A.B.C. of Relativity* by Bertrand Russell (1872–1972), *Three Men Discuss Relativity* by J. N. W. Sullivan (1886–1937), and *From Kant to Einstein* by Hervey de Montmorency (b. 1868).

Messmore Kendall (1872–1959), American lawyer, vice president of George Doran's firm from 1908 to 1929.

Tubby: unidentified.

Somerset Maugham (1874–1965) and wife Syrie had a house-warming party.

Tallulah Bankhead (1903–68), American actress, was a success on the English stage in these years.

Fay Compton (b. 1894) was starring in Maugham's *The Constant Wife*. She was in a film version of *The Old Wives' Tale* produced in 1920.

BERG / MS / 366
(*To Dorothy Cheston Bennett*)

Allasandri
Saturday 9.30 a.m.
16–4–27

My sweet sweet,

It takes a long time to tranquillise the spirit after 2 nights of 3 hours each. I was in a terrible state of nervous sensitiveness yesterday morning. But I very gradually recovered during the day. The English train was not full, & there was not much stir at Victoria, except a large placard announcing my 'new long novel' (*The Woman Who Stole Everything*) in Cassell's *Storyteller Magazine*. The boat was very full. I sent you a cable from Calais. I feared the Boulogne coach might miss the express at Paris; but we had 30 minutes in hand. Nothing but nerves on my part. Immense menus on the train. But it was Good Friday. No meat for lunch. And only a small bird (plus soup, fish, veg, salad, sweet, cheese, fruit) for dinner. I slept a lot. A fine car-conductor. The restaurant attendants are very good too. The carriages are 'Blue'. Made in England. Very small. I have a single compartment in the middle of the train. Some pleasure in the minute organising of this compartment all to myself, so as to save trouble & keep it clean etc. etc. I always forget to bring a duster with me. A duster is most necessary on a long journey. But I keep the window closed as much as possible in these trains.

I took a Norprine after dinner, & was in bed at 10.30. I slept heavily for stretches of about 1½ to 2 hours at a time. And by 6 o'clock had slept a good 6 hours in all. I shaved at some place—I forget where, & then ate an apple & an orange. I felt very reposed. Also—a heavenly morning. Blue & white sky. Very soft & warm air. Colour everywhere. Little villages on hill tops. Snow-topped Alps above them. Rivers rushing down with the train & so on. Curious how my registered trunk followed me like a dog. I saw it on the steamer. I saw it again at the Gare de Lyon hiding at the bottom of a truck on the platform. It had taken the truck to catch me up. Thought I didn't see it; but I saw it all right. Nothing whatever to do at the Customs at Modena, even for small baggage. No 'visite' at all. Why? We have just gone through Genoa. All the palaces. Glimpses of sea & Atlantic liners etc. behind. We shall soon be running along by the shore. I have just cabled you there, with the aid of an American Express agent. He brought me back the receipt for the payment. So I know the thing has gone off. After breakfast, I reclined, to read *The Brothers*. I soon felt heavy & went to sleep again, & yet again. I brought various books to read, chiefly French; but I couldn't resist beginning *The Brothers*, for the 4th time. Well, I am now thinking more highly of it than ever. So that's that. This book is not yet sufficiently appreciated—even by me. There is a middle-aged English woman next door to me, who is rather a bore. She talks both French & Italian fluently & badly, & reads the *New Statesman*. She was talking yesterday afternoon for about half an hour with an Italian. She gave a long description of an interview she had with Mussolini. 'Le grand homme, avec ces grands yeux.' I left to have tea, in the restaurant car. I took a long time over my tea, & when I came back she was still describing her interview with Mussolini, & she continued for a long time more. In fact I can't remember her finishing. The polite Italian said almost nothing. He looked very exhausted.

1. p.m. Just had another sleep. Just arrived at Spezia. Just going to have lunch.

6.15. We are now nearing Cività Vecchia. 2 hours from Rome now. Lovely day. I am still getting better. All went well, except that I had to have lunch opposite the terrible English-woman—& nobody else at the table. She is a fascist, & wears the insignia. The Italians are perfect; the French disgusting, & the English no good now. And so on. To show how much she knows of Italy & Italian, I will tell you that she saw on her bill the words '*Tassa di bollo*' & called the waiter & said: 'I haven't had a tassa of anything.' (*Tassa* means 'tax'.) I seem not to be able to keep you out of my thoughts. I am always wondering how you are getting on: in sole charge without me, of a car, a chauffeur, a friend—& yourself. But I doubt not you will be all right. When the Selwyns come please tell them I couldn't wait, & ask how the play is getting on, & give them my love. I sweetly kiss you good afternoon, my sweet sweet.

Little

I haven't read this through.

Love to Alick.

Train arrived punctually at 8.10. I have dined. Hotel full & noisy. Love & Love & Love.

366. *The Woman Who Stole Everything* was a long story. Bennett wrote it between 20 July and 11 August 1926. It appeared in the May 1927 issue of *Story-Teller* and was the title story for a collection of stories published on 9 June.
The Brothers Karamazov.
Alick: unidentified.

BERG / MS / 367
(*To Dorothy Cheston Bennett*)   San Domenico Palace Hotel
                                        Taormina (Sicilia)
                                        Wednesday 20–4–27
My sweet sweet,
    The more I think of it the more I am pleased with the way you *interpreted* that bit of Beethoven the other night. It was remarkable. The Otto party arrived at 6.30 last night. Otto had said he would arrive at 6.30 & he did, precisely. He says he is very pleased with the Scotch captain of the yacht. I know all the party except one (David Gray—part author of *The Best People*). Only I had forgotten that I knew them. Jo Davidson the sculptor & Dougherty the painter both reminded me of a previous meeting. Frank Crowninshields of course I knew. Kommer, as usual, seemed to know half the people in the hotel. I like all the party. (The French banker, Besnard, wasn't able to come—detained on business in South America. Our Austrian friend Polgar is to join the yacht at Athens. I shall be glad to see him again, & I hope he has learnt a bit of English.) I feel sure they are all extremely decent, as they are certainly intelligent. Jo Davidson has a bushy black beard, & at first I thought he was a Frenchman. He speaks French very fluently. Further, though it is a bit early to conclude thereupon, I think Otto is a very good host. He is bright, doesn't boss (though they all call him 'boss'), & is in favour of everyone feeling perfectly free. Kommer is a great advocate of freedom. When I said to the fellows that I hated sightseeing there was a great outburst of applause. It seems that Otto is a terrific sightseer,—never tired. I asked him last night: 'Well, what is the scheme for tomorrow?' He said: 'Well, I think we'll count tomorrow as a day of rest.' (General satisfaction.) 'But there is the Greek theatre to be seen

here.' (Apprehension.) I now feel pretty sure that this trip will
be all right. If the weather is all right. It hadn't been, up to this
morning. This morning is heavenly. I have a terrific view of
Etna from my window. It is about 10 times as imposing as
Vesuvius. There can be no question as to who is the best
dressed man in the party. There are only two men who are
dressed at all—Otto, and little Arnold. I fear, my sweet dear,
that I am once again held to be the most important personage
in the party. I see it on their faces. I am certainly the oldest.
Yesterday morning, all alone, without thee, I went forth
vaguely. I saw a village on a precipice high above this village. I
said: 'I shan't reach it, but I'll walk towards it.' Only a mule-
path, very steep & very bad. I stopped now & then for repose.
Then an Italian woman stopped me to sell me a fruit which
she called a 'mostarda'. It is rather like a *large* thin fig, blacker,
and very sweet. She said the 'villino' was only ten minutes
off. So I reached the village, Castelmola, & saw Americans
photographing themselves against the village war-monument.
Good God! That middle-west accent! Well, Castelmola is 750
feet above Taormina, & you may guess I was tired. Still I felt
very well. But as I walked down, mainly by the road—not the
path, I could feel a headache coming on. I said: 'It will be worse
after I've had my sleep.' It was. Not severe; but always there. It
is only just now going off (10 a.m.). This is of course a
constipating place. Life is a continual fight against the constipating softness of the climate. I've made a few (what I think)
interesting notes—I mean 'finished' notes ready for print. And
I've got far more material than I shall ever be able to catch up
with. No matter. We go to Siracusa tomorrow, & may (I fear)
see a Greek play—the Greek theatre there. Then the yacht
Friday morning. I should have much preferred to go by train
straight to Siracusa & join the yacht last Monday & sail
instantly. Still, the affair seems to have been pretty thoroughly
organised. Otto has here a valet, a secretary, a Sicilian guide,
and a Greek expert—all in his pay. All the gang are card
players—except me. That fact anyhow will give me some loose
time to fiddle with.

I slept another 6 hours last night, but it was much more
broken. A mosquito got within the curtain. Indeed I got up at
5.55 & looked around, & rearranged the curtains & went back

to bed, & slept about another 45 minutes. I was so hungry I had 2 eggs with my breakfast.

Well, how you are getting on without your rock to lean on and bite on? I bet you are all right. I send you my 45 different kinds of love, my sweet sweet.

Little

367. David Gray (1870–1968), American playwright and diplomat; Jo Davidson (1883–1952), American sculptor; Paul Dougherty (1877–1947), American painter; Frank Crowninshields (1872–1947), American author and editor; Alfred Polgar (d. 1955), Austrian dramatist and critic. For a letter to Jo Davidson and other references to him, see Vols. I and III.

Bennett wrote five articles about the trip. They ran in the *Sunday Express*, beginning on 24 July 1927, and they were reprinted as *Mediterranean Scenes* in 1928.

ELDIN / MS / 368
(*To Virginia Bennett*)

[Flying Cloud]
[postmarked 26 April 1927]

[no salutation]

With your classical upbringing, my dear child, comment upon this picture is needless for you.

Your father, A.B.

368. The postcard shows the Greek theatre at Syracuse.

BERG / MS / 369
(*To Dorothy Cheston Bennett*)

Flying Cloud
27–4–27

My sweetest sweet,

It is 10.50 p.m. I have written a lot of words today (cruising articles) & walked across Milo (where the Venus came from) & ridden on a mule, & listened to many stories, & seen the setting of all sails on this mighty ship; & before retiring to my bed, I wish to ask thee one question. Namely: would you care to come to Vienna for my birthday? *The Miracle* is to be done there. Kommer will be there certainly,—it is he who has begged me to go, & you too. Otto Kahn will probably be there. You would not have to leave London *before* the 18th May. I want you to wireless me two words: 'Yes darling' or: 'No darling'. You take the big express at Calais & don't change, & Kommer & I would meet you at the station at Vienna. I am inclined to think that it is an opportunity not to be missed. I shall have done enough work to justify me in this birthday escapade. But if you prefer not to come, I shall be quite content. All I want is a decision from you. If you say No, I shall be home about 21st or 22nd. If you say Yes, all arrangements will be made for you, & we should return home immediately after my birthday (27th). I've been trying to think of anything that I ought to say about the Richard position, but it seems to me that I can say nothing. I wrote to you last night. But we are many scores of miles off posts, & the letter is still on the ship. I have contracted with the *Express* to write only 10,000 words for £500, the price that young Pinker wanted me to write 20,000 for. The *Sunday Pictorial* have written me about more articles. They are also going in for short stories, & want 1 or 2 from me. They also want a serial from me. (That, I am afraid, they can't have.) This trip, my beloved creature, is *the* most marvellous thing, as regards scenery & archaeological remains, that I have ever been through. And, in addition, the running of the ship is mildly wanton. Dissatisfied (justifiably) with the chef, Otto cabled at once to Athens for a Greek chef. He has ended by having 2 Greek chefs. So that there are now 3 chefs on board, & a rare Babel of mutually uncomprehended tongues. We bathed this morning, off the yacht, after the Milo excursion. I have had a sore throat, with attendant head pains. That is now over, & I am very well. Constipation also is over. I arose at 5.30 this morning, & haven't felt short of sleep all day. But of course I'm tired now. Give my love & kiss to Virginia. (I'm glad she's growing up.) The same also to her mother, s.v.p.

Mon enf, je te bise bien.

Little

369. *The Miracle*, Max Reinhardt's spectacular drama.
Ralph Pinker (b. 1900), younger brother of Eric. For letters and other references to him see Vol. I.

BERG / MS / 370
(*To Dorothy Cheston Bennett*)

Flying Cloud
29–4–27

My sweet sweetest,

Take yesterday as a fair average day. I arose at 5.45, not needing any more sleep, and ate 2 apples & 1 orange, on the poop deck, talking to the officer of the watch. Neither the captain nor the other two officers are *really* interesting. The captain is young & energetic, but a bit boastful. Having eaten the fruit I return to my stateroom & write up the impressions of the day before in due form for print. It is really very easy. Shaving & bathing & so on is a great nuisance & consumer of time. Breakfast at 9. Rudolf is usually in his dressing gown. So is David Gray, the playwright; so is Kahn sometimes; so are others. Me never. The meal is very plenteous. The difficulty is not to eat too much. Cigarettes are always offered *before* the end of each meal. There are 2 or 3 stewards to look after us. They are great on offering bacon & eggs. The breakfast consists of grapefruit, porridge, bacon & eggs, liver & bacon, sausage, cold meats, various jams, tea, coffee, honey, and mineral waters. I alone have a cigar after it. The 'boss' (as they all call him except me—I always call him the 'commodore', he always calls me the 'vice-commodore') announces the time at which he proposes to leave for an excursion, but he will alter the time if asked. Yesterday we went ashore at Candia. Motor cars were waiting; they always are, & we drive off *instantly*, 3 miles to Knossos, the seat of Minoan civilisation. 3 palaces, one above another. Very interesting, but not *big* enough for my taste. Then we drove back to the museum, which is far more interesting, artistically, than the palaces. You should see the designs made over 3000 years ago! We return to the quay. The launch is waiting; it always is; we are back on the ship at 12.15. Decide to bathe. Lie in the sun on deck & dry. This does good. A steward comes round & asks what cocktail you have. Kahn won't have one. The first few days he was very self-indulgent; then he reined in sharply. In any spare time some of the fellows are *always* playing bridge or piquet. They continually miss scenery for bridge & piquet! Lunch. The talk at meals is very good; it is occasionally obscene, startling, & even bawdy; but very intelligent it assuredly is. All the fellows have been educated by experience. I retire to sleep. Yesterday I missed the 3 o'clock launch, through snoozing off again, but it came back for me, & I was in the town at 3.15. I would not go to the museum again, where Kahn was. I met Jo Davidson & Paul Dougherty in the port, intensely hot. We got back in instalments for tea—on deck. The tea is terrific. Bridge. Bridge. Bridge. At 6 p.m. the yacht weighs anchor for Santorin. Lovely dusk & night. Kahn reads a lot, & writes in his study. I go down & write a bit. I emerge at intervals to tease the cardplayers. I go out on the poop to see how the ship is getting along. Dinner at 8. Very plenteous. Too plenteous. I don't eat ½ of it. I devote most of my evening to a fine cigar. Bridge, bridge, bridge. Drinks come round. (Very little alcohol is drunk.) I read a bit & walk around. About 10.30 I bid good night to Kahn & nod to the others. Some go to bed also. Others continue playing cards. The ship's engines are always going. I turn out my light about 11.15, but sometimes I come out on deck again to look around. I'm reading a book written by Kahn. Full of sense.

My sweet sweetest, I kiss thee.

Little

Kisses to Virginia.

370. In some private notes in 1926 Bennett wrote: 'nothing gives me a purer pleasure than the first half of a fine cigar . . . ; I like nothing extremely, except a yacht'.

BERG / MS / 371
(*To Dorothy Cheston Bennett*)

[Flying Cloud]
2–5–27

My sweetest sweetest,

Got your 2 ink letters & 1 pencil. Apl 16 & Apl 21 & pencil 21 (later) this morning. Should have got them yesterday; but the mail was sent to Mytons, & the sea was too rough for the boat to call there. The mail came by special boat this morn. Your 2 letters are excellent. I agree with your plan of action re Richard—or rather of inaction. I doubt, however, if you are not crediting Richard with more powers of calculation than he possesses. They certainly are not going to get anything out of

me on this account. I am still leaving the affair in your hands.
Well, I am now counting on you for Vienna. I note what you
say about the end of *D.J.* No! Sanchez is put there on purpose
for expression, & not for silence. Sometime I must explain this
to you. I fear you may be forgetting the limitations of the
dramatic medium. This is not a letter. I am snatching a
moment before lunch. The posts are bad. This letter should go
with the previous letter by the Orient Express. 4 more letters of
yours have just come in this instant. I shall have to read them
afterwards. We have to go to the Acropolis after & the post
closes at 6 p.m. So far, I am up to date with the writing of my
Greek impressions. I note all you say, & I mainly agree. I know
I am reserved, & that it is a fault. But how to cure it. I think I
shall be less so if you are more so. Yesterday between tea &
dinner, having nothing to do I wrote the opening chapters of a
sensual, pornographic novel, solely for my own amusement.
You wouldn't like it so you won't see it. I'll write you a better
letter than this later. Love to V.

Little

No time to read through.

371. *Don Juan de Marana.*
On the pornographic novel see above, pp. 381–2.

BERG / MS / 372
(*To Dorothy Cheston Bennett*)

[Flying Cloud]
2–5–27

My sweetest sweet,

   I've read about 7 letters of yours today. All very good—
especially the one dated 22nd Saturday night. You must be
doing something that stops you from sleeping. Rudolph says
that the English rights of Čapek's play will be in the hands of
the International Copywright Bureau (Major Collins isn't it?)
who will give you all information and will probably be able to
get you a copy of the play. I return Ellis's letter. Deal with it
how you like. I leave it to you. I won't answer it myself. Tell the
fellow I have no address & have left you with full powers to act.
Your remarks about my story show an imperfect understand-

ing of creative methods. *No* good thing is produced with 'perfect detachment', or without passion. None of my work is detached or pretends to be. I have just come from the Parthenon. It is the purest classic stuff, & yet is full of passion. What you mistake for 'perfect detachment' is the result of an effort to avoid crudity & over-emphasis. I would not expect you to understand the genesis of my story. But I could show you in my books for years & years past, long before I knew you, the evidences of the feelings which inspired the story. Certainly one or two details (of a superficial nature, serving only as illustrations) are taken from your acts and doings; but the heroine is not at all like you; nor is the 'feel' of the thing the 'feel' that you produce. *Good* stuff is not produced in the way you think that this thing was produced. The procedure is vastly more subtle & more protracted, & the inspiration is never shown on the surface. (And so on and so on. But you will gradually find out for yourself.) I'm glad the story is liked. The phenomenon which finally precipitated the idea into execution was the Downs. It came over me all of a sudden as the only place for that girl really to show herself in. I have never known *well* a girl like her. But I have had chats with girls like that in the Riviera, chats which have produced everlasting resentment in my mind.

I think the word 'girlie' is the most odious and odiously sentimental term ever invented for a woman. My scorn of it cannot be decently expressed, except humorously.

I haven't heard from Tania, but I sent her a p.c. or a letter—I forget which.

I won't say any more nice things about you, for the present, lest you should again accuse me of politeness (insincerity). You don't understand me. But you will, because you are an exceptionally fine understander of people. (There I go again!) So am I. I willingly agree that there are grave gaps in me. But then I usually also agree with your criticisms of my work (& of me). I agree because I still have a very open mind about my work. Neither I nor anybody yet knows whether it is really good. I have discovered that the fellows here have *terrific* admiration for my stuff—all of them. They will not put H. G. or J. G. in the same street. They don't say so. But they imply it all the time. Their respect almost frightens me. I'm glad to say also that they are very fond of me. Otto not more than any of the others. I'm writing some not bad impressions. The Parthenon is *all* that is said of it. I shall describe it quite briefly. I now do *not* think that the climax of Greek sculpture was 400 B.C., the Phidias period. I think that 200 years earlier was finer. Anterior, etc. Tremendous! You have to see the blue sky & the seascape and the overpowering sunshine around the Parthenon. I shall most positively bring you to see it. You will probably be a damned nuisance over it at great length—bringing coals to Newcastle, but I shan't mind. You don't understand, yet, my feelings toward, and for, you. However, no politeness. I like the picture of Virginia throwing your underclothes about. We have met Arthur Rubenstein here. He lunched with us today. He was so enthusiastic about Constantinople that Kahn is greatly inclined to revert to his original plan of going there. I hope he will. No address possible yet.

Yes, it is all right.

Little

Duncan Grant is a distinguished 'little' artist. You only have to put him against the big French people to estimate him correctly. But he's all right.

A.B.

& so are you.

372. Dorothy's misgivings about *The Woman Who Stole Everything* are understandable. The setting is Amberley in West Sussex (called Cander in the tale) where Bennett and Dorothy spent several weeks after the birth of Virginia. Details in the description of the village and its surroundings are precise and evocative, and the heroine is a beautiful young woman who heedlessly wakes her husband in the middle of the night, lacks all sense of time and money, and commits adultery with pleasure. The chief male figure is not her husband but her kindly, forebearing, orderly, moral, and rich uncle. The woman gets away with everything in the story, and the uncle has to shrug his shoulders and say, 'There she was! Was he to criticize God?' The framework for the situation is the uncle's own situation: he is a bachelor who is on the point of deciding whether to take up with a woman who is interested in him. In spite of what he sees of his niece's intentions, and God's, he decides to go ahead with the affair.

Duncan Grant (1885–1978).

ELDIN / MS / 373
(*To Virginia Bennett*)

Orestantinople
11–5–27

[no salutation]
Je te bise, ma petite.

Ton père, A.B.

373. In 1934 Rupert Hart-Davis dealt with Dorothy in the arrangements for publication of her memoir. Many years afterwards he recalled the time in a letter to Frank Swinnerton.

One day she brought Virginia to the office (aged, I suppose, about 10). I gave her a children's book. She thanked me politely, then looked to see the number of pages, did some rapid mental arithmetic, and said 'I shall have read this in two-and-a-half hours'. Which reminded me immediately of A.B.'s counting all the words he wrote.

CAMBRIDGE / MS / 374
(*To Richard Bennett*)

Flying Cloud
Hotel Pesa Palace
Constantinople
11–5–27

My dear Rich,
    Your letter of the 2nd reached me here today. (Delay no doubt owing to uncertainty of address.) It will certainly be better if Stella is invited to return home. She may be more upset than either you or she thinks. You can never tell in these nervous affairs. Anyhow, I've no doubt that one way or the other things will settle down *somehow* now. Of course if Stella could get a decent & sure job, that would be best; but in default of that, & for other reasons, it would be best for her to return home—on proper terms. Glad you've got a bicycle that will. I certainly think that you ought to go to Cambridge for your MA, degree; but I think that you ought to do it as cheaply as possible. (The £5 is my affair; so are your fares.) Neither you nor Stella can properly afford to go to the race, & I hope that you will bear this in mind in the hours of temptation. It is of the greatest importance. I reckon on you not to forget that you are not yet keeping yourself.
    We left the yacht on Saturday last in order to get to Constantinople in 24 hours by a (relatively) fast steamer. We did. And we return to Athens tomorrow morning. I'm glad we came. It is exhausting but the reward is satisfactory. The one

drawback is that Turkish costume has completely vanished. What about Mohammedans praying & prostrating in mosques in cravats & collars & overcoats? What about a muezzin with a bowler hat of which the brim has been cut off so that he can touch the ground with his forehead? The women too are all free & go to afternoon teashops in European dress just like other folks,—and are served by exiled Russian waitresses. The night life is very poor. The fuss at the customs & over passports is terrific. But all that is done *for* me. I do *nothing*, except eat & allow myself to be removed from place to place. As a city Constantinople could hardly be beaten. The authorities also have humour. They have turned one of the Sultan's palaces into a casino municipal, where the chief doorkeeper, as you can tell at once by his voice, is an ex-Sultanic eunuch. The mosques are all that you have heard of them. The Golden Horn ditto. The Dardanelles ditto. You see Cape Helles and other Anatolian scenes on one side, but only a few miles away on the other side is Troy itself. In fact the prestige of names during the last 3 weeks has been overwhelming. We rejoin the yacht on Friday morning. Thank God! The yacht is by far the most luxurious & best-run hotel in either Italy, Greece or Turkey, & has the finest chef. We shall then go to Olympia & Delphi, & afterwards Corfu and up the Dalmatic coast to Venice. Whence Mr. Kommer & myself go to Vienna, where Dorothy will meet us for the solemn celebration of my birthday (60). The fellows in this party are all excellent, & one or 2 are brilliant, & we get on without the slightest friction. The holiday is the gold medallist of all my career as an idler. Not that I am totally idle, having averaged over 1,000 words per day since I left London. Doran is in London. Edgar Selwyn has been. Maurice Browne is,—and I am away therefrom. I gather that Dorothy is very busy trying to sell my plays.

> Loves,
> Your nursed uncle,
>
> A.B.

374. Maurice Browne (1880–1955), actor and manager, was interested in producing *Don Juan de Marana*.

BERG / MS / 375
(*To Dorothy Cheston Bennett*)

Flying Cloud
Saturday 4. p.m.
14th May 1927

My sweet sweet,

I've just wirelessed you that at Vienna we shall be at the Sacher Hotel. Apparently it is old-fashioned, excellent, quiet, & the best hotel in Vienna. This morning we went to Delphi, by motor cars (3) from the small port of Itea, which is about 11 hours from Athens by sea, via the Corinth canal, which is an artificial Canyon with sides about 250 feet high, & only 75 feet apart. Marvellous sunset last evening. Well, my dearest, you will have to see Greece, but it will be d. difficult without a yacht. By yacht is the only right way of seeing Greece, because Greece is all coast line. Delphi is on the lower slopes of Parnassus. Transcendent scenery; road climbing up in zigzags. Eagles wandering about overhead; we saw 9 eagles at once. Clouds wandering about the lower crests also, & entirely hiding the summit of the hill of the muses. I had a passion to see the house of the Oracle, which, as one would expect, was largely a political machine. I shall try to describe it in modern terms, after I've had tea. The museum at Delphi is the best Greek provincial museum we have seen in its arrangement (French), & has lovely things in it. Coming into Greek waters early yesterday (on the Teodora) morning was heavenly. There is no landscape like the Greek landscape. You remember Baia; multiply the classic feeling by 100, & you will get a notion of Greek landscape. Not only the forms but the colours of the hills! During our absence in the Constantinopolitan trip, Kommer worked 64 hours in 6 days, on a pantomime that he is doing for Reinhardt. He showed me the manuscript. He says he didn't shave, nor go off the ship at all for 5 days. This morning he condescended to go with us sightseeing to Delphi; but was soon tired. We visit Olympia tomorrow (15 hours sail from Itea, and then a special train). Kommer swears that he will not go to Olympia on any consideration. Mind you, sightseeing is exhausting work. Kahn is an engine. The tragedy is that he has no charm. Of course, he is very self-centred, rentré; I think he would like to be autocratic, but he is up against something a bit too much for him to do that. He is polite, ready to compromise, very vivant & full of go; but I doubt if anybody really *likes* him. Sometimes he talks admirably. He loves bathing. He has got the young Belgian sculptor Hélène Sardeau, to come with us for 2 days; he has also got Hill, the great Greek expert, who is a most decent fellow with real imagination, very modest, & stuffed with learning. I am already far better pals with Hill & Hélène than Kahn is. I thought Hélène might be 24. But she told me she is 27. I told her she'd better hurry up. I think she is still a virgin. In fact, I feel sure she is. Kahn calls her his darling. Both of these new guests leave tomorrow at lunch time, after seeing Olympia with us. Polgar is *exquis*. He knows both more French & more English now than he did in 1925. The man I like best in the gang is Jo Davidson the sculptor, & he has conceived a perfect passion for me. He much wants to do my bust & to give it to me! The price of his busts is ten thousand dollars. His wife is Yvonne Davidson, the French dressmaker. I learnt yesterday that the principal Norwegian newspaper, *Aftenpost*, is going to celebrate my 60th birthday by a special, 'richly illustrated' article on your husband. They asked me for a 'message to the Norwegian people': which I have sent! I bet anything no English paper will celebrate my *soixantième* in this way. I wirelessed Doran yesterday, to learn when he returns. Sweetest, I trust all is well with thee. Eleven days now, & I shall see thee (D.V.) I kiss, kiss, & kiss thee, & pay thee no compliments. Love to V.

Little

375. Max Reinhardt (1873–1943) ran the Deutsche Theatre in Berlin from 1895 to 1932.

Hélène Sardeau: not otherwise known.

George Francis Hill (1867–1948), later principal librarian of the British Museum.

Aftenpost published a photograph and a few lines, with a brief greeting from Bennett. In England the one known tribute was from Beaverbrook in the *Daily Express*.

CAMBRIDGE / MS / 376
(*To Richard Bennett*)

75, Cadogan Square
10–6–27

My dear Rich,

I very much disapproved of your going to the Café de Paris last night. I think, especially as Stella was staying here, that it would have been better for you to warn me beforehand of what you meant to do. It was only because of Stella that I made no comment on the spot. You were clearly told that the C. de P. is an expensive place. You have no economic right to do what you cannot afford to do. It is probably not your fault at all that you are still partly dependent on me, but the fact is there. You know your total means, & you must know that the notion of a man with your income taking a woman to the C. de P. is utterly ridiculous. I suppose that you saved more money from me than you expected, & that you at once decided to spend more. This is a wrong policy. It is not as if you were getting on worse financially than other men of your age. You are not. You are better off than lots of University men. Even allowing for the depreciation of money, you are earning & getting far more money than I was at your age. It is your business to save. I warned you at Christmas about the excessive cost of your visits to London. I know it is difficult for you not to contrast my expenditure with yours; but the two things have no connection, & you must get this into your head.

About Stella, the correspondence which you read seemed to me to be perfectly ordinary correspondence in the circumstances. I fully admit that the situation is very difficult for you both. I think, however, that it was a mistake for Stella not to answer her mother's last letter. I also think that Stella should decide definitely what she wants to do: whether to return home or to earn her own living. If the former, 'conditions' are impracticable. Even if they are agreed to, they would not be kept. If the latter, the thing should be arranged at once. I agree that the situation here must have influenced the Lisles; but I do not think that it has been by any means the sole factor in forming their attitude. I think that your manner, or what you say, is very often much more exasperating than you suspect. I don't like to hurt you, but I ought to tell you that your manner generally indicates a self-satisfaction which the facts do not justify, and that your continual facetiousness is less amusing than irritating. You know that I do not say a lot in the way of criticism, but when I say something I do mean it, & I try not to fall into exaggeration.

I should have thought better of you if, instead of going to the Café de Paris (which incidentally is a rotten place) you had spent the money on clothes for Stella.

Lastly I think that it is always well to show appreciation of anything that is done for you & Stella. This refers to Dorothy, who is really anxious to do what she can for both you & Stella. You should remember that Dorothy does not come from the harsh Midlands & that she must have some difficulty in understanding the current manners of our part of the world.

Love,
Your critical uncle,

A.B.

P.S. Dorothy likes Stella more & more.

A.B.

CAMBRIDGE / MS / 377
(*To Richard Bennett*)

75, Cadogan Square
20–6–27

My dear Rich,

Cut me finger in closing my penknife. Can't write very easily. Had to go to a chemist's last night after dining at Green Park Hotel, after it had been bleeding for 3 hours. All right, today, but it must be dressed again. Well, I must say I thought you were both a bit optimistic about a job for Stella. As for the eclipse, I shall see only the partial—if I am up. Lady Lisle wrote me again, but as she had nothing to say, the letter amounted merely to her laying her head on my shoulder & weeping into the folds of my new neck-tie. I entirely agree with Dorothy's view of the inadvisability of Stella taking a job at Wolverhampton unless she positively *wants* trouble. The notion seems to me to be well, you know. The gramophone is yours. Exchange it by all means. That efficient tall little thing, Mary Kennerley, has been so impressive at her job at Emile's in Hanover Square, that Madame Emile has offered her a partnership for next year if she'll go to Paris in the meantime; I mean a partnership without capital having to be provided! Some people have all the luck; but Mary is really the most efficient & the most passionately industrious kid I ever knew. She frightens me; because I always thought I was efficient & industrious. I now know that I am not. A wild life just now in this city. But we've taken a house at Winchelsea from July 22 till end of August. I drove down with Miss Nerney on Thursday & found the house. Folkestone road a marvel. I didn't take Dorothy because she said it couldn't be done in a day. I got back at 7.8 p.m. Tell me, why does an engine backfire when the mixture is weakened? I am too proud to ask Atkinson. Dorothy is exceeding busy, chiefly negotiating for the sale of *Don Juan*. She *may* do it.

Love,
Your wounded uncle,

A.B.

377. In August 1925 Bennett wrote to Edward Knoblock to ask if he could help in finding a suitable job for Mary Kennerley, 'who has a perfect passion for dressmaking, & a very marked talent for it, and a unique industry & force of character.... [She] would be invaluable to any firm, even from the start.' She began at Emile's, at 9 Hanover Square, as a paying apprentice (£25). After six months she became a 'hand' at 25 shillings a week. After her stay in Paris she returned as a fitter and cutter.

CAMBRIDGE / MS / 378
(*To Richard Bennett*)

75, Cadogan Square
1–11–27

My dear Rich,

Well well & Good God! These sudden relentings, however, are characteristic of an alcoholic temperament. My poor boy, you are marrying into a strange family, & once through the church, you will do well to keep away from the family as much as possible. I feel sure you will not expect me to attend the ceremony. I also feel sure that if you do expect me you will be disappointed. Your real parents can see to the ceremonials. Withal, I am very glad it has been settled, this affair. Of course it may be unsettled again. You can never be sure with the Lisles of this world. In view of the P.L.A. business I don't see how you can make any definite arrangements until after Christmas. Is Stella still the official cook of the household? I should say that the first official proof of repentance ought to be the replacing of Stella in the kitchen by some worthy member of the lower classes. She will cost more than Stella, of course, mais que veux-tu? I am very well, but very tired through imperfect sleeping &

a wild life. I went to see the Hill fight last night, & drank only
one tablespoon of champagne. It was a very good fight, &
aroused enthusiasm. Many first nights, concerts, & dinners.
There is a good dinner here tonight. Heaven knows what time it
will end, as Dorothy will not be in till after 11 p.m. *Paul I* is
coming off Saturday week & *Mister P* is coming on today
fortnight. May the blessings of God be invoked upon us all. I
find helping to run a theatre an awful bore, especially at night.
But I was born to be patient & helpful. Of this fact I am more &
more convinced by all my friends—I mean of their demands.

> Love,
> Your noble uncle,
> A.B.

378. P.L.A.: unidentified.
Johnny Hill, the British flyweight champion, defeated Petit Biquet at the National
Sporting Club.
Paul I, by Dmitri Merejkovsky, opened at the Court Theatre on 4 October. It was the
first work put on by Sloane Productions, to which Bennett contributed most of the
capital and of which he was chairman. Dorothy says in her memoir that Sloane
Productions came into being because Bennett and Mrs Patrick Campbell were
confident of her managerial as well as acting skills. In her long letter to Frank
Swinnerton (p. xxiv) she says she undertook the venture to help Bennett's finances.
Bennett's views on her managerial skills are given on p. 496, and there is little doubt not
only that the venture lost money but that Bennett thought it would. Dorothy and
Charles Laughton played in *Paul I*. Laughton then starred in *Mr. Prohack*, the second
production, which opened on 16 November for a brief but successful run. The footnote
in Vol. I, pp. 367–8, describing the history of Sloane Productions, was written by
Dorothy.

KENNERLEY / MS / 379
(*To Mary Kennerley*)

> 75, Cadogan Square
> 14–12–27

[no salutation]

  Well Mary my dear, I was very glad to hear from you—
especially to the effect that you are sticking it. But of course you
would. I've heard all about your disappointments, struggles,
fatigues, & grit, from your mother (who has sent us 2 mince
tarts). I hope that Madame Godebski (who must now be back)
will be able to do summat. Haven't seen Hughie for years! Is he
still fat? I know the carte d'identité is now in order. And that a

week today the attached family will invade Paris. We are very
well here, & hope to go to Brighton for 2 days at Xmas. Dorothy
can only be away for 2 days. The play is greatly liked. Weather
bad. Now less chilly, but rain-pouring. I should think it must be
nearly as bad as in Paris. Next week I have the vast job of
pleasing my various & varied relatives & others with missives
containing enclosures. Also books to send out, & 1 million
subscriptions to pay. No joke! But I'm used to it. Many
lunches, dinners, & functions such as concerts or plays. Do you
read the Continental *Daily Mail*, or are you contentedly out of
touch with Britain? Go on as you have before—I mean in
mood—& you will soon be all right. But contrive to remember
that Paris *is* the centre of the coutureic world, whatever you
may think of its defects.

Heureusement tu ne te mouches pas avec des tessons de
bouteille. (I hear you are very strong on French slang.) Donc,
tu réuissiras. Dorothy sends her love.

Your aff, well-wishing uncle,

A.B.

379. In Paris Mary Kennerley worked first for a small family firm and then for
Yvonne Davidson. Presently she began work for Chanel.
   Hughie: Hugh Ledward, one of Enid and Olive Ledward's brothers.

ELDIN / MS / 380
(*To May Beardmore Marsden*)

75, Cadogan Square
7–11–28

My dear May,
   Thanks for letter. I'm sorry about Edward. Damn him! Why
the hell doesn't he take better care of himself? I like him. He is a
wise, tolerant, & large-minded man, & yet he goes and gets ill!
All is well here. Just going to Paris for a few days. Virginia paid
a state visit to Auntie Tertia's yesterday. Great success. I have
a sort of suspicion I've written you this letter before, or
something like it. But I am enfeebled today. I saw *Macbeth* in
khaki last night, & it was so bad that I couldn't sleep after it. I
see too much, & sleep too little, but my health is marvellous. It

is the best health I've had for 30 years, & I'm 18 months older
than Edward in his pa's dressing-gown.

Our loves,
Yours ever,
A.B.

Maud came for tea last Thursday.

CAMBRIDGE / MS / 381
(*To Richard Bennett*)

75, Cadogan Square
20–2–28

My dear Rich,

Thanks for yours of yesterday. Well of course from now on
you will be having a rather trying time, but as you so ably say,
the ordeal will be short. I don't see how you can blame the
Lisles for making a big show of the affair. If you marry into a
family you must take the family as part of the bargain. It has a
perfect right to its own conventions which quite possibly in the
sight of God are no more absurd than ours. As regards the
'bankruptcy' I must say that I don't understand it. Hence you
have not made it as clear to me as you made the double-tides
clear at Southampton. I should *like* to understand it. As regards
the furniture, this is in Miss Nerney's hands. She will write to
you direct, and if necessary you will write to her. Her idea is to
send it by road. She says this will be cheaper & better. I really
forget now what hiccup is a sign of. I must look it up. But
somehow someone certainly ought to have sent for a doctor
long before the expiration of 60 hours. A father who hiccups for
even 12 hours without attending to the matter is entitled to
neither wifely nor filial respect & his wishes should be ignored.
I don't know about taking you to the 1st night of the revue.
Charlie is a great friend of mine. But in this excursion I have
rather forced myself upon him. He has insisted on giving me
one seat, though I wanted to pay for it. If I ask for another....
But I will see, & you shall hear. The company, including me, is
going up by special train on Sunday; but when the special train
starts or arrives I haven't the shadow of a shade etc. Dorothea is
robbing me of the car on Saturday next for 3 weeks; otherwise I

would have driven to Manchester. She's driving with Audrey Anderson from Boulogne to the Riviera—and back. I nearly had to promise to go & fetch her back; but I have escaped this. I should like it; but I am now in the midst of writing the greatest play ever written since God's drama of creation, & I should have hated to leave it. Your cousin John spent 2 hours with me yesterday. He has charm. He is 17 11/12th. I hear he is idle; but so were you at his age. And see what an exemplar of energy you have become since—snatching young maidens out of the fortresses of Wolverhampton & so on.

Loves,

Your theatrical uncle,

A.B.

381. *C. B. Cochran's 1928 Revue*, with 28 tableaux and 500 costumes, book and lyrics by Noël Coward. It opened in Manchester on 28 February and presently came to London.

Audrey Anderson: unidentified.

Bennett wrote *The Return Journey* from February to July 1928.

John Bennett, Septimus's son. He presently made his career in Lloyds Bank.

BERG / MS / 382   Midland Hotel
(*To Dorothy Cheston Bennett*)   Manchester
                                         Monday
                                         27–2–28

My sweet wanderer,

It is impossible to do anything else when you are away with a rehearsing revue company. Charles has good organisers. There were 90 people on his special train. I was his dandled pet. The largest saloon was labelled for us two. Even Noel was not put into it. However all was extremely promiscuous in the end, as we issued invitations & even had performances in the said saloon. 2 restaurant cars in the special train. I paid for nothing, not even the ticket. Photography of course at Manchester station. Couldn't help it, as Charles said it would be good publicity for his show. Florence Bennett, her son Vernon & his fiancée Lilian something came over without being asked on Sunday afternoon & I gave them tea. They went. Rehearsal began at 5.30. It ended at 2.5 a.m. Charles never left the theatre. Noel & I & two of his friends (not in the revue— mysterious lady & gent.—said to be Noel's 2 mistresses—

? aloha!]) came to the hotel for a short dinner & returned. There are 1 or 2 *very* fine things in this revue,—a few superlative artists. Noel is really wonderful in his width. His music isn't worth a damn, but he certainly has genuine ideas. Cochran is fine at rehearsals; I mean in his demeanour. There are 28 scenes & only 1 dress rehearsal. It—the D.R.—is expected to begin at 8.30 tonight (Monday) & to last 12 hours. The band is *not* good. The stage manager, dance-director, music overseers & the conductor are all extremely capable. Never a cross word. I had to see lots of journalists, & I observe this morn that I am the main point in the theatrical news of the Manchester papers. Very odd! Charles talked to me of his plans. He says that if this revue succeeds he will try to run an ordinary theatre. He seemed entirely to agree with me about you, of whom I discussed at some length. (Ah! What did I say!) Well after the rehearsal, we had supper at the hotel—about 15 persons (2.30 a.m.). I had nothing but bread & butter & hot milk. Charles had 2 lots of bacon & eggs. The artistes have to be on the stage made-up at 10.30 this morning. And they will then have about 24 hours on end. Lighting & scenery rehearsals during the day today. Tilly Losch stretched a ligament the other day at a rehearsal, & couldn't come to Manchester on Sunday. Terrific calmness of Charles under this blow. It is *hoped* that she will come today, for the rehearsal tonight. I am having a strange time, believe me. It is marvellous to see how all the girls (most of them insipid) really *enjoy* their work, revel in it. At the end of an $8\frac{1}{2}$ hour rehearsal, some of them stayed dancing on the stage for fun! Elsie April, who looks after all the musical side, is extremely capable. I said to her: 'Look here. There's a character named Elsie April in my book *The Regent*.' Said she: 'Yes. I thought it was such a lovely name that I took it for myself, & it's been a very lucky name for me.' Well, it's about time I expressed the hope that you and Audrey are faring according to plan, & that all is going smoothly, including the car. I spent 10 minutes with Virginia yesterday morning before leaving. She was in A1 form. Oh I forgot, I went to see *Warrior*. The first act was dreadful—false, sentimental, pretentious. I feared the absolute worst. M. Browne was *terrible*. And long residence in U.S.A. has spoilt his pronunciation, which is most deplorable. Such things as 'provadunce' for 'providence' all the time. Acts

II & III were better. In fact there were one or two *very* fine scenes. Maurice also was much better. The other two not good, at any time. The play is 'queer'—with brilliances. Cecil Lewis's translation is very bad. It is very refined, careful, full of deliberate effects which he thinks fine, but which are invariably 2nd rate. It is the sort of translation which lots of people, including critics, would call very fine. Sam Courtauld was of the party (I dined at Sybil's) also Elizabeth. He took us to the Café Anglais after for a drink etc. The Café Anglais is a perfectly dreadful place. Samuel came to me to exchange views about it while waiting for the women. We agreed absolutely. He is a nice quiet simple man who can't see my jokes.

Little

382. For a letter and other references to Noël Coward (1899–1973) see Vol. III. One of the songs in the revue was 'A Room with a View'. Tilly Losch (1907–75): Austrian dancer and choreographer. Elsie April was an orchestral arranger.

Vernon Bennett married Eunice Bradley.

The Unknown Warrior, translated from the French of Paul Raynal by Cecil Lewis, author some years later of a memorable account of his flying career in the War, *Saggitarius Rising*. The play starred Maurice Browne.

Samuel Cortauld (1876–1947), chairman of Cortaulds and trustee of the Tate Gallery.

Elizabeth Lewis; Sybil Colefax.

BERG / MS / 383
(*To Dorothy Cheston Bennett*)

75, Cadogan Square
1–III–28

My sweet wanderer,

Your letter from Avignon of Feby 28, which arrived this morning. The close of it, after all the excellent description. Frankness demanded. Yes. I consider that our life together is a considerable success, & I am sure that this now coincides with the general view. (The general view is not often wrong.) You expect more from life than most people do. I don't say it is a fault. You are utterly wrong—& this disturbs my trust in your general observation—in thinking that I care less for you than I did. *Quite the contrary is the case*. *I* think our life is very romantic, & on the whole I greatly enjoy it. Our social life is not excessive. It is on the whole less tiring than the average. Nor do I see how it can be cut down, nor do I think that you would really like it to

be cut down. You see you have a general tendency to exaggerate troubles & inconveniences. And our social life is by no
means the only thing that you exaggerate. I think you have still
something to comprehend about human relations. When you
ask me why I'm not the same bright thing at home that I am in
company, I really marvel at the question. I am not, for the same
reason that you are not, and that everybody is not. Because,
owing to circumstances & freedom of speech, it is impossible
and would be absurd even if possible. I think that you are
magnificent, comprehending, full of unusual reasoning power,
so long as you are calm. I think that you make tremendous
efforts to satisfy your conscience, & that you respond eagerly &
honestly to any similar effort in another. But I also think that
when you are not calm—when you are overcome by the sense of
a grievance or a trouble—there is absolutely no doing anything
with you. I was entirely staggered at the scene you made with
Miss Nerney over something so trifling that I cannot even recall
it. I discover every day that Miss Nerney is far from perfect. But
she has much common sense, she has been with me for about 18
years, she is completely devoted & completely faithful &
trustworthy. I am very dependent on her, you are very
dependent on her; if she left I should be in a hades of a mess. She
is older than you, she occupies a very important & a very
responsible position; and it was extremely painful to me to have
you talk to her as you did. And the more so, as you told her not
to do the very thing that a confidential secretary ought to do &
ought to be encouraged to do, namely argue with you. Arguing
is one of the chief jobs of a confidential secretary. No wonder
she was considerably upset for several days. Miss Nerney has,
rightly, got a great notion of her position; she gets £1 a day,
Sundays included; but she is priceless. I myself should never
dream of addressing her as you did—and all because you had
lost control of yourself. I don't *blame* you, because I know you
can't help it. Considering that we are both artists, & have quite
different work, I think that you & I get on wonderfully well. I
sometimes wish that you showed $\frac{1}{4}$ as much interest in my work
as I show in yours. Look at my last book. I put the early press-
cuttings out for you to read; after a week or two you did read
some of them; but since then you have shown no interest in the
reception of the book either commercial or artistic. Yet its

reception has some importance to us. I also wish to point out that, as regards nights, I have largely dropped the habit of going straight to bed when we are supposed to be going to bed. Night after night I lounge about in your room while you are composing yourself. And 5 nights of 6, just as I am leaving you, you begin some criticism of me, or some complaint as to the horrors of existence in this house. You are completely & demonstrably wrong in saying that you don't see me. You see more of me than 9 wives young or old out of 10 see of their husbands,—and a lot more. You certainly talk too much, & too great length over quite negligible details, and too loudly. When I am in my study I hear no one's voice but yours. When I went away to Greece you wrote several times insisting on the sense of freedom & relief which you experienced. I have exactly the same feeling. And it is natural. But it would be succeeded after a time by feelings of dissatisfaction & emptiness. Your health began to decline a fortnight before I returned, on your own statements—largely, I think, because you couldn't get yourself to bed in decent time, which was because I wasn't there. The Court season was too much for you, and it was too much for me. I wouldn't like to go through that experience again, because to me it was terrible, & if I had been engaged in any large work that work would have been ruined. I am now sleeping much better, simply because I go to bed quietly. I slept 7 hours last night—in your bed (mine is away). I don't demand that I should always go to bed quietly, but I ought often to go to bed quietly. For the last 3 or 4 months my sleeping has been worse than it has ever been. Now you asked for frankness, & you have it. I know I can trust you to receive it in the right spirit. You have, besides quantities of brains, sundry fine masculine qualities—when you are calm. I say nothing about my own faults, because your notion of them is at least adequate. The Milne play was a childish entertainment; in some respects not wholly evil; but wholly negligible. I have cleared up all accumulation & shall now proceed with my play. I *object* to your travelling at over 50 miles an hour. It is foolish. Atkinson's chill is much better. Virginia, apart from a very slight cold, is in splendid condition. I have just been playing with her. I love you.

Little

P.S. Annie is absolutely certain that she put the comb on the top of your suitcase. Miss Nerney is also absolutely certain that the Baedeker *went*. Surely it would have been simpler or easier to buy a comb in the first town you stopped at, than to have one sent out. Comb & another Baedeker have been sent out. But do you know the price of a Baedeker?

A.B.

383. *Mr. Pim Passes By*, by A. A. Milne (1882–1956), with Marie Tempest, was at the St Martin's Theatre.

BERG / MS / 384
(*To Dorothy Cheston Bennett*)

75, Cadogan Square
2–III–28

Siren,

Your Epistle of 6th only reached me this morn. Full of meat. I am distractingly occupied: but really only with my play, which is proceeding fairly well. (Virginia is playing in my study as I write this—10 a.m.) But of course this is the moment for my *World Today* article & then my *E.S.* article on Monday. You seem to be having a great time. I am *not* having a great time. My sleeping is not so good as it was, though not yet wholly evil. My play is eating me up. George arrives today. More distraction! & 7 of us are going to Leslie Vedrenne's play Sunday (Virginia is now sitting on my knees—that smudge is her fingering.) I looked in at the *Daily Mail* Ideal Home Exhibits—yesterday. There was a queue certainly 200 yards long to see the 'House of the Future', & I was told the queue is continuous all day & every day. I presented myself to the Manager, who showed me around instantly. It is very interesting. The booklet, of which part is enclosed, must be having a terrific sale. My family dinner on Wednesday went off with great tranquility & cheerfulness. Only Frank Beardmore stopped till 12.10 talking about the prospects of his literary son! I have no theatre news. I'm told *Mary Dugan* is a great success. I dined last night at the Other Club & heard a great deal from Winston Churchill, who said I was 'down in the mouth', & hoped it wasn't because I didn't like him. He said he couldn't *bear* me not to like him. I reassured him on both points. There will however be some caustic remarks about him in next month's *W. Today*. I note all you say, my sweet siren. I find Sybil's dinner is on 20th, so the 21st will do well, if you can come then; but I doubt if you will. (Don't come back with the curse.) And when you come don't forget to wear that blue skirt, & forget, *do* forget to wear anything else when you come upstairs of a night. I desire greatly to *see* thee. In fact, various things. I am very lonely in a certain way—not even a temporary mistress. Nothing. I think the flaw in your argument about the strain of life *here* is that you used to be in just the same state, (*but worse*,) when you lived alone. Still, live quietly by all means, & stay at home. I can go out, if urgency demands, by myself. I shall always return to you earlier—unless of course I stay out all night. I've had a word with Annie, but until you have a typewritten list of all usual things to be packed you will always have trouble. I don't advise you to meddle with Columbias at present. There is nothing in them either way. There is £112 waiting for you. I am now about to transfer my attention from the siren to the play. I must say I can see nothing whatever against my writing things like *The Vanguard* (quite apart, I mean, from finance). I *will not* always be writing grave & gloomy things. If I feel like writing things like *The Vanguard* I will write things like *The Vanguard*. See? But then, as you say, I am *never* wrong. That is an axiom. All is well here. Virginia is now bored by my lack of interest in her. Letter written under difficulties.

Little

P.S. I've told Miss C. about Hoffmansthal. Russell (broker) has just telephoned he will buy £200 more Columbia on Clyde's recommendation. So I have concurred.

A.B.

384. Bennett wrote eight monthly articles on 'Men and Events' for *World Today*. They began in November 1927. The attack on Churchill, who was then Chancellor of the Exchequer, was by James O'Connor, former Irish Attorney General, mentioned above, pp. 204, 205.

George: George Doran.

Leslie Vedrenne's play is not known.

The Trial of Mary Dugan, by Bayard Veiller, was showing at the Queen's Theatre.

The Strange Vanguard was published on 26 January 1928. It was published the preceding autumn in America under the title *The Vanguard*. Duplication of someone else's title forced the English change.

Miss C: Miss Colkbayer, Dorothy's secretary.

BERG / MS / 385
(*To Dorothy Cheston Bennett*)

75, Cadogan Square
10–III–28

My sweet seductress,

I have now taught your & my daughter to walk both up & downstairs with only the slightest help. This is news. Thanks for letter of 7th & two p.c.'s just received this morn. I have spoken to Annie. The said woman has evidently been much upset by the postcard accusation that she did not pack your comb. Whether she did or not I don't know. But she swears she did. She has looked everywhere for the blouse buttons & can't find them. Her theory is that, as the blouse had been worn before you took it away, the buttons ought to be in the blouse. Of course I declined to discuss this with her. I wish I had been able to tell her definitely that the comb was not packed; but your letter on this point was not clear. I told her about the elastic of the culotte. She had no excuse. When she gets resentful there is no doing anything with her. My opinion is that you will have to part company with this woman. She will never suit you. You have a wrong idea about her attitude to me: it is exactly the same as her attitude to you, & always has been. My advice to you is to get rid of her. She is incurable of the faults which annoy you. Such are my last words concerning this excellent, honest & faithful spinster who is also an obstinate & forgetful nuisance. You might get someone better; or someone worse. John mentioned the nurse question up at his other auntie's, but elicited no response. I have told him to do it again. George has arrived & is lunching with me today, here. I had a great & flattering compliment last night at the big dinner given to Capt. George Nicholls ('Quex' of the *Evening News*) at the Savoy. 175 persons. When I went in, I saw him first, & said 'Do you know where I'm sitting, Nicholls?' He said: 'You're sitting next to me, because I specially asked for it.' I said: 'Why?' (Because I don't know him at all well.) He replied: 'Because I knew I could trust you for moral support. It's a ticklish thing having a big dinner given to you & having to speak.' So I was pleased. Birkenhead was in the chair & made a most brilliant & impudent speech. Champagne was bad. Slight headache. Very busy on play & 2 articles all at once! Some life! I'm going with

Duff tonight to see *Beggar's Opera*. The pencil marks above are Virginia's daughterly contributions to this letter. Also the smudge.

Sweetest, I kiss & love thee.

Little

Sorry about Odette.

385. George Nicholls (d. 1933) signed social and political articles for the *Evening News* with the name Quex.

The Beggar's Opera was revived for a limited run at the Lyric Hammersmith, and continued there for two years.

Odette: possibly Odette Keun, H. G. Wells's current mistress, whom Dorothy might have seen on the Continent.

STOKE / MS / 386
(*To Margaret Beardmore*)

75, Cadogan Square
20–III–28

My sweet niece,

Well, the other night when I was talking about you with your adoring father, he did not know you were engaged. All he knew was that you were the goods. When Auntie Tertia called in this afternoon she said: 'Big Margaret's engaged.' I said: 'I know.' It is better to be engaged than not to be engaged. And it is better to be married than engaged. Hence I trust that the wedding will not be long postponed. In this Auntie Tertia powerfully agrees with me. As I know not Cyril I can't say much about the affair, except that if he has satisfied YOU he must be SOMEBODY. And this I flatly do say. My affection & my benevolence go very warmly forth to you—and to him. I *should* like to see Cyril & Roger; but we shan't be in town. You must write and tell Harriet Cohen (13 Wyndham Place, W.1.) who has always shown great interest in you. She is now touring the continent as a solo pianist. Poor thing, she is not well. Heaven keep you!

Love to all,

Your aff unc,

A.B.

386. Cyril Shingler was at this time a designer at Doulton's Pottery. Later he freelanced. After the Second World War he worked for Worcester Royal Porcelain, and became curator of their factory museum.

Roger Beardmore (b. 1904), the middle son of Frank and Fanny Gertrude. He began work in a pottery in Scotland when the family lived there. Later he worked for the BBC.

KENNERLEY / MS / 387
(*To Mary Kennerley*)

75, Cadogan Square
3–IV–28

[no salutation]

Well, Maria, we are charmed to hear from you, & this letter bears our Easter greetings upon the decease & resurrection of our Lord J.C. Greetings also to Margaret & Shelagh on the same occasion. *I* wish you were staying in Paris longer. But if you aren't staying, I quite agree that it would be absurd to come home earlier & then go back to a problematical Chanel's. You are, you know, very naughty not to announce & describe yourself as a 'first-hand'. In this detail I am against you. Don't go to the Folies Bergères—go to the Casino de Paris instead: it is much better. But in no case will you see in Paris a show finer than, or even equal to, the Noel Coward revue at the London Pavilion. Never have I witnessed its equal. Your mother called here yesterday to arrange for us to go down to Imbros Sunday fortnight. We shall go (D.V.). Virginia reached the old age of 2 on Friday week. She still doesn't talk, but she gets more alert daily.

Dorothy had 3½ weeks touring in France (depriving me thus of the car); she went everywhere except to Paris. She is now very busy again. So am I. We're going to Sidmouth for Easter. The only place in England where we could get rooms in a decent hotel! All others booked up! God keep you. I look forward to seeing you.

Loves from us both,
Your aff unc,

A.B.

P.S. Richard is to be married tomorrow.

387. Shelagh Bromly (d. 1950): Mary Kennerley's closest friend for many years.

A first hand in Paris was entirely responsible for any garment, apart from cutting out and fitting the customer. She would have one or more second hands or improvers working under her. Mary Kennerley was an improver.

Imbros: the house in Aldwick to which the Kennerleys came for holidays and to which Tertia and W.W.K. moved in 1939.

CAMBRIDGE / TS / 388
(*To Richard Bennett*)

75, Cadogan Square
4th June 1928

My dear Rich,

Very busy. Thanks for yours. The stuff you send is exactly the right kind of stuff for my purpose. You need not make it much longer. Keep down the ego, as far as you can. I hope you are not attaching too much importance to what I wrote. Its only importance springs from the fact that Keeble is an intimate friend of mine, and that he has asked me to take an interest in a protégé of his. Whether anything will or can be done, I do not in the least know. Let me have the stuff as soon as possible.

There was a garden party on Saturday afternoon at Putney to celebrate the return of Mary from Paris. Also her 21st birthday occurred next day. I saw many people whom I had not seen for years, and some of whom I had not seen for 20 or 25 years. Margaret Beardmore came up especially for the party and returned at 6 p.m. *Some* loyalty to the K. family! Joan Marsden (21 tomorrow) and Frederick Marriott were very bright.

Yesterday Dorothy and I went down to Beaverbrook's at Cherkley for lunch, and found a lot of gloomy and silent people there. We enlivened them somewhat, but not enough. However, we had a nice drive. Life here is rather running over. Both of us have too much to do.

It was a great relief to me the other day to learn from the managing director and the producer (Dupont) of British International Films Ltd that the film which I have written for them is absolutely perfect from their point of view. I have never before seen men so enthusiastic about any work of mine as they were. They immediately asked me to write another film for them. But my policy in such a case is always to hang fire, to make difficulties, to say that I cannot, etc. But I shall probably write them another film all the same. The difficulties and the delays only whet their appetite.

Virginia is getting very obstreperous and even naughty.

There was to have been some tennis today in the Square, but it is off on account of the indisposition of one of the players—a female. I am not sorry, as I had promised to play and am really too busy to find time to play.

Have I told you that Captain Prior is dead? Cancer of the Bladder.

I hope you read my article in the *Daily News* on Saturday. At any rate it was better than the article of the Bishop on Friday.

Loves,
Your fertile uncle,

A.B.

P.S. I did play 1 hours tennis after all.

A.B.

388. A. E. Dupont (1891–1956) was a producer for British International Pictures. Bennett wrote *Piccadilly* for him in April and May. The film had its first showing on 30 January 1929, with Anna May Wong, Gilda Grey, and Jameson Thomas in the leading roles. The story was published in book form in March 1929.

Bennett's article in the *Daily News* (amalgamated with the *Westminster Gazette*), 'Where are the Dead?' appeared on 2 June. He expresses little interest in congregations of spirits. In so far as he believes matter and spirit are inseparable, he thinks dissolution of material organization means dissolution of spiritual. But also in so far as matter is indestructible, there are no dead! The first article was by E. A. Knox, formerly Bishop of Manchester, who took a conventional Christian view of the afterlife.

ELDIN / MS / 389
(*To Joan Marsden*)

75, Cadogan Square
4–6–28

My dear Joan,

I heard months ago that your 21st birthday occurs & glorifies tomorrow. We wish you all success & all happiness. Please spend the enclosed according to your caprice of the moment, & oblige. Best wishes from Dorothy.

Your affectionate uncle (I am),

Arnold Bennett

KEELE / MS / 390
(*To Marguerite Soulié Bennett*)

[75, Cadogan Square]
7–7–28

Dear Marguerite,

Thanks for your letter of Monday, which I have only just received, as I have not been to the Club. I wish you would send your letters to the house. Nobody would open them but me. You may count on this absolutely.

I have also received copy of your note to Dorothy. She is at present away, but so far as I know she *never* gives the name of Mrs. Arnold Bennett. Of course tradesmen, seeing me with her sometimes, may make a mistake, but everything is done to avoid such mistakes. There can be no excuse for a tradesman sending a parcel to you. Dorothy does not even know your address. I quite realise the annoyance of these things to you, and I am sorry, but it is not the fault of either Dorothy or me. I shall do everything possible to avoid them in future, as in the past.

The bill was not enclosed in your letter.

Dorothy's *legal* name is 'Dorothy Cheston Bennett'. 'Dorothy Cheston' is only her stage name.

I really cannot imagine why anyone should tell you that I tell people that you and I are divorced. Such people are pure mischief-makers. They are also liars. I have never said any such thing; and you know me well enough to know that I would never say it. All our friends have been plainly told that Dorothy and I are not married, and they visit us, and we visit them, on that clear understanding.

Yours, A.B.

390. Bennett and Dorothy and Virginia went to France for the month of July. Bennett made a brief trip to London on the 6th.

KENNERLEY / MS / 391
(*To Tertia Kennerley*)

Villa M Coquille
Avenue Jules César
Le Touquet Paris Plage
23–7–28

My dear Tertia,

Thank you for cheque for £15 carrying interest up to July 20th. Fanny may be quite decent, but I feel I shall struggle on

satisfactorily if I don't see her. I thank God we've missed
Maud. John plays a very good game of tennis. This place is very
good. The house is small, but well fitted up, with running water
in the 3 house-bedrooms. Dining room & drawing room in one:
large. I have a small study, where I can carry on the business
side of my profession: necessary! Also there are 2 garden
bedrooms. Atkinson sleeps in one; the other is used for a dining
room by him & nurse. Kitchen good. Bathroom A.1. House
excellently planned. 5 minutes from sea. Too much sand. The
bathing is unsatisfactory. Sea goes out about 100 miles, & then
you have to wade another 100 to get out of your depth.
However, French people want only to wade. Poor dagoes! Also
there are various trenches in the beach. Hence dangerous for
fools at $\frac{1}{2}$ or high water. I counted the other day 1 motor boat &
2 row boats & 8 men in all, engaged by the town to protect
bathers. The air traffic between London & Paris passes over
head. Lots of it. Le Touquet & Paris Plage are now all one. The
fashionable part: 2 big hotels (highly costly) & casino & big
restaurant & fine shops: all in the forest, about 4/5 mile from us.
We have seen little of it, except we stayed one night at the
Westminster (one of the 2 big hotels). General Blaque-Belair,
Mimi's father-in-law, is a great figure up in the forest. He called
on us, but we weren't in. Mimi & husband are supposed to be
coming down to see us next weekend. Dorothy & I went to one
race-meeting, last Sunday but one, & lost 350 frs. at the
totalisator. We should have lost less, but we both forgot to
collect a win on a placed-horse. (I needn't say that I don't bet
on horses. Dorothy bets; I only pay.) It was agreeable enough. I
enclose a photo of Dorothy at the races. I am walking away, to
keep off the photographer. If he had got me the thing would
have been in all the English papers before you could say knife.
Our tenancy of the house expires the 30th, when we go to the
Grand Hotel (on sea-front) for about a fortnight, as Dorothy is
incapable of leaving the place. The Italian servant (who speaks
French as badly as Dorothy) is a marvel: A1 cook, great worker,
does everything, is fat, & always calm & efficient. The meals
are wonderful. They will be less so at the Hotel. Twice I have
had to go over to London to comfort Gerald. Like all theatrical
persons he does all his correspondence by telegraph. His wires
usually begin: 'Great Arnold, Help, help, help.' He rehearses

till the end of this week, then takes 3 weeks holiday; then about 2 weeks more rehearsal. Production supposed to be 30th August (but I doubt it). His production of the play is due to sheer accident. I was walking down Regent Street about 10 weeks ago, & an arm was put on my shoulder, & a voice said: 'Arnold, you'll get killed, if you moon along like that.' 'Gerald!' I said: 'I shan't. I know exactly what I'm doing. But I'm thinking out a play.' He said: 'It's mine!' Of course I said he couldn't possibly have it. This always sharpens their appetite. He wouldn't leave me alone. He sent Viola Tree to wheedle me. He offered to buy the play in the dark. I refused. At last I said he could read it when it was finished; but he must say Yes or No in 2 days. He did, & bought the play instantly. He will be very good in it. He knows he has only produced one good play in 15 years: *Dear Brutus*. And he is now getting alarmed for his prestige: wants to produce something by a good author. He is very nice to work with; but very nervoso if witty. I must say they all adore me, and are frightened of me. This is by no means all. I wrote a film for British International Pictures, with which B.I.P. is *enchanted*. It also is being done. Dupont is the producer. He enchants me, German-French. He really is an artist. He did *Vaudeville* and *Moulin Rouge*. Having taken delivery of the 1st film, *Piccadilly*, B.I.P. at once asked for another one. Of course I said: 'Out of the question.' And of course I graciously agreed in the end. This has to be delivered in the autumn too. Add to this that I have 11 short stories ordered but unwritten. Six special articles ditto, one article a month for the *Pictorial* & 1 a week for the *Standard*, & you will understand that my brain still has to function at intervals. Dorothy has finished a translation of a French play, & I have revised it. It is fine. Nothing yet settled about *her* schemes. She is always very busy. Her energy intimidates me. The nurse is splendid, & she & Virginia worship each other. The land at Aldwick is now ours; but I have no time yet to think about building. Tudor-Walters is going to see that I have all the architectural help we need. We have picked up a hint or two from the villas here, which, though often far too comically or grotesquely picturesque, are full of good ingenuities & gadgets. I think this is about all for the present.

Loves to all from all,

Yours, A.B.

P.S. My only important job is a long, dull, true novel, about the entire organisation & total entity of a big hotel (Savoy). I see no chance of beginning it this year.

A.B.

391. Fanny Bourne, daughter of Frances Edna and Ezra Bourne.

Gerald du Maurier (1873–1934) played the leading role in *The Return Journey*. It opened on 1 September.

The second film story was *Punch and Judy*, which Bennett worked on over more than a year. It was never produced. For Bennett's difficulties with Alfred Hitchcock and others over the film see Vol. III.

Dorothy translated Edouard Bourdet's play *Vient de Paraître*.

Bennett bought land at Aldwick very near to the Kennerleys.

John Tudor Walters (1868–1933) was a member of parliament for many years.

Imperial Palace had its origins in Bennett's earliest writings, well before *The Grand Babylon Hotel* of 1902. See p. 280 for the use of the Savoy Hotel in *Mr. Prohack*. In February 1924 he was shown over the hotel, and on 14 March 1927 he had lunch with Richmond Temple there and decided then to write the novel. He did not begin writing until 25 September 1929.

CAMBRIDGE / MS / 392
(*To Richard Bennett*)

75, Cadogan Square
25–9–28

My dear Rich,

Thanks for yours of yesterday. Today I am writing at 10.55 a.m. not 7 a.m. I am all in favour of maintaining friendly family relations; but it seems to me that if you & Stella have to spend 4 hours in travelling 40 miles, the least the ancestral roof can do (humming with Star cars as it is) is to send a car for you if they want you seriously & insist on wanting you. I fear it is the same in all firms with large staffs—they only pay at the pistol's point. I am once more very busy,—in full blast. My booklet about the religious situation is now nearly 1/2 done. I can approach it with a perfectly fresh eye because I know nothing about it, or God, or the Holy Ghost, or anything. This gives me a marked advantage over religious writers & experts. I saw my play on Thursday, & wondered why anyone should go see it at all—the last act is so *harrowing*. The audience are large, but only a small percentage of them understand what they are witnessing—that is obvious. Also the play is quite unlike all other West End plays—especially in tone, & people are therefore déroutés. Quite natural. Also there is present in it my accursed judicial detachment. However, the receipts are excellent—so far, though I can't understand how they can continue to be so. We yesterday received a 'Swedish housekeeper—cook' into this household. Young. Linguistic. Educated. Agreeable. And so on. But whether she can cook & keep house God alone yet knows. Of course we'd never seen her before. She arrived at Tilbury direct from Stockholm yesterday morning. Auntie Sissie is coming up to see the play next week. Auntie Emily sees it tonight. I may expect criticisms. Auntie Tertia has only just returned to London, & I haven't seen her. This is about all. I must turn towards God instantly, as I have to try on a new dressing gown at 12.15.

Loves,
Your seeking uncle,

A.B.

392. Bennett wrote *The Religious Interregnum* from 16 September to 20 October. He was invited to write the book by the Bishop of Liverpool, who had seen his article 'What I Believe' (one of a series by eminent people) in 1925. The book was published in March 1929.

W. J. Turner in the *New Statesman* described *The Return Journey* as 'rubbish'. It came off in November. It was never published in book form.

CAMBRIDGE / MS / 393
(*To Richard Bennett*)

75, Cadogan Square
4–12–28

My dear Rich,

Thank you. I will read the publicity stuff later. No time today. Got up late. Very busy. Bed late, after theatre. We saw Tallulah in *Her Cardboard Lover*. It is just an ordinary French farce, well anglicised by 'P.G.' But French farces are always *much* better than English. Tallulah very brilliant & very vulgar therein. Leslie Howard very brilliant & not vulgar. He played in *The Title* ten years ago, when he was nobody at all. We had Max Beerbohm & others to lunch on Friday. He was just the same as ever: that is to say, perfect, and the wonder of all beholders. Nurse fell down in the middle of the street yesterday (pram remained upright) and injured her tail-bone. She arrived at home in a state of collapse, & then fainted. Bed;

doctor; Annie had to look after Virginia; extra housemaid enlisted; quite a to-do. Last night she was fool enough to go to the lavatory. Fainted there. Fred carried her back to bed! She is better this morning, but she is bound to have to stay in bed for a time. I had a long séance with Dupont on Friday night at the Savoy, over the titles of *Piccadilly*. I have since written 122 titles. There are about 80 more to do. As you certainly don't know, the main scenes pass in a dance-club, called the 'Piccadilly Club' in Piccadilly Circus. The excellent Dupont, knowing not enough of this isle, had a piece of Piccadilly Circus erected at Elstree, & did a night scene with a huge electric-sign 'The Piccadilly Club'. When I pointed out to him that English clubs don't have electric signs, & that everybody would laugh at both him & me, he was electrified: such an idea had never occurred to him. The scene can't be done again, save at great expense. I am trying to get out of the difficulty by making the place a restaurant which merely *calls* itself a 'Club' in order to attract custom. It is a scheme, anyhow. Foggy here today. Tonight I'm dining with a group of eminent scientists & sociologists (including Sir R Gregory, the editor of *Nature*) apropos of a new monthly that is to be started, called the *Realist*. They want my advice. That is natural. But what *isn't* natural is that they want me to write the introductory article for the first number. This, my dear sir, is summat of a compliment to a mere all-round ignorant journalist who has no exact knowledge about anything.

> Loves,
> We are all well, except nurse!
> Your toiling uncle,
>
> A.B.

393. *Her Cardboard Lover.* Leslie Howard (1893–1943) produced as well as starred in it.

Richard Gregory (1864–1952) edited *Nature* from 1919 to 1939. The *Realist* had a short life. Bennett's article, 'The Progress of the Novel', appeared in the first issue, April 1929.

554 *10 December 1928*

ELDIN / TS / 394
(*To May Beardmore Marsden*)

75, Cadogan Square
10th December 1928

My dear May,

I am very glad to hear from you. But you are very naughty. What in hell did you mean by not coming to see us when you were last in London? I sent you a message that I expected you; and of course I expected you. This legend that I never have a moment to spare is partly invented by the newspapers and partly invented by me (to keep away nuisances). I have heaps of moments to spare. I waste hours.

It is excellent to hear that Edward is better. Let him continue in well-doing. Tell him that I should very much like to see him and that it is his duty to come to London once a year. The other day the *Sunday Chronicle* offered me £350 to go down to the Potteries and write my impressions of the same as they exist today. I declined. I see myself making a fool of myself in that way, don't you? Whatever I wrote, there would have been ructions and shindies throughout the glorious Midlands.

I can easily solve your difficulty about the notepaper. Send me *some* of it. I have a Victorian writing-case which needs it.

Loves,

Yours ever, A.B.

ELDIN / MS / 395
(*To May Beardmore Marsden*)

75, Cadogan Square
24–12–28

My dear May,

The sweet h.w.b. has arrived intact. I am acknowledging it because Dorothy is up to the nostrils in a new part in a play, & so we have divided the received-present-for-Virginia department into two halves. Your h.w.b. falls into my half. I would never have believed that that child would receive so many presents at the age of $2\frac{1}{2}$. The rooms are full of them. She has certainly had six times as many as I've had. The notepaper present from you is divine. I adore it. We are very grateful to you for both packages. I don't know whether Virginia is. I doubt if the little heathen has the least idea that tomorrow is the day on which the alleged Virgin was brought to bed of the Redeemer of us all. Further, she takes every present as a matter of course.

Our loves to you both,

Ever yours, A.B.

395. Hot water bottle.
The new play was *Byron*, by Alisia Ramsay.

CAMBRIDGE / MS / 396
(*To Richard Bennett*)

75, Cadogan Square
28–12–28

My dear Rich,

Thanks for thine. The tie & handkerchief, for which thanks also, are a *great* success. I have never told you that a black-&-white check handkerchief which you once gave me turned into a blue-and-white check after being washed. After shopping in the rain & in the King's Road with Dorothy on Saturday night, I had a chill, & stayed in the house on Sunday & Monday & in my thickest dressing-gown. I went out with Dorothy for lunch on Xmas day (Mayfair Hotel—good) & had a recrudescence of the chill. We had a few people in on Xmas night, for dinner & afterwards, & I received them in the same dressing-gown. Would they go home? No, they would not. And even when they did start to go there were terrible difficulties about taxis. On Boxing Night, I hear, the taxi-famine was much worse even. The chill completely upset my sleeping, which remains upset. Never mind, my film is duly delivered, & I have written 300,000 words this year. Dorothy is fantastically busy, rehearsing her part in *Byron*, & prosecuting her other schemes. She thinks she hates being too busy, but in fact she loves the same. Also she sleeps well. Virginia has had, in the shape of presents, the entire contents of all the big shops in the West End of London. Nothing could keep them out of the house. But she doesn't give a damn for any of them except a lamb on wheels & a tea-service. Most of them will have to be put away. Auntie May tells me that my Xmas article put old William Wood (84) into such a fury that he had to go to bed for 2 days. Edward

Beardmore is really not much better, I hear. Margaret Kennerley has got into Somerville College, & is now ill through
overwork or flu or both. Auntie Tertia says & confesses that she
has absolutely failed to prevent either Mary or Margaret from
overworking, & has now given up the attempt, definitely
defeated. It appears to me that the only vases of the Bennett
blood who don't overwork are your father & the undersigned. I
heard from your mother. Your parents were not so alone after
all on Xmas, seeing that I had greetings signed by six persons at
No. 7 Manley (or is it No. 9?). I am now going to write a short
story or so; I am terribly behind schedule with short stories. We
had a great dinner at Socrani's on Boxing Night with the
Roderick Joneses (Reuters). Max Beerbohm & spouse were
there. We dined at Socrani's because the Jones cook walked out
of their new house at 4 p.m. on Christmas Eve. Que veux-tu?
Les cooks sont comme ça. Our Swedish cook is fine. But if she
stays a year it will be the fulfilment of the outside hope of
Your well-wishing uncle for the N.Y.,
A.B.

Very sorry the glass broke.

396. William Wood, JP, master potter. He was one of the backers of the *Staffordshire
Knot*, in which Bennett published most of his earliest writing in 1888. His daughter Ada
was Tertia's great friend. Bennett's article, 'Santa Claus is Out', describes two sorts of
Christmas. In London the aim is to have a marvellous time by getting away from home
and Father Christmas and going to hotels and resorts. In the Midlands everyone stays
at home and the mistress of the house slaves all day and everyone is bored and envies
London but wants the old traditions to go on. Bennett can't decide which is the better
sort of Christmas.

BERG / MS / 397
(*To Dorothy Cheston Bennett*)

75, Cadogan Square
16–1–29

My dear girl,
    I hope I have made it clear that if I don't see the car here at
tea-time on Monday you won't see me at Portsmouth on
Tuesday. I am going solely to please you (no other purpose will
be served by my going), at a cost of at least 50/- in money & two
days time, neither of which I can spare, being very hard up for

both. I am delighted that you should work interestingly to yourself, & I am always ready to stand the mental racket which your work always entails. But I very strongly object to being flouted at the last moment, & to being put to expense. It costs 5^d a mile to run that car, so that the total cost of the present escapade will be at least £4 plus my own expenses. I like it not. I am fairly generous up to a point, but when my being set at naught involves me also in loss of money, my generosity dries up instantly. Morally it is your duty to pay for the car. I wish you every success. Please also give my good wishes & benedictions to Gwladys.

Yours, A.B.

P.S. We leave Waterloo (*subject to your actions*) on Tuesday at 3.50 & arrive at Portsmouth (town, *not harbour*) at 5.38.

A.B.

397. *Byron* ran for a few nights in Portsmouth before its London opening. Gwladys Wheeler directed.

BERG / MS / 398
(*To Dorothy Cheston Bennett*)

75, Cadogan Square
17–1–29

My sweet pet,
   Thy letter received this morn. I have written to both Cochran & Gerald. To write to the latter is a mistake; but you wished it, & I have written accordingly. Well, I think you are missing a point in the scene with Augusta, where you talk about being more Byron than the Byrons, & sinking to a 'lower hell'. It seems to me that if you had a swift, brief *outburst* here, showing the cauldron within, you could positively *frighten* the audience & get a great effect. But this is only my amateur notion of the way to treat the moment. Being terribly exhausted last night I took a Griffin drug, & slept 6 hours without a break. I attended the dinner at the Savoy last night to Raymond Needham. I have known him 20 years. I sat next to Reeves-Smith, who is *exceedingly* pleased with *Accident*. He says old Mrs. Lucass is one of the best characters I have ever drawn. As regards money you will have your salary tomorrow night. You must really finance yourself independently in these affairs. It

only needs preorganisation. The more I think of your performance as Anabella the more I like it. But the part is *not* a
sympathetic part. You make it one—that is all. The declaration
about 'saving' Byron renders it unsympathetic. London is
under snow. It was *intensely* cold yesterday afternoon. Less cold
in the evening. Less cold this morning. I have done no work
except oddments. I must get on with something sustained. I'm
going to the Queen's Hall concert tonight with Knoblock. I'm
now engaged every night till & including next Thursday—
when Thorpe & Co entertain me at the Savoy Grill about the
film. The article I wrote about stopping war has aroused
positive enthusiasm in the people who asked me to write it.
My sweet girl, I embrace thee.

Little

398. Raymond Needham (1877–1965). He and Bennett were involved in war work
together.
   Accident was published on 10 January 1929. Bennett wrote it between 26 November
1926 and 19 July 1927.
   J. C. A. Thorpe was a director of British International Pictures.
   The article about stopping war is unknown.

BERG / MS / 399
(*To Dorothy Cheston Bennett*)   75, Cadogan Square
                                              Thursday 8.30 a.m.
                                              22–1–29

My dearest, my author,
   Your letter dated 19th (Monday) reached me Wednesday
(last) night. Is it correctly dated? Also I fear you have not got
the letter I wrote to you Thursday last in the train, before Paris,
& that the Chicago man promised to post for me. If the fellow
forgot to post it or delayed posting it, I will not forgive him. I
think you are getting on all right, & I applaud you—especially
if you will continue to go to bed early at every opportunity of
doing so. Of course you were right to tell Maria Huxley that
you were writing. Why not, in God's name? I shall pass a
verdict on your short story only when it is finished & typed; but
in the meantime I may tell you that you are certainly a letter-
writer. Swinnerton came to lunch yesterday, & we talked
chiefly about Doran; subject rather gloomy; no conclusion
reached. I worked on the play in the morning alone & in the

afternoon with Knobby. At 5.45 we had done what we could do, and we sailed out, as I possessed a slight headache—it went off. We called on the Nicholsons, who were out, we then visited 2nd hand shops. I said I had to find a pair of cheap old good ear-rings for my niece Mary K. I need not say that Knobbo said he knew *the* place for old ear-rings. Well, he did, & we went to it. It is in Poland Street. It is the most interesting stone & jewel shop I ever saw, kept by a most amusing old man. I shall take you there. There are tens of thousands of loose stones in cases all over the counter, & immense stocks of antique jewellery, watches, fob seals etc. I soon got the ear-rings. I also bought a *most* curious & interesting 18th cent French (Louis XVI) hall-marked gold & turquoise ring, which I shall bestow where it will be appreciated. Then to dine & talk business with Duff at Garrick. Lyric prospects not too bright. I insisted that I was set on retiring from that affair at the end of the year (& the lease). He is most troubled, though I have been saying it for years.

10.25 a.m.

Breakfast, correspondence, massage & dressing accomplished. Just about to proceed with play. I have to lunch at Garrick with Glynne Williams (Chairman of *N. Statesman* Board) to settle about appointment of a new Director. Thence to Lyric. Knoblock is to be here at 5.30 for play. *I've nothing to do tonight* as yet. Glad about your frugality in wine. Except $\frac{1}{2}$ glass champagne I think I've had nothing since I arrived back. You will soon be going out more than I do.

I now softly & powerfully embrace thee with many & various x x x x x.

Your little A.B.

399. *Byron* opened at the Lyric in London on 20 January and ran for two weeks.
Maria Huxley (née Nys, d. 1955), Aldous Huxley's wife.
George Doran's firm was taken over by Doubleday in 1927, and Doran was now being forced out of the joint firm. He was also facing domestic divorce.
The play with Knoblock is unknown. From February to June 1929 Bennett wrote a new play, presumably on his own, perhaps with some advice from Knoblock. It was never produced or published.
Sir William Nicolson (1872–1949), the artist, and his wife Mabel. For a letter and other references to Nicolson see Vol. III.
Glynne (or Glyn) Williams helped to fund the *New Statesman*, along with Bennett and Shaw. He was a member of the Fabian Society from perhaps as early as 1904.

CAMBRIDGE / MS / 400
(*To Richard Bennett*)

75, Cadogan Square
19–2–29

My dear Rich,

Thanks for yours. Referring to your water leakages, we have only had one trouble—freezing of bath-waste down in basement. This was cured before our arrival last Thursday. I have been usually wearing *three* suits of underclothes. This dodge does me very well. It is much less than a year ago that I bought at 32/6. Someone advised me to. We have come to the conclusion that we don't want to build a house so close to the King at Aldwick. So I have just sold the land which I bought for £1,100 for £1,400 free of agent's commission. This leaves quite a fair profit in less than a year. However, my main triumph at the moment is that the Modigliani picture (over mantelpiece in hall) which I bought 10 years ago for £50 I sold yesterday for £1,000. I certainly had quite a sound instinct for Modiglianis. I ought to have trusted it more, for I could have bought 2 at the time instead of 1, equally good, at the same price each. Pity! I am not well & have not been. Disinclination to work, a sort of a chill in the head, & more acute insomnia. Yet quite well enough to go about. I am doing no work except articles. I don't know how long it will last. It's been lasting now about 3 weeks. The annoying thing is that everybody tells me how well I look! Margaret Beardmore brought her fiancé Cyril Shingler to lunch on Saturday. He is about 30, talks very well, & does designing for George Jones & Co. I was rather agreeably surprised in him.... Melba has just come back to England & rung me up. I have put her off, as I don't at the moment feel equal to her. We're very glad Stella has found a servant. Why, of course the little piece must have a servant! I learn that she created a most favourable impression again in the Potteries. I have to take the chair at the Board meeting here in 20 minutes from this instant.

Loves,
Your weakened uncle,

A.B.

400. King George V often visited Bognor Regis, staying at Craigwell House, west of Aldwick.

Amadeo Modigliani (1884–1920).
Dame Nellie Melba (1859–1931). For other references to her see Vols. II and III.

ELDIN / MS / 401
(*To May Beardmore Marsden*)

75, Cadogan Square
3–5–29

My dear May,

I must tell you the important news that I think that human nature *has* in many respects improved. May, love, I am convinced of it. I'm very sorry about Edward. He certainly ought to come to London & see a good man. I'll get you the name of one if you like.

Ever yours, A.B.

BERG / MS / 402
(*To George Cedric Beardmore*)

75, Cadogan Square
22nd May 1929

My dear Cedric,

I return your novel. It shows a very marked advance. It is an orgy of phrasing rather than a book, but there is very real imagination in it, and a lot of very good and original writing also. The plot is not good, and it is obscured by excessive description and capricious incident. Nevertheless the thing has distinction, and a good deal of promise. I agree with you that you ought not to make any attempt to get it published.

I am wondering whether you could explain to me why it is that this sort of subject makes such a strong appeal to you. And also whether you could tell me whether there is any immediate chance of you trying a less extraordinary theme.

Anyhow you are most assuredly a writer, and my hopes of you are multiplied.

Perhaps you will feel equal to the strain of putting yourself to the trouble of writing me frankly about your notions about the future of writing so far as they concern yourself.

Your aff unc,

A.B.

BERG / MS / 403
(*To George Cedric Beardmore*)   75, Cadogan Square
                                                             29–5–29

My dear Cedric,

Yes, I quite understand now why you wrote your novel. And I think you did well to write it. But the thought of Stoke Villas interests me much, much more. My personal idea is that you should go on as you are, and write something else of an 'earthy' nature, so that I can see how you are coming on. I don't see how I could get you a job in London that would be any better for your *work* than your present job. (I have not yet succeeded in getting the right sort of job for Richard—yet I thought I could.) You could not possibly do a publisher's reader's job. It needs great experience not only of books but of the book market. And anyhow it is ill-paid and uncertain (piece-work, you know, as a rule). I am beginning now to believe seriously in your future as a writer, & I am seriously anxious to do absolutely the right thing for you. It is not a question of money. What I am at present thinking is that in about a year's time, if your work improves, you might come to London & live at your Aunt Emily's, & I would give you enough to live on for a few years on the understanding that you gave me your earnings up to the amount of the total income I allowed you. I don't know whether this notion appeals to you, or whether it has any real drawbacks. You refer to what I did; but you must remember that I didn't get free of clerk's work till I was 25, nor free of journalistic office work till I was about 33, & that I was 40 before I had earned £1,000 in a year. I don't see much point in a similar experience for you. You had better think this affair over. And, if you can, begin on another book, or on a *series* of short stories. And write to me as often as you feel like it.

                    Your aff unc,

                                                             A.B.

P.S. I couldn't write before. I've been too busy.

                                                             A.B.

403. Cedric's book was entitled *Hilary*. A few days earlier he wrote to Bennett about it and about his career: 'I can't call it a novel, or a fairy-tale, or a history—it's an escape. I am tired of the subject and shall write no more about it. . . . How did you get your first

post? This writing before 9 o'clock in the morning and after 5 o'clock at nights is no sort of life. I have lots of things to ask you, if I could escape the office for a day or two.' He worked at an insurance office at the time.

CAMBRIDGE / TS / 404
(*To Richard Bennett*)

75, Cadogan Square
4th June 1929

My dear Rich,

Thanks for your letter of yesterday. Excuse typewriting. But between a vaccination pain in the arm and a crick in the back of the neck due to a draught at the Ritz on Saturday at lunch, I find it rather difficult to sleep with any sort of excellence, and so I have arisen late. Miss Nerney went quite a long journey by bus a week or two ago and was well satisfied with her experience.

The doctor has told me that I ought not to eat spinach—me who have been regarding spinach as the staff of life for many years past. The three doctors were not employed for vaccination, only one, and it was done in about a minute. That was eight days ago. The other two are for a general overhaul, with a view to improving sleeping. Both of them have advised me to take a drug called 'medinal' every night for at least four months. Both say that it is absolutely harmless, and so far as I can judge, it is.

Our party of over 90 people is understood to have been a very great success. We did nothing ourselves. Everything was done by Searcy & Tansley of Sloane Street, who are a first-rate firm. Tania, Kathleen Long, and Sheridan Russell all played admirably. We also had a dance band (Harrods) consisting of piano (1) and drum (1). I solemnly instructed them to play pianissimo and they did. I had a bit of a chat with them at 2 a.m. 'Do you do this sort of thing every night?' I asked. '*Every* night', said they. 'And when do you go to bed?' said I. 'As soon as we have finished,' said they. It was a good thing there was not a sudden fire in the house. If there had been, and the exit had been foozled, English literature would have been in a sad state and every newspaper in the land would have had a first-class front page item of news.

But our party was simply naught compared to the election

party of Gordon Selfridge on Thursday night. There must have
been about 2,000 people at that show. There was plenty of room
for them, plenty of loud speakers, two bands and as much
Cordon Rouge as the entire 2,000 could drink, besides solid sit-
down suppers for all who wanted it. I wanted it. The whole
affair was magnificently organised. I reached home before one;
Dorothy about two. I was quite well after it. Dorothy also is in
the hands of two or three doctors. She hath anaemia and other
things, and is already feeling better. When all the doctors have
been financially satisfied I will not tell you the total of their
demands. It might shock you. It will certainly shock me.

We are going away on the 30th June, and do not expect to be
back before the 28th August. During half of this time I shall be
at work as usual. During the other half I shall probably keep a
journal, which will be sold for the benefit of the doctors. A man
who is writing a biography of my works came to see me on
Saturday, and told me all sorts of interesting things that I did
not know about my own books. He predicts very high prices for
all the early first editions. He cannot get a copy of the first
edition of *The Old Wives' Tale* at less than £80, and so has not
bought it. I have no copy. But May has. And your father has.
These two collections will be worth quite a good deal in due
course. I have been putting together all my principal first
editions (of other authors), with a view to selling them and
buying Ecuadorian Corporation ordinary shares, as to which I
have received a private tip from one of the directors.

The Reform Club is a bit unelated about the elections, but is
bearing up nobly, as of course it would. The Club is full of
political talk at the moment, and I am getting rather tired of it.

Did you read my article in the Staffs *Sentinel*? It appeared also
in the Derby *Telegraph* and the Newcastle *Evening World*, which
all belong to Rothermere. It has annoyed a lot of people, for
which I am honestly glad. Others are very pleased with it. It is
of the sort known as 'trenchant'.

I have been forgetting to tell you that I do not think much of
Beer. I have been there one afternoon for tea. The beach is
negligible, and the service of the tea, in the principal hotel,
leaves much to be desired. Also it is not a pretty place, but there
are plenty of pretty places near it. St. John Ervines used to have
a place there, but they have now built a new one at or near

Seaton. Eden Phillpotts is leaving Torquay at last, and has bought a place near Sidmouth. This is about all, although there is lots more.

Loves,
Your drugged uncle,

A.B.

404. Sheridan Russell: unidentified.
Bennett and Dorothy went to France and Italy for six weeks on 30 June.
Labour won the general election with a minority vote.
' "Wake Up" Call to Industry' appeared on 29 May.

KENNERLEY / MS / 405   Celtic Hotel
(*To Tertia Kennerley*)   Sur la plage des Callots
     S. Cast
     28–7–29

My dear Tertia,

Got here yesterday. Cheque arrived today. Thank you. Incessant motoring from Lake Garda. Crossing Alps easy & fine. Big mail to deal with now—curse it! I don't think there is a great deal in John, but he is an agreeable youth. You may have heard that Rich has got a job in I.C.I. at £500 to start with. He has taken a houselet at Ealing at £120 a year. Seems not too dear. Your letter is long & interesting—very—& I would I could answer it fully. But my mail is very indigestible. I remember Armitage very well. I just *can't* remember the dining-room table. But I *thought* the whole thing was a suite. You must remember that the poor girl's articles have all been sadly cut. I haven't told her that she only sold them because I was in them; but so it certainly was. I quite agree that Margaret ought not to have gone back home. But from what she said to me it was a case of conscience. *I* would have seen Sissie in hades before I went back to such a home. Glad about Virginia. She is due here tomorrow morn at dawn; which means us motoring to Dinard at dawn. We had a great time at Lake Garda. Quite unspoilt. A perspiring heat all the time, but I don't mind that, though in the end it enervates you. We motored over the Alps. There is *nothing* in this feat; but it is very agreeable. I have, however, had enough motoring for the present.

Our loves,

Yours, A.B.

405. Richard made his career with Imperial Chemical Industries, and became head of their subsidiary Thorium Ltd.

Armitage: probably J. H. Armitage, who was headmaster of the Wesleyan Day School in Burslem in 1883–5. Bennett was at the school in 1875–6, and later he had lessons in Greek from Armitage.

Fanny Gertrude published several articles in the Manchester *Sunday Chronicle* in 1929. They describe past and contemporary life in the Five Towns, relying to some extent upon details of family life among the Bennetts and upon material in the novels.

BERG / MS / 406
(*To Dorothy Cheston Bennett*)   R.M.S.P. Arcadian
Monday
12 August 1929

My sweet pet,

Yes. I am thinking a great deal about you. Well, I hope you have found new friends & that all is well. I feel more than ever like a pauper. Max is worth about 5 millions. His younger brother, 38 and retired, a bachelor, very agreeable & with no illusions about Max's defects, is worth £750,000 & all made in a few years. Venetia Montagu came into half a million from her deceased spouse. Lady Louis Mountbatten is said by Max to have an income of £80,000 a year. Jean Norton is certainly poor. And I doubt if Captain Wardell earns more than £2,000 a year. Then there is poor me. Jean Norton gave Max a shoe with 9 packs of cards. So baccarat is played nightly (that is to say, 2 nights so far) in Max's sitting-room, & Max is the banker & Max is winning. He will not allow a higher stake than 10/-, though Jeanie & Lady L are always demanding it. He says that it is very dangerous in private playing to go beyond an agreed minimum. He is quite right. You never know where you'll end. I play because I have to play; but I find it rather tedious. Up to the present I have lost £2.18/-. A bit thick. Lady L & Venetia both have *excellent* brains, but I have never been able to perceive any in Mrs. Norton. All the rest have brains, lots. Max is in the most brilliant form, conversationally. But he says that I shout him down. When I said to Venetia that I wouldn't say another word about food, she said: 'But then you won't have anything to talk about, my dear Arnold.' Max can only talk well if he is not interrupted. When I interrupt him he doesn't say, 'If I could only be allowed to finish a sentence.' He says I shout him down. That man's memory & knowledge of history are really astonishing. On Saturday night he talked magnificently about John Knox, & then, when Mahomet was mentioned, he talked even better about Mahomet. The general company of passengers is just about on the stylistic level of the guests at the Celtic. They would make you 'uncomfortable and depressed'.

Another thing that would have annoyed you is the bugling for meals. The first bugle shook the ship at 8 a.m. on the first morning. On the 2nd morning it wasn't heard. Max had stopped it. I hear that it woke him on the first morning, & that he got into a perfect passion and sent for the purser. We have our meals 1 hour later than the hoi polloi. The food is indifferent rising in some ways to good. We left Leith yesterday at 1 p.m. & are due in Oslo tomorrow Friday at 8 a.m. Oslo is not named on the time-schedule & I didn't know we were calling there. The ship must be oldish; but she is decidedly good. She has a fine swimming bath, in which I swim. Up to now she has been as steady as a rock—well, nearly as a rock. Absolutely no inconvenience to anybody. Of course the 3 women, Max, & I are marked people, & the objects of terrible curiosity. Several times have I heard those exasperating words in a loud whisper: 'There's Arnold Bennett.' Manners! Manners! True, there is a goodish percentage of Midland & Northern accents about. Not that I think the southern accent shows any better manners. I don't. I can work on board; and do. From the plan of the decks I thought that I had a suite. But what I took for a dressingroom in the plan is a small independent cabin, entirely separate. Still with a double bedded room & a private bathroom & an A1 steward, I can struggle on very well. Anyhow I've written 2,000 words in 2 days; & yet wasted hours & hours of God's time in utter idleness. I felt quite unwell & very exhausted yesterday; also totally constipé. First day at sea! But I compelled myself to work between tea and dinner, & the malady (which must have been rheumatic) passed off. I think this is about all till Danzig, my sweet sir. Je te bise bien, & with renewed expression of the hope that all is well, and thanks to God that you exist. I am, dearest madam,

Little

406. Bennett went to Russia with Max Beaverbrook, leaving England about 10 August and returning about 31 August.

Dr Arthur Beaverbrook became a tuberculosis specialist in the United States.

Venetia Montagu (née Stanley, 1887–1948), Herbert Asquith's great friend, was widow of Edwin Montagu (1879–1924), who served in Asquith's government.

Lady Louis Mountbatten (1901–60).

Captain Michael Wardell came of a family with high social connections. He entered into employment with Beaverbrook in 1926.

BERG / MS / 407
(*To Dorothy Cheston Bennett*)

R.M.S.P. Arcadian
21–8–29

Sweetest pet,

I received your telegram & two letters (13th & 14th) tonight, on my return from Moscow. It is most distressing about your abscess being bad enough to send you home 4 days ahead of time. I have had lots of those abscesses in my time. So I know what they are, & can feel for you. You will feel easier about it in England, but I'm afraid the great Dowsett will be away. His partner is pretty good. Well, my thoughts are with you. As regards the money question, there is no question of not trusting you. I wrote out all the figures very carefully, *on the basis of what I myself had actually paid*, & I went through them with you carefully one by one. Now that I reflect I believe I did leave out the laundry; but on the other hand I left you with a margin of 3600 francs. As I wrote you last week, the notion of you depriving yourself of the use of the car and of proper teas etc, is monstrous, & there would be no justice in it, nor need for it— even if you had to get more money. But I think you will find at the end that you have more money even than you expected. I'm very sorry that you were worrying about money. It's the very last thing I want for you on a holiday. *I* am worrying about money on a big scale. However, we will leave the money question, seeing that in fact it is now over, so far as it relates to the holiday. I've already written to you about expenditure on the house. If I haven't got money, I haven't got it, & the fact is there and has to be faced. I know I *ought* to have money, but all these artists are alike—in the end! I am also much, even more, worried about my novel. But I am not worried about my articles on Russia etc, as I already have them in my head. We've had 2 nights on the train, & I've come through them as well as anybody. The Russian sleepers, however, are very good—better in fundamentals than the Blue Train, though worse in small details. We have had colossal meals. Max was enthusiastic about Russia on the first day. He is now enthusiastically *anti*-Russian. I have to strike a balance. Moscow is extraordinary. *However,* you will read my articles (D.V.). My insomnia is not better, but *I* am well. In addition to money & novel, I think quite a bit of a night—about that blue petticoat, etc. Que veux-tu! I bought a toy for Virginia, in the shape of a reproduction of a Russian monastery in many pieces in a box. The box got broken by porters, & the pieces of the toy are all over the place; but I think none of them is damaged. I've had a very enthusiastic letter from André Gide about *The O.W. Tale*. He & Martin du Gard have been revising the translation by Coppet. They are all 3 considerably knocked flat by the book. Odd! My sweet pet, be happy; then I shall; not otherwise. You see how selfish I am. I kiss thee very tenderly.

Little

407. Ernest Blair Dowsett (d. 1951), Bennett's dentist.
Bennett began writing *Imperial Palace* on 25 September.
Bennett wrote four articles on Russia. They appeared in the *Daily Express* on 4, 5, 6, and 9 September 1929. He wrote of Russia:

I sympathise with the original democratic ideals of the autocrats and their terrible exertions to abolish the scandalous social injustices of Czarism. But my brief glimpse of the Soviet regime has disappointed and disturbed me. As for its ultimate success, one can say no more than that the regime is holding together. It may succeed, but I very much doubt. Nor do I in the least desire its success. It presents itself to me as an extremely sinister business, based on a great ideal, but vitiated by prodigious lying and by blindness to the finer needs of ordinary human nature, conducted without scruple, and inevitably slipping back into the very evil which it was designed to cure. I departed from Russia with relief.

Un Conte de bonnes femmes, translated by Marcel de Coppet (b. 1881), was published in 1931. Gide and Roger Martin du Gard (1881–1958) reviewed the manuscript.

BERG / MS / 408   R.M.S.P. Arcadian
(*To Dorothy Cheston Bennett*)   Between Stockholm &
                                                            Copenhagen
                                                        Sunday
                                                        25–8–29

My sweetest pet,
    I have had little luck on this excursion. All your letters have been charged with trouble. The project of *Don Juan* at the Arts Club has disturbed me. Then I have a woeful letter from Richard. Then I learn that Rich Hayes the juggler is perform-

ing in London while I am away—damn him!! Then Geoffrey
Scott's death, which much saddened me. And so on till I dread,
almost, arrivals in ports with letters and newspapers awaiting.
I open the letters with trembling apprehensive hands. As
regards Richard, I have written to that youth telling him in
some detail that both he & Stella were absolutely in the wrong.
Still, they sin less from ungratefulness than from lack of habit in
expressing gratitude & from a general ignorance of London
manners. They have both a lot to learn. But I don't want a
permanent coolness or friction. The youth is my solemnly
adopted son, and a continuous jar would be very awkward for
yours truly. I've told him it is up to him & Stella to set the affair
right. (Monday) I dread also the end of this cruise. It will have
great compensations, the end will; but it will mean that *I must
really tackle that accursed novel*. And I know I shall have all sorts of
other worries in addition to that biggest one. That novel will
take a full six months of labour, concentration, & responsibility—I mean artistic responsibility. For that novel *must* be
something very striking indeed. If ever an artist needed the
moral, spiritual, & even physical cooperation of his wife, I am
now the man. There is just a chance that the novel *may be* rather
striking. I hate work. Well, I have come out of Russia. My
articles will not be very favourable. I'm sorry. I've written all of
them—four. And 2 more about Oslo, Danzig, Stockholm, &
Copenhagen; only I haven't written the Copenhagen bit yet, as
we shall not be there for another 90 minutes. (It is now 7.30
a.m., & I have ordered my breakfast.) Stockholm is a fine place.
The town hall is more than all that has been said of it in
architectural journals. I saw also a truly excellent revue,
admirably staged in every way, & often really beautiful. But the
most beautiful thing I saw was an act of Rimsky's *Sadko* at
Moscow. Exquisitely done. The 'Indian Love Song' was
absolutely re-created by the singer thereof. It raised me up so
much that I began to reach the moods necessary for novel
writing. Russia is rather sinister, I may say. Here is my
breakfast, my sweet pet. Heaven keep you. I wrote 5,000 words
Saturday & Sunday. I am still making a modest bit at baccarat.
Rain Saturday. Heavenly yesterday. I embrace thee much, my
dear. Remember me to Virginia.

                                                            Little

P.S.   Of course the mail has not yet arrived at the ship. I didn't hear from you at Stockholm but you must have been pretty busy.

408.   Geoffrey Scott (1885–1929), author of *The Portrait of Zélide*.
Bennett's articles on Oslo and Danzig, and Stockholm and Copenhagen, appeared in the *Daily Express* on 5 and 7 December 1929.
Rimsky Korsakov (1844–1908). *Sadko* was first performed in 1908.

CAMBRIDGE / MS / 409
(*To Richard Bennett*)

R.M.S.P. Arcadian
Hamburg
28–8–29

My dear Rich,
   Thanks for your letter of 26th. I am glad of its plainness. You may believe me there is nothing in the theory that Dorothy is 'taking advantage of' my absence. When you suggested that you & Stella should stay at 75, I asked Dorothy, because the handling of London servants etc etc is not so simple as it may seem, especially at holiday and cleaning time. Dorothy at once said that you must come & that she would send the instructions, which she did. It is of course true that I said years ago that 75 is your home; but this was when both you & I were single. The situation is not quite the same now. It is your home so far as possible, but this does not mean that you two have the right to use it untrammelled. Nor does it mean that you are not guests, with the customary obligations of guests. If you can't understand this, your understanding *is* 'insufficient'. When Dorothy & nurse & Virginia are at home, it is impossible for us to put up two people, and to put up one is not easy. I may tell you that Annie has given notice again & again. She always recants, however, because she is so attached to Dorothy. If Stella so rarely writes a letter, she will have to acquire the habit. An entirely different code prevails in London. I remember that when I first came to London I had just the same ideas about the London code as you & Stella have; & it took me years to get rid of them. At the same time I can well imagine that the settling in London is a tremendous strain on Stella, in every way. Judging from what I last saw of her I should say that she needs a complete rest for a time. In fact I am sure of it. I repeat, what I

said in my previous letter, that Stella definitely, & several times, promised to write, & ought to have written. She didn't write. The consequences of the Lisle family 'working themselves up about Dorothy' are no concern of Dorothy's. If our relations showed a complete decency in their attitude towards the situation, the Lisles ought to have had the decency to adopt a similar attitude. Mrs. Lisle's demeanour when she called on us was in the worst possible taste. If Stella hadn't been there, and if I had not been very anxious not to complicate the situation between the Lisles & you, I should certainly have ended the interview a long time before the end of the 2 hours which she chose to stay. I admit that I didn't expect any other demeanour from her, seeing what I know of her & Mr. Lisle's attitude to both you and Stella. The most wonderful forbearance was shown to Mrs. L at 75. Nobody who hesitates to come to 75 will be urged to do so. My difficulty, in regard to the Dorothy situation, has always been—right from the start—not to get people to come, but to keep them out. When Dorothy & Virginia first installed themselves Dorothy's health was decidedly upset by the siege of visitors, including a number of the best people in London. I fear that the Lisles' sense of perspective is a bit wrong. I know that Dorothy may sometimes be difficult, but I never yet knew a woman who wasn't. She has the defect of saying or writing impulsively all that passes through her mind. You & I are not like that; perhaps we are too much the other way. On the other hand Dorothy is full of generous impulses. And beyond question she has come very successfully through a situation infinitely more difficult than Stella's either at home or abroad.

We are now at Hamburg. It is possible that we shall go to Berlin for tonight & return tomorrrow morning. Max has been poisoned by some food or other, but is recovering. Stockholm is an A.1. place. I have finished all my articles on the cruise. At Copenhagen I was interviewed 3 times, photographed 4 times, & caricatured once, in a day. And simply couldn't help it.

Loves,
Your watchful uncle,

A.B.

P.S. I will write to you after I have seen Dorothy.

KENNERLEY / MS / 410
(*To Tertia Kennerley*)

75, Cadogan Square
8–9–29

My dear Tertia,

Would you like to have Virginia for a fortnight from the 17th. I only mention it because you seem to have a certain partiality for the child. If the suggestion doesn't suit you, you will of course decline it with one word. The reason is that Dorothy has been, and is, terribly racked with jaw-abscess trouble. The thing culminated in an operation, with doctor & dentist in league, jaw opened from the inside, about a pint of matter extracted, & a general high state of nerves. On the day before the operation the temporary cook walked out. On the day after Annie gave notice. And on the day after that the 2nd housemaid said she must go; & the kitchen maid wanted to go, but isn't going. A new cook came in yesterday; but she mayn't stay. Nurse must have a holiday. Annie has always acted as nurse in her absence, but that can't be now. The once-excellent Annie is suffering from change of life or something, & cannot be handled. Anyhow she too is in a high state of nerves & will shortly depart. She told me today that we had both been very kind to her, she was very grateful & devoted & so on: but that she *must* go. Well, well! And I'm supposed to be writing a novel! Dorothy is staying at the moment at the Savoy, with nurse & offspring. Thanks to my heavenly relations with the Savoy chiefs, they have insisted on giving her a fine suite for nothing! If you can't accept our suggestion of course we can get a temporary nurse. Dorothy has been suffering for about a month, & not long since she had a jaw like a football, & the extraction of a tooth seemed only to make it worse.

I hear that Pauline is coming up this week on her way to Crowborough.

I'm writing instead of Dorothy because Dorothy is hardly equal to it.

Loves,

Yours, A.B.

KENNERLEY / MS / 411
(*To Tertia Kennerley*)

75, Cadogan Square
27–10–29.

My dear Tertia,

Thank you. Some years ago Marguerite absolutely refused to consider the idea of a divorce, though I asked her to do so. Unless she has some reason of her own for divorcing, I am quite sure she won't. I don't know what she wants with you. All I know is that I am constantly doing things for her, & that if by chance she does want a divorce I shall not allow her to make any conditions about it before starting proceedings, either financial or otherwise. If she wants it, she must begin. But I don't think she does want it. The maximum sum she can get from me under the deed of separation is £2,000 a year. Up to now she has had this maximum. She has not had it invariably every year (2 exceptions, I think), but the amount short in one year has always been made up in a succeeding year. So that she has averaged the maximum—free of income tax & super tax.

She has made complaints at intervals about getting letters addressed to Mrs. Arnold Bennett which were meant for Dorothy. This is a legitimate complaint, if technical; but that it causes her any inconvenience is impossible. It only causes her to be aware that Dorothy is known in some places as Mrs. A.B. I have made every effort to stop the trouble, & I *have* very largely stopped it. But you cannot guard against other people's stupidity all the time. Some weeks ago, although Dorothy is officially known in the theatre as Miss Dorothy Cheston, a rehearsal call for her was sent to Mrs. A.B. at Marguerite's flat! (Marguerite has not yet complained about this to me yet). I always insist, & especially with tradesmen, on Dorothy being put down as 'Mrs. E.A.B.' and I am Mr. E.A.B. in all business affairs. I think this is about all. I expect I told you at the time that some years ago Marguerite wrote to me admitting that she has been in the wrong, & begging me to take her back.

Dorothy was all right on Friday night, thanks.

Yours, A.B.

CAMBRIDGE / MS / 412
(*To Richard Bennett*)

75, Cadogan Square
19–XI–29

My dear Rich,

Thanks for yours of y'day. You should take care of your cold. You will remember that your father has suffered very severely in that line, & the tendency is no doubt hereditary. Other people will be better judges than you of what you ought to do or not do. *The Matriarch* play is nothing; but Mrs. P.C. is fine in it. Dorothy only went because she had to. She is very thick with Mrs. P.C. *Bittersweet* I regard as exceedingly poor. Story sentimental & feeble; last act totally undramatic; music rotten; and jocularities 10th rate. The second act will just pass. Dorothy saw the *W Cargo* film. Didn't like it, of course. I agree with you about the play. My only exclamation on seeing it was 'Good God!' I am not going to any more concerts till next week, when I *have* to attend one, at 5.30 of the clock. I shall only stay for 45 minutes, as we *have* to attend the first night of *Tunnel Trench*. And after that I shall *have* to appear at a musical party given by Curtis Brown, who is one of my literary agents. And I am supposed to be writing a novel! I have now written over a third of it—that's something. I wrote a complete short story yesterday afternoon, & had an appointment which lasted 55 minutes, too. We had people to dinner which lasted till 12.30 a.m. I fear there is no news about people whom you know. However, I must tell you that Menetta Marriott is giving 'an hour of song' at FM's studio soon, & I much fear that I shall *have* to go there. She has absolutely no artistic feeling, & her performances are appalling. The power of suburbanism. But the Marriotts are terribly proud of her. It will be an infliction of a fantastic intensity. I shall be ill if I can. The worst of it is I see little hope of being ill. Despite imperfect sleeping, my health is excellent. I certainly need less sleep than I did even a year ago. Age! Age hath its compensations. If I knew Harty's size I would send him a dozen collars, with an expression of thanks for his exertions. I am lunching with 3 members of the top-staff of the Savoy today. I want a bit more Savoy atmosphere. I've just done a long chapter which I think is unique in the annals of the fictive art: namely, a full narrative of a general meeting of shareholders. But I am by no means sure that it is interesting. I got all the points in much detail from Beaverbrook, who is a great authority on the chicane of these affairs, & has presided at many general meetings. Dining with Gertrude Jennings tonight. Her brother, who does the excellent leaders in the *Daily Mirror*, & for some reason signs them W.M., lives with her, or she with him, and is a great book-collector. When I see his collection I feel that I have *no* books.

Loves,

Your reposing uncle,

A.B.

412. Mrs Patrick Campbell was playing in G. B. Stern's *The Matriarch* at the Royalty Theatre. *Bittersweet* was running at His Majesty's.

White Cargo, by Leon Gordon, had a long run as a play in the middle 1920s.

Tunnel Trench, by Hubert Griffith, opened on 25 November at the Duchess Theatre.

Curtis Brown (1866–1949), American founder of the international literary agency.

Menetta Marriott, the Marriotts' adopted daughter.

Harty: unidentified.

W.M.: Richard Jennings. He wrote leaders for the *Daily Mirror* for many years and was famous as a book collector.

CAMBRIDGE / MS / 413

(*To Richard Bennett*)

75, Cadogan Square

23–12–29

My dear Rich,

Thanks for yours. Exactly 1,000,000 parcels have come into this house during the last few days, but I have no memory of a parcel or parcels from you. Fred says you saw Miss Nerney. She isn't here yet. Anyhow we are greatly & vastly obliged to you & Stella. A bit trying about the scarletina. Your father & I once had scarlet fever together, about 50 years ago. He was ill, but I wasn't. I had to stay in bedroom but I got up everyday, & did drawings. I suppose there is no difference between scarletina & scarlet fever. I am already getting a bit tired of Xmas. There is a whole cupboard full of parcels for Virginia, waiting. And I have already opened some of her parcels. It takes me so long to keep level with my mail that I can't begin my work till heaven knows what time. However, I did a lot of work yesterday and Saturday. The weather, however, suits me not. I'm glad we aren't going away for Xmas. That's something, anyway. We were invited to dinner last night, at the Park Lane Hotel. It is dreadfully provincial, & might be in Piccadilly, Manchester, more suitably than in Piccadilly, London. But of course there are lots of provincial hotels in London. Only I never go into them. I propose to continue this policy as far as possible. The Ritz Hotel sent me some pâté de foie gras at every meal, as the stuff won't keep. Auntie Tertia & Margaret came on Friday with whole suitcase full of presents for Virginia, & Xmas pudding & mince tarts & cheese cakes. Their mince tarts are unsurpassed in my experience,—indeed unequalled. This means mince tarts at every meal. I can only get along by eating no meat, especially as I have had a lot of oat cakes given me: which monopolise my breakfasts. I *adore* oat cakes: yet was I glad to have eaten the last one this morning! We're going down to Beaverbrooks for next weekend. I couldn't easily get out of it; nor did I particularly want to get out of it. 2 1/2 days change will not harm us. *Any* change is good for Dorothy. Our consumptive 2nd housemaid has *not* got consumption. But yesterday afternoon, being in charge, she showed a man straight into my study, when I was hard at work, without even enquiring his name. It was Geoffrey Russell; but it might have been an assassin. And anyhow it ruined my work. Well, we call down God's blessings upon you, with thanks & wish you a good journey tomorrow, & no scarlet fever.

Loves,
Your greedy uncle,

A.B.

413. Geoffrey Russell (1877–1956), solicitor, a friend of Bennett's at the Reform Club.

KEELE / MS / 414
(*To Marguerite Soulié Bennett*)

75, Cadogan Square
3–3–30

Dear Marguerite,

Thanks for your letter & the cuttings. It seems impossible to stop these things entirely. Certainly I can take no responsibility for gossip-writers. They will say anything, & nothing can prevent them. I am constantly having the most ridiculous untruths said about me. As regards the Austrian reception, the practice seems to be, in all these big receptions, to print simply the list of people invited. The King does the same. Twice I have been reported as present at a Buckingham Palace reception, where I have never been & should never dream of going. I refused to go to the Austrian reception. I did not go, and nobody in this house went. I'm sorry, but I can't help it. I hope you're well.

Yours, A.B.

BERG / MS / 415
(*To George Cedric Beardmore*)   75, Cadogan Square
                                                  3rd March 1930

My dear Cedric,

I return *Dodd*. You are now approaching the printed stage. I think that *Dodd* is pretty good. I wish it was not so short. Another 20,000 words would have helped it a lot. The actual treatment is certainly good, and original too. The whole thing has an agreeable flavour, and it seems to me to be fairly true to life. In sum, I am decidedly pleased with the work. What do you feel about it yourself? Do you want it published as it is? I expect I could get a good publisher to publish it, though I do not want to use too much pressure in doing so. The brevity of the book is against it. Why don't you make things of a proper length? If you want to share your view of the world with the public, you must consider the habits of the public to a certain extent. I wish to have your ideas at large about *Dodd*.

There is a very considerable number of details of the mere writing which need revision.

But *Dodd* is an affair for which you ought not to blush. It has quality.

Your aff unc,

A.B.

CAMBRIDGE / MS / 416
(*To Richard Bennett*)

75, Cadogan Square
4–3–30

My dear Rich,

Thanks for yours, which entered post this morning. I have had a liver-attack, which was acutish for 2 days, but is now over, although I didn't get into bed this morning till 1.20, & was up at 7. I dined at Diana Cooper's last night. Never been to her Gower Street house before. It is fine. They have a complete house. Next door is a block of flats (converted). They have knocked a hole through the wall & added one of the flats to their home. An ingenious scheme. Dorothy arrived at 11.50. There was a delay over her smock, & not till 2.10 was she eating bacon & eggs & drinking champagne from a tray on her knee in the middle of a most rowdy crew. The house looks beautiful. But this is curious: Duff Cooper doesn't smoke ∴ there were no cigars: which pained me, not because I can't do without cigars, but because I disliked the argument. Yet Duff is a most delightful man. However, I am dining with the Duke of Marlborough on Thursday, & I hope that things will be better there. I have known him for 12 years, but at the Other Club last Thursday we became more intimate & he requested me to dinner. I go out every night unless I have a party here. I have never been able to stand solitary evenings; but I adore solitude during the day. I have now written 119,000 words, of you know what. If I hadn't been so infernally busy I should have gone to Manchester to see some more Cochran rehearsals. *Milestones* is still on the fence, & Dorothy still heartily believes in its ultimate glory. God keep her! I'm glad about the encounter of experts, & your share in it. There is nothing like this sort of thing. I agree about the Brahms. I am now proclaiming that that was the finest concert I ever heard. But the programme notes! Did you read them? I told Sam Courtauld that something ought to be done about them. He said: 'Don't tell me, I know. The writer of them is a very nice man!' Sunday we dined at the Colefaxes and saw the Ian Hamiltons again. Their ages united must reach about 140, but they are as young as you & Stella, & tremendously interested in all new things. Our new servants are now all installed. But when I wanted a bath last night (1.10

a.m.) the water was cold. This annoys Fred more than it annoys even me. His views on women (or rather girls) are gradually being soured. Wells & Shaw are coming to lunch on Friday. The top of the house has been painted & papered. We still have no idea where we shall move at the end of the year. The cost of the entire operation will be fantastic. Mrs. Thomas Hardy came for tea on Sunday. She is a very lively, podgy piece. She wants a flat in the Adelphi & we think we have found one for her. Auntie Sissie is coming for tea next Sunday. She is still exploiting my public interest to write articles about life at 205 Waterloo Road for the *Sunday Despatch*, & Auntie Tertia is furious thereat. Furious! She thinks I ought to stop it. I've tried. I can't. Cedric's novel is good. It *may* even be published, of tender years though he is. Going to the 1st night of *Lady with Camellias* tomorrow night with Mr. Tayler, who has been away lecturing on Scottish history in Scotland. He loves to do it. Did you see the exposure of Rothermere methods in the penultimate column of today's *Times* leader page? Magnificently funny.

Loves,
Your paternal uncle,

A.B.

416. Lady Diana Cooper (1892–   ), and Alfred Duff Cooper (1890–1954), Conservative politician and author.

Charles Richard John Spencer-Churchill, 9th Duke of Marlborough (1871–1934).

Charles Cochran followed up his 1928 revue with similar revues in 1930 and 1931.

Milestones, produced by Dorothy, opened at the Criterion on 28 January. It ran for two and a half months there, and then she took it on tour. She played Emily Rhead. The reviewer in *The Times* did not admire her performance.

Artur Schnabel played Beethoven, Mozart, and Brahms in a Courtauld–Sargent concert at the Queen's Hall on February 26th.

Hamiltons: possibly General Sir Ian (1853–1947) and Lady Hamilton (d. 1941). He led the British army at Gallipoli.

The Lady of the Camellias, Alexandre Dumas, opened at the Garrick Theatre on the 12th, with Tallulah Bankhead.

Rothermere was attacked in a letter from Beaverbrook.

CAMBRIDGE / MS / 417
(*To Richard Bennett*)

75, Cadogan Square
11-3-30

My dear Rich,

Thanks for yours of yesterday, which reached me only at lunch time today. I was beginning to think that you had gone to

India. Nobody wants to defeat the Labour Party at present, because nobody wants an election at present, because people are afraid that Labour might get in again. I have not heard of an increased Income tax; only of a lowering of the figure at which super tax is to begin. The Duke of Marlborough is the head of the Churchill family & the grand grand grand grandson of the greatest soldier in English history, to whom a grateful country presented Blenheim. Also he is a very nice, ignorant chap, and an ardent Roman Catholic. That is about all I know of him. Impossible for me to go to Manchester. Too busy. I am still toiling & moiling over my novel. I heard from your mother 2 days ago, in reply to mine. She gave the the history of her case, including some details that she said you didn't know. I told her in my letter, rather plainly, how difficult it had been to get any real news of her condition. I must have a look at the new I.C.I. building. I wish the architecture was better. Frank Baines seems to be an agreeable person, when I meet him, but to my mind not much of an architect. We went to the famous 'Box Office' dinner at the Savoy, Sunday. 640 people chattering & munching in 1 room at 1 time. Row terrific! It exhausted me. Leverton, the Haymarket Box Office Manager, was the best speaker. He is said to have been at the Haymarket for 50 years. I doubt that. But I have personally known him there for 30 years. His hair is a beautiful brown (probably not natural), and at the end of the speeches he sang and played comic songs very well. Varied servant troubles in this abode. Saturday morning I had to tell a kitchenmaid, who had almost certainly pinched £1 from one housemaid, and a pair of stockings from another housemaid, to go at once, under threat of police. It cost a pang, because kitchenmaids are as rare as emeralds. The 2 top floors of the house are now nearly re-decorated. Everything has been upset. Dorothy's latest notion is to take 2 flats at Chiltern Court. They are Underground property, & therefore, belonging to the traffic combine, ought to be better than the ordinary. But I fear the rooms will be too small. I pay a visit of inspection tomorrow probably. I suppose I haven't written to you since the Marlborough dinner. It was great fun. Enormous house. 22 covers at dinner. Soup & fish off silver plate. The Duchess (Bostonian & Parisian) collects French pictures. She said I was the first person who had shown *any* interest in them. I fastened on a certain superb picture, & asked the Duke whose it was. He said 'Van Gogh'. I said it wasn't. He said it surely was. He fetched the Duchess: 'This is by Van Gogh, isn't it?' he asked her. She said it wasn't. It was obviously a Cézanne. And so on. I enjoyed myself talking to her; but the bulk of the 20 guests seemed to me to have no interests whatever except sexual. I mean there were a few beautiful creatures. Well, that's all. Auntie Sissie & spouse took tea here on Sunday. Apparently they are coming to live in London! Well again, that's all, except sorry about cold.

Loves,
Your migratory uncle,

A.B.

417. Frank Baines (1877–1933), later director of works, HM Office of Works, in charge of Royal Palaces.
   W. H. Leverton (d. 1941).

CAMBRIDGE / MS / 418
(*To Richard Bennett*)

75, Cadogan Square
1st April 1930

My dear Rich,
   Thanks for yours. What were you up to at Mrs. Courtauld's? I can't go to the concert this night, as I must attend the 1st performance at the Lyric Hammersmith. Nor shall I attend the supper to which she invited us. Nor will Dorothy, who is in bed: chest, etc. She went to play at the matinee on Saturday, but came home without playing. Then to bed, where she has remained. It is really nothing but continuous overwork & run-downness. The doctor said privately to me: 'Can't you influence her?' I said: 'Not for more than about 3 hours.' She is better this morning. I had to go out to supper last night, after going out to dinner (not that I *ate* any supper) & I got home at 12.45. She was then as lively as a babe. In a few days I lay she will be working harder than ever. Still, every person has the right to go to the devil in his own way. Strange form of insanity, the Head of the River race! When I read of it in the paper, I simply didn't believe it.
   How ingenious you are about the *Milestones* advertisements! Dorothy is brimming over with new plans. I am *not* brimming

over with new plans for the remainder of my novel. I have
revised 140,000 words, & still have about 90,000 to do, I think.
Also I have brought my dictionary of the characters up to date.
There are 68 characters up to date. There will be more. The
chief phenomenon here is the painters in the house. They have
now got down to the dining-room. I eat in the hall—when I do
eat at home. Dorothy is not up yet. What with painters,
Dorothy indisposed, & new servants, this organism is not
exactly normal. However, we aren't entertaining; that's something. It is easier to be entertained; also cheaper. I was at Ciro's
last night. Very quiet. Savoy also; very quiet. I am going to the
Pavilion tomorrow night; also to bed. I note about your mother.
Strange story, her illness! I've been smoking too much; headache. Nevertheless, I go on smoking too much. Weak.

Love,
Your enduring uncle,

A.B.

418. Elizabeth Courtauld (née Kelsey).
Out of the Blue, an improvisation, with Nigel Playfair, Norman Page, and Eric
Portman.

CAMBRIDGE / MS / 419
(*To Richard Bennett*)

75, Cadogan Square
29–4–30

My dear Rich,
    T. for t. You refer to stagnation, but I shouldn't mind a bit
more of it. I am in need of it. Painters in, servants ill, Dorothy at
a hotel, arbitrations conducted by me between quarrelsome
authors & publishers, articles, reading, *and* my novel, to say
nothing of social engagements. Of course everything except my
novel would be nothing if there weren't the novel. 160,000
words now done. End still far distant. We all need a holiday,
but I *really* need one. Yet I had 6 days before Easter. Fred is
coming back next Monday. He wanted to come back on
Thursday, but I said No. Too soon. Nevertheless, it takes me $\frac{1}{2}$
an hour a day to do for myself what Fred does, as they say,
'about my person'. Norah is still in bed. I am charmed to hear
of the flowering of the garden. But the news renews my horror of
the damnable gardening of this square & of the garden behind

13 May 1930

the house. I have complained about it once, & I got some improvement, but of course it didn't last. I want to see you two, but I can't fix it yet. I am told by Auntie Emily that it is time I had a heart-to-heart talk with John. I don't want to, but I expect I shall. I know I am always beaten, which somehow reminds me that Dorothy is going today to an at home at Lady Melchett's. But not me. No. I was not beaten there. Many years ago I told Lady M to go to hell, & she did go & stayed there for ages. Then one night at a theatre she came up to me all honey & treacle, as if nothing had happened. Then she asked me to lunch. I went. Then again to lunch. I went. But no more. I have never had any friction with Melchett, who by the way is very stuck on Dorothy: as much by reason of her face as by what lies behind it. I went to *Brain* on Sunday night at the Savoy. The author called on me & begged me to go & gave me his box. Believe me, friends, it was *awful*. It gave me nervous dyspepsia for several hours. I mean its dullness did. The author is a charming youngish fellow; but he has the worst of all diseases: megalomania.

Loves,
Your striving uncle,

A.B.

419. Lady Violet Melchett (d. 1945), active in welfare work, wife of Sir Alfred Mond, 1st Baron Melchett.

Brain, by Lionel Britton, was put on for one night by the Masses Stage and Film Guild. The review in *The Times* on 28 April said, 'he is not afraid of being devastatingly dull'.

CAMBRIDGE / MS / 420
(*To Richard Bennett*)

75, Cadogan Square
13–5–30

My dear Rich,

Thanks for yours of yesterday. I am writing this at 7 a.m. in bedroom before starting my too-full day. I must have the day clear. Well, before I got your letter I looked up the name of your boss, & sent it to Keeble. I can quite understand that some people are frightened by him. But he is entirely all right. He is, scientifically, rather a bluffer, and is rather smiled at by his friends such as H.G. Wells & Julian Huxley. However, he has a lively and a broad mind. Jeanne de Casalis was here the other night, with the Keebles & *Aldous* Huxley, & she began on a comparison of the standards of average life in England & in France to the advantage of the latter, & the way those two demolished her in an immense survey of comparisons covering the entire world was very funny. Each of them seemed to know and have seen everything. I have requested that RDB's diary & the new Thornton Wilder be sent unto thee, though I doubt if the latter is 'in'. I have not had *Gallery of Women* & I have formed the idea that it is not very exciting. Be it known that I can always send you books. Congratulations on the issue of the Melchett–Richard prize-fight. Did I ever say that L.M.S. shares should be sold? That must have been on a general survey of Railway prospects. I have no inside information about railways, so my advice is worth naught. Still, I *did* sit next to Josiah Stamp at a little dinner not long since. He is about the most brilliant & the *fastest* brain I have met with. He certainly did not seem very bright about the L.M.S. future. Still, he told us that he had reduced the average time for reconditioning a locomotive from 3 months to 48 hours, & hoped to get it down to 46. Stamp is another man who knows everything. He telephoned me yesterday to go to lunch & meet Nicholas Murray Butler on Thursday. N.M.B. is President of Columbia Univ. I refused. And Lloyd George telephoned me yesterday asking me to lunch with N.M.B. & himself etc. at the H. of C. today. I refused. I first met N.M.B. 19 years ago, when I judged him to be an imposing facade with a first-rate bore behind. I sat next to him on Tuesday night last at the R.D.B. dinner to American Journalists (5) at the Carlton Club. My opinion of N.M.B. was there confirmed. The P. of Wales was at this trifling but rich dinner. I enjoyed it. I was leaving early (11 p.m.) & was just departing, hatted & coated, when 3 men, including Thomas Horder, ran after me & removed my hat & coat & brought me back to the whiskey-drinkers. The P. of W. had just gone. I've had a heavy week of American journalists, but it included a late visit to the *Daily Mail* offices, which *are worth seeing*. The *Express*, in their new building, will have to work hard to equal them. Dorothy is at Lewisham this week, & goes to Southampton next week. My novel is wearing me out. I *can't* ask you 2 out yet.

Loves,
Your flagging uncle,

A.B.

420. Julian Huxley (1887–1975), biologist and author.

Jeanne de Casalis (1898–1966), actress and dramatist. Some years earlier she had played in *The Bright Island*.

RDB: Ralph D. Blumenfeld, author of *RDB's Diary*, recently published.

Thornton Wilder (1897–1975), American dramatist and novelist.

Gallery of Women, a collection of tales about women, by Theodore Dreiser.

Josiah Stamp (1880–1941) served for many years with the Inland Revenue. He was connected with ICI and was president of London, Midland, and Scottish Railway.

Nicholas Murray Butler (1862–1947) became president of Columbia University in 1904.

BERG / MS / 421
(*To Dorothy Cheston Bennett*)

75, Cadogan Square
21–5–30

My sweetest pet,

I got your letter this morning. Thanks. You seem to be having a good time, except financially. But that was to be expected. I have only the very faintest hope of you *not* losing both at Southampton & at Birmingham. It is astounding, the number of people in a large city who are capable of *not* going to the theatre. You will have severe trouble financially, but in other respects you have emerged from this adventure with great credit & I am proud of you. Even on the business side, as to which you had had no experience, you have shown aptitudes. And above all you have really *worked*, and have shirked nothing. I say nothing as to your acting, as my views are well known to you & the world. But I was always against you combining the roles of actress & manageress. The strain of them is much more too much for you than you realise. I will not again agree to you combining them. If you insisted (I don't think you would), I should simply go on strike. Acting by itself breaks up domestic life, unless both partners are on the stage; but I am prepared to submit to that, being a person of the most ridiculous & remarkable self-sacrificingness. (I know I am a fool in this respect, but I can't help it.) I am not, however, prepared to experience again what I have experienced these last 3 months.

The greatest miracle of my life is the fact that I have been able to write my novel at all. I do not blame you; you can't help it. Over-fatigue not only makes you ill, but it intensifies your feminine 'emotional instability' (technical medical term) which even ordinarily is beyond the average slightly, I think. It certainly increases your slight tendency towards what is called 'persecution mania', and also your already very highly developed critical faculty. It gets you into a state in which nothing & no one is safe from your criticism, much of which is entirely unreasonable, as you generally recognise later. You probably don't realise what the atmosphere of this house is when you are over-tired, & what diplomacy is continuously needed to keep the yacht afloat. I know you have vastly improved in certain ways of demeanour to people under you. I have been delighted to observe your calmness of tone in correction & criticism. But you do undoubtedly emanate a feeling that you are dissatisfied & displeased & that you are bearing up heroically against the gross incompetence & even the ill will of your dependents. Believe me, my sweet pet, this is so. Everyone, including me, thinks that to please you is frequently impossible. I will give you one instance, in scores. The other evening I went up to your bedroom. You were comatose. You said: 'I gave orders to be called at *ten* minutes to seven.' I said: 'Well, it's twelve minutes to!' You rang the bell. Instantly Norah comes in. You said to her, in your most martyrised tone: 'I asked to be called at a *quarter* to seven.' Norah said that Nurse told her to call you at ten minutes to. You made no amends. You went on being a martyr. This kind of atmosphere spreads through a house like wildfire. What do you suppose servants talk about downstairs? Nobody will stay in such an atmosphere if it can be avoided. The atmosphere is altogether too discouraging. Half an hour later you burst out against Norah's carelessness in sending you downstairs without your hat. But Norah had given you your hat & it was in the dining-room. This kind of thing is continually occurring, & its effect is certain. The mere fact that you should say to Norah 15 minutes to 7, when you had just said 10 minutes to me, & when 10 was undoubtedly what you did say to nurse, shows that when you are over-fatigued, the fatigue shows itself in an inner *necessity* to grumble. Exactness is nothing to you when you are very tired. You exaggerate, or even invent, before you know what you are saying. Your dignity with servants is compromised. The servants feel resentment, & nothing but a thoroughly bad effect is produced. Also when you are over-tired your orders become more & more confused, lengthy, & difficult to follow. And you have no mercy on me. For instance, you come to lunch 25 minutes late, & then burst into the room with an explosion of grumbling at servants. Do you realise the effect of this on the meal? It is absolutely desolating. Servants ought never to be unfavourably discussed at meals. At the same time I wish to say that your demeanour to *me* is immensely more agreeable & thoughtful than it used to be. I don't suppose that servants are always punctual, but as I told you long ago, no mistress who is always unpunctual herself can reasonably expect punctuality in her staff. The habits of the mistress are always catching. And thus your unpunctuality is catching, and so is your critical habit. Servants become critical & dissatisfied themselves. You keep on saying that I always take the side of the servants against you. This is not so. What I take is the side of common sense & reasonable justice, having severely suffered myself. As regards servants, you are decades behind the times. You are living in the stuffy Victorian eighties, my girl. No experienced servant will accept the canon that all orders must be obeyed. They won't do it. No other class of employees will do it, and they won't. The servant problem is bound to go from bad to worse. For the conditions of domestic service are still awful. They might easily be remedied by careful organisation. What will people say 30 years hence of the conditions under which, in 1930, young girls could not go out of the house for several days at a time? Well, the people of 1960 will be staggered, that's all. The situation is kept together solely by the fact that when you are not over-strained you can exercise such extraordinary charm. Hence it is that I will never again agree to you trying to do more than any woman can safely try to do. You have done wonders, but of course you have not done the impossible. I don't like telling you all this, but I am bound to give you my views; it is my duty to do so. No room for anything else, my pet. I am working all right & sleeping all right, and I am very busy & I look forward to seeing you on Sabbath next.

Little

421. In his memoir Frank Swinnerton says that Winifred Nerney told him that often in the house 'she would hear screams and discover that Dorothy, in a paroxysm of rage, had thrown herself face downward on the stairs and was beating them with her clenched fist'.

BERG / MS / 422
(*To Dorothy Cheston Bennett*)

75, Cadogan Square
23–v–30

My sweetest pet,

Thanks for epistle.

Anyway you are having a bit of a change now & then in the daytime. On which I congratulate you. I am very busy with my novel, which is a continuous source of anxiety, & often I cannot keep my mind on it.

Theatre. You enclosed nothing from Gibbons. If you knew the facts you would smile sadly as I do at the idea of suppressing repertory & amateur performances for the sake of an occasional tour. I should not dream of stopping such performances, nor would Knobby. They are a small but regular source of income—and far better than tours. When people don't go to the theatre, managers frequently say that the fault is repertory or amateur. This merely is not so. And the Southampton man has a nerve to suggest it. There is no repertory in Southampton or district, & I have not yet traced any amateur performances either. *All these people are the same.* They will not look facts in the face. They are always absurdly hoping. On Monday, Wednesday is the great day. And till Saturday, Saturday will be the great day. Etc. Except for well-*done* musical plays, and for stars with big names, the provincial theatre is ruined. Damn it, I have said this for years; & it is continually being re-demonstrated. It is all exceedingly trying for you, & I am very sympathetic, but you have to make up your mind to it. And you would do much better to listen to me, and do as I say, than listen to any stage-person in London. Optimism is a great quality, but it may be darned expensive. As regards Birmingham, *no London manager will go there to see you.* It is too much to ask of them. Imagine it to be some other person than yourself, & you will see the point. Managers don't do these things. They ought to, perhaps, but they won't. Do you suppose that Cochran, with all his schemes at full pressure, could or would give a day to go to Birmingham? Or Gilbert? Buda Pesth—oh yes! They'll go there to see new plays—& rotten plays they are—but they have no interest in anything that appertains to old plays, and as for consecrating a day to see a mere actress! Good God! My sweet girl, where is your sense of proportion? Lonsdale is not in town, or if he was he wouldn't go to Birmingham. You don't understand how these people's minds work. I do. Your sense of proportion is a bit wrong.

House. I doubt if 'the first thing' is to get a good staff, & to make them work harder than the present staff does.

You have at least three excellent workers & very decent people on the present staff. You simply will not & cannot get more out of a staff than you do get. You expect too much. You are far too critical and you constantly give the impression to your servants that their misdoings are atrocious & painful. The 'first thing' to do is to alter your attitude to servants, talk less to them, criticise less, and be cheerful & brief when you do criticise. Servants can choose their places & they will not stay long in a house where they are too often made to feel that they are not giving anywhere near satisfaction. And things will be no better in the flat unless the attitude is changed. And this is very trying for you, for you have a tender conscience. It is also trying for me. I have no room, nor time, now, for my own doings and not-doings. My sweetest pet, despite my defects, & my sharing with servants the defect of not being an archangel, it is perhaps not a bad thing that you have me at your side, & my love too.

Little

422. Arthur Gibbons (1871–1935), manager, founding member of the Touring Managers Association.

Gilbert Miller (1884–1969), the producer, with whom Bennett negotiated for productions of *Don Juan de Marana* and *Flora*.

Frederick Lonsdale (1881–1954).

BERG / MS / 423
(*To Dorothy Cheston Bennett*)

75, Cadogan Square
28–5–30

My sweetest pet,

Your letter received this morn was a very good one. I hope you won't expect me to show my feelings too much, because I can't. Each of us has his own way of existing. And although I am young for my years, this does not help me much because you are still younger for your years than I am for mine. You are the youngest young thing for your years that I have ever come across. And yet, despite this, I do not consider myself the most gloomy or sad person in this house. No! I don't. I admire your charm, your frequent lovingness, your beauty, and your terrific energy & initiative. The things in you that pull me up are your general complainingness, your air of being a martyr, which air spreads a feeling of dissatisfaction throughout this house, your self-centredness, and your growing unpunctuality. Diana was 30 minutes late for the Heineman lunch yesterday. The lunch was ruined. Some years ago she told me that she had been obliged to reform herself because Duff was 'such a beast' about unpunctuality. But now the poor thing has backslidden, I fear. Elizabeth told me the other night that George had cured her of her terrible unpunctuality by wearing her out with reminders. I can't do this; I am too soft-hearted, curse me! When you make a 75 minute speech, & then are asked to fix your own time for dinner, and arrive for it 25 minutes late, & then demand of an exhausted man that he shall adore & coax you, the exhausted man finds it a bit thick. Believe me, I am still tired. As for your speech, of course I agree and have always agreed, with a lot of it, though it was vitiated by exaggeration & by the fact that continually reiterated complainings about all manner of things must inevitably exhaust the springs of sympathy. Has it occurred to you that, quite apart from servants, something is always going wrong for you, and that nine times out of ten the fault according to you is somebody else's? No more things go wrong with you than with other people, but you make far more fuss about yours. Your speech did not touch my previous (written) remarks, which were based solely on what I myself have seen. I know perhaps more of your difficulties than you imagine. I gather them from Fred's brief but hostile remarks about servants. But I am absolutely convinced that you are too hard on servants, that you expect too much from them, and that your attitude towards them continually discourages them. If you are unjust to me, as you often are, naturally you are unjust to servants, & to others. However, I do admit that your manner to servants has *much* improved. I admit also my own faults of deportment. I can only say, not in justification but in explanation, that I have been rather worn out by (1) the serious damage to domestic life during the last few months (2) worry about my enormous novel (3) still graver worry about finance (which by the way is worrying everybody—I mean everybody who has the final financial responsibility (4) your defiance of my advice. I really do not know what the financial future will be. As for domestic life, I have often said, & I still say, that I prefer it to anything. Lastly, I will say with my dying breath that I have done my utmost to help you in your career, and at great personal self-sacrifice. I agree with you that you & I deeply understand one another, so *that I am convinced that everything will be all right*, although at present I am certainly going through a very rough time indeed, and I have still quite 40,000 words of my novel to write. I shan't be able to resume it for a few days, as my ideas are not in order. I have no desire to complain; I hate complaining, & assuredly I complain infinitely less than you do; but no good can come of trying to hide one's feelings completely. I glimpsed Freddie Lonsdale at lunch-time yesterday—he had just arrived straight from Hollywood; and he turned up in the club at dinner (me also) so he sat with Duff and me & dined, & we had a delicious evening, & I was home before 11. He may be, & is, unreliable; but he has marvellous charm & is very witty and for some strange reason he has a perfect infatuation for me. I hope it will be all right for Hammersmith, but in your place I wouldn't count on that absolutely. There has been some fuss lately about the committee of the Garrick selling valuable manuscripts. Members said it was the thin end of the wedge & they would be selling the pictures next. The Committee swore never to sell a picture. Arthur Wontner said to Freddie: 'Do you think that if I put up Gilbert Miller for membership the committee would accept him?' Freddie answered: 'They would sooner sell a picture.' I am having a dinner tonight, chiefly for the Ellis Robertses. Doran will be here, & Gertrude Jennings & I forget who else. I am lunching with Eric Pinker today at his club. He is over on a flying visit. He hasn't told me, but I surmise it must be about a project of Doubleday, Dorans, & other publishers to reduce the price of novels from 2 or 2½ dollars to one dollar! This is fairly serious. Freddie is giving a dinner tomorrow night at the Club, at which Knobby & I will be present.

Your last train on Sunday leaves Birmingham (*Snow Hill*) at *11.40* & arrives Paddington at 1.40 (luncheon car). I will send the car to meet you, but I doubt if I shall come myself, as I must try to squeeze in a snooze. (So if I am not visible, don't make me visible; I shall attend you as quickly as poss. The concert is at 3. We must be punctual.)

This letter is not gloomy. It is merely honest. I understand you all right, as you are aware, with your intelligence, which should also inform you of my tender, ceaseless feelings towards you.

Little

Virginia being in the house makes a great difference. I play much with her, & she is a great waster of my time.

A.B.

423. Elizabeth Lewis married George Wansbrough in 1928.
Arthur Wontner (1875–1960), actor and manager.
Ellis Roberts (1860–1930), Staffordshire-born artist, and Eliza (née Glover).

CAMBRIDGE / MS / 424
(*To Richard Bennett*)

75, Cadogan Square
3–6–30

My dear Rich,

Thanks for yours. The Toscanini, on Sunday, despite Albert Hall acoustics, was the greatest musical experience I have ever had. And the Q. Hall concert last night easily surpassed it. The *Enigma Variations* item was absolutely overwhelming. I saw Elgar afterwards at the Savoy Grill (which was full), & congratulated him. He said he never went to hear his own music. He said also that he wrote the thing 31 years ago, when it was

called 'silly', & now people talked about its 'profound psychological import' etc. He is now rather a silly & disgruntled old
man. Even 8 years ago, when I last had him to dinner, I said I
would never ask him again, because of his affectations.
However.... I know naught of the map of Europe, except what
can be gained from looking at a simplified map, such as you see
in windows of Travel Agencies. Very useful things, these
windows! I quite agree with you about both statistics. I know
little of the *News–Chronicle* business, except that the editors of
both papers were absolute duds. Unless a new editor is
obtained, there will be no 'large Liberal daily'. I should say that
the fusion was 'effected' for the reason that the *Chronicle* had no
further cash resources to meet losses. When I attended the
dinner given by about a dozen of us to Sir Josiah Stamp some
weeks ago at the Reform Club (I sat next to him), he laid more
stress than on anything on the widening abyss between
wholesale & retail prices, & said that one of the first & chief
things to be done was to narrow the difference. He gave the
percentages, but, having no head, I have quite forgotten them.
Dorothy does not go to Liverpool. Her tour ends at the King's
Hammersmith July 9–14. Then she is going down to Cornwall
by car for a day or two to look for rooms for us for the summer.
We have decided not to go abroad. It would be too much of an
effort, & also too costly. And I want a change from abroad.
Dorothy returned from Birmingham (not a good week) on
Sunday in great form. We have now a new cook & new upper
housemaid, from both of whom great things are expected. We
shall go to the 10th anniversary of *Beggar's Opera* on Thursday.
So far as I am affected by it, the London season is now at its
height. And so is my novel. But I refuse everything I can. I
leave this epistle to run to the novel.

> Loves,
> Your acrobatic uncle,

A.B.

424. Arturo Toscanini (1867–1957) conducted the New York Symphony Orchestra,
of which he was then principal conductor. The Queen's Hall concert offered the
Colonne Orchestra of Paris, conducted by Gabriel Pierne. Edward Elgar (1857–1934).
The *News Chronicle* merged with the *Daily News-Westminster Gazette*.

STOKE / MS / 425
(*To Margaret Beardmore*)

75, Cadogan Square
11–6–30

Sweet niece,

I was glad to hear from you at length. You couldn't expect the *Sentinel* to publish Cyril's ode. Sarcasm about a place is not understood *in* the place, unless the place is a very large place. Then it is understood by about .001 p.c. of the pop. I thought the ode was quite funny, but of course that kind of thing is very easy to do in a loose form if you have a sardonic mind. I may say that we are probably nearly as much interested in our removal as you are in yours. I hope ours will be a success. We have joined 2 flats together. There are about 12 rooms (not *counting* 3 bathrooms), all in a row, & all with southern aspect. The total length of the abode is equal to about three cricket pitches—if you know how much that is. Even so, however, we shan't have the space that we have here, & a lot of the furniture will have to be sold. Also I am going to have a modern study, with decorations & furniture presided over by McKnight Kauffer. (I don't expect you to know of him). My novel is not yet done. I am on page 1,056 of the manuscript, and every page holds 200 words. I hope with God's help to finish by the end of June. I say God's help; but all I ask of Him, really, is that he shall leave me alone. I think we shall go to Cornwall for a holiday. I should prefer the Continent; but I shall be so tired after my book that I don't feel equal to the responsibility of taking a family & a car across the channel and then miles & still miles. Too complicated. I will go later to the continent with Dorothy alone. That girl is very busy—too busy, & not at all well. Her tour of *Milestones* ends on Saturday at Hammersmith, & both of us will be much relieved. She working in the evening & me in the morning: not an arrangement that is divinely satisfactory, is it! But it can't be helped. She is now busy on other schemes. Her energy frightens me, though I reckon to have a bit of energy myself. You needn't worry: I shan't offer you any advice about marriage. All I say is that if you don't do something more than keep house, either the house will be marvellous beyond earthly words, or you will soon have a funny feeling inside you; not indigestion but discontent arising from unemployed vital force.

This is a certainty. But I doubt not that you will do something. Virginia is marvellous. You think I am making a noise like a father. Not at all. Everybody says so. Auntie Tertia is quite 'gone' on her, & has her down to Putney for tea at every opportunity. She is very naughty, and she talks too much. Her health is perfect, & she deeply enjoys life. I heard her say on the stairs: 'Damn,—I mean dash!' She is exquisitely ignorant, thank God. I believe that at four I could read, and think what trouble my ability to read has brought upon me! On Monday I met the manager of the Aga Khan's racing-stables in the Park. Young man. He may be able to read, though I doubt it. Yet what a grand, fine, expensive life he leads. He is always somewhere else. I am always here. Nothing would have induced me to attend the Potteries fandango & fêtes. But my refusal to show has got me into calm & deadly disfavour with the nobs down your way. They can't understand it. They think I am conceited, whereas I'm the most modest of created uncles. Well, love to everyone. My benedictions on you two, etc.

Your aff unc,

A.B.

425. Margaret Beardmore married Cyril Shingler on 17 October 1930.
    E. McKnight Kauffer (d. 1954), American designer and artist, made his career in England. He did illustrations for limited editions of *Elsie and the Child* and *Venus Rising from the Sea*.

CAMBRIDGE / TS / 426
(*To Richard Bennett*)

75, Cadogan Square
1st July 1930

My dear Rich,
    Thanks for yours of yesterday. This is my supreme week. Either I shall have finished my novel on Sunday next or my death will be in the papers. I feel the strain considerably, but I am nothing if not persevering. Dorothy is better but not cured. On Sunday she had to go down to Brighton to see her mother, who has been ill for a very long time. She returned in a state of considerable exhaustion. As regards the books, you can certainly have some or most of them. I think that the last story

in *Brief Candles* is very good. I have not read the rest. I think that I have no rubber shares. If I have, they are not worth talking about. I meant to go to Lords on Saturday, but I could not fix it anyhow, so I remained at home and worked. Ditto Sunday. Ditto everday.

But believe me, I am getting exhausted.

And I cannot write any more.

Except to say that I am reading the new Wells novel. I will send it to you in due course. *I* think it is rather good.

> Loves,
> Your expiring uncle,

> > > A.B.

426. *Brief Candles*, by Aldous Huxley.
Wells's novel was *The Autocracy of Mr. Parham*.

CAMBRIDGE / TS / 427
(*To Richard Bennett*)

> 75, Cadogan Square
> 15th July 1930

My dear Rich,

Thank you for your letter of yesterday. I am now laid low with neuralgia, which I suppose is one of the sequels of writing a long novel. We ought to have gone away to Cornwall today, but business of Dorothy's prevented this, and we are going on Thursday instead. Nurse and Virginia have just gone by themselves. Atkinson went yesterday morning in the Chrysler car which we have hired because the Rolls is a size too large for the Cornish lanes. The Chrysler seems to be a rather fine vehicle.

Your books will be posted to Stocks Hotel, Sark, on Thursday as requested. The matter with Sark is that it is so small. You can walk all over it in about half an hour. Nevertheless some of the scenery is marvellous.

You had better change your tailor, if what you say is strictly true. How much do you pay for a suit?

At the moment I am engaged, despite neuralgia, in writing a few articles in advance for the *E.S.* Fortunately they are very easy to do.

On Sunday we went for the day to Sonning, and boated, and

practised sloth there. Also we met Gilbert Frankau, whose first word was that he had lost thousands and thousands on the Stock Exchange in the recent slump. He was gloomy, but hoped for the best from his new book, which was being advertised by sandwich men outside Harrods yesterday. I went to the barber's at Harrods yesterday, and saw Gilbert there again—rather more cheerful, and full of enthusiasm for Virginia, whom he had closely observed at Sonning. Gilbert is a very nice fellow, but his niceness is impaired by a certain Jewish coarseness. His mother was a great friend of mine.

We have seen two bad plays:—*Cynara* and *The First Mrs. Fraser*. On each occasion I had acute neuralgia, but my judgment on them is sound, believe me.

Auntie Sissie is in bed with a heart attack.

Fanny Bourne has returned to the Potteries. I regard it as almost certain that before long she will be in a lunatic asylum. She has illusions; the latest of which is that she is followed by policemen. She wrote to me asking that I should do something about it. It was from Hampstead. I advised her to leave Hampstead. I saw one of her letters to Auntie Tertia. It was a most astonishing production, but it gave enough domestic detail about the life she has led in places as a housekeeper or something to make a novel.

This is all. Except that we hope that your holiday will be fine and the passage both ways smooth.

> Loves,
> Your pained uncle,
>
> A.B.

427. Bennett finished writing *Imperial Palace* on 5 July. It proved to be his longest novel, 243,000 words as against 200,000 for *The Old Wives' Tale*, and almost 100,000 longer than he expected when he started it.

·Gilbert Frankau (1884–1952), author and journalist; his mother Julia Frankau (1864–1916) wrote under the name Frank Danby.

Cynara, by H. M. Harwood and R. Gore Browne, was at the Playhouse Theatre. *The First Mrs. Fraser*, St John Ervine's play, was in a new production at the Haymarket.

BERG / MS / 428
(*To Dorothy Cheston Bennett*)   The Falmouth Hotel
Falmouth
Tuesday morn, 9–8–30

My sweetest pet,

Your long letter was not too long. It had not arrived at Fowey at 12.30 yesterday. I had it sent on to Falmouth. It is curious that I *did* get your telegram (about me deserving a holiday etc)—on Sunday morning at Fowey. I am rather troubled about your being 'frazzled'. I wish you could manage not to be. Nothing to be frazzled about. As regards the voyage, I can't possibly say to Alfred: 'You mustn't go to so-and-so because Dorothy is nervous.' There is nothing whatever to be nervous about. We came here from Fowey yesterday afternoon in 4 hours. *Heavenly* day. Sea was flat. The nuisance was that there was no wind, & we had to motor all the way. Helford is only round the corner, & we shall get there tomorrow in 1½ hours. *If* we go! No wind today, but continuous rain. The ship is having her hull scraped free of weed & barnacles, so we have left her for the day. We have marooned ourselves at this hotel (in a taxi) hoping for the rain to stop, & we rejoin the ship at 6 p.m. Movement tomorrow will depend on weather. I do hope you will go to the D.R. of *The Honeymoon*, as in these matters I have much faith in your judgement. I hope that the cutting will not be done by some idiot. Boucicault spoilt it by his damned cutting. I am annoyed by the friendly fool Walpole having said in an American article that my novel is about the Savoy. I've told him to withdraw the statement. But Doubledays have seized on his remark & want to use it for publicity! I have written drastically to stop them. As nearly all the characters are either directors or employees of the hotel, imagine the trouble that would ensue if the Imp. Palace is officially identified with the Savoy! Reeves-Smith having a liaison with a girl in Paris! The grill-room manager falling in love with a floor-house-keeper! Etc. etc. It would be awful. The Imp. Palace is an imaginary hotel. What I say is: Curse Hughie and Doubledays. It is all very interesting about Virginia. Like you, I have often thought that nurse is too severe on Virginia. But supposing she wasn't, what kind of an inferno would result? And the fact remains that Virginia is devoted to nurse. Also, Virginia's character is much too strong to be much affected, in its roots or in its future, by anything that anybody does to her. What I say is: *Correct*; but do not *resent*. The child is not *naughty*, she is only natural. No! I had not heard a word of the accident to M.M.B. Forget it. Alfred & I are in the smoking-room of the hotel. All the other public rooms are full of visitors who want to go out, but can't because of the rain. My sweet girl, you are all right, & I love you. Very amusing about Higham.

Little

428. Bennett sailed with A. E. W. Mason, the author (1865–1948).
The Honeymoon had a brief run in September at the Everyman Theatre.
Dion Boucicault (1859–1929) starred in the original production of *The Honeymoon* in 1911.
Higham: unidentified.

KEELE / MS / 429
(*To Marguerite Soulié Bennett*)

75, Cadogan Square
1 Sept 1930

Dear Marguerite,

Thanks for your letter of the 10th August. You are completely mistaken in supposing that I stopped the sale of your book. Both the editor of the *Express*, and Cassells, the publishers of the book, asked me before they agreed to publish, whether I had any objection. I replied that I had no objection whatever. And I had not. I have done *nothing* to stop the sale of the book. Anybody who tells you the contrary is a malicious liar. Good wishes.

Yours, A.B.

CAMBRIDGE / MS / 430
(*To Richard Bennett*)

75, Cadogan Square
30–9–30

My dear Rich,

Thanks for thine. But I wish you would put your address on your letters. This is quite the usual thing to do. Even women do it. I can never remember your address with any certainty. You seem to be in a pretty satisfactory state at the office (except for salary) & the state of the Rochdale branch of your family is not surprising. I must say that your mother's courage, cheerfulness & energy *are* surprising. Well perhaps they aren't, in *her*. I haven't yet seen any proof that free trade is a cause of unemployment. There is as high a percentage of unemployment in U.S.A. as here. And what about Germany? And what about Australia? Nor do I regard dumping as an *unmixed* evil. The point of view of the consumer never seems to interest these political arguers. Trade is bad throughout the world, & this gives a chance to every supporter of a method untried in this country to find the reason of unemployment here in the untriedness of that method. The arguments in favour of free trade have never yet been answered—not even by J. M. Keynes in my ear at dinner when explaining his changes of opinion! I am now getting gradually drowned in the great affair of preparing the flat for habitation. It is a heavy business, & demands endless conferences and discussions. Also the cost is fantastic. Further, I am still deeply in the dentist's parlour—curse it. Fortunately I am only working on light stuff—the libretto of *Don Juan* for Goossens' music; I have done 3 acts out of 4. My next novel is all in my head, but I shall do nothing in the fiction line except short stories until we are in the flat, tidily. 2 first nights last week; 2 this. Coward's play is a terrific lark; but without him in the chief role it would be *nothing*, & that is why Cochran is taking it off when Coward leaves the cast—in 3 months time. Coward is an incomparable performer in his own plays. Without him *Private Lives* would be unendurable. I saw Coward in his dressing-room after the 1st night, & I spoke unto him these words *only*: 'But of course you can act'. He comprehended & laughed like anything. This is about all for today.

Loves,
Your torn uncle,

A.B.

430. Bennett wrote the libretto for *Don Juan* in September and October 1930. The opera was produced at Covent Garden on 24 June 1937.

The next novel, *Dream of Destiny*, was begun on 25 November 1930. Bennett left off writing it on 26 December. It was published unfinished in June 1932.

Private Lives, with Noël Coward and Gertrude Lawrence, opened at the Phoenix Theatre on 24 September.

KENNERLEY / TS / 431
(*To Mary Kennerley*)

75, Cadogan Square
9th October 1930

My sweet niece,

Lady Victor Paget had lunch with me today, and I had a long talk with her. I gave her a rather impressive but quiet account of you. I specially refrained from asking her whether she could find a job for you. I only asked her, to begin with, for advice. She herself suggested that you should call and see her at her establishment (10 Grafton St.). When you write be careful to say that I have told you that Lady Victor very kindly offered to see you, and ask for an appointment. Make this plain, because all her letters are opened by her manageress (who appears to me to run the show in all details). Lady V. expects to be able to see you towards the end of next week. She is rather disturbed at the present moment by the fact that one of her children has just had an operation. I very much doubt whether she will be able to give you a job, but anyhow it cannot do any harm to see her, and it may do good. She was evidently somewhat intrigued by my remarks about your capabilities, etc.

                    Your aff unc,

                                        A.B.

431. Lady Victor Paget, wife of Lord Victor Paget (1889–1952).

BERG / TS / 432
(*To George Cedric Beardmore*)

75, Cadogan Square
24th October 1930

My dear Cedric,

I enclose copy of a letter which I have received from Mr. Flower, managing director of Cassells.

Today I have discussed terms with him. He will pay you 15% royalty on the first 5,000 copies and 20% after 5,000. (The price will be 7/6d). He will pay you £100 in advance of royalties on the day of publication. These, I may say, are very good terms, but Mr. Flower offered them himself, so that there was no argument. The contract would be for three novels, the same terms for each novel separately.

If you sell 2,000 copies of your first novel you will be very lucky.

I am now thinking of America, and I have a faint hope that I may be able to place the book there also. But do not count on this at all.

I telegraphed you last night to know if you had a second copy, because I should like to send the copy I have to U.S.A. at once.

Cassells want to publish in February. Though, if America is secured, I doubt whether this will be possible.

With regard to Mr. Flower's suggestions, I fully agree with them. (You will remember that I objected from the first to the introductory chapter.) You will hate to do it, but I want you to lay aside your present novel and revise *Dodd*, the matter being rather urgent. When you have revised it, I must go through the book myself in order to correct a vast amount of mere phrasing that simply will not do as it stands. I have not yet decided whether it would be better for me to do this alone or whether you should come up to London and go through it with me, as I should not wish to make a lot of verbal changes which you disliked. Some of the phrasing is provincial, even local, e.g., the use of the word 'road' for 'way'.

Loves,
Your aff unc,

A.B.

P.S. Thanks for your telegram and letter. If you have already sent the second copy I will return it. I want you to go through it yourself in the light of Mr. Flower's letter, immediately. We will then consider the question of phrasing.

I am sending my copy of your book to America next week.

A.B.

432. *Dodd the Potter* was published by Cassell in 1930. Doubleday published it in America. George Cedric Beardmore eventually made a career as an author. *Dodd the Potter* was the only work he published under the name Cedric Beardmore. He published a couple of novels under the name Cedric Stokes, and three under the name George Wolfenden. After 1950 he published exclusively under the name George Beardmore. The latter titles include a dozen books for young people. He wrote for *Girl* and *Eagle* for many years, in association with Marcus Morris and Chad Varah. Among his books for adults, *A Lion Among Ladies* is notable for its warmth and humour. In 1984 his book *Civilian at War*, an account of his years from 1938 to 1947, was published for the first time.

BERG / TS / 433
(*To George Cedric Beardmore*)   97, Chiltern Court
                                                  [Clarence Gate, N.W.1]
                                                  14th November 1930

My dear Cedric,

Thanks for your letter of yesterday. The sooner I receive the amended *Dodd* the better. With regard to your remarks on *IP*, I am glad you like it. I never reply to critics except on matters of fact. You are entirely wrong in thinking that I have never felt a passionate interest in any character since the servant girl in *Riceyman Steps*. Indeed you were never more wrong in all your long life.

Any novel written on 'an intellectual plane and without abandonment' could not possibly be good, or even interesting.

I never knew that I used the word 'naughty' any oftener than other people.

                                    Loves,
                                    Your aff unc,

                                                        A.B.

433.   Bennett and Dorothy moved into Chiltern Court on 9 November.

CAMBRIDGE / MS / 434
(*To Richard Bennett*)

                                                  97, Chiltern Court
                                                  17–11–30

My dear Rich,

I don't want you to have the refectory table. Anyhow, it's too large for you, & I desire to sell it. You can have all the other things you mention. The sooner you clear them out the better. Dorothy is staying for a few days at the Great Central Hotel close by, to have quiet & seclusion for studying her part! This does not prevent her from spending much time telephoning to most of the staff here, at considerable length. She is now much better. For weeks before coming here she was complaining of insomnia & fatigue. Still, considering she has only had her part a week today, she has done very well. She has an absurd idea that despite five hours a day, or more, at the theatre, she can do everything she was doing here! Well, she can't! I am gradually getting the pictures hung. They *may* be finished today. If not today, tomorrow. After dinner last night, when Dorothy went off to rehearse with Martin Walker, I went up to Wells's wigwam. Both daughters-in-law were there; also Frank, but not Gyp. Also C.E.M. Joad, & the Williams Ellises and a Glasgow man whose name I have forgotten. Also Anna-Jane Blanco White, a School of Economics girl to whom H.G. is godfather. I stayed miscellaneously yarning till midnight, when my announcement of departure broke up the party. And a good thing too. Frank & Peggy had to drive to Welwyn Garden City. I like both Marjorie & Peggy. My study is not in order, but it has a superficial air of being in order. Have I told you—no I haven't—that Dorothy's mother died at Brighton on Saturday morning. She was over 70 and her death was fully expected, & as she was no good to anybody, even to herself, her decease is not an unmixed evil. She had been unconscious for three days. So far as I know Dorothy is not going down to the funeral. If she isn't, I certainly am not. There is the usual ferocious warfare (about jewelry etc., this time) between her and her sister Gladys, whom I have no use for whatever since she once said to me: 'India would be all right if it wasn't for the natives.' Gladys is one of the executors. Dorothy isn't. But her brother Harry, who is excellent, is an executor. He comes down from Newcastle tonight. I wrote my first article in this flat yesterday—for next Thursday. I shan't do any more actual literary composition till next Sunday. Nevertheless I appear to be frightfully busy.

> Loves,
> Your arranging uncle,
>
> A.B.

434. Dorothy played Cecilia Flinders in *The Man from Blankley's*, by Frederic Anstey. It opened on 26 November at the Fortune Theatre.

Martin Walker (1901–55) played Mr Poffley in the play.

C. E. M. Joad (1891–1953), philosopher and author.

William Ellis (1860–1945) was a member of the governing body of the Imperial College of Science and Technology.

Anna-Jane Blanco White was actually the daughter of Wells by Amber Reeves. Wells and Amber Reeves broke off their relationship during her pregnancy, and she married George Rivers Blanco White. In his biography, Anthony West says that Wells was forbidden to have any contact with Anna-Jane until 1932.

CAMBRIDGE / MS / 435
(*To Richard Bennett*)

97, Chiltern Court
27–11–30

My dear Rich,

Your recital of misfortune is distressing. However, do you know any of our family with a good set of teeth? We pray God to give you strength—& especially strength not to faint again. The first night passed off very well and enthusiastically last night. Playing good; production absolutely rotten. Play too long; ought to be cut. I think the *Times* criticism pretty fair-minded. I don't know who did it. I didn't see Morgan there. After the show there was a simply frightful gathering on the stage, with speeches from person after person standing on a chair. And they nearly all said: 'The proudest moment of my life, career,' etc. Frightful! It was 1.45 before I got into bed. Such is the theatre. Dorothy gave an excellent performance. If you join the People's Theatre (2/6) you can get stalls at 2/4^d each. The whole thing seems to me to be immoderately insane. But they have got 25,000 subscribers, & 25,000 half crowns make the whole of their capital, I think. I have begun my new novel. A French author (excellent), Jacques Chardonne, whom I don't know personally, has written me to assert that *IP* is the greatest novel of this age, & that I am one of the greatest authors of any age. This will do to go on with. Dorothy is sleeping. Auntie Tertia called yesterday on her own business. She is pretending not to be disturbed by uncle William's retirement, but of course she *is* disturbed, & ought to be. Auntie Emily is disturbed about John, & keeps on writing. Auntie Sissie is disturbed about Cedric, & Cedric is disturbed about Auntie Sissie. And Auntie Maud is merely a blasted trying nuisance. And I am the head of the family. Still, I shirk nothing. Dorothy was charmed with your wire. Between Wolverhampton & Rochdale, I judge not!

Loves, & get better,
Your sturdy uncle,

A.B.

---

435. *The Times* thought that the play was old-fashioned and unsatisfactory. It praised Guy Newall, who played Lord Strathpeffer, but made no mention of Dorothy. Morgan: unidentified.

Jacques Chardonne, pseudonym of Jacques Boutelleau (b. 1884), prolific novelist and essayist, also a publisher.

CAMBRIDGE / MS / 436
(*To Richard Bennett*)

> 97, Chiltern Court
> 2–12–30

My dear Rich,

Thanks for interesting epistle. If I were you I should not leave those doubtful teeth over-long. You will save money & trouble by not doing so. It may comfort you to reflect that almost *everyone* has a lot of worry through teeth. This is why dentists are so busy. I can appreciate Auntie Emily's attitude about 'Auntie'. She is always like that. Somehow rather ashamed of being nearly 60! But practically all women are like that also. There must be something sound in the attitude. I have now looked into the Emily v. John Bennett feud, & I have concluded that John is not very blameworthy, though perhaps a little. Dorothy is still worried about this place & her not being able to sleep properly therein because of the vibrations. She is at the moment sleeping at the Savoy, but not for long. For myself I sleep better here than I have slept anywhere for years. We are not yet 'settled in'. Something is done everyday, but things always remain to be done. I hesitate to estimate the cost. I've only had one or two bills yet. The affair is like a diarrhoea of money. I've just had a cable from Doran that he will arrive on the 10th. Trouble ahead there. We had a great evening the other night with his friends the Messmore Kendalls at Claridges. Unfortunately it continued till 2.30 a.m. However I worked all right next day. I have now fairly begun my new novel, & I toil at the same everyday except Sunday (when I write my *Evening Standard* article). Time is not being lost. I was at the first night of the *Man from Blankley's* & at the stage orgy afterwards (which was terrible). The play is very good, but the production was very bad, & Mr. Duff T. & I had to stifle sundry yawns. Tonight I spend in the sweet society of Freddie Lonsdale. Last night I was at Ethel Sands' and had a great pow-wow with Virginia Woolf. (Other guests held their breath

to listen to us.) Virginia is all right. And I was at home by 11.30.
I trust you are now out of pain.

Loves,

Your ceaseless uncle,

A.B.

436. John Bennett had lodgings with Emily at this time.

In her memoir Dorothy says that although she was the one to learn of the available
flat at Chiltern Court, she did not care for it and wanted something in Richmond or
Hampstead, but she yielded to Bennett's liking for it. When they moved in she
discovered that the place 'was inimical to our particular kind of person and to our type
of existence'. She wanted to leave immediately, and said to Bennett that going or
staying was 'a matter of life and death'. Frank Swinnerton says that she said of the
vibration from the underground trains: 'it went right up my rectum'.

Virginia Woolf (1882–1941) wrote of the occasion that she and Lord David Cecil
'taunted the old creature with thinking us refined'.

CAMBRIDGE / MS / 437
(*To Richard Bennett*)

97, Chiltern Court
16–12–30

My dear Rich,

Thanks for yours of yesterday. Well, I fear no spectacle of
any kind would draw me to Twickenham on a crowd day. Mr.
Tayler goes, but he curses afterwards. (He cannot learn.) All
cross-country routes are inferior to main routes, & must be, and
when a cross-country route becomes rapid, it also becomes a
main route. Odd! I sympathise with you in the matter of
salaries. But millionaires & shareholders have to live. I don't
envy your Christmas. It may be all right, though I object to all
family-Xmases except my own. We were going away to Jo
Davidson's for Xmas. But as Dorothy is working till, &
including, the 27th we can't. So we go on the 29th, & God keep
us en route, because we shan't arrive till 10.30 p.m. You may
say a journey of 12 hours. Not that that is anything. Dorothy, in
the matter of nerves, is far from well, & not improving.
Overwork. She *may* last out till 27th without a collapse. While
her own bedroom is being altered she is staying at the Savoy.
Sunday-Monday night at 1.15 a.m. she rang up with the news
that she had a serious heart-attack. (I didn't hear of it till next
morning.) She wanted nurse to go down in the middle of the
night. Nurse, having seen her in these 'heart' attacks

(flatulance only) before, & having sat up with her, happily didn't go. Dorothy had immediately afterwards gone to sleep & slept 8 hours right off! Still, she needs a lot of watching. She has it. The flat is not yet done; but it is proceeding. Your auntie Tertia was here on Saturday morning. Miss Nerney wouldn't let her come into my study while I was at work, in order to see the same. I saw A.T. afterwards, but I was full of my work & must have seemed a bit dreary to her. I do wish people wouldn't call in the mornings, however excellent their intention. It seems that Mary K is bang full of work—12 hours a day, on her own. I'm dining out most nights. I saw Augustine Birrell last night. He stayed later than I did, & seems as young, & he is over 80. May heaven sustain you both through Xmas. I'm glad about that garden path. It is a good work.

> Loves,
> Your philosophic uncle,

> > > > > A.B.

437. Davidson's home was near Tours.
Augustine Birrell (1850–1933), essayist, professor of law, member of parliament.

CAMBRIDGE / MS / 438
(*To Richard Bennett*)

> > > 97, Chiltern Court
> > > 21–12–30

My dear Rich,
   Here is a trifle to take the sharp edge off Xmas. And God save you both, & don't get drunk. Last night's film was really, on its own plane, about the best I have witnessed. Dorothy is in bed. I am working.

> > Loves & best wishes,
> > Your unChristmassy uncle,

> > > > > A.B.

438. *Disraeli*, with George Arliss, made a couple of years earlier.

CAMBRIDGE / MS / 439
(*To Richard Bennett*)

97, Chiltern Court
23–12–30

My dear Rich,

Thanks for thy missive. My information from Sir George Paish is that things will improve in 1932. He was right in 1928 in his predictions of what would happen in 1930. He is usually very gloomy, but has of late become much less pessimistic. *I* haven't seen any parcel from you. But as there are about a million parcels in this house & more arrive every hour this does not surprise me. I doubt not that I shall ultimately perceive the parcel, & anyhow the thanksgivings of this community are heartily despatched to you herewith. I always keep my presents down to the smallest limit. In fact, outside the family I only give about two gifts. The family presents a field sufficiently large for me. Miss Nerney says that this year she is giving between 40 & 50 presents. Well, what I say is, let her! My Xmas cheer is improved by the discovery that electricity here costs 3/4ᵈ a unit, against 6ᵈ in Cadogan Square. I doubt whether lighting & heating here will cost more than £25 a year, against about £180 at 75, despite the fact that Dorothy adores electricity & has a fearful down on steam-heating. Further the hot water is *always* very hot. I saw the sun (red) here yesterday morning, walked out & in 10 minutes was in a thickish fog. But it has been nothing like so bad near here as at H.P. Corner & certain other places further off. Yes, I should say that Sark was well spent, & I was very glad that you have kept yourselves solvent. I doubt if I shall do as well. I say with feeling: God keep us all, knowing well that he won't. Still, I am working & sleeping better here, far better, than at 75. Dorothy is not. She is far from well & needs a change much more than I do. The dining-room has been decorated. A good holiday to you both.

   Loves,
   Your productive uncle,

          A.B.

439. Sir George Paish (1867–1957), writer on economic affairs.

ELDIN / MS / 440
(*To May Beardmore Marsden*)

97, Chiltern Court
23–12–30

My dear May,

How timely you are! I adore them. Thank you very much, & all our good wishes unto you & Edward Harry. The flat is a great success so far as I am concerned, & Virginia & everyone except Dorothy. On the second morning here she was wakened by a steam-drill (which vanished after a few days of road-repairs) & she has never got over this. But she has been, & still is, working too hard, & acting (in *The Man from Blankley's*) has gotten on her nerves, through troubles in the theatre; & she has been very unwell & is still rather unwell. That's all. We go to France for a change on Monday next. Toys have been a bit thick. All good wishes to all of you, again, including Joan.

Ever yours, A.B.

KENNERLEY / MS / 441
(*To Tertia Kennerley*)

97, Chiltern Court
26–12–30

My dear Tertia,

Christmas is now over, and I have come to the conclusion that the spot-light on it is your mince tarts, of which I have now eaten three. (Pudding not yet opened.) I enjoy these mince tarts as much as anything in the year (except possibly oatcakes). Dorothy does too. I didn't go to sleep till 2.30 on Xmas morning, & I didn't go to sleep till 2.45 on Boxing Day morning. But Dorothy slept till 11.20 on Boxing Day morning. She is much better. I am very well & very productive. She has 2 performances today & 2 on Saturday, & on Saturday night she will be less well. And on Sunday night, what with packing & playing with Virginia, she will be still less well. We leave for Paris on Monday morn. Virginia's parties are only outnumbered by her parcels, of which there are about a million and a quarter. I am delighted that Xmas is over; but I watch the

diminishment of the mince tarts with sadness. *Imp Palace* is at
the moment the top of the 'best-sellers' in U.S.A.

Loves, and Dorothy's, to you all and sundry,
Yours, A.B.

CAMBRIDGE / MS / 442
(*To Richard Bennett*)   Hôtel Matignon
                                                   Paris
                                                   9–1–31
My dear Rich,

    Thanks for yours of 1st which reached me today only. I don't
know what it has been doing. I look at your balance sheet in a
broader way than you do. What I see is that for this last year
your expenditure exceeded your income by over £20. So I regret
to say that I don't find it very satisfactory. The next increase of
salary you have *must* come off my allowance to you. It is high
time that somehow you were entirely keeping yourself. Of
course income tax is a great nuisance. North Harrow is also a
great nuisance, though this is between ourselves. The weather
is also a great nuisance, here as in England. It is very cold, &
this afternoon it snowed. And we're only just emerging from flu.
Dorothy was until recently much worse than I was. She is now
better than I am. We haven't yet been able to go out in the
evening. But tonight I think we shall attend a theatre. You
don't know Jo Davidson, at whose house on the Indre Dorothy
was ill in bed *all* the time, so I can't talk to you about him. He is
just about finishing my bust, & I shall thank God when it *is*
finished. We met James Joyce yesterday. Nearly blind, &
totally self-centred: a very strong personality indeed. I should
hardly like to be his wife. He looks quite boyish but has 2 adult
children, one married; and still a strong Irish accent. We
haven't seen the Godebskis or Mimi or André or any of my
friends. I did 3 hours shopping with Dorothy today. I left her at
it, after lunch, & went to bed, being dead, & was just asleep
when the concierge rang me to say that Madame would not be
in till between 5 & 6! So my sleep was ruined. A parcel of books
has *not* arrived from the *Standard*, & therefore I can't do my
proper article for next week. However, I may write a story. I

must do something to keep the wolf out of the hotel. The hotel is very good—and cheap. We like it better than ever before. *Très sympathique*. I saw the outskirts of Joffre's funeral procession on Wednesday, & could write a diverting article thereon, but I am too idle.

Loves,
Your French uncle,

A.B.

442. North Harrow: where the Frank Beardmores lived.
James Joyce (1882–1941).
The funeral procession for Marshal Joffre (b. 1852), Commander in Chief of French forces in the War, went from Notre Dame to the Invalides.

CAMBRIDGE / MS / 443
(*To Richard Bennett*)   Hôtel Matignon
Paris
14–I–31

My dear Rich,
    Thanks for yours. Of course I don't want any graspingness to decrease your salary. What you suggest will be agreeable to me, and the sooner it happens the better—that's what I say! We are living a terrific life here. Dorothy is shopping without cash, & sometimes I go with her, & a considerable fatigue it is. And we lunch & dine with friends, or they with us, & we go to the theatre most every night. I have seen five things, including the big revue at the Casino de Paris, & I haven't yet seen one piece at which I was not most markedly bored. But the acting is marvellously better than London acting. It is superb. The Godebskis we have had once to lunch & tonight we dine with them & go to the theatre. Mimi & spouse we have seen 3 times. She is still unique, that girl is. Her infant is aged 2. I have had the august visits of André Gide, James Joyce, & Valéry Larbaud almost all at once. And now the hotel has found out at last who I am. I mean the management of the hotel has found out. Which is a pity, for I have always come here disguised as E.A.B. But when celebrated persons arrive and ask for A.B. the cat is bound sooner or later to leap out of the bag. It has done. Jo Davidson has finished my bust, & he is going to do André Gide next. I am rather suffering from visits—but not from

Gide's and Larbaud's. I don't think now that we shall *really* get home till Tuesday. *I* put it off one day because of a party at Godebskis on Sunday night. And now Dorothy wants to put off the departure for another day. And who am I to refuse? The weather has been chiefly awful. But today is beautiful, though it won't 'stay put', I feel sure. Still, I don't care. We continue to like the hotel more & more. I live in dread of the inevitable visit to North Harrow, and in greater dread of North Harrow's visit to Chiltern Court. I can get on fine with Uncle Frank, & pretty well with A. Sissie if she keeps off her own affairs, (which she doesn't). I don't know Roger. I am perfect with the all-conquering Cedric, who is destined to some thin times in London, I fear. Yes, Melchett's last words were pathetic (if true). However, Beethoven did *not* say as he expired 'I shall hear'. That legend has long since been destroyed. If the control of factories does come your way, of course everything will be all right & we ought all to buy shares. But what about my Australian Trustee Stocks? All dropped to pieces! Queensland! Still, the interest still arrives. Dorothy is steadily getting better. Logically, she ought to get steadily worse, as she runs all sorts of after-flu risks all day every day. But women are not men. This is the greatest of all truths.

Loves,
Your dashing uncle,

A.B.

443. For letters to Valéry Larbaud (1881–1957) see Vols. II and III.

Lord Melchett, head of ICI, supposedly said, 'Run along now, I am tired.'

In a letter to Winifred Nerney on the 17th Bennett wrote, 'I have written a complete short story (5600) in 5 mornings while waiting for Mrs. B. to get up.'

CAMBRIDGE / TS / 444
(*To Richard Bennett*)

97, Chiltern Court
26th January 1931

My dear Rich,

Thanks for your letter which I received last Tuesday on our return from Paris. I have not replied to it because from the moment of our arrival I was struck all of a heap by 'flu', and I have got up for the first time this afternoon (Saturday, I mean) for a few hours. Not a severe attack, but quite enough for my taste. I expect to be at work today. In fact, I shall be. We had a great but very exhausting time in Paris. Indeed, the 'time' left me with insufficient strength to defeat the germs floating about. This is all I can write now. But no doubt I shall write again some day. Oh yes, some day I shall write.

> Loves,
> Your convalescing uncle,
>
> A.B.

STOKE / S.Tr. / 445
(*To William Kennerley*)

> [97, Chiltern Court]
> [about 26 January 1931]

My dear William,

Thank you. I hope that the enterprise will succeed. I have for the present lost all interest in stock markets. I have no money and am indeed ruined by income tax and flat installation. When I have some available money again—if ever—I will inform you of the great fact. I have all manner of worries. F.C.B. has lost his job. Richard is coming to see me about that situation tomorrow, Sunday. Florence has written to me. Even F.C.B. has written to me, although he never wrote to me, nor said a word to his family until the day before he actually left his office. Characteristic.

I am convalescing, but unable to do anything beyond short articles and chores, and I feel like nothing at all. Dorothy is not well. She will have to go away.

> God keep us,
> Loves to all,
>
> Yours, [A.B.]

CAMBRIDGE / TS / 446
(*To Richard Bennett*)

> 97, Chiltern Court
> 27th January 1931

My dear Rich,

Thank you for your faithful letter. I am very glad that you are about to travel at the expense of I.C.I. I personally adore having my expenses paid. I am now still more considerably convalescent. In fact this morning I felt what is called 'a different man', and I shall in all probability go to the Schnabel concert tonight. I managed to write an article, and to deal with a certain amount of correspondence yesterday, but I shall not really begin to use my brain until next week. The article appearing in the *Daily Express* today I must have written more than a year ago. I had forgotten all about it. I have not read any of the other articles in the series; but I am convinced that none of them could have been very much better than mine. A pleasing thought. We trust that your cold is well and truly killed.

    This letter is merely an acknowledgment of yours.

Our loves,
Your true uncle,

A.B.

446. Artur Schnabel (1882–1951), the pianist. In a journal entry Bennett remarks that Schnabel's playing of Mozart and Brahms 'was very great'.

    Bennett's article in the *Daily Express* was entitled 'Thinking as a Science'. It was one of a series in which eminent people answered the question 'What I Think About'.

KENNERLEY / MS / 447
(*To Tertia Kennerley*)

97, Chiltern Court
2–II–31

My dear Tertia,

    Thank you. Yes, in my first letter to F.C.B. I was wrong (lack of brain after flu) & I wrote him the next day to apologise. I saw Richard yesterday, & arranged with him his line of action when he gets to Rochdale next week. There are 4 people to divide old Mrs. Barlow's bit of money. *I* am sorrier for Florence than for Frank, because Frank has extremely little sense of responsibility, & will glide through anything. Frank's greatest asset is Flo. I had a very cheerful letter from William, which bucked me much. I agree about the moral influence of flu. I am going to see a physician this morning about my heart—& generally. Also, I have only 2 teeth in my head. One broke off last night, and now my lower plate is floating around! Slightly distressing. Fred's wife is ill, & he had to rush off this evening urgently & goodness knows when he will be back. Dorothy's illness is nervous, & due to overwork & undue worry over nothings. But she is now a bit better. Acting is very bad for her, & I shall ban further acting as much as I decently can. When she has a part, she quickly gets infinitely worse, indeed acutely. And she is one of your household worriers. I should like to see you, but not mornings. Tea is the time. I'll send you a notelet. I haven't seen Sissie, thank God! She is hanging over me. Further, Emily wants to come. I shan't know till 10 a.m. tomorrow how deeply I am involved with the dentist. I'm doing *no* work, except my weekly article, which I always regard as more lark than labour. But of course I have to keep my correspondence in order. Miss Nerney is marvellous. Ditto Fred. Virginia has been in bed 2 days. Tummy. Now up again, & very obstreperous.

Yours, A.B.

CAMBRIDGE / TS / 448
(*To Richard Bennett*)

97, Chiltern Court
4th February 1931

My dear Rich,

Thanks for your letter of yesterday. Unfortunately my health is not a bit better, and I cannot do anything at all. Even to write a letter exhausts me. So I will ask you to excuse me for the present.

Loves,
Your obsolescent uncle,

A.B.

448. Winifred Nerney sent this letter with an accompanying note:
Dr. Griffin says Mr. Bennett must stay in bed, & I have cancelled all his engagements. He is very queer today, temperature just over 101....
Bennett died of typhoid fever on 27 March. He apparently contracted the disease either at Jo Davidson's house or at a Paris restaurant. It was not properly diagnosed until February.
In his memoir Frank Swinnerton says that he believes that Bennett returned from France with the conviction that he must separate from Dorothy and that Dorothy on her part was demanding a settlement equal to Marguerite's as the price. If this view is questionable (see the Introduction, p. xxxv), what is certain is that there was enormous dislike of Dorothy among Bennett's friends and family. The dislike was expressed in extraordinary tales about her that circulated for many years. One of them was that she was sexually involved with Richard and was caught with him even as Bennett lay dying, another that she was directly and consciously responsible for Bennett's death.

Swinnerton rejects the first and accepts the second metaphorically. On the second matter he records two details. He himself stood with Dorothy in the room where Bennett lay dead, and he saw her suddenly observe a ring on the little finger of Bennett's left hand. 'To my horror', he says, 'she moved quickly across the room, wrenched the ring from his finger, and said, "I'm sure he'd wish me to have this."' Some minutes later, at her request, he went up to Wells's flat to ask Wells to come down to see her. He found Wells in tears. 'He almost screamed "No! I *won't*! She's a bitch; and she killed Arnold!"'

In May 1933 the third and final volume of the *Journals* was published, and after the last entry came a note that said that Bennett 'died in London on March 27, 1931, of typhoid fever contracted in France'. The note prompted a letter from Tertia to Fanny Gertrude, who replied:

Dear T.,

I have hunted up the facts of Arnold's death in my Diary and find them to be as follows.

For a week previous to his death I had been constantly on the phone to Chiltern Court receiving only evasive replies either from Fred, the butler, or Miss Nerney, the secretary, who were evidently acting under orders to give nothing away. From time to time I visited Miss Nerney and was more successful in obtaining news as to progress; on such occasions, if D. entered the room she disregarded me and was indeed barely civil.

However on Thursday evening March 26th 1931, you telephoned to me with the news that having met Sir Wm. Wilcox in the corridor of A.B.'s flat you had obtained permission for us to visit A.B. and I promptly put on my hat & coat and went, remaining there until midnight of Friday March 27th.

Arnold was unconscious and never regained consciousness, gradually growing more and more quiet.

I saw nothing of D. all Thursday night and was told she had gone to bed. Early next a.m. I went to bed, in a room at the far end of the corridor, for a short time, and when I rose I found you already about. We had some difficulty (you will remember) in obtaining food, D.'s pretext being that the staff were extremely overtired. D. had already on the previous evening pressed me to leave the flat, this in the presence of my son Cedric, but I was resolved that Arnold should pass out with his family about him and I remained.

At 6.30 in the evening of the 27th I was turned out of A.B.'s room by the doctors who were making a final effort to save him. After a long wait I went across the road to have dinner and returned into A.B.'s presence at 8.15. At 8.30 D. came into the room but stayed only for 5 minutes or so. As the end was very near A.B. was visited for the last time by Frank C.B., Mr. Doran and one or two others. You also were in a considerable time. At the moment of death the sister in charge (Treloar?) and myself alone were present. I remained in the room only 5 minutes longer and in the corridor discovered D. lying on the breast of some young man or other whom I did not know.

Richard and my son Roger were in the study. Roger took me home by the midnight train. . . .

Conclusions. Cause of illness typhoid in France where A.B. drank water & ate oysters. Previous attacks of colitis & intestinal trouble predisposed to severity of typhoid attack. Temporary improvement Mch 1st–Mch 15th was not a subsidence of the illness as anaemia & delirium cont'd. The acute inflammation of gall bladder was the seat of infection & responsible for relapse & reinfection. Meaning Dorothy.

INDEX

Numbers in parentheses refer to translated material on pages where there is no reference in French.